C000045615

JOURNAL FOR THE STUDY OF THE OLD TESTAMENT SUPPLEMENT SERIES
165

Sheffield Academic Press

The Psalms in the Early Irish Church

Martin McNamara

Journal for the Study of the Old Testament
Supplement Series 165

Copyright © 2000 Sheffield Academic Press

Published by
Sheffield Academic Press Ltd
Mansion House
19 Kingfield Road
Sheffield S11 9AS
England

Typeset by Sheffield Academic Press
and
Printed on acid-free paper in Great Britain
by Bookcraft Ltd
Midsomer Norton, Bath

British Library Cataloguing in Publication Data

A catalogue record for this book is available
from the British Library

ISBN 1-85075-925-1

CONTENTS

PREFACE

Some years ago at public function a colleague made mention of the number of essays I had published on the Psalms in the Early Irish Church and suggested that I write a book on the subject. I reflected on the idea, but came to the conclusion the time was hardly yet ripe for such a work, and in any event most of what I would have to say could be read in the essays already written or soon to be published. In my view, what would be more useful at this juncture would be to bring together in one volume the essays I had already published on the topic, and make them available in print with a minimum of updating—provided, of course, that a publisher willing to take on the task could be found. I was very glad when David Clines indicated that Sheffield Academic Press would be happy to do so.

The present volume contains a slightly updated reprint of eight essays published in various journals and books between 1973 and 1999—that is over 27 years in all. The first (1973) is a general survey of the area, together with an introduction and a study of some of the questions involved. This initial survey indicated that the material to be studied was extensive, both with regard to biblical texts of the Psalter and commentary material. The title of the article ('Psalter Text and Psalter Study...') was intended to indicate what the essay contained and what was omitted. It did not treat of aspects of the psalms in the Irish Church beyond the biblical texts and Psalm interpretation. In this reprint attention has been paid to studies on individual topics that have appeared since 1973 (e.g. the Springmount Bog tablets), critical editions of major texts (e.g. Cummian's Paschal Letter; of the Latin translation of Theodore's commentary, and the epitome of this), the likely date and place of origin of the epitome of Julian's translation, and the transmission of the Julian translation and the epitome of this in the West. There is clear evidence of the attention paid to Greek and the Greek Psalter by Irish peregrini on the continent in the ninth century. The knowledge of Greek in Ireland before the ninth century is a matter that has engaged the minds of scholars for some time. I take occasion of the section on the Greek and Greco-Latin Psalters to include a bibliographical indication on later writing on this topic. The original essay (here reprinted) had a section on 'the influence of Theodore of Mopsuestia on Irish exegesis', which is in part but another way of saying 'the influence of Antiochene historical exegesis on Irish psalm interpretation'. Scholars have more recently once again brought to our attention that the Antiochenes did not neglect spiritual interpretation, and at the appropriate place I insert a new section in this essay on 'spiritual exegesis' in the School of Antioch and the likelihood of its influence on Irish tradition.

The contents of the second essay (1998) here reprinted are indicated in the title. It is a survey of the most recent research on the Irish Psalter text and commentaries, with special attention to two Psalters from the BL Cotton collection (Codex Vitellius F. XI and Codex Galba A.5), and to the so-called Psalter of Charlemagne. The treatment of the Cotton codices significantly updates what was said concerning them in the 1973 essay, especially so with regard to Codex Galba A.5. Here, too, there have been some changes to ensure clarity and expression and in order to update with regard to bibliography and to publication of texts.

The third essay (originally 1986) has to do with a detailed analysis of the oldest Hiberno-Latin commentary on the psalms known to us, namely that found in Codex Palatinus Latinus 68 of the Vatican Library. It situates this particular work in the context of Irish psalm exegesis.

The fourth essay (1984) concentrates on the tradition Ireland inherited with regard to the Psalter text, Psalter prefaces and commentaries on the psalms, and examines the manner in which Irish exegetical activity articulated and developed this inheritance.

The oldest Irish Psalter text we possess is that known as the Cathach of St Columba (of Iona). In fact it is the second oldest Latin Psalter text we know. It has a series of headings which interpret the individual psalms in a spiritual manner, as referring to Christ, the Church, the judgment, to Christian life, to eternal life and such like. This is the oldest, and best attested, series of psalm headings to Latin Psalters. Hitherto the tradition or traditions on which the Columba Series depends has not been identified. In the fifth essay (1998, 1999) an attempt is made to identify some of the traditions with which this Series seems related. What indications there are point towards a relationship with south-eastern Gaul in the late sixth century.

The Psalter stood at the very centre of monastic life. The sixth essay (1983) takes a look at the use of the Psalter in early Irish monastic spirituality.

Christian use of the Bible went hand in hand with Christian theological reflection on the person of Christ, and on the Christian mystery. Theodore of Mopsuestia had his own particular theological stance and availed of his Psalm commentary to treat of this in the psalms he took as direct prophecies of Christ (Psalms 2, 8, 45[46], and 109[110]). The Latin translation of his exposition of two (Pss 2, 8) of these psalms has come down to us, and the Latin text is glossed heavily in Old Irish. A question arises as to whether the early Irish scholars were aware of the theological questions involved. This issue is discussed in the eighth essay (1998), where there is also a consideration of the christological interpretation of the Psalms in the early Irish Church.

The final essay (1990) has not to do directly with the Psalms in the Irish Church at all. It is about the contents of the Vatican Codex, Reginensis latinus 49, now commonly known as the *Catechesis Celtica*. This work has come to be regarded as having close Irish connections, how close remains to be yet exactly determined. The work is a collection of items on various topics, some homilies, others exposition of Scripture. One of these is a comment on Psalm 1 which is almost entirely in the peculiar Irish tradition. For this reason the entire essay is reproduced here.

From various sources we know that the chief study in the early Irish monastic schools was the Bible. From early sources and from monastic traditions consigned to writing in later Lives of Irish saints we also know that the important element in an ecclesiastic's education was the reading of the Scriptures, and especially the reading of the Psalms. From the evidence examined in the essays here published we now know how seriously the study of the Psalms was carried out in these schools, and by Irish scholars on the Continent. In Ireland, and from an early date, the revision of the Latin Psalter made by Jerome and also Jerome's new Latin version of the Hebrew Psalter were being used. On the Continent scholars of the ninth century paid serious attention to the Greek Psalter. For an understanding of the psalms these early scholars drew on the work of such western Fathers as Eucherius, Jerome, Augustine and Cassiodorus. The chief exegetical influence in Irish schools, however, was the Psalm commentary of Theodore of Mopsuestia, as translated into Latin by Julian of Eclanum, and in particular the summary or abbreviation (epitome) made of this. The epitome, and sections of the full translation, were used directly and commented on in Old Irish, and other commentaries drawing liberally on the epitome were in use. This Antiochene commentary stressed the historical approach to the Psalms, and interpreted only four of them as direct prophecies of Christ. Together with this we have clear evidence that the early Irish schools had another quite distinct historical approach to the interpretation of the Psalms, one concentrating on understanding them of David and his times, and taking none of them as a direct prophecy of Christ. Together with these two main expository approaches, there is another well attested Irish tradition that combines both of them, and also includes a combination of the historical and Christian, Christological, understanding of the Psalms.

The Irish material examined here spans the period from c. 650 to 1200, the exegetical texts 650 to c. 1100. For this period there is evidence that the Irish scholars were heavily influenced by imported texts, but creatively moulded the traditions they received to produce fresh understanding of the Psalms. This Irish tradition drinks deeply from the exegetical approach of Antioch in the East, which it combines with the historical, literal and spiritual inheritance of the western Church. Through Antiochene influence it retains an echo of a very old Jewish understanding of Psalm 109(110) in which the psalm is understood to speak of Abraham.

Antiochene historical exegesis was intended as an aid to an intelligent choral recitation of the Psalms, in accord with Ps. 47.7 (LXX 46.8): 'Sing praises *maskïl*', which the LXX translates as 'Sing psalms with understanding' (*synetôs*; Vulgate, *sapienter*; RSV: 'Sing praises with a psalm'; REB: 'Sing psalms with all your skill'). The author (probably Diodore of Tarsus, died c. 390) of a psalm commentary in an introduction to his work expresses himself as follows:

> I have thought fit to give a brief exposition of this most necessary work of Scripture, the Psalms, as I myself have received it, an exposition of the subject matter of each psalm and their literal interpretation. In this way the brothers (and sisters), when they are singing the psalms will not be merely carried along by the sound of words nor, for lack of understanding, their minds occupied with other thoughts; rather by grasping the sequence of thought in the words, they will sing 'with understanding' (*synetôs*), as it is written (Ps. 46.8, LXX), that is from the depths of their minds and not with mere lip-service and superficial sentiment.

We can presume that the Irish tradition remains faithful to that of Antioch. One series of psalm headings combined this historical tradition with another giving the spiritual, Christian or Christological sense of the psalm.

One naturally asks how and when this Antiochene exegetical tradition reached Ireland. The date depends on that to which we may assign the composition of the epitome of Julian's translation of Theodore's commentary. This must have been somewhere between Julian's translation (about 420) and the first attested use of it in Ireland (between 650 and 700). There are some indications that the epitome originated in a region in southern Gaul contiguous with Mozarabic Spain, or in Mozarabic Spain itself. There are also some affiliations between the Columba Series of Psalm headings (from 600 or so) and an exegetical tradition active in south-eastern Gaul (probably Provence). This tradition was also interested in referring the psalms to the life of David, and it may also have influenced the Irish tradition of psalm exegesis.

It appears that two distinct traditions of historical psalms exegesis were introduced into Ireland at an early date (possibly c. 600 if not earlier), namely the Antiochene tradition through the translation of Julian (and the epitome of this) and another understanding the psalms principally as referring to David and his times. The approach understanding the psalms as speaking principally of David and his times, and interpreting none of them as direct prophecies of Christ, is found in particular in the expository material on Psalm 16 in the Double Psalter of St Ouen (Rouen, Bibl. mun. 24 [A. 40]). Dr Luc De Coninck has done pioneering work on the 'glosses' on these psalms in this Psalter. In a recent communication to me (November 1999) he has noted that for the scholia on these psalms it would be preferable not to use the term 'gloss' but to speak of 'elements of a pre-existing anonymous Antiochene-like commentary on Pss. 1.16–16.11 of non-Irish provenance' on the one hand, and 'parts of another literal and historical commentary reflecting the practice of "classical" Irish exegetical schools c. 700 A.D. on the other'. (Dr De Coninck's researches on the Double Psalter of St Ouen material will be treated of in greater detail further below. Both the Theodorean-Julian Antiochene Psalm exegesis and this other 'Antiochene-like' Psalm exegesis, extant for Pss. 1.1–16.11, seem to have come to Ireland from abroad. The Hiberno-Latin commentary on the psalms, now extant in the Vatican codex Palatinus latinus 68 seems to blend both of them. Once established, Irish psalm exegesis continued to be transmitted and to develop right down to the twelfth century. This 'home' branch of the Irish tradition is well represented by Irish and Latin texts. We know from at least three Latin texts of the ninth century that it also reached the continent, where it was probably at home for some time in Irish centres.

In the early Irish Church, then, there was a tradition of serious psalm study. The same holds good for the Pauline epistles, on which we have Latin commentaries and extensive glossing in both Irish and Latin. In 1954 Bernhard Bischoff published an important study of manuscripts with biblical commentaries from the early Middle Ages which he believed were or Irish origin or with Irish connections. His thesis has since been questioned. In the ongoing discussion of this issue now taking place, note must be taken of the solid Irish tradition in the field of Psalm study, both at home and on the continent.

One may ask what bearing, if any, these early exegetical exercises have with regard to the modern scene. In one sense they are not so far removed from the present-day discussion on the Bible *in ecclesia*, and the Bible in academe. Not so far removed, since I believe the question of the Bible in both academe and in the church is not specifically modern. The problem would have occurred in any situation in which the Bible was approached as literature by scholars who also regarded Scripture as the word of God and the New Testament as a whole, or sections of it, as having been foretold or foreshadowed in the Old. The Antiochenes admitted the problem, and refused to accept the typical Alexandrian allegorical approach. Together with their better-known historical interpretative method, the Antiochenes also had a spiritual exegetical method, known as theoria, through which they believed that at least for certain important texts of the Old Testament the inspired authors saw two historical realities—one contemporary or future in the history of Israel, another in the life of Jesus. Thus, for instance, the prophecy of the entry of the royal saviour gently to Jerusalem in Zech. 9.9, was understood as probably referring in the first instance to Zerubbabel but seen in vision of the future (theoria) to include Jesus' entry into the city (Mt. 21.1-6). We do not know whether such Antiochene spiritual exegesis directly influenced Ireland, which country, however, like the medieval west in general, has its own theory of spiritual exegesis (in general a triple one) which it attempted to link with the basic, historical, interpretation.

At the outset I noted that the very title of the first essay in this collection indicated that the study attempted was only a partial examination of a larger reality. The same can be said for this entire work. Research in the area is ongoing and a number of issues have not been addressed at all, or if so only in passing. More work needs to be done on the biblical texts of the Psalms, both Vulgate and Hebraicum. The entire body of Irish glosses and commentary material has not yet been published. Some treatment of the construe marks in Irish manuscripts has been given in the introduction to Codex Pal. lat. 68. A study of the much richer system of construe marks in the Double Psalter of St Ouen still remains to be published. The evidence from iconography on the influence of the Psalter on Irish art probably requires further exploration. The role of the Psalter in Irish liturgy and in Church life also merits consideration. And there surely are other questions besides these that can call for our attention.

It remains for me to acknowledge my debt to many people who have helped me in my study of the psalms in the Irish church, and have been involved in the publication of these essays, down through three decades. Of these I may mention Ludwig Bieler, Maurice Sheehy, Leonard Boyle (who as Vatican Librarian saw the edition of Pal. lat. 68 through the press), the anonymous readers for various essays, Sheffield Academic Press, in particular David Clines, who kindly accepted the work for publication, the other persons at the Press involved in the production of this work, and in a very special way Rebecca Cullen for her patient and thorough attention to the various stages of the proofs before they were finally submitted to the printer.

ACKNOWLEDGMENTS

The publishers and author are grateful for kind permission to reproduce the following articles:

'Psalter Text and Psalter Study in the Early Irish Church (A.D. 600–1200)'. First published in *PRIA* 73C (1973), pp. 201-98. Reprinted with permission.

'The Psalms in the Irish Church: The Most Recent Research on Text, Commentary, and Decoration—with Emphasis on the So-Called Psalter of Charlemagne'. First published in John L. Sharpe III and Kimberley van Kampen (eds.), *The Bible as Book: The Manuscript Tradition* (The British Library and Oak Knoll Press, 1998). Reprinted with permission.

'Introduction to the Glossa in Psalmos: The Hiberno-Latin Gloss on the Psalms of Codex Palatinus Latinus 68' (Studi e Testi, 310; Vatican City: Biblioteca Apostolica Vaticana, 1986). Reprinted with permission.

'Tradition and Creativity in Early Irish Psalter Study'. First published in *Irland und Europa: Ireland and Europe. Die Kirche im Frühmittelalter. The Early Church* (Klett-Cotta, 1984), pp. 328-89. Reprinted with permission.

Some Affiliations of the St Columba Series of Psalm Headings: A Preliminary Study. First published in *Proceedings of the Irish Biblical Association* 21 (1998), pp. 87-111; 22 (1999). Reprinted with permission.

The Psalter and Early Irish Monastic Spirituality. First published in *Monastic Studies* 14 (1983). Permission sought.

The publisher and author are grateful to Four Courts Press for permission to reproduce 'Christology and the Interpretation of the Psalms in the Early Irish Church', which first appeared in *Studies in Patristic Christology*, edited by Thomas Finan and Vincent Twomey (Dublin, 1998).

'The Irish Affiliations of the Catechesis Celtica'. First published in *Celtica* 21 (1990), pp. 291-333. Reprinted with permission.

ABBREVIATIONS

BL	British Library
CCSG	Corpus Christianorum, Series Graeca
CCSL	Corpus Christianorum, Series Latina
CLA	E.A. Lowe, *Codices Latini Antiquiores* (Oxford: Clarendon Press, I, 1934; II, 1935; III, 1938; vol. IV, 1947)
CSEL	Corpus scriptorum ecclesiasticorum latinorum
DIL	*Dictionary of the Irish Language*
HTR	*Harvard Theological Review*
Irish Art I	Françoise Henry, *Irish Art in the Early Christian Period, to 860 A.D.* (London, 1965)
Irish Art II	Françoise Henry, *Irish Art during the Viking Invasions (800–1020 A.D.)* (London, 1967)
Irish Art III	Françoise Henry, *Irish Art in the Romanesque Period (1020–1170 A.D.)* (London, 1970)
JRSAI	*Journal of the Royal Society of Antiquaries of Ireland*
JTS	*Journal of Theological Studies*
OIT	K. Meyer, *Hibernica Minora, being a fragment of an Old-Irish Treatise on the Psalter* (Anecdota Oxoniensa, Medieval and Modern Series, 8; Oxford: Clarendon Press, 1894)
PG	J.-P. Migne, *Patrologia cursus completa... Series graeca* (166 vols.; Paris: Petit-Montrouge, 1857–83)
PL	J.-P. Migne, *Patrologia cursus completus... Series prima [latina]* (221 vols.; Paris: Petit-Montrouge, 1844–65)
PRIA	*Proceedings of the Royal Irish Academy*
PSAS	*Proceedings of the Society of Antiquaries of Scotland*
RB	*Revue biblique*
Rbén	*Revue bénédictine*
RC	*Revue Celtique*
RIA	The Royal Irish Academy
RSR	*Recherches de science religieuse*
SBLMS	Society of Biblical Literature Monograph Series
SC	Sources Chretiennes
SE	*Sacris Erudiri*
SLH	Scriptores Latini Hiberniae

Thes. Pal.	W. Stokes and J. Strachan (eds.), *Thesaurus Palaeo-hibernicus: A Collection of Old-Irish Glosses, Scholia, Prose and Verse*. I. *Biblical Glosses and Scholia* (2 vols.; Dublin Institute for Advanced Studies; Dublin, 1975)
ZAW	*Zeitschrift für die alttestamentliche Wissenschaft*
ZCP	*Zeitschrift für celtische Philologie*

PSALTER TEXT AND PSALTER STUDY IN THE EARLY IRISH CHURCH (600–1200 CE)*

Writing on the Bible in the early Irish Church in 1929, James F. Kenney[1] could note that 'scholars are hampered, in spite of the vast amount of study that has been expended on biblical texts, by the fact that accurate information is not at their disposal regarding much of this Irish, or semi-Irish, material: only a small number of the manuscripts have been described by persons having modern expert knowledge either of Irish palaeography or of Irish biblical texts'. Since then Professor Bernhard Bischoff has published his major work on early Irish exegesis,[2] a study in which he revealed the rich literary output of the Irish schools between 650 and 800 CE. The manuscripts of many of the works identified as Irish compositions by Bischoff were not written by Irish scribes. He bases his identification of them as Irish works on certain characteristics which give them a family similarity: the recurrence of certain questions, the use of certain stock words and phrases, the quest for etymologies of certain words in 'the three sacred languages' (Hebrew, Greek and Latin), etc.[3]

Dr Bischoff has certainly opened up a new field of research. What

*   I wish to express my sincerest thanks to Dr Ludwig Bieler for the interest he has shown in this study, for having read the entire manuscript with meticulous care and for the corrections and suggestions he has made.

1.   J.F. Kenney, *The Sources for the Early History of Ireland: Ecclesiastical* (New York: Columbia University Press, 1929; repr. Dublin: Four Courts Press, 1997), p. 625.

2.   B. Bischoff, 'Wendepunkte in der Geschichte der lateinischen Exegese im Frühmittelalter', *SE* 6 (1954), pp. 169-281 (= Mittelalterliche Studien, I [Stuttgart: Hiersemann, 1966, pp. 205-73]); trans. by C. O'Grady, 'Turning-Points in the History of Latin Exegesis in the Early Middle Ages', in M. McNamara (ed.), *Biblical Studies: The Medieval Irish Contribution* (Proceedings of the Irish Biblical Association, 1; Dublin: Dominican Publications, 1976), pp. 74-160.

3.   Bischoff, 'Wendepunkte', pp. 202-10.

now remains to be done is to study in depth and edit the texts he has brought to our attention, many of which are as yet unpublished. One could approach the problem in either of two ways: the texts could be studied and edited in chronological order irrespective of the books of the Bible with which they deal, or one could select a particular book of the Bible and study all the Irish material treating of this, The second approach has a distinct advantage in that is it more likely to reveal to us the continuity of tradition—or its absence—within the Irish schools.

In the present study I follow this second approach. I have chosen the Psalter as my subject of study because of its central place in the early Irish monastic system,[4] owing to its place in the divine office. Of all the books of the Bible the Psalter was the one read most. And because of the difficulties encountered in understanding its text it was also the book most studied. All this is true both of the Church in general and of the early Irish Church.

My purpose has been to glean from the available material all the information one can on the place of the Psalter in the early Irish Church, that is, from the beginnings down to the twelfth-century reform. In order to proceed in an orderly fashion I shall first speak of the place of the psalms in Irish monastic training (1). I shall then proceed to give a survey of the extant material on the Psalter texts and the commentaries on it (2). Next, I shall treat of the sources for the study of the psalms available in Irish monasteries (3). I shall then comment on the interpretation of the psalms in the Irish schools (4). After this I shall treat of the text of the Psalter used in Ireland (5) and also of the critical work on the Psalter text done in Ireland (6). I shall finally (7) say something on various aspects of Irish Psalters. Appendices will give selected excerpts from Hiberno-Latin commentaries on the psalms which have hitherto remained unpublished.

1. *The Psalms in Irish Monastic Training*

For information on early monastic training and the central place in this training enjoyed by the Psalter we have to rely in good part on incidental scraps of information, drawn mainly from the Lives of Irish saints.

---

4.   A glance at the entry under *salm* (with its compounds and derivations) in the RIA *Dictionary of the Irish Language* (col. 42, line 53 to col. 44, line 11) will give some idea of this central role of the Psalter in the early Irish Church.

1.1. *Elementary Training*[5]

In the monastic settlement itself there was a central building (*schola*) surrounded by cells. In the life of a certain St Daig who studied at Devenish, mention is made of a little monastery (*monasteriolum*) which adjoined the main one and which served as a school (*schola*).[6] Here Daig learned his letters and the art of writing.

As a general rule the child was taught to read before being handed over to the monks for further instruction. Seven years must have been a common age for beginning this elementary study, as it is mentioned more than once in the Lives of Irish saints.[7]

As everywhere in Western Christendom during the Middle Ages, the child learned his reading from the Latin Psalter. We have abundant evidence of this in the lives of the Irish saints.[8] The child learned both the psalms and the canticles and was thus prepared to take part in the litur-

5. Cf. Louis Gougaud, *Christianity in Celtic Lands* (London: Sheed and Ward, 1932; reprinted Dublin: Four Courts Press, 1993), pp. 244-47; John Ryan, *Irish Monasticism: Origins and Early Development* (Dublin: Talbot Press, 1931; reprinted Dublin: Four Courts Press, 1993), pp. 377-83.

6. *Acta Daggaei* I, 5 in C. de Smedt and J. de Backer (eds.), *Acta Sanctorum Hiberniae ex Codice Salmanticensi* (Edinburgh, 1888), col. 891-94 = W.W. Heist (ed.), *Vitae SS. Hiberniae ex Codice olim Salmanticensi* (Brussels, 1965), pp. 359-60.

7. See texts collected by C. Plummer, *Vitae Sanctorum Hiberniae* (2 vols.; Oxford: Clarendon Press, 1910; reprinted Dublin: Four Courts Press, 1997), I, p. cxv n. 13; C. Plummer, *Bethada Náem nÉrann, Lives of Irish Saints* (2 vols.; Oxford: Clarendon Press, 1922; repr. Oxford: Clarendon Press, 1968), II, pp. 326, 362; cf. also Gougaud, *Christianity*, p. 244 n. 5; Ryan, *Irish Monasticism*, p. 377 n. 1.

8. Cf. Gougaud, *Christianity*, p. 244 and the sources cited by him in n. 6; Ryan, *Irish Monasticism*, p. 379; thus for instance in the *Tripartite Life of St Patrick* (*ro lég Macc Nisse a shalmu ic Pátraic*) (ed. K. Mulchrone, *Bethu Phátraic: The Tripartite Life of Patrick* [Dublin: Royal Irish Academy, 1939], p. 97) (Pars secunda, line 1880), which is explained in *DIL* (s.v. *salm*, col. 42, lines 69-71) as: 'i.e. he learnt Latin, the Psalms being the medium of instruction for beginners'. In this context we may also refer to the 'alphabets' (*abgitir, abgitrech*) said to have been written by St Patrick. Mulchrone (ed.), *The Tripartite Life* (p. 69, lines 1245-46) says he wrote one for Ernaisc (*scribais Pátraic abgitir dó*), while a chronological tract in the *Leabhar Breac* (p. 220, col. 1; W. Stokes [ed.] in *The Tripartite Life of Patrick* [Rolls Series, part II; London, 1887], p. 552 n. 5) says he wrote three hundred 'alphabets' (*trí cét apgitrech roscrib*). What *abgitir* in these contexts means is not clear. *DIL* (letter A, 1964, col. 8) understands it as a 'set of alphabetical symbols'. It is possible that what is meant are alphabetical psalms. On these see section. 7.f below.

gical services.[9] It appears that he not only learned to read and write from the Psalter but that he also learned by heart the one hundred and fifty psalms (or the 'three fifties' as they are called in Irish).[10]

To the evidence available from other sources for both these customs we can now add that of the Irish *Reference Bible* (2.10 below). Citing Cassiodorus[11] the author speaks of the young student learning to read from the Psalter and also speaks of the psalms being consigned to memory for chanting.

1.2. *Wax Tablets*

Parchment was a rare and precious commodity. In any event it was ill-suited for elementary instruction. Instead of parchment the pupils were provided with wax tablets. For this again we have abundant evidence from the Lives of Irish saints.[12] Wax tablets were also used by teachers and others for making notes and preparing works to be written on parchment. It was on tablets that Adamnan of Iona wrote down Arculf's account of the holy places he had visited.[13]

We are fortunate in possessing a set of such wax tablets, and this it would appear from a very early period—about 600 CE (below, 2.2 and Appendix I). These tablets were probably used for such elementary education, although the scribe in this instance was probably a teacher, not a student. And as a teacher he appears to have been more interested in teaching his pupils how to write and read than in transcribing the psalms correctly, since his text bears evidence of slips of memory. The

9.   See Gougaud, *Christianity*, pp. 244-45 with sources p. 245 n. 1; cf. also text of *Rule of Céli Dé* cited in 1.2.c.

10.   E.g. Rule of Ailbe, stanza 17 in J.O. Neill (ed.), 'The Rule of Ailbe of Emly', *Ériu* 3 (1976), pp. 92-115 (97-98); Rule of St Carthage, no. 19 in Mac Eclaise (pseudonym, ed.), 'The Rule of St. Carthage', *Irish Ecclesiastical Record* 27 (1910), pp. 495-517 (506-507); the *Féilire Óengusso*, *epil.* 179 in W. Stokes (ed.), *Félire Oengusso* (London: Henry Bradshaw Society, 1905), p. 272. See further 7.5 below.

11.   Cassiodorus, *Expositio psalmorum*, Praefatio XVII end. Reproduced in Appendix 4 below.

12.   References in Ryan, *Irish Monasticism*, p. 292 n. 1. The evidence from the Lives of the Irish saints is collected by Plummer, *Vitae Sanct. Hib.*, I, p. cxv n. 11. See also P.W. Joyce, *A Social History of Ancient Ireland* (2 vols.; Dublin: Gresham Publishing Co., 1913), I, pp. 482-85.

13.   *De Locis Sanctis*, Prologue in Denis Meehan (ed.), *Admanan's De Locis Sanctis* (SLH, 3; Dublin, 1958), pp. 36-37; p. 12 n. 2.

biblical text of the psalms in question is the Gallican with some Old Latin readings. This in itself is evidence that even at this early date Irish pupils were initiated to reading and writing through the Gallican Psalter, not through the earlier Old Latin text.

1.3. *The Teacher's Remuneration*[14]

In the monastic schools the teacher (called *magister, praeceptor, didascalus, sapiens* or *lector*—this last term corresponding to the Irish *fer légind*) was remunerated for his labours by the family of the pupil. His fee consisted in a cow, a heifer or a pig. This usage is illustrated by the following text from the *Rule of the Céli Dé*[15] which also gives interesting information on matters referred to above.

> Anyone, moreover, with whom the boys study who are thus offered to God and to Patrick, has a claim to reward and fee at the proper season, namely, a milch-cow as remuneration for teaching the psalms with their hymns, canticles and lections, and the rites of Baptism and communion and intercession, together with the knowledge of the ritual generally, till the student be capable of receiving Orders. A heifer and a pig and three sacks of malt and a sack of corn are his fee every year besides tendance and a compassionate allowance of raiment and food in return for his blessing. But the milch-cow is made over immediately after the student has publicly proved his knowledge of the psalms and hymns, and after the public proof of his knowledge of the ritual the fee and habit are due. Moreover, the doctor or bishop before whom proof of the psalms has been made is entitled to a collation of the beer and food for five persons the same night.

The *Rule of the Céli Dé* is preserved in the *Leabhar Breac* (9b-12b), where it is presented as a prose paraphrase of the metrical composition of Maelruain. W. Reeves assigned the prose paraphrase to the twelfth or thirteenth century. From a study of certain aspects of the language, however, J. Strachan concluded that in substance it was an earlier composition, belonging probably to the ninth century. In Kenney's view, the rules found in this work 'might have been written for any of the monastic communities founded in the sixth and seventh centuries'.[16] The usages quoted above may be taken to represent the practice of early

14. Cf. Gougaud, *Christianity*, pp. 245-46 (with indication of sources).

15. Ed. E.J. Gwynn in *The Rule of Tallaght, Hermathena* 44 (second suppl. vol.) (1927), p. 83.

16. Kenney, *Sources*, p. 472.

monastic Ireland. One of them is graphically illustrated by the story of the good cow that accompanied Ciarán, the future abbot of Clonmacnois, on his way to Clonard to study under Finnian.[17]

1.4. *Advanced Studies*[18]

After his elementary education the pupil went on the higher studies, the *studia maiora* as Bede calls them when speaking of the Irish schools.[19] In an old Irish monastery the monks lived in their separate cells or huts, and so apparently did the students. Rather than think of a central lecture hall in which lectures were given to groups, we should envisage the students going from cell to cell seeking information from those monks who were renowned for their learning. Bede,[20] speaking of the great plague of 664, writes of the Irish schools as follows:

> Many of the nobles of the English nation, and lesser men also, had set out thither (i.e. to Ireland), forsaking their native land for the sake of sacred learning or a more ascetic life. And some of them, indeed, soon dedicated themselves faithfully to the monastic life; others rejoiced rather to give themselves to learning, going about from one master's cell to another (*circumeundo per cellas magistrorum*). All these the Irish willingly received and took care to supply them with food day by day without cost, and books for their studies, and teaching free of charge.

1.5. *Oral Teaching and Written Texts*

The instruction, it would appear, was in the main oral.[21] The students got their information by word of mouth from their masters, rather than from written texts. This oral character of the instruction imparted in early Irish schools is emphasized by most writers on the subject. It would be a grave mistake, however, to assume that written texts did not exist. The contrary, in fact, has been demonstrated by Dr Bischoff's researches. And 'the works' (which he has identified as the products of the early Irish schools)

---

17. *Vita Ciarani de Cluain* 15 in Plummer (ed.), *Vitae Sanct. Hib.*, I, p. 205; R.A.S. Macalister, *The Latin and Irish Lives of Ciaran* (London, 1912), pp. 23, 45-46; a similar instance in *Vita Tathei*, in W.J. Reeves (ed.), *Lives of Cambro-British Saints* (Llandovery: 1853), p. 258.

18. Cf. Gougaud, *Christianity*, pp. 247-49; Ryan, *Irish Monasticism*, pp. 378-83.

19. *Hist. Eccl.* 3.27.

20. *Hist. Eccl.* 3.27.

21. Cf. Gougaud, *Christianity*, p. 245.

among which there are nine commentaries on Matthew alone, are still only a fraction of the total amount... Anonymity and a real mass production of works seem to have predominated in Ireland. The aim was not originality in the production of scientific scholarly works, to the composition of which but few are called. There was no aversion to repetition, and many apparently owed their origin to the mere transcription of other works, or to the new formulation of widespread scholastic teaching. In fact, school literature, with a different presentation of similar material, constitutes a great portion of this writing. What is remarkable is that so much of it has been written down.[22]

What Dr Bischoff says here on the character and content of these exegetical writings applies in a very special way to the Hiberno-Latin commentaries on the psalms, in particular to the introductions: 'different presentation of similar material'. The exegetical material on the psalms we present here probably represents what was commonly taught in the early Irish schools.

1.6. *Irish Monastic Libraries and Scriptoria*[23]

Irish sources speak of 'the host of the books of Erin',[24] of a *copia librorum*.[25] The evidence of the texts we are to study would appear to bear

22. Bischoff, 'Wendepunkte', p. 213; see also p. 198.

23. Cf. K. Hughes, 'The Distribution of Irish Scriptoria and Centres of Learning from 730 to 1111', in N.K. Chadwick (ed.), *Studies in the Early British Church* (Cambridge: Cambridge University Press, 1958), pp. 243-72; H. Graham, *The Early Irish Monastic Schools* (Dublin: Talbot Press, 1923), pp. 101-18; Gougaud, *Christianity*, pp. 361-70; Joyce, *Social History*, I, pp. 485-86.

24. The phrase is from the *Félire Oengusso*, p. 270.

25. Cf. Ryan, *Irish Monasticism*, p. 380 n. 5; Gougaud, *Christianity*, p. 259; K. Meyer, *Learning in Ireland in the Fifth Century and the Transmission of Letters* (Dublin: School of Irish Learning and Hodges, Figgis and Co., 1913), p. 11. *Ethicus Ister* (*Cosmographia*: D'Avezac [ed.], *Ethicus et les ouvrages cosmographiques intitulés de son nom* [Mém. présentés par divers savants à l'Acad. Des inscr. et belles letters, 1st ser., II; Paris, 1852], p. 469) spent much time among the ancient Irish 'turning over their books' (*eorumque volumina revolvens*), evidence of the fame enjoyed by 'the books of Ireland' in the milieu in which the author wrote (between 518–742 CE according to one writer; cf. Kenney, *Sources*, pp. 145-46). We should note, however, that according to H. Löwe ('Ein literarischer Widersacher des Bonifatius: Virgil von Salzburg und die Kosmographie [des Aethicus Ister]', *Abhandlungen der Akademie der Wissenschaften und der Litterature in Mainz, 1951* [Mainz, 1952]) 'Aethicus Ister' is none other than Virgilius of Salzburg (latter half of eighth century).

out the truth of this statement. An analysis of the sources used in the
Old-Irish Treatise on the Psalter (2.11 below) led R.L. Ramsay to
write:[26]

> The subjects treated, and still more the authorities used and named, give
> a very flattering impression of the state of Irish learning and Irish lib-
> raries at the time. Nearly every Latin commentator on the psalter whom
> we know to have written before 750[27] is mentioned and quotations made
> from his work; and there are a number of references which can no longer
> be identified and which perhaps are to works that have perished.

An analysis of the sources of the other works here studied leads more or
less to the same conclusion, although we cannot always be sure whether
citations were drawn directly from the earlier commentaries themselves
or from catenae or collections of excerpts (*eclogae*) from these works
which had already been made. We shall return to this point later.

The reproduction and multiplication of works required scriptoria,
which only the richer monasteries could afford.[28] It would be enlightening to trace our texts to known scriptoria and monasteries. It would be
both interesting and enlightening to know what works were used in
which Irish schools. In this way we could determine whether a particular monastic school followed or favoured the literal interpretation of the
Bible rather than the 'mystical', or vice versa.[29] Françoise Henry[30] has
been able to localize certain Irish manuscripts on the evidence of their
illumination, and I am happy to use her conclusions in what follows.
We are justified in associating the verse rendition of the *Old-Irish
Treatise* on the Psalter (2.17 below) with the school of Ros Ailithir. The
Milan commentary on the psalms (2.7), which came to Milan from
Bobbio, was probably used in the monastery of Bangor.[31] The illumina-

26. R.L. Ramsay, 'Theodore of Mopsuestia in England and Ireland', *ZCP* 8
(1912), pp. 452-97 (466).

27. The date earlier assigned to the *Old-Irish Treatise*. It is now dated somewhat
later, 800–850 CE (see 1.2.k).

28. Cf. Hughes, 'Distribution', esp. pp. 251-59.

29. One should also bear in mind the friendly interrelations between certain
Irish monasteries; on this see Ryan, *Irish Monasticism*, pp. 323-27.

30. In her three-volume *History of Irish Art*, I–II; in 'Remarks on the Decoration of Three Irish Psalters', *PRIA* 61C (1960), pp. 23-40 and in 'A Century of Irish
Illumination (1070–1170)', *PRIA* 62C (1962), pp. 101-64 (this last work in conjunction with G.L. Marsh-Micheli).

31. Lowe (*CLA* III, no. 326) thinks it could also possibly have been written in
Leinster.

tion has led Henry to assign the glossed so-called Psalter of Caimin (2.25 below) to Clonmacnois or Inis Cealtra. Yet there remains much more we would like to know on the texts actually used in the several Irish schools.

1.7. *The Interpretation of the Psalms*

Aldhelm[32] tells us that together with grammar, geometry and natural philosophy, the *allegorical* interpretation of Scripture was also taught in Irish schools. It is probably this evidence that leads some writers to say that the type of biblical exegesis followed in Ireland was allegorical rather than historical or literal. Such a statement as that of Aldhelm must, however, be considered against the available evidence. Allegorical exegesis was very prominent in the medieval Church and was held in high regard by Cassian and Bede among others. It was also followed in Ireland. As far as the interpretation of the psalms is concerned, however, the prevailing if not the sole method followed was the historical not the allegorical. Extant texts put this beyond reasonable doubt. This is a point to which I shall return later (4.2 below). Grammar, much beloved of the early Irish, also influenced the exegesis of the psalms, with the result that we find some of the texts pass from a consideration of what the author meant to a grammatical or etymological analysis of words. Two of the native authorities mentioned in the Milan commentary, that is, Coirbre and Mailgaimrid, seem to have interested themselves principally, if not solely, in grammar. To this also I shall return later (4.5, 6 below).

2. *Survey of Extant Material on Psalms in the Irish Church* (c. 600–1200 CE)

I list here in chronological order all our known sources of information on the text and the interpretation of the psalms in the early Irish Church. I also make a brief study of each of these sources. Most of the texts were written or composed by Irishmen. I include, however, a few items which, although not the work of Irishmen, have a direct bearing on the subject.

---

32. R. Ehwald (ed.), *Epistola ad Ehfridum* (*Monumenta Germaniae historica*, Auctores antiquissimi, 15.3, pp. 490-91). Aldhelm (c. 640–709 CE) received his early education at Malmesbury from an Irishman named Mael-dubh or Mael-dún.

2.1. *The Cathach of St Columba (Sixth–Seventh Century)*

MS: Dublin, Royal Irish Academy (*s.n.*)

Edition: H.J. Lawlor, 'The Cathach of St Columba', *PRIA* 33 C (1916) pp. 241-443 (with six plates; text, with detailed description and study of the MS itself and of questions connected with it); *Liber Psalmorum* (full collation of the MS made from photographs supplied by the RIA for the critical edition of Jerome's Vulgate Psalter). A digitized version on CD-ROM, accompanied by a printed introduction, in preparation by the Royal Irish Academy.

Studies: H.J. Lawlor, 'The Cathach' (with an appendix on 'The Shrine of the Cathach', by E.C.R. Armstrong, pp. 390-96; and W.M. Lindsay, 'Palaeographical Notes', Appendix II, pp. 397-403); E.A. Lowe, *CLA* II, no. 266; H. de Sainte-Marie (ed.), *Sancti Hieronymi Psalterium iuxta Hebraeos Edition critique* (Collectanea Biblica Latina, 11; Rome: Abbaye Saint-Jérome; Vatican City: Libreria Vaticana, 1954), pp. xxiii-xxiv; Henry, *Irish Art*, I, pp. 58-61; F. Henry, 'Les débuts de la miniature irlandaise', *Gazette des Beaux Arts* (1950), p. 5; Carl Nordenfalk, 'Before the Book of Durrow', *Acta Archaeologica* 18 (1947), pp. 141-74, esp. 151-59 (a study of the decoration); Kenney, *Sources*, pp. 629-30 (no. 454); M. Esposito, 'The Cathach of St. Columba', *County Louth Archaeological Journal* 4 (1916), pp. 80-83.

The Cathach is our oldest Irish manuscript of the Psalter. The extant text contains only 58 of the original 110 (or so) folios, bearing the text of Pss. 30.10–105.13 (in the Vulgate numbering). The remainder has been lost somewhere along the chequered history of the MS. The text is written *per cola et per commata*. Each psalm is preceded by a rubric, added by the scribe of the Psalter text in spaces left to receive them. These rubrics contain the Vulgate psalm titles, followed by a liturgical direction on when the psalm is to be read, and a heading giving the mystical or spiritual interpretation of the psalm. Only some of the psalms have the liturgical direction. I shall consider the 'mystical' headings in greater detail later—(2.3.a below). The biblical text of the Cathach is that of Jerome's correction of the Latin Psalter according to Origen's Hexapla, known as the *Gallicanum*. The Cathach (*C*) presents a very pure form of Jerome's original work and is one of the five codices on which the Benedictine editors base their critical edition. Another of these five codices is the *Gallicanum* text of the Irish Double Psalter of Rouen (2.18 below). Like Jerome's work, the Cathach is provided with the critical signs of the asterisk and the obelus. I shall consider the use and the significance of these later (6.2).

The Cathach was traditionally believed to have been the work of St Columba of Iona (migrated to Iona, 563 CE; died, 597) of the northern branch of the Uí Néill. The work was already somewhat damaged when it was put in its *cumhdach* (a wooden box covered with metal) at the end of the eleventh century. It was then in the possession of the O'Donnells of the same branch of the Uí Néill. It gets its name *An Cathach* ('The Battler') from the fact that it used to be carried into battle by the O'Donnells. As Manus O'Donnell says in his Life of Columba (compiled 1532 CE),[33] '(The Cathach) is the chief relic of St. Columba... It is in a silver gilt box which must not be opened. And each time it has been carried three times, turning towards the right, around the army before a battle, the army came out victorious.' After the Treaty of Limerick (1693) it was taken to France by one of the O'Donnells, but was brought back to Ireland in 1802. In 1813 it was given on loan to Sir William Betham who opened the coverings and after much difficulty separated the pages of the manuscript which had become stuck together by the damp. Some time later it was deposited in the library of the Royal Irish Academy.

It is hard to say whether or not the Cathach can be ascribed to St Columba. Lawlor believed that we have very good reasons to assume that Columba is the scribe.[34] He was even of the opinion that the Cathach is the actual copy which Columba surreptitiously made of the work of Finnian (of Moville).[35] In this case, the Gallican Psalter would have been the work, or at least among the works, brought by Finnian from Rome some time previously and the Cathach would have been transcribed some short time before the battle of Cúl-dremne in 561. Although this identification is now discredited, palaeographers find no difficulty in assigning the Cathach to Columba's day. In Lindsay's opinion there seems to be no valid reason for not doing so.[36] According to Lowe 'the early date (i.e. 561 CE) for the MS is palaeographically

---

33. A. O'Kelleher and G. Schoepperle (eds.), *Betha Colaim Chille: Life of Columcille compiled by Maghnas Ó Domhnaill in 1532* (Urbana: University of Illinois, 1918; repr. Dublin Institute for Advanced Studies, 1994), Irish text on p. 181. An inexact English translation on facing p. 182.

34. Lawlor, 'The Cathach', pp. 291-307.

35. Lawlor, 'The Cathach', pp. 307-29.

36. Lindsay, 'Palaeographical Notes', p. 397.

possible'.[37] We may possibly find corroborative evidence for Columban authorship in Adamnan's *Life of Columba* (written before 704) which more than once tells us that the saint worked as a scribe during his sojourn in Iona. In fact, at his death Columba was engaged in the transcription of a Psalter and had arrived as far as the words *inquirentes autem Domino non deficient omni bono* (Ps. 33.11). Books in the handwriting of Columba were still in the monastery of Iona in Adamnan's day and miracles were believed to be worked through them. This belief which is mentioned more than once by Adamnan[38] could explain the use of the Cathach in battle.

Another possible argument in favour of the Columban authorship of the Cathach is the presence of the asterisks and the obeli in the text. An old Irish tradition associates the Saint of Iona with just such critical work on the Psalms. In the *Amra Coluim Chille*, composed very soon after the saint's death, we read of him: *Gais gluassa gle, glinnsius salmu*. Unfortunately for our purpose, however, the text of the *Amra* is notoriously obscure. The above text has been translated:[39] 'He obelised glosses well, he ascertained the psalms.' Later Irish glosses on the *Amra* are more explicit. The first part is glossed as follows: '...he probed the glosses, i.e. he was a sprig (*gas*) at explaining the glosses well: that is, Columba was a good key to make glosses or questions easy...' The second part is glossed: 'i.e. he learned the psalms, i.e. or he made the psalms sure, i.e. *he separated them under obelisk and asterisk* (*ro[s]terbae fo obeil ⁊ astreisc*), or under titles and arguments, or under

---

37. *CLA* II, no. 266.

38. A.O. Anderson and M.O. Anderson (eds.), *Adomnan's Life of Columba* (London: Nelson, 1961); Preface (4a), II, 8; II, 9; II, 16; II, 29; II, 44; II, 45; III, 15 and III, 23 (128ab in Anderson and Anderson).

39. Whitley Stokes (ed.), 'The Bodleian Amra Choluimb Chille', *Revue Celtique* 20 (1899), pp. 252-53; for a slightly different translation see J.H. Bernard and R. Atkinson, *The Irish Liber Hymnorum* (2 vols.; London: Henry Bradshaw Society, 1898), II, p. 67. Compare text and glosses of the *Amra* with *Adomnan's Life of Columba* III, 18 (Anderson and Anderson, *Adomnan's Life*, pp. 502-503) on a three-day visitation of the Holy Spirit to Columba at Iona: 'Moreover, as he afterwards admitted in the presence of a very few men, he saw, openly revealed, many of the secret things that had been hidden since the world began. And almost everything that in the sacred scriptures is dark and most difficult became plain, and was shown more clearly than the day to the eyes of his purest heart. And he lamented that his foster-son Baithene was not there, who...would have written down...a number of interpretations of the sacred books.'

sym-psalms and *dia*-psalms, or he divided them according to the decades of Augustine'. While granting that the glosses on the *Amra* may be no more than the guesswork of later glossators, it is possible that in this instance the glossators were going on genuine tradition. Columba may have been renowned even during his life for such critical work on the Psalter text.

These arguments, however, do not amount to anything like certainty. And there are difficulties to Columban authorship of the Cathach. One derives from the text of Adamnan already cited. If the biblical text of Ps. 33.11 '...*non deficient omni bono*') transcribed by Columba was that given by Adamnan, then the saint was copying an Old Latin Psalter, not the Vulgate which reads *minuentur* where the former has *deficient*. The critical signs (the asterisks and the obeli), too, create difficulty. These, as we shall see below (6.3), as used in the Cathach represent a critical revision of the Gallican text to have it conform with the Irish family of the *Hebraicum*, that is, Jerome's rendering from the Hebrew. It is difficult to assume that these represent the work of Columba. They are more likely to be the work of a school than of an individual. We may finally note that D.H. Wright dates the Cathach to 630 CE, some decades after Columba's death. What is important in our study of the Cathach is not who composed it but what evidence it provides of the biblical text in Ireland and the critical work of the early Irish schools. It is in this light we shall return to it later (6.3).

2.2. *Wax Tablets from Springmount Bog (Seventh Century) (Appendix I)*

Editions: E.C.R. Armstrong and R.A.S. Macalister, 'Wooden Book with Leaves Indented and Waxed Found near Springmount Bog, Co. Antrim', *JRSAI* 50 (1920), pp. 160-66; new edition below, Appendix I, by Dr Maurice Sheehy.

Studies: Armstrong and Macalister, 'Wooden Book'; Henry, *Irish Art*, I, p. 58; J.N. Hillgarth, 'Visigothic Spain and Early Christian Ireland', *PRIA* 62C (1962), pp. 167-94 (p. 183 n. 78, p. 184); D.H. Wright, 'The Tablets from Springmount Bog, a Key to Early Irish Palaeography', *The American Journal of Archaeology* 67 (1963), p. 219 (summary of a paper presented to the Sixty-fourth General meeting of the Archaeological Institute of America at Baltimore, December 1962); CLA Supplement 1684; B. Bischoff, *Latin Palaeography: Antiquity and the Middle Ages* (trans. D. Ó Cróinín and D. Ganz; Cambridge: Cambridge University Press, 1990), p. 14 n. 43; B.T. Schauman, 'The

Emergence and Progress of Irish Script to the Year 700' (PhD disser-
tation, University of Toronto, 1974), pp. 308-10; B. Schauman, 'Early
Irish Manuscripts: The Art of the Scribes', *Expedition* (The University
Museum Magazine of Archaeology/Anthropology, University of
Pennsylvania) 21 (1979), pp. 33-47 (35-37); T. Julian Brown, 'The
Irish Element in the Insular System of Scripts to circa A.D. 850', in
H. Löwe (ed.), *Die Iren und Europa im Frühmittelalter* (2 vols.; Stutt-
gart: Klett-Cotta, 1982), I, pp. 101-19 (104); T. Julian Brown, 'The
Oldest Irish Manuscripts and their Late Antique Background', in P. Ní
Chatháin and M. Richter (eds.), *Irland und Europa: Ireland and
Europe. Die Kirche im Frühmittelalter. The Early Church* (Stuttgart:
Klett-Cotta, 1984), pp. 311-27 (312, 320, 321); W. O'Sullivan, 'The
Palaeographical Background to the Book of Kells', in F. O'Mahony
(ed.), *The Book of Kells: Proceedings of a Conference at Trinity Col-
lege Dublin 6–9 September 1992* (Atlanta: Scholars Press, 1994),
pp. 175-82 (177-79).

These tablets were found in Springmount Bog, about half a mile from
the village of Clough, Co. Antrim, and seven miles north of Ballymena.
They were purchased by the National Museum of Ireland in 1914 from
Mr W. Gregg of Clough. They probably come from an ancient monastery.

The tablets contain the text of Psalms 30–32 (in the Vulgate numbering). The text is Gallican, with some readings due to the influence of
the Old Latin, and others, arising, it would appear, from carelessness in
transcription or from the fact that the writer depended on his memory.

The tablets were probably used in primary instruction, to initiate a
pupil into the arts of reading and writing through the Psalter, as was the
custom (cf. 1.b above). The scribe in this instance was probably the
schoolmaster. The purpose of the tablets will explain the inaccuracies
of transcription.

The original editors made no attempt to date the tablets. Dr Bernhard
Bischoff, in a letter to J.N. Hillgarth, noted that the script of the tablets
has the same cursive characteristics as the fragments of Isidore in MS
St. Gall 1399 a. 1 (seventh century) and Codex Usserianus Primus
(Trinity College, Dublin 55; beginning of seventh century), both of
which are in Irish script. The tablets would thus be of a seventh-century
date. In a more detailed study, D.H. Wright dated them to about 600 CE.

Since Wright's contribution studies on the palaeography of the tablets
have been made by T. Julian Brown (1982, 1984), W. O'Sullivan
(1994), and particularly by B. Schauman (1974, 1979). With regard to

the date to be assigned to them, Bischoff,[40] with reference to Wright,[41] says that they may be dated around 600. According to Schauman[42] the archaic features of the script argue against a date as late as the seventh century and in favour of a rather early date for the tablets. In her opinion it is not unreasonable to place them in the sixth century, and indeed, she believes they may well represent a type of hand common in Ireland as early as St Patrick's day. In T. Julian Brown's opinion[43] the tablets cannot be dated by internal evidence and it is perhaps enough to ascribe them to the first half of the seventh century.

In these tablets we possibly have the oldest extant specimen of Irish writing. They provide precious evidence that even at this early date pupils were being initiated into the arts of reading and writing through the Gallican text of the Psalter, not through the Old Latin. And, in fact, it is the Gallican text, and it alone, we find as the biblical text used in all later Irish commentaries.

2.3. *Psalm Headings*

In the Hebrew text of the Bible, headings are prefixed to all but 34 of the psalms. These headings or titles tell us of the poetic nature of the piece; the author or the person to whom it is ascribed or with whom it is associated; the presumed occasion of its composition; the kind of instrument and air to which it is to be sung; its liturgical use, for example (Ps. 3): 'A psalm of David when he fled from Absolom his son.' The Greek Septuagint and Latin renderings took over these headings and added some more.

The Syrian Church rejected the psalm headings as non-authentic. The Latin Church found them insufficient for an understanding of the psalms, particularly for a Christian understanding of them. When the Jewish Psalter became the Prayer Book of the Christian Church it was natural that the psalms came to be related to Christ, to the Church and to Christian life. It was difficult to use them as Christian prayer while looking on them as speaking of events in the life of Israel. This gave rise to psalm headings which interpreted or applied the psalms in different ways. In the Latin Church alone at least six series of such psalm

---

40. *Latin Palaeography*, p. 14 n. 43.
41. 'The Tablets from Springmount Bog', p. 219.
42. 'Early Irish Manuscripts', p. 37.
43. 'The Irish Element', p. 104.

headings (*tituli Psalmorum*) were composed, each with its own special tradition behind it. These have been collected from manuscripts, studied and edited by Dom Pierre Salmon in his excellent work *Les 'Tituli Psalmorum' des manuscrits latins*. The first of these series given by Dom Salmon is that of St Columba (studied below, 2.3.a). Series II is that of St Augustine of Canterbury. Series III is one inspired by the Writings of St Jerome. Series IV is translated from the Greek; it is derived from the commentary of Eusebius of Caesarea. Series V is inspired by Origen while series VI, the Cassiodorus series, represents an adaptation of the excerpts of Cassiodorus's commentary made by Bede (see 2.3.c below). The Cassiodorus series has been edited by Dom Salmon from two Milan Psalters and from the Psalter of Nonantola (Vat. lat. 84, tenth to eleventh centuries), which carry the Roman Psalter. (For the use of some of its headings in Ireland see 2.25 below.) Some Psalters have more than one series of psalm headings, for example, that of Nonantola has series I, III and VI. Here we treat only of those series of psalm headings which are of interest for the study of the Psalter in Ireland.

An excellent study of the history and theology behind these headings has been made by Liam G. Walsh, O.P., 'The Christian Prayer of the Psalms according to the Tituli Psalmorum of the Latin Manuscripts' (Pars Dissertationis ad Lauream in Facultate S. Theologiae apud Pontificiam Universitatem S. Thomae de Urbe; Dublin, 1967); earlier in Placid Murray, O.S.B. (ed.), *Studies in Pastoral Liturgy*, III (Maynooth: The Furrow Trust; Dublin: Gill and Son, 1967).

a. *The Columba Series of Psalm Headings*

> MSS, Editions and Studies: Dom Pierre Salmon, *Les 'Tituli Psalmorum' des manuscrits latins* (Collectanea Biblica Latina, 12; Rome: Abbaye de Saint-Jerôme; Vatican City: Libreria Vaticana, 1959), pp. 47-74; H.J. Lawlor, 'The Cathach of St Columba', *PRIA* 33 C (1916), pp. 413-36.

This series of psalm headings was given its name by Dom Salmon for the reason that the oldest MS in which they are found is the Cathach of St Columba. It is also, to judge from the evidence of manuscripts, the earliest and the one most widely attested to of all the six. In Dom Salmon's view an the witnesses to this series derive, through England and the insular missions on the Continent, from a text used in Ireland in the sixth century. Its earlier history is, of course, another question. This

series is generally found with the Gallican Psalter text. Notable exceptions are the Codex Amiatinus (written about 700 CE at Wearmouth-
Jarrow) and Karlsruhe Cod. Aug. CVII in both of which the series is
found with the *Hebraicum*. These two MSS, however, derive from an
insular ancestor (see 5.4 below), which was close to the exemplar of the
Cathach; their psalm headings are derived from a Gallican text.

A characteristic of the St Columba series is its Christological orientation. Most of the psalms are understood as spoken by Christ, by the
Church or by the apostles: *Vox Christi ad Patrem* (Pss. 3, 6, 12 etc.),
Christus ad Patrem (5); *Vox ecclesiae post baptismum* (22), *Ecclesia
laudem dicit Christo* (9); *Vox apostolorum, quando Christus passus est*
(59).[44] Only 24 psalms are placed on the lips of the psalmist-prophet
himself and even then for the greater part only to announce the work of
Christ, for example, *Propheta adventum Christi adnuntiat* (67). This
manner of looking on the psalms as prophecies of Christ and his work
is exactly what we find in the introduction to the *Old Irish Treatise* on
the Psalter (no. 11 below.)

A number of the headings of the Columba series carry liturgical
instructions, bearing especially on the reading of a particular psalm in
conjunction with a stated book or passage of Scripture, for example,
Psalm 2: *Legendus ad evangelium Lucae*; Psalm 27: *Legendus ad lectionem Danihelis prophetae*; Psalm 44; *Legendus ad evangelium
Matthei, de regina Austri* (Mt. 12.42). A study of these particular
rubrics may shed some light on the use of certain psalms in the liturgy
and possibly also on the use of certain other readings from Scripture in
the Divine Office.

Each of the six series of psalm headings has a tradition behind it and
depends on a particular understanding of the psalms. Series III-VI are
connected with well-known commentators on the psalms. The exact

---

44. Cf. Hilary, *Tractatus in Psalmum I, Clavis sive Introitus in Psalmum I.
Argumentum* 1 (*PL* 9, cols. 247-48): '*Principalis haec in psalmis intelligentia est,
ex cuius persona, vel in quem ea quae dicta sint intelligi opporteant, posse discernere. Non eni—uniformis et indiscreta est eorum constitutio, ut non et auctores
habeant, et genera diversa. Invenimus enim in his frequenter personam Dei Patris
solere proponi, ut in octogesimo octavo psalmo, cu—dicitur:* Exaltavi electum de
plebe meo... *Personam vero Filii in plurimis fere introduci: ut in decimo septimo
psalmo:* Populus quem non cognovi, servavit mihi; *et in vicesimo primo:* Diviserunt
sibi vestimenta mea...'

tradition that gave rise to the St Columba series has yet to be determined. Some of the headings can be connected with patristic exegesis.
Psalm 1, for instance: *De Joseph dicit qui corpus Christi sepelivit* can
be traced back through Jerome (*Commentarioli in Psalmos*) to Tertullian (*De spectaculis* 3. 4). The headings for Psalms 7, 8 and 13 also
have points of contact with earlier patristic and liturgical tradition.
Those for Psalms 48, 50, 56, 60, 86, 90 and 115 can be compared in
certain respects with Augustine's *Enarrationes in Psalmos*. Further
research may determine in greater detail the exegetical origins of the
series and its bearing on other Irish exegetical works.

b. *The Theodorean Psalm Headings*

> MSS and Edition: Willem Bloemendaal, *The Headings of the Psalms in
> the East Syrian Church* (Leiden: E.J. Brill, 1960) (critical edition of
> Syriac titles without translation).

> Studies: Bloemendaal, *The Headings*, pp. 1-31; R.L. Ramsay, 'Theo-
> dore of Mopsuestia and St Columba on the Psalms', *ZCP* 8 (1912), pp.
> 421-26; R.L. Ramsay, 'Theodore of Mopsuestia in England and
> Ireland', *ZCP* 8 (1912), pp. 452-97 (452-65); R. Devreesse, *Essai sur
> Théodore de Mopsueste* (Studi e testi, 141; Vatican City: Biblica
> Apostolica Vaticana, 1948); R. Devreesse, *Le commentaire de Théo-
> dore de Mopsueste sur les Psaumes (I–LXXX)* (Studi e Testi, 93;
> Vatican City: Biblioteca Apostolica Vaticana, 1939), p. xxvii.

The headings to the psalms in the Hebrew Bible do not appear to have
belonged to their original composition; they were most probably added
at a much later time. In his commentary on the psalms Theodore of
Mopsuestia rejected most of the psalm headings of both the Hebrew
Text and the Septuagint as not inspired and false. In his commentary
Theodore begins his exposition of each psalm by considering it first as a
whole; he gives what he thinks is the guiding idea and the meaning of
the psalm, that is, its *argumentum* (in Greek: *hypothesis*; see his introduction to Psalm 32.[45]

The East Syrian Church also rejected the Hebrew and Greek psalm
headings. They are consequently not found in their Psalters. In their
stead new headings were introduced, drawn from or dependent on the
commentary of Theodore. This Theodorean series of psalm headings,

---

45. Devreesse, *Essai*, pp. 69-70.

found in a number of Syriac Psalters, has been collected and critically edited by Willem Bloemendaal (*The Headings*), with a good introduction but unfortunately without translation.

At an early period a Latin translation of psalm headings drawn from Theodore's commentary must also have been made. We find them in the *Tituli Psalmorum* attributed to Bede, in the Milan commentary (2.7 below) and in other Latin works connected with Ireland. The origins of this series remain to be determined.

c. *The Work* De Titulis Psalmorum *Attributed to Bede*

MSS: See F. Stegmüller, *Repertorium Biblicum Medii Aevi* (2 vols.; Madrid: Consejo Superior de Investigaciones Científicas, 1940–80), II, no. 1665 (pp. 189-90). See also below p. [297]. Edition: *PL* 93, cols. 477-1098.

Studies: H. Weisweiler, 'Die handschriftlichen Vorlagen zum Erstdruck von Pseudo-Beda, In Psalmorum Librum Exegesis', *Biblica* 18 (1937), pp. 197-204; Dom Pierre Salmon, *Les 'Tituli Psalmorum' des manuscrits latins* (Collectanea Biblical Latina, 12; Rome: Abbaye de Saint-Jerôme; Vatican City; Libreria Vaticana, 1959), pp. 47-48; R.L. Ramsay, 'Theodore of Mopsuestia in England and Ireland', *ZCP* 8 (1912), pp. 452-97 (453-58); J.W. Bright and R.L. Ramsay, 'Notes on the "Introductions" of the West-Saxon Psalms', *JTS* 13 (1912), pp. 520-58; see Stegmüller, *Repertorium*; see now B. Fischer, 'Bedae de titulis psalmorum liber', in J. Autenrieth and F. Brünholzt (eds.), *Festschrift Bernhard Bischoff zu seinem 65 Geburtstag* (Stuttgart: Hiersemann, 1971), pp. 90-110.

Among the works of Bede (673–735 CE) printed in the Basel edition reproduced by Migne there is one entitled *In Psalmorum librum exegesis*. In this work the exegesis of each psalm is divided into three sections: (i) a brief *Argumentum*, (ii) an *Explanatio* dealing with the psalm in general, followed by (iii) the *Commentarius* proper. The third section goes only as far as Psalm 121 whereas the *Argumenta* and *Explanationes* continue to the end of the Psalter.

The commentary itself has nothing to do with Bede and its association with the *Argumenta* and *Explanationes*, which originally circulated independently of it, is purely fortuitous. It is only these latter which interest us here. The *Explanationes* depend almost entirely on the introductions which Cassiodorus prefixed to the psalms in his commentary (see 2.12 below). The *Argumenta*, which occur for all 150, are composite. Though brief, each *Argumentum* can be divided into three sections.

Section (a), a historical explanation, is present for every psalm except Psalm 87 and almost invariably stands first. There the psalm in question is understood as speaking of the trials of David, of Hezekiah or of the Maccabees. Section (b), introduced by *aliter*, gives the mystical meaning and occasionally a liturgical note. What we find in this section is simply the St Columba psalm headings, with occasional variants from the other witnesses of the series. Section (c), when present, gives a brief moral application, drawing on Jerome or Arnobius.

Ramsay ascribes the *Argumenta* and *Explanationes* to Bede, on the grounds that in the *Old-Irish Treatise on the Psalter* (2.11 below) both are cited for Psalm 1 as the work of Bede.[46] The same writer notes that the combination of historical, christological (mystical) and moral interpretation found in the *Argumenta* also forms the basis of a number of Irish homilies, for example, some of those in *Leabhar Breac*. The structure of these *Argumenta*, then, is scarcely arbitrary; it would seem to derive from an approach to Scripture very much at home in Ireland.

My chief concern is with the (a) sections or the historical explanations. Ramsay has shown that they are all Theodorean; in his view they are borrowed directly from the Milan commentary (2.7 below), even if occasionally rephrased.[47] If Bede is the real author of the *Argumenta* it would follow that the commentary now found in the Milan Codex was used in the British Isles in the seventh century, or at latest in the eighth.

While this is highly probable, we should not too hastily conclude that the 'Theodorean' headings depend directly on the Milan commentary. Even though the psalm headings of the latter reproduce the exegesis of Theodore, they differ more than once from the headings—equally Theodorean—of Bede. Devreesse has wisely remarked that the headings (titles) and the *Argumenta* of the Milan commentary are better considered apart from the commentary proper.[48] It is very probable that the former once existed independently of the commentary itself. Both they and the Bedan (c) sections of the *Argumenta* represent a Latin series of Theodorean psalm headings, or rather two series differing somewhat in details. When, where and by whom this series of Latin Theodorean psalm headings was made, whether in the British Isles or elsewhere, is hard to determine. They may have been made directly from a Latin translation of Theodore's commentary. They could depend

46. Ramsay, 'Theodore of Mopsuestia', pp. 460-62.
47. Ramsay, 'Theodore of Mopsuestia', p. 454.
48. Devreesse, *Le commentaire*, p. xxvii.

on general Theodorean exegesis. They could even have been made from some Syriac text.

The latter, however, would not have been the Syriac Series of headings edited by Bloemendaal. While agreeing with these in substance, the Latin headings are more elaborate. Whatever the origins of the Latin series of Theodorean headings, we may presume that, like the St Columba series, it already existed before it was incorporated into the Bedan *Tituli Psalmorum*.

2.4. *Catena on the Psalms of Codex Palatino-Vaticanus 68 (Eighth Century) (Appendix II)*

MS: Vatican, Pal. lat. 68, fols. 1-46 (Pss. 39.11–151.7).

Editions (partial and facsimiles): W.M. Lindsay, *Early Irish Minuscule Script* (Oxford: James Parker & Co., 1910), pl. 12 (fol. 46); E.A. Lowe, *CLA*, I no. 78 (facs.; portion of fol. 27v); below Appendix II (fols. 1; 46r). Complete edition: M. McNamara (ed.), *Glossa in Psalmos: The Hiberno-Latin Gloss on the Psalms of Codex Palatinus Latinus 68 (Psalms 39.11–151)*. Critical edition of the text together with Introduction and Source Analysis (Vatican City: Biblioteca Apostolica Vaticana, 1986). Introduction, pp. 165-238 in this volume.

Studies: Bischoff, 'Wendepunkte', p. 105. For further studies and editions of glosses see Kenney, *Sources*, p. 637 (no. 465); Lindsay, *Early Irish Miniscule*, pp. 67-70 (study of abbreviations).

The beginning of this work is lost. The text now opens abruptly with a comment on the last words of Ps. 39.11: '*a concilio multo idest toto Israel praedicabo*'. It ends with comments on the apocryphal Psalm 151. The commentary has the form of a catena, that is, a series of citations from earlier authorities. The greater part of these are from a text almost identical with the Milan commentary (2.7 below) although there are occasional differences. This text might thus help in the emendation of the occasionally corrupt Milan codex. It also contains a number of excerpts from Jerome. The presence of passages from Hilary has also been noted.

Each psalm has its Vulgate heading, with occasional additions. Next follow the opening words of the psalm, which are connected (by *haeret*) with some verse in the preceding psalm.[49] Other psalms headings fol-

49. For this use of *haeret* as an Irish 'symptom' see Bischoff, 'Wendepunkte...', no. 22.

low: the mystical headings of the St Columba series (2.3.a above), headings relating to a psalm to an incident in the life of David, and the 'Theodorean', headings of Bede and the Milan commentary (2.3.c above), thus combining the mystical headings referring the psalms to Christ or the Church and the 'historical' headings referring them to David or later Jewish history. In the commentary itself interest in the historical aspect predominates, the psalm being interpreted as referring to David or to Jewish history.

The Codex Palatinus was written in the eighth century. The colophon reads: *Sicut portus opportunus navigantibus, ita vorsus* (= *versus*) *novissimus scribentibus. Edilberict filius berictfridi scripsit hanc glosam.* Edilberict was a Northumbrian scribe who may have been educated in Ireland. The text contains both Irish and Northumbrian glosses, both running continuously with the text but distinguished from it by apices. The manner in which the glosses are incorporated into the text suggests that our MS may be only a copy of Edilberict's work.

It is difficult to say whether the original was composed in Northumbria or in Ireland. In either case the work is evidence of the learning of both regions. It shows the early presence of the Milan commentary in Ireland. For this and other reasons the text should be published *in toto*.

2.5. *The Abbreviated Psalter of the Book of Cerne (Eighth Century)*

MS: Cambridge University Library, Ll. 1. 10, fols. 87b-98a; Headed: 'Hoc argumentum forsarii (i.e. versarii) oedhelwald episcopus decerpsit.' Begins: '*Beatus uir qui non abit*' (Ps. 1.1).

Edition: A.B. Kuypers, *The Prayer Book of Aedeluald commonly called the Book of Cerne* (Cambridge: Cambridge University Press, 1902), pp. 174-98.

Studies (of the book in general): Kenney, *Sources*, pp. 720-22 (no. 578); Henry, *Irish Art*, II, pp. 60-63.

MS Ll. 1. 10 of Cambridge University Library, that is, 'the Book of Cerne', contains within one cover three originally independent codices. Here we are concerned only with the central one, known as 'The Book of Aethelwald the Bishop', a work of 99 leaves. In fols. 1-40a we have the accounts of the passion and resurrection of Christ from each of the four Gospels. Then (fols. 40b-87b) comes a collection of 74 prayers; this is followed (on fols. 87b-98a) by the abbreviated Psalter which is the present item. After this comes an apocryphal dialogue between

Christ and Adam and Eve in *limbo patrum*,[50] ending on the last folio (99b) of our MS (in its present state). The original work was presumably longer.

The surviving copy of the Prayer Book of Aedeluald would appear to have been written in northern England, most probably in Lindisfarne. Mlle Henry finds its decoration similar to that of the Vatican Gospel-book MS Barberini lat. 570 which was written for a certain Uigbald, probably Wigbald, Abbot of Lindisfarne from 760 and 803. She dates the transcription and decoration of both works between the years 770 and 790. The decoration links both closely with Ireland, and in Lindisfarne there were then both Irish scribes and artists. The Aedeluald whose name the book bears was probably Aedeluald, Bishop of Lindisfarne from 724 to 740. Our present text would be a copy of an earlier one made for him.

The reason for including evidence from the Prayer Book of Aedeluald here is the undoubtedly close relationship it has with Celtic Christianity. The work, in fact, is accepted as one of the chief representatives of the Celtic liturgy. The abbreviated Psalter is composed of verses from consecutive psalms, strung together so as to form a continuous prayer (e.g. Pss. 1.1, 2; 2.11; 3.4; 5.2 etc.). We have another early example of such an abbreviation of the Psalter in the *Collectio Psalterii Bedae* found in Migne's edition of Alcuin's works (*PL* 101, cols. 569-79). I shall consider a later example from Ireland below (2.24). The abbreviated Psalter of the Book of Cerne, like the other items in the Prayer Book of Aedeluald, was most probably intended for private devotion.

Despite the Irish connections of Aedeluald's Prayer Book, the text of this abbreviation of the Psalter is not Gallican but rather the *Romanum*. The Old Latin Psalter of the Roman type was probably brought to England by St Augustine of Canterbury in 597 CE. It later became very common in England but does not appear to have been used in Ireland (see 5.2 below). The use of the Roman rather than the Gallican Psalter text seems to indicate that this abridgment of the Psalter is of English origin.

---

50. I make a study of this work in *The Apocrypha in the Irish Church* (Dublin Institute for Advanced Studies, 1975), pp. 72-74 (60). The apocryphal piece has prayers composed from texts of the Psalter; these are all from the Old Latin, not from the Vulgate.

2.6. *Turin Fragments of the Latin Translation of Theodore's Commentary on the Psalms (Eighth–Ninth Century)*

MS: Turin, Biblioteca Nazionale, MS F.IV.I, fasc. 5-6.

Edition: Devreesse, *Le commentaire*, pp. 85-111, 112-259.

Studies: Devreesse, *Le commentaire*, pp. xiii-xxiv; R. Devreesse, 'Le commentaire de Théodore de Mopsueste sur les psaumes', *RB* 37 (1928), pp. 340-66; 38 (1929), pp. 35-62; Kenney, *Sources*, pp. 665 (no. 515); Lowe, *CLA*, IV, no. 452.

In Devreesse's words these are two rather large fragments of one and the same book written in two columns to the page (of 44-47 lines) in an insular hand of the eighth or ninth century, like that of Amb. C 301 inf. (2.7 below).[51] Fasc. 5 contains eight leaves; fasc. 6 has six. Devreesse gives the order of the fragments and their contents as follows: (fasc. 6, fol. 1-6a) a continuous commentary on Pss. 13: 7-16; 15; (fasc. 6, fol. 6b) the *argumentum* of Psalm 37; (fasc. 6, fol. 6c-d) the commentary of St Augustine on Psalms 57 and 62; (fasc. 5, fol. 7-14a) sequence of interpretations of different verses of Psalms 17 (argument) to 40.13a.[52]

The contents of fasc. 5 are practically identical with MS Amb. C 301 inf., fols. 4a-13d. Both contain portions of a Latin translation of the genuine commentary of Theodore of Mopsuestia. Fasc. 6 is composed almost entirely of fragments of a Latin translation of the genuine commentary of Theodore, of which practically identical texts occur in Amb. C 301 inf. These Turin fragments carry the same Latin translation of Theodore as do the corresponding sections of the Milan Codex. This could be explained by assuming that both are copies of the same original. Lowe, however, thinks that the Turin fragments may be a direct copy of Milan Amb. C 301 inf.

The manuscript of which the Turin fragments are survivors belonged, like Amb. C 301 inf., to the monastery of Bobbio. It was written either in the Bobbio scriptorium or in Ireland; probably at Bobbio according to Lowe. Both the Turin fragments and the Milan Codex show that the genuine commentary of Theodore (or at least portions of it) was known and studied in Irish monastic circles. We shall return to this point in our study Amb. C 301 inf.

---

51. Devreesse, *Le commentaire*, p. xxiv.
52 *Le commentaire*, p. xxiv.

2.7. *The Milan Commentary, Amb. C. 301 inf (Eighth–Ninth Century)*

MS: Milan, The Ambrosian Library, MS C 301 inf. (146 folios).

Editions: G.I. Ascoli (ed.), *Il codice irlandese della Ambrosiana* (= Archivio glottologico italiano, 5; Rome: Loescher, 1878, pp. 1-160) (a careful diplomatic edition of the text and glosses); R.I. Best, *The Commentary on the Psalms with glosses in Old Irish preserved in the Ambrosian Library*. Collotype facsimile with introduction (Dublin: RIA, 1936) (with an excellent introduction); *Thes. Pal.*, I, pp. 7-483 (text and English translation of the glosses together with their Latin context). Devreesse, *Le commentaire* (contains the genuine Theodorean material found on fols. 4-13 and 14-39; with valuable introduction). L. De Coninck and J. d'Hont (eds.), *Theodori Mopsuesteni Expositionis in Psalmos Iuliano Aeclanensi interprete in Latinum versae quae supersunt* (CCSL, 88A; Turnhout: Brepols, 1977): A critical edition of Julian's Latin translation with the Epitome of this, from all known texts, together with a lengthy introduction (pp. vii-xlv) on the various questions relating to the work.

Studies: R.L. Ramsay, 'Theodore of Mopsuestia and St Columban on the Psalms', *ZCP* 8 (1912), pp. 421-51; and 'Theodore of Mopsuestia in England and Ireland', *ZCP* 8 (1912), pp. 452-97; A. Vaccari, 'Nuova opera di Giuliano eclanese: Commento ai Salmi', *La civiltà cattolica* 67 (1916), pp. 578-93; A. Vaccari, 'Il salterio ascoliano e Giuliano eclanese', *Biblica* 4 (1923), pp. 337-55; A. Vaccari, 'Note lessicali', *Archivium Latinitatis Medii Aevi* (Bulletin du Cange, 1; Paris, 1924), pp. 184-86 (185); Dom G. Morin, 'Le "Liber S. Columbani in Psalmos" et le Ms. Ambros. C. 301 inf...', *RBén* 38 (1926), pp. 164-77; R. Devreesse, 'Chaines éxégetiques grecques', *Supplément* to *Dictionnaire de la Bible*, vol. 1 (1928), col. 1131; Devreesse, *Le commentaire*, pp. xxi-xxvi; Lowe, *CLA* III, no. 326; further studies in Kenney, *Sources*, pp. 200-203 (no. 47). 'Irish Transmission of Late Antique Learning: The Case of Theodore of Mopsuestia's Commentary on the Psalms', in P. Ní Chatháin and M. Richter (eds.), *Texts and Transmission* (Dublin: Four Courts Press, forthcoming). The contents of this large manuscript are as follows:

I.   (fol. 1). Two Old-Irish poems (*Thes. Pal.*, II, pp. 291-92).

II. (fol. 2a-b). Jerome's preface to the Gallican Psalter: *Incipit praefatio (Hieronimi) psalmorum...Psalterium Romae dudum possitus...de purissimo (ebreo) fonte potare*. With Irish glosses (Ascoli [ed.], *Il codice irlandese*, pp. 3-4; *Thes. Pal.*, I, pp. 7-8). For the preface see Stegmüller, *Repertorium*, I, no. 430.

III.   (fol. 2b-c). Pseudo-Bede's preface to the Psalter: *Incipit pro-*
        logus psalmorum. Dauid filius Iessae...canticum graduum XV.
        With Irish glosses (Ascoli [ed.], *Il codice irlandese*, pp. 4-5;
        Thes. Pal., I, pp. 8-9). For preface see Stegmüller, *Reperto-*
        rium, I, no. 414.

IV.   (fol. 2c-3a). Jerome's preface to his translation of the psalms
        from the Hebrew: *Incipit prologus Hirunimi ad Suffro-*
        nium...Scio quosdam putare psalterium...laudem vel uituper-
        ationem tecum esse commonem. Finit. Amen. With Irish
        glosses (Ascoli, *Il codice irlandese*, pp. 5-8; *Thes. Pal.*, I, pp.
        9-10). For preface see Stegmüller, *Repertorium*, I, no. 443.

V.   (fol. 3a-4a 16). St Basil's preface to the Psalter in the transla-
        tion of Rufinus: *Incipit praefatio psalmorum uel laus psalterii.*
        Hirunimus dicit: Omnis scriptura diuinitus inspirata...uide-
        amus tandem quid etiam ipsa psalmi indicentur initia. Finit.
        Amen. Finit. Without Irish glosses. For preface see Stegmüller,
        Repertorium, I, no. 411 (edited from other MSS in *PL* 36, cols.
        63-66).

VI.   (fol. 4a 17-21). An invocation and a commentary on Ps.
        16.11b.

VII.   (fol. 4a 22-13d 20). Commentary on Psalm 17 (*argumentum*)
        to Ps. 40.13a.

VIII.   (fol. 14a-146). Continuous commentary on Psalms 1–150.

The Latin text and the glosses, apart from a few additions by a corrector, are the work of a single scribe who in the colophon signs himself
'Diarmait': 'The end. Amen. Diarmait has written it. Pray for that sin-
ner.' This same Diarmait also wrote the Latin text and Irish glosses of a
commentary on Mark, fragments of which are now in Turin.[53]

In our commentary on the psalms (fol. 44b, gloss 10), Diarmait himself refers to the exposition of Mark which he ascribes to Jerome,
although it is very probably the work of an Irishman Cummeanus
(seventh century).[54] Two native authorities, Coirbre and Mailgaimrid
(cf. 4.4 below) are cited in the Irish glosses on the Milan commentary.
The latter, in the opinion of many, is almost certainly to be identified

53. Cf. Kenney, *Sources*, pp. 660-61.
54. Cf. Bischoff, 'Wendepunkte', no. 27.

with the Mailgaimrid *scriba optimus et ancorita, abbas Bennc[h]air* (Bangor), who died in 839. The scribe of the Milan Codex may possibly be the Diarmait grandson of Áed Rón, described as *anchorita et religionis doctor totius Hiberniae*, who died in 825. The language of the glosses dates the work to the beginning of the ninth century, although some glosses seem to be slightly earlier, namely, from the end of the eighth. These were probably copied by Diarmait from his exemplar. Scholars are divided on whether the manuscript was copied in Ireland and brought thence to Bobbio or whether it was copied at Bobbio itself. Lowe[55] holds that it was written in Ireland, probably at Bangor or possibly in Leinster, while Kenney[56] thinks it was probably written at Bobbio from an exemplar of Irish origin.

In fol. 2 (top) the work is described as *Liber sancti Columbani de Bobio*, whereas in fol. 1, as in a catalogue of the monastery of Bobbio drawn up in 1461, it is presented as a commentary of Jerome. In listing the work as a commentary by Jerome the catalogue of 1461 may very well have been going on very old tradition. Already in the Irish *Eclogae tractatorum in Psalterium* (2.9) of the late eighth century it is extensively cited as a work of Jerome (*hir. in his.*). It may even have been known to Diarmait, its scribe, as a work of Jerome.

In point of fact the only material that can be ascribed to Jerome are items II and IV of the list given above. The commentary material in items VI and VII represents a Latin translation of the commentary of Theodore of Mopsuestia. The authorship of the main commentary of the Milan Codex (fols. 14a to the end, our item VIII) has been the subject of much scholarly debate and thus requires more detailed consideration. Jonas, the biographer of St Columbanus, tells us that while still a young man in Ireland the saint composed a commentary on the psalms in elegant language (*elimato sermone*; see 2.29 below). The fate of this commentary is unknown. No trace of it could be found in the libraries of St Gall or Bobbio in the seventeenth century. In the following century Muratori discovered the Milan commentary and published some extracts from it, refusing to admit it was a work of Jerome. In that same century Domenico Vallarsi suggested that its true author was Columbanus. Later such scholars as Peyron, Zeuss, Nigra and Ascoli agreed with this opinion, Not so, however, B. Krusch in his critical edition of

---

55. *CLA*, III, no. 326.
56. *Sources*, p. 200.

Jonas's *Life of Columbanus*.[57] As early as 1896, and in later studies, G. Mercati pointed out that the Milan commentary derived from the celebrated commentary of Theodore of Mopsuestia. The excellent latinity led him to date the work to the fifth century. While not holding Irish origin as altogether impossible, Mercati doubted it very much. Yet as late as 1912 R.L. Ramsay still defended Columban authorship. While granting that the work was basically Theodorean, Ramsay maintained that the Milan commentary represented an abbreviation of Theodore's work made by Columbanus. In his abbreviation, according to Ramsay, Columbanus removed objectionable features of the original. A new approach was made in 1916 by A. Vaccari who claimed to have identified in Amb. C 301 inf. a lost commentary of Julian, the Pelagian Bishop of Eclanum, or at least an adaptation of Theodore made by Julian. In 1926 Dom G. Morin returned to the assumption of Columban authorship. In his opinion besides the ideas of Julian (who was possibly dependent on Theodore), the Milan Codex contained the commentary, or more precisely the compilation, on the psalms made by St Columbanus.

This was the situation when Robert Devreesse, a specialist on Theodore of Mopsuestia, came to devote his attention to the problem. All students prior to him assumed that the Milan commentary proper (Amb. C 301 inf. fols. 14a-146) is a homogenous work. Devreesse showed that this is not the case. The commentary on Pss. 1.1–16.11a (fols. 14a-39d), he notes, is different from the exposition on the remaining psalms (fols. 39d to the end). The commentary on Pss. 1.1–16.11a is a Latin translation of the genuine commentary of Theodore and represents the same translation as that found in the Turin fragments. Both are copies of the same Latin translation and are in fact the only known texts of this rendering. In the comment on Ps. 16.11 (fol. 39d), however, there occurs a change; cf. Devreesse:

> Here, in the very centre of fol. 39d, exactly at line 23, there is a break; the copyist—for it is the same hand that continues to the end of the volume—has changed his method or, to be more precise, his exemplar. For a few more lines he will remain close enough to the complete translation of Theodore, but for the remainder of the work he will be content to tran-

57. Bruno Krusch (ed.), *Ionae Vitae Sanctorum Columbani, Vedastis, Iohannis* (Hannover: Hahn, 1905), pp. 29-30.

scribe a few abbreviated fragments, often separated from one another by long spaces filled by other forms of exegesis.[58]

Devreesse goes on to remark that for the remainder of the commentary (on Pss. 16.11–150) the exposition proper should be considered apart from the headings and *Argumenta*, which once probably enjoyed an independent existence. Devreesse himself was not particularly interested in the question of the authorship of the commentary on Pss. 16.11b to the end, beyond having proved that it is not the work of Theodore. Its author, he remarks, may well have been Julian of Eclanum. The exposition may also contain traces of the editorial work of Columbanus.

With Mercati, Devreesse agrees that the translation was made in the fifth century and, in his opinion, probably in northern Italy. There, he concludes,[59] it remained until a scribe who had come from Ireland copied it three centuries later.

The question of Columbanus's possible connection with the Milan commentary, in whole or in part, does not concern us here. (I shall return to Columbanus's work later—2.29 below.) I shall concentrate, instead, on certain aspects of Devreesse's position and its implications. To begin with, he accepts that the Milan Codex was written in Bobbio (northern Italy), not in Ireland. This, as we have seen, is by no means certain. No less an authority than Lowe thinks it was written in Ireland. Then again, Devreesse's position presumes that prior to the copy made in northern Italy in the eighth (or ninth) century the commentary, or at least the genuine Theodorean section of it, was unknown in Ireland. This runs counter to our available evidence. If, as is shown by the Theodorean Series of Psalm headings (2.3.b above), Theodorean exegesis was known in the British Isles in the seventh century, there is no reason why the Theodorean section of the Milan commentary should have been unknown. The Vatican Catena on the Psalms (eighth century; 2.4 above), which, we may recall begins only at Psalm 39, proves that the non-Theodorean section of the commentary was known and used in Ireland in the eighth century. The Irish *Eclogae tractatorum in Psalmos* (2.9 below), composed about 800 CE, quotes both the Theodorean and the non-Theodorean portions of the Milan commentary. These are strong grounds for arguing that the composite work of Theodorean and

58. Devreesse, *Le commentaire*, p. xxxvi.
59. Devreesse, *Le commentaire*, p. xxviii.

non-Theodorean material now found in the Milan commentary was used in Ireland prior to the date of the copy transcribed by Diarmait.

This militates against another of Devreesse's assumptions, that is, that the change of exemplar and the change from the genuine commentary of Theodore to a non-Theodorean work at fol. 39d (Ps. 16.11) was due to Diarmait, the scribe of the Milan text. The composite work would appear to have been known in Ireland before the Milan copy was made; Diarmait probably followed a single exemplar throughout. Where and when did this composite commentary originate? Some light is probably shed on this problem by the glosses on the *Hebraicum* of the Irish Double Psalter of St Ouen (tenth century; 2.18 below). These glosses on Psalms 17 onwards are from the Milan commentary. Glosses on a number of the earlier psalms (Pss. 8, 9, 10, 15 and 16), however, have been shown not to derive from the Milan commentary, but from some other, unidentified source. A fuller study of the St Ouen glosses should prove rewarding. Even with Devreesse's authoritative study the last word on the Milan commentary had not yet been spoken.

The critical edition by De Coninck and d'Hont of what remains of Julian's translation, and the Epitome of it represented a major step forward. The author, date and place of the Epitome of Julian's work, which constitutes the greater part of the Milan Commentary, still remain unclear. It is generally assumed that the author of the Epitome, if not Julian himself, was not an Irishman. The date must have been between 1120 or so (the date of Julian's translation) and c. 700 (date of first attested use of it in the Commentary in Pal. lat. 68). P. Ó Néill favours an origin in Visigothic Spain or Southern France.[60]

The Latin text of Amb. C 301 inf. is heavily glossed in Irish. These glosses probably represent notes made by a teacher for the instruction of his students. They are thus important evidence of the manner in which the Psalter was expounded in some eighth-century Irish school, probably at Bangor or in some place associated with Bangor. The glosses range from a simple translation of the Latin to remarks on textual corruptions, on the biblical text used, and so on. Unfortunately, they have so far been studied almost exclusively from the philological point of view. However, they deserve serious attention also as evidence

---

60. P. Ó Néill, 'Irish Transmission of Late Antiquity Learning: The Case of Theodore of Mopsuestia's Commentary on the Psalms', in *Ireland and Europe: Texts and Transmission* (Dublin: Four Courts Press, forthcoming).

of early Irish learning. I shall later (Section 4; 6.2 below) consider them in a small way under this aspect.

2.8. *The Breviarium in Psalmos of Pseudo-Jerome*

MSS: In Stegmüller, *Repertorium*, III, p. 60 (no. 3333); the oldest of the MSS are from the ninth century.

Edition: *PL* 26, cols. 871-1346.

Studies: E. Dekkers, *Clavis patrum latinorum* (Turnhout: Brepols, 1995), p. 218 (no. 629); G. Morin (ed.), in *S. Hieronymi Presbyteri Opera. Pars I: Opera Exegetica* (CCSL, 72; Turnhout: Brepols, 1959), p. 166.

The *Breviarium in Psalmos* found in MSS as a work of Jerome, and printed in Migne with Jerome's other works, is pseudo-hieronymian. Among other sources it makes use of Jerome's *Commentarioli in psalmos* and of his *Tractatus sive homiliae in psalmos*. It also draws on other authors. Its present form, which may in fact result from a long period of development, shows certain Irish characteristics, such as the repeated designation of certain verses of the psalms as *vox Christi, vox ecclesiae*. (See the Columba series of psalm headings, 2.3.a above.) This exegesis is Christocentric. The psalms are preceded by headings which differ from any of Dom Salmon's six series (2.3 above). Yet in a number of instances these headings and the commentary itself are close to the exegesis implicit in the St Columba series. In the commentary on Psalm 15 the *Breviarium* incorporates Jerome's *Commentariolus* but then goes on, in Irish fashion, to speak of the inscription (*titulus*) which was on the cross in 'the three languages', Hebrew, Greek and Latin. The *Commentarioli* are also incorporated into the commentary on Psalm 21. In the comment on Ps. 21.7 (*Ego sum vermis et non homo*) the *Breviarium* gives Jerome's reference to Isa. 41.14 but goes on to explain this through Christ's virginal birth (without a father, like the worms!) exactly in the manner found in the Irish Augustine's *De mirabilibus sacrae scripturae* (3.2).[61]

---

61. The Irish Augustine possibly depends for this on the genuine Augustine or on Ambrose, both of whom make mention of it. (I owe this information to Dom Gerard MacGinty, O.S.B.). Even if this were so, use of the material in the *Breviarium* would still be suggestive of Irish influence. Dom Bonifatius Fischer assures me that the *Breviarium in Psalmos* in its present form is an Irish product; see now Fischer, 'Bedae de titulis psalmorum liber', p. 93); see also H.J. Frede, *Pelagius,*

2.9. *Eclogae Tractatorum in Psalterium (c. 800 CE) (Appendix III)*

MSS: St Gall, Stiftsbibl. 261, pp. 147-274, saec. IX[1] (see A. Bruckner, *Scriptoria medii aevi Helvetica*, III (Genf: Roto-Sadag, 1938, 88); in this MS the *Eclogae* are preceded by excerpts from Jerome, Eucherius and others on the Psalms: Jerome, Epp. 30 and 26); Munich, Clm 14715, fols. 1r.-56v, saec. IX[2] (see B. Bischoff, *Die südostdeutschen Schreibschulen und Bibliotheken in der Karolingerzeit*, I [Wiesbaden: Otto Harrassowitz, 3rd edn, 1974], p. 253). The first and last folios of this MS are missing; fol. 1 begins towards the end of the prologue = St Gall, p. 156 (the exposition of Ps. 1 begins on fol. 2v).

(prol.) Inc.: *Prophetia est aspiratio divina, que eventus rerum...*
Expl.: *...ex brevitate sermonum longumque sensum habent.*
(Ps. 1.1) Inc: *'Beatus vir'. Moralis psalmus est...*
Expl.: *...Sic multis divisionibus per mare huius seculi transitur ad dominum.*

Editions: Below Appendix III (fols. 1-3; 21, 36 of Clm 14715: part of prologue, and exposition on Pss. 1.1–2.1; 35–40; 67.28–70.15); critical edition of the Preface from both manuscripts, together with Flemish translation and discussion by P. Verkest, 'De *Praefatio* van de *Eclogae tractatorum in Psalterium* (Ierland ca. 800)' (MA dissertation, Director Professor Dr L. De Coninck, Katholieke Universiteit Leuven, Fakulteit van de Letteren en de Wijsbegeerte, Academic Year 1992–1993; both manuscripts derive from an original written in Ireland).

Studies: Bischoff, 'Wendepunkte', p. 233; P. Verkest, 'De *Praefatio*' (codicological and grammatical data, indications of Irish origin; source analysis; general introduction).

The title *Ecloga* occurs over selections of passages from existing compositions. The title of the present work possibly echoes that of the *Egloga de Moralibus Iob* by the Irish writer Latchen (Laid-cend; died 661 CE). According to Bischoff the script of both MSS, written on the Continent, shows Irish symptoms. A further Irish symptom is the title of the book of Psalms being given, in Irish style, 'in the three languages' (Hebrew, Greek and Latin), as it is in the introduction to the psalms in the Irish *Reference Bible* (2.10 below). Even a partial analysis of the sources used and a comparison of the work with the *Reference Bible* seems to place the Irish origin of the *Eclogae tractatorum in Psalterium* beyond reasonable doubt.

der irische Paulustext, Sedulius Scottus (Freiburg: Herder, 1961), p. 76. Only a detailed study will reveal how 'Irish' it really is.

The work consists of a prologue and an exposition of the entire Psalter by means of excerpts from earlier writers. Very often the sources are cited in the margins in abbreviated form. In the introduction, the sources so noted are Hilary, Cassiodorus, Isidore, Augustine, Josephus, Junilius, Eucherius, Jerome and Ambrose. For the commentary proper the sources indicated are for the greater part Jerome, cited in abbreviated form as *hir. int.*, *hir. in his.*, *hir. in psal.*, *hir. in trac.* These sources require analysis with a view to determining the individual works quoted and the compiler's dependence on particular recensions where such exist.

Restricting myself to the material here published, I have failed to identify the following citation from Ambrose and Hilary (fol. 2 v): *Am. Si toto effectu inuestigaueris psalmos multum laborem arripies. Nam etiam intellectu historico duplices sensus latent uel habent. Hil. Lege psalmos historico intellectu ubi diuersos modos inuenies.* It seems worth noting that the same words, under the same names, are quoted in the *Reference Bible* (Clm 14276, fol. 95r). On fol. 2r Jerome's Preface *Scio quosdam* is cited, which is found also in Cod. Amb. C. 301 inf. (2.7 above).

In the commentary proper *hir in trac.*, I presume, refers to Jerome's *Tractatus in librum Psalmorum*. All references to *hir. int.* in the portion published below are to Jerome's *Commentarioli in Psalmos*. The author, then, apparently knew these two works as distinct, not combined as in the pseudo-hieronymian *Breviarium in Psalmos* (2.8 above). His *hir. in psal.* stands for Jerome's rendering of the Hebrew Psalter (the *Hebraicum*). Much more interesting is *hir. in his.* (= *Hirunimus in historica inuestigatione?*) In the texts published in Appendix III this always refers to the Milan Commentary (2.7 above). Most of the excerpts so labelled, whether from the beginning or the later part (Pss. 35–40; 67–70), are verbatim as in the Milan text. The author of the *Eclogae*, therefore, must have had before him the genuine text of Theodore (for Pss. 1.1–16.11), combined as in the Milan Codex with the non-Theodorean material. This is evidence in support of the view that the composite Milan text was known and used in Ireland. A glance at the Appendix III will show that the chief source, often not even expressly referred to, for the commentary proper is the Theodorean Commentary. For many psalms all that is given is the Theodorean psalm heading. This commentary was known to the author as a work of

Jerome. The Bobbio Catalogue of 1461 CE (see 2.7 above) was thus going on old tradition.

2.10. *Introduction to the Psalter in the* 'Reference Bible' *(c. 800 CE) (Appendix IV)*

MSS: Munich, Clm 14276, fols. 94v-99r (saec. IX, in.; cf. Bischoff, *Die südostdeutschen Schreibschulen*, I, p. 194; Paris: Bibl. Nat. Lat., 11561, saec. IX med.-2).

Edition: Below Appendix IV (fols. 94v-99r of Munich MS).

Study: Bischoff, 'Wendepunkte', pp. 226-27.

The *'Reference Bible'* (*Das Bibelwerk*) is the name Bischoff gives to a long Hiberno-Latin commentary on all the books of the Bible from Genesis to the Apocalypse. (The Paris MS of the work has 217 folios: a Vatican codex with Genesis alone has 106.) It is a kind of biblical encyclopedia. Its late eighth-century compiler, an Irishman who had lived some time on the Continent, had behind him a century and a half of Irish exegetical activity. He depends on earlier writings and also, probably, on the oral tradition of the Irish schools. His composition has numerous Irish characteristics. It is

interspersed with a considerable number of comparisons between Hebrew, Greek and Latin words. And when somebody does something for the first time or when something happens for the first time (in the biblical narrative) the pedantic questions (as to who was the first to do such a thing, etc.) are particularly obtrusive'.[62]

The type of exegesis depends largely on the compiler's sources. Sometimes he works citations into his exposition; at other times excerpts are merely placed side by side and their origin is not always correctly indicated. This may be due to the use of such second-hand sources as catenae or *Eclogae*.

In Irish fashion, the treatment of the Psalter is in the form of question and answer. There are 33 questions: on the designation of *psalmus* in the 'three languages' (Hebrew, Greek and Latin); on the difference between *psalmus cantici* and *canticum psalmi*; on the first and last psalm composed (*cantatus*); on the distinction between *psalmus, canticum, hymnus* and *laus*; on the first authors of the psalms; whether we

62. Bischoff, 'Wendepunkte', p. 211; *MS* I, p. 222; *idem*, 'Turning-Points', p. 88.

should read the psalms in the historical or the mystical sense (*sensus*); who gave the psalms their (present) order; why the 'p' is written in *psalmus* although not pronounced; why the psalms alone are learnt by heart; who was the first to sing the psalms in the New Testament; the name of the Psalter in the 'three languages'; in what section of the Canon are the psalms; why are they not classed among the Prophets in the Hebrew Canon; whether they were originally in verse or prose; on the definition of prose; on the class of teaching they contain; on Alleluia; why unlike Osanna, Alleluia is repeated in the chant; on *diapsalma* and *sinpsalma*; the meaning of *diapsalma* and the psalm in which it first occurs; who first sung *diapsalma*;[63] the title of the psalms; how many psalms have no title; why have they not; how many are the psalms of David; why the titles are not chanted; the meaning of *in finem* or similar in the titles; whether the Psalter has five books or only one; why there are Hebrew letters before some psalms; how many sang with

---

63. Questions as to who was the first to do something in the Bible, which is the first occurrence of a word, etc., are characteristics or early Irish exegesis and are especially frequent in the *Reference Bible*; see Bischoff, 'Wendepunkte', p. 211. Bischoff recalls how interest in such 'problems' exposed the Irish scholar Cadac-Andreas to ridicule at the court of Charlemagne, Cadac being asked by Theodulf and an unnamed bardling the sarcastic question: 'Who was the first among the Irish to paint his face at a funeral?' These lines occur after a similar attack on Irish curiosity in *diapsalma* and *synpsalma*:

> Dic etiam, sine mente pecus, cornuta capella,
> cum Grecis qualis legitur nam littera prima,
> *Dic, insane caput, quid sit diapsalma vel in quo*
> *psalmis synpsalma legitur, stultissime vatum.*
> Dic etiam, Scotte, qui sottus corpore constas,
> inter 'sic' et 'ita' quae sit discretio sensus.
> Impie, die etiam fallax deceptus in arte,
> quis primus Scottus stravis pinxisset in oras.

('Versus ad quendam Scottum nomine Andream', ed. B. Bischoff, *Historische Jahrbuch* 74 [1947], p. 96). The *OIT* (no. 11, 11) also treats of *diapsalma* and *sinpsalma*. The Psalm Prologue of Bede found in the Milan Commentary (Amb. C. 301 inf., fol. 2c) gives the number of the Psalms of David as 150, '*deabsalma lxxv*' (thus Ascoli [ed.], *Il codice irlandese*, p. 5; *Thes. Pal.*, I, p. 9 has 'LXXII'), on which an Irish gloss (*Thes. Pal.*, I, p. 9) comments: 'i.e. seventy-five times is dia-psalma present in the Psalter, or, there are seventy-five psalms of which diapsalma is the superscription'.

the king; on the obelus and asterisk; why Psalm 151 (*Pusillus*)[64] is not canonical, why are the names of different authors indicated in the psalm titles; meaning of psalter and psalm; why there are only 150 psalms; why the first psalm is without title. Before the third last question there are two sections not introduced as questions. The work ends with an abbreviated form of part of Cassiodore's preface to his commentary on the psalms.

This analysis will have made it obvious that the compiler has imposed no great order on his material. Nor does he appear to have had a command of it. Unlike the great expositors of the psalms such as Jerome, Hilary, Augustine, Cassiodorus, he does not seem to take a stand and maintain a fixed position on a given problem. Thus, for instance, in section V he says that ten persons 'sang' (*cantaverunt*) the psalms in the first instance: Moses, David and others, whereas in section XXVII citing Cassiodorus he maintains that David alone was the author of all the psalms. More than once it is difficult, if not impossible, to get the point the compiler is making—if he really intends to make one. Sometimes the lack of clarity is due to over-abbreviation of his sources. A good example of this is section XXXIIII (fol. 98v) where the compiler's words become clear only after reading Cassiodorus's longer treatment of the question. Perhaps the compiler was working against time—such a long work as the *Reference Bible* must, after all, have entailed quite an amount of research.

The questions asked in this introduction to the psalms are similar to those in the *Old-Irish Treatise* (2.11 below). The answers, however, are not always the same. That the introduction of the *Reference Bible* is closely related to the *Old-Irish Treatise* is evident. Both probably represent the teaching common in Irish schools of the period. The introduction is related also to the *Eclogae* (2.9 above): both give the same definition of *psalmus* in the 'three languages' and contain an unidentified quotation attributed to Ambrose and Hilary.

2.11. *Treatise on the Psalter in Old Irish (800–50 CE)*

MSS: Oxford, Bodleian Library, Rawl. B. 512, fols. 45-47 (fifteenth century); British Library, Harley 5280, fols. 21-24 (sixteenth century). Begins: '*Is hé titul fil i n-dreich ind libuir se*'; ends (*imperfect*): '*Ab eo didiu, úad immthiag...*'

---

64. On the *Pusillus* see 7.9.

Edition: Kuno Meyer, *Hibernica Minora, being a fragment of an Old-Irish Treatise on the Psalter*, with translation, notes and glossary, and an appendix containing extracts hitherto unpublished from 3,18 Rawlinson B. 512 in the Bodleian Library. Edited with a Facsimile (Anecdota Oxoniensia, Mediaeval and Modern Series, 8; Oxford: Clarendon Press, 1894).

Studies: Heinrich Zimmer, 'Anzeige der Hibernica Minora', *Göttingische Gelehrte Anzeigen* (1896), pp. 376-409 (with valuable comments); K. Meyer, 'Erschienene Schriften', *ZCP* 1 (1897), pp. 496-97 (observations on some of Zimmer's comments); R.L. Ramsay, 'Theodore of Mopsuestia in England and Ireland', *ZCP* 8 (1912), pp. 421-97 especially pp. 465-74 (on Theodorean material in the Treatise); Robin Flower, *Catalogue of Irish Manuscripts in the British Library* (Dublin Institute for Advanced Studies: Dublin, 1992), pp. 302-303.

The two MSS of this text are copies of the same exemplar; both end with the same word in the middle of a sentence. While our present copies are late, the original must be dated, on linguistic grounds, well into the Old Irish period. It was dated by its first editor to about 750 CE.[65] This date was at the time assigned to the Milan glosses, the language of which is similar. The latter are now dated somewhat later, to about 775–850; accordingly the *Old-Irish Treatise* is dated to the first half of the ninth century.

All that survives of the original treatise is a long introduction to the Psalter and part of the comment on Ps. 1.1. The work is mainly in the form of question and answer: the names of the psalter; what is the book's name in Hebrew, Greek and Latin?; whence this?; description of a psalter (the musical instrument); whether there are many (five) books in the Psalter or only one; the division of the Canon of Scripture to which the psalms belong; to what kind of sacred literature (*historia, prophetia, proverbialis species, simplex doctrina*)[66] do the psalms belong?; on 'the three well-known things found in every composition' that is, place, time and author, with regard to the psalms (here are juxtaposed two contrary views, one ascribing the psalms to various authors and the Psalter to David through *synekdoche*, another ascribing all the psalms to David); whether the psalms were 'sung' (composed) in prose or metre; the alphabetical psalms (this question is treated twice, in

---

65. *OIT*, p. xiii.

66. The division is that of Junilius: *De partibus divinae legis*, 1.1–6; *PL* 68, cols. 15-49, esp. 16D.

almost identical words); the 'order' obtaining among the psalms now; the order or state in which they were originally; unity and multiplicity in the Psalter; the psalm headings (*tituli*); why written when not sung?; why written in red?; on the *argumenta* and division of the psalms, on *titulus, diapsalma* and *sympsalma*; on the fourfold sense of the psalms (first story, second story, [mystical] sense and morality); on the object of the prophecy in the psalms; on the translations of the Psalter, including Jerome's critical work 'under dagger (*obelus*) and asterisk' on the first Psalm; which was the psalm first sung? (it was the apocryphal psalm 151); the *argumentum* of Psalm 1; why it has no title; grammatical and etymological considerations of certain words and phrases.

This analysis shows the similarity of this introduction with that of the *Reference Bible* (2.10 above). The introduction of the *Old-Irish Treatise* is, however, much more detailed. If, as was Kuno Meyer's view, we now possess but the first quaternion of the commentary, it must have been quite long. Ramsay has advanced strong arguments for the view that the Irish commentary is the translation of a Latin original which supplied the glosses found in the margins of the Southampton Psalter (2.21 below). Ramsay also maintained that it was used by the author of the tenth-century West-Saxon version of the first 50 psalms. The Irish commentary or its Latin original would then still have been used in the tenth and early eleventh centuries. In 982, Airbertach Mac Coisse rendered the Old Irish prose introduction into verse (see 2.17 below). We cannot say whether he knew of the entire commentary or only our present fragment. The introductory portion of it at least was known in the southern school of Mac Coisse at Ros Ailithir (present-day Rosscarbery in south-west Cork) a little over a century after its composition. What other schools the *Old-Irish Treatise* served remains unknown.

Authorities cited by name in the introduction are Jerome (nine times), Isidore and Hilary (twice each), Gregory, Augustine and Sebastianus (?; MS. *sapaist*) (once each); in the commentary on Psalm 1, Isidore, Hilary and Gregory (twice each), Jerome, Ambrose, Cassiodorus, Bede and Sergius (once each). Even when the author does not mention his sources he is heavily dependent on earlier writers. As has been noted, some of his sources can no longer be identified (see 1.7 above).[67] Occasionally his indication of a source is faulty. At least twice (on the number of books in the Psalter, lines 415 and on the Davidic authorship of

---

67. Cf. M. Adriaen (ed.), *Magni Aurelii Castiodori expositio* (CCSL, 98; Turnhout: Brepols), p. viii.

the psalms, lines 1341-42) he attributes views to Hilary that are the direct opposite of those held by the saint. There is need of a new edition of the *Old-Irish Treatise* accompanied by an up-to-date study of its sources.

2.12. *Copy of Commentary on the Psalms by Cassiodorus (800–50 CE)*

MS: Laon, Bibliothèque municipale 26 (with Irish glosses).

Edition of Irish glosses: K. Meyer, 'Neu aufgefundene altirische Glossen', *ZCP* 8 (1912), pp 175-76; edition of Cassiodorus's commentary: M. Adriaen (ed.), *Magni Aurelii Cassiodori expositio psalmorum* (CCSL, 97-98; Turnhout: Brepols, 1958) (critical edition with introduction).

Studies: Adriaen, *Magni Aurelii Cassiodori* (on Cassiodorus and his commentary); Kenney, *Sources*, p. 666 (no. 517). See also 2.3.c above.

Cassiodorus was a senator who enjoyed an honoured position in the Gothic kingdom. He abandoned Ravenna and secular life to retire to Vivarium in southern Italy where he devoted himself, among other things, to a serious study of the psalms. At the beginning of the year 548 he praised a work of Facundus in defence of the Three Chapters (*pro Defensione Trium Capitulorum*) presented to the Emperor Justinian (cf. conclusion to his comment on Ps. 138). A little later he presented his commentary on the Psalter to Pope Vigilius who condemned the Three Chapters on April 11 that same year. About 560 he published his renowned *Institutiones divinarum litterarum* and some time later (between 560 and 575) a second edition of his commentary on the psalms in which he added some extra bibliographical material and a few other items. He tells us that in his commentary he has limited himself to making a resumé of the *Enarrationes* of St Augustine. An analysis of his sources, however, reveals that he has gone far beyond this and has drawn on many other writers besides.

His commentary was to become immensely popular in the western Church. The first attested use of it, however, is in Bede (on Ezra 2.7; *PL* 92, col. 849C). We have seen that the work is used in the Bedan *De Titulis Psalmorum* (2.3.c above), in the *Eclogae* (2.9), in the Irish *Reference Bible* (2.10) and in the *Old-Irish Treatise* (2.11). The earliest series of excerpts would appear to be in the *Eclogae*.[68] In his critical

---

68. Cf. Adriaen (ed.), *Magni Aurelii*, p. viii.

edition of Cassiodorus's commentary Adriaen notes (p. ix) the existence of MS Laon 26. He has not, however, collated it. The MS deserves such collation, to determine its place in the history of the text and to see how it compares with the excerpts made from Cassiodorus in Irish works. This Laon MS was written by an Irish scribe, whether on the Continent or in Ireland one cannot say. It has a number of Irish glosses, edited by Meyer.[69] They are of the irrelevant, 'aside' character—on the nature of the parchment, on the weather—with no bearing on the text itself.

a. *Fragmentary Psalter of Codex Paris (Early Ninth Century)*

> MS: Paris, Bibl. Nat. Fr. 2452, fol. 75-84. In these folios we have fragments of an Irish text of the *Hebraicum* (on which see 2.18 and 5.4 below). The fragments are from a manuscript written in the early ninth century and thus represent the oldest Irish text of the *Hebraicum* we know. I know of these fragments only from a reference by Fischer,[70] who in turn was informed of their existence by David H. Wright. I am not aware that any study has been made of them. They deserve examination to determine their precise relation to the Irish *Hebraicum* family.

2.13. *The Basel Greco-Latin Psalter (Second Half of Ninth Century)*

> MS: Basel, Universitätsbibliothek MS A. vii. 3.

> Editions (in facsimile): *Psalterium Graeco-Latinum: Codex Basiliensis A. VII. 3* (Umbrae Codicum Occidentalium, V; Amsterdam, 1960), with introduction in German, pp. v-xxii, by L. Bieler; A. Baumeister, *Denkmäler des klassischen Altertums*, II (Munich: R. Oldenberg, 1887), pp. 1132-33 (fol. 23r with Pss. 29.10c–30.6b; with palaeographical observations on Greek text); A. Bruckner, *Scriptoria Medii Aevi Helvetica*, III (Genf: Roto-Sadag, 1938), table xiv (fol. 23r); J. Smits van Waesberghe, *Muziekgeschiedenis der Middeleeuwen*, II (Tilburg, 1942), App. 15 and 18 (fols. 23r and 58r, this latter with Pss. 72.17a–73.2b).

> Studies: L. Bieler, *Psalterium Graeco-Latinum*, introduction (a detailed examination of the MS from points of view of palaeography, text, etc.; with further bibliography on p. xxii); A. Rahlfs, *Verzeichnis*

---

69. Meyer, 'Neu aufgefundene'.
70. 'Bedae de titulis psalmorum liber' (see 2.3.c above), p. 28.

der griechischen Handschriften des Alten Testaments (Berlin: Weide-
mann, 1914), p. 25 (our MS is given the no. 156 among Greek texts);
H.J. Frede, *Altlateinische Paulus-Handschriften* (Aus der Geschichte
der lateinischen Bibel, 4; Freiburg: Herder, 1964), pp. 50-77 ('Der
Codex Boernerianus'); 78-79 (Greek studies at St Gall); 67-69, 73-75
(our MS); Bruckner, *Scriptoria medii aevi Helvetica*, III, pp. 27-29, 31;
S. Berger, *Histoire de la Vulgate* (Paris: Librairie Hachette, 1893; repr.
New York: Burt Frankler, 1961), pp. 115-16, 376; M. Esposito, 'Hib-
erno-Latin Manuscripts in the Libraries of Switzerland', *PRIA* 28 C
(1910), pp. 62-95 (69-70); Kenney, *Sources*, no. 364 (pp. 557-58);
Lindsay, *Early Irish Minuscule*, pp. 47-50 (on the abbreviations in the
Latin text); B. Bischoff, 'Das griechische Element in der abendländ-
ischen Bildung des Mittelalters', *Byzantinische Zeitschrift* 44 (1951),
pp. 27-55, especially p. 42 (reproduced in *Mittelalterliche Studien*, II
[Stuttgart: Hiersemann, 1967], pp. 246-75 [see esp. p. 260];
B. Bischoff, 'The Study of Foreign Languages in the Middle Ages',
Speculum 36 (1961), pp. 209-24 (reproduced in *Mittelalterliche Stu-
dien*, II, pp. 227-45, esp. 231-35). See also M.W. Herren and
S.A. Brown (eds.), *The Sacred Nectar of the Greeks: The Study of
Greek in the West in the Early Middle Ages* (Kings College London
Medieval Studies, 2; London: University of London, 1988).

This codex has 99 folios. Originally it must have had more: the Psalter
proper ends with Ps. 146.2 in the middle of a word. On fols. 1v-3v it
contains prayers and what appears to be a form of a Celtic Office. Fols.
4r-97v are a bilingual Psalter—the Greek text with interlinear Latin
translation. On fol. 98r in a narrow column at the left are the remnants
of two Ambrosian hymns; on the right the apocryphal psalm 151 in
Greek with interlinear Latin translation.

The Psalter proper is written by two different hands. Hand A wrote
fols. 4r-12v, line 8 (the remainder of this page is occupied by a prayer)
with Pss. 1.1–17.28, and fols, 50v, middle-97v (i.e. the end of the
Psalter). Hand B wrote the remainder, that is, fols. 13r-50v with Pss.
17.25 (sic)–62 (end). Fol. 13, with which B commences, begins a new
quire. The scribe began the folio in the middle of a Greek word (ὀφθα-
λμον; *recte*: -μων, written correctly by A on fol. 12r) and repeats both
the Greek text and interlinear translation of full three verses with thirty
words of the biblical text. Since both his Greek text and interlinear
translation for these verses differ from that of A, B must have copied
from a different original. It appears that A as well as B wrote both the
Greek text and the interlinear Latin translation.

The psalms are preceded by the Septuagint psalm headings in Greek with Latin translation and are numbered by Greek letters and Roman numerals, the Greek headings and letters being in red ink, the remainder in the ink of the text. The Greek headings and the Latin versions of these were each written by two different hands, none of them being the hand of the Psalter text itself. The name *martianus* occurs on fol. 48r near a psalm heading and in the same hand as the Latin translation of the heading. He would appear to have been the scribe of the greater part of the Latin translation of the psalm headings and also of the following marginal note on fol. 23r: *hucusque scripsi hic incipit ad marcellum nunc*.[71] This marginal note occurs at the end of Psalm 29 and opposite the heading for Psalm 30. In Bieler's opinion it refers to a copy to be made from our present text, not to the copying of the text I am considering.[72] Marcellus would then be the scribe of a copy made from this text, not of the text itself.

The script of the Psalter is Irish and is palaeographically similar to that of Codex Sangallensis 48 of the four Gospels and to Codex Boernerianus (Dresden A 145b) of the Epistles of St Paul, both accompanied by an interlinear Latin translation. All three in fact may have originally have formed but parts of one large codex. Bieler goes a step further and surmises that the scribe of both these manuscripts was hand A of the Basel Psalter.[73] All three codices were probably written in the monastery of St Gall.

The Greek text merits collation to determine its position within the history of the Septuagint. Bieler notes that it is close to that written by Sedulius Scottus (1.2.n).[74] I have compared the text of Psalm 151 (written as I have noted in a different hand) with that of Sedulius and found certain differences (readings of the Basel Psalter given first): v. 1: ἐποιμαινον—ἐποιμενον; v. 2: δακτιλοι—δακτυλοι; v. 3: εἰσακουει—εἰσακουσει (*exaudiet*); v. 4: ἐλεη (= ἐλεει; Vulgate: *misericordia*)—ἐλαιω (*oleo*). The evidence of fols. 12v-13r indicates that the Basel Psalter was copied from two slightly different originals.

The Latin interlinear 'translation' is basically the Gallican, revised to have it conform to the Greek. Sometimes two Latin translations of a Greek word are given, the Vulgate one and a more literal rendering, for example, Ps. 2.1: *ut quid-quare* (Greek: ἱνα τι). In Psalm 151 the inter-

---

71. Cf. Bieler, *Psalterium Graeco-Latinum*, pp. xiii-xiv.
72. *Psalterium Graeco-Latinum*, pp. xiii-xiv.
73. *Psalterium Graeco-Latinum*, p. xix.
74. *Psalterium Graeco-Latinum*, p. xx.

linear translation is also basically Vulgate, but with more correction—
due partly to the fact that the Greek text used differed from that on
which the Vulgate was made.

After transcription this Psalter must have been examined by critical
eyes as marginal references draw attention to false translations of Greek
words and to Greek words left untranslated.[75] On fol. 24v in the margin
attention is drawn to a *varia lectio*, the text itself having ἀνομιαν written above ἁμαρτιαν (Ps. 31.5). ἀνομιαν in this verse is the reading of
Codex Alexandrinus, ἁμαρτιαν that of Sinaiticus.

The Basel Psalter is generally considered to have come from the circles of Sedulius of Liège. In Bieler's opinion this contention is quite
uncertain. Nonetheless, he continues,[76] the Basel Psalter is evidence of
the highest order for the study of the Greek Bible, and with it of Greek
in general, among the continental Irish of the ninth century.

While there is agreement among scholars with regard to the interest
of certain Irish *peregrini* on the Continent in Greek in the ninth century,
and their competence in the language, matters are different with regard
to the knowledge of Greek in Ireland itself in this and in the preceding
centuries. Scholarly opinion varies. Some deny that the Irish had any
knowledge of Greek; others admit a minimal, or limited knowledge,
derived from glossaries.[77] More recently D. Howlett has defended the
view that even before the *peregrini* of the ninth century Irish and
British scholars were acquainted with Hellenic learning and competent
in Greek.[78]

75. See Bieler, *Psalterium Graeco-Latinum*, p. xi.

76. *Psalterium Graeco-Latinum*, p. xxi.

77. See M.W. Herren. 'Hiberno-Latin Philology: The State of the Question', in
M.W. Herren (ed.), *Insular Latin Studies: Papers on Latin Texts and Manuscripts
of the British Isles*. 550-1066 (Papers in Mediaeval Studies, 1; Toronto: Pontifical
Institute of Mediaeval Studies, 1981), pp. 1-22 (at 10-11); W. Berschin, *Greek Letters and the Latin Middle Ages from Jerome to Nicholas of Cusa* (trans. J.C. Frakes;
rev. edn; Washington, DC: Catholic University of America Press, 1988), pp. 95-
101; W. Berschin, 'Griechisches bei den Iren', in H. Löwe (ed.), *Die Iren und
Europa im frühen Mittelalter* (2 vols.; Stuttgart: Klett-Cotta, 1982), I, pp. 501-510.

78. D. Howlett, 'Hellenic Learning in Insular Latin: An Essay on Supported
Claims', *Peritia* 12 (1998), pp. 54-78; see also A. Ahlqvist, 'Notes on the Greek
Material in the St. Gall Priscian (Codex 904)', in M.W. Herren and S.A. Brown
(eds.), *The Sacred Nectar of the Greeks*, pp. 195-214.

2.14. *The Greek Psalter of Sedulius Scottus (Ninth Century)*

MSS: Paris, Bibliothèque de l'Arsenal 8407 (no. 2 of Greek series); fols.1-55; this MS earlier belonged to the monastery of St Nicholas-du-Pré at Verdun.

Editions (partial and in facsimile): Bernard de Montfaucon O.S.B., *Palaeographia graeca*, III (Paris: Apud Ludovicum Guerin, 1708; repr. Westmead, England: Gregg International, 1970), pp. 7, 235-36 (Pss. 101–102); H. Omont, 'Inventaire sommaire des manuscrits grecs', *Mélanges Charles Graux* (Paris, 1884), p. 313 (fol. 55, with Pss. 149.3–Ps. 151 and colophon).

Studies: Victor Gardthausen, *Griechische Paläographie* (1st edn, Leipzig: Teubner, 1879), p. 427; (2nd edn, II, Leipzig: 1913), pp. 257-62 (pp. 257-62: Greek in West, pp. 258-60: mediaeval Greek MSS and bilingual Psalters, p. 258: the Arsenal MS); Henri d'Arbois de Jubainville, *Introduction à l'étude de la littérature celtique* (Paris, 1883), p. 380 n. 2; L. Traube, *O Roma nobilis* (Munich, 1891), pp. 344-45, 359 (pp. 338-63 are on Sedulius and his circle; on their knowledge of Greek and on MSS written by them); Berger, *Histoire de la Vulgate*, pp. 116, 411; Kenney, *Sources*, p. 557; Gerard Murphy, 'Scotti Peregrini', *Studies* 17 (1928), pp. 39-50, 229-44; M. Esposito, 'The Knowledge of Greek in Ireland during the Middle Ages', *Studies* 1 (1912), pp. 665-83 (at 677) (repr. Mario Esposito, *Latin Learning in Medieval Ireland* [ed. M. Lapidge; London, 1988]); M. Esposito, 'A Bibliography of the Latin Writers of Mediaeval Ireland', *Studies* 2 (1913), pp. 495-521 (at 505; further works on Sedulius).

The Psalter itself is entirely in Greek, without Latin translation. (Berger and Kenney are misleading in this regard.) After the Psalter (fols. 55v-63v) there follow Canticles and the Our Father in Greek and Latin. The psalms are numbered by Greek letters and Roman numerals. They are preceded by psalm headings and the opening words of the psalms in Latin are given. Both the Greek and Latin headings of the apocryphal Psalm 151 are given.

After Psalm 151 comes the following colophon (written in Greek capitals):

ΕΥΧΑC Θ(Ε)Ω ΕΓΩ ΑΜΑΡΤΩΛΟC ΠΡΑΞΟ…
CΗΔΥΛΙΟΧ CΚΟΤΤΟC ΕΓΩ ΕΓΡΑΨΑ

This Sedulius Scottus who says he wrote the Psalter is generally identified with Sedulius of Liège who arrived there from Ireland about

848 CE. He had a particular interest in the Psalter[79] and probably had some knowledge of Greek before arriving on the Continent.

The Arsenal Psalter deserves study to determine its exact position among MSS of the Septuagint. Where it was transcribed by Sedulius is hard to say. One naturally thinks of Liège. Before coming to Paris it was at Verdun. This we know from a note on the last folio, now lost but

---

79. Cf. Murphy, 'Scotti Peregrini', p. 237. One may also note that there is an echo of the Greek text of Ps. 109.1 in a prayer of the Irishman Martin of Laon (or possibly of Johannes Scottus) for Charles the Bald (MS Laon 444, fol. 297v; ed. by L. Traube in *Monumenta Germaniae historica, Poetae aevi carolini*, III, p. 697). The Greek Psalter (*epi petron pedas mu*, Ps. 39.3) is also cited in the Hiberno-Latin Commentary (Ps.-Hilary) on the Catholic Epistles, on 1 Pet 1.1 (MS Vienna 750; ed. *Spicilegium Casinense* 3, 1897, p. 225; *PL Supplementum*, III, fasc. 1, 1963, col. 83; R. McNally [ed.], *Scriptores Hiberniae Minores* [2 vols.; CCSL, 108B; Turnhout: Brepols, 1975], I, p. 77, line 10). In the passage concerning Mount Thabor in *De Locis Sanctis* (11. 27. 6; [ed.] D. Meehan, pp. 96-97) Adamnan remarks: 'At this juncture it should be noted that the name of that famous mountain ought to be written in Greek letters with θ and long Ω thus, θABΩP. Whereas in Latin letters it ought to be written with aspiration (*cum aspiratione*) and long o—Thabor. The orthography of this word was found in Greek books (*in libris Grecitatis*).' What the *libri Grecitatis* are is uncertain. P. Geyer (*Itinera Hierosolymitana saeculi IIII-VIII* [CSEL, 39; Vienna, 1898], p. 353) takes it that Greek works of Jerome (*Grecitatis libri s. Hieronymi*) are intended. B. Bischoff, however (in a letter to Dr Bieler), expressed the view that the reference might be to some bilingual Psalter (cf. Ps. 88.13). The citation, in part at least, seems dependent on Eusebius's *Onomastica Sacra* as translated by Jerome (*De situ et nominibus locorum hebraicorum liber* (P. de Lagarde [ed.]; Göttingen, 2nd edn, 1887]), a work which Adamnan uses extensively and once quotes (cf. Meehan, *De Locis Sanctis*, p. 13). At the end of the section on names beginning with *T* Jerome explicitly remarks that all these names begin with a simple *T* (*per T simplicem literam*), i.e. with T representing Hebrew *Teth*, not Hebrew *Tau*. He then goes on to give names in which the *T* represents the Hebrew *Tau*: '*quoniam non ex Teth, sed ex Tau, id est Theta Greco scribuntur,* cum aspiratione *legere debemus*' (de Lagarde [ed.], *De Situ*, p. 156). Under such words he treats, both in Greek and Latin, of Thabor. Book 11.27 of *De Locis Sanctis* is probably dependent on the *Onomasticon*: both use the expression *mira rotunditate* of Thabor. The *Onomasticon*, being bilingual, is thus probably the work intended by Adamnan, The *Onomasticon*, however, does not speak of the long *o* in Thabor. In the Basel Psalter (1.2.n) the short *o* (omicron) is often substituted for the long (*omega*) and vice versa (cf. Bieler, *Psalterium Graeco-Latinum*, 2.13 above). In Ps. 88.13 (fol. 68r, line 22), as a matter of fact, Greek Thabor is written there with a short *o*!

fortunately published by Montfaucon and reproduced from Montfaucon by Omont.[80] It was as follows:

Iste liber est beati Nicolai in Prato Virdunensi (fifteenth century).

Further on the note reads:

Anno salutis Christianae 1503 prima novembris apostolica sede bis eodem anno per Alexandri VI et Pii III Romanorum Pontificum obitum pastore carente, liber hic psalmorum, ex bibliotheca monasterii divi Nicolai de Prato extra muros Virdunenses mihi Johanni Colardo, prae-posito beatae Mariae Magdalenae et archidiacono de Vepria, Vir-dunensium ecclesiarum ejusdem sedis apostolicae pronotario, precario datus est: quem quidem restitui decima mensis decembris 1503, anno sanctissimo D.N.D. Julii papae II. Theô charis: hôrion. Joan. Colardi.

2.15. *Letter of a Scot on Translation of Psalter from Greek (Ninth Century)*

MSS: Munich, Staatsbibliothek 343 (ninth century), fols. 1v-9v; Cod. Vatican 82 (ninth–tenth centuries), fols. 2v-12v; Cod. Vatican 83 (ninth century), fols. 1-9v.

Editions: A.F. Vezzosi, *Ios. Mariae Thomasii Opera Omnia*, II (Rome, 1747), pp. xx-xxvi (from Vatican 82 and Munich 343); E. Dümmler, in *idem* (ed.), *Monumenta Germaniae historica, Epistolae*, VI (Berlin, 1902), pp. 201-205 (from all three MSS). Studies: G. Morin, 'Une revision du psautier sur le texte grec par un anonyme du neuvième siècle', *RBén* 10 (1893), pp. 193-97; S. Hellmann, *Sedulius Scottus* (Munich, 1906), p. 95 n. 2; M. Manitius, *Geschichte der lateinischen Literatur des Mittelalters*, I (Munich: Beck'sche Verlagsbuchhandlung, 1911), pp. 317-18; Kenney, *Sources*, p. 569 (no. 376); R. Hayes, *Manuscript Sources for the History of Irish Civilisation*, IV (Boston: G.K. Hall Co., 1965), p. 397 (sub 'Sedulius'); M. Esposito, 'Notes on Mediaeval Hiberno-Latin and Hiberno-French Literature', *Hermathena* 16 (1910), pp. 58-72 (64).

This anonymous treatise on the translation of the Psalter is headed: *Scottus quidam in territorio mediolanensi commorans Graecae linguae gnarus de psalterio in linguam Latinam transferendo atque emendando disserit.* ('A certain Scot with a knowledge of Greek, residing in the territory of Milan, treats of the translation of the Psalter into Latin and of

80. *Palaeographia graeca*, p. 236 ; Omont, 'Inventaire', p. 313.

its emendation.') What we have in the extant MSS, all of them written in Milan, is explicitly presented as a brief preface (*praefatiuncula*) to an emended text of the Psalter. The emended text is apparently extant in Berlin, Deutsche Staatsbibliothek, MS Hamilton 552, a ninth-century Greco-Latin Psalter.[81]

The author of the preface has taken it on himself, so he tells us, to emend the text of the Psalter for persons he addresses as 'most beloved brethren'. This emendation, he continues, he will do by 'rejecting what is superfluous and inserting what is fitting' (*reprobare superflua et inserere congrua*) in the Psalter, so as to have the psalms conform to the truth, that is, to the Greek text. He finds such an emendation necessary in view of the discrepancy between the Latin translation and the Greek. He invites anyone doubting the exactness of his rendering to consult the Greek Psalters. He has also been informed by people in many areas that such discrepancy exists.

The corrector had been provided with a number of Latin and Greek Psalters for this task. He does not, however, consider himself free to emend at will. Having the highest regard for St Jerome he is at pains to have his own emendation conform as far as possible with Jerome's rendering. He is also anxious to make sure that his revision will not repel people by reason of its novelty.

The author classes the errors in the Latin translation—which he emends under four headings: omission (*detractio*), addition (*adiectio*), change (*mutatio*) and transposition (*transmutatio*). As examples of these respectively he instances Pss. 6.7 (*meis*), 1.2 (*fuit*), 4.8 (*tempore*) and 5.9 (*in tua iustitia*, instead of *i. i. tua*). From the biblical texts he gives it is clear that the Psalter he emends is not the *Gallicanum*. It is the Old Latin of the Ambrosian family used in Milan.

The extant preface, as already said, was intended to accompany an emended text of the psalter. This emended psalter, the preface informs us, was provided with five critical signs: Θ (Theta), Ψ (Psi), ℞ (Chrismon), ꝛ (Et) and Ɔ (Diastole). Theta marked additions, passages not found in the Greek or in Jerome; Psi marked a *mutatio*; Chrismon indicated an *omissio*; an Et the omission of the conjunction *et* in Latin, although present in the Greek and in Jerome. The Diastole was used in conjunction with the Theta and Psi to indicate the extent of the passages

---

81. Cf. Hayes, *Manuscript Sources*, IV, p. 397.

which were superfluous or had been changed, that is, it corresponded to the two points after the obelus and the asterisk in Jerome's system. The author requests that nothing be added or changed in his emended psalter without first consulting the Greek Psalters or those emended by Jerome. Proper use of the critical signs noted in the preface would require direct consultation of his emended text which accompanied his preface.

This text is important for the light it sheds on one aspect of Irish continental scholarship of the period, and indeed of continental scholarship generally. Apart from the author's acquaintance with the Greek text, he was also familiar with Jerome's works, Jerome being for him the great authority (*qui celeberrimus in sancta Ecclesia per totum orbem proficum habetur*).

He mentions Jerome's *Tractatus (in Psalmos)*, which he must have known directly and not through the *Breviarium* (cf. 2.8 above). He makes rather liberal use of Jerome's letter 106 to Sunnia and Fretela on the emendation of the Psalter. From this letter (par. 44) he cites the evidence of Aquila, Symmachus, the Quinta, the Sexta, the Hexaplaric Septuagint and Theodotion. He knows of Jerome's preface to the Gallican Psalter and of the asterisks and obeli in this latter. He also knew of, and used, Jerome's rendering from the Hebrew (the *Hebraicum*). He cites from Jerome's letter (no. 112) to Augustine on the rendering from the Hebrew; likewise from Jerome's commentary on Matthew and from his preface to the Life of the Egyptian monks. He also seems to have known Isidore's *Etymologies* and Quintilian's *Institutes of Oratory*.

Who was the remarkable Irishman who gave us this work? His name must have been unknown to all three more or less contemporary scribes who copied his preface. Morin believed it was Sedulius of Liège, an opinion which Hellmann considered to be based on insufficient evidence. Manitius, however, favoured Morin's position. We have no evidence that Sedulius ever went as far as Milan. There was, however, an Irish colony in that city and if this preface is not the work of Sedulius it could well have been written by one of his disciples or by a student from the circle associated with him. It shows the same interest in the Greek Psalter text as do the other two works considered under 2.13 and 2.14. It would be interesting and possibly informative to compare the Greek text used by the Scot in question with the Basel and the Arsenal Psalters.

2.16. *Psalter of Codex BL Vitellius F. XI (about 920 CE)*

MS: British Library, MS Cotton Vitellius F. XI, 59 fols.

Studies: J.O. Westwood, 'On the Particularities Exhibited by the Miniatures and Ornamentation of Ancient Irish Illuminated Manuscripts', *Archaeological Journal* 7 (1850), pp. 17-25; L. Gougaud, 'Répertoire des fac-similés des manuscrits irlandais', *RC* 35 (1914), pp. 415-30 (423-24); J. Romilly Allen, 'On some Points of Resemblance between the Art of the Early Sculptured Stones of Scotland and Ireland', *PSAS* 31 (1897), pp. 326-27; F. Henry, 'Remarks on the Decoration of Three Irish Psalters', *PRIA* 61 C (1960), pp. 23-40; Henry, *Irish Art*, II, pp. 106-108; Anne O'Sullivan, 'The Colophon of the Cotton Psalter (Vitellius F. XI)', *JRSAI* 96 (1966), pp. 179-80; *Facsimiles of the National Monuments of Ireland*, part II (London, 1878), p. 24, pl. xlviii (fol. 29v, 38v; Pss. 84, 85, 101). (For this text see also later M. McNamara, 'The Psalms in the Irish Church: The Most Recent Research on Text, Commentary and Decoration—with Emphasis on the So-Called Psalter of Charlemagne), pp. 143-64 below.

This manuscript was damaged in the disastrous fire of Sir Robert Cotton's Library, then at Ashburnham House, in 1731. The beginning and the end are lost; what has survived is mostly shrunken and discoloured. The Codex contains a Psalter in Irish script and with Irish decoration, divided in typical Irish style (see 7.5 below) into the 'three fifties'. The text of the Psalter is Gallican.

Henry has published a study of its decoration, made possible even for the most damaged parts through infra-red photographs and special printing. The illuminations have a violence of style which closely connects them with the carvings on the tenth-century high crosses. There is a particularly close connection between the painting of David killing Goliath at the beginning of the third fifty and the same scene on the cross of Muiredach at Monasterboice. The Muiredach in question is most probably the one who became abbot about 887 and died in 923. Taking the two works as contemporary, Henry dates the Psalter to the early tenth century, as had already been done by J.O. Westwood on palaeographical grounds.

Henry's dating is confirmed by the colophon of the Psalter.[82] Although this colophon no longer exists in the Psalter itself, it had fortunately been copied, prior to its loss, by James Ussher and is now

---

82. See O'Sullivan, 'The Colophon'.

found in his notebooks in the Bodleian Library (MS Add. A. 91-S.C. 27719). It runs as follows (in O'Sullivan's rendering):

> The blessing of God on Aluiredach, bright fulfillment,
> may the scholar (probably = head of monastic school) be successful
>   and long-lived here,
> may his time here not be short;
> may the outstanding (?) abbot without falsehood
> be a dweller in the kingdom of heaven.

The Muiredach of this colophon, even though he might possibly be a contemporary abbot of Dromiskin or Duleek, or even of Bangor, is most probably the abbot of Monasterboice who died in 923.

2.17. *Airbertach Mac Coisse's Verse Rendition of the Introduction of the Old-Irish Treatise (982 CE)*

> MS: Oxford, Bodleian Library, Rawlinson B. 502, fol. 46a-b (twelfth century).

> Edition: K. Meyer, 'Erschienene Schriften', *ZCP* 1 (1897), pp. 496-97 (of small portions only, without translation); K. Meyer, 'Mitteilungen aus irischen Handschriften. Aus Rawlinson B.502 fo. 46a', *ZCP* 3 (1899), pp. 20-23 (complete text, without translation). Facsimile edition: K. Meyer, *Rawlinson B. 502: A Collection of Pieces in Prose and Verse in the Irish Language* (Oxford, 1909) (cf. p. vi).

> Studies: R.L. Ramsay, 'Theodore of Mopsuestia in England and Ireland', *ZCP* 8 (1912), pp. 474-76 (with translation of four quatrains by Eleanor Hull); Henry, *Irish Art*, III, p. 48 (on the artistic associations of Rawl. 502 with Clonmacnois), Kenney, *Sources*, p. 682; Thomas Olden, 'On the Geography of Ros Ailithir', *PRIA*, NS 16 (1854–88), pp. 219-52 (on Mac Coisse's geographical text from same MS).

Rawl. 502, fol. 46, contains religious poems by Airbertach Mac Coisse, the composition or the original writing of which is dated in the text as 21 December 982. After an introductory poem of 3 quatrains, there comes our text with 36 quatrains, subdivided into several sections. Next there is a poem on Adam's head, followed by 5 other quatrains.

Airbertach Mac Coisse (also called Airbertach mac Coisidobrain) was *fer-légind* or head of the monastic school of Ros Ailithir ('Ross of the Pilgrims'), present-day Rosscarbery in south-west Cork. The Annals of Inisfallen tell us that in 972 (*rectius* 991) he was taken prisoner by the Northmen when they destroyed Ros Ailithir. He was later rescued by Brian Boru at Scattery Island. He died in 1016. Apart from the poems listed above he composed, also in Irish, a versified compendium of geography. He was also very probably the author of a poem in 25 quatrains on Israel's war with the Midianites and of another in 61 quatrains on the kings of Israel. Professor Gearóid Mac Eoin believes Airbertach is also the author of *Saltair na Rann*, an Irish versified account of sacred history from creation to Doomsday, generally believed to have been composed in 988.[83]

The poem we are considering is a verse rendering of the introduction to the Psalter in the *Old-Irish Treatise* (2.11). That the verse account derives from the Old-Irish prose text is beyond doubt; there is even frequent verbal agreement, apart altogether from the content of both, which is the same. We cannot say whether Airbertach knew more of the *Old-Irish Treatise* than the introduction. His versification, as his other poems, most probably served as a help to memorization for his students at the school in Ros Ailithir.

2.18. *The Double Psalter of St Ouen (Tenth Century)*

MS: Rouen, Bibliothèque municipale 24 (A.41).

Editions: *Liber Psalmorum* (complete collation for the critical edition of the *Gallicanum* of St Jerome); H. de Sainte-Marie, *S. Hieronymi Psalterium iuxta Hebraeos* (Collectanea Biblica Latino, 11; Rome: Abbaye Saint-Jérôme; Vatican City: Libreria Vaticana, 1954) (complete collation of text of *Hebraicum* for the critical edition of Jerome's rendering from the Hebrew). For both texts our MS is signed I.

Studies: *Liber Psalmorum*, p. ix; H. de Sainte-Marie, *Psalterium iuxta Hebraeos*, pp. viii, xxiiff.; Kenney, *Sources*, p. 650; L. Bieler and G. MacNiocaill, 'Fragment of an Irish Double Psalter with Glosses in the Library of Trinity College, Dublin', *Celtica* 5 (1960), pp. 25-39; F. Henry, 'Remarks on the Decoration of Three Irish Psalters', *PRIA* 61 C (1960–1961), pp. 23-40 (at 37-40); Henry, *Irish Art*, II, pp. 59, 106. L. De Coninck, 'The Composite Literal Gloss of the Double Psalter of St. Ouen and the Contents of MS. Val. Pal. Int. 68', in T. O'Loughlin (ed.), *The Scriptures in Medieval Ireland: Proceedings of the 1993 Conference of the Society for Hiberno-Latin Studies on Early Irish Exegesis and Homilectics* (Instrumenta Patristica, 31; Steenbrügge: Abbatia St Petri–Turnhout: Brepols, 1999), pp. 81-93.

---

83. Professor James Carney disagrees with the date 988 and suggests the second half of the ninth century for the composition of the *Saltair* ('Notes on Early Irish Verse', *Éigse* 13 [1970], pp. 291-312 [291-92]).

Before coming into possession of the Municipal Library of Rouen this MS belonged to the church of St Ouen and earlier to the church of St Evreult. Script and illumination are Irish. The MS was written in Ireland, most probably in the tenth century. It was still in its homeland in the following century and has some Irish glosses of that date. It was in France, however, before the end of the twelfth century, a fact proved by the existence of some additional glosses in a twelfth-century French hand.

It is a Double Psalter containing the *Gallicanum* and the *Hebraicum* in verse facing it *in recto*. The codex now counts 160 folios (24 cm by 16 cm); three folios were lost—between pp. 242 and 243, 284 and 285, 306 and 307. The texts of both *Gallicanum* and *Hebraicum* belong to the Irish families; both have been fully collated for the above-mentioned critical editions. The Gallican text is one of the five which form the basis of the Roman edition (another is the Cathach; cf. 2.1 above). The *Hebraicum* of our MS is the purest representative of the Irish family.

The text is heavily glossed, the *Hebraicum* interlinearly and in the margin, the *Gallicanum* only between the lines. There are two different sets of marginal glosses, which seem to be written in different hands.[84] One set of these has been identified, in part at least, as an abbreviated form of the Milan commentary (2.7 above); the other is from a different source.[85] The relationship of the glosses to the Ambrosian commentary deserves further study. It is clear that many of those from Psalm 17 onwards are drawn from it. A check of the glosses for Psalms 1–18 has produced interesting results. None of the glosses checked for Psalms 7, 8, 9 and 16 are from the Milan commentary, whereas all those for Psalms 17 and 18 are. This would seem to be of extreme importance in view of Devreesse's discovery (see 2.7 above) that the Milan commentary at Ps. 16.11 changes text from a Latin translation of Theodore to another, non-Theodorean commentary. Do the glosses on Psalms 1–16 in the Rouen MS represent the first portion of the commentary found in the latter part of the Milan manuscript? Only more detailed study will show. An edition of these glosses on Psalms 1–16 is called for, and indeed of all the glosses of the Double Psalter of Rouen. The glosses on Psalms 1–16 may well turn out to depend on some early patristic commentary otherwise unknown; possibly even on a work of Julian of Eclanum.

---

84. Cf. Bieler and MacNiocaill, 'Fragment', p. 29.
85. Cf. Bieler and MacNiocaill, 'Fragment', p. 29.

2.19. *Fragment of Sister Codex of St Ouen Psalter (Tenth Century)*

MS: Dublin, Trinity College, MS 1337 (H. 3. 18), fols. 2*-3*.

Edition and Study: Bieler and MacNiocaill, 'Fragment', pp. 28-39
(with photo of fols. 2*v-3*r).

The manuscript 1337 (H. 3. 18) is a miscellany of law texts transcribed
by different scribes in the sixteenth and seventeenth centuries. Three
unpaginated leaves are bound in at the beginning of the codex. The first
(1*) contains legal matter. Next come two pages, a bifolium which was
the second from the centre of a quire. This carries fragments of a
Double Psalter—with the *Hebraicum* and *Gallicanum* texts as follows:

> 2*r: Ps. 71 (70).9-20a (*Hebraicum*);
> 2*v: Ps. 70.20b–71. 9a (*Gallicanum*);
> 3*r: Ps. 73 (72).3-17a (*Hebraicum*);
> 3*v: Ps. 72.17b—73. 2a (*Gallicanum*).

There are glosses on the Gallican text—some interlinear, but mostly
marginal. These glosses are derived from the Milan commentary (2.7
above).

In both text and glosses the Dublin fragment is closely related to the
corresponding portion of the Double Psalter of St Ouen (2.18). The two
mauscripts can be assigned to the same period, that is, probably the
tenth century. They were both written in Ireland, but unlike the Psalter
of St Ouen, now at Rouen, it does not appear that the Psalter to which
the Dublin fragments belong ever left its country of origin.

Both are copies of an earlier Irish Double Psalter, presumably with
glosses, which, it would appear, derived in the main from the Milan
commentary. Since the gloss on the Dublin fragment is on the *Gallicanum*—not, as in the Rouen Codex, on the *Hebraicum*—and since the
Gallicanum is a more suitable text for the gloss than the *Hebraicum*, it
may well be that in the parent text both the interlinear and the marginal
gloss were on the *Gallicanum*. The scribe of the St Ouen Psalter would
then have transferred the marginal gloss and the psalm headings (the
tituli psalmorum) to the margins of the *Hebraicum* and added another
marginal gloss of a completely different type from some other source;
of this second marginal gloss we have already spoken when considering
the Psalter of St Ouen.

2.20. *Psalter of Codex Vat. Lat. 12910 (Eleventh Century)*

MS: Vatican Latin, 12910.

This is a fragmentary text of an Irish Psalter,[86] a number of the original folios being lost; for example, the text passes from Ps. 5.5 on fol. 2v to 17.36C on fol. 3r. The biblical text is Gallican, of a type that can be determined only by a complete collation. A collation of Pss. 2.1–5.5 and 17.36-48 (fols. 1v-3r) with the critical edition shows that while it does on occasion agree with the Irish family of Gallican texts (5.5—*non volens deus*), in a number of instances it agrees with others (e.g. the Alcuin recension) against the Irish family. A complete collation of the MS is called for. (Since the foregoing passage was written the Psalter has been studied in detail by L. Bieler, 'A Gallican Psalter in Irish script, Vaticanus Lat. 12910', in P. Gambert and H.J.M. de Haan (eds.), *Essays Presented to G.I. Lieftinck.* II. *Texts and Manuscripts* (4 vols.; Amsterdam: van Gend, 1972), pp. 7-15.

2.21. *The Southampton Psalter (Beginning of Eleventh Century)*

MS: Cambridge, St John's College, MS C.9.

Edition (of glosses): *Thes. Pal.*, I, pp. xiv, 4-6 (of Irish glosses); R.L. Ramsay, 'Theodore of Mopsuestia in England and Ireland', *ZCP* 8 (1912), pp. 471-74 (of Latin glosses on Ps. 1 and some others). Facsimiles: Henry, *Irish Art*, II, pls. M, N, O; see also L. Gougaud, 'Répertoire des fac-similés des manuscrits islandais' (*RC* 35 [1914], pp. 415-30, 416).

Studies: Ramsay, 'Theodore of Mopsuestia', pp. 471-74 (on the Latin glosses and their relationships); F. Henry, 'Remarks', *PRIA* 61C (1959–61; paper published 1960), pp. 23-40 (33-36); Henry, *Irish Art*, II, pp. 106-108 (on decoration and the Psalter's relationship to Vitellius F. XI and to Psalter of St Ouen); see further Kenney, *Sources*, pp. 645-46 (no. 476); E.H. Zimmermann, *Vorkarolingische Miniaturen* (Berlin: Deutscher Verein für Wissenschaft, 1916), p. 111, pls. 212-13.

This is an illuminated Psalter intended for liturgical use or at least derived from one so intended. In the Irish style it is divided into the 'three fifties', with a picture page at the beginning of each: David

---

86. I wish to thank Dr Bieler for having brought the existence of this manuscript to my attention.

killing the lion, the crucifixion and David killing Goliath. A rhyming prayer and canticles are inserted after each of the three fifties.

The biblical text of the Psalter is Gallican. It has both interlinear and marginal glosses, some in Irish, the vast majority in Latin. The first page is more heavily glossed than the others. All the Irish glosses have been published but the Latin ones, apart from those edited by Ramsay, remain unedited.

Throughout, the Psalter reproduces the *Argumentum* for each psalm and the *Explanatio* for some of them. (On these see 2.3.c above.)

The Psalter is in an excellent state of preservation, as regards both its text and the colours of its decoration. Henry observes that the illuminator was inspired by Vitellius F.XI (2.16 above). His style, however, is more formal and less natural: in the representation of David and Goliath, for instance, he hardly understands what he is copying. On artistic as well as on linguistic grounds Henry believes that the MS was probably written at the beginning of the eleventh century. A tenth-century date would appear too early in view of the illumination.

Ramsay has made a special study of the glosses as bearers of Theodorean material.[87] The *Argumenta* reproduce such material, he notes, especially of the type found in the Milan commentary (2.7 above). However, in the *Argumentum* for Psalm 87 (fol. 61b) we have a Theodorean *Argumentum* found in the Syriac version of Theodore, but not in the Milan commentary. The Milan commentary was, then, not the sole source through which Theodore was known in ancient Ireland.

Ramsay finds that the glosses on Psalm 1 correspond exactly to the commentary on this psalm in the *Old-Irish Treatise* (2.11 above). This, he believes, 'makes it practically certain that the Psalter glosses must have been copied from the commentary or from its immediate source',[88] which we may recall was, in Ramsay's opinion, a Latin one. If this is so in the case of Psalm 1, we may presume the same of the remainder. These glosses, then, give us an idea of the lost portion of the *Old-Irish Treatise*.

I have collated the sections of the Psalter reproduced in plates by Henry (Pss. 51.3-8a in Pl. O; 99. 1-5 and 100. 1-7a in Pl. 48) and edited in the *Thes. Pal.*[89] In Ps. 51.3 (*gloriaris*) Southampton agrees with most MSS (including Cormac, 2.28 below) against the Cathach and the criti-

---

87. 'Theodore of Mopsuestia', pp. 471-74.
88. 'Theodore of Mopsuestia', p. 471.
89. I, pp. 4-6.

cal edition. In five cases it agrees with the Cathach and/or the Psalter of St Ouen against the critical text (51.3—omits *est*; 51.6—*lingua dolosa* for *-uam -osam*; 53.7—adds *tuo* to *tabernaculo*; 100.2—*innocentiam*; 100.7—*habitat* for *-abat*). In two of these cases (51.3; 100.7) the readings are attested only in these three MSS. In another (100.2) only one other MS has the same reading. The evidence from these readings would seem to indicate that Southampton belongs to the Irish family of Gallican texts. The texts published in the *Thes. Pal.* point in the same direction. Three readings are proper to the Irish family: Ps. 18.8 (*dei* for *domini*); 47.5 (adds *terrae*); 80.9 (*contestificabor* for *contedabor*, the former reading being found only in the Cathach, Psalter of St Ouen, Coupar-Angus Psalter and Southampton). We should note, however, that a number of the readings given in *Thes. Pal.* are unique (70.18; 73.6; 73.14; 77.6 [5]; 74.54). In Ps. 135.14 this MS goes with the Irish family and the best Gallican tradition in reading *rubrum mare* for *m.r.* A full collation of the biblical text of the Southampton Psalter is called for. Only in this way can we really determine where it stands within the family of Gallican manuscripts. Its entire body of glosses should also be published.

2.22. *The Edinburgh Psalter (about 1025 CE)*

MS: Edinburgh, University Library, MS 56 (142 folios).

Edition (in facsimile): *Celtic Psalter, Edinburgh University Library MS 56*, introduction by C.P. Finlayson (Umbrae Codicum Occidentalium, 7; Amsterdam: North-Holland Publishing Company, 1962).

Studies: Finlayson, *Celtic Psalter*, pp. v-xxxii (physical description, handwriting, decoration, text, later additions, provenance); Henry, *Irish Art*, II, pp. 58-59, 106; Henry, *Irish Art*, III, p. 120.

This is a pocket 'Hebrew' Psalter written in Irish miniscule and with Irish decoration. It contains 10 original quires, mostly of 14 leaves each, together with a quire of two leaves supplied in the fifteenth or sixteenth century. Fol. 50r has English eleventh-century illumination of the 'Winchester' style. Of the original Psalter the text of Pss. 1.1-2 and 148.14–150.6 (end) has been lost, but was supplied in the fifteenth–sixteenth century from a *Hebraicum* text of a different tradition. The text of Pss. 101 (102).1-3 and 120 (121).2–128 (129).5, also lost, has not been supplied. The loss of the latter section can be explained by the loss of an entire quire. It would appear that the original work remained in the form of separate unbound quires for a considerable period as the outermost pages of the quires are darkened. The present binding is modern.

To save space in this pocket Psalter the scribe resorts occasionally to arbitrary suspensions, mainly at the end of verses. On such occasions words can even be reduced to their initial letters, or occasionally omitted altogether, the omitted word being represented by a dot.[90] Such modes of abbreviation, however, are only resorted to when the text of the *Hebraicum* coincides with the more familiar *Gallicanum*. (See also 2.25 below.)

The Psalter text, as I have said, is Jerome's Latin rendering from the Hebrew, with the psalms, however, numbered according to the Septuagint and the *Gallicanum* (in the Hebrew the psalms between 9 and 136 are generally one in advance of the Septuagint and Gallican text). In Irish fashion the psalms are divided into the 'three fifties', each beginning with a special page of decoration. There are no psalm headings, biblical or otherwise. Nor were there any prayers originally, although a prayer has been supplied in a Gothic hand at the end of the first fifty (fol. 49).

The Irish script and decoration date the work to the eleventh century, as does the 'Winchester' style illumination. The work cannot be much later than the Southampton Psalter which its decorations closely resemble. For this reason Henry dates it to about 1025 CE.[91] The work was in Scotland before the end of the eleventh century. It could have been composed there. But if this is so, it proves close scholarly intercourse between Celtic Scotland and Ireland as 'all the elements of the Psalter's script are found in contemporary native Irish manuscripts, especially in those associated with Clonmacnoise'.[92] It is more natural to assume that it was written in Ireland in the Clonmacnois region (Clonmacnois or Inis Cealtra) and taken to Scotland by some visiting scholar.

The biblical text of the Psalter belongs to the Irish family (represented by the manuscripts with the sigla *AKI*) of *Hebraicum* manuscripts (cf. 5.4 below), a family characterized by certain omissions. Some of these omissions are found in all three MSS, and therefore derive from the common ancestor of *AKI*; others are found in *AK* only,

---

90. Familiar passages are abbreviated in a similar fashion in Irish Gospel-Books.
91. *Irish Art*, II, pp. 28-29.
92. Finlayson, *Celtic Psalter*, p. xxx.

which descend from a common ancestor inferior to *I*. Now, while the peculiarities common to *AKI* are almost all present in the Edinburgh Psalter, those peculiar to *AK* are almost all absent. (Ps. 21.2—*exultavit*—is an exception; cf. also Ps. 69.20—*reverentiam*—in which the Edinburgh MS agrees with *AK* against *I*). There are some instances, however, in which Edinburgh 56 agrees with the critical edition of Jerome's genuine text against *AKI*, for example, Ps. 104.12 (*nemorum*); 13.16 (*exultabit*; *AKI*: -*avit*); 66: 7 (*gentes*; *AKI*: *in gentes*). Edinburgh 56, then, represents an early tradition within the Irish family of *Hebraicum* manuscripts but appears to have undergone slight corrections to make it conform to other *Hebraicum* texts. Where exactly it stands within the Irish family can be determined only by detailed study.

2.23. *The Psalter of Ricemarch (soon after 1055 CE)*

MS: Dublin, Trinity College, MS 50 (A. 4. 20).

Edition: H.J. Lawlor, *The Psalter and Martyrology of Ricemarch* (2 vols.; London: Henry Bradshaw Society, 1914).

Studies: Lawlor, *The Psalter and Martyrology*; J.O. Westwood, 'Notice on a Manuscript of the Latin Psalter written by John, brother of Rhyddmarch', *Archaeologia Cambrensis* 1 (1846), pp. 117-25; H. de Sainte-Marie, *S. Hieronymi Psalterium iuxta Hebraeos* (Rome: Abbaye Saint-Jérôme; Vatican City: Libreria Vaticana, 1954), p. xli; Henry, *Irish Art*, II, p. 108; Henry, *Irish Art*, III, pp. 3, 56, 121; N.K. Chadwick, 'Intellectual Life in West Wales in the Last Days of the Celtic Church', in N.K. Chadwick, K. Hughes, C. Brooke and K. Jackson (eds.), *Studies in the Early British Church* (Cambridge: Cambridge University Press, 1958), pp. 121-82 (126-27, 165-71).

This Psalter is indirectly connected with Ireland in that it was written and decorated by sons of Sulien, a Welshman who had studied in Ireland. In a poem on Sulien one of his sons says:

> *Exemplo patrum commotus more legendi*
> *ivit ad Hibernos sophia mirabile claros.*

> Moved by the example of his fathers, eager for learning he went to the Irish, renowned for their marvellous wisdom.

This is a witness to the renown enjoyed by Ireland immediately after the defeat of the Danes. Sulien reached Ireland in 1045 and remained there for about ten years to study and be trained as a scribe and illuminator. On returning to Wales he imparted to others the learning he had acquired in Ireland. Among his students were four of his own sons, two of whom (Ricemarch and John) have given us the present Psalter, which is evidence of the Irish illumination of the period.

In the Irish fashion the Psalter is divided into three 'fifties', but there are neither canticles nor collects. This can be explained by its text, which is the *Hebraicum*. (Among texts of the *Hebraicum* it is listed as no. 47 by Dom de Sainte-Marie and as R by J.M. Harden, an earlier editor of this translation.) The *Hebraicum* of the Ricemarch Psalter belongs to the Irish family *AKI* (cf. 5.4 below), but represents the later form found in *K* (Codex Augiensis XXXVIII, now at Karlsruhe), the text of which it invariably follows. Whether Sulien took this *Hebraicum* text with him from Ireland or whether his sons copied it from a manuscript being used in Wales is difficult to decide.

2.24. *Abbreviated Psalter of the Irish* Liber Hymnorum *(Late Eleventh Century)*

> MS: Dublin, Trinity College (MS 1441 E. 4.2), fols. 22b-31a. Headed: '*Incipiunt MCLXV. orationes quas beatus papa Grigorius...congregauit*' Begins: *Deus in adiutorium...*'*Exsurge domine, saluum me fac deus meus*' (Ps. 3.7). Ends: '*Et eripe me de manu filiorum alienorum*' (Ps. 144.11).

> Edition: J.H. Bernard and R. Atkinson, *The Irish Liber Hymnorum* (2 vols.; Henry Bradshaw Society, 13 and 14; London: Henry Bradshaw Society, 1898), I, pp. 144-56 (text); II, pp. 216-18 (notes).

> Studies: Henry, *Irish Art*, III, pp. 56-59; see also Kenney, *Sources*, pp. 716-18 (both on the *Liber Hymnorum*).

The Irish *Liber Hymnorum* is extant in two MSS, that of Trinity College and that of the Franciscan Library, Killiney, County Dublin. The abbreviated Psalter is found only in the Trinity MS. Otherwise the two MSS are very similar in text and seem to go back to a common exemplar whose date on linguistic grounds can be assigned to the early eleventh century. The Trinity copy, from the evidence of language and decoration, can be dated to the late eleventh century, the Killiney one to the early twelfth.

The abbreviated Psalter consists of verses from the psalms in consecutive order, from Ps. 3.7 to Ps. 144.11. In the heading we are told that the number of prayers given from the Psalter is 365. In the extant text, however, we find only 240. This is so because there evidently is a gap in our MS between fols. 24 and 25, as the sequence passes suddenly from Ps. 42.3 to 69.6. Another indication of a lacuna is that the first and third 'fifty' is each introduced with an antiphon (*Deus in adiutorium*) and that the second and third 'fifty' end with the *Pater Noster*. This abbreviated Psalter was evidently divided in Irish style into the 'three fifties', each section having its own opening and ending.

The abridgement of the Psalter is in the tradition of that of the Book of Cerne and the others noted in 2.5 above. This particular one is attributed to St Gregory. It was apparently intended as a substitute for the entire Psalter and is further presented in the text as efficacious for the souls of the departed.

The Psalter text is the Gallican; it differs, however, in certain details from the critical edition of the Benedictines. Sometimes it agrees with the Irish witnesses of the *Gallicanum* against that edition (e.g. Pss. 24.11; 26.4; 26.9; 30.18; 32.22; 37.23). Occasionally its readings are unique. These details, however, are for the textual critic; the work merits examination to determine its exact relationship to the families of the Gallican Psalter, particularly to the Irish family.

2.25. *The So-Called Psalter of St Caimin (about 1100 CE)*

MS: Franciscan Library, Killiney, County Dublin, MS A.I; 6 fols.

Studies: M. Esposito, 'On the So-called Psalter of Saint Caimin', *PRIA* 32 C (1913), pp. 78-88 (with 1 plate: fol. 3b, p. 6); Kenney, *Sources*, pp. 646-47; *Thes. Pal.*, I, pp. xiv, 6 (edition of Irish glosses); F. Henry and G.L. Marsh-Micheli, 'A Century of Irish Illumination (1070–1170)', *PRIA* 62 C (1962), pp. 101-64 (esp. 117-19); Henry, *Irish Art*, III, pp. 41, 48, 50.

The extant part of the so-called Psalter of St Caimin consists of a quire of six folios (numbered as pages 1-12) with portions of Psalm 118 (Vulgate numbering), that is the *Beati*. On these folios we have verses 1-16 and 33-116 (the entire psalm has 176 verses). The folios measure 10 inches by 131. The biblical text is written in beautiful majuscule with 14 to 18 lines per page. The biblical text at the centre of the page in majuscule is the Gallican. At the top of each page the corresponding section of the *Hebraicum* is written in minuscule and in an abbreviated form, the words agreeing with the *Gallicanum* being represented only 'by their initial letter (cf. 2.22 above). Very wide margins are left on either side of the pages. These margins are glossed, the left-hand ones very heavily. Psalm 118 in the Hebrew is alphabetic, and is divided into

22 sections according to the number of letters of the Hebrew alphabet, each verse of a group beginning with the appropriate Hebrew letter. This division is followed in the Psalter of Caimin; the initial word of each section begins with an ornamental capital. Each section is also preceded by a long psalm heading, for which ample space is left in the manuscript. These headings would appear to have been written before the text of the corresponding section: the script of the headings does not in the least look crowded. Together with the marginal glosses there are also glosses between the lines.

If this is but a section of an entire Psalter written in the same way as the six folios we now have, the complete work must have consisted of 216 or more folios. It would have been one of the finest of later Irish manuscripts. It could well be, however, that the original work contained only Psalm 118 with its glosses. In this case the original would have consisted of some twelve folios. The *Beati* was an extremely popular psalm in Ireland (it was even referred to in Irish as the *Biait*) and was often recited alone. That the latter was the case may be argued from the long introduction prefixed to v. 1.

The manuscript (fol. 2a)[93] has a note by Michael O'Clery (died 1645 CE) saying that he got the leaves from Flann and Bernard MacBruaidedha (Mac Brody) who, like their ancestors before them, resided in Termonn Caimin. According to the tradition they had received, the MS was written by St Caimin (died 664) of Inis Cealtra (Holy Island). In 1639 this fragment was in the Franciscan Convent in Donegal. Soon afterwards it was taken to the Franciscan Convent of St Anthony in Louvain. During the French Revolution part of the MS was taken to St Isidore's, Rome, and another part to Brussels. In 1872 the MS was transferred to Dublin and in recent times to the Franciscan House of Studies, Killiney, County Dublin, where it now is.

The MS was written long after the time of St Caimin. The language of the Irish glosses (on fols. la, 3a, 4a, 5a, 5b, 6b), the script and the decoration all point to about 1100 CE, a date assigned to it by J.A. Brunn in 1897.[94] Henry dates it to the late eleventh century. From the ornamentation she assigns its composition to the monastery of St Caimin at Inis Cealtra, or possibly to that of Clonmacnois further up the Shannon.

The text of the Psalter itself is Gallican. Esposito has attempted a collation which, unfortunately, is useless because of the inferior texts he

93. Reproduced by Esposito, 'On the So-called Psalter', p. 79.
94. Cf. Esposito, 'On the So-called Psalter', p. 81.

used for comparison.[95] Many of the 'deviations' he notes are in fact really genuine Gallican readings. I have collated the entire MS against the critical edition of the *Gallicanum* and find it impossible to connect it with a particular family of Gallican texts. For the verses in question the 'Irish' family, as represented by *I* (i.e. the Psalter of St Ouen; 2.18 above) has seven deviations from the critical text. In three of these (vv. 53: *pro*; 62 *iustitiae*; 100: *exquisiui*) Caimin agrees with *I*; in the remainder it agrees with the critical text against *I*. It has five readings common to *I* and *F* (Codex Corbiensis). It also has some readings of the Paris recension represented by the Coupar-Angus Psalter (2.27 below) and has readings peculiar to itself (vv. 11: *abscondidi*; 16: *in tuis iustificationibus* for *i. i. t*; 48: *mirabilibus* for *iustificationibus*; 71: *quod* for *quia*; 110: *a* for *de*). Together with this it has some obeli that are attested in no other text: vv. 34, 40, 50, 66, 67, 68, 69, 81, 95, 105, 116. There also appear to be two asterisks in the same category (vv. 40, 112).

A collation of the *Hebraicum* text of Caimin against the readings peculiar to the Irish family *AKI* shows that Caimin agrees with *AKI* against the critical text in vv. 14, 58, 59, 70 (twice); with *AK* in vv. 42, 62, 72, 73, 80, 81; with *A* in v. 77 and with *K* in v. 98. On the other hand it goes against *AKI* in v. 57 (*mea*); against *AK* in vv. 80 and 81; against *AI* in v. 70; against *I* in vv. 56, 57, 70, 85 and 88; against *A* in vv. 56, 76, 82, 83, 84, 85, 93 and 114 (twice) and against a reading proper to *K* in v. 76. The *Hebraicum* text of Caimin, then, would appear to belong basically to the Irish family (*AKI*) of texts but does not represent it in a pure state. The task of determining the exact family of Caimin is here rendered more difficult by its abbreviated writings and by the very real possibility of contamination from the *Gallicanum* which the *Hebraicum* accompanies. Some aberrant readings in the *Hebraicum*, which I have noted, are possibly scribal errors. Whatever of the exact biblical text, the manuscript is clear evidence of the use of the *Hebraicum* at Inis Cealtra or Clonmacnoise in the eleventh century. We have further evidence of this from the Edinburgh Psalter (2.22 above).

What I take to be clear instances of the obelus (and possibly of the asterisk) Esposito reckons as 'ornamental signs used here and there to fill up space'![96] The signs are clearly obeli—the division sign ($\div$) followed by the colon (:). I have already listed those proper to Caimin. In

95. Esposito, 'On the So-called Psalter, p. 83.
96. Esposito, 'On the So-called Psalter', p. 82.

seven other occurrences (vv. 39, 49, 51, 77, 92, 99 and 105) of the obelus, it marks words so marked also in the second hand of Codex Sangallensis 20 (ninth century); the words *sub obelo* in v. 39 are also *sub obelo* in the second hand of Codex Reginensis, eighth century, and that of v. 92 is written *manu secunda* in *I*. In no other MS of the *Gallicanum* listed in the critical edition is any of these words *sub obelo*. This seems to indicate some relationship between Caimin and Codex Sangallensis, written in the ninth century by the scribe Wolfcoz. The purpose of the obeli in Caimin is clear. It is to correct the text in accord with the*Hebraicum*. The words obelized are nearly always absent in all texts of the *Hebraicum*. In v. 40 it marks a word (*tua*) omitted only in *AI* of the Irish family. (The word *is* in the *Hebraicum* text reproduced by Caimin!) On the other hand in v. 68 it marks a word (*es*) absent from all *Hebraicum* texts *except AK* and that of Caimin. In v. 95 it marks a word (*me*, 20) absent only in Codex Legionensis[2] of the *Hebraicum*. In vv. 67, 69, 81, and 105 it indicates words not found in any *Gallicanum* MS except Caimin. In v. 105 it actually marks two words (*tuum Domine*), the last one absent from the *Hebraicum* and the Gallican in general— probably being the only word on which it should be.

What appears to be an asterisk (a cross with four dots in the angles accompanied by the colon) in vv. 40 and 112 is found in no other Gallican MS. Nor does there appear to be any grounds for it, the words under the asterisk being in the Septuagint. If this mark is really an asterisk it presents the same problems as some of those in the Cathach (1.2.a above).

I now pass to the psalm headings which introduce each section of Psalm 118. That to the first section is composite, it begins (lines 1-4) with some unidentified text, continues (to line 7) with a text basically from Jerome's *Commentarioli* (on Ps. 118), found also in the *Breviarium in Psalmos* (its reference to Ps. 114 being alphabetic is found in neither), then gives Cassiodorus's *Divisio* and ends with the Cassiodorus's psalm heading (cf. 2.3 above). The headings to the other sections are also from Cassiodorus, in the main a combination of his commentary and the psalm headings derived from it. Together with these psalm headings in large minuscule there is another series in small minuscule, directly above the first line of each section. This series is practically identical with that of the Nonantola Psalter (tenth–eleventh centuries; with Roman Psalter as text). This Psalter, it may be noted, has conjoined these particular headings to the Columba Series for

Psalm 118; it also has the Cassiodorus Series. The Psalter of Caimin may in some way be connected with it.

I have noted that the Psalter of Caimin is heavily glossed. I have failed to identify the source of the interlinear glosses and of those in the right-hand margins. Of those in the left-hand margin, some at least are composite. Apart from those listed below, I have failed to identify them in the commentaries of Jerome (including the *Breviarium*), Augustine, Cassiodorus, Hilary or the Milan commentary: for example, p. 2: gloss 2 in part from Milan commentary; gloss 3 in part from Milan; p. 5, gloss 1 from Milan; p. 5, gloss 9 from Milan; p. 6, gloss 5, from Milan; p. 9, gloss 3 (on *sicut gelv*, v. 83), cf. Milan; p. 9, gloss 5, from Milan; p. 11, second last gloss, from Milan; p. 12, first part from Milan.

The Milan commentary refers this psalm to the Jews in the Babylonian captivity. It is worthy of note that many of the glosses on the left-hand margins, even when not found in the Milan commentary, mention the Babylonian captivity, the Chaldeans, and so on (cf. p. 3, gl. 5, 6, 8; p. 5, gl. 2, 6, 7; p. 6, gl. 6, 8; p. 7, gl. 4; p. 9, gl. 1: on *defecit* of v. 81: *Vox electorum in Babilonia captivorum magno desiderio desiderantium de captiuitate salutem*; gl. 6; p. 10, gl. 8; p. 11, gl. 10-11; p. 12, gl. 9.

Some of the glosses also refer to Saul, Absalom, Achitophel; for example, p. 5, gl. 3; p. 7, gl. 4; p. 11, gl. 10-11; gl. 3-4 (refers to David's love for Saul); gl. 5-6 (refers to Susanna); p. 12, gl. 4 (Saul, Absalom and captivity). In thus combining references to the life of David and to the exile, these glosses are reminiscent of the catena of the Vatican Palatino 68 (2.4 above). Indeed, the glosses may well be related to this earlier work. A comparison of the glosses in the Psalter of Caimin and in Vat. Pal. lat. 68 as well as in the Psalter of St Ouen (2.18 above) and the Southampton Psalter (2.21 above) is called for.

In conclusion I can say that the six folios of the so-called Psalter of Caimin, even if but a fragment of the original work, present very valuable information on the study of the psalms in some monastery on the Shannon in the eleventh century. Publication of its rich body of glosses would help us to get a better understanding of the sources on which its compilers drew.

2.26. *The Psalter of Ms Cotton Galba A.V. (Twelfth Century)*

MS: British Library, Codex Galba A.V. (35 folios).

Studies: *Facsimiles of the National Manuscripts of Ireland*, part II (London, 1878), p. xxiv (description), pl. xlix; F. Henry and G.L. Marsh-

Micheli, 'A Century of Irish Illumination (1070–170)', *PRIA* 62 C (1962), pp. 101-64 (at 141-43) (pl. xxiii); Henry, *Irish Art*, III, p. 47; Kenney, *Sources*, p. 647; Thomas Smith, *Catalogus Librorum manuscriptorum Bibliothecae Cottonianae* (Oxford, 1696), p. 61 (brief description). (For this text see 1998 revision in this volume; pp. 154-56 below.)

This MS was severely damaged by the fire of 1731 (see 2.16 above). It now has only 35 folios, turned brown. Among the lost pages is the one written in Irish which, according to Smith, was at the end of the manuscript.

The MS is of the twelfth century. The psalter is divided in Irish style into the 'three fifties', with canticles and collects at the end of each division. Each of the three parts is introduced by a decorated page.[97] The biblical text appears to be Gallican

2.27. *The Coupar-Angus Psalter (about 1170 CE)*

MS: Vatican, Pal. lat. 65, fols. 197.

Editions and facsimiles: *Liber Psalmorum*; (siglum: V, complete collation); F. Ehrle and F. Liebart, *Specimena Codicum Latinorum Vaticanorum* (Bonn, 1912), pl. xxiv; J.B. Cardinal Pitra, H. Stephenson and I.B. de Rossi (eds.), *Codices Palatini Latini Bibliothecae Vaticanae*, I (Rome, 1886), p. 11; *Codices e Vaticanis selecti phototypice expressi*, series minor, I (Rome, 1912).

Studies: *Liber Psalmorum*, p. x; H.M. Bannister, 'Specimen Pages of Two Manuscripts of the Abbey of Coupar-Angus in Scotland', in Pitra, Stephenson and de Rossi (eds.), *Codices e Vaticanis selecti*); H.M. Bannister, 'Irish Psalters', *JTS* 12 (1910–1911), pp. 280-84; H.M. Bannister, 'Abbreviations &c in MS Vatican-Palat.-Lat. 65', *ZCP* 8 (1912), pp. 246-58 (on abbreviations and date of MS); Henry and Marsh-Micheli, 'A Century of Irish Illumination', pp. 157-59, pl. xxxiii and xxxiv; Henry, *Irish Art*, III, pp. 47-48; Dom D. de Bruyne, 'La reconstruction du psautier hexaplaire latin', *RBén* 41 (1929), pp. 297-324.

The Psalter, which bears a thirteenth-century *ex libris* of the Scottish Cistercian abbey of Coupar-Angus, is connected in script and decoration with the products of northern Ireland, particularly with MS 122 of

---

97. An example is given by Henry and Marsh-Micheli, 'A Century', pl. xxiii..

the Library of Corpus Christi College, Oxford (written probably at Bangor about 1140).

In the opinion of Henry, the Coupar-Angus Psalter was written at the monastery of Viride Stagnum (Soulseat, Wigtownshire, Scotland), which appears to have followed the Cistercian rule. On his journey from Bangor to the Continent in 1148 St Malachy visited this monastery and left some monks there under an abbot who had been a monk at Bangor. Viride Stagnum disappeared soon afterwards and its books would have passed to the Cistercian monastery of Coupar-Angus. From Scotland the Psalter passed to Heidelberg and thence, during the Thirty Years' War, to the Vatican.

The book is of large format (9 ins. by 12¼ ins.). The Psalter is divided into the 'three fifties' and has the canticles. The first page of each 'fifty' is written in Irish majuscule, the remainder in minuscule. The text is accompanied by the *Maior (Magna) Glossatura* of Peter the Lombard. This gloss, completed in 1142–43, is based on that of Anselm of Laon. Although the gloss on the Coupar-Angus differs in places from the Lombard's work, the completion of the latter provides a terminus a quo for the former. Bannister dates our MS as not before the second half of the twelfth century, Henry before 1170.

The text of the Psalter is Gallican. It represents, as Dom de Bruyne[98] has ascertained, the recension used in the University of Paris in the thirteenth century. As regards both text and gloss, then, the Coupar-Angus Psalter represents the new learning, whose introduction into these islands is seen to be associated with the Cistercians. Its exemplar may have been either Scottish or Irish.

2.28. *The Psalter of Cormac (1150–1200 CE)*

MS: British Library, Additional MS 36929 (fols. 197).

Editions (of individual folios, in facsimile): F. Henry and G.L. Marsh-Micheli, 'A Century of Irish Illumination', pl. xxxviii (Ps. 1, Part); pl. xx3D (Ps. 51, part); pl. xl (Ps. 101, Part); pl. xli (fols. 31v-32r; Pss. 30.25–32.2); Henry, *Irish Art*, III, pl. 14 (fol. 60, Ps. 51.3-4); pl. 15 (fol. 122, Ps. 101.4); plates A + B (between pp. 56-57, fols. 5b-6a, Pss. 6.2–7.6).

Studies: *Catalogue of Additions to the Manuscripts in the British Museum in the Years 1800–1905* (London, 1907), pp. 259-60; H.M.

---

98. 'La reconstruction'.

Bannister, 'Irish Psalters', *JTS* 12 (1910–1911), p. 282; E.H. Zimmermann, *Vorkarolingische Miniaturen* (Berlin, 1916), p. 109, pl. 216a; Henry and Marsh-Micheli, 'A Century', pp. 161-64.

This small volume (7 ins. by 5¹/₂ ins.) which before binding was somewhat larger, now has 179 folios out of its original 182; one folio was cut off at the beginning and two at the end. The Psalter is divided into the 'three fifties'. Each fifty is followed by collects and canticles. The psalms as far as Psalm 57 inclusive are provided with series of allegorical headings in the place of the biblical ones. The colophon, after the first 'fifty', (fol. 59r), reads thus: *Cormacus scripsit hoc psalterium ora pro eo. Qui legis hec ora pro sese qualibet hora*. The Psalter proper is preceded by three texts. The first, headed *Expositio sancti Augustini in Psalmos*, is generally attributed to Alcuin (*PL* 101, col. 466). The second, headed *Absolutio Bernarddi*, is a formula of a well-known twelfth-century type. This is accompanied by some staves of music for which we have parallels in Cistercian MSS of the twelfth century. The third text *Ante psalmos oremus* is found in psalters from the tenth to the fifteenth centuries. The script and decoration of the Psalter are Irish.

The British Library purchased the Psalter in Munich in 1904. It must have been in Germany for some time as its binding, of the late sixteenth or early seventeenth century, is German. That the MS is Irish is indicated by script and decoration as well as by the scribe's name, Cormac. Henry and Marsh-Micheli believe that it was written in Ireland, rather than by an Irish scribe in Germany. Together with the Book of Leinster they place the composition of the Psalter in a scriptorium of the centre of Ireland. It was probably written in and for a Cistercian house. Various indications permit us to date it to the late twelfth century.

The text of the Psalter is Gallican, but its exact place within the families of Gallican texts can be determined only by a complete collation. In the published portion of the text I have noted some readings typical of the Paris Recension (e.g. Pss. 7.5; 101.4), of which the chief representative is the Coupar-Angus Psalter (2.27). This is not surprising in view of its Cistercian associations. The allegorical headings also require study. The two known from the plates noted above (to Pss. 7 and 51) belong to Dom Salmon's series II (2.27 above). The Psalter of Cormac, then—like the Coupar-Angus Psalter, probably—represents the later recension of the *Gallicanum* whose introduction to Ireland can be associated with the Cistercians.

2.29. *Columbanus's Commentary on the Psalms*

> Studies: See Kenney, *Sources*, pp. 200-201 (no. 47); to which add:
> Dom G. Morin, 'Le "Liber S. Columbani in Psalmos" et le Ms.
> Ambros. C. 301 inf...', *RBén* 38 (1926), pp. 164-77 (see 2.7 above);
> Michele Tosi, 'Il commentario di S. Colombano sui salmi', *Columba*
> (Bobbio) 1 (1964), pp. 3-14; G.S.M. Walker (ed.), *Sancti Columbani*
> *Opera* (SLH, 3; Dublin: Dublin Institute for Advanced Studies, 1957),
> p. lxiv-v; G.F. Rossi, C.M., 'Il commentario di S. Colombano ai Salmi
> ritrovato a Bobbio in un codice della fine del secolo XII', *Divus*
> *Thomas* 67 (1964), pp. 89-93. F. Nuvolone, 'Le commentaire de S.
> Columban sur les psaumes rentre-t-il définitivement dans l'ombre?',
> *Freiburger Zeitschrift für Philosophie und Theologie* 26 (1979),
> pp. 211-19.

In his *Life of Columbanus* Jonas tells us that the saint left his native
Leinster to study under the holy man Sinilis (generally assumed to be St
Senell of Cleenish in Lough Erne) before he went on to Bangor to live
the religious life under Comgall. Having spoken of his progress in
learning under Sinilis, Jonas goes on to say: 'So great were the trea-
sures of the divine scriptures held in his breast that even at a youthful
age he (Columbanus) expounded the book of Psalms in elegant language' (*elimato sermone*).[99] While it does not follow from Jonas' words
that Columbanus composed this work as a student of Sinilis, it is
implied that he compiled it when still in Ireland.

The commentary apparently was taken to the Continent; it probably
is referred to in the ninth-century St Gall catalogue as *Expositio sancti*
Columbani super omnes psalmos volumen I and in the tenth-century
Bobbio catalogue as *Liber sancti Columbani in psalmos II*. The significance of 'Volumen I' and 'II' is hard to determine. It may be that
there were two volumes in the commentary, the first of which was at St
Gall and the second at Bobbio. It is, however, also possible that the
commentary was in one book, of which the Bobbio Library had two
copies.

The fifteenth-century inventories of the Bobbio Library, however,
make no mention of Columbanus's work. Nor could Patrick Fleming
find any trace of it in either Bobbio or St Gall when he searched for it in
the seventeenth century. In 1740 Domenico Vallarsi put forward the

---

99. Krusch (ed.), *Ionae Vitae Sanctorum Columbani*, p. 158; cf. pp. 29-30 on
Columbanus and Codex Amb. C 301 inf.

view that Columbanus's work was preserved in the Milan commentary (2.7 above), an opinion later defended, as we have seen, by Ramsay and Dom Morin. An attempt has even been made to identify Columbanus's commentary with the *Breviarium in Psalmos* (2.8 above).

A new possibility was advanced by Don Michele Tosi,[100] archivist of the Bobbio episcopal archives, in 1964, and this appropriately in the first issue of a new review, *Columba*, bearing Columbanus's original name. Don Tosi there reports his discovery of a commentary on the psalms in the Bobbio archives which may possibly be the one composed by Columbanus in his youth. The MS (of 194 folios) was apparently written in the late twelfth or early thirteenth century and, to judge from its miniatures, at Bobbio. Certain abbreviations characteristic of the eighth century, Don Michele remarks, are suggestive of an earlier exemplar.

The commentary in question is inspired to a large extent by the commentary of Cassiodorus (see 2.12 above), who is once cited by name. Its biblical text, written in the centre of each page with a large margin below, is the Gallican. The commentary, in the form of glosses, is written on the sides and also between the lines.

A note on fol. 1 in an eighteenth-century hand says that, so far as one can believe, the commentary is the work of Columbanus. While granting that this may be so, Don Tosi tells us that he has set himself the task of determining the real author. Rossi expresses reservations on Columban authorship without a more detailed examination of the work.[101] I am not aware that Don Tosi has written on the matter since.

Only with difficulty, indeed, can one accept that the commentary discovered by Don Tosi is the work of the young Columbanus. The most serious objection is the use of Cassiodorus's commentary, completed in 548, which was hardly known to Columbanus. Unfortunately the chronology of the saint is uncertain. One school dates his birth and his departure from Ireland to 540 CE (or 543) and 575 respectively, another to 559/56 and 590. It is unlikely that Cassiodorus's commentary was known in Ireland even by the end of the sixth century. The earliest attested use of it in England was made by Bede (seventh–eighth centuries); in Ireland there is no evidence of such use before the eighth–ninth centuries (cf. 2.9, 10, 11 above). There certainly is no trace of

100. 'Il commentario', p. 12.
101. 'Il commentario', p.12.

Cassiodorus in those writings of Columbanus which are accepted as genuine.[102]

While Columbanus's authorship of the commentary in this Bobbio manuscript would remain uncertain for the reasons given, identification of the gloss it carries as deriving from the *Glossa ordinaria super psalmos* (twelfth century?) puts beyond doubt any connection of the work with Columbanus.[103]

2.30. *Marianus Scottus (died 1080) and the Psalter*

> Literature: See Stegmüller, *Repertorium*, III, no. 5454 (p. 535); Kenney, *Sources*, pp. 616-18 (no. 444); the Bollandists' *Acta Sanctorum*, February II (Paris and Rome, 1864), pp. 361-72.

The real name of Marianus Scottus was Muiredach mace Robartaig. The Maic Robartaig (Maic Roarty or Rafferty) family in Donegal were the hereditary custodians of the Cathach (2.1 above) of the O'Donnells. In 1067 Muiredach with two companions set out on pilgrimage to Rome, but remained in Ratisbon, where he died in 1080.

a. *Psalters written by Marianus Scottus*. In the *Life of Marianus* (written in 1184/85) we are told that

> with his own hand he wrote the Old and New Testaments with their expository comments. Moreover during the same time he had written many books and many manuals of the Psalter for poor widows and clerks of the same city (Ratisbon), for the benefit of his soul, without any hope of earthly reward.

No manuscripts of such Psalters are listed by Stegmüller.

b. *Commentary on the Psalter by Marianus Scottus (1074)*. In the *Acta Sanctorum* (February, II, p. 363; introduction no. 12) the following passage is transcribed from the *Annals of Bavaria*[104] (Book 4) of Aventinus (who died at Ratisbon 1534 CE):

---

102. Columbanus's great authority on scriptural matters was Jerome; see his letter (*Ep* I. 5) to Pope Gregory, in Walker (ed.), *Sancti Columbani Opera*, pp. 8-9.

103. See Nuvolone, 'Le commentaire'.

104. *Annales Boiorum* (editio 1554), *lib*. 5, p. 554. The text is also cited in Latin by J. O'Hanlon, *Lives of the Irish Saints*, II (Dublin: James Duffy; London: Burns, Oates & Co.; New York: The Catholic Publishing Society; no date; but preface I 1875), p. 422 n. 5.

At Ratisbon (Regenburgi) in the lower monastery are to be found the divine hymns of David with commentaries, written on parchment, the work of Marianus. Its preface runs verbally as follows: 'In the year of Our Lord's Incarnation 1074, Henry the Younger being Emperor, Mactilda the abbess of St. Mary's, Marianus Scottus, in the seventh year of his pilgrimage gathered these ripples *(modicas undas)* from the deep sea of the Fathers, i.e. from the works of Jerome, Augustine, Cassiodorus and Arnobius and from the minor works (opusculis) of St. Gregory, and put them together in one book in honour of Our Saviour, the Lord Jesus Christ, of his Mother the ever-Virgin Mary, and of St. Herhardus the Confessor'.

As far as we know this commentary no longer exists. A copy of St Paul's epistles from the pen of Marianus (written 1079 CE) is now at Vienna.[105]

2.31. *Irish Psalters and Psalm Commentaries in Medieval Continental Libraries*

Editions of catalogues: G. Becker, *Catalogi bibliothecarum antiqui* (Bonn, 1885); T. Gottlieb, *Über mittelalterliche Bibliothekwesen* (Leipzig, 1890). See further Kenney, *Sources*, pp. 620-21 (no. 449); G. Murphy, 'Scotti Peregrini', *Studies* 17 (1928), pp. 39-50, 229-224 (for these wandering scholars in general; pp. 49-50 for their scribal activity).

Some of the material I have considered is now found in libraries on the Continent. The presence of books in the peculiar Irish script did not pass unnoticed by mediaeval librarians and is recorded in some extant catalogues. To mention only references to the Psalms: the catalogue of the monastery of St Remacle at Stavelot (1105 CE) registers *psalterium scotticum*, that is a psalter in Scottic (Irish) script; the twelfth-century catalogue of St Maximin at Trèves includes *Expositio psalterii scottice conscripta*.[106]

3. *Material for Psalm Study Available in Irish Monasteries*

Irish psalm study, as mediaeval studies in general, was repetitive rather than original or creative. Its value will, therefore, largely depend on the

105. Kenney, *Sources*, pp. 618-19.
106. In mediaeval catalogues there are also references to unspecified books in 'Scottic' script, some of which may have been Psalters or commentaries on the Psalms.

sources used by individual writers or compilers. We are still far from having a comprehensive picture of the knowledge and use of the litera- ture of Christian antiquity in early Ireland. As a first step the sources of each individual Irish writer will have to be analysed in detail. Only then shall we be in a position to determine when, and possibly where, a par- ticular work was introduced. We may even be able to identify the text used in Ireland with a particular recension of that work. Here I limit myself to the sources available for the study of the psalms.

3.1. *Psalm Prefaces*

The Milan commentary (2.7 above) proper is preceded by two prefaces of Jerome, by the preface attributed to Bede and by the preface of Basil, in the Latin translation of Rufinus. The first three were widely used in the western Church. The Irish glosses that accompany them indicate that they were used also in the early Irish schools. The preface of Basil, in Rufinus's version, was often attributed to St Augustine; in the Milan commentary, however, it is introduced: *Hirunintus dicit*. As it has no Irish glosses, we cannot be sure that it was used in Ireland. The prefaces of Jerome give information on the Gallican and Hebrew versions, on the obeli and asterisks, and on the various Greek translations of the Psalter. Both supplied much information to the early Irish commenta- tors, as did the preface of Bede. Jerome's preface to the *Hebraicum*, *Scio quosdam*, is cited in the *Eclogae* (2.9). Both of Jerome's prefaces were known to the Irish author of the letter on the translation of the Psalter from the Greek (2.15).

3.2. *Psalm Headings*

I have considered above the St Columba series of psalm headings (2.3) which relate the psalms to Christ, to the Church and to Christian life. These headings testify to an approach to the psalms which we find reflected in the introduction to the psalms in the *Old-Irish Treatise* (2.11; lines 320-29).

3.3. *The Fathers*

The Vatican Catena on the Psalms (2.4) contains excerpts from Hilary, Jerome, Theodore and the Milan commentary (possibly the work of Julian of Eclanum). The *Eclogae* (2.9) use Hilary, Cassiodorus, Isidore, Augustine, Josephus, Junilius, Eucherius, Jerome and Ambrose in the introduction, and in the commentary proper Jerome's *Commentarioli* and *Tractatus*, but principally the Milan commentary, which the compiler believed to be a work of Jerome. The *Old-Irish Treatise* (2.11) cites much the same names in the introduction (Jerome, Isidore, Hilary, Gregory, Augustine and Sebastianus [?]; it also uses Junilius without citing by name) to which in the partial commentary on Psalm 1 it adds Ambrose, Cassiodorus and Bede. The introduction to the Psalter in the Irish *Reference Bible* (2.10) uses much the same sources and some of the same texts as the *Eclogae*. The Double Psalter of St Ouen (2.18) and its sister codex (2.19) excerpt from the Milan commentary; the former draws also on some unidentified source. The Psalter of Caimin (2.26) uses Theodorean material, probably through the Milan commentary, but draws on Jerome and some unidentified works besides. In the Coupar-Angus Psalter (2.27), we find the later learning of the *Glossa Maior*.

All the great writers on the psalms, then, were known in Ireland. In many instances, however, it remains to be determined whether the Irish had the original commentaries before them or knew them indirectly through catenae or *eclogae*. It would seem that the Irish did have the Milan commentary and possibly also that of Cassiodorus (cf. 2.12). Future research on this problem should not be confined to glosses and similar on the Psalter but should extend to the study of the Fathers by Hiberno-Latin writers in general. Attention must also be paid to errors of ascription in citations (cf. 2.9 and 2.10 above).

3.4. *The Influence of Theodore of Mopsuestia on Irish Exegesis*
No writer on the psalms influenced Irish exegesis more than Theodore of Mopsuestia. A Latin translation of his commentary on the psalms is preserved in the Turin fragments (2.6) and in part of the Milan Codex (2.7); the remainder of the Milan commentary (on Pss. 16.11 to the end) is Theodorean at least in inspiration. Indirectly his thought was probably transmitted through Junilius, who is cited in the *Eclogae* (2.9) and used in the *Old-Irish Treatise* (2.11).

Theodore's influence is seen also in the Bedan psalm headings (2.3). The Milan commentary heavily influences the Vatican Catena (2.4) and is virtually the sole source for the exposition of the psalms in the *Eclogae*, at least in the sections which I examined, and in the Psalter of St Ouen and its sister codex. Theodorean matter, as already noted, is found in the Psalter of St Caimin. Theodore has influenced the commentary of the *Old-Irish Treatise* and through it, it would appear, the glosses of the

Southampton Psalter (2.21). His influence on early Irish Psalter exegesis is, in fact, all-pervading—almost as much so as is that of Pelagius on the exposition by the Irish of the Pauline Epistles. This is all the more striking in that the Theodorean commentary on the psalms seems to have been unknown in the West outside of Irish circles. The connections of Pelagianism with Theodore's teaching may explain the introduction of his work into Ireland.

Theodore (died 428 CE) belonged to the Antiochene School of exegesis, a school which, in reaction to the allegorizing tendencies of Alexandria, insisted on the literal and historical sense of the Scriptures, refusing to see prophecies or types of Christ in almost everything in the Old Testament. Theodore composed his commentary as a young man of 20 and did so strictly in accord with the principles of the Antiochene school. He took David to be the author of all the psalms. Each psalm, in his opinion, refers to some situation which can be determined from a consideration of the psalm as a whole. This situation could be from the life of David or from some later age which David would have seen in prophetic vision. His division of the psalms seems to have been as follows: 4 messianic psalms (Pss. 2, 8, 44, 109; Septuagint and Vulgate numbering); 17 didactic psalms; 19 psalms referring to David and his time; 1 psalm concerning Jeremiah; 25 referring to the Assyrians; 67 to the Chaldeans and 17 to the Maccabees.[107]

Long after Theodore's death the Emperor Justinian, partly for political reasons, had some propositions ('chapters') from his writings and those of Theodoret of Cyrus and Ibas of Edessa (propositions known as the 'Three Chapters') drawn up for condemnation. He got Pope Vigilius to condemn Theodore as a heretic in 548 (in Vigilius's *Constitutum*). Vigilius withdrew his condemnation in 551, but in 553 the second Council of Constantinople condemned the 'Three Chapters', including Theodore's interpretation of Psalms 8, 15, 21 and 68. Vigilius at first declined to ratify the Council's condemnation but finally did so on 8 December 553 and 23 February 554. A storm blew up in the West over Vigilius's action and the ecclesiastical provinces of Milan and Aquileia refused for some time to recognize the Council. This was the state of affairs Columbanus found when he reached Milan. It inspired him to write his letter to Pope Boniface IV 612/613 CE.

Pelagius (late fourth–early fifth centuries) may have become

---

107. Cf. Bloemendaal (ed.), *The Headings*, pp. 15-16 (with further references).

acquainted with the teaching of Theodore through his contact with Rufinus the Syrian who had come from Bethlehem to Rome in 399. A closer link between Pelagianism and Theodore was forged through Julian, Bishop of Eclanum, who when expelled from his see because of Pelagian teaching in 418 lived for some time with Theodore and Nestorius in Constantinople. Julian was a systematic exponent of Pelagianism and in his exegesis followed the Antiochene school. (We have seen that the greater part of the Milan commentary, 2.7 may be his.) The work of Theodore was also made known to the Latin world through Junilius Africanus, *quaestor sacri palatii* at the court of Justinian. About 542 Junilius translated and edited the work of a Persian, Paul of Nisibe, under the title *Instituta regularia divinae legis*—an introduction to the Bible which faithfully reflects the ideas and method of Theodore of Mopsuestia.

It may, then, be assumed that Theodore's commentary and probably that of Julian of Eclanum were introduced into Ireland through Pelagian circles. Theodore's commentary reflects some of the theological questions of his age. It would be interesting to see how much, if at all, the Irish expositors and glossators were aware of these theological problems. A study of the Milan glosses and of other early Irish exegetical and theological literature under this aspect might be rewarding. One thing, however, is certain: Theodore's approach to the psalms and his emphasis on the supremacy of the literal and historical sense made a very deep impact on Irish exegesis. To this we shall presently turn.

3.5. *'Spiritual Exegesis' in the School of Antioch and the Likelihood of its Influence on Irish Tradition*

Antiochene exegesis is often presented as having been interested only in the historical meaning of the text, unlike Alexandria, not looking for a hidden meaning, but for the sense intended by the inspired author. The Antiochenes, however, did have a spiritual exegesis.[108] Like all Christian scholars they did face the question of the harmony of the two Testaments. While rejecting allegory and allegorization as used by the Alexandrians, they centred their own spiritual exegesis around what they called *theoria*, even though the Antiochene scholars differed among themselves on the precise meaning of this term. One view was

---

108. See B. Nassif, ' "Spiritual Exegesis" in the School of Antioch', in *idem* (ed.), *New Perspectives on Historical Theology: Essays in Memory of John Meyendorff* (Grand Rapids, MI: Eerdmans, 1995), pp. 343-77.

that an Old Testament sacred writer had in mind a fulfilment of a prophecy both in Israel's history and in Jesus Christ, for instance the fulfilment of Zech. 9.9-10 (Israel's king riding on a donkey) fulfilled in Zerubbabel and in Jesus (Mt. 21.25; Jn 12.15)—thus Theodore of Mopsuestia; or Hos. 1.10 ('You are not my people...') fulfilled in the return from Exile and in the union of Jew and Greek in the Church (Rom. 9.27-28)—thus Julian of Eclanum. Julian is a representative of the Antiochene School. Through *theoria*, at least in one understanding of it, some texts would have, if not quite two senses, at least two points of reference with regard to fulfilment, one within Israel's history, the other in Christ and his Church. Special attention has been paid to Antiochene spiritual exegesis in modern times. In a recent essay, B. Nassif gives a history of scholarship in the field from 1880 to the present. In his conclusion[109] he notes that much work remains to be done and suggests six directions in which future studies of Antiochene *theoria* may profitably proceed. A fourth line of such inquiry, he writes, needs to discover the influence that Antiochene methods of messianic interpretation exerted on Irish exegesis in the West from the seventh to the twelfth centuries. Then, with reference to an essay by the present writer, he says that Diodore and Theodore's theory of a twofold historical sense clearly appears in early Irish scholars. This is a subject worthy of further investigation. Through the Psalms Commentaries we have evidence of the influence of one Antiochene text. The emphasis on the historical sense did of necessity influence the understanding of the spiritual sense, or senses, of the Scriptures in Ireland. I do not believe that there was any direct influence of *theoria* of Antiochene spiritual exegesis on Irish tradition. Julian's other works do not appear to have been known in Ireland and the Psalm Commentary was not known under his name or that of Theodore. The Irish twofold historical sense does not appear to have arisen under influence of the Antiochene *theoria*. Its origins seem to be due to the combination of two distinct traditions of historical exegesis of the Psalms—one understanding them mainly of David and his times, the other under the ultimate influence of Theodore of Mopsuestia. An alternative fourfold sense of *littera, allegorica, morale, anagogia* seems to go back to a formulation of Cassian.

109. See Nassif, 'Spiritual Exegesis', pp. 374-76, with a citation from J.P. Mackey (ed.), *An Introduction to Celtic Christianity* (Edinburgh: T. & T. Clark, 1989), pp. 428-29; This citation is from an essay by M. McNamara, 'Celtic Scriptures and Commentaries' in Mackey (ed.), *An Introduction to Celtic Christianity*, pp. 414-40.

4. *Interpretation of the Psalms in the Irish Schools*

4.1. *The Fourfold Sense of Scripture*

The whole of mediaeval exegesis is dominated by the belief in a manifold, generally in a fourfold, sense of Scripture, as expressed in the well-known distich (according to some by Augustine of Dacia, O.P., died 1282, according to others by Nicholas of Lyra):

> *Littera gesta docet, quid credas allegoria;*
> *moralis quid agas, quo tendas anagogia.*

A fourfold sense was known also in Irish exegesis of the psalms and is thus expressed in the *Old-Irish Treatise* (lines 312-20):

> There are four things that are necessary in the psalms, to wit, the *first story* (*cétna stoir*), and the *second story* (*stoir tánais*), the *sense* (*síens*) and the *morality* (*morolus*). The first story refers to David and to Solomon and to the above-mentioned persons (Asaph, Heman, Jeduthun, etc. mentioned in lines 158ff.?), to Saul, to Absalom, to the persecutors besides. The second story to Hezekiah, to the people, to the Maccabees. The *sense* to Christ, to the earthly and heavenly Church. The *morality* to every saint.

A similar schema is found in the Irish glosses of the Milan commentary. It must have been generally accepted in Ireland about 800 CE. In glosses on Psalm 1 we read: '*prima facie*, i.e. of the histories (*inna-stoir*), for it is the *history* (*instoir*) that is most desirable for us to understand' (14d7); '*occasiones maioris intellegentiae*, i.e. the *sense* (*sens*) and the *morality* (*moralus*)' (14d9); '*aliqua addere.* i.e. it is thus we shall leave to them (i.e. to other expositors) the exposition of the *sense* (*sens*) and the *morality* (*moralus*) if it not be at variance with the history that we narrate' (14d10). In 44b4, 6 (on Ps. 21) instead of the contrast *stoir/síens* we have *stoir/rún*; *mad dustoir* (44b4)—*madurúin, rún* being the Irish for *mysterium*, the regular Latin word for the mystical sense of Scripture. *Sens/síans* represents the Latin *sensus*. I have failed to find this Latin term used with the meaning of the mystical sense of Scripture in Latin texts, except perhaps in the *Eclogae* (Clm. 14715, fol. 2v) and the *Reference Bible* (Clm. 14276, fol. 95 r), both Irish works (cf. App. III and IV below) where *historia* and *sensus* are contrasted. It is used with this meaning in a homily of the *Leabhar Breac*.[110]

---

110. R. Atkinson (ed.), *The Passions and the Homilies from the Leabhar Breac*

4.2. *The Primacy of the Historical Sense*

The mutual relationships of the senses of Scripture, and in particular the relation of the others to the literal or historical sense, were questions that engaged the minds of medieval writers. The solution that came to . be accepted was thus formulated by St Thomas Aquinas (*Summa theologica* 1a, 1, 10): 'All the senses of Scripture are based on one, namely the literal sense. From this alone can arguments be drawn (in theological reasoning)'.[111] Aquinas's words were anticipated in the two glosses I have already cited. 'It is the history (i.e. the literal or historical sense) that is most desirable for us to understand' (14d7). The other senses (for example, the mystical and moral senses) are legitimate only when not at variance with this historical, literal meaning (14d10).

Irish interest in the historical sense is evidenced by the extensive use made of the Milan commentary. The historical sense also predominates in the Vatican Catena on the psalms (2.4). While this work reproduces the mystical psalm headings of the St Columba Series, it refers the psalms, in the commentary itself, to the life of David or to later Jewish history. The same interest in the historical sense of Scripture is found also in Irish homilies, a number of which are built up according to the manifold senses of Scripture, the first in order being the historical.[112]

4.3. *Interpretation of Messianic Psalms in the Milan Glosses*

We have seen that Theodore accepted only four psalms as messianic (Pss. 2, 8, 44, 109, Vulgate numbering). In 553 the *Constitutum* of Vigilius and the second Council of Constantinople anathematized certain explanations of Theodore on Psalms 8, 15, 21 and 68—the alleged heterodox doctrine on the natures of Christ in his commentary on Psalm 8 and his absence of messianic reference in the others. The glosses on Psalms 8 and 15 in the Milan commentary represent Theodore's exegesis. For Theodore Psalm 15 was composed 'in the person of the people of Israel', and he maintained that in Acts 2.25-28, 31 Peter merely applies to Christ by accommodation words not originally intended as a messianic prophecy. This view is repeated in gloss 36b3: 'The apostle

(Todd Lecture Series, 2; Dublin: Royal Irish Academy, 1887), line 6848, pp. 232 (Irish), 469 (Latin), a bilingual Irish-Latin homily which may well be an Irish composition.

111. See also Beryl Smalley, *The Study of the Bible in the Middle Ages* (Notre Dame: University of Notre Dame Press, 1964), p. 41.

112. Cf. Ramsay, 'Theodore of Mopsuestia', pp. 452-97 (469).

did not apply it according to the sense in which the prophet uttered it.' Although the non-Theodorean heading refers Psalm 21 to Christ's Passion, the commentary proper, which represents Theodore's exegesis, interprets the psalm as being about Absalom's conspiracy against David. The glosses reflect the exegesis of both the heading and the commentary. The passage in Theodore's comment on Psalm 68 (v. 22) condemned by the *Constitutum* of Vigilius and the Council is also found in the Milan commentary, and is reproduced in an Irish gloss (86d16). In all probability the glossator was interested merely in explaining what the text said, not in its conformity with conciliar teaching—if he knew of it.

4.4. *The Mystical Sense*
That the existence of a mystical sense in Scripture was recognized in Ireland is clear from the texts cited in 4.2 above. This approach dominates the St Columba Series of psalm headings (2.3.a above). It prevails also in the *Breviarium in Psalmos* (2.8), but not in the majority of our texts.

4.5. *Grammatical Interest*
Exposition of the Scriptures and the study of Latin Grammar were the two main preoccupations of the early Irish schools. Irish exegesis itself often shows the expositor's interest in grammar. Points of grammar make up a good portion of the comment on Psalm 1 in the *Old-Irish Treatise*. A grammatical interest is seen also in a number of glosses in the so-called Psalter of Caimin (2.25). Some Irish expositors of the Bible were probably also grammarians, for example, the two native authorities mentioned by name in the Milan glosses, that is, Coirbre and Mailgaimrid.

4.6. *Coirbre and Mailgaimrid*
We are far better informed on the scribes of Irish manuscripts than on the authors whose works they copied. With regard to these latter anonymity was the prevailing rule. The names of Irish teachers, too, are transmitted but rarely and incidentally, as when the Irish Augustine in *De mirabilibus sacrae scripturae* mentions Bathanus and Manchianus, and the anonymous Irish author of the commentary on the Catholic Epistles gives us seventh-century Irish scholars Breccanus, Bercannus filius Aido, Manchianus, Bannbannus, Lodcen and Lath.

Two native authorities—Coirbre and Mailgaimrid—are cited in the

Milan glosses, the former in 68c14, and 94a5, the latter in 46b12, 56b33, 68c15, 85b11, and 85b14. The observations of both as recorded in the glosses are brief and of a grammatical nature, observations it would appear made on the Latin text of the Milan commentary. Both of them had probably commented on this in Ireland and were well known to the main glossator.

Mailgaimrid of the Milan glosses is very probably to be identified with the Mailgaimrid *scriba optimus et ancorita, abbas Bennc(h)air* who died in 839. He was probably a scribe of the Culdee movement. Such Culdee 'scribes' were scholars, not merely copyists, and were often put in charge of the larger monastic scriptoria.[113]

The identification of Coirbre is less certain. He is probably the same Coirbre who worked at the St Gall copy of Priscian (St Gall MS 904), and who in a gloss (p. 194a, marg. inf.) is said to have come from Inis Maddoc (*do inis maddoc dún .i. meisse 7 coirbbre*). The identification of Inis Maddoc is uncertain. From the preface to Sanctàn's hymn (probably ninth century) we know that it was west of Clonard. Eugene O'Curry identified it with Inch in Templefort Lake, County Leitrim, which however, as E. Hogan remarks,[114] is north-west, not west, of Clonard!

5. *The Biblical Texts of the Psalter in Ireland*

When Patrick came to Ireland all the major Latin translations and revisions of the psalms had already been made: the Old Latin versions before Jerome; Jerome's revision of the Old Latin (the *Gallicanum*), and his direct translation from the Hebrew (the *Hebraicum* or *Juxta Hebraeos*). Here I shall first consider the Psalter quotations in early Irish theological literature, and then study the texts of the Psalter known and used in Ireland.

5.1. *Historical Survey*
Dr Ludwig Bieler has made a detailed examination of the biblical text of St Patrick.[115] He shows that Patrick's Psalter text is univocally Gallic

---

113. Cf. K. Hughes, *The Church in Early Irish Society* (London: Methuen, 1966), p. 175; Hughes, 'Distribution', p. 265.

114. *Onomasticon Goidelicum* (Dublin: Hodges, Figgis & Co.; London: Williams & Norgate, 1912), p. 467.

115. L. Bieler, 'Der Bibeltext des heiligen Patrick', *Biblica* 28 (1947), pp. 31-58; 236-63.

(that is, Old Latin of the type used in Gaul), but younger than the Gallic text at the time of St Hilary. There is no certain trace of Hieronynian readings.[116]

What the biblical text of St Columba of Iona (died 595) was we cannot say. We may, however, note that according to Adamnan[117] Columba died while transcribing *inquirentes autem dominum non deficient omni bono* (Ps. 33.11), which is the Old Latin text, the Gallican reading being *minuentur*, not *deficient*.

The Psalter text of Columbanus (died 615) as analysed by G.S.W. Walker[118] is mainly Gallican (15 out of a total of 26 readings). Three citations are Old Latin, four are uncertain and four more are peculiar to Columbanus.

The Psalter is cited four times in Cummian's paschal letter (written 632/33).[119] No conclusion can be drawn from the evidence, since the text for three of the citations (Pss. 132.1; 120.6; 70.3) is identical in both the *Gallicanum* and Old Latin, and furthermore occur in citations from patristic sources. Psalm 73.14 (*qui datus est) in escam populis Aethiopibus* is adapted to its new context and as cited in Cummian's letter has peculiarities both of the Old Latin (*in*) and the Gallican (*populis*).

In *De mirabilibus sacrae scripturae* (composed 655 CE) the Irish Augustine has references to Psalms 21, 104, 120 and 147 and quotes from Psalms 77, 84, 98, 103, 109, 120 and 148 (all Vulgate numbering). His text is Gallican with a few personal deviations. Psalm 103.4 in the Irish Augustine is difficult to identify but seems to be Gallican, with, however, *suos...suos* (of the Old Latin and Alcuin's recension of Gallican) for *tuos...tuos*. Psalm 148.7-8 is Gallican, but substitutes *qui* for

---

116. Bieler, 'Der Bibeltext', p. 257.

117. Anderson and Anderson (eds.), *Life of St Columba*, III, 23, p. 524.

118. Walker (ed.), *Sancti Columbani Opera*, pp. lxix, 216.

119. The most recent edition is *Cummian's Letter De Controversia Paschali* edited by M. Walsh and D. Ó Cróinín, *together with a related Irish Computistical Tract De Ratione Conputandi, edited by D. Ó Cróinín* (Studies and Texts, 86; Toronto: Pontifical Institute of Mediaeval Studies, 1988); earlier edition by James Ussher, in *Veterum epistolarum Hibernicarum sylloge* (Dublin, 1632), pp. 24-35, epistola 11; reproduced in Migne, *PL* 87, cols. 974-75. The texts of Pss. 132.1; 120.6 and 70.3 are respectively in Walsh and Ó Cróinín (eds.), *Cummian's Letter*, lines 170-71, 174-75, 198-99; *PL* 87, cols. 974C, 975B; Ps. 73.14 is in Walsh and Ó Cróinín (eds.), *Cummian's Letter*, line 106; *PL* col. 975B. There is a study of the biblical text of Cummian's letter in Walsh and Ó Cróinín (eds.), pp. 222-25.

quae (as does the Irish Psalter of St Ouen, 2.18). Ps. 120.6 as given by him (*nec sol per diem nec unquam luna per noctem exurit*) is probably a paraphrase; it is found in none of the Latin translations. Otherwise the Irish Augustine's biblical text for the Psalter is pure Gallican.[120]

An analysis of the texts from the Psalter in the *Antiphonary of Bangor* [121] (compiled between 680 and 691) reveals 14 as distinctly Gaelican. There are some 20 others in which the Gallican and Old Latin are identical. Four agree with the Mozarabic Old Latin, and in seven the textual form is uncertain. Otherwise there is scarcely a text of the *Antiphonary* that can truly be called Old Latin.

In *De locis sanctis*[122] Adamnan (died 704) gives only four quotations from the psalms (Pss. 88.21 and 44.8 in Bk. III. 5. 9; 73.12 in Bk. I. 2. 4 and 77.16 in II. 3. 3), insufficient material on which to base a judgment on his Psalter text, particularly in view of the identity or similarity between the Gallican and the Old Latin in the passages in question. The portion of Ps. 77.16 cited is identical in the Gallican and Old Latin. Ps. 73.12 as cited by him has a peculiarity both of the *Gallicanum* (*saeculum*) and Old Latin (*salutem*); yet, the Codex Corbeiensis and the Mozarabic of the Old Latin have *saecula* and later Gallican texts *salutem*. Psalm 44.8 could be Old Latin or Gallican, apart from *participibus* which is found in neither, except in the Veronensis of the Old Latin. This text in Adamnan, however, may be from Heb. 1.9 or at least influenced by it. Ps. 88.21 as cited by Adamnan (*In oleo sancto meo linui eum*) is interesting, containing as it does a reading (*linui*) of the Irish Gallican family, found also in the Corbeiensis (*prima manus*) and Mozarabic of the Old Latin.

There are nine Psalter quotations in the *Collectio Canonum Hibernensis*[123] (eighth century).[124] Of these nine, six could either be Old Latin or Gallican, the texts of both being identical in the sections quoted. Two

---

120. The above is almost entirely from information kindly supplied to me by Gerard MacGinty, O.S.B., who has completed a study and a critical edition of *De mirabilibus*.

121. Ed. F.E. Warren (Henry Bradshaw Society, IV and X; London, 1893, 1895).

122. Meehan (ed.), *Adamnan's*. Adamnan had a considerable portion of Jerome's Vulgate at his disposal; see Meehan (ed.), *Adamnan's*, p. 14.

123. The psalm texts of the *Hibernensis* have been kindly communicated to me by Dr Maurice Sheehy who was preparing a critical edition of the work.

124. See Kenney, *Sources*, pp. 247-50.

citations (Ps. 36.25 in Bk. 36. 9 and Ps. 9.20 in Bk. 61. 3) are clearly Gallican. The ninth example (Ps. 102.8 in Bk. 67.4) is the reading of Sangermanensis (of the Gallic Old Latin), but is also found in the Old Latin Roman Psalter.

The Psalter text of the Vatican Catena on the Psalms (2.4 above; eighth century) is entirely Gallican. So too, with one exception, are the psalm *incipits* of the *Old-Irish Treatise*, the exception being Ps. 50.1 (3) with *mihi* of the Gallic Old Latin (Sangermanensis and Corbeiensis) where the Gallican and other Old Latin texts have *mei*. One gets the impression from the *Treatise*, in fact, that the *Gallicanum* was the sole Latin rendering known to its author. It is the only one he instances in answer to the question 'What is the translation that is of the psalms?' (lines 329-30). All the quotations save one in the introduction to the Psalter contained in the Irish *Reference Bible* (about 800 CE; 2.10 above) are also from the *Gallicanum*. The exception this time is Ps. 4.4 where the *Reference Bible* has *admirabilem fecit Deus* as against the Gallican *mirificavit Dominus*. In reading *admirabilem fecit* the *Reference Bible* agrees with the Codex Veronensis of the Old Latin; in reading *Deus* for *Dominus* it is unique. We might also note that the *Reference Bible* (Clm MS fol. 97v) reads *loquitur* for *loquetur* which, however, may be a mere difference in spelling (due to Irish influence). *Loquitur*, on the other hand, is an Old Latin reading of the Gallic family; it is found in the Corbeiensis and in the Psalter of St Zeno.

The Psalter text of the Irish glossator of the Milan commentary (2.7) was the *Gallicanum*. He repeatedly notes that the biblical text of the Latin commentary disagrees with this; cf. 6.2 below. The glossator also seems to have known the *Hebraicum*; see 6.2 below.

All this goes to show that very soon after the days of St Patrick the Psalter text most commonly used in Ireland was the Gallican. The evidence from Irish theological literature is confirmed by the Irish Psalter texts which we still possess (cf. 5.3 below).

5.2. *The Old Latin Psalter in Ireland*

This, as we have seen, was the Psalter used by St Patrick and, we might presume, by the other early missionaries. The 'Gallican' revision of Jerome (died 420) could hardly have established itself so early. No Irish copies of the Old Latin Psalters are known to have survived. The Old Latin Psalter would appear to have been superseded by the Gallican so completely that the former ceased to be copied. All the same, a few words on the major families of the Old Latin would seem to be in place here.

a. *The Gallic Old Latin*. This was the type of Psalter used by Patrick (1.5.a). The chief representatives of the Gallic Psalter are the Codex Sangermanensis, the Codex Corbeiensis and the Psalter of St Zeno of Verona. Some of these may have been used in early Ireland as readings from them are found in Irish Gallican texts.

b. *The Roman Psalter* (the Romanum). A copy of this Psalter was brought to England by St Augustine, and from it stems an entire English family of the *Romanum*. There is no Irish manuscript of the Roman Psalter, unless we consider the 'Psalter of St Salaberga' (MS Hamilton 553 of the Staatsbibliothek, Berlin) as Irish. Script and ornamentation of this eight-century Psalter are insular, that is, either English or Irish, but it has yet to be determined which of the two countries may claim it. In the opinion of Kenney it probably is English;[125] Dom R. Weber, too, in his critical edition of the *Romanum* classes it with the English family.[126] We cannot say whether the *Romanum* ever reached Ireland. The (Irish) Gallican text of the Cathach is contaminated by readings from it, but this phenomenon, which is a feature of all early Gallican texts, need mean no more than that the Gallican exemplar of the Cathach had already undergone such influence. More significant is the contamination by the Roman Psalter of the Irish family (*AKI*) of the *Hebraicum*. In his critical edition of the *Hebraicum* Dom Henri de Sainte-Marie explains 25 variant readings of the Irish family by the influence of the *Romanum* and remarks that the Irish family *AKI* is 'assez fortement contaminé par Ro(manum)' ('Rather strongly contaminated by Ro[manum])'.[127] If the 'Irish' family of the *Hebraicum* originated in Ireland, then the *Romanum* must also have been used there and this at a very early date since A (the Codex Amiatinus), which was written before 716 CE, represents an inferior text at some removes from the original. And yet the *Romanum*, if known in Ireland, does not appear to have left any evidence either in manuscripts or in peculiar readings, apart from the *Hebraicum* and the Cathach. True, the abbreviated

125. Kenney, *Sources*, p. 658.
126. p. xxii.
127. pp. xxii, xxvi.

Psalter of the Book of Cerne (2.5 above) has the *Romanum* text, but in this it is probably a witness to English rather than to Irish tradition.

c. *The Ambrosian (Milan) Psalter.* This was the Psalter corrected by an anonymous 'Scot' in the ninth century (2.15). He can be presumed to have first come into contact with it in Milan. There is no evidence of its use in Ireland.

d. *The Mozarabic Old Latin Psalter.* I noted above possible influence of the Mozarabic Old Latin Psalter on Irish texts. Any such influence should be studied against the background of the contacts between Visigothic Spain and Early Christian Ireland.[128]

5.3. *The Gallican Psalter in Ireland*

The Irish Psalter *par excellence* was the *Gallicanum*. The literary evidence shows that it was the Psalter most, if not exclusively, used from the late sixth or early seventh century onwards. It is the only Psalter text in nine of the MSS listed in 2.1, 2, 16, 23, 25, 26, 27 and 28. It is copied together with the *Hebraicum* in two others (2.18, 19; cf. also 2.25), whereas only two Psalters (2.22 and 2.23) have the *Hebraicum* alone.

We do not know for certain when the Gallican Psalter was introduced into Ireland, but there is evidence to show that it was not later than the first half of the sixth century. Columbanus must have known it at Bangor. It appears to have been used to introduce pupils to reading and writing about 600 CE (cf. 2.2). The literary evidence shows that by the seventh century it had become the established text in Ireland.

The Irish texts of the *Gallicanum* which I have studied represent at least two diffierent recensions. First, there is the 'Irish' family of the Cathach, the Psalter of St Ouen and its sister codex. In this 'Irish' family of texts we have a very early and a very pure form of Jerome's original work; both the Cathach and the St Ouen Psalter are fundamental for the critical edition of the *Gallicanum*. The later 'Parisian' recension is represented by the Coupar-Angus Psalter (2.27). The place within the Gallican tradition of the other texts (2.16, 20, 21, 24, 25, 28) can be determined only by a complete collation; such a collation may shed some light not only on Irish biblical tradition but also, possibly, on Ireland's relations with continental Europe.

128. On which see J.N. Hillgarth, 'Visigothic Spain and Early Christian Ireland', *PRIA* 62C (1962), pp. 167-94.

5.4. *Jerome's Rendering from the Hebrew (the Hebraicum)*

This rendering is represented by six of our texts: the fragmentary Psalter of Codex Paris, Bibliothèque Nationale Fr. 2452 (2.12.a), the Double Psalter of St Ouen (2.18), its sister codex (2.19), the Edinburgh Psalter (2.22), the Psalter of Ricemarch (2.23) and the so-called Psalter of St Caimin (glosses; 2.25). I have spoken more than once of the Irish family of *Hebraicum* texts (*AKI*) of which Dom H. de Sainte-Marie had made a detailed study.[129] A is the Codex Amiatinus, now in Florence, written at Jarrow-Wearmouth before 716 CE.[130] *K* is Cod. Aug. XXXVIII, a ninth-century MS now at Karlsruhe, while *I* is the siglum for the Psalter of St Ouen. *I*, although of the tenth century, represents the Irish family in its comparatively purest form. Even the ancestor of the family, however, was already corrupt. The exemplar of *A* was more corrupt than either *I* or *K*.[131]

Jerome's 'Hebrew' rendering must have been in these islands for a considerable time prior to 716. It probably came to Ireland as early as the *Gallicanum*. And yet, early literary sources do not give us much information on its presence there, although its text does seem to have been known to the Irish glossator of the Milan commentary (see 6.2 below). The Irish form of the text was faithfully transmitted to reach us in the Psalter of St Ouen (and also, it would appear, in the Edinburgh Psalter; cf. 2.22 above). It must have been used in Inis Cealtra or Clonmacnois in the eleventh century, when its text was copied in the margins of the *Gallicanum* in the Psalter of St Caimin (2.25). The Edinburgh Psalter (about 1025 CE) appears to be connected with the same region.

---

129. In his critical edition of the Hebraicum: de Sainte-Marie, *Sancti Hieronymi*, pp. xxii-xxvi.

130. That the Psalter in the Amiatinus (inserted between Paralipomena and Proverbs, fols. 379-418 v) derives from an Irish text is proved, *inter alia*, by the presence of the St Columba series of psalm headings (cf. 2.3.a above) in a form paralleled only in the Cathach. Besides, the insular *per*-symbol (in SEMPER) occurs nowhere in the Amiatinus outside the psalms (see Lowe, *CLA*, III, p. 299). On the textual sources of the codex see now B. Fischer, 'Codex Amiatinus and Cassiodor', *Biblische Zeitschrift* 6 (1962), pp. 57-79 (74 ff.), reproduced in B. Fischer, *Lateinische Bibelhandschriften im frühen Mittelalter* (Freiburg: Herder, 1985), pp. 9-34 (29-33).

131. de Sainte-Marie, *Sancti Hieronymi*, pp. xxiv, xxvi.

6. *Critical Study of the Psalter in Ireland*

6.1. *The Quest for Good Manuscripts*

Irish monastic libraries of the eighth and ninth centuries, as has been said above (1.6), were rich in books of high quality. Whether the same may be said of the sixth and seventh centuries is not so clear. Some of the texts available in the seventh century were inferior, and Irish scholars, conscious of this, went in quest of better ones. Thus a certain Calmanus (lege: Colmanus?), whom Bischoff [132] believes to have lived in the seventh or eighth century, tells us his 'most dear and learned son Ferodad' (Ferodach?) that his community had obtained a number of manuscripts from the 'Romani' (i.e. Irish writers following the Roman Easter computus). These manuscripts, Calmanus continues, had much better texts than those owned by himself and his students. He goes on to complain of the defects of one copy of the *De officiis ecclesiasticis* in which almost four pages had been omitted; likewise of the text of the *Carmen paschale* of Sedulius, the first part of which, he says, had in the earlier manuscript been corrupt and the second part was hardly known at all. This letter reveals an interest in good manuscripts, the basis of any serious study. To what monastery Calmanus belonged is uncertain. Kathleen Hughes[133] tentatively identifies him with Colman, the Bishop of Bangor who, according to the Annals of Ulster, died 680 CE.

The Columban community of Iona, as represented by Adamnan in his *Life of Columba*, was conscious of the need of the careful, even meticulous, copying of manuscripts. We read (I. 23) of Baithene bringing to Columba for correction a copy of a Psalter he had written. And at the end of his own work (III. 23) Adamnan adds the following subscription, modelled on a passage which Jerome (*De viris illust.*, ch. 35) had translated from Irenaeus: 'I beseech all those who may wish to copy these books, nay more I adjure them…that after carefully copying they compare them with the exemplar from which they have been written, and amend them with the utmost care; and also that they append this adjuration in this place.'

---

132. 'Il monachesimo irlandese nei suoi rapporti col continente', in *Il monachesimo nell'alto medievo e la formazione della critica occidentale* (Settimane di studio del centro italiano di studi sul alto medio evo, 4; Spoleto, 1957), pp. 121-33 (128) (= *MS* II, pp. 195-205 [199]). The letter has been published in *Bulletin de l'Académie Royale de Bruxelles* 10 (1843), p. 368.

133. Hughes, *The Church in Early Irish Society*, p. 93.

6.2. *Critical Approach in the Milan Glosses*

The Milan commentary on the psalms (2.7 above) was probably used as a textbook in some Irish school, or at least as a manual for teachers in their exposition of the psalms. The Irish glosses on the Latin text show us how some Irish teacher approached this; they give examples of the questions he put himself and of the observations he made. From these glosses we can learn a good deal about the intellectual interests of Irish scholars and students in the eighth century. I shall consider some of these here.

First of all comes the Latin text itself. The glossator often notes that the text he is commenting on is probably corrupt. (See the list drawn up in *Thes. Pal.*, I, p. xvi.) Sometimes he leaves it at that. Occasionally, however, he emends the text or offers an alternative reading, for example, fol. 74d1 (on *peccator*): '*uel* precator. i. *gessidi*' (= suppliant). Again in 74d10 (on *probate uitae*): '*uel* probitate uiuendi *uel* pro breuitate *uel* in probitate'. We cannot say whether these emendations were the glossator's own or whether he was correcting the corrupt text from other copies. A comparison of the Milan text with the excerpts from it in the Catena on the psalms (2.4), in the *Eclogae* (2.9) and in glosses on other Psalters may have some light to shed on this question. Such glosses as these, in any event, are proof of an interest in textual criticism.

The glossator was also anxious to identify the biblical text used in the Latin commentary. His own text was the *Gallicanum* but he was also familiar with Jerome's rendering from the Hebrew. The biblical text of the Latin commentary presents a problem. In the portion containing Theodore's genuine work there is no trace of the *Gallicanum*, but 18 occurrences have been identified as Old Latin of the *Romanum* and Sangermanensis type.[134] In the remainder of the manuscript many passages from the Psalter are also Old Latin; Jerome's 'Hebrew' rendering is used 40 times, being introduced by name (as *ebreus* or *in ebreo*) 25 times.[135] Its 'Hebrew' text is nearly always that of the older manuscripts.[136]

Confronted with these facts, the Irish glossator repeatedly remarks that the commentary has a different text, that is, one that differs from the *Gallicanum* which he occasionally refers to as the 'Septuagint' (as

---

134. Cf. Devreesse, *Le commentaire*, p. xxvii.

135. The Psalter text has been studied by A. Vaccari, 'Il salterio ascoliano e Giuliano eclanese', *Biblica* 4 (1923), pp. 337-55.

136. See de Sainte-Marie, *Sancti Hieronymi*, p. xlviii.

does also the *Old-Irish Treatise*, lines 329-39). For instance, on *docebit mansuetos* (= *Hebraicum*) of Ps. 24.9 (fol. 46c5) he notes: 'This is a difference of rendering, for it is *mites* that is in the Septuagint version.' On Ps. 67.5 (fol. 83b12) he notes that the commentary has *laetamini* instead of *exultate* (of the *Gallicanum*). (For a full list of textual differences see *Thes. Pal.*, I, p. xvi.) The glossator also notes an inverted order in a biblical citation (fol. 47a14). The commentary on Ps. 81.4 has a curious combination of biblical texts: the Old Latin of the Mozarabic type (v. 4*a*) and the *Hebraicum* (v. 4*b*) not introduced as such. The Irish glossator notes the 'difference of rendering' in 4*a* and also remarks (103d26) that the text commented on in 4*b* is the translation of Jerome (the *Hebraicum*), not the 'Septuagint' or *Gallicanum*. The commentary on Ps. 129.4 cites Jerome's rendering; the Irish gloss (136a13) notes where this rendering ends.

Occasionally the glossator confesses that he fails to see the point being made by the commentator (e.g. 111d1). He even gives different understandings of particular texts (e.g. 131c3) which would seem to indicate that the Latin commentary had been commented on by earlier scholars and in places had been variously understood.

6.3. *The Obeli and Asterisks in the Cathach of St Columba*[137]

I have already stated that Jerome provided his correction of the Psalter (later known as the *Gallicanum*) with obeli and asterisks so as to indicate the relationship of its text with the Septuagint and the original Hebrew. An obelus indicated a passage in the Septuagint but not in the Hebrew; an asterisk words not in the Septuagint but added from the Hebrew. In the preface to his correction (*Psalterium Romae dudum positus*) he tells future copyists to reproduce his critical signs along with the text itself. That this critical work of Jerome was known to the Irish we learn from the Irish glosses on this preface (Amb. 301 inf. 2a6), and from the *Old-Irish Treatise* (lines 329-43). It was also known to the Irishman who left us the letter (2.15 above) on the translation of the Psalter. He imitated it in his own work.

Despite Jerome's direction to copyists his critical signs were more

---

137. See de Sainte-Marie, *Sancti Hieronymi*, pp. xxiii-xxiv; H. de Sainte-Marie (ed.), *Liber Psalmorum ex recensione Sancti Hieronymi* (Rome: Vatican Polyglot Press, 1953), p. xiv; H.J. Lawlor, 'The Cathach of St Columba', *PRIA* 33C (1916), pp. 257-58; A. Rahlfs, *Septuaginta-Studien* (3 vols.; Göttingen: Vandenhoek & Ruprecht, 1904–11), II, pp. 128-33.

often than not omitted, with the result that not all of them can now be restored with certainty. Of the basic *Gallicanum* MSS, Codex Reginensis (*R*) alone reproduces most of them in their correct position. Two others omit them altogether. The Irish texts *C* and *I* have obeli and asterisks, but not always as intended by Jerome. Obeli and asterisks are found in later MSS of the *Gallicanum*, notably in those of the Alcuin recension. Alfred Rahlfs[138] has shown, however, that in many instances, these signs do not represent Jerome's original work but rather a later collation of the *Gallicanum* with the *Hebraicum*. I am now going to study the use of these signs in the Cathach; their use in the Psalter of St Ouen would require a special examination.

In the Cathach there are about 19 occurrences of the obelus, and 21 of the asterisk. I shall first examine the use of the obelus. In two instances (Pss. 33.10; 84.11) it corresponds to an obelus in Jerome's original. In all the other cases, as Dom H. de Sainte-Marie has noted,[139] the obelus in the Cathach represents not Jerome's original but a later revision of the *Gallicanum* against Jerome's *Hebraicum*. He instances Pss. 35.5; 50.7, 20; 52.7; 57.12; 64.2; 67.5; 80.6, 12; 84.12; 88.11. To these texts we can add *omnes* at 88.48, given *sub obelo* by Lawlor but marked as *sub asterisco* in the critical edition of the Benedictines. A check against the original shows that Lawlor has transcribed faithfully. Dom de Sainte-Marie further points out that, in the Cathach, the *Gallicanum* was revised against the *Hebraicum* in its peculiarly Irish text form. The Irish family, as we have noted (above 2.22), is characterized by certain omissions; sometimes only single words are omitted, at other times entire phrases. In the Cathach we find the phrase *et opera manum tuarum dirige super nos* of Ps. 89.17 *sub obelo*, indicating its absence from the Hebrew text. The only reason for this obelus is that the corresponding phrase is absent from the Irish family of the *Hebraicum*, represented by the MSS *AKI* (to which we can now add the Edinburgh Psalter, 2.22 above). The phrase in question is in the Hebrew text and in the genuine text of Jerome's *Hebraicum*. The same applies to the obelus on the second occurrence of *in cithara*, Ps. 97.5. The words are repeated in the original Hebrew and in Jerome's genuine *Hebraicum*; they are absent only in the Irish family *AKI*. To these two instances noted by de Sainte-Marie we add the obelus on both occurrences of *quoniam* in Ps. 91.10. The corresponding word (*enim*), while in the genuine *Hebraicum*,

---

138. Rahlfs, *Septuaginta-Studien*, pp. 128-33.

139. de Sainte-Marie, *Sancti Hieronymi*, pp. xxii-xxvi.

is absent from the Irish family. There is a fourth instance in Ps. 95.9, where *me* of *probaverunt me* is *sub obelo* (although the obelus sign is written above the line, between the words).[140] The word *me* is absent from *AKI* and some other texts of the *Hebraicum*; likewise from the *Romanum* and the Mozarabic Old Latin.

The Cathach, then, is evidence of a collation of the *Gallicanum* with the *Hebraicum*, two centuries or so before the similar recension of Alcuin (730–804 CE). It also proves an early origin of the Irish family of *Hebraicum* texts. Where was this critical work on the *Gallicanum* done? The collation against the Irish family of the *Hebraicum* would point to Ireland. If such was really the case, one or other Irish school must have turned to a critical study of the Psalter text at a very early date in the sixth century at the latest.

Nine of the 21 asterisks in the Cathach correspond to asterisks in Jerome's original Gallican text.[141] Five other passages under asterisk (Pss. 34.20; 53.5; 70.8; 77.21; 88.45) contain material in the Hebrew but not in the Septuagint, yet are not under asterisk in the critical edition of the *Gallicanum*. Of these 34.20 may have had an asterisk in Jerome's original. The words under asterisk in the four other places were probably not in the original of Jerome's *Gallicanum* at all; they are absent from the critical edition. The asterisks on these words would then represent a correction of the faulty Cathach text or of its exemplar against a better text of the *Gallicanum* or against a text of the Old Latin. All the words in question are absent also from the Codex Veronensis of the Old Latin.

The remaining seven Cathach passages marked with an asterisk (i.e. Pss. 34.15; 49.7; 58.6; 65.7; 85.4; [85.12?]; and 103.7) present a greater problem. In these we find asterisks placed before words which are in the Septuagint (including the Basel Psalter; 1.2.m). The words under asterisk in 34.15; 58.6; 65.7; 85.4 and 103.7 are found in all other texts: the Hebrew, the Septuagint, Old Latin and the *Gallicanum*. *In aeternum*, under asterisk at 65.7, is likewise *sub asterisco* in *R*, the chief manuscript of the *Gallicanum* (falsely, however, in the Benedictine editor's opinion), in the Psalter of Charles the Great, in Codex Sangallensis 20 and in some manuscripts of the Alcuin recension. It might have been in the exemplar of the Cathach. The *et* under asterisk at 49.7 is

---

140. The critical edition is again wrong in reading an asterisk here. A check against the original manuscript shows Lawlor's edition extremely accurate.

141. In Pss. 31.5; 67.13; 69.2; 73.15; 83.3; 88.19; 92.3; 103.27; 105.7.

omitted in the Sangermanensis of the Old Latin (cf. 1.5.b.i above) and in the Codex Bovinensis of the *Gallicanum*; it is likewise *sub asterisco* in Codex Sangallensis 20 of the *Gallicanum*. The asterisks of this group possibly represent 'corrections' of the Gallican text against some faulty manuscript of the Gallican or Old Latin Psalter. Their presence could also be due to some careless scribe. An examination of both the obeli and asterisks in Irish manuscripts in the light of the principle enunciated in the *Reference Bible*, no. XXV (fol. 98r; Appendix IV below) may help us solve these enigmas.

7. *Certain Aspects of Irish Psalters and Psalm Study*

In this final section I treat very briefly of certain aspects of Irish Psalters and certain questions connected with the use and study of the psalms in the early Irish church. Some of the problems would deserve much more detailed consideration.

7.1. *Purpose of Psalter Texts*
Some at least of the Gallican Psalter texts were probably written for use in choir.[142] The Psalter of St Caimin with the *Beati* may have been written for private use or for use in a monastic school. The Edinburgh Psalter (2.22) was probably for devotional use.

7.2. *Double Psalters*
Two of the Psalters we have studied (2.18, 2.19) are Double Psalters, both 'Gallican' and 'Hebrew'. A number of such Double Psalters with

---

142. In this study I have on purpose refrained from going into such questions as the *cursus psalmorum* used in Ireland and the actual manner in which the psalms were recited in choir. To do so would take me into the vexed question of the composition of the Breviary and of the variety and evolution of the Divine Office in Ireland. The interested reader will find a wealth of information on the matter from the Lives of Irish Saints collected by Plummer in *Vitae Sanctorum Hiberniae*, I, p. cxvi n. 1 (see n. 7 above). The order of *psalmista* (psalmist and senior-psalmist) in early Ireland likewise deserves study. In his *Liber de statu ecclesiae* (*PL* 159, col. 97711) Gilbert (Gilla-easpaic) of Limerick says that the *psalmista* (or cantor) is not reckoned as one of the *gradus Ecclesiae*, i.e. one of the (Minor) Orders. Writing as he is with a view to reforming Irish practice (cf. *PL* 159, cols. 995-96), we can presume that in his day it was still so reckoned in Ireland, and had been for centuries before the early twelfth century. A more detailed study of the Psalms and the Divine Office in the early Irish Church would need to take note of all this.

these same texts are known, but mainly from the twelfth and thirteenth centuries. There were also Triple Psalters, which add the *Romanum*, dating from the eighth to the fifteenth century. Cod. Aug. XXXVIII (*K*) with the later form of the Irish *Hebraicum* text (ninth century) is such a Triple Psalter. Quadruple Psalters were formed by the addition of the Greek Psalter (in Latin letters) to a Triple Psalter of the type found in Cod. Aug. XXXVIII.

7.3. *Greek and Greco-Latin Psalters*

The Psalters of this kind which I have studied (2.13, 14) are from the ninth century. These texts and the letter of an Irishman on the translation of the Psalter from the Greek (2.15) pose the question whether Greek was studied in some monasteries in Ireland and whether Greek or Greco-Latin Psalters were used there and later taken to the Continent. The prevailing opinion is that the Irish scholars came into contact with these on the Continent, where they would also have mastered the Greek language. But in view of the interest of the *Scotti Peregrini* in Greek and in the Greek Psalter, and considering the citation from the Greek Psalter in a Hiberno-Latin commentary on the Catholic Epistles, the whole question of the study of Greek in early Ireland and of the possible use of the Greek Psalter there should be reconsidered. Not indeed that Greek would have been widely known or studied in all the schools; the evidence is against this. But it may well have been done in some of them.

7.4. *Psalters Written* per Cola et Commata

The Irish Psalters are written *per cola et commata*. Summarizing a passage of the Divine Institutions of Cassiodorus, the Irish *Reference Bible* (fol. 98v-99r; Appendix IV below) seems to refer to Psalters written in a different fashion. Perhaps the Irish author was more interested in summarizing Cassiodorus than in describing Psalters used in Ireland.

7.5. *The Psalms Divided into 'Three Fifties'*

Most of the Psalters listed in 1.2 are divided into three parts of fifty psalms each. Gallican Psalters so divided are II: 16, 21, 24, 26, 27 and 28; Hebrew Psalters, II: 22 and 23 even though the division is suited only to the numbering of the Gallican Psalter.

On the grounds that the tripartite division is not found in the Cathach nor mentioned in the *Old-Irish Treatise*,[143] Henry[144] assumes that its use spread in Ireland only in the course of the eighth and ninth centuries and may conceivably derive from divisions into three books of such commentaries on the Psalter as those of St Augustine or Cassiodorus. There is, however, evidence of a much earlier date for this division both in Ireland and outside. As has been pointed out by Bernard and Atkinson in their edition of the *Liber Hymnorum* (II, p. 217) the tripartite division was known to Hilary who treats of it in the *Prologue to the Book of Psalms* (no. 11; *PL* 9, col. 239). As a matter of fact, Psalters divided into three fifties appear to be the only kind he knew; he gives mystical reasons for this division, which he attributes to the Greek translators (cf. his *Tractatus in Ps. 150*, no. I; *PL* 9). A tripartite division of the Psalter must also have been known to St Augustine (cf. *Enarratio in Ps. 150*, especially nos. 1, end, and 3; *PL* 37, cols. 1960–62), and to Cassiodorus.[145]

The tripartite division is mentioned explicitly in the Irish *Reference Bible* (fol. 98r; Appendix IV below) in a passage most probably dependent on Hilary's *Prologue* no. 11, and again at the end of the same introduction to the psalms in a passage dependent on Cassiodorus. This Hiberno-Latin text, compiled about 800 CE, represents the teaching of the Irish schools during the preceding centuries. The tripartite division is actually presumed in the *Old-Irish Treatise*.[146] The Irish forms of the phrase (*na tri cóicait*) is found as early as 'The Old Irish Table of Commutations' (nos. 2, 9, 20, 24, 32A; cf. also 25, 32), a work composed in the second half of the eighth century.[147] The tripartite division must, then, have been known in Ireland from an early date.

---

143. Actually the *OIT* presupposes this tripartite division as it mentions (lines 110-125) 'the first fifty' and 'the middle fifty'; cf. *OIT*, pp. 24-25.

144. 'Remarks on the Decoration', pp. 26-27; *Irish Art during the Viking Invasions (800–1020 AD)* (London: Methuen, 1967), p. 105.

145. M. Adriaen (ed.), *Expositio Psalmorum*, Praefatio (CCSL, 97; Turnhout: Brepols, 1958), pp. 3-4; *PL* 70, col. 9; . The Latins probably got the tripartite division from the Greeks. For the tripartite division in Greek Catenae on the Psalms see Devreesse, *Les anciens commentateurs grecs des psaumes*, p. xviii and in 'Chaines exégétiques grecques', in *Supplément* to *Dictionnaire de la Bible*, I (Paris: Letouzey, 1928), cols. 1116-1117.

146. See n. 63 above.

147. See now D.A. Binchy, 'The Old-Irish Table of Commutations', in L. Bieler (ed.), *The Early Irish Penitentials* (SLH 5; Dublin Institute for Advanced Studies, 1963), pp. 277-83 (introduction, English translation, with references to editions of

7.6. *Alphabetic Psalms*

Psalms 24 (25), 33 (34), 36 (37), 110 (111), 111 (112), 118 (119) and 144 (145) are alphabetic in the Hebrew Text, that is, each verse or group of verses begins with a successive letter of the 22-letter Hebrew alphabet. This was noted by Jerome, and through his writings this information passed into medieval introductions to the psalms. It is given in the *Old-Irish Treatise* and in the Irish *Reference Bible* (fol. 97v-98r; Appendix IV below), even though only Psalms 36, 110, 111, 118 and 144 are listed as alphabetic. Jerome prefixed the names of the relevant Hebrew letters (in Latin transliteration) to each of the group of verses in Psalm 118 in the Gallican text. Later MSS introduced it into other alphabetic psalms as well. The *Gallicanum* of the Psalter of St Ouen has the Hebrew letters (even in Hebrew characters) for Psalms 36, 110 and 111; in Psalm 118 it has the names of the Hebrew letters in Latin transliteration. The names of the Hebrew letters (with Latin translations) are found also in the Psalter of Caimin. The Hebrew names in Latin transliteration are also found in the Basel Psalter (2.13) for Psalms 24 and 118.[148] In his rendering from the Hebrew Jerome prefixed the names of the Hebrew letters (in Latin characters) to the relevant verses of Psalms 37, 111, 112, 119 and 145—the psalms described in the *Old-Irish Treatise* as alphabetic. The names are found in this form also in the Amiatinus (*A*) and Augiensis (*K*) of the Irish *Hebraicum* family, and in the *Hebraicum* of the Psalter of St Ouen for Psalms 111 and 119. They are not noted in the Edinburgh Psalter; however, in Psalm 118 (119) each of the 22 groups is marked by an especially large initial.

7.7. *Psalter Glosses*

A number of the Psalters I have studied are heavily glossed both in the margins and between the lines (2.18, 19, 21, 24 and 27). The purpose of these glosses, of course, was to elucidate the text for students and also probably (in some cases at least) for those reciting the psalms during

---

Irish texts of the work). For further occurrences of *na tri cóicait* see texts noted in n. 10 above.

148. Together with the Latin names of the Hebrew letters (Aleph, Beth...) found in the text before each section, in the left-hand margin for Ps. 118 the Basel Psalter has figures which are probably intended as imitations of the Hebrew letters themselves.

the divine office, the slow pace of which would permit the monks to reflect on the words and their meaning.

7.8. *Psalm Readings*

These gave the substance of the psalms or the manner in which they could be referred to Christian life. The St Columba Series, in particular, would help those reciting the psalms to turn these ancient Jewish poems into Christian prayer. They guided the mind.[149]

7.9. *The Apocryphal Psalm 151 (*Pusillus)

Psalm 151 (*Pusillus eram*) is a non-canonical psalm found in the Septuagint but not in the Hebrew text. In the Septuagint it is headed: 'This psalm is a genuine psalm of David, though supernumerary, composed when he fought with Goliath'. From the Greek the psalm was translated into Latin and is included in some Old Latin and Gallican Psalters. We now know that the Greek text represents a rendering from the Hebrew, or more precisely that it probably is an amalgam of two distinct Hebrew psalms, of which the first (dealing with the anointing of David) and part of the second (on the combat with Goliath) have been found in Qumran.[150]

Psalm 151, without its heading, is added in the Gallican section of the Psalter of St Ouen after the canticles and in a different hand from the remainder of the manuscript. It is also found (with, heading) in the Codex Amiatinus, the only copy of the *Hebraicum* to have it. The text of the Amiatinus is purer than the St Ouen text which differs in a few readings. The psalm is found in Greek (with the Latin heading of the *Gallicanum* and Old Latin) in the Psalter of Sedulius. It is found in Greek also in the Basel Psalter, accompanied with an interlinear Latin translation (see above 2.13). It must have been well known in early Ireland: it is discussed in the *Old-Irish Treatise* (lines 343ff) and in the

---

149. It is interesting to note that in the modern Roman Catholic vernacular Breviaries the psalms are again provided with headings. The new Breviary (*The Prayer of the Church*) draws most of these headings from the New Testament. At least one, however (that for Ps. 53), is from Cassiodorus.

150. See J.A. Sanders, 'Ps 151 and 11QPss', *ZAW* 75 (1963), pp. 73-86; J.A. Sanders, *Discoveries in the Judaean Desert of Jordan*. IV. *The Psalm Scroll of Qumran Cave 11 (11 QPsᵃ)* (Oxford: Clarendon Press, 1965), pp. 49 (Hebrew text of Ps. 151) and 53-64 (study of the Apocryphal psalm); P. Sheehan, 'The Apocryphal Psalm 151', *The Catholic Biblical Quarterly* 25 (1963), pp. 407-409.

Reference Bible (fol. 98r; Appendix IV below), and is commented on in the Vatican Catena on the Psalms (2.4 above).

7.10. Spitamis-P[s]almus

The Irish *Reference Bible* (MS Clm fol. 94v; Appendix IV below) gives the equivalents of *psalmus* in the 'three languages' as: *Spitamis in Ebrea, psalmus in greca, laus in latina.* The *Eclogae* (MS St Gall, p. 147) has a similar derivation: *Haec sunt nomina huius libri apud Hebraeos: ...spitamis; cum grecis...psalmus...cum Latinis uero...laus.* For *spitamis* and *psalmus* Bischoff[151] refers to Eucherius, *Instructiones* II: *Spitames palmus*(!).[152] In this passage Eucherius is comparing obscure words of an older Latin Bible translation with the more intelligible renderings of a recent one (that of Jerome). From the latter part of the book of Ezekiel he instances *spitamis palmus*, which can only mean that where the older rendering has *spitamis*, the other has *palmus*. The text in question is Ezek. 43.13, where the Vulgate has *palmus* ('a span') and the Greek (and older Latin translation) has its Greek equivalent *spitames* (*spitamis*).

The use of *spitamis-palmus* (the former a Greek word taken over as a loanword into Latin; the latter its Latin equivalent) in Eucherius is clear. But is it possible that this is the origin of the 'Hebrew' etymology of 'psalm' found in Irish sources? It looks very much like it, as *spitamis* is a genuine Greek word. It is possible that the 'etymology' arose from lists of Hebrew and Greek words accompanied by their Latin equivalents. *Spitamis* would have been mistaken for a Hebrew word and then *palmus* read as *psalmus*. The etymology, in any event, is a good instance of some of the pseudo-learning of early medieval Ireland, particularly in regard to equivalents for a number of terms in the 'three languages'.

---

151. 'Wendepunkte', p. 233.

152. C. Wotke (ed.), *Eucherii Opera Omnia* (CSEL, 31; Vienna: F. Tempsky, 1894), p. 149, lines 19 (= *PL* 50, col. 816 D).

APPENDICES I–IV

Maurice Sheehy

Appendix I
*Wax Tablets From Springmount Bog**

The Springmount wax tablets (National Museum, Dublin, No. S.A. 1914: 2) which were found in a bog in County Antrim, consist of a book of six wooden 'leaves', inlaid with wax on both sides of each (except the two outer ones which have no wax on the outside). The six tablets when found were bound together as a book by a thong of leather stitching which passed through holes perforating one edge of the tablets thus forming a loose spine; two bands of leather were placed around the book, at the top and the bottom. The tablets measure approximately 21cm by 7.7cm and each is 6 to 7mm thick. The wax inlay leaves a variable ungrooved margin around the edges of each side lywch measures from 1.2cm. to 1.6cm.[153]

Since the outside of the two outer 'leaves' have no wax inlay and thus form the cover of the book, the writing begins on fol. 1v and continues through fols. 2r–v, 3r–v, 4r–v, 5r–v to 6r, that is ten sides in all. Where it is undamaged, the writing on the wax pages is clear and legible. The cursive characteristics, which resemble the cursive minuscule of the seventh-century Irish manuscripts, date the writing on the wax tablets to the seventh century.[154] Unfortunately, most of the writing is damaged beyond repair; in some places the wax has melted and the writing surface decomposed but mostly the damage was caused when the leaves were being separated. Blocks of wax on opposite pages became stuck together and were drawn out of their original inlay. Since then, pieces of the wax have been chipped off. On the positive side, the identification of the text, Psalms 30, 31 and 32 (Vulgate numeration) greatly facilitates the reading.

Each 'page', except the first (fol. 1v) is divided into two columns with a rough and badly centred dividing line. On fol. 1v, the writing continues right across the page.

The following is the text as I have been able to read it.[155] The punctuation follows the Vulgate edition of the Psalms. Square brackets indicate editorial emendation: angle brackets indicate mutilation and other forms of illegibility, the text within the brackets being supplied from the Vulgate version of the Psalms—without prejudice to the fact that an older Latin version of the Psalms was among the sources of our text.

---

    *   Permission sought.

  153. See Armstrong and Macalister, 'Wooden Book', *JRSA 1* 50 (1920), pp. 160-66.

  154. See Hillgarth, 'Visigothic Spain', pp. 183-84.

  155. The Armstrong-Macalister readings have been relied upon to some extent where the text has been obliterated since 1920. In other places I have found the text legible where it was illegible to them. Photographs, taken some time ago, have been helpful.

Folios 4v, 5r-v and 6r are almost entirely illegible. Some words of Ps. 32.8-9 are decipherable in column 2 of 4v. No attempt could be made to reconstruct the text on these four sides.

Fol. 1v
In te, Domine, [s]peravi, non confundar in eternum: in iustitia <tua> libera me. Inclina ad me <aur>em tuam, adcelera ut eruas me, <es>to mihi in Deum protectorem et <in domu>m refugii, ut salvum me facias: quoniam fortitudo m<ea et refugium me>um es tu et propter no<men> tuum deduces me et inutries <me. Edu>ces me de laqueo [h]oc que<m abscon>derunt mihi, quoniam tu es <protecto>r me<us>. In manus tuas D<omin>e <com)mendo spiritum meum: re<dimisti me, Domine Deus> veritatis. Odisti observantes vanetates supervacue; ego autem[156] in Domino speravi.

Fol. 2r   *col. 1*
Exultabo et le[ta]bor in misericordia tua,
quoniam respexisti humilita<tem meam>,
salvasti di nicessi <tatibus animam meam>,
nec conclusisti me in man<ibus inimici>;
statuisti in loco spatioso <pedes meos>.
Miserere me[i] Domine quo<niam tribulor>;
<conturba>tus est in ira ocul<us meus>,
anima mea et venter meus.

                        col. 2
Quoniam defecit in dolo<re vita mea>,
et anni mei in gemitibus;
<infirma>ta est in paupertate <virtus mea>,
<et ossa mea> conturbata sunt.
<Super> omnis inimicos meos
<factu>s sum obprobrium,
et vicinis meis valde, et timo<r>
notis meis; qui videbant me
foras fugerunt a me.
Oblivioni datus sum,

Fol. 2v   *col. 1*
<tanquam mortuus a> corde;
<factus sum, tanqu>am vas perditum.
<Quoniam audi>vi vituperationem multorum

---

156. Interlineated.

<commora>ntium in cir<cuitu: in eo dum convenirent simul adversus me accipere animam meam consilitati sunt. Ego autem in te speravi, Domine, dixi: Deus meus es tu; in manibus tuis sortes me>. Eripe me de manu inimicorum meorum et a persequentibus me>

col. 2

Inlostra fuciem tuam super ser-
vum tuum,[157] salvum me fac in miseri-
<cordia tua>. Domine, nec confundar,
quoniam vocavi te.

Er<ubescant impi>i et de<ducantur in   infernum; muta fiant labia dolosa, que loquentur adversus iustum iniquitatem in superbia et in abusione>.

Fol. 3r   *col. 1*

Quam ma<gna multitudo dulcedinis tue,   Domine, quam abscondisti timentibus te. Perfectisti eis qui sperant in te, in con-spectu filiorum hominum. Abscondes eos in abscondito faciei tue a conturba-tione hominum, proteges eos>

.... in <taber>naculo
tuo a contradictione linguarum. Benedictus Dominus,
<quoniam mirifica>vit misericordiam suam mihi in
<civitate muni>ta. Ego[158] autem dixi in <excessu>

col. 2

mentis mee; proiectus sum a facie
oculorum tuorum; ideo exaudisti vocem orationis mee,
dum clamarem ad te. <Dili>gete omnes <sancti> Deum
quoniam veritatem requiret Dominus
et retribuit hie qui habundant in
superviam.[159] Viriliter agite
et confortitur cor vestrum
omnes qui speratis in Domino.

Fol. 3v   *col. 1*

<Beati, quoru>m remisse sunt iniquitates
<et quoru>m tecta sunt peccata.
<Beat>us vir cui non inpotavit Dominus peccatum,
<n>ec est in spiritu eius dolos. Quoniam t<a>cui in-

157. Interlineated.
158. *eogo.*
159. *agant* added above Une, see Old Latin version.

<ve>teraverunt in me ossa mea d<um cla>ma-
rom tota die. Quoniam die ac nocte
gravata est super me m<anu>s t<u>a,
conversus sum in er<?>omna mea,
dum configitur mihi spina.

col. 2

Dilictum[160] meum cognitum tibi fe<ci>
et iniustiam meam non absco<ndi>.
Dixi: confitebor adversus me [iniustitiam meam Domino] et <tu>
rimisisti impietatem peccati mei.
Pro hac orabit ad te omnis[161] sanctis in
tempore oportuno,
verumtamen in diluvio aquarum
multarum ad [eu]m non proximabunt.
Tu es refugium meum

Fol. 4r   *col. 1*

<a t>ribulatione que circumde<dit me>:
exultatio mea, <erue me a circumdantibus me.>
Intellectum tibi dabo et in<struam te>
in via [h]ac qua gradieris firmabo s<uper>
<te> oculos meos. Nolit<e fieri sicut equus et> mulus,
<qu>ibus non est intellectus, in camo et fre-
<no ma>xillas eorum constringe,
<qui non> proximant ad [te]. Multa
<flagella peccatoris>

col .2

sperantem autem in
Domino misericordia
circumdabit.
Letamini in Domino
ex exultate iusti
et gloriamini
omnes recti corde.

---

160. dilectum.
161. omnes.

Appendix II*
Catena on the Psalms

MS Vaticanus Pal. lat. 68 fol. lr and 46r. These extracts are edited from photocopies which do not permit the inclusion of marginal notes or glosses. There are few corrections; angle brackets are used to indicate blurring or folds in the parchment—the words in brackets may be quite legible in the original. The capitals used in this edition for the psalm headings and verses are not so identified in the manuscript. The punctuation is largely that of the manuscript.

fol. 1r

A CONCILIO MULTO[162] id est toto Israel predicabo. INIQUITATES MEAE id est causam malorum[163] dicit. ET NON POTUI UT VIDEREM id est adtollere faciem atque oculos elivare nequivi pro magnitudine pudoris vel more fumi oculos excecat. MULTIPLICATI SUNT id est adfligentium, me multiplex infinitusque, numerus.[164] SUPER CAPILLOS id est quia capilli fragiles sunt et innumerabiles ita inimici. ET COR MEUM id est virtus mea. DERELIQUIT ME id est pro timore. CONPLACEAT[165] id est sit tibi hec voluntas ut omnia quae me adfligunt adversa disolvas.[166] CONFUNDANTUR ET REVEREANTUR id est Saul cum semine suo ut in montibus Giluae factum est. CONVERTANTUR RETRORSUM id est pro pudore intueri non audeant.[167] QUI VOLUNT MIHI MALA id est dolum et insidias. QUI DICUNT MIHI id est qui in vocem letitiae meis adversis erumpunt. EUGE EUGE id est 'ait ait', id est adverbium optantis.[168] EXULTENT id est ore. ET LAETENTUR id est in vassis salmorum. SUPER TE OMNES id est ego et socii mei. QUI QUERUNT TE id est in oratione. MAGNIFICETUR DOMINUS id est in virtutibus cultu et honore cunctorum.[169] SALUTARE TUUM id est adiutorium. MENDICUS SUM id est cibo et vestimento. PAUPER id est in viris. ET PROTECTOR MEUS id est quia ipse semper auxiliatus est nulla dilatione inpedente.[170]

BEATUS QUI INTELLIGIT (Ps. 40) haeret DOMINE AD[171] ADIUVANDUM (Ps. 39, 14). In finem salmus David pro erumnis a Saul. Vox Ezechiae de infirmitate et curatione eius atque occasione langoris qualiter latentes inimici eius detecti

---

*   Permission sought.

162. *multa.*

163. *molorum.*

164. Cf. the Milan Commentary, in Ascoli (ed.), *Il codice irlandese*, p. 233—almost verbatim.

165. *conplaceāt.*

166. Ascoli (ed.), *Il codice irlandese*, p. 233.

167. Ascoli (ed.), *Il codice irlandese*, p. 233.

168. Ascoli (ed.), *Il codice irlandese*, p. 233.

169. Ascoli (ed.), *Il codice irlandese*, p. 233.

170. Ascoli (ed.), *Il codice irlandese*, p. 234.

171. ei or et.

sunt.[172] Vox Christi de passione et Iuda traditore. Vox aeclesiae in tribulatione. QUI INTELLIGIT id est sicut David vel Ezechias. IN DIE MALA id est in tempore discriminum suorum Dei auxilio protegetur.[173] CONSERVET EUM id est a malo. ET VIVIFICET EUM id est in multis diebus. ET BEATUM id est divitem. ET NON TRADAT id est non patietur eum inimicis suis subieci et arbitrio eorum potestatique permitti. INIMICORUM EIUS id est Saul et sociorum eius vel Assiriorum. DOMINUS OPEM FERAT ILLI id est ut contigit Ezechiae et sub eius exemplo cunctis similiter meritis non dificulter eveniet.[174] STRATUM EIUS VERSASTI id est ita velociter egrotationem eius solvisti quam cita est strati conversio.[175] MISERERE MEI id est in infirmitate mea. SANA ANIMAM id est per sanitatem animae sanabitur corpus. INIMICI MEI DIXERUNT MALUM id est Saul et socii eius vel inimici Ezechiae sub infirmitatis vexatione discrimine constitutus inimicis meis fui gladio.[176] QUANDO MORIETUR id est haec sunt mala quando privabitur a luce et in aeterna oblivia trudetur.[177] ET SI INGREDIEBATUR reliqua, id est visitare iacentem, id est quilibet amicorum si firmus an[178] infirmus esset. VANE LOQUEBATUR id est fictis verbis consulationem simulabant.[179] INIQUITATEM SIBI id est dolum. EGREDIEBATUR FORAS id est ac si diceret eadem que coram tegebatur ficte seperatim loquibatur liberius quando morietur.[180] SUSSURABANT id est qui sussurat non audet palam loqui.[181] OMNES INIMICI MEI id est Saul cum socis vol inimici Ezechiae. NUMQUID QUI DORMIT reliqua, id est somni enim instar est Deo curante gravis infirmitas.[182] ETENIM HOMO PACIS MEAE reliqua, id est Abisolon vel amicus quilibet. QUI EDEBAT PANES id est Achitophel vel amicus quilibet, si ad Christum Iudas Chariotham intellegimus. ET RESUSCITA ME id est a dormitatione. ET RETRIBUAM EIS id est sicut mihi rediderunt. QUONIAM VOLUISTI ME id est in regem sicut promisisti in visionibus Samuelis. QUONIAM NON COGNOSCEBIT id est si amoveris causas quibus insultare putaverunt inimici.[183] PROPTER INNOCENTIAM id est innocentiam vocat nullum ledere et puras omnibus amicitias exhibere.[184] BENEDICTUS DOMINUS id est qui talia prestit invocanti. FIAT FIAT id est vox familiae David

172. Ascoli (ed.), *Il codice irlandese*, p. 234.
173. Ascoli (ed.), *Il codice irlandese*, p. 234.
174. Ascoli (ed.), *Il codice irlandese*, p. 235.
175. Ascoli (ed.), *Il codice irlandese*, p. 235.
176. Ascoli (ed.), *Il codice irlandese*, pp. 235-36.
177. Ascoli (ed.), *Il codice irlandese*, p. 236.
178. āñ.
179. Ascoli (ed.), *Il codice irlandese*, p. 236.
180. Ascoli (ed.), *Il codice irlandese*, p. 236.
181. Ascoli (ed.), *Il codice irlandese*, p. 236.
182. Ascoli (ed.), *Il codice irlandese*, p. 237.
183. Ascoli (ed.), *Il codice irlandese*, p. 238.
184. Ascoli (ed.), *Il codice irlandese*, p. 238.

consummationem salmi videntes. Aliter vox David cum sensiret spiritum recedere. In Ebrio scribitur 'amen amen' id est vere et fideliter.[185]

QUEMADMODUM (Ps. 41) haeret TU AUTEM DOMINE MISSERERE MEI (Ps. 40, 11). In finem, intellectus filis Choraid est cur—.[186] Hic aliquid[187] dificile videtur ut hunc salmum filii Chore cantarent, dum in eo habetur FUERUNT MIHI LACRIMAE MEAE PANES DIE ET NOCTE (Ps. 41, 4). Et cum alibi dicitur numquam cantaverunt filii Chore aliquid triste. Et ita sanatur filii Chore id est filii Calvariae ac si dixisset conveniens est hic salmum apostolis et martiris qui a persequtoribus decalvantur... (fol. lv).

fol. 46r

CONFESSIO EIUS SUPER CAELUM ET TERRAM (Ps. 148, 14) id est <confitemini in cantico laudabili in aera> sussum et in extrema terrae. EXALTAVIT CORNU POPULI SUI <id est...magna> fecit virtutem faciet populo suo. HYMNUS, OMNIBUS SANCTIS EIS id est <prebet imnus laudis> suae pro his omnibus beneficis. FILIIS ISRAHEL id est meruit filios Israhel ut laudent eum. ADPROPINQUANTI SIBI id est adpropinquanti templo eius et a<r>ae.

CANTATE DOMINUM CANTICUM NOVUM (Ps. 149) haeret QUIA EXALTATUM EST NOMEN EIUS SOLIUS (Ps. 148, 13). Alleluia, vox David, vox Christi de futuro <et de resurrectione>[188] id est in aeclesiasticorum, id est patriarcharum. LAETETUR ISRAHEL IN EO QUI FECIT EUM id est cum laetitia factorem vestrum regemque laudate. ET FILII SION <id est> sacerd<otes>. EXULTENT id est in vassis salmi. IN TIMPANO ET SALTIRIO SALLANT EI id est haec sunt vassa laud<atio>nis regis. LAETABUNTUR IN CUBILIBUS id est quia post maximos labores in stratis locisque prosp<...>is quiescere nos fecisti. EXULTATIONES DEI id est laudes Dei. ET GLADII ANCIPITES[189] id est ter<ribiles> nos hostibus fecisti.[190] AD FACIENDAM VINDICTAM id est omnibus gentibus quae nostr<...>um morabantur.[191] IN MANICIS FERREIS id est in vinculis. IUDICIUM CONSCRIPTUM id est u<ltio ta>m magna ut tradi literis debeat.[192]

LAUDATE DOMINUM IN SANCTIS EIUS (Ps. 150) haeret GLORIA HAEC EST OMNIBUS SANCTIS EIUS (Ps. 149, 9). Alleluia, vox David hortantis popu-

185. Cf. G. Morin (ed.), Hieronymus, *Commentarioli in Psalmos* (CCSL, 72; Turnhout; Brepols), p. 208. All references are to the CCSL volume unless otherwise stated.

186. cūr.

187. -d *interl.*

188. Psalm heading of St Columba series: *Vox Christi ad fideles de futuro et de resurrectione* (BM Cotton Vitellius E XVIII: surrectione).

189. corr. from ace-

190. Cf. Milan Commentary, Ascoli (ed.), *Il codice irlandese*, p. 609, *terribiles nos hostibus retidisti.*

191. Ascoli (ed.), *Il codice irlandese*, p. 609, *quae nostrum reditum morabuntur.*

192. Ascoli (ed.), *Il codice irlandese*, p. 609, *quae ultio tam magna est quam memorabilis, ut tradi literia debeat.*

lum laudare Domini. Vox Christi post saeculum in regno laetantis. LAUDATE DOMINUM id est levitis dicit. IN SANCTIS EIUS id est in vassis templi vel in templo et in altaris eius, vel laudate eum in mirabilibus quae fecit per sanctos suos. IN FIR[MA]MENTO VIRTUTIS id est hoc est in templo ubi multas virtutes fecit vel in tabernaculo. IN VIRTUTIBUS EIUS id est in <r>egibus, principibus, tribunis quos unxit. IN SALTERIO reliqua, id est saltirium in modum q<u>adrati clepei de sussum habens ratem decem chordis; cithara autem quattuordecim chordis; timpanum minima res, quae in manu mulieris portari solet. Chorus pellis simplex duabus cicutis aenis. IN CHORDIS ET ORGANO id est pro duobus pellibus camellorum. IN CIMBALIS id est duae tabulae aeneae modulatae voce concinnantes. IUBILATIONIS id est iubilatio post victoriam sit. OMNIS SPIRITUS LAUDET DOMINUM id est voces hominum vel omnis creatura in suo ministerio debet laudare Dominum. Amen. Amen. Amen.

PUSSILIUS ERAM.[193] Hic salmus proprie David scriptus extra numerum. Cum pugnabat contra Goliath.[194] Vox Christi saeculum exhortantis.[195] Hic salmus pro Ebreos primus. In cantico victoriam indicat cum Goliath et ideo in fine ponitur quia alia sequentia in hoc salmo puerilia sunt cantica. PUSSILLUS ERAM INTER FRATRES id est in tribu Iuda vel inter filios Issai. ET ADOLISCENTIOR IN DOMU PATRIS MEI id est de septem fratribus meis ego octavus. PASCEBAM OVES PATRIS id est opus aptum puero. MANUS MEAE FECERUNT ORGANUM id est duo genera organorum sunt, unum maius quod duodecim viri saltant, aliud minus quod unus vir saltat. ET QUIS ADNUNTIAVIT DOMINO MEO id est ac si diceret *badethbir do cini fesed*,[196] personam meam minimam. IPSE DOMINUS IPSE OMNIUM id est magnorum et parvorum. IPSE MISIT ANGELUM SUUM id est Samuelem ad me ordinandum. ET UNXIT ME IN MISERICORDIA id est in unctione enim donum misericordiae continetur. FRATRES MEI BONI id est fortes. ET MAGNI id est corpore. EXIBI OVIAM ALIENIGENAE id est Goliath de Philistinis. ET MALEDIXIT MIHI IN SIMULACRIS id est in idulis suis. ET ABSTULLI OBPROPRIUM DE FILIS ISRAHEL[197] id est per quadraginta dies provocabat nos ad bellum.

Finit liber psalmorum in Christo Ihesu Domino Nostro; Lege in pace. sicut portus oportunus navigantibus, ita vorsus novissimus scribentibus Edilberict filius Berictfridi scripsit hanc glosam, quicumque hoc legat oret pro scriptore. Et ipse similiter omnibus populis et tribubus et linguis et universo generi humano aeternam salutem optat.

In Christo. Amen. Amen. Amen.

193. The Apocryphal Psalm 151, on which see above pp. 114-15.

194. The heading of the Septuagint and Latin Manuscripts.

195. The heading of the St Columba series in the Codex Amiatinus and the Karlsruhe Codex Aug. CVII, with the omission of *ad* before *saeculum* as in the Paris MS lat. 13159.

196. 'It were right for him that he should not know.'

197. *De* instead of *a* as in the Codex Amiatinus and Codex Reginensis Lat. 11.

Appendix III
*Eclogae Tractatorum in Psalterium**

MS Clm 14715 fol. 1r-3v; 21r-v; 36r-v. Part of the introduction to the psalms is missing. The extant portion of the manuscript begins on fol. 1r line 1 with the line: *ubi aliquid de ebreica veritate defuisse radiat*. The first extract edited here begins on line 2. On the top margin, running into the right-hand margin, in a separate hand is written: *super psalterium a psalmo Beatus vir usque ad psalmum Memento Domini* (Pss. 1–131). In the outside margins the sources are identified by author's name. Some of the corrections in the text are made in a near contemporary hand, and often consist in interlinear expansions of correctly abbreviated words. The psalm headings and verses, here printed in capitals, are not so iden-tified in the manuscript. The division into paragraphs usually follows the use of maiuscule initial letters.

cas   'Inter expositores psalmorum de hoc nomine[198] quaedam noscitur pro-venisse diversitas.

Hieronimus ebraeicae[199] linguae doctissimus inquisitor continuationem Spiritus Sancti esse confirmat,[200] ob quam "diapsalma" significat "sem-per". Beatus autem Augustinus rerum obscurarum subtilissimus indaga-tor vel ardua sine offensione discurrens, hanc potius partem elegisse cognoscitur, ut magis divisio esse videretur, nominis ipsius discutiens qualitatem. "Sympsalma"[201] quippe dicitur greco vocabulo vocum adi-mata copulatio, "diapsalma" vero sermonum rupta continuatio, docens ubicumque repertum fuerit, aut[202] personarum aut rerum fieri permuta-tionem.[203] Merito ergo tale nomen illic interponitur, ubi vel sensus vel personae dividi conprobantur. Unde[204] et nos divisiones congruas facie-mus, ubicumque in psalmis "diapsalma" potuerit inveniri'.[205]

hir   'Zesalla' vel 'sella' in ebraeice, 'diapsalma' in greco, 'semper' sonat in latino[206]

isd/ag   —intervallum orationis profetae. Diapsalma quidam ebreum verbum esse volunt

---

*   Permission sought.

198.   -min- *interl.*

199.   1st -a- *interl.*

200.   corfirmat.

201.   -p- *interl.*

202.   -ut *interl.*

203.   -u- *corr. from* -o-.

204.   -de *interl.*

205.   Cassiodorus, *Expositio Psalmorum*, Prefatio, pp. 14-15.

206.   corr. from latina. Cf. Hieronymus, *Epistolae* 28. 203, *PL* 22, cols. 433-34; *Com-mentarioli in Psalmos*, Ps. 4.4, pp. 184-85.

quo significatur semper, id est, quod illa quibus hoe interponitur sempiterna esse confirment.

ag   Quidam vero grecum verbum // (fol. 1v) existimant 'quo significatur intervallum, psallendi ut psalma sit quod psallitur,[207] diapsalma vero interpositum in psallendo[208] silentium. Ut quemadmodum sinpsalma[209] dicitur vocis copulatio cantando, ita[210] diapsalma disiunctio earum ubi quedam[211] requies distincta continuationis ostenditur'.[212] Unde illud probabile est non coniungendas sententias in psallendo, ubi diapsalma interposita fuerit; qui ideo interponitur ut conversio sensuum vel personarum esse noscatur.

eucheri   'Quid sibi vult illud quod frequenter in psalmorum titulis inscribitur "in finem. psalmus David"? Responsio: quod psalmi in finem mundi bonorum repromissione respiciunt vel quod ea quae Iudei obtinere se posse in principio crediderunt nos consequamur in Christo quem venisse confitemur in fine'.[213]

hela   'Psalmi igitur quibus inscribentur "in finem", ita intelligendi sunt ut ex perfectis atque obsolutis bonorum aeternorum doctrinis et speciebus[214] existant, quia ad ea quae in his dicuntur,[215] fidei se nostrae cursus extendat, et in his doctrinis nullo ulteriore procursu in ipso suo obtate et adepte beatitudinis fine requiescat';[216] id est quo spes nostra[217] bonorum aeternorum doctrinis existat, quo fides nostra[218] tendat.

hila   'De his autem qui sine [diversorum] auctorum // (fol. 2r) nominibus sub diversis superscriptionibus habentur, antiquorum vororum ista traditio est, quod ex eo psalmo, [cuius] auctor in superscriptione preponitur, qui deinceps sine auctorum superscriptione succedunt,[219] huius[220] esse existimandi sunt, qui anterioris[221] psalmi auctor inscribitur, usque in eum psalmum [in] quo nomen[222] auctoris alterius preferatur;[223] ut si

---

207. corr. from psalletur.

208. -p- *interl.*

209. -p- *interl.*

210. cantando. Ita.

211. -ue- *interl.*

212. Augustinus, *Enarratio in Psalmos*, Ps. 4.4. See also the Irish Reference Bible Appendix IV, below, p. 294.

213. Eucherius Lugdunensis, *Intructio ad Salonium*, p. 89 (*PL* 50, cols. 786-87).

214. spebus.

215. dicentur.

216. Hilarius, *Prologue in Librum Psalmorum* 18, *PL* 9, col. 244.

217. -r- *interl.* between *na*.

218. -r- *interl.* between *na*.

219. corr. from succi-.

220. -uiu- interl.

221. *anteprioris* corr. from *antepriores*.

222. -n interl. above ñō.

223. corr. from pro-.

psalmi alicuius superscriptio talis sit "psalmus David", caeteri qui sine titulo consequantur, David esse credantur, donec profetae alterius nomen[224] in superscriptione ponatur'.[225]

'Scio quosdam putare psalterium in quinque libris[226] esse divisum, ut ubicumque apud Septuaginta interpretes scriptum est: ΓΕΝΟΙΤΟ ΓΕΝΟΙΤΟ[227] id est, "Fiat Fiat"—finis librorum sit pro quo in ebreo legitur "Amen Amen". Nos autem ebreorum auctoritatem sequuti, et maxime apostolorum qui semper in Novo Testamento psalmorum librum nominant, unum volumen adserimus psalmosque omnes eorum testamur auctortun qui ponuntur in titulis David, scilicet Asab et Iditum, filorum Chore, Eman Ezraitae,[228] Moysi et Salamonis et reliquorum, quos Hesdras[229] uno volumine comprehendit; nam et titulis ipse ebraeicus[230] ΣΕΦΕΡ ΘΑΛΛΙΜ,[231] quod interpretatur volumen ymnorum, apostolice auctoritati congruens non plures libros sed unum volumen ostendit'.[232] // (fol. 2v).

am   'Si toto effectu investigaveris psalmos multum labor arripies; nam etiam
hil   intellectu historico duplices sensus latent vel habent'.[233] 'Lege psalmos historico intellectu ubi diversos modos invenies'.[234]

cas   'Commemoratio historiae de Regum tracta volumine, in ipso limine posita, virtutes noscitur indicare psalmorum.[235]

hir   'Historico intellectu psalmos investioavi et certas personas in his consideravi'. Iterum dicit: 'me totum divino labori reddidi inseruique psalmos historico ordine'.[236]

Sciendum quot species historiae sint et que de his in psalmis repperitur?

isd   XI Historie species variae ac diversae videntur. Nam simplex historia est, multiplex historia, commonis historia, prosalis historia, metrica historia, canonica historia, profetica historia, proverbialis historia, historia

---

224. -n interl. above ñō.

225. Hilarius, *Prologue in Librum PL* 9, cols. 233-34.

226. corr. from libros.

227. CHNOϒTΩ CHNOϒTΩ

228. essas architae.

229. corr from hestras.

230. -a- *interl.*

231. CHΠHP ΘΑΘϒM.

232. lower margin. Hieronymus, Psalm preface *Scio quosdam*. It is also found in Ascoli (ed.), *Il codice irlandese*, pp. 5-8. See also above pp. 50-51

233. abent.

234. Unidentified texts, cited also in the Reference Bible, see below Appendix IV, p. 113.

235. Cassiodorus, *Expositio Psalmorum* 21.

236. Unidentified texts, cited also in the Reference Bible, see below Appendix IV, p. 133.

nuda, historia stricta, historia explanati, reliqua.[237] Historia autem profetica in psalmis[238] est.

Incipiunt in nomine Ihesu Christi argumenta Hieronomi in psalmis.[239]

hila   Argumenta sunt quae causas ostendunt ex brevitate sermonum longumque sensum habent.

BEATUS VIR. Moralis psalmus est quod ex his quae sequuntur apparet,
in quibus et de virtutum appetitu et de errorum abstinentia disputatur. //
(fol. 3r). In Ioas proprie convenire non potest[240]—ut putant Iudei.[241]
Parvulus enim per illud tempus in quo Ioada[242] pontifice nutritus est,
neque meditationem legis iudicio suo curare poterat, qui ad omne studium pro nutrientis arbitrio ducebatur.[243] Ideo etiam in presenti psalmo
ante dogmata[244] disciplina moralis indicitur. Nam obesse profecto fidei
morum vitia apostolo testante discamus, qui ait ad Chorinteos: 'Non
potui loqui quasi spiritualibus sed[245] quasi carnalibus, et quasi parvulis
in Christo.[246] Non est nobis propositum latius psalmos prosequi, sed[247]
strictum dictorum omnium sensus atingere. Ista enim in psalmis veri
intellectus preceptio est, ut secundum[248] historiae fidem tenorem expositionis aptemus, et concinnent ea que dicenda sunt proferamus.[249]

hisid/int   'Quidam dicunt hunc[250] psalmum quasi[251] prefatio Spiritus Sancti
[esse], et ideo titulum. non habere. Alii in eo quod primus sit ordinis sui,
habere principium et pleonasmorum[252] esse vitium, eum primum dicere,
ante quem nullus sit. Aliter: apud ebreos et primus et secundus unus est
psalmus, quod in apostolorum quoque Actibus comprobatur. Denique

237. Cf. Junilius Africanus, *De partibus divinae legis* 1.1, 6, *PL* 68, cols. 16D. The passage is also cited in *OIT*, p. 22. See also above p. 55 n. 66.

238. corr. from -os.

239. corr. from -os. On the text of Hieronymus used see above p. 51.

240. Cf. Ascoli (ed.), *Il codice irlandese*, p. 10.

241. Cf. Hieronymus, *Commentarioli in Psalmos*, p. 180 '*Iudaei hunc psalmum dictum
esse estimant de Iosia*'.

242. 1st -a- and -ia *interl.*

243. Cf. Ascoli (ed.), *Il codice irlandese*, p. 10.

244. Ascoli (ed.), *Il codice irlandese*, p. 11 'ante documenta fidei'.

245. -ed interl.

246. 1 Cor. 3.1—also cited in Ascoli (ed.), *Il codice irlandese*, p. 11.

247. -ed interl.

248. 2nd -u- added.

249. Cf. Ascoli (ed.), *Il codice irlandese*, p. 12.

250. -un- interl.

251. que.

252. pleon asinorum.

quia [a] beatitudine coeperat in beatitudine disevit, dicens: BEATI
OMNES QUI CONFIDUNT IN EO'.[253]

cas 'Primus, hic psalmus // (fol. 3v) ideo non habet titulum, quia[254] capiti
Domino nostro Salvatori, de quo absolute dicturus est, nihil debuit ante-
poni. Dum ipsum rerum omnium constat esse principium, quidam tituli
quidam prefationis locum eum tenere dixerunt; sed licet a quibusdam
omni iusto videatur aptatus, nulli tamen preter Domino Christo potest
veracissime convenire'.[255]

hlrl/int 'Beatus qui non cogitavit, non fecit, non docuit mala.'
ET IN VIA PECCATORUM NON STETIT. 'Non dixit: in via peccatorum

hir/int non ambulavit; hoc quippe impossibile est, quia nullus absque peccato,
[ne][256] si unius quidem hora fuerit vita eius;' 'sed[257] IN VIA PECCA-
TORUM NON STETIT, hoc est, qui non perseveravit in delicto, sed[258]
per penitentiam ad meliora conversus est'.

hir/int ET ERIT TANQUAM LIGNUM, reliqua. 'Lignum autem cui vir beatus,
conparatur, sapientiam puto, de qua et Salomon loquitur: "Lignum vite
omnibus his qui adprehendunt eam".'

hir/int NON SIC IMPII NON SIC, 'Id quod[259] secundo dicitur NON SIC in
ebreis voluminibus non habetur, sed[260] ne in ipsis quidem Septuaginta
interpretibus: nam exempla Originis in Caesariensi[261] biblioteca
relegens semel tantum scriptum repperi'[262]

QUARE FREMUERUNT GENTES.[263] In secundo psalmo David pro-
fetans omnia quae a Iudeis passionis Dominice inpleta[264]//
(fol. 21r) potestatem insidiator venisset, ab eiusque internicione tem-
perasset, sublato tamen scipho et hasta pro manifestatione negotii, in ore
suo opus ad verba retulit.[265]

---

253. Hieronymus, *Commentarioli in Psalmos*, pp. 178-79. St Jerome wrote *pleonasmou*
in Greek characters—this has been variously corrupted to *pleonasmor, pleonasmorum*, etc.

254. -a interl.

255. Cassiodorus, *Expositio Psalmorum*, p. 27.

256. erasure.

257. -ed. interl.

258. -ed. interl.

259. followed by in erased.

260. -ed. interl.

261. 1st -i- interl.

262. These comments are all taken from Hieronymus, *Commentarioli in Psalmos*,
pp. 179-80. The *exempla* in the text is a corruption of St Jerome's *hexaplous*, written in
Greek characters.

263. interl.

264. Cf. Ascoli (ed.), *Il codice irlandese*, p. 17.

265. Cf. Ascoli (ed.), *Il codice irlandese*, p. 207—*more* for *in ore*.

NOLI EMULARI. Quoniam[266] plerique mortalium, pro adflictione bonorum et prosperitate impiorum turbantur, ut inremuneratis[267] in hac vita virtutes deserant et vitia consectantur felicia, ad huiusmodi depellendum errorem iste conponitur psalmus.[268]

DOMINE NE IN FURBORE TUO. Sicut unum argumentum est sexti psalmi et presentis, ita par idemque principium.[269]

DIXI CUSTODIAM. Angentibus sub Saule meroribus atque periculis hunc psalmum cecinit, qui plurimam speciem doctrinae, non tantum deprecationis de se preferret, quantum in profecto audientium.[270]

hir/in his   OBMUTUI usque A BONIS. Inmanitate persequentis coactus in latebras; bonorum ussu audituque ut mutus carui, qui accipiendi reddendique sermonis expers est.[271]

EXPECTANS. In personam populi gratias agentis ob reditum de Babilone hoc carmon formatur.[272]

hir/in his   TUNC DIXI usque DE ME. Pro volumine cuiuslibet profete qui tam de captivitate mea quam de reversione predixi.[273]

hir/in psal   BEATUS QUI INTELLEGIT. // (fol. 21v). In volumine libri scriptum, est de me.[274] Predicitur hoc psalmo de infirmitate Ezechie, et curatione eius, atque occasione languoris eius, qualiter inimici latentes detecti sunt insultando quoque ipsa egrotatio[275] in devotionem[276] eius coarguerit.[277]

QUEMADMODUM. Ea que erat Iudeorum populus in Babilonia captivitate passurus, beatus David providens et predicens, ex persona populi ipsius presens, carmen instituit. Talem formans orationem que tempori illi captivisque conveniat.[278]

IN VOCE EXULTATIONIS usque ILLI, id est iterum agam gratias quo supradixerat quando ingrediebar templum.[279]

---

266. vel quia interl.
267. corr. from -atus.
268. Ascoli (ed.), *Il codice irlandese*, p. 212.
269. Ascoli (ed.), *Il codice irlandese*, p. 220.
270. Ascoli (ed.), *Il codice irlandese*, p. 225—*anguentibus* for *angentibus*.
271. sunt in margin opposite caret. Ascoli (ed.), *Il codice irlandese*, p. 225.
272. Ascoli (ed.), *Il codice irlandese*, p. 229.
273. Ascoli (ed.), *Il codice irlandese*, p. 232—*praedixit* for *predixi*.
274. Ascoli (ed.), *Il codice irlandese*. Hieronymus, *The Hebraicum* Ps. 40.8.
275. -ne erased after -io.
276. erasure between -o and t-.
277. Ascoli (ed.), *Il codice irlandese*, p. 234. Irish gloss on *latentes* of *Cod. Amb.* 301 inf. suggests *laetantes* for *latentes*. This passage also cited in the Catena, Appendix II above p. 120.
278. Ascoli (ed.), *Il codice irlandese*, p. 238.
279. Ascoli (ed.), *Il codice irlandese*, p. 240—*qui* for *quo* and *quoniam* for *quando*.

hir/in psal   IN VOCE EXULTATIONIS. In voce laudis et confessionis multitudinis
cas   feste celebrantis.[280] 'Sequitur SONUS EPULANTIS. Definitio brevis
                 quid sit "exultatio et confessio", id est "sonus epulantis"; qui[a] sonus
                 ipse animam pascit et epulas illi suavi dilectatione concedit. Quid enim
                 dulcius quidve, salubrius [quam] Deum laudare et se semper arguere?'[281]
hir/in his   PROPTEREA MEMOR ERO TUI DE TERRA IORDANIS. 'Comme-
                 moratione, montis et fluminis totam terram repromissionis ostendit'.[282]
                 ET ERMONIM A MONTE MODICO. Expressit autem[283]
hir/in psal   (fol. 36r) Ibi Beniamin parvulus contenens eos.[284]
                 A TEMPLO TUO, id est propter templum tuum.[285]
hir/in his   INCREPA FERAS usque ARGENTO. Acsi diceret reppelle a nobis ini-
                 micos nostros crudeles multos ac fortes ut non excludantur hii qui pro-
                 bati sunt
hir/in psal   argento, virtutibus pretiosos proturbant ac terreant.[286] Congregatio for-
                 tium in vitulis populorum calcitrantium, contra rotas argenteas.[287]
hir/in his   QUI ASCENDIT usque AD ORIENTEM. 'Acsi diceret ab initio sive a
cas   principio quod nihil ante Deum. sed Deus ante omnia ostendit'.[288] 'AB
                 ORIENTE vero, quod dicit, Hierusolimam evidenter ostendit, que est in
                 Orientes partibus collocata: unde Dominus apostolis videntibus, ascendit
                 ad celos. Terra multis plena miraculis ubi fidelium credulitas plus
                 aspectibus quam lectionibus eruditur.'[289]
                 SUPER ISRAHEL MAGNIFICENTIA EIUS—subaudi ostenditur.[290]
hir/in psal   ET VIRTUS EIUS IN NUBIBUS. Id pro elimentis partem pro toto
                 posuit,[291] et fortitudo eius in celis.[292]

                 SALVUM ME FAC. In temporae[293] Machabeorum profetali spiritu hoc
                 carmen scribitur, et persoms causisque eiusdem aetatis conveniens apta-
                 tur[294] oratio.[295]

---

280. Hieronymus, *The Hebraicum* Ps. 42.5—*feste*, for *festa*, with Irish family *AKI*.
281. Cassiodorus, *Expositio Psalmorum*, p. 382.
282. Ascoli (ed.), *Il codice irlandese*, p. 241.
283. autem repeated in margin in Insular abbreviation.
284. Hieronymus, *The Hebraicum* Ps. 68.28.
285. Cf. Ascoli (ed.), *Il codice irlandese*, p. 340.
286. Ascoli (ed.), *Il codice irlandese*, p. 341—with *detererent* for *terreant*.
287. Hieronymus, *The Hebraicum* Ps. 68.31.
288. Ascoli (ed.), *Il codice irlandese*, p. 342.
289. Cassiodorus, *Expositio Psalmorum*, p. 602.
290. Ascoli (ed.), *Il codice irlandese*, p. 342.
291. Ascoli (ed.), *Il codice irlandese*.
292. Hieronymus, *The Hebraicum* Ps 68.35.
293. -a- interl.
294. corr. from abtatur.
295. Ascoli (ed.), *Il codice irlandese*, p. 349.

hir/in his ADPONE INIQUITATE usque EORUM.[296] Id adflictionem quam meretur iniquitas ut est illud donec transeat iniquitas, id est vindicta.[297]

hir/in his DELEANTUR DE LIBRO usque NON SCRIBANTUR. Erat prisce consuetudinis apud Iudeos ut scriberent nomina clarorum virorum, non solum viventium sed etiam mortuorum, quod et nunc apud nos observatur // (fol. 36v) in aeclesiis, cum mortui, inquit, fuerint, non sunt digni iustorum numero copulari, id est, ab omnibus bonis prorsus[298] alieni.[299]

DEUS IN ADIUTORIUM. In finem[300] psalmus David in rememorationem quod salvum fecit eum Deus; in discrimine regni salutisque deductus quod ei a filio suo Absolon suscitatum, David beatus hunc psalmum posuit, qui vicem possit orationis inplere.[301]

IN TE DOMINE SPERAVI. Ipse David filiorum Ionadab et eorum qui primi in captivitate ducti sunt; predicit ea que erat populus in Babilone passurus, et quod ad emendationem erant profutura ipsa captivitatis adversa, reditum etiam populi pollicetur. Nec umquam mala ita ventura pronuntiant[302] ut non eis etiam statim spem consolationis adiungeret;[303] propter infirmitatem populi, ne disperatione fractus studium emendationis abiceret;[304] omnia autem ex consuetudine sua personae eorum aptat, quos in huiusmodi verbis captivitatis erat necessitas coactura.[305]

hir/in his QUONIAM NON COGNOVI LITTERATURAM.[306] Etiam si continua inquit te gratiarum actione concelebrem, neque[307] ita potero beneficia tua velud in summa[308] redacta comprehendere ac laudibus exequare, neque, enim beneficia tua possunt in numero contineri.[309]

cas Negotiatores ergo illi adhominabiles estimantur...[310]

---

296. id est vindictam interl.

297. Ascoli (ed.), *Il codice irlandese*, p. 343.

298. prarsus.

299. The Milan Commentary, Ascoli (ed.), *Il codice irlandese*, p. 349. This passage is also cited in the *Catena*.

300. id est currit interl.

301. Ascoli (ed.), *Il codice irlandese*, p. 351.

302. 3rd -n- interl.

303. adiungat and -ere- interl.

304. abieciat and -ere- interl.

305. Ascoli (ed.), *Il codice irlandese*, p. 351—with *conectura* for *coactura*, *verba* for *verbis*, *adiungat* for *adiungeret* and *abieciat* for *abieceret*.

306. vel negationis interl.

307. Neque.

308. id est numero interl.

309. Ascoli (ed.), *Il codice irlandese*, p. 356.

310. Cassiodorus, *Expositio Psalmorum*, p. 635.

Appendix IV*
Introduction to the Psalter in the Irish Reference Bible

MS Clm 14276 fol. 94v-99r. The title and sub-titles as well as the identification of sources are rubrics in red in the manuscript; we print them in italics. These rubrics are rarely legible in photocopies; they have been transcribed from the original by Fr Thomas Wilson M.S.C. with the help of the Librarian of the Staatsbibliothek in Munich. The psalm headings and verses here printed in capitals are not so identified in the manuscript. The text is not divided into paragraphs; the punctuation too, in the printed version of this extract, is largely the work of the editors. Besides the interlinear and other corrections in a later hand, there are numerous erasures which do not bear examination in a photocopy.

fol. 94 v

INCIPIUNT PAUCA DE[311] *PSALMIS DAVID REGIS ISRAEL*

I Psalmus quomodo vocatur in tribus linguis, id est, ebrea et greca et latina?
Spitamis in ebrea, psalmus in greca, laus in latina.[312]

II Cur dicitur 'psalmus cantici' et 'canticum psalmi'?[313]

'Psalmus cantici' est quando subpsalmiste[314] prius cantabant ore et postea cantabat David psalterio. *SENATOR CASSIODORUS*[315] 'Canticum' vero 'psalmi' quando David cantabat prius psalterio et postea subpsalmiste ore.

III HILA[RIUS]. Quis psalmus primitus cantatus est de psalmis et quis novissimus?[316]

EXSURGAT DEUS primitus cantatus est, vel verius DOMINE REFUGIUM, quia Moyses illum cantavit. Primus vero psalmus David BENEDICTUS DOMINUS DEUS MEUS QUI DOCET. Novissimus palmus DEUS IUDICIUM TUUM vel NISI DOMINUS quia Salamon cantavit illos. Novissimus psalmus David PUSILLUS.

IIII Quid interest psalmum[317] et canticum et hymnum et laudem?

Psalmus in psalterio cantatur, canticum, ore cantatur; hymnum vero quicquid in laude Dei, laus autem aliquando Deo aliquando homini cantatur.

V ISID[ORUS]. Quot[318] sunt auctores[319] qui cantaverunt psalmos[320] primitus?

---

   *   Permission sought.

311.   interlineated in black.

312.   Cf. *OIT* 21 lines 1-8. See also above 2.10.

313.   Cf. Ascoli (ed.), *Il codice irlandese.* 31 lines 272 ff.

314.   p- interl. Cf. Ascoli (ed.), *Il codice irlandese; Thes. Pal.,* I, p. 8, where *subpsalmista* is glossed *fochetlaidi* = subsingers.

315.   SENATUS G. blur IS.

316.   corr. from -is. Cf. *OIT* p. 29, lines 110-125.

317.   p- interl.

318.   corr. from que.

319.   -c- interl.

320.   corr. from -us.

Decem[321] auctores[322] cantaverunt psalmos,[323] id est Moyses, David, Salamon, Asaph, Ethan, Idithun, Eman, Asir, Elcana,[324] Abiasaph; alii dicunt Hesdras,[325]

fol. 95 r

Ageus // Zacharias.[326]

VI AMB[ROSIUS] Utrum secundum historiam an secundum sensum legendi sunt psalmi?

Secundum sensum legendi[327] sunt psalmi ut Ambrosius dicit: 'Si toto affectu investigaveris psalmos multum[328] laborem arripies, nam etiam intellectu historico duplici sensu latent'.[329] *HIERO[NIMUS]* 'Historico intellectu investigavi psalmos et certas personas in his consideravi'. Item dicit: 'me ideo divino labori reddidi et[330] inserui psalmo historico ordini'.[331] *HILAR[IUS]* 'Psalmos lege historico intellectu ubi diversos modos invenies'.[332]

HIER[ONIMUS] VII Quis posuit ordinem psalmorum?

Hesdras[333] vel Septuaginta[334] posuerunt[335] ordinein psalmorum secundum sensum et non secundum ordinem cantandi et ante Hesdram[336] sparsi fuerunt usque ille collegit in unum librum.[337]

VIII Cur .p. primo scribitur in psalmo cum non sonat?

Ideo[338] ut indicat quia nomen grecum est; quia .F. aput ebreos .q. aput grecos et sic sonatur .psi., et sic numerat[339] .DCC., et sic interpretatur laus latine, et per .p. apud latinos et sic scribunt grece ΨΑΛΜΟC; et nos non[340] possumus sonare illam litteram[341] grecam nisi per .p-s. ut dicamus Ψ psalmos[342] sed per grecam figurem illam litteram semper debemus scribere.[343]

---

321. X.
322. -c- interl.
323. corr. from -us.
324. hel. canna.
325. corr. from hestr-.
326. Cf. Hilarius, *Prologus in Librum Psalmorum*, PL 9, col. 233 and *OIT*, p. 25.
327. corr. from legenda.
328. -l- interl.
329. 6 Cf. *Eclogae* Appendix III above, p. 126, equally attributed to Ambrose.
330. interl.
331. Cf. *Ecloges* Appendix 3 above, 126, attributed to St Jerome.
332. Cf. *Ecloges* Appendix 3 above, p. 126, attributed to St Hilary.
333. corr. from hestr-.
334. LXX.
335. corr. from posuit.
336. corr. from hestr-.
337. Cf. Hilarius, *Prologus in Librum*, PL 9 col. 238.
338. interl.
339. -nu- interl.
340. interl.
341. 2nd -t- interl.
342. p- interl.
343. Cf. *OIT*, p. 20, lines 33ff.

VIIII Cur psalmi[344] cantantur memoriter et non lex Moysi neque Isaias neque evangelia?

Ideo quia in carmine cantati sunt primitus et ideo levius parare illos alia historia quam omnia in psalmis continentur, quia de futuris prophetant et presentia corrigunt,[345] moralia imperant, demones fugant,[346] angelos[347] in adiutorium invocant.[348] Ideo ipsi in consuetudine cantantur,[349] vel quia conveniunt unicuique [350]persone que eos cantat.[351]

fol. 95 v

X Quis primus // cantavit psalmos in Novo Testamento?

Christus vel apostoli dederunt auctoritatem cantandi. Psalmus primitus in Novo Testamento est[352]: DIXIT DOMINUS DOMINO MEO; primus psalmus cantatus est in Novo Testamento et Christus cantavit.

XI Quomodo vocatur psalterium in tribus linguis?

Nablum in ebreo, psalterium in greco, organum vel laudatorium in latino.[353]

XII In quo ordine sunt psalmi?

In ordine canonis, in ordine agiographorum,[354] id est sancta scripta secundum ebreos. *UT HIER[ONIMUS] DIXIT* in prologo Librorum Regum; secundum vero Iunilium[355] et Isidorum[356] inter prophetas[357] sunt quia quatuor sunt ordines canonis: lex, prophete et sancta scriptura[358] et dubia scriptura.[359]

XIII Cur psalmi[360] non sunt inter prophetas secundum ebreos?

Ideo quia ipsi plurissime de passione Christi prophetant quem illi ebrei crucifixerunt. Ideo illi dicunt psalmi[361] quod sancta sit[362] scriptura[363] tantum et non propheti aut non de Christo prophetassent.

344. p- interl.

345. corr. from corregunt.

346. corr. from fugunt.

347. over erasure.

348. Cf. Basilius, *Preface to the Psalms* (trans. Rufinus) attributed to Augustine. *PL* 36, col. 63f. See also above pp. 44 and 90.

349. over erasure.

350. over erasure.

351. over erasure.

352. interl.

353. Cf. *OIT*, p. 20, lines 9ff. See also Cassiodorus, *Expositio Psalmorum*, p. 12.

354. ariospatiopom.

355. Junilius, *De partibus divinae legis* 1, *PL* 68, col. 16D.

356. Isidorus, *Libri Etymologiarum* 6. 1, *PL* 82, col. 233.

357. -s interl.

358. -ur- interl.

359. -ur- interl. Cf. *OIT*, p. 23, lines 76ff. 'There are four kinds in the canon of the Old Testament, i.e. *historia, prophetia, proverbialis species, simplex doctrina*'.

360. -p interl.

361. -p interl.

362. interl.

363. -ur- interl.

XIV Utrum per metrum cantati sunt psalmi primitus an per prosam?

Per metrum,—*UT ISID[ORUS]DICIT* 'Omnia prius versibus condebantur; prose vero studium[364] sero viguit; prosa quid sit? producta oratio soluta a lege metri'[365]— vel per prosam. Primitus cantati sunt psalmi nisi sex: id est NOLI EMULARI et DIXIT DOMINUS et CONFITEOR...IN CONSILIO et BEATUS VIR QUI TIMET DOMINUM et BEATI IMMACULATI et EXALTABO TE DEUS MEUS REX—ipsi tantum cantati sunt per metrum.[366]

XV Que species de speciebus canonis continetur in[367] psalmis, id est, utrum istoria an prophetia an proverbium an simplex doctrina?[368]

Id est prophetia principaliter continetur in psalmis.[369]

fol. 96 r

XVI Quot psalmi habent 'Alleluia' et quomodo // in ebreo et in greco et in latino 'Alleluia', et quis primus cantavit 'Alleluia' et cur iteratur 'Alleluia'? Psalmi viginti[370] habent 'Alleluia'. et David cantavit quando vidit bestiam in deserto, id est leonem. 'Alleluia' in ebreo, prologus faccio in greco, laus Dei in latino; vel tribus modis conponitur 'Alleluia', id est 'alle'—canta, 'lu—illi, 'ia' qui est Deus, vel 'salvum me fac Domine'.[371] Ideo pro certo non possumus interpretari[372] quia sic angelus ad Iohannem sonavit ebreica lingua; 'Alleluia' enim et 'Osanna' et 'Amen', et nomen tetragrammaton de antiqua ebrea que fuit ante Hesdram[373] remanserunt,[374] pro honore eorum sicut homo qui tollit[375] et radit silvam et spinas de suo agro relinquid ligna que plus decorem habent in memoriam quod fuit silva ante, sic ebrei alia verba ebreica de antiqua ebrea relinquerunt—que sunt in usu usque hodie in memoriam quod habuerunt aliam ebream ante; de illis verbis misticis sunt 'Alleluia' et 'Ossanna' [et][376] 'Amen' in psalmis.

XVII Cur iteratur in cantando cum, non iteratur 'Ossanna' neque 'Amen' in psalmis.[377]

Ideo ut laus Dei, id est prima 'Alleluia', terminat primum psalmum[378] et ut psalmus[379] secundus incipiat laudem Dei, id est 'Alleluia'.

---

364. vī.
365. Isidorus, *Libri Etymologiarum* 1.38, *PL* 82, col. 117.
366. Cf. *OIT*, p. 26, lines 175-206.
367. interl.
368. Cf. n. 14 above.
369. followed by erasure. *OIT*, p. 23, '*Prophetia*...nothing is more sacred'.
370. XX.
371. Cf. Cassiodorus, *Expositio Psalmorum*, p. 942.
372. corr. from -are.
373. corr. from stram.
374. Cf. Hieronymus, *Epistolae* 26. 3 and 25.2, *PL* 22.
375. corr. from tullit.
376. blur.
377. possibly erased.
378. p-interl.
379. p- inserted before s-.

XVIII Quot psalmi[380] habent diapsalma et quid est diapsalma et sinpsalma[381] et quis primitus cantavit diapsalma et in quo psalmo primitus ponitur diapsalma?[382] Septuaginta quinque[383] habent psalmi.[384] Quomodo interpretatur et in quo psalmo primitus invenitur? *AGUS[TINUS] DICIT* in tractatu CUM INVOCARUM in versiculo SCITOTE QUONIAM ADMIRABILEM FECIT DEUS SANCTUM SUUM: 'Sed interpositum diapsalma vetat istam cum superiore coniungi, sicut enim ebreum est verbum, sicut quidam nolunt, quod significatur "Fiat Fiat"; sive grecum quod significat

fol. 96 v

intervallum psallendi ut psalma sit // quando psallitur,[385] Diapsalma vero interpositum in psallendo ut quemadmodum sinpsalma dicitur vocum in cantando coniunctio[386]. Ita diapsalma disiunctio earum ubi quedam requies distincte[387] continuationis ostenditur. Sive ergo illud sive hoc aliut sit certe illud probabile est non recte continuum et coniunge sensum ubi diapsalma interponitur'.[388] 'Sela' in ebrea, 'diapsalma' in greca, 'semper' in latina.[389]

XIX HELAR[IUS] DICIT Quis primus cantavit diapsalma et cur non cantatur et cum non cantatur cum psalinis cur scribitur?[390]

Id est subpsalmiste[391] vel Hesdras[392] primitus diapsalma posuit, ut Elarius dicit in Annalibus Istoriographis, poni solent linee adherentes, hoc modo visus est Hesdras[393] propheta psalmos conponere cum diapsalma et sinpsalma. *ITEM HIERO-[NIMUS] DICIT* 'Diapsalma indicium silentii esse non possit. Hoc verbo superiora

---

380. p- interl.

381. p- interl.

382. corr. from diapsalmo.

383. LXXV.

384. A gloss on the Psalm Preface-attributed to Bede—found in the Ascoli (ed.), *Il codice irlandese* (cf. pp. 42-43 above), reads: 'Seventy five times is diapsalma present in the Psalter', see the Ascoli edition p. 5; *Thes. Pal.*, I, p. 9. See also above p. 53 n. 63.

385. p- interl.

386. 2nd -c- interl.

387. -c- interl.

388. Cf. Augustinus, *Enarratio in Psalmos* 4.4, pp. 15-16 'Sed interpositum diapsalma vetat istam cum superiore coniungi: sive enim hebraeum verbum sit, sicut quidam volunt, quo significatur fiat; sive graecum, quo significatur intervallum psallendi, ut psalma sit quod psallitur, diapsalma vero interpositum in psallendo silentium; ut quemadmodum sympsalma dicitur vocum copulatio in cantando, ita diapsalma disiunctio earum, ubi quaedam requies disiunctae continuationis ostenditur: sive ergo illud, sive hoe, sive aliud aliquid sit, certe illud probabile est, non recte continuari et coniungi sensum, ubi diapsalma interponitur'. See also the *Eclogae*, Appendix III above pp. 124-25 and *OIT*, p. 31 'Augustine says: dipsalma intervallum psallendi, vel in psallendo, sinpsalma vocum coniunctio'.

389. -n- interl.

390. Cf. *OIT*, p. 26 ff. lines 207-215.

391. -p- interl.

392. corr. from stras.

393. corr. from stras.

pariter et inferiora connectere aut certe dicere sempiterna esse que dicta sunt; in fine librorum aput ebreos unum et tribus solere subnecti, aut 'amen' aut 'Sela' aut 'Salomon' quod exprimit pacem: unde Salamon pacificus dicitur. Igitur ut nos solemus completis opusculis ad distinctionem rei alterius sequentes medium interponere 'explicuit' aut 'feliciter' aut 'Amen', et iam ut ebrei que scripta sunt roborantes[394] dicunt[395] 'Amen' aut 'sempiterna' scribenda comemorent ut ponent 'Sella'[396]; aut transacta feliciter protestantur pacem in ultimo submotantes; diapsalma, observavi diligenter in ebreo et cum greco contuli, inveni quia ubi lingua

vol. 97 r

ebrea 'Sella' greca vero 'diapsalma' // latina 'semper' habetur'.[397]

XX Quis primus posuit titulos ante psalmos et quid eat titulus?[398]

Subpsalmiste vel Hesdras[399] primitus cantaverunt titulos.[400] Titulus[401] enim grece significatio interpretatur eo quod significat sensum psalmi sequentes[402], vel titulus[403] grece incendium latine quia incendit intellectum psalmum sequentem.[404] Quot sunt psalmi[405] qui non titulos habent? Quattuordecim[406].Cur illi non habent? Quia titulus[407] psalmi precedentis[408] convenit psalmo sequenti, ideo[409] non iteratur.[410] Quot aunt psalmi David? Septuaginta quattuor.[411] Asaph, Agegi et Zacharic duo[412], Ithithun unus[413], Solomon duo.[414]

DEUS IUDICIUM TUUM et NISI DOMINUS, Moyses duo[415] EXSURGAT

---

394. corr. from roborentes.

395. corr. from dicant.

396. corr. from over erasure.

397. Hieronymus, *Epistolae* 28 Ad Marcellam nos. 2-6 *PL* 22, cols. 433-34 and *idem*, *Commentarioli in Psalmos* Ps 4, p. 184. See also *Eclogae*, Appendix III above pp. 124-25.

398. corr. from titulos.

399. corr. from hestras.

400. Cf. *OIT*, p. 28, lines 208-215.

401. corr. from titulos.

402. corr. from sequentes.

403. corr from titulos.

404. Cf. *OIT*, p. 30 lines 269-271.

405. p- interl.

406. XIV.

407. corr. from titulos.

408. corr. from -tes.

409. interl.

410. See, for example, Hilarius, *Prologus in Librum Psalmorum* 3, *PL* 9, cols. 233-34— a text quoted in the *Eclogae*, Appendix III above pp. 125-26.

411. LXXIV. Different numbers in *OIT*, p. 24, lines 110-125 and in Ascoli (ed.), *Il codice irlandese*, p. 4; *Thes. Pal.*, I, p. 8.

412. II.

413. I.

414. II.

415. II.

DEUS et DOMINE REFUGIUM, filiorum, Chore undecim[416], canticum graduum quindecim[417].

XXI Cur non cantantur[418] tituli cum psalmis cum coniuncti[419] sunt eis, et cur coniunguntur[420] illis cum non cantantur?

Ideo non cantantur cum psalmis[421] quia non per Spiritum Sanctum cantati sunt, sicut diapsalma et sinpsalma et psalma[422], sed secundum intellectum.[423]

Ideo vero iunguntur quia indicant sensum psalmi sequentis.[424]

XXII[425] Quid indicat in titulos[426] quando dicitur 'in finem' vel 'in carminibus' vel 'psalmus ipsius David' vel 'psalmi[427] ipsi David'?

Ubicumque dicitur in titulis 'in finem' ad Christum pertinet—qui est finis legis, ut apostolus dicit: 'Finis legis Christus est ad iustitiam omni credenti.[428]

Item senator[429] Cassiodorus dicit: 'Quoties in titulis psalmorum "in finem" reperis, ad Christum aciem mentis intende, qui est finis legis sine fine'.[430] Ubi dicitur 'in carminibus', in peregrinatione cantatus eat ille psalmus. Ubi

fol. 97 v

'psalmus David' vel 'ipsius David' vel 'ipsi David', ad Christum pertinet // quia David significat Christum; sicut David occidit leonem et ursum, ita Christus diabolum et Antichristum.

XXIII Utrum unus liber sit psalterium an quinque libri, ut sunt quinque 'fiat' in psalterio[431]?

Unus liber certe psalterium quia legitur in Actibus Apostolorum 'sicut in libropsalmorum dicitur'.[432] Ideo vero quinquies invenitur in psalterio 'fiat fiat' quia subsalmiste[433] semper in diebus quinque cantabant psalmos[434]; ab initio usque BEATUS QUI INTELLEGIT ubi dicitur 'fiat fiat' in primo die: in secundo die usque DEUS IUDICIUM TUUM ubi finit[435] 'fiat fiat': in tertio die usque MISERICORDIAS

---

416. XI or possibly XV.
417. XV.
418. can- interl.
419. 2nd -n- interl.
420. corr. from cun-.
421. p- interl.
422. p- interl.
423. Interl.
424. Cf. *OIT*, p. 28 lines 229-39.
425. black ink in margin only.
426. corr. from titulus.
427. p- interl.
428. Rom. 10.4.
429. corr. from titulus.
430. Cassiodorus, *Expositio Psalmorum*, Prefatio, p. 1.
431. p- interl.
432. Cassiodorus, *Expositio Psalmorum*, p. 15. See also *OIT*, p. 22, line 57.
433. p- interl.
434. p- interl.
435. corr. from finet.

DOMINI ubi finit 'fiat fiat': in quarto[436] die usque, CONFITEMINI...QUIS LOQUITUR ubi in fine 'fiat fiat': in quinto die usque LAUDATE DOMINUM. 'Amen' in ebreo, 'pisticen' in greco, 'fiat' vel 'fideliter' vel 'semper' in latino.[437] *XXIV* Cur littere aebreice anteponuntur aliis psalmis?[438]

Ideo *UT HIER[ONIMUS] DICIT* quia tu dum requiris legere vel psallere versum, literam titulatam in capite versus invenies per quam in numerum cognoscis.[439] Quot et quanti voce psallebant cum[440] rege? Rex enim incipiebat et numerus litterarum tot voce cordarum cum timpanis, reliqua.[441] Igitur cognoscis de his[442] octoginta quattuor[443] qui per singulas litteras canebant. Isti enim incipiebant et populus respondebat qui erat numero septuaginta.[444] David enim rex nocte ymnificabat et populus respondebat et mane interrogabat rex notarios suos, id est Asaph et Eman et Ethan[445] et[446] Ithitun quod ymnificabat populus illi[447] adnuciabant[448] ei sicut tu locutus es nocte. Ita populi

fol. 98 r

ymnificabant[449] vel ideo ponuntur littere ante psalmi versus quia con//venit interpretatio littere ad sensum versus aequentis.

CAS[SIODORUS] XXV Cur inveniuntur alia verba in psalmis[450] sub obolo que sunt in ebreo et alia sub asteriscis que non sunt in ebreo?[451]

Ideo quia non contra ebreum sefe < > sed consideravit Hieroninius Theodocian priusquam vidit, quia dissonans fuit secum contra Septuaginta[452] et invenit primum scriptorem, deinde posuit obelum super quod est in Septuaginta[453], quod non fuit in Theodocian, et posuit[454] astariscum in Theodocian, deinde convertit ad veritatem ebricam.[455]

---

436. IIII.

437. Cf. Hieronymus, *Commentarioli in Psalmos*, p. 208 and *Epistolae* 140 no. 4.

438. p- interl.

439. -os- interl. Cf. Hieronymus, *Epistola* 30, *PL* 22, cols. 441-45.

440. corr. from com.

441. Unidentified.

442. h- interl.

443. LXXXIV.

444. LXX. Cf Ascoli (ed.), *Il codice irlandese*, p. 5 line 7.

445. eman et han.

446. interl.

447. corr. from ille.

448. -u- corr. from -o-.

449. 2nd -n- interl.

450. p- interl.

451. See above 6.3.

452. LXX.

453. LXX.

454. corr. from possuit.

455. corr. from ebreic-. Cf. *OIT*, p. 32 and Ascoli (ed.), *Il codice irlandese*, p. 3; *Thes. Pal.*, I, p. 7.

XXVI Cur PUSILLUS extra numerum, ponitur et utrum secundum[456] auctoritatem[457] accipitur et si spiritalem sensum. recipit cur in fine ponitur?

Ideo sciendum est quod in veritate ebrica[458] habetur, et in Septuaginta[459] sicut trium puerorum ymnus et fabula Susanne et liber Tobie, reliqua. Hic psalmus scribitur et ideo non cantatur quia non per Spiritum Sanctum cantatus est et quia ultra tria[460] quinquaginta sit; non habet fidem Trinitatis neque figuram penitentie quinquagesimi psalmi.[461]

XXVII Cur nomina quasi diversorum auctorum in titulis psalmorum recipiuntur?

In libris Paralippomenon dicens David cum senuit quattuor ex Israel elegit[462] 'qui psalmos organis, citharis, nablis, tympanis, cimbalis, tubis propria voce personarent',[463] tactu flatu voce in significatione Trinitatis quos David una inspiratione protulit in figuram unitatis. 'Ex quo numero sepe nomina indita in titulis reperimur ut Asaph, Ethan, Ithithun et filii Chore, reliqua. Non quia illi auctores fuere psalmorum sed quoniam prepositi artificibus ministratores earum predictarum probabiles exstiterunt ad canendum'.[464] David

fol. 98 v

vero solus psalmigraphus historie fuit.[465] // De hoc dixit Iohannes in Apocalipsi: 'Haec dixit sanctus et verus qui habet clavem David qui aperit et nemo claudit; et qui claudit et nemo aperit'.[466] Item in [evangelio] etiam Dominus dixit: 'Quomodo David in Spiritu vocat eum Dominum dicens: DIXIT DOMINUS DOMINO MEO'[467] reliqua. Unde probatur David totos psalmos cantavisse si in titulis alii psalmi aliis deputantur.

XXVIII Quid sit psalterium et quid sit psalmus?

'Psalterium, est' *UT HIER[ONIMUS AIT]* 'in modum delde littere formati ligni sonora concavitas, obesum ventrem in superioribus habens, ubi chordarum fila ligata disciplinabiliter plectro percussa suavissimam dicuntur reddere cantilenam. Huic cithare positio videtur esse contraria dum quod ista in imo continet, illud versa

456. interl.

457. -c- interl.

458. corr. from ebreic-.

459. LXX.

460. corr. from trea.

461. On the 'three fifties' see above 7.5. Compare also Hilarius, *Prologue in Librum Psalmorum*, *PL* 9, col. 233, and *OIT*, p. 26, line 199.

462. Cf. the Psalm preface of Pseudo-Bede in Ascoli (ed.), *Il codice irlandese*, p. 4; *Thes. Pal.*, I, p. 8 '*David filius Iesse cum esset in regno suo IIII elegit viros qui psalmos facerent, id est, Assab, Eman, Ethan, Idithun*'.

463. Cf. Cassiodorus, *Expositio Psalmorum*, p. 9.

464. *Ibid.* p. 10.

465. Cf. Cassiodorus, *Expositio Psalmorum*, p. 10.

466. Rev. 3.7. See also Cassiodorus, *Expositio Psalmorum*, p. 10 and Hilarius, *Prologus in Librum*, p. 236.

467. MT 22, 43-4, Seo also Cassiodorus, *Expositio Psalmorum*, p. 10 and Hilarius, *Prologus in Librum*, p. 237.

vice gestat in capite'.[468] Carmen[469] id est quod desuper venit de superno culmine resonat quod Christo convenit. *UT IOH[ANNES] DICIT* 'Qui de terra est de terra loquitur, qui de celo venit de celo loquitur et super omnes est'.[470] Psalmus grece dictus est apotopsauin, hoc est, a tangendo.[471]

XXIX De inscriptione titulorum que in psalmo[472] non invenitur.

Cum non invenies in psalmis ea que in titulis continentur ad tropicum intellectum accomodet ut est cum[473] fugit David a facie Abisolon.[474]

XXX De cantu psalmorum vel lectione.

'Athanasius Alaxandrinus: Quicumque psalmi verba recitat quasi propria verba decantat[475] et tanquam a semetipso conscripta'.[476] Ideo tyrones Christi non a Genesi, non ab evangelio, non ab apostolo, sed a psalmis initium legendi accipiunt.[477]

XXXI Cur non per metrum legimus psalmos cum, per metrum primitus cantati sint?

Ideo non per metrum nos legimus psalmos cum per metrum primitus cantati

fol. 99 r.

sint apud // ebreos ne fastidium faciat per cola et comata procedens ad deponendum sensum.[478]

XXXII Cur centum quinquaginta[479] sunt psalmi et non plus vel minus?

Ideo centum quinquaginta[480] sunt numerati psalmi ex quibus genus humanum peccatis suis pollutum redditur absolutum sicut centum quinquaginta diebus diluvio supradicto criminibus suis terra diluta est.

XXXIII Cur primus psalmus non habet titulum?

Ideo 'qui[a] capiti[481] Christo de quo absolute dictus est nihil debuit preponi, dum rerum omnium constat[482] esse principium, ut est: "Ego sum principium propter quod et loquor vobis"';[483] item 'Ego sum alfa et o[mega]', reliqua.[484] 'Merito capud operis sancti ponitur qui princeps esse monstratur'.[485]

DE LAUDE PSALTERII

Post tantam copiam sancti patris Augustini qui avidos populos ecclesiasticis dapibus

---

468. Cf. Cassiodorus, *Expositio Psalmorum*, pp. 11-12.

469. carmen

470. Jn 3.31-32 quoted in Cassiodorus, *Expositio Psalmorum*, p. 12.

471. Cassiodorus, *Expositio Psalmorum*, 'ἀπὸ τοῦ ψαύειν hoc est, a tangendo'.

472. p- interl.

473. corr. from com.

474. Ps. 3, quoted in Cassiodorus, *Expositio Psalmorum*, p. 14.

475.

476. Cassiodorus, *Expositio Psalmorum*, p. 22.

477. Cassiodorus, *Expositio Psalmorum*

478. Unidentified; cf. however Cassiodorus, *Expositio Psalmorum*, p. 18.

479. CL.

480. CL.

481. followed by Domino erased..

482. corr. from constet.

483. Jn 8.25 quoted in Cassiodorus *Expositio Psalmorum* 1, p. 27.

484. Ap. 1, 8.

485. Cassiodorus, *Expositio Psalmorum*, p. 28.

fluentes tam magne predicationis emanans saciavit, ego memor infirmitatis mee mare tam magnum psalmorum defusum multis fontibus divinis, Deo adiuvante, in rivulos vadosos conpendiosa brevitate deduxi, uno codice tam defuso conplectens que illi in decadas quindecim, explicavit. Sed ut quidam de Homero dicit: 'tale est de eius sensu aliquid subripere quale Ercolis de manu clavim tollere'.[486] Ille litterarum omnium magister et fons purissimus, nulla fece pollutus, in fide perseverens catholicus. Et ego post eum istum librum per quinquaginta[487] psalmos cum prefationibus suis trina divisione sum, partitus. Vere curruscus liber, sermo lampabilis, cura cordis saciati, favus[488] interioris hominis, pinax spiritalium, lingua virtutum, inclinat superbos, humiles erigit.[489]

486. Macrobius, *Saturnalia* 5.3.16 quoted by Cassiodorus, *Expositio Psalmorum*, p. 3.
487. L.
488. fanis.
489. This entire paragraph is culled mainly from Cassiodorus, *Expositio Psalmorum*, pp. 3-4.

THE PSALMS IN THE IRISH CHURCH: THE MOST RECENT RESEARCH ON TEXT, COMMENTARY AND DECORATION—WITH EMPHASIS ON THE SO-CALLED PSALTER OF CHARLEMAGNE

In early Irish history the Psalter of David was very much at the centre of Christian life, indeed of the life of the literate community. In the schools children of seven learned reading itself from the Bible. In fact what appears to be the earliest specimen, of writing we have from Ireland are the so-called Springmount Bog tablets from the early seventh century—wax tablets with Psalms 30–32 used, it would appear, to initiate the pupils into the arts of reading and writing. The Psalter as a book in Ireland was loved and venerated. It was at the very centre of the monastic liturgy and Irish learning.

In 1973 I gave an account of the Irish Psalter text and the study of the Psalter in Ireland from the beginnings up to about the year 1200 CE.[1] Since then a certain amount of work has been done in this field. In this paper I will not repeat what I have said there. Instead I propose to report what progress has been made in the field since then, and to indicate what I believe are areas deserving of further investigation.

1. *Text*

Only two Irish manuscripts with the *Gallicanum* text have been fully collated. These are the Cathach of St Columba (Dublin, RIA; MS with siglum *C*) and the *Gallicanum* of the Double Psalter of Rouen (Rouen, Bibl. mun., MS 24 [A. 41], with siglum *I*). These two manuscripts have good *Gallicanum* texts and are used in the Roman critical edition of the Vulgate. Seven other Irish *Gallicanum* texts await full collation, a collation necessary to determine the relation of later texts to the earlier Vulgate, and also the relationships of these later texts among themselves.

---

1. See the previous article in this volume.

The only Irish text of the *Hebraicum* to be fully collated for the critical edition is that Rouen Double Psalter (to which we may add Karlsruhe Codex Aug. XXXVIII which has the typically Irish-form *Hebraicum* text [siglum *K*]). Five other Irish *Hebraicum* texts await full collation.[2]

2. *Commentaries*

We have a relatively rich commentary literature on the psalms from the early Irish Church, both in Latin from about 700 CE onwards and in vernacular Irish from about 800. In all these sources stress is laid on the importance of interpreting the psalms historically, within Jewish history, whether in the life of David and his contemporaries or as referring to later Jewish history, for example, Hezekiah, the exile, return from Exile, the Maccabees. The basic commentary used was that of Theodore of Mopsuestia in the translation of Julian of Eclanum, and in an epitome of this. There is evidence that together with this Theodorean and Antiochene historical exegesis, there emerged early in Ireland (probably before 700) another form of historical exegesis which interpreted the psalms principally of David and his time. There is no evidence for such exegesis outside Ireland, and it may have originated within Ireland itself, or possibly in Iona-Northumbria.[3]

This historical exegesis has been transmitted in various ways. The Theodorean commentary and the epitome are found in the Milan Commentary, together with Irish glosses (Milan, MS Amb. C 301 inf.). Excerpts from it are found in the *Eclogae tractatorum in Psalterium* (c. 800; composed apparently in Ireland). The historical exegesis has also been transmitted in the *Tituli Psalmorum* attributed to Bede, preserved in two manuscripts traditionally known, written on the Continent, that is Munich Clm 14387 (s. IX) and Paris, Bibl. Nat., lat. 12273 (s. XI), and in two others more recently identified, that is Paris, Bibl Nat. lat. 2384 (s. IX) and Rheims, Bibl. mun. 118 (s. IX). We may presume that these Tituli came to the Continent from Northumbria. A special commentary

2.   On both text-forms see McNamara, 'Psalter Text', pp. xx-xx.

3.   See McNamara, 'Psalter Text'; also McNamara, 'Tradition and Creativity in Early Irish Psalter Study', reprinted below pp. 239-301; M. McNamara (ed.), *Glossa in Psalmos: The Hiberno-Latin Gloss on the Psalms of Codex Palatinus Latinus 68 (Psalms 39.11–151.7)* (Studi e Testi, 310; Vatican City: Biblioteca Apostolica Vaticana, 1986). Introduction reprinted below, pp. 165-238.

with Davidic interpretation has been partially preserved in Vatican MS. Pal. lat. 68 (for Pss. 39.11–151.7). In the so-called Psalter of Charlemagne (Paris BN, lat. 13159) we have psalm headings which correspond to the Vatican commentary. I shall return to this manuscript further below. Dr Luc De Coninck is presently preparing for edition the glosses of the Double Psalter of St Ouen (Rouen, Bibl. mun. 24 [A. 40]) which serve as a complement to the commentary of MS Pal. lat. 68. He notes that there are two glosses on the *Hebraicum in the Double Psalter of Rouen.*[4] One of these two glosses consists of pre-existing Bedan or pseudo-Bedan collections or excerpts (the *Explanationes* and the *Interpretatio psalterii artis cantilenae*, see *Clavis Patrum Latinorum* no. 138).[5] The other, which he refers to as 'the second *Hebraicum* gloss', is relatively well known among scholars of Hiberno-Latin exegesis for two of its three component parts, that is for its anonymous Antiochene-type explanation of Pss. 1.1–16.11 and for the comments on Pss. 16.11 to Psalm 150 quoted from the epitome of Theodore of Mopsuestia's commentary. The third component part is found in hundreds of additional scholia. Some of these scholia establish contextual correlations or explain peculiarities of biblical language and imagery, others specify persons and events that are supposed to be involved in the psalms. These scholia belong to the historical type of exegesis. They focus on events from David's life (the 'first story' of the Psalms according to Irish hermeneutics) as well as on later Jewish history (the 'second story'). This exposition appears to follow the viewpoint—though seldom the wording—of the Epitome or the anonymous Antiochene-like exegesis. Thus it happens that material derived from the Theodorean/ anonymous commentary appears twice in the second *Hebraicum* gloss: first as an excerpt in its own right and afterwards as an alternative to David explanations in the 'composite', 'mixed,' supplementary gloss. De Coninck goes on to note that 'historical' exegesis on the Psalms very closely related to these scholia have been transmitted in the literal headings in the pseudo-Bedan *De titulis Psalmorum*, in the commentary

---

4. McNamara (ed.), *Glossa in Psalmos*.
5. L. De Coninck, 'The Composite Literal Gloss of the Double Palter of St. Ouen and the Contents of MS. Val. Pal. lat. 68', in T. O'Loughlin (ed.), *The Scriptures in Medieval Ireland: Proceedings of the1993 Conference of the Society for Hiberno-Latin Studies on Early Irish Exegesis and Homiletics* (Instrumenta Patristica, 31; Steenbrugge: Abbbatia S. Petri-Turnhout: Brepols, 1999), pp. 81-93 (81-82).

of Pal. lat. 68 and in the headings of the Psalter of Charlemagne. A comparison with Pal. lat. 68 indicates that these additional scholia show impressive analogies to the commentary preserved in Pal. lat. 68. This is true for all its types of scholia, linguistic as well as contextual and historical ones, which for L. De Coninck, implies that the whole stems from the same scholarly tradition as the Vatican commentary—though probably not from the same redaction, as it shows no trace of allegorism. The Double Psalter of St Ouen dates from the tenth century. If the date for c. 700 is accepted for the composition of the commentary of Pal. lat. 68, this implies that the method of the Irish/Northumbrian school tradition in question changed little in the intervening period.

Professor De Coninck is also editing the gloss (mainly with the spiritual sense) on the *Gallicanum* of the Double Psalter of St Ouen, to be published in the *Corpus Christianorum* (Turnhout: Brepols) in a new 'Scriptores Celtigenae' sub-series. This draws on Cassiodorus, Augustine, Hilary, the *Glosa Psalmorum ex traditione seniorum*, and for Psalm 100 onwards on Prosper of Aquitaine (who commented only on Pss. 100–150). The gloss is also rather closely related to that of the Southampton Psalter (Cambridge, St John's College, MS C.9) (see 1.2.u). One question arising from the evidence he produces will be the need to determine the date of the introduction of Prosper's work into Ireland, whether it was there at an early date or came only in the tenth century, when this double Psalter seems to have been composed. P. O'Neill is completing an edition of the glosses of the Southampton Psalter, to be published in the *Corpus Christianorum* (Turnhout: Brepols) in a new 'Scriptores Celtigenae' sub-series.

The completion of these critical editions should help immensely in the study of the origins and development of psalm exegesis in Ireland. The evidence we have points to the involvement of the Irish schools in Northumbria and Ireland. From Northumbria the exegesis seems to have influenced southern England and West Saxon territory before 900 (the West Saxon prose translation of Psalms 1–50 by King Alfred). The introductory material in the Psalter of Charlemagne (795–800) and the Continental manuscripts of the *Tituli Psalmorum* of (Pseudo-?) Bede (MSS s. IX) indicate that at least the principles governing it were taken to the Continent, possibly from Northumbria. We know that the Irish-Northumbrian commentary of Vatican MS Pal. lat. 68 reached Rome from Germany (probably Lorsch). What, if any, impact this approach to the psalms made on the Continent is difficult to say. Apparently it was very little. There is evidence that texts of Julian's translation were known in Normandy, and also that the Theodorean-Julian commentary was known to Remigius of Auxerre (c. 841–908 CE) or his circle and that parts of it found their way into an earlier edition of Remigius's commentary, but not in a later one.[6]

3. *Decoration*

F. Henry has made a special study of the decoration of the three Irish Psalters: BL, Cotton MSS, Vitellius F. XI, Cambridge, St John's College, MS C. 9 (the Southampton Psalter), and Rouen, Bibl. mun., MS 24 (A. 41).[7] The Cotton manuscript was damaged in the fire of 1731. It has two miniatures, David and Goliath and David playing the harp (or *David Rex*), now bound at the beginning of the Psalter. Henry has shown that they were once located at Psalms 51 and 101, at the beginning of the second and third 'fifties', where they framed initial pages as was the case in the Southampton Psalter.[8] The artist of the Southampton Psalter imitates the Vitellius, but is less original. The Southampton Psalter has three portraits: facing Psalm 1 David killing the lion; facing Psalm 51 the crucifixion of Christ; facing Psalm 101 David and Goliath. Henry comments that as for the crucifixion portrait heading the second section, it is not in itself a strange choice and it corresponds to the growing tendency to illustrate Psalters with scenes from the life of Christ. Psalm 53 being one of the psalms closely connected with the Passion, a representation of the crucifixion would come quite normally at the beginning of the section which contains it.[9] In the Rouen Double Psalter the decoration consists mainly of capitals at the beginning of each psalm. There are about three hundred of them, all of the knotted-wire type. They are finely drawn and the little animal heads are often of exquisite design. In addition there are designs in the margin and the text of a few pages, some of which are probably nothing more than

---

6. See A. Vaccari, 'Il genuino commento ea salmi di Remigio di Auxerre', *Biblica* 26 (1952), pp. 52-99 (98-99) (=A. Vaccari, *Scritti di erudizione e di filologia*, I (Rome: Edizioni di storia e litteratura 18, 1952), pp. 283-329 (327-28).

7. F. Henry, 'Remarks on the Decoration of Three Irish Psalters', *PRIA* 61C (1960–61; published 1960), pp. 23-40.

8. Henry, 'Remarks', p. 31.

9. Henry, 'Remarks', pp. 35-36.

'doodles', while others may be intended to refer to the content of the biblical text.[10] In a later study on a century of Irish illumination (1070–1170) F. Henry and G.L. Marsh-Micheli[11] examine the illumination of four later Irish Psalters or fragments of Psalters: the so-called Psalter of Caimin (MS Franciscan House, Killiney, County Dublin); BL, Cotton MSS, Galba A. V; BL, Additional MSS, 36929 ('The Psalter of Cormac') and Vatican MS Pal., lat. 68. They note that the decoration of the Psalter of Cormac consists in three introductory pages with framed pages opposite each of them. The frame of the first fifty is filled by a text headed '*absolutio bernarddi*' (*sic*); the two other frames are empty except for a *Dextra Dei* appearing in the corner of that facing '*Quid gloriaris*' (Ps. 51). It is likely, they continue, that they were meant to contain figure drawings which would then correspond with those in two other Irish Psalters, BL, Cotton MSS, Vitellius F. XI and MS C. 9 in the library of St John's College, Cambridge.[12]

In an unpublished doctoral dissertation on the Tiberius Psalter for the University of Toronto, K.M. Openshaw has in chapter 5 made a special study of the illumination of the Southampton Psalter and its cultural background.[13] In 1992 she published the substance of her work in an essay in the review *Arte medievale*.[14] Although she draws on the work of F. Henry, G.L. Marsh-Micheli, and the others who have written on the subject, she has done much personal research. The Psalter of Cormac she regards as an archaic Irish Psalter of the early twelfth century, which appears to provide further evidence for the continuity of the Irish approach to the Psalter decoration she has been studying, even though in some details of ornament it betrays the impact of new artistic influences. She says that the pages facing Psalms 51 and 101 were originally decorated with full-page figures. Regrettably the figures have been scraped off and we do not know their iconography for sure. However,

10. Henry, 'Remarks', p. 38.

11. F. Henry and G.L. Marsh-Micheli, 'A Century of Irish Illumination', *Proceedings of the Royal Irish Academy* 62C (1961–62; published 1962), pp. 101-65 (161-63 for the Psalter of Cormac).

12. Henry and Marsh-Micheli, 'A Century', p. 163.

13. K.M. Openshaw, 'Images, Texts and Contexts: The Iconography of the Tiberius Psalter, London, British Library, Cotton MSS, Tiberius C. iv' (unpublished doctoral dissertation; University of Toronto, 1990).

14. K.M. Openshaw, 'The Symbolic Illustration of the Psalter: An Insular Tradition', *Arte Medievale* NS 6 (1992), pp. 41-60.

an examination carried out by her under infra-red light suggests that at Psalm 101 there was a laterally viewed image of David enthroned, much like the picture in the Vitellius Psalter. The Psalm 51 image is less easy to construe, though it seems possible that there were two upright figures, one of which was helmeted on the same style as David and Goliath in the Southampton Psalter. A strong vertical line divides the two figures, and this could well be David's staff that is so prominent in the Southampton and Vitellius David-and-Goliath pictures. On balance there is a fair likelihood that the Psalm 51 picture depicted David and Goliath, and that figural decoration of the Psalter followed in the tradition clearly seen in the Vitellius and Southampton Psalters.[15]

She lays stress on David as the image of Christ in this tradition, using the evidence of the Durham Cassiodorus (Durham, Cathedral Library, MS. B 1130) with the figure of David as image of Christ as Psalm 51, and recalls the figure of David, albeit in different iconography, in the same position (Ps. 51) in the Vitellius Psalter. Three statements can be made, she writes, about the Durham Cassiodorus manuscript. First, the decoration of the manuscript is symbolic. These splendid full-page figures do not illustrate the text that they face in any specific way and they clearly do not represent a narrative sequence. Secondly, the decoration most emphatically emphasizes the typological relationship between the psalmist David and Christ, by unique and economical means. Finally, the triumph over evil is an important element of the decoration; and here, as in the Southampton Psalter, it is the triumph both of the psalmist and of Christ.[16] What is said of the Cassiodorus manuscript holds good for the Irish Psalter tradition. Openshaw[17] does not agree with Henry's explanation of the choice of crucifixion scene facing Psalm 51 in the Southampton Psalter, an explanation seeking, without success, relationships between the Irish Psalter pictures and adjacent and nearby texts, and with regard to the positioning of this particular picture invoking a growing tendency to illustrate Psalters with scenes from the life of Christ.

The final section of her essay[18] is devoted to some suggested ideological sources for the symbolic and typological Psalter programmes of

15. Openshaw, 'Symbolic Illustration', pp. 47-48.
16. Openshaw, 'Symbolic Illustration', p. 48.
17. Openshaw, 'Symbolic Illustration', p. 46.
18. Openshaw, 'Symbolic Illustration', pp. 53-57.

the Insular world. One must consider the thought-world, she notes,[19] within which this art was created, and examine the Psalter exegesis that reflects it. Some of the early Irish exegesis of the psalms, she continues, displays a much more consistent view of the Davidic and christological typology of the Psalter than the standard patristic commentaries. For instance, in their prefaces Hilary and Cassiodorus make statements of the general christological relevance of the Psalter, but they tend not to see the book as relating to David in any broad sense. By contrast, in some eighth- and ninth-century Irish exegetical texts there is a more pronounced uniformity of approach in giving each psalm a historical interpretation first, and then a spiritual or christological one, as part of unique Irish variants of the standard mediaeval fourfold exegesis. Knowledge of such Psalter exegesis might very well have predisposed scribes to the use of unified typological programmes of decoration in their Psalters.

Openshaw concludes by noting that, although it was a product of Irish scholarship, the tendency towards what is effectively a typological interpretation of the Psalter was not reserved to Ireland. This particular facet of the Irish world-view was absorbed and enhanced in Anglo-Saxon England. The enhancement is evident in the Anglo-Saxon prose translation of the first 50 psalms, now confidently ascribed to King Alfred, and executed in West Saxon territory just before 900. She also sees its influence in the Tiberius Psalter (BL, Cotton MSS, Tiberius C. vi). The kernel of the ambitious picture cycle of this Psalter is clearly the symbolic and typological programme seen in the earlier Southampton Psalter; the cycle presents the psalmist David as a prefiguration of Christ, and his battles as forerunners of those of Christ. In the Tiberius Psalter, however, this earlier plan is expanded. Thus the Tiberius Psalter stands as a watershed in western Psalter illustration, marking the transition from the symbolic and typological Psalter schemes of earlier Insular Christianity to the elaborate historically oriented schemes of the Romanesque and Gothic, and marking also the assimilation of this particular Insular approach to Psalter decoration into the European mainstream.[20]

19. Openshaw, 'Symbolic Illustration', p. 54.
20. Openshaw, 'Symbolic Illustration', p. 57.

4. *Manuscript Studies: Two BL Cotton Psalters (Vitellius F. XI; Galba A. V) and the So-called Psalter of Charlemagne (Paris BN, Lat. 13159)*

a. *Introduction*

There are two Irish Psalters in the Cotton Collection of the British Library (Vitellius F. XI and Galba A. V). The Collection was brought together by Sir Robert Cotton (1570–1631), passed to his son John and later to public ownership. It was ravaged by a fire in 1731, and became part of the British Museum (now British Library) at its foundation in 1753. The collection was catalogued by Thomas Smith in 1696 and later by J. Planta in 1802. The collection comprises 25,000 distinct articles in Planta's catalogue.

James Ussher (1581–1656) was on friendly terms with Robert Cotton and made regular use of the library, beginning, it would appear, around 1606. Ussher's biographer Richard Parr[21] tells us that after 1609:

> he [Ussher] constantly came over to England once in three years, spending one month of the summer at Oxford, another at Cambridge, and the rest of the time in London, spending his time chiefly in the Cottonian Library, the noble and learned Master of which affording him free access, not only to that but his own conversation.

Parr prints a letter of Cotton to Ussher, then Bishop of Meath, dated 26 March 1622, in which he mentions the return of eight manuscripts of his which Ussher had.[22]

Possibly it is to this early period of his career that we should date the manuscript of Ussher now in the Bodleian Library, Oxford, with the shelfmark Add. A. 91 (S. C. 27719). This text is a study by Ussher of certain Latin Psalters. Two of these, to which he gives the sigla F and G, are the two Irish Psalters from the Cotton library. He describes F (=Vitellius F. XI) as follows (Add. A. 91 [S. C. 27719], fol. 72v):

> *Psalterium admodum antiquum in Hibernicis literis quadratis (Hibernicis seu Saxonicis) descriptum. habetur in eadem Bibliotheca. In fine additur:* **Bendacht dé formúiretach/comall glé robsen sutin sunn**

---

21. R. Parr, *The Life and Times of the Most Reverend James Usher late Lord Arch-Bishop of Armagh Primate and Metropolitan of All Ireland* (London, 1686), p. 11.

22. Parr, *Life*, p. 79.

insúi niropdutham sunn/ haré intapthanth[é] ha[superscript 'o']*btbaid/ flatha de* [written over a crossed-out *'il'*][23]

Immediately afterwards Ussher describes the manuscript with the siglum G, which is clearly Galba A. V:

> G *Psalterium charactere* [following word unclear but apparently *uetustissimo*] *Hibernico descriptum in eadem Bibliotheca. Cui praefixa fuerunt haec verba is liber oswini deirorum regis.*

Thomas Smith, describes F. XI as follows:[24]

> Vitellius F. XI
> 1. *Psalterium vetustum cum canticis Mosis ad filios Israel characteribus Hibernicis exaratum.*
> 2. *Quaedam Hibernica, charactere Hibernico.*
> 3. *Oratio in benedictione panis novi.*

He thus describes the other Psalter:

> Galba A. V.
> *Psalterium Davidis, characteribus Hibernicis vetustissimis, cum cantico Mosis, Hannae & trium puerorum. Additur in fine folium, Hibernice. Dicitur fuisse liber Oswini regis.*

Smith apparently wrote after personal examination of the manuscripts. There is no indication that he knew of Ussher's work. The *Quaedarn Hibernica* in the description of Vitellius F. XI probably indicates the Irish text at the end noted by Ussher. A new element in his description of Galba A. V is the mention of a page in Irish at the end of the manuscript.

Planta did not have access to Vitellius F. XI, damaged in the 1731 fire. Under this heading he simply entered 'Desideratur'. He thus describes Galba A. V:[25]

> Galba A. V.
> *Codex membran. in 8vo minori, constans hodie foliis 35 igne et madore nimium corruptus.*
> *Psalterium Davidis characteribus Hibernicis vetustissimis; dicitur fuisse liber Oswini regis.*

---

23. A. O'Sullivan, 'The Colophon of the Cotton Psalter (Vitellius F. XI)', *Journal of the Royal Society of Antiquaries of Ireland* 96 (1966), pp. 179-80.

24. *Catalogus Librorum Manuscriptorum Bibliothecae Cottonional* (Oxford, 1696), p. 103.

25. J. Planta, *A Catalogue of the Manuscripts in the Cottonian Library deposited in the British Museum* (London: Hansard, Printer, 1802), p. 42.

As we shall see, Planta's description bears little resemblance to the Galba manuscript, yet it has influenced later descriptions.

b. *Cotton Vitellius F. XI*

In modern times the first serious study of Vitellius F. XI was made by J.O. Westwood.[26] Westwood notes how it had only been recently discovered in the British Museum after the disastrous fire of 1731, and was carefully mounted under the direction of Sir F. Madden. Westwood compares the illumination (David's combat with the lion; David's combat with Goliath) with the Psalter of St John's College, Cambridge (MS C.9, the Southampton Psalter). He regarded the script and the illumination of both to be the same and believed that Vitellius F. XI was by the same scribe as that of the Southampton Psalter. With regard to date, he considered that the drawing of Vitellius F. XI may be referred to the ninth or first half of the tenth century.

F. Henry published a study of the illumination of the Psalter in 1960.[27] The illuminations, she notes, have a violence of style which connects them closely with the carvings on the tenth-century high crosses. There is a particularly close connection between the painting of David killing Goliath at the beginning of the third 'fifty' and the same scene on the cross of Muiredach at Monasterboice. The Muiredach whose name is on this cross was probably the person who became abbot about 887 and died in 923. Taking the two works as contemporary, Henry dates the Psalter to the early tenth century, as Westwood had earlier done. In the same study Henry examines the illumination of the Southampton Psalter which, with others, she dates to the beginning of the eleventh century. She believes that the illuminator was inspired by Vitellius F. XI. His style, however, she remarks, is more formal and less natural: in the representations of David and Goliath, for instance, he hardly understands what he is copying.

Later A. O'Sullivan drew attention to the Irish text at the end of the Psalter, given by Ussher.[28] It confirms Henry's connection of the work with Muiredach. O'Sullivan translates the Irish text as follows:

26. J.O. Westwood, 'On the Peculiarities Exhibited by the Miniatures and Ornamentation of Ancient Irish Illuminated Manuscripts', *Archaeological Journal* 7 (1850), pp. 16-25.

27. Henry, 'Remarks'.

28. O'Sullivan, 'Colophon'.

> The blessing of God on Muiredach, bright fulfilment!
> May the scholar be successful and long-lived there,
> May his time here not be short;
> may the outstanding(?) abbot without falsehood
> be a dweller in the kingdom of God.

A closer examination of this Psalter is called for since this is one of the few Irish manuscripts from the tenth century.[29]

There are two interlinear glosses in the text. The first is to *multiplicasti filios hominum* of Ps. 11.9 and reads: *id est in Adam corporaliter in Christo spiritualiter* (fol. 3v). The same gloss is found to these same words on the *Gallicanum* in the Double Psalter of St Ouen. The orthography *spiritualiter* (clearly with a *u*) indicates a post-900 date for the entry of the gloss in Vitellius F. XI. The other gloss is in fol. 42r, over *Beel Phegor* of Ps. 105.28. The gloss (read by fibre-optic reader) over *Beel* reads *id est idulum*, and that over *Phegor id est ciuit(as) ut* (read: *est) terrae Moab et Ammon et Midian*. This is identical with the gloss of the commentary in Vatican Pal., MS lat. 68 on these words.[30] The Double Psalter of St Ouen has the gloss *idulum* to *Beel*, but not the other gloss.

This manuscript merits palaeographical consideration (abbreviations system, and so on). A partial collation of the biblical text shows agreements with I (*Gallicanum* of Rouen Psalter) and sometimes with specific readings of the Southampton Psalter. A full collation is called for, to determine its agreements with, and deviations from, the Irish *Gallicanum* text, and also with that of the Southampton Psalter, with which it is very close in the illumination.

c. *Cotton Galba A.V.*

Planta's description of this manuscript is very misleading. It is not badly damaged by fire and damp *(igne et madore nimium corruptus)*; in fact it is in an excellent state of preservation, apparently in no way affected by the 1731 fire. It has 62 folios (in present foliation), not the

---

29. The others are 'The Lambeth Commentary', London, Lambeth Palace, MS 119); the Double Psalter of St Ouen (Rouen, Bibl. mun., MS 24 [A. 41]); fragments of the sister codex of this in Dublin, Trinity College, MS 1337 (H.3.18), fols 2*-3*; Vatican Pal., lat. 49 (if written in Ireland), in Continental script. Professor Denis Brearley was kind enough to examine the text for me in June 1994, noting that about 60 per cent of the text seemed legible. In August of that year and again in January 1995 I had an opportunity to examine the text.

30. McNamara, *Glossa in Psalmos.*

35 of Planta's catalogue, with an additional unnumbered folio Irish at the end.

F. Henry and G.L. Marsh-Micheli published a study of the illumination of the codex in 1962. Their opening description of the codex seems dependent on Planta:

> It is no more than the ruin of a book, its pages having been turned brown, shrunk and split by the 1731 fire which ravaged the Cotton Library. It consists now of thirty-five folios, 5 in. by about 3 in., but it probably shrank considerably in the fire.[31]

This description seems to have been written before a personal inspection of the codex. The essay goes on to give the results of the authors' personal inspection of the work, including reference to the illuminated initial of Psalm 101 in fol. 48r. They consider the work to be of artistically inferior quality, and believe that the painter was copying indiscriminately from several manuscripts. This Psalter, they say, is likely to be a fairly late imitation (twelfth century?), impossible to localize.

I had the opportunity to examine the codex rapidly in August 1994 and January 1995. As already said, the Psalter text is in an excellent state of preservation. The present manuscript Galba A. V has a continuous foliation from 1 to 63. The Psalter text ends at fol. 62v, at Ps. 148.14. Fol. 63rv contains an Irish text. There is evidence for an earlier foliation, or foliations, for most folios. The contents of the present codex are as follows:

Fol. 1r Outside. In three colours, blue, brown and yellow, with some writing, not legible to naked eye. Not in Irish script.

Fol. 1v Small page with writing; 17 lines to page. Latin. Illuminated initials. Not in Irish script.

Fol. 2r The same Latin text. Not in Irish script.

Fol. 2v Writing. 17 lines to page. Some rubrics, with words *quomodo psal*...preceded in black ink by words: *te populo tuo* and followed by what seems to be a prayer.

Fol. 3r This seems to have been the outer cover of a book.

Fol. 3v Inside cover apparently; faded; whitish grey colour. Has some writing, hard to decipher. Above (apparently): *Catalogus. In isto (?) volumine*. Below this, but in page partly torn: *charac-*

---

31. Henry and Marsh-Micheli, 'A Century', pp. 141-42; see also below, pp. 82-83.

tere Hibernicoluetustissimo (/) olim erat/ haec uerba Liber oswim (=oswini) regis.

Fol. 4r   (older foliation fol. 1). Psalter text in Irish script begins: *Beatus uir.*

This Irish Psalter is divided according to the 'three fifties'. Some of the original folios are now lost, as is the last folio with Ps. 148.15-150 (or 151). A page in Irish has been added at the end (as fol. 63).

It would appear that the present fols. 1-2 and the final fol. 63 are additions to the codex known to James Ussher, who makes no mention of a folio in Irish at the end. This final page would seem to have been there when T. Smith examined it (1696). The Irish text of fol. 63 has been identified by Aoibheann Nic Dhonnchaidh of the School of Celtic Studies, Dublin, as a computus text, and part (of folio 4) of the Cotton manuscript Cotton Appendix LI (written 1589 CE). It would appear to have been added as a kind of end cover.[32]

d. *The So-Called Psalter of Charlemagne (Paris BN, lat. 13159)*

The work referred to as the 'Psalter of Charlemagne' was written 795–800 CE in some centre in northern or north-eastern France.[33] It contains the Gallican Psalter preceded by headings and introductory material. On the outer margins of the manuscript, at the beginning of each psalm, a triangular cartouche contains the Series III of psalm headings. Each psalm has an illuminated capital. At the end of each psalm there is a Psalter collect, from the African Series. The manuscript also contains Litanies.

The date of transcription is assured by the prayer for Pope Leo (III) (795–816) and *pro rege Carolo* (not yet emperor, 800 CE). The place of transcription is not agreed on by all. F. Masai[34] believed it was tran-

---

32. On this manuscript see S.H. O'Grady, *Catalogue of Irish Manuscripts in the British Museum*, I (London: British Museum, 1926; repr. under title *Catalogue of Irish Manuscripts in the British Library [formerly British Museum]* [Dublin: Institute for Advanced Studies, 1992], pp. 285-37). This fine Irish Psalter still awaits proper palaeographical examination. It also merits full collation to situate it within the history of the Psalter text in Ireland.

33. Lowe, *CLA*, V, no. 651. On this Psalter, together with the works cited below, see V. Leroquais, *Les psautiers manuscrits latins des bibliothèques publiques de France*, II (Macon: Protat Frères, 1940–41), no. 338 (pp. 112-15).

34. F. Masai, 'Observations sur le psautier dit de Charlemagne (Paris lat. 13159)', *Scriptorium* 6 (1952), pp. 299-303.

scribed for the abbey of St Riquier, probably at Corbie. M. Huglo[35] maintained it was written at St Riquier. E.A. Lowe[36] describes as follows: 'Written in a centre with insular connections situated somewhere on the Rhine or in Belgium or East France, to judge by the local saints mentioned in the litanies.' B. Bischoff says that details in the Psalter's litany point in particular to the border region between north-east France and north-west Austrasia,[37] noting (against Masai's view) that this codex is utterly different from everything that we know of Corbie's script and book decoration. It belongs to the same group (and presumably is from the same scriptorium) as the Essen Münsterschatz Gospels in minuscule, the ornamentation of which is dominated by the same wild inventiveness, tamed only by the draughtsman's skill. B. Fischer explicitly rejects St Riquier or Corbie origin, and opts for one in the Rhein-Maas-Gebiet region, without possibility of more precise localization.[38]

What is granted by all is that, whatever the precise place of composition, the work depends on an Insular original. Lowe[39] notes the misuse of *s* typical of Insular scribes: *hierussalem, abysus, dissolauerunt (desolauerunt)*. The extent of this dependence must be determined for each of the elements. An attempt should also be made to determine as precisely as possible the nature of the 'Insular' influence, for instance, whether it came from Ireland or Northumbria. (The 'Insular' influence is clearest in the decoration and I shall return to this point. However, the litanies represent, in the main, Continental devotion, pointing to

35. M. Huglo, 'Un tonaire du graduel de la fin du VIIIe siècle, Paris, B. N. lat. 13159', *Revue Grégorienne* 31 (1952), pp. 176-86; 224-33.

36. Lowe, *CLA*, V, p. 652.

37. B. Bischoff, *Manuscripts and Libraries in the Age of Charlemagne* (ed. and trans. M. Gorman; Cambridge Studies in Palaeography and Codicology, 1; Cambridge: Cambridge University Press, 1994), p. 29, with reference to M. Coens, 'Litanies carolines de Soissons et du Psautier de Charlemagne', in *Receuil d'études bollandiennes, Subsidia Hagiographica* (Brussels, 1963), pp. 296-98 (297).

38. B. Fischer, 'Bibeltext und Bibelreform unter Karl dem Grossern', in Wolfgang Braunfels (ed.), Karl der Grosse, *Lebenswerk und Nachleben*. II. *Das geistige Leben* (ed. B. Bischoff; Düsseldorf: Pädagogischer Verlag Schwamm-Bagel, 1965), pp. 156-216; reproduced in B. Fisher, *Lateinische Bibelhandschriften im Frühen Mittelalter* (Aus der Geschichte der lateinischen Bibel, 11; Freiburg: Herder, 1985), pp. 101-202 (167).

39. Lowe, *CLA*, V, no. 652.

north-east France or north-west Austrasia in M. Coens's opinion.[40])

The *Psalter text* is *Gallicanum*. It is Q of the Roman Benedictine edition.[41] Its text is of an inferior quality, replete with errors, probably due to pressure of time for completion.[42] This Psalter text seems to represent influences from various text forms, for instance the Palace School model, represented by W of the Benedictine edition (Vienna, Österreichische Nationalbibliothek, MS 1861). This Psalter by the scribe Dagulf (and known as Dagulf's Psalter) was written 783–93 CE.[43] It was presented by Charlemagne to Pope Hadrian I,[44] is of the Stuttgart-Alcuin Type and shows Irish influence.[45]

It is difficult to say whether the *psalm headings*, Series III, in cartouches in the margins, derive from an Irish original. This Series has been edited by P. Salmon[46] according to a Spanish tradition of *Iuxta Hebraeos* (*Hebraicum*) Psalters. The Series, however, was not originally composed for the *Hebraicum* text, nor inspired by the *Hebraicum*. It is a well-constructed text, rich in ideas, directing the mind to the New Testament, but without attributing the greater part of the psalms to Christ himself. Outside of Spanish texts it is found in two Swiss Psalters (Zürich, Stadtbibl. Rh. 34, and Stadtbibl. C. 12) as well as in the Psalter of Charlemagne. H.J. Lawlor[47] made a collation of the Psalter in BL, MS Egerton 1139, a Gallican Psalter written in England about 1140. The headings in this are inspired, often somewhat freely, by Series III. Salmon notes that the Series III headings of Paris 13159 often agree with Zürich, Stadtbibl. Rh. 34 (assigned the siglum D) against the Spanish tradition. In Series III, then, the Psalter of Charlemagne may represent Continental (French) rather than Irish or Insular tradition.

40. See Coens, 'Litanies'.

41. *Liber Psalmorum ex recensione Sancti Hieronymi* (Biblia Sacra iuxta Latinam Vulgatam Versionem ad codicum fidem, X; Rome: Vatican Polyglot Press, 1953), pp. ix-x.

42. P. Salmon, *Les 'Tituli Psalmorum' des manuscrits latins* (Collectanea Biblica Latins, 12: Rome: Abbaye Saint-Jéremie; Vatican City: Libreria Vaticana, 1959), pp. 31-32.

43. Lowe, *CLA*, X, p. 1504.

44. *Liber Psalmorum*, p. x; Fischer, 'Bibeltext', pp. 166-67.

45. Fischer, 'Bibeltext', p. 167.

46. Salmon, *Les 'Tituli'*, pp. 97-113.

47. H.J. Lawlor, 'The Cathach of St. Columba', *PRIA* 23 C (1916), pp. 413-36.

With regard to the *psalm collects* (of which there are three series), the Psalter of Charlemagne is the only manuscript that has the African Series (Series I). Each of these three series has its own particular orientation. In comparison with the other two it has been noted that the African Series has a more pronounced theological character and that it issues from a doctrine influenced by Augustinian thought. In the domain of christology it stresses the historical redemptive work of Christ and its great stages, leaving in the shadow the dogmatic reflections on his human-divine being.[48] The African Series, the oldest and most original of the three, has been transmitted by this single manuscript. It is called the African Series because the African Psalter text, represented principally by the *Veronensis*, is the principal text used. Brou[49] thinks that this Series I was composed by an African in a time of persecution, probably by the Vandals, during the century after the death of Augustine of Hippo. There may have been a variant form of this text intended for times of peace. Brou[50] believes that the text in the Psalter of Charlemagne derives from an Insular original. 'All that remains now is to find the Insular manuscript that serves as a model for the scribe of Saint-Riquier' (where he believes Paris BN, lat. 13159 was written). Since these psalm collects, for the greater part at least, are collective prayers of petition under the inspiration of the individual psalm, it seems difficult to detect in them an influence of any particular exegetical approach, historical or christological. With regard to the place of composition, one may, I believe, query the need for an African origin. The *Veronensis*, after all, is a north-Italian manuscript (s. VI-VII), and Series I might conceivably have originated there. From there the Series could have come to Ireland and Northumbria with the Julian commentary and the epitome of this, works which stand behind the psalm headings in the Psalter of Charlemagne.

48. Salmon, *Les 'Tituli'*, p. 55.

49. L. Brou, 'Les collectes du Psautier: Introduction', in A. Wilmart and L. Brou (eds.), *The Psalter Collects from V–VIth Century Sources* (ed. with introduction, apparatus criticus and indexes by Dom Louis Brou; London: Henry Bradshaw Society, 1949), pp. 9-26 (18-24); *idem*, 'Etudes sur les collectes du Psautier', *SE* 6 (1954), pp. 73-95. On these collects see further T.S. Ferguson, 'Africana Psalm Collects and the "Psalter of Charlemagne": African or Carolingian?', *RBén* 108 (1998), pp. 44-57.

50. Brou, 'Etudes', p. 94 note.

With regard to the *psalm headings*, the composite introduction prefaced to each psalm contains first of all the opening words of the psalm, which is then often described as *Psalmus Dauid*. One or more historical headings is then given, after which there generally comes the mystical heading. Occasionally certain important words of the psalm are then explained. In *almost* every one of these elements the introductory material of the so-called Psalter of Charlemagne is very closely related to the corresponding material in the Hiberno-Latin psalm commentary of the Vatican MS Pal. lat. 68. This holds for peculiarities of the historical references and a peculiar form of the Series 1 mystical headings.[51] This introductory material, or psalm headings, of the Psalter of Charlemagne presupposes a certain unified approach to the understanding of the psalms, an entire commentary on the Psalter. This commentary has come down to us in the psalm gloss of Vatican Pal. lat. 68 and in the glosses on the *Hebraicum* of the Double Psalter of St Ouen (Rouen, Bibl. mun., MS 24 [A. 41]). The comments on the individual words of the Psalms are often drawn from, or dependent on, the Psalms commentary, recently published, entitled *Glosa Psalmorum ex traditione seniorum*, compiled in Southern France about 600 CE.[52]

The *psalm grouping*, or the division of the Psalter of Charlemagne, merits special consideration, because it might yield valuable evidence on the traditions lying behind it. In Irish literary texts from the eighth century onwards the Psalter is commonly referred to as 'The Three Fifties', which might lead one to believe that Psalters known to Irish writers were so divided. This is the case for the second-oldest Irish Psalter we know, BL, Codex Vitellius F. Xl, from the early tenth century, and for all later Irish Psalters, where each of the divisions (at Pss.

---

51. See McNamara (ed.), *Glossa in Psalmos*, pp. 43-45.

52. The introductory material, including the psalm headings and comments of the individual verses, for Ps. 40 to Ps. 151 has been critically edited by K. Ceulemans: 'Scotti (?) anonymi Tituli psalmorum in psalterio Caroli Magni traditi (= cod. paris. BN lat. 13159). Argumenta, opschriften en woordverklaringen bij psalmen 40-151. I. Inleiding, kritische tekstuitgave en vertaling'. II. Tekstkritische aantekeningen en inhoudelijke commentaar' (Dissertation for Licentiate in Greek and Latin classics, Katholieke Universeit Leuven, 1997). For an non-exhaustive list of the (verbal) agreements with the *Anonymi Glosa Psalmorum ex traditione Seniorum* 20 see I, xxx, instancing Pss 62.5; 79.15–17.20; 91.12; 97.6-10; 99.5-7; 100.21-26; 103.8-9; 104.24; 106.6-8; 109.6-10; 110.4-5; 111.8-9; 112.5-6; 117.6-9. For the *Anonymi Glosa Psalmorum ex traditione Seniorum* see below.

1; 51; 101) was preceded by a special illuminated page. However, our oldest Irish Psalter, the Cathach (c. 650 CE) has no tripartite division, and perhaps had no division at all (the text has not been completely preserved). Another division of the Psalter known from the eighth century onwards (found in both Gallican and *Romanum* Psalters) is an eightfold division, again noted by special illuminated initials.[53] This division would appear to have corresponded to the psalms assigned to the night hours of the office according to the Roman usage.[54] In this the psalms for the night hours were to be drawn from Psalms 1–108, with 12 psalms for each of the days of the week and (in some traditions at least) twice 12 psalms for the Sunday night hours during the winter period. This eightfold division is clearest in the Vespasian Psalter (BL, Cotton MS Vespasian A.I; England, probably Canterbury, St Augustine's Abbey, c. 720–30).[55] In this an elaborately decorated incipit marks the beginning of certain psalms: thus for Psalms 17, 26, 38, 52, 68, 80, 97, 109, and 118. The last of these is clearly intended to be less elaborate than the others; the first lacks the pointed background of the others, but its size is the same as that of the following incipits.[56] Of these, Psalms 26–97 inclusive are the opening psalms for the night hours of Monday through Saturday in the Roman office. The special illumination of Psalm 109 indicates the psalm for Sunday vespers. Verses of Psalm 118 were used during the hours of terce, sext and none. Psalm 17 was the beginning of the second group of psalms for the night office on Sunday.

Two other English Psalters have both a threefold and eightfold division, namely Berlin, Deutsches Staatsbibliothek, Hamilton 553 (the

---

53. On this point see U. Kuder, 'Die Initialen des Amienspsalters (Amiens, Bibliothèque municipale MS 18)' (unpublished PhD dissertation, Ludwig-Maximilians-Universität, Munich, 1977), pp. 67-83 (67-74).

54. See M. Righetti, *Manuale di storia liturgica*. II. *L'anno liturgico, il breviario* (2nd edn; Milan: Ancona, 1955), §§351-61, pp. 499-517. In his chart on the distribution of psalms in the Roman office (facing 352), Righetti gives the following as the first psalm: Sunday Noct. 1 Ps. 1; Noct. 2, Ps. 15; Monday Ps. 27; Tuesday Ps. 39; Wednesday Ps. 53; Thursday Ps. 68; Friday Ps. 80; Saturday Ps. 96.

55. On this Psalter and its divisions see D.H. Wright and A. Campbell, *The Vespasian Psalter* (Early English Manuscripts in Facsimile, 14: Copenhagen, 1967); p. 47 for the Psalter decoration.

56. Wright and Campbell, *Vespasian Psalter*, p. 47.

Salaberga Psalter, *Psalterium Romanum et Cantica)*,[57] Northumbria, first half of eighth century; and New York, Pierpont Morgan Library, MS M. 776 (*Psalterium Romanum*), England, and probably southern England, middle of the eighth century. In the Psalter of Charlemagne there is no trace of any threefold division (with special initials for Pss. 51 and 101). It does, however, have special illumination for Psalm 1, no particularly large initial for Psalm 17, but very specially decorated large initials for Psalms 26, 38, 52, 68, 80 and 97. There are also large initials for Psalms 109 and 118. The Psalter of Charlemagne thus belongs to the tradition of the eightfold division represented by the English Psalters, and that of Northumbria as represented by the Salaberga Psalter. It goes with the Roman office usage for the night hours, and our available evidence indicates that this usage was not followed in Ireland.[58]

It would appear, then, that in the eightfold division of the Psalter Paris BN, lat. 13159 does not represent Irish tradition. The Roman tradition it represents would seem to have been mediated through a Northumbrian, or possibly even directly from a Roman model, since Charlemagne in his *Admonitio generalis* of 789 says his father Pepin had ordained that the night hours and the gradual office be celebrated in accord with Roman usage and the will of the apostolic see.[59] Unfortunately, we have no early Roman or French examples of Psalters with an eightfold division. On balance, the model used by the Psalter of Charlemagne for this division would seem to have been Northumbrian or English.

All that remains to be studied of this Paris manuscript is the illumination, the decorated initials. That the decoration of the Psalter is Insular, or at least of Insular inspiration, is admitted by all who have examined it. F. Masai speaks of 'sa décoration d'inspiration insulaire

57. On the Salaberga Psalter see D. Ó Cróinín, *Psalterium Salabergae: Staatsbibliothek zu Berlin—Preussischer Kulturbesitz Ms. Hamilt. 553* (Codices illuminati medii aevi, 30; Colour Microfiche Edition; Introduction and Codicological Description by D.Ó Cróinin: Munich: Edition Helga Lengenfelder, 1994); on the special initials, p. 17 (for Pss. 17, 118, 26, 38, 52, 68, 80, 97 and 109).

58. For the divine office in Ireland see M. Curran, *The Antiphonary of Bangor* (Dublin: Irish Academic Press, 1984), pp. 159-91; for the Iona tradition see A.O. Anderson and M.O. Anderson, *Adomnan's Life of Columba* (London: Nelson, 1961), pp. 121-22.

59. '*ut cantum romanum pleniter discant et ordinabiliter per nocturnale uel graduale officium peragatur...ob unanimitatem apostolicae Sedis*' (*Monumenta German. Legum*, sect. 2, tom. 1, 61. Cited in Righetti, *Manuale*, §360, p. 513.

(une lettrine au début de chaque psaume)' ('its decoration of Insular inspiration [a dropped initial at the beginning of each psalm]');[60] 'L'atelier qui l'a decoré témoigne...d'une forte influence insulaire' ('The workshop that decorated it bears witness...to a pronounced Insular influence').[61] Masai (arguing for an origin at Corbie) remarks that the Psalter of Amiens (Amiens, Bibl. mun. 18), from the renowned Abbey of Picardie, is the closest known relation of our codex from the point of view of decoration.

G.L. Marsh-Micheli examined the illumination of the manuscript in some detail in 1939,[62] in a study in which she considers in particular the cross-channel influences on the three manuscripts: the Essen Gospels, the Psalter of Charlemagne, and the Amiens Psalter. In these three works she sees the presence of strong cross-channel influences. She notes the giant initials of the Psalter of Charlemagne, arranged with a sense of articulated composition transmitted by Insular works. Some are isolated and alone; more often they are double, with intertwining. This she compares with the cross-channel gospel-books, in those of Lindisfarne or Durham. She considers the abundance of illuminated letters surprising, although interlace predominates. The initials with birds are of the traditional type of Corbie.[63]

In his treatment of the manuscript, E.A. Lowe writes with regard to the illumination:[64]

> Numerous initials of curious design, skilfully drawn in pen and ink, showing the plait motif, imaginary dog-like beasts, birds (fols. 52v, 74v, 79r, 156v) serpents and a mermaid (fol. 13v) here and there with a dart of red, yellow or green; the form of many initials is manifestly copied from Insular models... A pen-and-ink drawing of Christ and two angels at the end of fol. 118v seems a slightly later addition.

J. Porcher[65] notes the 'initiales grandes et petites, certaines rehaussées de rouge, de style insulaire' ('large and small initials, some embellish-

---

60. F. Masai, 'Observations sur le psautier dit de Charlemagne (Paris lat. 13159)', *Scriptorium* 6 (1952), pp. 299-303 (299).

61. Masai, 'Observations', p. 303.

62. G.L. Micheli, *L'enluminature du haut moyen age et les influences irlandaises: Histoire d'une influence* (Brussels, 1939), pp. 84-87, 132-33.

63. Masai, 'Observations', pp. 84-85.

64. Lowe, *CLA*, V, p. 652.

65. J. Porcher, J., *Bibliothèque Nationale: Les manuscrits à peinture en France du VIIᵉ au XIIᵉ siècle* (Paris: Bibliothèque Nationale, 1954), no. 18.

ments with red, of Insular style'). U. Kuder has devoted a doctoral dissertation to the initials of the Amiens Psalter, which he considers quite different from Paris BN, lat. 13159.[66] Apart from this observation and a summary of the discussion of its place of origin[67] he has very little to say on the Psalter, although he does note the mermaid in fol. 13v.[68]

The illumination of these initials of the Psalter of Charlemagne merits detailed examination, to determine if possible the predominant tradition behind it, whether this is Continental (Merovingian France) or Insular, and if Insular, whether this is Northumbrian or Irish. The two differing forms of illumination for Psalm 109 on fol. 119r and the facing fol. 118v may indicate a clash of cultures—the animal initial *D* of *Dixit* representing the 'Insular' tradition, the pen-and-ink drawing of Christ (added later, but contemporaneously) indicating local interests. For a study of the Psalter's illumination we have rich variety in the initials, since the same initial opening letters or words are differently treated in the different occurrences.[69] As already noted, each of the eight divisions of the Psalter is introduced by a specially large illuminated letter, occupying from a half page (the *DNS* of Ps. 16; fol. 28) to almost an entire page (the *S* of Ps. 68, fol. 70r).

With such a study of the Psalter's illumination we should have advanced a step further towards determining the traditions behind the Psalter of Charlemagne, the relationships between Merovingian France and Britain, and the interrelationships of Ireland with both.

66. Kuder, 'Die Initialen', p. 35 n. 2.

67. Kuder, 'Die Initialen', p. 35 n. 2.

68. Kuder, 'Die Initialen', p. 249.

69. The following is the frequency of occurrence of the Psalm initials: the letter D with 43 occurrences; C with 15; B with 11; I with 11; L with 10; Q with 10; A with 7; M with 7; N with 5; S with 5; V with 4; U with 3; P with 2; O with 1; T with 1.

INTRODUCTION TO GLOSSA IN PSALMOS: THE HIBERNO-LATIN
GLOSS ON THE PSALMS OF CODEX PALATINUS LATINUS 68

Codex Palatino-Latinus 68 of the Vatican Library is a *glossa* on the Psalms.

Due to the loss of the first section it begins imperfectly with Ps. 39.11d: 'a *concilio multa*'. It ends with the apocryphal psalm 151. The Latin commentary or gloss follows on the *lemma*. There are 25 glosses in Old Irish and five in Old English.[1] All are written as part of the text though (with two exceptions) marked off from it by apices. We can presume that this particular codex was taken to Rome with the remainder of the Palatine collection in 1623.

1. *Review of Research*

The codex was briefly described by H. Stevenson Jr in 1886 in the catalogue of the Palatine collection.[2] He assigned it to the eighth century, a date arrived at after consultation with I.B. de Rossi.

Soon afterwards the vernacular glosses received the attention of scholars, those in Old English being studied by A.S. Napier[3] and those

---

1. See N.R. Ker, *Catalogue of Manuscripts Containing Anglo-Saxon* (Oxford: Clarendon Press, 1957), no. 388.

2. *Codices Palatini Latini Bibliothecae Vaticanae descripti, recensuit et digessit Henricus Stevenson Iunior, recognovit I.B. De Rossi...* I (Rome, 1886; repr. 1975), p. 12; pp. cxxxf. for date of manuscript.

3. A.S. Napier, 'Old Northumbrian Glosses in the Vatican', *The Academy* 35 (1889), p. 342; A.S. Napier, 'The Old Northumbrian Glosses in MS. Palatine 68', *The Academy* 35 (1889), p. 449. Albert S. Cook, on the other hand in 'The Old Northumbrian Glosses in MS. Palatinus 68', *The Academy* 36 (1889), pp. 10-11, drew attention to the form Edilberict and Berictfridi in the colophon, and surmised that the rare form *berict* might be a partial confirmation of Stevenson's eighth-century date. Napier later edited the Northumbrian glosses in his book *Old-English Glosses, Chiefly Unpublished* (Anecdota Oxoniensia, Mediaeval and Modern Series, 11; Oxford, 1900), pp. xxii, xxxi, 220.

in Old Irish by W. Stokes.[4] Both these scholars cast doubt on the eighth-century date assigned to the codex, the latter expressing the belief that it was more probably from the ninth or tenth centuries. Sir E. Maunde Thompson,[5] assigned the manuscript to the ninth century. On the basis of language, however, the Old English glosses were reckoned to be no later than the early eighth century,[6] and those in Old Irish to be as old, possibly, as the glosses of the chief glossator of the Würzburg Codex Paulinus (which are now assigned to c. 750 CE).[7] In his monograph on *Early Irish Minuscule Script* (1910),[8] W.M. Lindsay opted for a date from the eighth to the ninth century for the manuscript, noting that the script and the abbreviations point to the eighth century or to the beginning of the ninth at the latest. A point noted by B. Güterbock[9] was that the Latin glosses of the commentary, and some of those in Old Irish as well, were related to those of the commentary found in Codex Ambrosianus C 301 inf. (a work copied by the Irish scribe Diarmait about 800 CE). In his study of the use made of Theodore of Mopsuestia's commentary on the Psalms in England and Ireland, R.L. Ramsay[10] built on these earlier studies and, further, remarked that G. Mercati had informed him in a letter that the excerpts in the catena were drawn from the works of Hilary, Jerome and Theodore, as well as from other commentaries on the Psalms.

In 1920 L. Gougaud[11] listed the manuscript as an eighth-century

4.   W. Stokes, 'The Old-Irish Glosses in Palatine 68', *The Academy* 35 (1889), pp. 361-62; *idem*, 'Hibernica. I. The Glosses in Palatine 68 with Commentary', *Zeitschrift für vergleichende Sprachforschung* 33 NS 11 (1892), pp. 232-36; *Thes. Pal.*, I, pp. xiv, 3, 715.

5.   On the opinion of Sir E. Maunde Thompson, see Napier, 'The Old Northumbrian', p. 449.

6.   Thus Napier, *Old-English Glosses*, p. xxxii.

7.   See R. Thurneysen, *A Grammar of Old Irish* (revised and enlarged edition; ET by D.A. Binchy and O. Bergin; Dublin Institute for Advanced Studies, 1946), p. 4.

8.   W.M. Lindsay, *Early Irish Minuscule Script* (Oxford: James Parker and Co., 1910), pp. 67-70.

9.   B. Güterbock, 'Aus irischen Handschriften in Turin und Rom', *Zeitschrift für vergleichende Sprachforschung* 33 NS (1895), pp. 100-102.

10.   R.L. Ramsay, 'Theodore of Mopsuestia and St Columban on the Psalms', and 'Theodore of Mopsuestia in England and Ireland', *ZCP* 8 (1912), pp. 421-51 and 452-97; 428 and 453 for Pal. lat. 68.

11.   L. Gougaud, 'Répertoire des fac-similés des manuscrits irlandais (3e partie)', *Revue Celtique* 38 (1920), pp. 1-14 (9).

work. J. Kenney (1929)[12] and B. Bischoff (1954)[13] have nothing significant to add to earlier researches, but accept an eighth-century date for
the manuscript. So, too, does E.A. Lowe in his palaeographical description of the codex.[14] Lowe remains non-committal with regard to the
country of origin, but believes it was the north of England rather than
Ireland. T.A.M. Bishop treats of the manuscript in passing, in his palaeographical study of the Cambridge manuscript, Trinity College B. 10.
5 (together with British Library Cotton Vitellius C.VIII),[15] a codex in
Anglo-Saxon minuscule from the first half of the eighth century and
most probably, in his view, written in an Irish centre in Northumbria.
Bishop sees remarkable similarities between this Codex and Pal. lat. 68;
he considers both to be contemporary and assumes that Pal. lat. 68 is an
Anglo-Saxon production. In his *Catalogue of Manuscripts containing
Anglo-Saxon Glosses* (1957)[16] N.R. Ker assigns the date saec. VIII to
both manuscript and Old English glosses in Pal. lat. 68. In an essay
(1971) on the *Tituli Psalmorum* of Pseudo-Bede Bonifatius Fischer[17]
remarked on the close relationship between these and the corresponding
headings in the so-called Psalter of Charlemagne (MS. Paris, Bibl. Nat.
lat. 13159) and in the Codex Pal. lat. 68. In the same essay he expressed
the view that in some places the exegesis of the glosses in Pal. lat. 68 is
more radical than that of Theodore of Mopsuestia. In 1973, in a study
of the Psalms in the early Irish Church,[18] the present writer treated

12. J. Kenney, *The Sources for the Early History of Ireland: Ecclesiastical*
(New York: Columbia University Press, 1929; later reprints; Dublin: Four Courts
Press, 1997), p. 637.

13. B. Bischoff, 'Wendepunkte in der Geschichte der lateinischen Exegese im
Frühmittelalter', *SE* 232 (ET C. O'Grady, 'Turning-Points in the History of Latin
Exegesis in the Early Middle Ages', in M. McNamara [ed.], *Biblical Studies: The
Medieval Irish Contribution* [Proceedings of the Irish Biblical Association, 1; Dub-
lin: Dominican Publications, 1976], pp. 74-160 [105]).

14. *CLA*, I, no. 78, bibliography, p. 42; and Supplement (Oxford: Clarendon
Press, 1971), p. 44.

15. T.A.M. Bishop, 'Notes on Cambridge Manuscripts. Part VII. Pelagius in
Trinity College B.10.5', *Transactions of the Cambridge Bibliographical Society*, 4,
part 1 (1954), pp. 70-74; pp. 72-73 for Pal. lat. 68.

16. Ker, *Catalogue of Manuscripts*, no. 388, pp. 457-58.

17. B. Fischer, 'Bedae de Titulis psalmorum liber', in J. Autenrieth and F. Brün-
holtz (eds.), *Festschrift Bernhard Bischoff zu seinem 65* (Stuttgart: Hiersemann,
1971), pp. 90-110, especially pp. 96-97.

18. M. McNamara, 'Psalter Text and Psalter Study in the Early Irish Church

briefly of the manuscript and noted the relationship between some of its glosses and those of the later (eleventh century) so-called Psalter of Caimin. He also expressed the view that the text should be published *in toto*. As an Appendix to the same study, Dr Maurice Sheehy published the opening and closing folios of the Codex.

Lucas De Coninck and M.J. d'Hont collated the manuscript for their critical edition (1977)[19] of Julian of Eclanum's Latin translation of Theodore of Mopsuestia's commentary on the Psalms and of the Epitome of this Latin translation. He notes that the compiler has throughout used the Epitome, not the full translation itself—even in places where both are extant: the excerpts contain additions and formulations proper to the author of the Epitome. In the places where the compiler wished to reproduce his source textually we find that there are numerous errors and conjectural emendations. Despite this, however, the manuscript of the Epitome from which the excerpts are drawn was a much better one than the text in the Milan Codex, Amb. C 301 inf. The manuscript used by the compiler contained, as part of the text itself, readings which in the Milan text figure *in margine* or *supra lineam*. De Coninck and d'Hont also make mention of Mgr Mercati's remark to Ramsay of the presence in the catena of the influence of Hilary, but very wisely comment that the situation in this matter is very complex. With 'most recent writers' De Coninck and d'Hont take the manuscript to date most probably from the second half of the eighth century.

The present writer completed a critical edition of the text in 1976 and published an essay on it in 1979.[20] In 1981 Patrick O'Neill published a study of the obscure Old English gloss *brondegur̄* (found at Ps. 77.46)[21] and also a summary of a paper of his on the vernacular glosses of the manuscript.[22] He takes the date of the work to be the early eighth century and believes that the scribe of our present manuscript did not

(A.D. 600–1200)', pp. 19-142 in this volume; see especially pp. 120-23 for M. Sheehy's edition of fols. 1r and 46r.

19. L. De Coninck and M.-J. d'Hont (eds.), *Theodori Mopsuesteni Expositionis in Psalmos Iuliano Aeclanensi interprete in latinum versae quae supersunt* (CCSL, 88A; Turnhout: Brepols, 1977), pp. xli-xlii.

20. M. McNamara, 'Ireland and Northumbria as Illustrated by a Vatican Manuscript', *Thought* 54 (1979), pp. 274-90.

21. P. O'Neill, 'Old English *brondegur̄*', *English Studies* 62 (1981), pp. 2-4.

22. P. O'Neill, 'The Vernacular Glosses of MS. Vat. Pal. 68: Evidence for Cultural Links between Ireland and Northumberland in the Early Eighth Century', *Old English Newsletter* 14 (1981), pp. 47-48.

understand Old English and was copying from an original in which, presumably, the Old English glosses stood above the lines of the Latin text or in the margins.[23]

This brief survey takes the history of research over the past century (from 1886) as far as 1981. In my view two major studies still remain to be done on Codex Vaticanus Pal. lat. 68, each of which will probably have significant contributions to make with regard to the date, as well as the cultural milieu, of the composition of the present manuscript.

The first of these studies would concern itself with the codex as such, concentrating on such elements as the parchment, the lining, the ink, handwriting, punctuation, marginal notations such as *diple*, diminuendo effect and elements of decoration. The study of these and other relevant details of the codex in the light of what is known of Irish and British calligraphy and book production during the eighth and ninth centuries should help us situate more closely the composition of the codex in place and time.

The other study I refer to is linguistic. This would concentrate mainly on orthography, but would also examine questions of grammar in so far as is permitted by the nature of this work, which is in the main a collection of excerpts from other writings. An important part of the grammatical study, in fact, would be an examination of the manner in which the work changes the orthography of the original sources in keeping with a peculiar grammatical structure.

Even a cursive reading of the Codex Pal. lat. 68 reveals that orthographically, both in the *lemmata* and the glosses, it contains most of the characteristics one associates with Hiberno-Latin works and with writings of the early Middle Ages, especially of the Merovingian period. Without in any way aiming at being exhaustive I instance some of these characteristics, as set out by the authorities in the field: in consonants, assimilation and dissimulation, syncope and its absence, absence of *n* in *coiux,* frequent haplography and dittography, especially with regard to certain consonants, confusion or interchange of certain consonants (*p/b, b/w* consonantal, *c/k* or *qu, d/t, g/c, ph/f*), *c* or *q* for *qu,* insertion of *p* between labial and dental (*in solempnitate semptimbris,* Ps. 45.5).

There is also the frequent interchange of certain vowels; *o/u, a/o, a/e, e/i;* we have *ae* for e (universal in *aeclesia*), *u* for *uu, u* for *au, a* for *au, i* for *ii.* Some instances of such occurrences in the codex may be due to

---

23.   Cf. O'Neill, 'Old English *brondeguī*', p. 4.

scribal errors. This may be the case in some cases of the use of *a* for *o* and vice versa. Rather than emend the text, however, I here list these occurrences in Pal. lat. 68, including page reference of the present edition:

Use of *a* for *o*

Word	Psalm reference	Page number
arganorum	136.2	290
carda	50.15	112
cohartatur	131.6	268
continua	88.22	188
dua	74.9	157
meditabar	118.117	257
multa	39.11	91
tabernacula	60.5	126
ulla	138.12	294

Use of *o* for *a*

Word	Psalm reference	Page number
auersabor	118.85	254
hoc	71.6	147
louoraui (=laboraui)	48.9	106
matutino	142.8	300
meorum	68.34	143
mirabor	72.19	151
molorum	39.13	91
obsolutionis	66.3	135
obsoruet	57.10	122
operiantur (=ap–)	140.3	297
saluos	71.13	148
sancto	133.2	287

2. *Description of the Manuscript*

The manuscript is thus described by E.A. Lowe:[24]

> *Glossa in Psalmos.* Anglo-Saxon minuscule saec. VIII. Foll. 46; ca. 310 × 190 mm. (ca. 267 × 150 mm.) in 40-43 long lines. Ruling after folding, several leaves at a time; single bounding lines. Prickings in both margins guided ruling. Gatherings normally of tens, signed by a Roman numeral

---

24. Lowe, *CLA*, I, no. 78.

in the centre of the lower margin of the last page (once on the first page), standing apparently over older marks. Scribe's signature at the end of the MS. (fol. 46) in the script of the text. Main pauses marked by ·.·, lesser pauses by the mere point; at the end of the Psalm :– or ..— is used, often repeated to fill out a line. Citations marked in the left margin by , or ., . Accents on monosyllables. Abbreviations of Insular type and very numerous; ...tur has the Anglo-Saxon form ꝥ...

Parchment thick, of Insular type. Written in rapid and expert fine minuscule. Each psalm begins with an uncoloured initial of strikingly angular Insular type, followed by a group of larger letters often in majuscule... In the text occur vernacular glosses marked by oblique apices.

Written by Edilberict, son of Berictfrid (fol. 46), probably in the north of England. The tur-symbol ꝥ points to an English scriptorium, as do the vernacular glosses, but script and decoration point to Ireland. Later in Germany, probably at Lorsch: a pen-trial 'CUNIBRAHT' is found on fol. 46v.

The present text begins with the *lemma* and gloss for Ps. 39.11d: '*A concilio multa*'. i. *toto Israhel praedicabo*. The first part of the commentary, and possibly also an introduction accompanying it, has been lost. The 46 folios that remain are in an excellent state of preservation. There is a tear in the parchment from the top left downwards and inwards on fol. 3[25] and a hole right through the parchment in fol. 16.[26] The continuity of the text in both cases makes it clear that both faults existed before the text was added. The final folio is rent at the top and slightly creased further down.[27] The interference with the text indicates that both tear and crease came after parchment had been written on. The text in general is very legible, although in a few cases the ink has faded and the writing has blurred (for example, 5r, IIV).[28]

3. *Marginal and Interlinear Markings and Glosses*

3.1. *Marginal Citation Marks:* Diple

Most lines of the commentary proper (that is, outside of the introductory material) are accompanied in the left-hand margin by the following

25. M. McNamara (ed.), *Glossa in Psalmos: The Hiberno-Latin Gloss on the Psalms of Codex Palatinus Latinus 68 (Psalms 39:11–151:7)* (Critical Edition of the text together with Introduction and Source Analysis; Studi e Testi, 310; Vatican City: Biblioteca Apostolica Vaticana, 1986), pp. 102, 105.

26. McNamara (ed.), *Glossa in Psalmos*, pp. 170, 173.

27. McNamara (ed.), *Glossa in Psalmos*, pp. 308-10.

28. McNamara (ed.), *Glossa in Psalmos*, pp. 114, 116, 148.

signs:[29] , (a large comma sign), ., (point and large comma), .., (two points and large comma). The second of these (., point and large comma) can appear singly or be repeated twice, three times or occasionally even four times. From fol. 19r (lower part) onwards only the first of these (, — a single large comma) occurs. I fail to find an explanation of the change, but it may in some way be connected with the fact that the latter half of the manuscript has fewer marginal signs than the earlier part.

It appears that these signs are the *diple* of which Isidore speaks (*Etym.*, 1, 21, 13, PL 82, 97B): '*Diple...hanc scriptores nostri apponunt in libris ecclesiasticorum virorum ad separanda, vel demonstranda testimonia sanctarum scripturarum.*' The *diple* in the margin would be placed against a *lemma* in the text; two, three or four *diple* would indicate the corresponding number of *lemmata*. In our manuscript, however, not every *lemma* has a corresponding *diple*; on more than one occasion, lines with more than one *lemma* have only a single *diple*, even in the folios before 19r.

We have no way of knowing whether these present marginal signs (*diple*) were in the original work or have been added later.

3.2. *Marginal Source References*
In the left-hand margins we also find *hir* 15 times[30] and the letter *h* about 33 or 34 times,[31] this latter often accompanied by one or more dots (*h. – .h. – .h..– h ...*). Source analysis indicates that hir stands for *hirunimus:* it stands opposite material ascribed to Jerome. The letter *h* in most instances seems also to indicate a source believed to be Jerome's, since it often stands in the margin opposite such texts. However, I fail to understand this twofold form of reference *hir* and *h*, for the same author. It may be that these marginal source references were added to the manuscript at different times and by different scholars. This would also help to explain two occurrences of a marginal *h* opposite texts which the compiler (and presumably the tradition he repre-

29. They are, presumably, the citation marks noted by Lowe, *CLA*, I, no. 78.
30. Fols. 3r (twice). 4r (three times), 4v, 7v, 11r, 22r, 23r, 23v (twice) 25v, 32r, 37r; McNamara (ed.), *Glossa in Psalmos*, respectively pp. 105, 108, 110, 113, 128, 147, 199, 205, 207, 216, 245, 265.
31. Fols. 1v, 2v (five times), 3v, 7r, 8r (twice), 8v, 9r (five times), 9v (three times), 10r, 10v, 12v (three times), 13v, 17r, 18v (three or possibly four times), 19v, 24r, 25r, 29v, 30v, 40v.

sented) seems to have attributed to Hilary (that is, at Pss. 73.14 and 131.1, in second and allegorical exposition). In these two cases *h* seems to be intended as indicating *hilarius*. There are also a few cases in which *h* stands opposite unidentified texts. In these cases the letter may now be misplaced.

While the dots accompanying the *h* are scarcely without purpose, I have failed to identify their raison d'être. They may have something to do with the number of citations from a given author, although this does not appear to be the case.[32]

3.3. *Marginal Indication of Senses of Scripture*
Occasionally the form of exegesis given in the text is indicated in the left-hand margin. Thus: *hist* (*historia, historice* or *historialiter*), fols. 2v,[33] 18v (twice),[34] 29v,[35] 30r,[36] *Mor* (38v)[37] or *M* (= *Moraliter*), several occurrences,[38] chiefly on fols. 37v-41r, in the second exposition of the Gradual Psalms.

3.4. *Marginal Annotations and Glosses on the Text*
The following glosses or annotations on the text occur in the margins. In fol. 19r, left-hand margin, at Ps. 87.12,[39] we have the remark: *per hironiam haec dicuntur*. In fol. 20v,[40] left margin, we have a gloss on a single word of a text, both the gloss and the relevant word (*transeat* of Ps. 89.5) carrying the reference sign ⸪. (This verse is also heavily glossed interlinearly.)[41] In fol. 25r a gloss in the left margin: *haec*

---

32. A similar problem exists regarding the purpose of the Roman numerals i, ii to the left of the letter *h* in the margin of fol. 10v (heading of Ps. 70); see McNamara (ed.), *Glossa in Psalmos*, p. 145.

33. McNamara (ed.), *Glossa in Psalmos*, p. 100.

34. McNamara (ed.), *Glossa in Psalmos*, p. 183.

35. McNamara (ed.), *Glossa in Psalmos*, p. 234.

36. McNamara (ed.), *Glossa in Psalmos*, p. 235.

37. McNamara (ed.), *Glossa in Psalmos*, p. 270. The *or* of *Mor* is, however, a later addition.

38. Fols. 3v, 9r, 9v (three times), 10r (three times), 10v, 12v, 17r, 18v (four times), 22r, 29v, 37v (five times), 38r (three times), 39r (twice), 39v (twice), 40r (twice), 40v (three times), 41r, 41v (twice), 42r, 42v.

39. McNamara (ed.), *Glossa in Psalmos*, p. 186.

40. McNamara (ed.), *Glossa in Psalmos*, p. 192.

41. McNamara (ed.), *Glossa in Psalmos*, p. 192.

omnia iuxta alligoriam conueniunt,[42] indicates a preference for allegorical exegesis, possibly over against the text's mainly literal exposition
of the psalm in question (Ps. 103). In fol. 26r (on *misit* of Ps. 104.28)[43]
a marginal note, with reference sign ⸺ over both, notes that this is the
first plague; the remaining seven plagues are indicated by Roman
numerals in the left-hand margins of fol. 26rv, without any reference
sign in text or margin. The eight *beneficia* which follow are noted in the
margin, the first occurrence having the reference sign ⸺⸺ over the
marginal note and over *eduxit* of the text (Ps. 104.37).[44] The remaining
beneficia are indicated by Roman numerals without any reference signs.
Meta, with the sign ⸺ above it, occurs in the left margin of fol. 28r,
where the text (at Ps. 106.23)[45] without any sign has *per metaforam.*

The composite gloss, in Old Irish and Latin, *.i. anoirdes ab hierū*
occurs on the top right-hand margin of fol. 11v, and is probably intended to be taken as part of the text of the comment on Ps. 71.10 inad-
vertently omitted. A note (dot; full-stop sign) in the text (*duae Arabiae
sunt .i. anairdes . ab hiru*), although apparently wrongly placed, seems
to indicate this.[46]

A gloss in the right-hand margin of fol. 9r appears to be intended as
supplying an omission.[47]

3.5. *Probationes Pennae*
What appear to be pen trials appear in fol. 8v, thus: in the left-hand
margin *iv* (with a *v*, not a *u*), four times;[48] in lower margin *i* twice (one
of these probably a gathering number) and *pheb*; in left-hand margin
what appears to be *G.*

3.7. *Interlinear Glosses and Corrections of Text*
In fols. 1-20v and in fol. 40v occasional interlinear glosses and corrections of the text occur. Sometimes it is difficult to determine whether
the interlinear glosses are intended to supply passages that have been

---

42. McNamara (ed.), *Glossa in Psalmos*, p. 213; see also below 12.1.
43. McNamara (ed.), *Glossa in Psalmos*, p. 218.
44. McNamara (ed.), *Glossa in Psalmos*, p. 219.
45. McNamara (ed.), *Glossa in Psalmos*, p. 227.
46. See further McNamara (ed.), *Glossa in Psalmos*, pp. 21-22. and Apparatus I
to Ps. 71.10, p. 148.
47. See McNamara (ed.), *Glossa in Psalmos*, p. 137.
48. McNamara (ed.), *Glossa in Psalmos*, p. 135.

omitted or are additional glosses. The interlinear material can be classed
as follows:

(1)   *Insertion of omitted letter or letters.*[49] The omission is gener-
       ally indicated by a dot between the letters where the omission
       occurs, and also after or before (sometimes both and after) the
       letter or letters added interlinearly.

(2)   *Insertion of omitted word or words.* The omission is indicated
       in the text by a dot (.) or colon (:) inserted between two words,
       with the same sign repeated before and after the inserted
       words. Thus: fols. 12v (Ps. 73.11, colons),[50] 14r (Ps. 76.17,
       dots),[51] 16v (Ps. 80, heading; colons),[52] 20v (Ps. 89.5, several
       glosses; dots).[53]

(3)   *Explanatory glosses, possibly not intended as corrections.* In
       these instances we have neither colon or dot to indicate an
       omission. Some of the glosses in this class identify the person
       intended in the text, for example, fol. 7v: *.i. Dauid*, on *inmacu-*
       latum of Ps. 63.5.[54] Some are grammatical notes, for example,
       giving the case of a particular noun, for example, fol. 7r, *dati*
       <uus> on *parieti* of Ps. 61.4.[55] In fol. 15r the commentary on
       Ps. 77.43 interprets *in Aegipto signa* as the ten plagues.[56] The
       Roman numerals i-uiii placed interlinearly over words in
       verses 45 (*misit, ranam*),[57] 46 (*dedit, labores*), 49 (*missit*) and
       51 (*percussit*) number these plagues. (We have seen already[58]
       that the plagues are numbered in the margin for the parallel
       passage of Ps. 104.)

49. Occurrences in fols. 2r (Ps. 443), 2v (Ps. 453), 3v (Ps. 48.12), 4r (Ps. 49.7),
5v (Ps. 54.19; 55.8), 13r (Ps. 73.20), 13r (Ps. 74; heading); 13v (Ps. 763). 40v (Ps.
129, heading); McNamara (ed.), *Glossa in Psalmos*, respectively pp. 99, 102, 106,
109, 117, 156, 159. 279.
    50. McNamara (ed.), *Glossa in Psalmos*, p. 153.
    51. McNamara (ed.), *Glossa in Psalmos*, p. 161.
    52. McNamara (ed.), *Glossa in Psalmos*, p. 173.
    53. McNamara (ed.), *Glossa in Psalmos*, p. 192.
    54. McNamara (ed.), *Glossa in Psalmos*, p. 130.
    55. McNamara (ed.), *Glossa in Psalmos*, p. 127.
    56. McNamara (ed.), *Glossa in Psalmos*, p. 166.
    57. McNamara (ed.), *Glossa in Psalmos*, p. 166.
    58. See 3.3.d above.

(4)   *Other interlinear additions.* The interlinear additions in fols. 131 (Ps. 74.4, 9),[59] 14v (Ps. 77.25),[60] 17v (Ps. 8.34)[61] and 20v (Ps. 89.5)[62] are full glosses which may have been absent from the copyist's exemplar and added to the present manuscript from some other source. A gloss in fol. 3r (Ps. 47.3),[63] that is, *inpēr* (= *inperatiuus*, if the reading and expansion are correct), above *fundatur* and below *monte* of the biblical text, seems to take the verb *fundatur* as imperative. (The same interlinear gloss occurs again in fol. 31r, at Ps. 114.7.)

3.7. *Construe Marks*[64]

A characteristic of Hiberno-Latin manuscripts is various critical signs, consisting of points, commas, semicolons, dashes and similar placed over and under words, generally in pairs—construe marks apparently intended as a guide for the student through the intricacies of a Latin text, indicating which words went together, and such like. In Pal. lat. 68 there are five cases of markings or critical signs on words, which we may very probably regard as construe marks. These are as follows:

(1)   fol. 2r (heading of Ps. 44):[65] '*In finem salmus Dauid' .i. de se ipso et Salomone. 'Pro his qui commotabuntur' .i. de exilio in requiem. 'Ad intellectum filis Chore canticum pro dilecto'.* The corresponding text of Cod. Amb. C 301 inf. (fol. 64b, 31-32) has two of these three markings (and another besides):[66] '*In finem pro his qui commotabuntur / filiis Chore canticum ad intellectum'.* A similar text in Cod. Amb. C 301 inf. (fol. 101b,

59. McNamara (ed.), *Glossa in Psalmos*, pp. 156-57.
60. McNamara (ed.), *Glossa in Psalmos*, p. 164.
61. McNamara (ed.), *Glossa in Psalmos*, p. 178.
62. McNamara (ed.), *Glossa in Psalmos*, p. 192.
63. McNamara (ed.), *Glossa in Psalmos*, p. 104; p. 241 for Ps. 114.7.
64. On these marks in Hiberno-Latin manuscripts see M. Draak, 'Construe Marks in Hiberno-Latin Manuscripts', in *Mededelingen der honinkliike Nederlandse Akademie van Wetenschappen, ald. Letterhunde* (Nieuwe reeks, Deel 20, no. 10; Amsterdam, 1957), pp. 261-82; R.I. Best, 'Introduction', in *The Commentary on the Psalms with Glosses in Old-Irish preserved in the Ambrosian Library (MS. C 301 inf.)* (Collotype Facsimile; Dublin: Royal Irish Academy, 1936), p. 29.
65. McNamara (ed.), *Glossa in Psalmos*, pp. 98-99.
66. The markings of this and the following text of Cod. Amb. C 301 inf. are reproduced in Best's collotype edition.

15-16), in the heading to Ps. 79 has similar markings: *'In finem̄ psalmus pro his qui commota/buntur testim̄onium assab. pro assirio'*.

(2) What appears to be another occurrence of construe marks is found in fol. 2v (Ps. 93.3-4):[67] *'Uṣquequo peccatores' .i. pro mag/nitudine doloris geminatur vox. 'Ëffabuntur et loquentur iniquitatem'* ... The idea behind these signs may be to indicate that *usquequo* and *effabuntur* go together.

(3) The signs found in the following text in fol. 22v (Ps. 96.12)[68] may also have been intended to serve a similar purpose. *'Laetam̄ini iusti in Domino' .i. in u̇assis salmi.*

(4) The same reason may also stand behind the signs in fol. 31r (Ps. 113.10):[69] *'super misericordia tua et ümeritate' .i. per quam beneficus es nobis et per qüam uindicas nos de inimicis tuis.*

(5) The same may be true of this other occurrence of signs in fol. 45v (Ps. 148.7):[70] *'Lauḍate Dominum de terra' .i. hucusque de caelo canit el de mirabilibus eius... 'Drächones et omnes'* ...

3.8. *Transposition Signs*

What must be regarded as transposition signs are found in fol. 7v (Ps. 63, heading: *De .ipso se)[71]* and fol. 14r (Ps. 77, in *heret: 'populum tuum sicut oues').[72]*

3.9. *Omission Signs over* Lemmata

In the *lemmata* capricious abbreviations frequently occur, indicated by a stroke over the letters. In the *lemmata* strokes also occur where no word abbreviation is present. In these cases the strokes indicate the omission of part of the biblical text and are the equivalent of *usque* or (when occurring at the end of a *lemma*) *et reliqua* of other mediaeval commentaries.

67. McNamara (ed.), *Glossa in Psalmos*, p. 197.
68. McNamara (ed.), *Glossa in Psalmos*, p. 202.
69. McNamara (ed.), *Glossa in Psalmos*, p. 239.
70. McNamara (ed.), *Glossa in Psalmos*, pp. 307-308.
71. McNamara (ed.), *Glossa in Psalmos*, p. 130.
72. McNamara (ed.), *Glossa in Psalmos*, p. 161.

4. *Later Additions to the Text*

In the top margin of fol. 1r, above the beginning of the present text, stand the words *Supras ps* (with uncertain letter above *ps) dauid*, possibly a mistaken writing for *Supra Psalmos Dauid*. In the bottom margin of this page, to the left, *codex sancti* is clearly legible, and below this slightly to the right, the number 23 in Arabic numerals. This number is cancelled by two strokes through it. To the right of this we have the stamp of *Bibliotheca Apostolica Vaticana*, with 68 Palat to its right. The Vatican Palatine collection came from the Rhenish Palatinate in 1623. Our codex was probably in the monastery of St Nazarius at Lorsch, the most prominent monastery in the area, from which most of the manuscripts in the Palatine collection came. Possibly *Nazarii* once stood after *Codex sancti* of fol. 1r. As is evident, all these entries in fol. i were made in an already acephalous codex.

Lowe[73] has noted that the codex is in gatherings normally of tens, signed by a Roman numeral in the centre of the lower margin of the last page; once on the first page. These Roman numerals are as follows: i (fol. 8v; written twice, once apparently over earlier number); ii (18v); iii (28v), iiii (38v), v (written as *v*, not *u*; 39r). Since these mark the gatherings of the present acephalous text which begins with Ps. 39.11d, it is clear that they do not belong to the original eighth- (or ninth-) century text although, as Lowe observes, they are apparently over older marks.

What are described by Lindsay[74] as 'scribblings' in fol. 46v (the very last page) are of different kinds. On the top right we have in majuscule *Cunibraht exaudiat te Dñs̄*. On the top left we have *(Deus?) eorum palmas semper*; underneath this downwards the numbers i-xiii (with u, ui, uii, uiii, uiiii) in Roman numerals. There are some resolutions of suspensions and abbreviations, presumably those found in the codex itself: *ū uero; hs̄ huius; cs cuius* (twice), *d̄r dicitur; d̄t dicit; (em* added to *dicit); q̄re quare*. There are also suspensions and abbreviations without solutions. The biblical names Eman, Ethan, and Idithun occur; also *M* and *Modorum* with the peculiar Greek *M* of *Moraliter* as found in the margins and text of the codex. There are some further scribblings

73. Lowe, *CLA*, I, no. 78.
74. Lindsay, *Early Irish Minuscule Script*, p. 68.

besides, and some faded writing apparently in the same hand that wrote *Cunibraht.*

Some of the additional writing in fol. 8v has already been noted.[75] To this may now be added a large *D* in the upper left-hand margin. In line 1 of this folio *facite* is rewritten over this word in the text in a hand different from that of the text. It is possibly this same hand that has added *Psalmus D-D* in a space left vacant at the end of Psalm 66. It may be intended to go with the heading of the following psalm. It is possibly the same hand that has added *r i* interlinearly over *faciamus* in the last line of the glosses on Psalm 66, without any apparent reason.

Psalmus D-D is also added at the end of Psalm 54 (fol. 5v) in vacant space, but undoubtedly intended to go with the heading of Psalm 55. It is also added at the end of the heading of Psalm 57 (fol. 6r). In both cases it is probably by the hand that added it in fol. 8v. The numbers i, ii are written to the left of *h..* (= *hirunimus*?) in the left margin of fol. 11v (to the heading of Ps. 70), with what significance if any I cannot say, unless they are intended to indicate the number of citations from *h* in the line.

5. *Vernacular Glosses*

There are 25 Old Irish Glosses in the codex and 5 Old English ones. While the Old Irish glosses are distributed throughout the manuscript right from the first folio (1r) to the last (46r), three of the Old English are concentrated in the same page and in three verses of the same psalm (Ps. 77.45, 46, 47). Eleven of the 25 Old Irish and 3 of the 5 Old English are the sole glosses on the Latin *lemma.* Two at least of the Old Irish glosses seem to be intentionally composite, with the Latin and the Irish text not merely juxtaposed and independent one of the other. In nine of the Old Irish and in one of the Old English (fol. 12v, on Ps. 73.14) there is a combination of Latin and the vernacular but of such a nature that either part could stand alone. Apart from one marginal (fol. 11v, on Ps. 71.10) and one interlinear gloss (fol. 20v, on Ps. 89.6), all the glosses in Old Irish now form part of the text of the commentary, as do all the Old English glosses. With the exception of two Old Irish glosses (fol. 15r, on Ps. 77.44 and 20v on Ps. 89.6—an interlinear gloss) the vernacular glosses are set off from the Latin text by means of apices, just as the

---

75. See above, p. 178.

Old Irish glosses are in the Book of Armagh and in the Schaffhausen manuscript of Adomnan's *Vita Columbae*, this latter work written at Iona.

Scholarly opinion is still divided as to whether the vernacular glosses were from the beginning part of the text or whether they have been introduced into it from the margins. The evidence seems to favour the former view, at least with regard to the genuinely composite glosses and those which are the sole comment on the Latin *lemmata*.

5.1. *The Old Irish Glosses*

The 25 Old Irish glosses, with an English translation, are as follows:[76]

1. (fol. 1r). '*Euge, euge*' (Ps. 39.16) *.i.* ait ait *.i. aduerbium optantis.* The Irish word *ait (aitt)* as an adjective means 'pleasant, agreeable'. It is here used as an interjection. See also gloss no. 10 below.

2. (fol. 1v). '*erue me*' (Ps. 42.1) ba em carat. '*Incedo...*' (42.2). 'It were indeed (the part) of a friend.'

3. (fol. 2r). *De quo dicit* '*eructuauit cor meum uerbum bonum*', (Ps. 44.2), *.i.* cridescel. '*Vox Dauid de Salomone.*' *Cridescel* literally means 'heart-tidings'.

4. (fol. 2r). '*Dico ego opera mea regi*' (Ps. 44.2) *.i.* tuasilbiu. '*Lingua mea calamus.*'

tuasilbiu means 'I present, put forward, set forth'.[77]

5. (fol. 4r). '*Numquid manducabo carnes*' (Ps. 49.13) *.i.* isara fia dom. "*Imola Deo...*" (Ps. 49.14).'

The Irish gloss means: 'I have it in my power'.[78]

6. (fol. 5r). '*Tu uero homo*' (Ps. 54.14) *.i. conuertit sermonem ad Achitophiel qui consiliarius fuit Dauid, quasi dixisset* badito. (baditos or baditor?)...friom (or: frium?)[79]

---

76. Edition of the glosses with translation of the 12 more difficult ones in *Thes. Pal.*, I, p. 3.

77. Cf. *DIL* s.v. *do-aissilbe* (**to-ad-selb-*). The regular form is with initial *du-*. The initial *t-* is the archaic form. According to Thurneysen, *A Grammar of Old Irish*, §178.2, p. 111, the change to *d-* took place about the end of the seventh century. A text from about 750 CE, however (cf. J. Pokorny, 'Über das Alter der Würzburger Glossen', *ZCP* 10 [1915], p. 36) has several forms of *to-* instead of *do-*. The form *to-* of itself, then, does not prove that this gloss of Pal. lat. 68 is early (say pre-700).

78. Cf. *DIL* s.v. *arafial-fie* (col. 376, 31). The older spelling is *arafie*. See *DIL* s.v. *arafia/-fie* , and *Thes. Pal.*, I, pp. 661, 570, 516 for translation given.

79. Güterbock, 'Aus irischen Handschriften', p. 102, would read: '*baditos* (wohl

Part of the text is illegible (c. 23 mm of the entire Old Irish gloss's 45 mm), because it has been erased and the meaning is consequently uncertain. The gloss itself, however, is clearly composite, the Irish being introduced by *quasi dixisset.*

7. (fol. 7v). '*scrutinio*' (Ps. 63.7) *.i.* o scrutunt. '*Accedit homo.*'

The Irish gloss, the only one the *lemma*, says that the Latin word is derived from (*o*) a term meaning *scruta(i)n*, that is, 'the act of examining, pondering, studying, meditation, thought'.

8.   (fol. 8r). '*germinans*' (Ps. 64.11) *.i.* inti siligfes. '*Benedices coronam anni*' (Ps. 64.12).

The Irish gloss means: 'he who will sow'.

9. (fol. 10r). '*raucae*' (Ps. 68.4) *.i.* truisc. '*Defecerunt oculi mei.*'

truisc is apparently the name of some disease.[80]

10. (fol. 10v). '*euge, euge*' (Ps. 69.4) *.i.* he, he sirson sirson. '*Euge ad indicium laetitiae pertinet.*'

Both *he (e)* and *sirson* are exclamations denoting surprise or amazement. *Sirsan sirsa(n)* glosses *euge, euge* of Ps. 34.21 in Cod. Amb. C 301 inf. (55a 15).

11. (fol. 11v). '*Reges Tarsis*' (Ps. 71.10) *.i. Tarsis nomen maris in Mari Terreno, et a nomine regionis nominatur Tarsum. Nomine Tarsis itaque litorias ciuitates uocat.* '*Reges Arabum*' *.i. duae Arabiae sunt. .i.* anairdes *ab Hirusalem; .i.* anoirdes *ab Hierusulem.* '*Et Saba dona adducent*' *.i.* aneordes, *.i. tus et aurum.*

Both *anairdes* and *anoirdes* mean 'from the south-east', the latter being a later form. The third gloss is *aneordes (= aniardes,* 'from the south-west'); the third letter (*e*) is certain but written over an erasure.[81]

---

eher *-tor) .a...it friom*'. On the understanding of the Psalm as speaking of Ahitophel, see below, n. 263.

80. Cf. *DIL*, s.v. *trosc.* The same Irish word (under the form *druisc*) glosses the same word of Ps. 68.4 in the Southampton Psalter. P.P. Ó Néill ('Some Remarks on the Edition of the Southampton Psalter Irish Glosses in *Thesaurus Palaeohibernicus*, with Further Addenda and Corrigenda', *Ériu* 44 [1993], pp. 99-103 [102]) translates in both cases as 'hoarse, parched'. The Southampton gloss, he believes, depends on Pal. lat. 68, or on a common source, dating back to the eight century at the latest.

81. Güterbock, 'Aus irischen Handschriften', p. 102, reads the manuscript as *aneordes*, where Stokes could only read *an..rdes.* (cf. *Thes. Pal.*, I, p. 3 n. c). In 'Addenda et Corrigenda' (*Thes. Pal.*, I, p. 715), Strachan admits that *aneordes* may be right, *eo* being a peculiar spelling of diphthongized *ē*; *aneordes* is the reading accepted in *DIL*. s.v. *aniar(dess)*, col. 347.19. In the introduction (*Thes. Pal.*, I,

The gloss *'anoirdes ab Hierusalem'* (in the MS as *.i. anoirdes ab hierū*) is actually on the top right-hand corner of the page, and may be intended as inserted above, or possibly for insertion after *'nominatur Tarsum'*.[82]

12. (fol. 12v). *'ascia'* (Ps. 73.6) .i. taal. *'Deiecerunt eam...'* taal means 'adze'. The same Latin word in this verse is also glossed by *tal* in the Milan commentary (Ml92d8, 92d10) and Southampton Psalter.[83]

13. (fol. 15r). *'imbres'* (Ps. 77.44) .i. dructae. *'Misit'* (Ps. 77.45). No apices are visible over *dructae,* the plural of *druct,* 'dew'.

14. (fol. 16v). *'propagines'* (Ps. 79.12) .i. clanda. *'Ut quid dis-truxisti...?'* (Ps. 79.13). *clanda* means 'offshoots'.

15. (fol. 17v). *'sicut stipullam'* (Ps. 82.14) .i. *instabiles,* etrom, lasomuin. *'Ante laciem uenti...'* The Irish words mean 'light, flaming/blazing'.

16. (fol. 20v). interlinear gloss over *'mane sicut herba'* (Ps. 89.6) .i. fer .i. *iacintinum'*.

p. xiv) the editors note that the Irish of the glosses of Pal. lat. 68 may be older than that of the chief glossator in the Würzburg Codex (c. 750 CE) if *aneordes* is the right reading.

82. The disturbed state of the gloss makes both reading and interpretation difficult; see Apparatus I to the edition of Ps. 71.10, McNamara (ed.), *Glossa in Psalmos,* p. 148. Güterbock ('Aus irischen Handschriften', p. 102) regards *aneordes,* the gloss on *Saba,* as a mistaken repetition of *anairdes,* the gloss on *Arabiae.* The uncertainty of where to insert the marginal gloss *anoirdes ab Hierusalem* also complicates matters. The interpretation found in the glosses is probably connected with the compiler's (or glossator's) system of geography. The early Greek and Roman writers generally had a twofold division of Arabia: Arabia Deserta (*hê erêmos*), between Syria and the Euphrates (including Petra), and Arabia Felix (*hê eudaimôn*) or the whole of the Arabian Peninsula. Following on Ptolemy a threefold division became current: Arabia Deserta, Arabia Felix and Arabia Petraea. The Irish scholar Dicuil (fl. c. 814–25), in *Liber de mensura orbis terrae,* 11. 5, depending on a defective source, also knows of a threefold division: 'Arabia Eudemon Phlecmea...Trogoditen Arabiam...Vab (= Nabataea) Arabia' (*Dicuili Liber de mensura orbis terrae* (J.J. Tierney [ed.], with contributions by L. Bieler; SLH, 6; Dublin Institute for Advanced Studies, 1967), p. 52.

83. See *Thes. Pal.,* I, pp. 134 and 135 respectively. The lengthening shown through the doubling of the vowel in *taal* (found also in *noon* on Ps. 118.164; below Irish gloss no. 23) is characteristic of archaic Irish texts; see Thurneysen, *A Grammar of Old Irish,* pp. 20-21. It is also frequent, however, in the Würzburg glosses and is also found in the Irish glosses of the Book of Armagh, written in part before 807 CE and completed before 846.

There are no apices visible over the Irish word *fer*, 'grass'.

17. (fol. 23v). '*sicut gremium*' (Ps. 101.4) .i. brosne crin. '*Percussus sum ut foenum*' (Ps. 101.5).

brosne crin means 'a withered bundle of firewood'.

18. (fol. 27v) '*per desertum in tabernaculis*' (106.4) .i. botha. '*Essurientes et sitientes*' (Ps. 106.5).

botha means 'tents'.

19. (fol. 28r). '*et mirabilia eius in prolundo*' (Ps. 106.24) .i. *tempestas et tranquilitas;* .i. tuile et aithbe. '*Dixit*' (Ps. 106.26).

tuile et aithbe means 'flood et ebb'.

20. (fol. 28v). '*libes (=lebes) spei mei*' (Ps. 107.10) .i. *libes* .i. fiund caire; '*id est coquet mihi carnes*'.

fiund caire means 'fair (*fiund*) cauldron'. The same Irish word occurs twice in Cod. Amb. C 301 inf. in glosses on this same verse, although not directly on *libes* (*afindchoriu*, Ml126c16 and *findchoire*, Ml126c17).[84]

21. (fol. 29r). '*nutantes*' (Ps. 108.10) .i. fulmaini. '*Et mendicent*'.

fulmaini, the pl. adjective of *fulmain,* means 'fluttering, moving rapidly'.

22. (fol. 30v). '*retrorsum*' (Ps. 113.3) .i. frituile. '*Montes exultauerunt*' (Ps. 113.4).

frituile means 'against the flood'.

23. (fol. 37r). '*septies in die laudem dixi tibi*' (Ps. 118.164) .i. antert, tert, sest, noon, fescer, midnoct, maten; *quod conuenit quia septies in die cadit iustus*'.

The Irish gloss contains the names of the seven canonical hours: prime, terce, sext, none, vespers, midnight, matins.[85]

24. (fol. 43v). '*Dirigatur oratio mea*' (Ps. 140.2) .i. *sic mea oratio in conspectu tuo placida fiat quemadmodum incensum suauissimi odoris*

---

84. Cf. *DIL* s.v. *findchoire*, col. 138.

85. For other occurrences of the canonical hours in Irish literature, see the entries in *DIL* under *anteirt, teirt, sest, nóin, fescor, matan, maiten*, but especially under *íarmérge*. The seven canonical hours are also mentioned by Alcuin in his gloss on the verse: '*Matutinum, Tertia, Sexta, Nona, Lucernaria, Completorium, Nocturnum*'. For the divine office in the Irish Church, see L. Gougaud, *Christianity in Celtic Lands* (London: Sheed and Ward, 1932; repr. Dublin: Four Courts Press, 1993), pp. 329-34 (p. 332 for text of Pal. lat. 68), and M. Curran, M.S.C., *The Antiphonary of Bangor* (Dublin: Irish Academic Press, 1984), especially Chapter 19, 'Cathedral and Monastic Office in Ireland'; pp. 248-49 n. 33 for Pal. lat. 68 text.

fit quod uespere per manus sacerdotis offerri solet; .i. luib *cuius fumus rectus est ad caelum.*'

luib means 'herb, plant'.[86]

25. (fol. 46r). '*Et quis adnuntiauit domino meo*' (Ps. 151.3) .i. *ac si diceret* badethbir do cinifesed *personam meam minimam.*'

The Irish can be translated: 'it was natural for him that he should not discover (*personam meam minimam*)'.[87]

We have seen that in 1901 W. Stokes and J. Strachan expressed the opinion that the Irish of these glosses may be as old as that of the chief glossator of the Würzburg Codex Paulinus (that is, c. 750 CE), and possibly older if Güterbock was right in reading *aneordes* (in gloss no. 11 above), with *eo* as a peculiar orthography for diphthongized *e*.

The Irish glosses of Pal. lat. 68 have not received much attention in recent years, but the scholars who have examined them from the point of view of assigning a date to them are of the opinion that they do not have sufficient specific features to enable us to determine this.[88]

5.2. The Old English Glosses

The following are the five Old English glosses in Pal. lat. 68:[89]

1. (fol. 12v). '*Dedisti eum escam*' (Ps. 73.14, alternative explanation). i. *eo quod limore eius pisces ad terram Aethiopiae ueniunt. Timet enim et manducat unumquodque animal in mari alterum, et dicunt quod uii minoribus saturantur maiores, ut* VII *fiscas selaes fyllu, sifu selas hronaes fyllu, sifu hronas hualaes fyllu. Spiritaliter: capud draconis...*

The Old English (in this case Northumbrian) gloss is rendered: 'seven fishes are a seal's food, seven seals are a (sperm?) whale's food, seven (sperm?) whales are a whale's food'.[90]

---

86. *luib* glosses the Latin *tus* in Sg 46a13; see *Thes. Pal.*, II, p. 100.

87. *Thes. Pal.*, I, p. 3 renders as: 'reason had he not to know'. For the rendering of *badethbir* as 'it was natural', see *DIL* s.v. *deithbir*, col. 14.31-62; for rendering of *cinifesed* (from *ro-finnadar*) as 'that he should not discover' see *DIL* s.v. *ro-finnadar*, cols. 86-88 (Pal. lat. 68 text noted in col. 87.18). While both meanings, 'to discover' and 'to know' are possible (*DIL* s.v. *ro-finnadar* col. 87.18), the former seems to suit the context better.

88. E.g. Professor B. Ó Cuív in a private communication on the point: 'I can see nothing in the glosses in *Thes. Pal.* I, p. 3 [with glosses of Pal. lat. 68] which would enable us to determine their date'.

89. For the text of the Old English glosses see Napier, *Old-English Glosses Chiefly Unpublished*; see above, nn. 3, 4, 5.

90. *Hron* and *hwael* are generally used indifferently for 'whale'. Here, however,

2. (fol. 15r). '*et ranam*' (Ps. 77.45) .i. frosc. '*Et dedit erugini*'
The Old English gloss is rendered as 'frog'.

3. (fol. 15r). '*Et dedit erugini*' (Ps. 77.46). *id est* brondegur̄. '*Et labores eorum locustae. El occidit in grandine.*'

Brondegur̄ is an obscure word for which no accepted explanation has been found.[91] It may contain an erroneous combination of the Old English *brond (brand)*, 'mildew' and a corruption of *erug*, the abbreviation of the Latin *erugini*;[92] or of *brond*, 'blight causing leaves and so on to look as though burnt', and *aerugo*;[93] or of *brond*, 'blight' and the Old English *egor/eagor* (dative pl. *egurum*), 'water/sea', 'flood, cataclysm'; *brond* being the proper gloss on *erugini,* and *egur* a misplaced one on *grandine.*[94]

4. (fol. 15r). '*et murus (=moros) eorum*' (Ps. 77.47) .i. pro omni feraci arbore possuit; .i. aliquando fructus eius albus, aliquando rulus, aliquando niger,* .i. herutbeg. '*Et tradidit grandini...*'

In the words of A.S. Napier,[95] *herutbeg* is synonymous with *heorotberge,* in the NE dialect 'hartberry'.

5. (fol. 20v). '*usquequo*' (Ps. 89.13) .i. nu du hiru scaealt. '*Repleti sumus mane*' (Ps. 89.14).[96]

The Old English (and Northumbrian) gloss is rendered: 'now indeed thus shalt'.

We have already seen[97] that the scholars who examined the Old English glosses at the end of the last century and at the beginning of this were in agreement that they could not be later than the early eighth century; that some of them were specifically Northumbrian, and that the spelling of the proper names Edilberict and Berictfrid in the colophon

---

hron evidently designates a smaller species; possibly the sperm whale; see Napier, 'Old Northumbrian Glosses', p. 342.

91. On this gloss see the earlier studies of Napier, 'Old Northumbrian Glosses', p. 342; Napier, 'The Old Northumbrian', p. 449; O'Neill, 'Old English *brondegur*', *English Studies* 62 (1981), pp. 2-4.

92. Cf. Cook, 'The Old Northumbrian', p. 89.

93. Cf. T.N. Toller, *An Anglo-Saxon Dictionary Supplement* (Oxford, 1908–1921), p. 104.

94. Cf. O'Neill, 'Old English *brondegur*', pp. 2-4.

95. Cf. Napier, *Old-English Glosses*, no. 54; Napier, 'The Old Northumbrian', p. 119; likewise, H. Bradley, 'The Old Northumbrian Glosses in MS. Palatine 68', *The Academy* 36 (1889), p. 154.

96. Cf. Napier, *Old-English Glosses*, no. 54.

97. See above, p. 166.

bore out this conclusion. The inference to be drawn from this is that, if the present manuscript is from the later eighth or from the ninth century, the Old English glosses must have been copied from an earlier original.

6. *Layout of the Commentary*

The exposition of each psalm is rather uniformly arranged. Each begins with the *incipit* or opening words of the psalm. To the left of this, in the margin, there is generally a cross. (Pss. 48, 120, 121, 123, 150 and 151 are exceptions.) The psalms are not numbered. After the *incipit* the particular psalm is linked to some words of a verse of the preceding one by the word *heret.*[98] After the *heret* passages we have the biblical psalm heading. Next we generally have a historical heading taken from, or related to, the Epitome of Julian.[99] Sometimes, together with this, or instead of it, there is a psalm heading relating the psalm to David and to his times. Next comes the mystical series of psalm headings, almost always from Series I, that is, the St Columba Series. Exceptions to this general rule is the introduction to the 15 gradual psalms prefaced to the *incipit* of Psalm 119 and the fact that in Psalm 44 the psalm heading comes before the *incipit*.

The exposition follows on this introductory material. There is no verse division. The *lemma*, that is, the biblical text to be commented on, is first given (often in abbreviated form) and then expounded in a gloss which may consist of anything from a single word to a long passage. The explanatory gloss is in Latin, apart from the vernacular glosses already noted. There is only one case of a *lemma* without any gloss (Ps. 77.46).[100] The glosses, particularly the brief ones, must be taken in conjunction with the *lemmata* commented on, the form of verbs and cases of nouns and so on being occasionally determined by the operative word in the *lemma*. The *lemmata*, generally brief, may be intended

---

98. Abbreviated as *hēt* in general; as *hēēt* in Ps. 76 (McNamara [ed.], *Glossa in Psalmos*, p. 75). Written in full as *heret* (but with stroke over ēr) in Ps. 91 (McNamara [ed.], *Glossa in Psalmos*, p. 195). Bernhard Bischoff regards the connection of two biblical passages through the simple *haeret* as typically Irish; see 'Wendepunkte'.

99. On this work see below, 11.3.a.

100. McNamara (ed.), *Glossa in Psalmos*, p. 166.

to recall the larger context, as occasionally the expository gloss is not on the *lemma* but on adjacent biblical words.

In Psalm 118 (the Beati, held in especial regard in ancient Ireland) each of the 22 subsections is treated in its layout as if it were an independent psalm. Each has its own *incipit, heret*, headings, and so on.[101] The gradual psalms (Pss. 119–33) have a special introduction and receive a twofold exposition, the second introduced as *Moraliter*.[102] In Psalms 119 and 120 this is given in the exposition of the relevant verses, in Psalms 121 and 131 in two blocks within the psalms; in the other psalms, however, it is given at the end of each psalm, being introduced in the text as *aliter* and noted in the margins as *Moraliter*.

7. *The Colophon*

At the end of the entire exposition we have a colophon which is given as part of the text, not set off from it. It reads as follows:[103]

> *per .xl. dies prouocabat nos ad bellum. Finit liber psalmorum in Christo Ihesu Domino/ nostro. Lege in pace. Sicut portus oportunus nauigantibus ita uorsus/ nouissimus scribentibus. Edilberict filius Berictfridi scripsit hanc glosam./ Quicumque hoc legat oret pro scriptore; Et ipse similiter omnibus populis/ et tribubus et linguis et uniuerso generi humano aeternam salutem optat/ in Christo. Amen. Amen. Amen.*

This colophon is very similar to that of the Cambridge, Trinity College manuscript B. 10. 5 (+ BL Cotton Vitellius C. VIII),[104] written about

101. See further below, 6.
102. See further below, 12.8.
103. McNamara (ed.), *Glossa in Psalmos*, p. 311.
104. Manuscript described by Bishop, 'Notes', pp. 70-76. The colophon occurs at the end of Hebrews, and again runs on as part of the text: '*cum omnibus uobis*': (Heb. 13.25). *Finit amen Deo Gratias: – Sicut portus oportunus nauigantibus ita scriptoribus nouuisimus uersus.* A similar colophon is found in the Burchard Gospels (MS. Würzburg, Universitätsbibliothek, M.p.th. f. 68), saec. VII-VIII (Italy and Wearmouth-Jarrow) fol. 170v/a; see P. McGurk, *Latin Gospels from A.D. 400 to A.D. 800* (Paris-Brussels, Anvers-Amsterdam, 1961), no. *80, pp. 1-76 (75-76). The portion with the colophon is Italian. The colophon reads: '*Sicut navigantibus proximus est portus, sic et scriptori novissimus versus*'. Other similar colophons, published in the volume of anonymous colophons, in Bénédictins du Bouveret (eds.), *Colophons de manuscrits occidentaux des origines au XVIe siècle* (Spicilegii Friburgensis Subsidia, 7; Fribourg Universitätsverlag, 1982), pp. 505-506 are: '*Sicut portus oportunus navigantibus, ita versus novissimus scribentibus. Amen.*

the same time and most probably in an Anglo-Irish centre in Northumbria. It belongs, however, to a fairly common form of colophon not specifically connected either with Ireland or Northumbria and is consequently not decisive with regard to the place of origin of the manuscript.

As noted already, this colophon in our present text was most probably copied with the text from an earlier original, belonging apparently to the early eighth century. The forms of the proper names indicate this. The colophon itself may be a full century older than the present manuscript.

Edilberict was a Northumbrian scribe. This does not prove, however, that he wrote the work in Northumbria. He could have been a Northumbrian scholar resident in an Irish monastery. By *glosa* he means the commentary or gloss found in our present manuscript. The word *scripsit* seems to imply that he was a scribe rather than the original author or compiler of the gloss.

8. *Some Characteristic Features of the Work*

The gloss I am studying consists of a collection of excerpts from different writings. For this reason it reveals little or nothing of the personality of the compiler. The nature of the excerpts chosen, of course, may show us the form of exegesis preferred by him or the tradition which he represents. From this point of view we can say that the compiler of Pal. lat. 68 was chiefly interested in the historical interpretation of the Psalms. It is good, however, to attempt to pass beyond the excerpts themselves to the personality of the compiler. Traces of his personal position may possibly be visible in the manner in which he disassociates himself

---

Finit. Pax legentibus (MS. Milano Amb. I.99 sup. saec. 8-9, fol. 128, Bobbio); '*Sicut navigantibus dulcis est portus, sit scriptori novissimus versus*' (Vatican Regin. lat. 316, saec. 7-8, fol. 245); '*Sicut navigantibus optimus portus, ita scriptori novissimus versus*' (Oxford, Bodl., Laud. misc. 48, saec. 9); '*Sicut naviganti dulcis est portus, ita scriptori novissimus versus*' (Paris: Bibl. Nat. lat. 6842 A, saec. 12-13, fol. 64v). (Information kindly supplied by François Huot, O.S.B., Monastère St-Benoit de P.V., Le Bouveret, Suisse). See further W. Wattenbach, *Das Schriftwesen im Mittelatter* (Graz, 4th edn, 1958), pp. 278-83, with the Greek equivalent of the colophon. M. Maurice Haenni has kindly brought to my attention the presence of a similar colophon in the following numbers of Bénédictins du Bouveret (eds.), *Colophons*: 262; 2,541; 3,699; 3,920; 4,784; 4,915; 5,527; 7,098; 8,376; 12,387; 12,875 (?); 13,323; 13,940.

from the historical exegesis of Psalms 44 and 109,[105] which interpretation he describes as *inertialis historia*, or *historialis inhertia*, a clumsy or foolish historical interpretation. His preference for Augustine's allegorical exegesis may have occasioned the marginal gloss on Ps. 103.15 (if it is from the compiler): *haec omnia iuxta alligoriam conueniunt.*[106]

Certain phrases occurring with greater or lesser frequency throughout the gloss are apparently to be attributed to the compiler rather than to his sources. The most frequently used of these is *uassa salmorum, in uassis salmi,*[107] (of musical instruments used in psalmody). The phrase is sometimes found alone, but is more often accompanied by such phrases as *in canticis* (as in Pss. 56.8; 67.4; 99.4) or *in ore.*[108] All three are found in the gloss on Ps. 99.2: *in uassis salmi, in ore, in canticis.*

Another set of terms which occurs frequently is *in fili(i)s, in nepotibus.*[109] What appears to be a variant of this—*in genelogi(i)s*—also occurs (for example, 47.15; 51.7; 105.23). The terms *terra repromissionis*[110] and *uindicta*[111] are also rather frequently encountered. As in other Irish commentaries, we have reference to *doctores*[112] and comparisons through the term *more.*[113]

Occasional attention is paid to points of grammar, for example, the form of a verb: *inperatiuus* (44.2); the nature of a sentence: *interrogatiue,*[114] *yperbolice* (104.8; 106.26); *per tropum* (83.4); the nature of a

105. See below, 12.3; texts in McNamara (ed.), *Glossa in Psalmos*, pp. 99, 235.

106. McNamara (ed.), *Glossa in Psalmos*, p. 213.

107. The phrases gloss a variety of words in the biblical text and occur in the following places: Pss. 39.17; 46.7; 56.8; 65.2, 4; 67.4; 78.13; 80.3; 85.12; 94.1, 6; 96.12; 97.4; 99.2, 4; 100.1; 149.2.

108. E.g. at Pss. 56.10; 85.12; 91.2; 107.4.

109. The occurrences are: Pss. 43.9; 44.18; 47.14; 48.12; 51.10; 60.7; 66.7; 71.5; 76.9; 79.10; 83.45; 84.6; 88.5; 101.19, 20; 144.2, 4, 11; 145.10; cf. 89.1.

110. Occurrences at: Pss. 49.12; 51.7; 58.12; 64, 5, 8, 10, 11; 66.3, 5; 71.8, 17; 73.2; 75.9, 10; 77.53; 80.17; 83.6; 85.11; 88.12; 92.1; 93.2; 95.12; 96.1; 97.9; 101.15; 104.23; 105.47; 106.7, 37; 113.2; 114.9; 118.122; 119.5; 124.1.

111. Occurrences at: Pss. 57.8, 10; 58.11, 12; 63.7; 73.3, 9, 18; 74.9; 77.21, 35, 38, 50, 62; 79.17; 82.16, 18; 83.7; 86.4; 88.8; 93.1; 93.23; 96.4; 98.38; 117.10; 118.69, 78, 84, 138.

112. E.g. at Pss. 118.161, heading; 121.1; 124.2; 131.6, 12.

113. The term occurs rather frequently in Pal. lat. 68. For use of this term in Hiberno-Latin texts see Bischoff, 'Wendepunkte', p. 207.

114. Occurrences at Pss. 52.5; 59.12; 72.13; 73.1, 10; 76.8, 9; 78.5; 88.36, 47. In Pss. 73.10, 76.9 and 88.47 it glosses *in finem* of the biblical text. In Ps. 73.10 it is written in full, but is abbreviated as *intēr* in the other two cases.

word: *monoptoton* (77.70); *aduerbium* (39.36); the subject and object of a verb are given (cf. 109.1-3) or the construction of a passage explained for example, 61.12; 94.10); *ita disponitur (textus)* (86.1).

9. *Analysis of the Biblical Text*[115]

Analysis of the Psalter text of Pal. lat. 68 in order to ascertain whether it is basically *Gallicanum* or *Romanum* (Old Latin) is rendered difficult by a variety of factors. One is the brevity of the *lemmata*, which may be identical in both the genuine *Gallicanum* and *Romanum* traditions. Another is the fact that there has been a mutual contamination between the *Gallicanum* and *Romanum* traditions, some manuscripts of Ga having Ro readings and vice versa. Then, there is the possibility that in any given case the compiler of the gloss in Pal. lat. 68 may have borrowed a biblical text from the commentary from which he was excerpting rather than directly from a Psalter. However, the fact that, despite the mutual contamination, we still possess some specifically Ga and Ro readings in the manuscript tradition makes an analysis of the biblical text of Pal. lat. 68 possible.

9.1. *The Basic Text of Palatino- Latinus 68 is Gallican*
There are sufficient specifically Gallican readings in Pal. lat. 68 to warrant the conclusion that the basic text used by the compiler was the *Gallicanum*. We have a good example in the opening *lemma: a concilio multa* (Ps. 39.11).[116] The *Romanum* has: *a synagoga multa*.

---

115. In this analysis the following critical editions have been used: *Liber Psalmorum ex recensione Sancii Hieronymi cum praelationibus et epistula ad Sunniam st Fretelam* (Biblia Sacra iuxta latinant versionem ad codicum fidern iuxta Pii pp. XII cura et studio monachorum Abbatiae Pontificiae Sancti Hieronymi in Urbe Ordinis Sancti Benedicti edita, X; Rome: Vatican Polyglot Press, 1953); R. Weber, *Le Psautier Romain et les autres anciens Psautiers latins* (Collectanea Biblica Latina, 10; Rome: Abbaye de Saint-Jérôme; Vatican City: Libreria Vaticana, 1953); H. de Sainte-Marie, *Sancti Hieronymi Psalterium iuxta Hebraeos* (Collectanea Biblica Latina, 11; Rome: Abbaye de Saint-Jérôme; Vatican City: Libreria Vaticana, 1954).

116. McNamara (ed.), *Glossa in Psalmos*, p. 91. The ancient Psalter of Lyons (with siglum L for its Old Latin readings) has the reading: *a consilio multo*. It is known, however, that this Psalter has a mixture of Old Latin and Vulgate readings.

Another is Ps. 107.13: *quia uana salus hominis*[117] (Ro: *et uana salus hominis*). Texts of this nature could be multiplied. In Ps. 107.10 the *lemma* has the specifically Gallican *libes*[118] (= *lebes*), where Ro has *olla*. The gloss repeats *libes*. Very telling, too, are the instances where we have only vernacular glosses, without anything in Latin. Here there can scarcely be any question of commentary influence on the text-form of the *lemmata*. A number of such *lemmata*, however, are specifically Gallican, for example, *germinans* (Ps. 64.11),[119] where Ro has *dum exorietur*; Ps. 77.44, with *imbres*[120] (Ro *pluuiales aquae*); Ps. 101.4, with *gremium*[121] (Ro *in frixorio*). The vernacular glosses in the above cases are in Old Irish. In 89.13 we have an Old English gloss on the Gallican reading *usquequo*[122] (Ro *aliquantulum*).

Also very indicative with regard to the primacy of the *Gallicanum* as the compiler's text is the fact that on occasion we find the *Gallicanum* used as a *lemma* and glossed by the *Romanum*, for example, Ps. 77.45: *cinomiam* (Ga) glossed as *musca canina*[123] (Ro). Likewise Ps. 61.5: *praetium* (Ga) glossed by *honorem*[124] (Ro). In Ps. 104.28 we find a *Gallicanum lemma* glossed by Ro which in turn is glossed by the *Hebraicum* rendering: '*Et non exacerbauit sermones* (Ga), *id est in noua enim translatione non exacerbauerunt* (Ro), *id est non fuerunt enim increduli uerbis Moisi*' (cf. Heb.).[125]

There are about nine instances in Pal. lat. 68 where the same brief Psalter text is repeated twice. In four of these the repeated text is identical in both cases and in one of these four the text is Gallican, namely, Ps. 117.26: *Benedictus qui uenturus est*[126] (Ro has: *Benedictus qui uenit*). (I shall consider the significance of these repeated texts presently.)

While this evidence seems sufficient to justify the conclusion that the compiler's basic Psalter text was the Gallican, it is not adequate to

117. McNamara (ed.), *Glossa in Psalmos*, p. 230.
118. McNamara (ed.), *Glossa in Psalmos*, p. 230.
119. McNamara (ed.), *Glossa in Psalmos*, p. 132.
120. McNamara (ed.), *Glossa in Psalmos*, p. 166.
121. McNamara (ed.), *Glossa in Psalmos*, p. 207.
122. McNamara (ed.), *Glossa in Psalmos*, p. 193.
123. McNamara (ed.), *Glossa in Psalmos*, p. 166.
124. McNamara (ed.), *Glossa in Psalmos*, p. 127.
125. McNamara (ed.), *Glossa in Psalmos*, p. 219; see also below 9.2.
126. McNamara (ed.), *Glossa in Psalmos*, p. 244.

permit us situate this text within the Gallican family. At times the gloss has good Gallican readings, coinciding with Jerome's original as reconstructed by the Benedictine editors.[127] On the other hand, however, it often goes with the tradition of inferior readings against Jerome's original.[128] On some occasions it has readings proper to the Irish family of *Gallicanum* texts[129] (the CI of Gallican manuscripts). On the other hand it very often disagrees with the peculiar readings of this family.[130] It has some readings proper to the so-called Psalter of Charlemagne (the Q of Gallican manuscripts),[131] with which it is closely related in the introductory material prefixed to each psalm.[132] However, it very often disagrees with the peculiar readings of Q.[133]

The explanation of what evidence the text presents may be that, while the compiler was working within the tradition of the Gallican Psalter, he does not appear to have followed any Gallican manuscript or family of manuscripts known to us. He may even have used more than one Gallican text.

9.2. *Old Latin Readings in Palatino-Latinus 68*

The presence of Old Latin readings in Pal. lat. 68 has already been noted. It does not follow that these were always, or even in the majority of cases, drawn directly from Psalter texts. In some cases, at least, they seem to have come through commentaries such as the Epitome of Julian or the *Enarrationes* of Augustine.

This seems to be the case with regard to Ps. 104.28, where the *Romanum* is used to gloss the *Gallicanum* and the *Hebraicum* in turn used to gloss the *Romanum*. The combination here seems to be due to the Julian Epitome, in which the *Hebraicum* glosses the *Romanum* and where the same peculiar reading (*non exacerbauerunt*,[134] found also in Codex

127. *Liber Psalmorum*. We have instances at, e.g., Pss. 50.6; 53.7; 55.3; 57.10; 60.8; 64.3. In these cases it also agrees with the Irish (CI) Gallican tradition.

128. E.g. at Pss. 46.10; 48.21; 50.10; 58.14; 71.15 (with Ro).

129. E.g. at Pss. 47.1; 49.3; 51.9; 64.9 (with Ro), 76.11, 81.7; 87.10.

130. E.g. at Pss. 39.13; 40.7; 44.1; 45.3; 48.19; 51.3; 54.10; 55.9; 73.3; 80.17; 82.7; 83.6; 83.13 (twice); 85.4; 88.21, 39. It also contains words omitted by C (the Cathach), e.g. at Pss. 47.8; 51.3; 63.8; 70.3.

131. E.g. at Pss. 49.2, 65.4.

132. See below, 10.1, 10.8.

133. E.g. at Pss. 56.5, 6; 62.10; 70.20; and with Q, *prima manu*, at Pss. 40.7; 55.6; 64.1; 70.9; 84.9.

134. See De Coninck and d'Hont (eds.), *Theodori*, pp. 340, 115-16.

Corbeiensis) occurs. Other Ro texts have *quia exacerbauerunt*. At Ps. 77.45 the Julian Epitome[135] also has the *Romanum musca canina* as *lemma*. The presence of the Old Latin reading of the Veronensis type in Ps. 132.3 (*super mont<es> Sion*)[136] is to be explained through the compiler's dependence on Augustine, who used a Veronensis-type Psalter. The same may be true of the presence of the rare Old Latin variant *quoniam* (for *quia* of Ga and Ro) of the Veronensis found in Ps. 148.5.[137]

There are some cases of repeated texts in which one of the occurrences is the *Gallicanum* and the other the *Romanum*. Thus, for instance, in Ps. 102.21 in the *lemma* we have the *Romanum* reading *Benedicite Dominum*[138] whereas in the *haeret* to Psalm 103[139] this text appears in its specifically Gallican form: *Benedicite Domino*. The same *Romanum* reading *Benedicite Dominum* occurs twice in Pal. lat. 68 at Ps. 133.2,[140] where the true Gallican text has *b. Domino*. In this instance, however, the *Romanum* reading has penetrated many inferior manuscripts of the Gallican tradition. We have three instances (two of them within the gradual psalms) with the Gallican reading in the first occurrence (Pss. 118.49; 119.1; 125.5)[141] and the *Romanum* reading in the other occurrence (the *incipit* in Ps. 118.49; 119.1, and in the alternative interpretation in 125.5).[142] In the case of 125.5[143] the use of the *Romanum* is probably through Augustine whose *Enarrationes* (or an abbreviation of them) are being used in the context.

Psalm 119.4 in Pal. lat. 68 has the reading *sagitae potentes acutae*,[144] where the critical editions of both Ga and Ro read *sagittae potentis acutae*. The glosses on the *lemma* show that *potentes* is taken as plural, not as an orthographic variant of *potentis*. The reading is that of the *Romanum* of the manuscripts being used in England in the eighth century (MSS AHNS of the critical editions), and also of the Montpellier

135. See De Coninck and d'Hont (eds.), *Theodori*, pp. 283, 213.

136. McNamara (ed.), *Glossa in Psalmos*, p. 286 see also below pp. 214-15.

137. McNamara (ed.), *Glossa in Psalmos*, p. 307. A gloss on Ps. 148.7 may depend on the *Enarrationes*.

138. McNamara (ed.), *Glossa in Psalmos*, p. 211.

139. McNamara (ed.), *Glossa in Psalmos*, p. 211.

140. McNamara (ed.), *Glossa in Psalmos*, p. 287.

141. McNamara (ed.), *Glossa in Psalmos*, respectively, pp. 250, 265, 274. (To these we may add Ps. 94.7, with Ro reading in *incipit* of Ps. 95.)

142. McNamara (ed.), *Glossa in Psalmos*, respectively, pp. 250, 265, 274.

143. McNamara (ed.), *Glossa in Psalmos*, p. 274, with source indication.

144. McNamara (ed.), *Glossa in Psalmos*, p. 265.

Psalter.[145] It is also that of the Codex Sangermanensis and Codex Corbeiensis of the Old Latin and is the text used and glossed by Eucherius.[146] The presence of the reading in Pal. lat. 68 may be due to an
influence from the Roman Church in Britain. In Pss. 117.6 (*adiutor est*)
and 129.4 (*verbum tuum*) we have two Old Latin readings that do not
appear to have been due to the influence of the commentaries being
used in the glosses.

It would be too much to conclude from all this that the compiler had
access to a complete Old Latin Psalter, whether of the kind being used
in the Roman Church of Britain or elsewhere in the West, although of
course he may well have had.

9.3. *The Use of the* Hebraicum *in Palatino-Latinus 68*

The occurrence of the *Hebraicum* as a gloss in Ps. 104.28 has already
been noted. Its use in this instance is probably due to the influence of
the Epitome of Julian. The presence of a *Hebraicum* text in Ps. 108.4
(*pro eo quod eos diligebam aduersabantur mihi*)[147] may be explained
in the same manner. No such influence can explain the presence of the
Hebraicum in Ps. 54.20 where its text (*qui iudex est ab initio*)[148] is used
to gloss *Qui est ante saecula* (= Ga, Ro). The gloss on the preceding
verse (*qui fuerunt aduersum me*)[149] may also be dependent on the *Hebraicum* (*multi enim luerunt aduersum me*). The purpose of the *Hebraicum* as a *lemma* in Ps. 87.11[150] and its corresponding gloss (*aut
gigantes*—Heb.—glossed as *id est non*) is hard to explain, since the corresponding Gallican (and Old Latin) text *aut medici* had just been commented on.

This evidence, limited though it be, seems to indicate that the compiler had access to, and used a copy of, Jerome's rendering from the
Hebrew. That he should have is not at all surprising. The text was early

145. F. Unterkircher (ed.), *Die Glossen des Psalters von Mondsee (vor 788)*
(Montpellier, Faculté de Médecine MS 409) (Spicelegium Friburgense, 20; Freiburg; Universitätsverlag, 1974), p. 448.

146. C. Wotke (ed.), *Instructionum libri duo*. I. *De Psalmorum Libro* LIII (CSEL,
31; Prague, 1894), p. 100, 16-23.

147. McNamara (ed.), *Glossa in Psalmos*, p. 231; see De Coninck and d'Hont
(eds.), *Theodori*, pp. 349, 19-20.

148. McNamara (ed.), *Glossa in Psalmos*, p. 117.

149. McNamara (ed.), *Glossa in Psalmos*, p. 117.

150. McNamara (ed.), *Glossa in Psalmos*, p. 186.

known in Ireland and seems to have been current there in its peculiar Irish text form before the Gallican Cathach text was written (about 600–30 CE).[151] The evidence of the Hiberno-Latin *Eclogae tractatorum in Psalterium* shows that it was being used in Bible study in Irish schools before the end of the eighth century.[152]

9.4. *Deviant Psalter Readings in Palatino-Latinus 68*

Together with the texts from the *Gallicanum*, *Romanum* and the *Hebraicum* just considered, there are in Pal. lat. 68 a few Psalter readings not attested in any of these three. Two of those have to do with the presence of small additions of *Domine* in Ps. 118.72[153] and *et* in Ps. 139.11.[154] One is a slight difference in wording—*ex me scientia* for *scientia tua ex me* in Ps. 138.6.[155] Two more may involve a mere question of orthography—*consummatione* for *consummationi* in Ps. 118.96[156] and *redemet* for *redemit* in Ps. 135.24.[157] A final unique reading in Ps. 131.1 in the alternative interpretation (*in atris domus Domini* for *in atris domus Dei*, as in earlier *lemma*)[158] may be due to the presence of *in domo Domini* in the first part of the verse. The insertion of *in* before *Hirusalem* in 121.6 may be due to a scribal error.

10. *Analysis of Psalm Headings*

It has earlier been remarked[159] that the commentary on each psalm in Pal. lat. 68 is preceded by introductory material, or psalm headings, which generally follows the following order: (a) the biblical psalm heading; (b) a historical heading referring the psalm to David and his times; (c) a historical heading (generally Theodorean and drawn from the Epitome of Julian) referring the psalm to later Jewish history; (d) a mystical heading. I shall now proceed to analyse each of these in turn.

151. See McNamara (ed.), 'Psalter Text', pp. 263-64.
152. See McNamara (ed.), 'Psalter Text', pp. 226-27.
153. McNamara (ed.), *Glossa in Psalmos*, p. 252.
154. McNamara (ed.), *Glossa in Psalmos*, p. 296.
155. McNamara (ed.), *Glossa in Psalmos*, p. 293.
156. McNamara (ed.), *Glossa in Psalmos*, p. 255.
157. McNamara (ed.), *Glossa in Psalmos*, p. 290, in *heret* Ps. 136.
158. McNamara (ed.), *Glossa in Psalmos*, p. 287.
159. Above, 6.

10.1. *The Biblical Psalm Headings*

Strictly speaking, the biblical psalm headings, being part of the biblical text, should be analysed as part of the biblical text itself. They merit separate consideration, however, since in the tradition represented by the gloss (found also in the so-called Psalter of Charlemagne) they are treated more freely than the biblical text. They differ quite often from the accepted texts of the *Gallicanum* and *Romanum*, and have occasionally inserted into them, or attached to them, references to David and his times. In fact it is not always easy to ascertain whether these expanded headings of the catena were really intended as part of the biblical text, as biblical headings proper, or as interpretative expansions. Perhaps in the tradition in which they stood no such distinction was made.

Some of these biblical headings have readings identical with those found in one or other of the two representatives of the Irish Gallican tradition (that is, in MSS C and I), or with some of those of the Codex Amiatinus (which also represents Irish tradition). Instances of this can be seen in the headings for Psalms 42, 50, 71, 81, 88, 143.

A matter worthy of note is the manner in which these expanded biblical headings of Pal. lat. 68 agree with those of the so-called Psalter of Charlemagne (sigled Q for its biblical text). The following examples will illustrate this:

Gallicanum, ed. cr.	Pal. lat. 68; Psalt. Charl. (Q)
(Psalm 43)	
In finem filiis Core ad intelleclum	*In finem salmus Dauid*
(Psalm 44)	
In finem pro his qui commutabuntur filiis Core ad intellectum canticum pro dilecto	*In finem salmus Dauid. id est de ipso et Salomone. Pro his qui commotabuntur. id est de exilio in requiem. Ad intelleclum filis Chore canticum pro dilecto. id est de regno iusti.*
	(Q. In finem salmus Dauid de se ipse et Salomon. et de his qui commutabunt de exilio in requiem ad intellectum filiis Core).
(Psalm 45)	
In finem pro filiis Core pro arcanis psalmus	*In finem salmus Danid pro erumnis a Saul.*

Gallicanum, ed. cr.	Pal. lat. 68; Psalt. Charl. (Q)
(Psalm 46) *In finem pro filiis Core psalmus*	*In finem intellectus filis Core. Vox Dauid accepto regno.* (Q: *In finem Psalmus Dauid accepto regno.*)
(Psalm 52) *In finem pro Melch intellegentiae Dauid*	*In finem salmus Dauid de Saul intellegentia Dauid pro Abimelech* (Q om. *Dauid* 1°; has '*De Amalech*')
(Psalm 75) *In finem in laudibus psalmus Asaph canticum ad Assyrios*	*In finem de laudibus salmus Asaph pro uictoria Dauid et pro uictoria Ezechiae*
(Psalm 94) *Laus cantici David*	*Laus cantici ipsi Dauid ueniens in regnum* (to which V adds from Psalm 95: *quando domus aedificabitur*).
(Palm 120) *Canticum graduum*	*Canticum gradum. Vox Dauid proerumnis Saul*

10.2. *Special Headings Referring to David and to Saul*

Whereas David is frequently mentioned in the biblical psalm headings, Saul is only rarely so (Pss. 17, 51, 53, 56, 58). A characteristic of the gloss of Pal. lat. 68 is the frequency with which it introduces the names of David and Saul into the introductory material, and into the very biblical psalm headings as we have just seen. The explanation of this must lie in a tradition which interpreted the psalms in question of David and his contemporaries. The psalms in question are generally interpreted in the same manner in the glosses of the commentary itself.[160] I set out the headings in question as follows:

---

160. On this interpretation see further below 12.2.

Vox Dauid	Pss. 41, 50, 61, 96, 109, 111, 112, 144 (*laudatio Dauid*), 149
Vox (oratio) Dauid pro (de) socis (suis)	Ps. 89; cf. also Ps. 90
Vox Dauid in exilio	Pss. 70, 105
(Vox Dauid) pro erumnis (a) Saul	Pss. 45, 56, 63, 68, 120, 140
(Vox Dauid), (Salmus Dauid) de Saul	Ps. 52, 58, 73, 119
Querela Dauid pro Saul	Ps. 42
Vox Dauid cum fugeret a facie Saulis	Ps. 55
Vox (Salmus) Dauid de (sua) reuersione (in regnum, regno)	Cf. Pss. 60, 65, 84, 94, 114, 115
(Salmus) Dauid cum coepisset profisci ad terram repromissionis	Ps. 64
Vox Dauid de gratulatione post praelium contra Abisolonem	Ps. 95
Vox Dauid de Abisolon filio suo	Ps. 108
Vox Dauid de iustis qui rapti sunt in Babiloniam	Ps. 118
Vox Dauid de liberatione (reditu) populi	Cf. Pss. 80, 83, 86, 127, 135, 145, 146, 147
Vox Dauid de gratiarum actione	Ps. 74; cf. Ps. 148
Vox Dauid orantis	Cf. Ps. 142
Vox Dauid ad ortationem populi	Ps. 104
Vox Dauid hortantis populum	Ps. 150
Vox Dauid commemorantis beneficia (antiqua)	Pss. 77, 91; cf. 43, 79
Vox Dauid de priscis	Ps. 113
Vox Dauid et Asaph de persequtoribus Israel	Ps. 82

10.3. *Theodorean Psalm Headings*

About one third of the glosses in the commentary itself are derived from the Epitome of Julian.[161] In like manner, the chief source of inspiration for the historical headings in the work is the same Epitome or rather the *argumenta* prefixed to the exposition proper in this commentary. The Epitome has influenced the headings in two ways. In many cases the historical headings in Pal. lat. 68 reproduce verbatim the text of the Epitome.[162] In other cases, however, the substance of the heading

161. See below, 11.3.a.
162. E.g. at Pss. 40, 45, 46, 47, 53, 54, 59, 60, 62, 66 (a long text), 68, 70 (a long

in Pal. lat. 68 is that of the *argumentum* of the Epitome, although the wording is different.[163] In some instances there is a mere reflection of the text of the Epitome.

10.4. *Other Historical Psalm Headings*

Together with the historical headings thus far considered, there are some others in Pal. lat. 68 which have a bearing on the historical interpretation of the particular psalm but do not fall under any of the two classes thus far considered. They are as follows: *Vox Ezechiae,*[164] *Vox plebis (populi),*[165] *Vox Moisi confirmantis populum suum.*[166]

10.5. *The Columba Series of Psalm Headings*

The mystical Series of psalm headings in the gloss belongs in general to Series I, the Series of St Columba, edited by Dom Pierre Salmon.[167] As we shall see later,[168] within this, the series of Pal. lat. 68 is very closely related to the peculiar readings of the mystical headings in the so-called Psalter of Charlemagne (given the siglum *i* in Dom Salmon's edition).[169]

---

text), 72, 100, 121, 122 (almost verbatim identical), 123 (almost verbatim identical), 132, 134, 138, 139 (a very long text), 141–44.

163. E.g. Pss. 42, 64, 65, 69, 85, 87, 88, 90, 92, 94, 96, 97, 98, 101, 102, 103, 105, 106, 108, 114, 118, 126, 137, 145–48, 150. With regard to the headings for Pss. 137, 145–18, 150 the influence of the Epitome of Julian is at best faint.

164. Pss. 47, 76.

165. Pss. 45, 46, 59, 63, 124.

166. Ps. 90. A gloss of the Montepellier Psalter notes on this psalm: '*Hapud hebreos titutulum* (sic) *non habet, ut sciat quia moses est*' (Unterkircher, *Die Glossen*, p. 350).

167. Cf. P. Salmon, *Les 'Tituli Psalmorum' des manuscrits latins* (Collectanea Biblica Latina, 12; Rome: Abbaye de Saint-Jérôme; Vatican City: Libreria Vaticana, 1969), pp. 45-74.

168. See below, 10.8.

169. Cf. Salmon, *Les 'Tituli'*, pp. 31-32, 49. Pal. lat. 68 agrees with the peculiar headings of *i* in the following psalms: 43; 45; 48; 55; 62; 65; 68; 72; 73–76 (with minor variants); 77–81; 88; 89; 92; 95; 97; 97 (with minor variants); 98; 100; 113; 114; 117; 118 (in headings to all the 22 subsections); 119; 120; 123–25; 128; 129; 141 (no heading in the St Columba Series); 143; 151 (with variant *exhortantis* for *exoperantis*).

10.6. *Mystical Headings not from Series I*
Some of the mystical psalm headings of Pal. lat. 68 are not found in any
representative of the St Columba Series. Most of the headings in question, in fact, are not found in any of the six series of headings edited by
Dom Salmon,[170] although some of them are similar to known headings.[171]

10.7. *The* Romani *Mentioned in Psalm Headings*
In three different psalm headings mention is made of the manner in
which the particular psalm is interpreted by *Romani*. In all three cases
the word is written in full, not abbreviated. The occurrences are as follows:

> (Psalm 49). *Deus deorum Dominus... In finem salmus Dauid. De mira-*
> *bilibus mundi hic salmus ad Iudeos conponitur qui uirtutem neglegentes*
> *solas curarent hostias ligalium iusionum; in priore salmo sermonem ad*
> *omnes direxit, in praesenti ad Iudeos tantum* (= Julian Epitome). *Vox*
> *Spiritus de aduentu Christi.* Hic salmus secundum Romanos de iudicio
> futuro canitur.

The first part of this heading (*De mirabilibus...ad Iudeos tantum*) is
drawn for the greater part from the Julian Epitome. The mystical heading seems to understand the psalm of the first coming of Christ. The
understanding of the *Romani* disagrees with this. Actually, the understanding of the *Romani* has nothing exceptional about it. It is that found
in Series I (*De aduentu Christi propheta dicit et de iudicio futuro*) and
is similar to the heading of Series III (*Vox apostolica de secundo*
Christo aduentu). It is simply impossible with the little information at
our disposal to determine why the *Romani* understood the psalm in this
way. It may have something to do with a theory of interpretation and
may be connected with the biblical psalm heading, which for this psalm
in the genuine Gallican and *Romanum* tradition is 'Psalmus Asaph',
although Pal. lat. 68, with other Gallican and *Romanum* texts take it as a
Psalm of David.

---

170. For instance in Pss. 40; 51.1; 55; 58.2; 59; 72.1; 98; 107; 129; 140; 145.
171. Thus, for instance, the headings in Pss. 41.2 (cf. Series I, II, III); 52 (cf.
Series II, III, IV); 53 (cf. Series II, III, IV); 62 (cf. Series II); 68 (*Vox Ionae*
prophetae do sua persona; cf. Series I); 70 (cf. Series III); 72 (cf. Series III); 73
(*Vox populi post uindictam crucis*; cf. Ps.-Bede of Series I) 80 (*Vox Christi ad*
Pentecosten; cf. Ps.-Bede of Series I); 93 (cf. Series II, III); 112 (cf. Series III).

> (Psalm 52). *Dixit insipiens...In finem. Salmus Dauid de Saul. Intellegentia Dauid pro Abimelech. id est pro choro. Vox Ezechiae de Rabsace, et de his temporibus quae in illis gesta sunt.* Secundum Romanos pro insidis Saul et occissione sacerdotum in Nouae decantatur. *Vox Christi de Iuda traditore.*

The genuine biblical heading for this psalm in the Gallican and *Romanum* tradition is *In finem pro Melech intellegentiae (intellectus) Dauid.* The tradition represented by Pal. lat. 68 (and the so-called Psalter of Charlemagne) has read *Salmus Dauid de Saul* into the biblical heading. For *Melech* Pal. lat. 68 has 'Abimelech', as have many other MSS. We simply cannot say what reading the Psalter of the *Romani* had. Their interpretation, however, does not follow the Theodorean one of the Epitome of Julian, which understands the psalm of Hezekiah and the Assyrian general (cf. 2 Kgs 18.17 and elsewhere). They interpret it rather of the slaughter of the priests of Nob (*Nouae*) mentioned in 1 Samuel 21–22. David's visit there and to the priest Achimelech (called Abimelech in Pal. lat. 68 and other corrupt texts) is the subject of the biblical heading for the preceding psalm (Ps. 51). It may well be these two psalm headings which had the *Romani* opt for the reference to David and his times rather than to later Jewish history. Their interpretation has been read into the very biblical psalm heading of Psalm 52 (*Salmus Dauid de Saul, Intellegentia...pro Abimelech*) and is also found in the explanatory glosses (for example, vv. 1, 3, 5, 6, 7).

> (Psalm 54). *Exaudi Deus orationem...In finem in carminibus intellectus Dawid. Vox Honiae sacerdotis expulsi de sacerdotio a regibus Grecorum quod emit Simon quidam propincius Honiae; inde Honias fugit in Aegiptum et Deum ibi coluit iuxta mores Hierusolimorum.* Hic salmus secundum Romanos pro erumnis Saul cantatur. *Vox aeclesiae de Christo.*

In interpreting the psalm as speaking of the persecution of David by Saul, rather than of Onias and Maccabaean times as the Theodorean tradition and the Epitome do, the *Romani* may once again have been guided by the biblical heading of the preceding psalm which connects Psalm 53 with the report of the Ziphites to Saul that David was hiding among them. They may even have been influenced by the mention of David in the heading of the present psalm. The glosses, we may note, seek to combine this *Romani* interpretation with the Theodorean one at least as far as v. 9. From v. 10 onwards a third form of interpretation enters, understanding the psalm of Ahitophel's counsel and Absalom's revolt—the understanding of the psalm found in the glosses of the Montpellier Psalter.[172]

It is obvious that the *Romani* referred to in these texts were a clearly identifiable group in the communities in which the gloss of Pal. lat. 68 was compiled, or at least in which the tradition it enshrines was formed, which in the view proposed in this work was in Columban monasteries of either Ireland or Northumbria.

Who precisely these scholars were is less easy to define. The most obvious solution would be to identify them with the *Romani* of the Paschal controversy.[173] These from about 630 onwards advocated the adoption of the Roman celebration of Easter. A scholar of the *Romani* is mentioned in connection with computation tables.[174] The *Romani* are also mentioned in the *Collectio Canonum Hibernensis*[175] (made at the beginning of the eighth century) and in the Canons of Adamnan.[176]

The *Romani* appear to have been most active from c. 620 CE to 670 or 700. They may also have been involved in the exegetical field at the same time, so that the relic of the Psalm interpretation now preserved in Pal. lat. 68 may represent actual exegetical work that took place around 630–50.

172. Unterkircher (ed.), *Die Glossen*, pp. 226-30. See also above p. 180 (Irish gloss no. 6).

173. On these *Romani* of the Paschal controversy see Gougaud, *Christianity*, pp. 185-201; Kenney, *Sources*, pp. 210-16; K. Hughes, *The Church in Early Irish Society* (London: Methuen, 1966), pp. 103-10.

174. Thus, for instance, in MS. Würzburg, M.p.th.f. 61, in an additional folio (fol. 29) attached to a Hiberno-Latin commentary we read that '*Mosinu maccu Min, scriba et abbas Benncuir primus Hibernensium compotem a graeco quodam sapiente memoraliter dedicit. Deinde Mocuoroc maccu Minsemon quem Romani doctorem totius mundi nominabant alumnusque praefati scribae in insola quae dicitur Crannach Duin Lethglaisse hanc scientiam literis fixit ne memoria laberetur*' (see text in *Thes. Pal.*, II, p. 285. Mosinu's obit is variously given as 609, 610, 612 CE. See now D. Ó Cróinin, 'Mo-Sinnu moccu Min and the Computus of Bangor', *Peritia* 1 (1982), pp. 281-95 (283 for our text).

175. H. Wasserschleben (ed.), *Die irische Kanonensammlung* (Leipzig: Verlag von Bernhard Tauchnitz, 2nd edn, 1885), pp. 62, 159-60, 163, 183, 194, 211, 212.

176. L. Bieler (ed.), *The Irish Penitentials* (SLH, 5; Dublin: Institute for Advanced Studies, 1963), pp. 178-79, 254.

10.8. *Psalm Headings of Palatino-Latinus 68 and of Psalter of Charlemagne*

The close relationship that exists between the psalm headings in Pal. lat. 68 and in the Psalter of Charlemagne has already been touched on more than once.[177] It must now be examined in somewhat greater detail.

The manuscript referred to as 'The Psalter of Charlemagne' (that is, Paris, Bibl. Nat., lat. 13159) was written 795–800 CE in some Continental centre with Irish connections. Irish saints are included in the litanies given in the Psalter and its illumination shows clear Irish influence. It has Psalter collects of the African Series at the end of each psalm. On the outer margin of the manuscript a triangular cartouche contains the Series III of psalm headings.[178]

Each psalm is preceded by introductory material, most of which has been mentioned in passing in the preceding pages. The composite introductions prefaced to each psalm contain first of all the opening words of the psalm, which is then often described as *Psalmus Dauid*. One or more historical heading is then given, after which there generally comes the mystical heading. Occasionally certain important words of the psalm are then explained.

In practically every one of these elements the introductory material of the so-called Psalter of Charlemagne is very closely related to the corresponding material in Pal. lat. 68. The heading of Psalm 42, given below, is typical of this relationship.

Pal. lat. 68	Psalter of Charlemagne
In finem salmus Dauid. De gratulatione reuersionis in regnum; uel querila Dauid pro Saul. Vox plebis in Babilonia. Vox Christi ad Patrem. Vox aeclesiae.	*In finem psalmus Dauid. Gratulatio reuertente in regnum; uel queralla Dauid pro Saul. Vox plebis in Babilonia. Vox Christi ad passionem et Ecclesiae ad Christum.*

Needless to say, there are differences as well as resemblances between these two texts. I give some examples of both here.

---

177. The Pseudo-Bedan Psalm Titles are also related to both these. On the entire question see Fischer, '*Bedae de*', pp. 90-110, especially 96-97.

178. The Paris manuscript has been collated for Series I (already mentioned) and III by Dom P. Salmon for his edition, *Les 'Tituli'*; see pp. 98, 31.

Both texts have some *biblical Psalm headings* proper to them-selves.[179]

With regard to the *Theodorean material*—both draw what they have of it from the Epitome of Julian. In a number of instances the material in both texts is identical both in the wording and in the amount bor-rowed from the Epitome.[180] In other cases, however, while the text car-ried by both is identical, the Psalter of Charlemagne draws more exten-sively on the Julian Epitome than does Pal. lat. 68.[181] Evidently, the Psalter of Charlemagne does not depend directly on the present text or the original of Pal. lat. 68.

There are about 45 instances in which Pal. lat. 68 has historical headings not drawn from the Epitome. Thirteen or so of these headings are also in the Psalter of Charlemagne.[182]

Mention has already been made of the special headings of Pal. lat. 68 referring to David and Saul.[183] Some of those are also found in the Psal-ter of Charlemagne.[184] Of the other historical headings in Pal. lat. 68 which do not come under any of the above headings (eight in all)—five of them occur in identical wording in the Psalter of Charlemagne.[185]

The close relationship between Pal. lat. 68 and the Psalter of Charle-magne is clearer still in the St Columba Series of Mystical Psalm Head-ings (Series I). Within this St Columba Series, as noted already by Dom Pierre Salmon, the Psalter of Charlemagne has certain peculiarities not

179. Examples in Pss. 44; 49; 52; 66; 70; 86; 90; 92; 94; 95; 100; 102; 139. Occasionally it can be doubted whether the heading in question can really be clas-sed as 'biblical', e.g., in Ps. 52.

180. Instances are at Pss. 42; 64; 85; 87; 92; 97; 101; 103; 118 (in the heading to the entire psalm); 126; 128 (texts here merely similar).

181. Instances at Pss. 88; 90; 145. Together with this it should be noted that the Psalter of Charlemagne occasionally has texts from the Epitome of Julian which are not in any way in Pal. lat. 68, e.g., at Pss. 65; 69; 73; 74; 94; 96; 102; possibly at 105 (text faded); 106 (a very long text from the Epitome); 137; 146; 147; 150.

182. The 13 instances are: at Pss. 43; 44; 86; 104; 107; 111; 115; 117; 126; 129; 131; 136; 151.

183. Above, 10.2.

184. Instances (following order of former list) at Pss. 41 (similar); 111 (com-parable); 70; 45; 56; 63 (Psalter of Charlemagne faded, but same at least in part as Pal. lat. 68); 68; 120; 140; 52; 73; 119; 60; 65; 84; 94 (Psalter of Charlemagne Similar to Pal. lat. 68); 114; 115; 64; 108; 118; 127; 145; 146; 147; 148; 142; 104; 150.

185. They are: Pss. 47; 45; 46; 59; 90.

found in the other witnesses.[186] Occasionally the Psalter of Charlemagne omits the St Columba heading altogether. In both these ways
Pal. lat. 68 goes along with the Psalter: in the peculiar headings,[187] and
by omitting the St Columba heading where the Psalter omits it.[188]

This close connection between the two texts is nowhere more in evidence than in the headings of the 22 subsections of Psalm 118. Both
Pal. lat. 68 and the Psalter of Charlemagne are unique not only in having lengthy and composite headings to each of these subsections but
more so in that these rare and complex headings are practically verbatim identical in both.

One final piece of evidence on the relationship between the two texts
is that both have the references to the *Romani* interpretation in the
headings to Psalms 49, 52 and 54, although the garbled manner in
which part of the heading of Psalm 52 is reproduced in the Psalter of
Charlemagne seems to indicate that the European scribe of MS. Paris.
Bibl. Nat. lat. 13159 failed to understand the peculiar Irish manner of
spelling Nob (that is, *Nouae*).[189]

The conclusion to be drawn from this evidence is that the exegetical
tradition found in the Pal. lat. 68 psalm headings (a tradition at home in
schools of Ireland and Northumbria) must have been taken to the Continent some time before the so-called Psalter of Charlemagne was written in the dying years of the eighth century. How much earlier than
795–800 CE it was taken there remains to be determined.

---

186. These are noted in the apparatus of Salmon, *Les 'Tituli'*.

187. See n. 169 above.

188. E.g. at Pss. 86; 87; 115; 127.

189. In the heading for Ps. 52 the text corresponding to '*pro...occisione sacerdotum in Nouae* (= Nob) *canitur*' of Pal. lat. 68 (see 3.10.g above) in the Psalter of
Charlemagne is: '*pro...occisione sacerdotum in nouo cantico*'. In most instances
the words following immediately on *secundum* in the Psalter of Charlemagne are
faded but can be presumed to be the same as Pal. lat. 68. There is a further reference
to *Romani* in the heading to Ps. 73 in the Psalter of Charlemagne (not found in Pal.
lat. 68): *Hic psalmus secundum Ebre<um> de Machabeorum periculis...Romani
dicunt* (...text following on this faded, but following words in part legible) ...*non*
(?) *habere (historiam?) ex aduerso nisi in* (some letters illegible) ...*tur transferatur.*
Compare the heading of Ps. 128 in the same Psalter: *Hic psalmus secundum
Ebreum pro commonibus inimicis canitur et transfertur ad personam populi*; cf.
heading to Ps. 128 in Pal. lat. 68.

11. *Source Analysis of the Commentary in Palatino-Latinus 68*

We are helped to a certain extent in the identification of the compiler's
sources by the source ascriptions given in abbreviated form in the margins,[190] and in abbreviated form or written out in full in the text itself.
Both of these have limitations in that they are in part erroneous. A further reason for caution in the use of the marginal ascriptions is that we
are not always sure to which precise text they are intended to refer,
since many lines have more than one text, or indeed whether due to
copyists' errors the ascriptions any longer stand opposite the proper line
or text. In all cases the marginal and text source ascription must be
verified through source analysis, which remains our chief way of identifying the works on which the compiler drew.

11.1. *Sources Noted by Abbreviation in Margins*
As already noted, these marginal source indications are *h*, *hir* and *hil*.
They are identified as follows:

(1)   *h opposite genuine works of Jerome.* In a number of instances
        the abbreviation *h* stands opposite passages drawn from
        Jerome's *Commentarioli in Psalmos*.[191] In one instance (at Ps.
        41.8) it stands opposite a text from Jerome's *In Psal. XXXXI,
        ad Neophytos*. Once (Ps. 44.8) it stands opposite what resem-
        bles a text from Jerome's *Tractatus de Psalmo 44*.

(2)   *h opposite Pseudo-Jerome Texts.* In one instance (Ps. 88.28) *h*
        stands opposite a text from the Epitome of Julian, which the
        compiler appears to have taken as a work of Jerome, an identi-
        fication made throughout the Hiberno-Latin *Eclogae tracta-
        torum in Psalterium* of the late eighth-century.[192] In one
        instance (Ps. 64.10)[193] *h* stands opposite an unidentified text
        which may be compared with *Breviarium in Psalmos*, in Ps.
        64.10.

(3)   *h (=Hilarius) opposite texts from Augustine's* Enarrationes. In
        two places (Pss. 73.13; 131, in second and allegorical exposi-

190. On these see also above, 3.2–3.4
191. Pss. 59.9; 66.7; 67.10; 67.13; 67.17 (in text *hir*); 67.24 (in text *hir*); 68.5;
75.6; 81.7; 86.3; 102.5; 103.20; 109.3 (in text *hir*).
192. Cf. on this McNamara (ed.), 'Psalter Text', pp. 225-27.
193. Cf. McNamara (ed.), *Glossa in Psalmos*, p. 132.

tion) *h* stands opposite texts almost certainly dependent on Augustine's *Enarrationes in Psalmos*, or an abbreviation of them. The same may be true for *h* in the margin at Ps. 73.13. It is likely that *h* in these instances is intended to stand for *Hilarius* whom the compiler or his tradition seems to have regarded as the author of the *Enarrationes*.[194]

(4)   *h opposite unidentified texts.* Together with the above, there are some instances in which I have failed to identify the text accompanying a marginal source ascription *h*.[195] This may be due to the fact that the marginal ascription mark has been misplaced either in the original or by a later copyist.

(5)   *hir opposite texts from Jerome's* Commentarioli. There are four instances of this.[196]

(6)   *hir opposite texts from the Epitome of Julian.* There are six or seven instances of this.[197]

(7)   *hir opposite a biblical Psalter text.* At Ps. 94.3[198] *hir* stands opposite a Gallican-*Romanum* Psalter rendering of Ps. 95.5, given as a gloss on Ps. 94.3. It is possible that *hir* in this instance was intended to indicate the preceding gloss which is for the Epitome of Julian.

(8)   *hir opposite unidentified texts.* At Pss. 49.2; 93.3 (and possibly 101.11) *hir* stands opposite unidentified texts. In the case of Ps. 101.11, texts from the Epitome of Julian precede and follow.

(9)   *hil opposite texts from Augustine's* Enarrationes. This is so for the beginning of the second and allegorical exposition of Ps. 133.[199] *Hil* in this instance stands for Hilarius, the presumed author of the *Enarrationes*.

194. See below, 11.3.e; for texts see McNamara (ed.), *Glossa in Psalmos*, p. 53 n. *248.

195. At Pss. 44.10, 11, 13, 15; 48.8; 64.8; 67.6, 7, 18; 70, heading; 86.5; 103.20.

196. At Pss. 71.3; 104, heading; 118, heading; 119.1.

197. At Pss. 47.14, 15; 49.3; 49.22 (apparently); 51.10; 101.10 and possibly 101.12 (see McNamara [ed.], *Glossa in Psalmos*, p. 207).

198. McNamara (ed.), *Glossa in Psalmos*, p. 199.

199. McNamara (ed.), *Glossa in Psalmos*, p. 287.

11.2. *Sources Mentioned in Full or by Abbreviation in the Text*

(1)   *hir* occurs five times before excerpts from Jerome's *Commentarioli in Psalmos.*[200]

(2)   *hir* occurs once (at Ps. 131.10)[201] before a text from the Epitome of Julian.

(3)   *Hierunimus* is written in full in the heading to Ps. 104,[202] where it probably refers to a statement attributed to Jerome in a psalm preface.

(4)   *Hilarius* is written out in full at Ps. 86.1[203] in reference to a statement which almost certainly depends on Augustine's *Enarrationes in Psalmos* or an abridgement of them, and also in the heading of Ps. 104,[204] presumably with reference to a statement attributed to Hilary in some psalm preface.

(5)   *Eucherius* is written out in full in a comment on Ps. 90.6,[205] and introduces some words from Eucherius's *Formulae spiritalis intellegentiae.*

(6)   The names *Agustinus* and *Grigorius* occur in the heading to Ps. 104.[206] The words attributed to them appear to have been drawn from a psalm preface rather than from genuine works of theirs.

11.3. *Authorities Revealed through Source Analysis*

11.3.a. *The Julian Epitome.* Analysis reveals that the chief source used by the compiler was the work that has already in these pages been often referred to as the Julian Epitome, or the Epitome of Julian, that is, the abbreviated commentary on the Psalms based on Julian of Eclanum's translation of the commentary of Theodore of Mopsuestia.[207] This work is preserved principally in the Milan Codex Amb. C 301 inf. In this codex, fols. 14a1-146d34, we have a Latin commentary on the Psalter

200. At Pss. 67.17, 24; 68.22; 73, heading; 109.3.
201. McNamara (ed.), *Glossa in Psalmos*, p. 282.
202. McNamara (ed.), *Glossa in Psalmos*, p. 216.
203. McNamara (ed.), *Glossa in Psalmos*, p. 182.
204. McNamara (ed.), *Glossa in Psalmos*, p. 216.
205. McNamara (ed.), *Glossa in Psalmos*, p. 194.
206. McNamara (ed.), *Glossa in Psalmos*, p. 216.
207. De Coninck and d'Hont (eds.), *Theodori*; review by M. McNamara in *Irish Theological Quarterly* 46 (1979), pp. 305-308.

with Theodorean exegesis. It has been established by scholars, and by Mgr R. Devreesse and A. Vaccari in particular, that this commentary is actually composite. In fols. 14ai-39d22 we have a full Latin translation (by Julian of Eclanum) of Theodore's Greek commentary on Ps. 1.1–16.11a. At fol. 39d23, at Ps. 16.11a, the form of exegesis changes abruptly and without the reader being notified. From there to the end of the commentary we no longer have the full translation, but instead a briefer treatment of the subject, an abbreviation or Epitome which is based on Julian's translation but is not by Julian himself. It is natural to presume that this Epitome once covered the entire Psalter. The first portion of it apparently got lost and was replaced in the tradition represented by Codex Amb. C 301 inf. by the full translation of Theodore.

While the fullest text of the Epitome is found in the Milan Codex, we have excerpts from it in a number of works: the Hiberno-Latin *Eclogae tractatorum in Psalterium* (second half of eighth century);[208] the introduction to the Psalter in the one-volume Hiberno-Latin commentary on the entire Bible designated 'Das Bibelwerk' (late eighth century) by Dr Bernhard Bischoff; in the Irish Double Psalter of Rouen (MS Rouen, Bibl. mun. 24 [A.40 [tenth century]; in a Dublin fragment (MS Trinity College, TCD H 3 18) from a sister Codex of this; in a fragment of Ps. 13.6, 7 in a codex (Oxford, Bodl. 826 [S. C. 27151]) written in Normandy in the eleventh century; and in our codex, Pal. lat. 68. Together with these we may also include the evidence of the introductory material in the *Tituli Psalmorum* of Pseudo-Bede and in the so-called Psalter of Charlemagne.

From Ps. 16.11b onwards all these works are witness of one and the same Epitome. Texts from this in the *Eclogae tractatorum in Psalterium* are introduced as *hir. in his.* and in 'Das Bibelwerk' under the rubric *Iosepus*.

With regard to the corresponding commentary on Pss. 1.1–16.11a in these same texts, the tradition divides into two. On the one hand we have the Milan Codex, Amb C 301 inf. and the *Eclogae tractatorum in Psalterium* (introduced as *hir. in his*)[209] with the full translation of Theodore's commentary. On the other hand we have the Psalter of

---

208. See McNamara, 'Psalter Text' (reprinted above) for these various Latin texts: for the *Eclogae*, above pp. 50-51; 'Das Bibelwerk', pp. 42-44; Double Psalter of Rouen, and Dublin Codex, pp. 58-61; excerpts from the *Eclogae* edited by M. Sheehy above pp. 124-31.

209. See preceding note.

Rouen and 'Das Bibelwerk'. In the former of these we have not a single trace of the Theodorean commentary in the glosses before Ps. 16.11b,[210] although it is extensively used from there in the end. The same is true of 'Das Bibelwerk': the excerpts under the rubric Iosepus for psalms before Ps. 16.11b[211] are identical with those of the Psalter of Rouen, in so far as these latter are decipherable. The same, it would appear, holds true for the Psalms 1–16 in the *Tituli Psalmorum* of Pseudo-Bede and in the so-called Psalter of Charlemagne: these so far as can be ascertained

---

210. As already noted by the present writer, 'Psalter Text', p. 240, and amply demonstrated by De Coninck and d'Hont (eds.), *Theodori*, pp. xlii-xliv.

211. The excerpts in 'Das Bibelwerk' for Pss. 4–17 under the rubric Iosepus are as follows (citations from the Paris MS. Bibl. Nat. lat. 11561): 'IOS. iiii. *"Irascimini et nolite peccare"* (Ps. 43). *id est in uos ipsos furorem conuertite, quia uana idola dilexistis. "Et nolite peccare". id est Dei potentia'* (some letters—apparently IOS—stroked out after this) (fol. 56v, col. 2,28)—*"uiiii. IOSEPUS. 'Periit memoria eorum cum sonitu et Dominus"* (Ps. 9.7). *id est sicut sonitus aliquis cito pertransit aures audientium ita memoria peccatorum obliuioni tradetur'* (fol. 57r, col. 2, 11). An identical gloss on Ps. 9.7 is to be found in the Psalter of Rouen (p. 15, last gloss, left margin). In 'Das Bibelwerk', fol. 57v, col. 1, 12-29 we have a series of glosses from *Iosepus* on Pss. 15–17, i.e. on Pss. 15.4; 16.4; 16.14; 17.26; 17.46. The first two of these (before Ps. 16.11b), also in the Rouen Psalter (pp. 27 and 29), are not from the commentary found in Cod. Amb. C 301 inf. Those on passages after 16.11b are either identical with texts from the Epitome or to be compared with them. The text of 'Das Bibelwerk', fol. 57v, col. 1, reads: '*IOSEPUS. "Non congregabo conuenticula eorum de sanguinibus"* (Ps. 154). *id est non ibi conuenticula collegam ubi cotidie sanguinis effusio exercetur. "Ut ne loquatur os meum opera hominum"* (Ps. 16.4). *id est ut nullo timore coactus in hominibus uel in operibus eorum. id est in idolis, confidam, quorum spes uana est. XVI. "Domine a paucis de terra diuide eos"* (Ps. 16.14). *id est disperge eos malos a paucis sanctus. "De absconditis"* (16.14). *id est suppliciis* (3rd i interl.). *"Saturatis filii"* (Ps. 16.14). *id est hoc uult dicere: Ita illos puni, ut neque ipsis filiis parcas, sed reple miseriis* (3rd i interl.). *XVII. IOSEPUS. "Cum sancto sanctus eris" reliqua* (Ps. 17.26). *Mitis sis bonis et seuerus malis; "filii alieni mentiti sunt mihi"* (Ps. 17.46). *id est metu et necessitate conpulsi, dixerunt nihil uelle nisi seruire.'* For gloss 2° and 3° on Ps. 16.4, see the Epitome of Julian, De Coninck and d'Hont (eds.), *Theodori*, pp. 88, 222-27; on Ps. 17.26, De Coninck and d'Hont (eds.), *Theodori*, pp. 95, 145-46 (on Ps. 17.27), on Ps. 17.46, De Coninck and d'Hont (eds.), *Theodori*, pp. 97, 234-35. The remaining texts of 'Das Bibelwerk' under the rubric '*Iosepus*' are all from the Epitome. They are as follows: Ps. 20.13 (fol. 58rl); Ps. 28.3, 7 (fol. 58v1); Ps. 38.7 (fol. 59rl); Ps. 44.2 (fol. 59v1); Ps. 47.9, 10 (fol. 59vl); Ps. 50.6, 7 (fol. 59v2); Ps. 59.8 (fol. 60r2); Ps. 61.12 (fol. 60r2); Ps. 63.7; 67.5 (fol. 60vi); Ps. 73.5, 12, 15 (fol. 61r1-2); Ps. 75.11 (fol. 61r2); Ps. 86 (fol. 61v1-2); Ps. 77.20 (fol. 6 2r2).

correspond to the headings and the glosses of the corresponding section of the Psalter of Rouen.[212]

In his critical edition of Julian's commentary, L. De Coninck had shown that the Theodorean material in Pal. lat. 68 came to the compiler through the Epitome,[213] not through the fuller translation. The same scholar has studied the quality of the text of the Epitome used by the compiler. He notes that the compiler makes numerous mistakes and conjectural corrections in the places where he intends to transcribe his source textually. Nonetheless, De Coninck believes that at the basis of the compiler's excerpts there lies a manuscript much more exact than that of Codex Amb. C 301 inf., one which contained some readings which in the Milan Codex are found *in margine* or *supra lineam*.

About a third of the Latin glosses in Pal. lat. 68 are from the Epitome. In fact there are only two or three psalms in the gloss which have not borrowed something from it (Pss. 96, 160; cf. Ps. 98). The amount borrowed varies from a brief text or two (Pss. 82.2; 86.1, 14; 116, heading 124.7; 133.1; 135.8) to practically the entirety of the glosses (in Pss. 137–39).

The source ascription within the text itself indicates that the compiler believed this commentary to be a work of Jerome, since a text from it in Ps. 131.10 is introduced as *hir*. The marginal source ascriptions *hir* and *h* confirm this, at least as far as the transmission history of the text is concerned. The fact that a text from it at Ps. 86.4 carries the marginal ascription *hist* shows that the tradition was aware of the nature of its

---

212. The *Tituli Bedae* are published in *PL* 93, cols. 477-1104. For the manuscripts see Fischer, 'Bedae de Titulis psalmorum liber', pp. 90-110, especially 95-97. For the Psalter of Rouen, see De Coninck and d'Hont (eds.), *Theodori*, especially p. xliii n. 245. The historical sections of this Psalter's Tituli have yet to be published. I print some of them here, together with the corresponding texts of the so-called Psalter of Charlemagne: Ps. 1 (only partly legible in photocopies from a microfilm)...*docet quae merces bona opera...et de Ioseph posse intelligi qui corpus Domini sepelibit et de his qui ad spectacula...' Ps. — Bede*; Psalter of Charlemagne illegible. — Ps. IX (in left-hand margin): '*Orat Dauid Dominum pro dolosis cogitationibus filii sui gratias agens quod eas non sequeretur effectus; uel Ezech(ias) de interritu assirii exercitu*' (= *Tituli Psalmorum* of Ps. — Bede). The Psalter of Charlemagne: *Ita inscribitur: Pro ocultis Absalon. Depraecatus est Deum gratiasquae Deus reddidit quod (?) eos affectus potentiae Deo proibente non secutus sit. Siue persona Ezechiae ostenditur gratias agentis Deo qui tanta in populum Dei molestus est. Vox Ezechiae (lege: ecclesiae?) dicentis laudes Deo.*

213. De Coninck and d'Hont (eds.), *Theodori*, p. xlii.

exposition. In both these points, I may note again, the gloss of Pal. lat. 68 agrees with the *Eclogae tractatorum in Psalterium* of the late eighth century where this commentary is described as *hir. in his.*

11.3.b. *Jerome's* Commentarioli in Psalmos.[214] The compiler of the gloss must have had access to a copy of this work. Source analysis reveals that he used it rather extensively,[215] especially in view of the brevity of the *Commentarioli* and the number of psalms which they leave without any comment. The compiler also knew it as a work of Jerome, citing it as *h* and *hir*. He also appears to have known it as an independent work, not as part of a larger one (such as the *Breviarium in Psalmos*) which it was later to become. This we can deduce from the use made of it in the heading to Psalm 72, in which Pal. lat. 68 cites the relevant section of the *Commentarioli* and goes on (as the *Commentarioli* do) to comment on part of v. 7. Pal. lat. 68 then gives glosses on vv. 1-7 from other sources, citing another text from the *Commentarioli* for v. 7.[216]

11.3.c. *Jerome's* Tractatus siue Homiliae in Psalmos.[217] A text introduced in the comment on Ps. 83.2 as coming from Jerome (*Hirunimus ait*)[218] seems to depend on the *Tractatus in Psalmos*. The same text is already referred to in the heading to Psalm 41.[219] A gloss on Ps. 132.1 also seems to depend on the *Tractatus*, as do some other glosses. A major difficulty in identifying texts from the *Tractatus* is that there is no

214. G. Morin (ed.), *Commentarioli in Psalmos* (CCSL, 72; Turnhout: Brepols, 1959), pp. 177-245.

215. Texts occur in glosses on Pss. 40.11, 41 heading; 43.7; 44.1; 50.6; 55 heading; 57.4, 7, 9; 58.7; 59.9; 61.12; 66.7; 67.10, 14, 15, 17, 24, 26, 34; 68.14, 15, 22, 24, 26; 76.11, 19; 81.7; 83.7; 86.4, 5; 88.16; 89.9; 95.11; 96.10; 102.5; 103.20, 26, 104 heading; 108.6; 109.1 110 heading; 111 heading; 112 heading; 113.24; 115.11, 15; 117.27, 118 heading, 119 heading (introduction to Gradual Pss.); 1; 122 heading, 133.1 134.7; 136 heading, 2, 3, 4, 7 (in the second exposition of this psalm), 138.7-8, 143.3; 144; heading. The extent of the borrowing is all the clearer when we recall that Jerome has no *Commentarioli* on 23 Psalms: Pss. 42, 45–46, 49, 52–54, 56, 60, 63, 69–70, 91, 127, 129–130, 137, 141–42, 147–150.

216. McNamara (ed.), *Glossa in Psalmos*, p. 149.

217. G. Morin, *Tractatus sive homeliae in Psalmos* (CCSL, 78; Turnhout: Brepols, 1958).

218. McNamara (ed.), *Glossa in Psalmos*, p. 178.

219. McNamara (ed.), *Glossa in Psalmos*, pp. 93-94.

verbatim citation from them in Pal. lat. 68. The *Tractatus*, which are homiletic and verbose, do not lend themselves to verbatim citations.

11.3.d. *Jerome's* Liber interpretationis[220] *and Letters 30 and 73.*[221] Since Adamnan of Iona very probably had access to a copy of Jerome's *Liber interpretationis hebraicorum nominum*,[222] we may presume that the author of a work like that under consideration (which appears to have originated in the same milieu) would also have had access to a copy. There is a possibility that it influenced glosses on Psalms 103[223] and 127.[224] The influence, if any, however, may have been only indirect. The same may have been the case with regard to Jerome's Letters nos. 30 and 73—the former on the meaning of the letters of the Hebrew alphabet, which may have been used in Psalm 118,[225] the latter on Melchizedek, which may have influenced a gloss on Ps. 109.4.[226]

11.3.e. *St Augustine's* Enarrationes in Psalmos.[227] St Augustine is mentioned by name (*Agustinus*) with regard to the explanation of *Alleluia* in Psalm 104: *Secundum Agustinum 'Alleluia', 'Saluum me fac Domine'*, This however, is the explanation of Hosanna, not of Alleluia and is drawn from some psalm preface, rather than from a work of Augustine.

Source analysis does reveal that the compiler has made extensive use of Augustine's *Enarrationes in Psalmos*,[228] or possibly an abbreviation

220. P. de Lagarde (ed.), *Liber interpretationis hebraïcorum nominum* (CCSL, 72; Turnhout: Brepols, 1959).

221. I. Hilberg (ed.), *Hieronymi Epistulae* (CCSL, 54 and 55; Vienna, 1910, 1912).

222. See D. Meehan (ed.), *Adamnan's De locis sanctis* (SLH, 3; Dublin Institute for Advanced Studies, 1958; repr. 1983), p. 13.

223. See McNamara (ed.), *Glossa in Psalmos*, pp. 212, 214.

224. See McNamara (ed.), *Glossa in Psalmos*, p. 277.

225. See McNamara (ed.), *Glossa in Psalmos*, pp. 245-63.

226. See McNamara (ed.), *Glossa in Psalmos*, p. 234.

227. E. Dekkers and J. Fraipont (eds.), *Sanctus Augustinus: Enarrationes in Psalmos* (CCSL, 38–40; Turnhout: Brepols, 1956).

228. As indicated in the source analysis of Pss. 50.6; 52, heading; 57.5; 73: heading, 2, 12, 14, 15, 13-14 2nd exposition (McNamara [ed.], *Glossa in Psalmos*, pp. 154-55); 74.9; 77.3, 34, 37; 86.1, 3, 5; 87: heading; 103.4, 15, 19; 118: heading; 118.17 heading (p. 247); 119.4, 6 and in the second exposition of the Gradual Psalms: 120 (p. 266); 121 (pp. 267-69); 122 (pp. 270-71); 123 (pp. 271-72); 124 (p. 274); 125 (p. 273); 126 (pp. 275-76); 127 (pp. 277-78); 128 (p. 279), 129 (p. 280), 130 (p. 281), 131 (pp. 281-82), 132 (pp. 283-85); 134.4, 3, 7, 10; 135.4; 148.11.

of them.[229] Dependence on the *Enarrationes* is clearest in the second exposition which the gloss gives for the gradual psalms (Ps. 119–33). Nowhere do we have a direct citation from the *Enarrationes* in the gloss. They are, in any case, generally too lengthy for this. The probable use of the *Enarrationes* is indicated by the theology and terminology of the passages in question. From probability we pass practically to certainty in the gloss on Ps. 132.3:[230] '*Sicut ros Hermon*'. id est lumen exalt<ta>tum interpraetatur, supernam gratiam Christi significat. 'Sitper mon<tes> Sion'. id est aeclesiam.

The peculiar interpretation of *Hermon* as *lumen exaltatum* is that given by Augustine in his comment on the passage.[231] Even though Augustine says that he got his interpretation *ab his qui illam* (that is, the Hebrew) *linguam noverunt*,[232] it is an explanation I have failed to find in any other interpreter on the Psalms. The classical interpretation of *Hermon* (or Ermon), that given by Jerome,[233] Hilary,[234] Cassiodorus,[235] is *anathema, damnatio anathema tristitiae, anathema moeroris*. The dependence of Pal. lat. 68 on Augustine is rendered more probable still by the reading *super mont(es) or mont(em) Sion*. *Super montes* is the reading of Augustine; *super montem* that of the Veronensis and the Mozarabic. The *Gallicanum* and the *Romanum* both have *in (monte, montem)* instead of *super*.

Nowhere in the work is any of these texts ascribed to Augustine. As already noted, on one occasion within the commentary one of the texts

229. If an abbreviation was used, it was not that of Prosper of Aquitaine, his *Expositio Psalmorum* (*PL* 51, 277-426).

230. McNamara (ed.), *Glossa in Psalmos*, p. 286; see Dekkers and Fraipont (eds.), *Sanctus Augustinus*, p. 1933, 1-9 (no. 11).

231. Dekkers and Fraipont (eds.), *Sanctus Augustinus*, p. 1933, no. 11, 6-8.

232. Dekkers and Fraipont (eds.), *Sanctus Augustinus*, p. 1933. Yet in his *Enarratio* (no. 12) on Ps. 41.7 Augustine understands differently: '*Hermoniim anathematio interpretatur*' (Dekkers and Fraipont [eds.], *Sanctus Augustinus*, p. 469, 30). Similarly in the *Enarratio* (no. 13) on Ps. 88.12: '*Hermon autem interpretatur Anathema eius*' (Dekkers and Fraipont [eds.], *Sanctus Augustinus*, p. 1228, 11-12).

233. Lagarde (ed.), *Liber interpretationis*, pp. 86, 93, 119: *Commentarioli in Psalmos* 132.3 (CCSL, 72, p. 240); *Tractatus in Psalmos* (CCSL, 78, pp. 281, 177-78).

234. Hilary, *Tractatus super Psalmos* (A. Zingerle [ed.]; CSEL, 22; Vienna, 1891), pp. 689, 9-10.

235. M. Adriaen (ed.), *Magni Aurelii Cassiodori expositio* (CCSL, 98; Turnhout: Brepols), in Ps. 132.2.

(Ps. 86.1) is ascribed to Hilarius (the name written in full), while another has *hil* written opposite it in the margin (Ps. 133.1). It seems that the compiler believed that the work from which he was excerpting was by Hilary.

11.3.e. *Eucherius of Lyons.*[236] Eucherius is mentioned by name in a gloss on Ps. 90.6: *demonio meridiano.* Eucherius (written in full) a *demonio manifesto.* The text is from Eucherius's *Formula spiritalis intellegentiae.*[237] The same work probably influenced other glosses in the work.[238] The compiler also knew and used Eucherius's other work, *Instructionum libri duo.* He has a citation from Book I at Ps. 102.5 and from Book II at Ps. 61.10. A gloss on Ps. 79.14 seems to depend on Book I.

11.3.f. *Letter 23 'Ad Dardanum' of Pseudo-Jerome.* The work headed '*Ad Dardanum*': '*De diversis generibus musicorum*', printed in Migne[239] as no. 23 of the spurious letters of St Jerome, is considered by modern scholars to be a composition of the Carolingian age. It has even been tentatively ascribed to Rabanus Maurus (776–856 CE).[240] It has a rich manuscript tradition: B. Lambert[241] lists 61 manuscripts, the oldest being of the ninth century.

Irish evidence has a direct bearing on the date and the presumed authorship of this work. There is a long citation from it (agreeing verbatim with the text printed in Migne) in the St Gall manuscript of the Irish *Eclogae tractatorum in Psalterium* (late eighth century), containing a

236. C. Wotke (ed.), *Sancti Eucharei Lugdanensis* (CSEL, 31; Vienna, 1894).

237. Wotke (ed.), *Sancta Eucharei*, p. 31, line 7.

238. E.g. Pss. 120.1; 125.6.

239. *PL* 30 (1st edn, 1846), cols. 213-215 (2nd edn, 1865, cols. 219-223).

240. Cf. E. Dekkers, *Clavis patrum latinorum* (SE, 3; Steenbrugge: Abbatia Sancti Petri; Brugge: C. Beyaert; The Hague: M. Nijhoff, 2nd edn, 1961), no. 633, p. 145, who refers to R. Hammerstein's opinion (in *Archiv für Musikwissenschaft* 15 [1959], pp. 117-34) that it was the work of Rabanus. H. Robbins Bittermann, however, believes that Rabanus merely copied an earlier text (cf. 'The Organ in the Early Middle Ages', *Speculum* 4 [1929], pp. 390-410, especially 398-99). In the 3rd edition of the *Clavis* (Turnhout: Brepols; Steenbrugge: Abbatia Sancti Petri, 1995), p. 221 agrees with the view that it is slightly older than Rabanus.

241. B. Lambert, *Bibliotheca Hieronymiana manuscripta: La tradition manuscrite des oeuvres de Saint Jérôme*, 4-3A (7 vols.; Instrumenta Patristica, 4; Steenbruge: Sint-Pietersabdij, The Hague, M. Nijhoff, 1970), no. 323, p. 108.

description of the organ, and carrying AG. (presumably Agustinus) as marginal ascription.[242] Substantially the same text on the organ is found in the Irish 'Bibelwerk' (likewise late eighth century),[243] where it is ascribed to ORIG. presumably Origen (MS. Clm 14267, fol. 34r-v). This evidence tells against Rabanus' authorship of the work and the presumed Carolingian date of composition. The same letter is the source of some of the glosses in Pal. lat. 68 (Pss. 80.1; 107.2; 150.3, 4), a fact which obliges us to push the date of composition back further still.

11.3.g. *Adamnan's* De locis sanctis.[244] This work by the man who was to become the ninth abbot of Iona in 679 was composed about 683–86. The account it provides of Arculf's description of Jerusalem seems to be the source for a variant explanation of Ps. 45.5 in Pal. lat. 68. The texts are as follows:[245]

Pal. lat. 68	*De Locis sanctis* I, i, 8-10.
Aliter: 'Fluminis inpetus'. id est in solempnitate semptimbris concuinat tur (?) urbs a multis et plateae eius equorum stercore; et dehinc pluiae magnae fiunt, et de monte Sion torrens erumpit qui mundat ciuitatem; sic aduentus Christi mundauit aeclesiam gentium.	*Diuersarum gentium undique prope innumera multitudo duodecimo die mensis Septembris anniuersario more in Hierusolimis conuenire solet ad commercia motuis uenditionibus et emtionibus peragenda. Unde fieri necesse est ut per aliquot dies in eadem hospita ciuitate diuersorum hospitentur turbae populorum; quorum plurima camelorum et equorum asinorumque numerositas nec non et boum masculorum, diuersarum uectores rerum, per illas politanas plateas stercorum abhominationes propriorum passim sternit, quorum nidor herentum non medio-*

242. MS. St. Gall, Stifsbibliothek 261, p. 148. This section is missing in the Munich MS. (Clm 14715, fol. 1r-56v) of the *Eclogae*.

243. MS. Clm 14276, fol. 34r-v. In 'Wendepunkte', p. 229, Dr Bischoff draws attention to this noteworthy description of the organ, without identifying the source.

244. Meehan (ed.), *Adamnan's*.

245. Meehan (ed.), *Adamnan's*, pp. 40, 24-37; McNamara (ed.), *Glossa in psalmos*, p. 102.

> *criter ciuibus inuehit molestiam, quae*
> *et ambulandi inpeditionem praebent.*
> *Mirum dictu, post diem, supra mem-*
> *oratarum recessionis cum diuersis*
> *turmarum iumentis nocte subsequente*
> *immensa pluuiarum copia de nubibus*
> *effusa super eandem discendit ciuita-*
> *tem, quae totas abstergens abhomin-*
> *abiles de plateis sordes ablutam ab*
> *inmunditiis fieri facit cam.*

I have failed to find any other text outside of *De locis sanctis* on such a cleansing of Jerusalem, nor have the editors of the work indicated any.

11.3.h. *Hilary, Gregory the Great, Isidore of Seville.* Hilary and Gregory are mentioned by name. I have failed to find any evidence of the use of their works in the gloss, including in this Paterius's collection of the biblical texts of Gregory. The author does not appear to have had access to them. The same holds true for the works of Isidore of Seville. The gloss does have a number of etymologies but not one of these seems to be derived from Isidore.[246]

12. *Biblical Interpretation in Palatino-Latinus 68*

12.1. *The Senses of Scripture*
On one occasion (on Ps. 44.2) mention is made in the gloss of a three-fold sense of Scripture. Elsewhere, however, we have a twofold schema, in which the historical sense in contrasted with another, variously called

---

246. The sources of the etymologies used (when identifiable) can be seen in the apparatus to the individual occurrences: *saltirium, cithara, timpanum* (Ps. 150.3; 80.3; 107.2); *Alleluia* (Ps. 104.1); *aquila* (Ps. 102.5); *aspis* (Ps. 57.5); *basiliscus* (Ps. 90.13); Beboth (= Behemoth) and Leviathan (Ps. 103.26); *bruchus, eruchus* (Ps. 104.34); *ceruus* (Ps. 41.2); *cinomia* (Ps. 77.45); *cuturnix* (Ps. 104.40); *draco* (Ps. 148.7); *erinacius* (Ps. 103.18); *hirodius* (Ps. 103.17); *leo* (Ps. 57.7; 90.13; 103.21); *necticorax* (Ps. 101.7); *passer* (Ps. 123.7); *pellicanus* (Ps. 101.7); *ranae* (Ps. 104.30); *scinifes* (Ps. 104.31); *turtur* (Ps. 83.4); *murus* (Ps. 77.47); *ramnus* (Ps. 57.10); *crystallum* (Ps. 147.17); *topazion* (Ps. 118.127); *angelus et spiritus* (Ps. 103.4); *dedrachma* (Ps. 61.10); *deplois* (Ps. 108.29); *Deuteronomium* (Ps. 118.32); *oleum* (Ps. 108.24); *saraphin* (Ps. 103.4); *tabula* (Ps. 118.25); *melch* (Ps. 52, heading). No single source seems to have been followed by the compiler for his etymologies.

the spiritual, moral or allegorical—all three apparently meaning the
same thing in this work. We have the threefold sense in a gloss on Ps.
44.2:[247] '*Haec quae sequntur conueniunt Salamoni historialiter, et
Christo* spiritaliter *et sancto* moraliter.'

This is very close to the explanation of these three senses in the four
fold sense as set forth in the *Old-Irish Treatise of the Psalter.* 'The first
story refers to...Solomon, the *síens* (spiritual sense) to Christ...the
morality to every saint'.[248] The only term used to designate the historical sense, or literal interpretation, of a passage is *historia*, most often
used adverbially as *historialiter*. In some texts *historialiter* is contrasted
with *spiritaliter*, either explicitly or more often implicitly. Thus on Ps.
109.3 '*ante luciferum*'. *id est ante Saul.* Spiritaliter *haec Christo conueniunt, ut Hirunimus dicit.*[249] The words introduce a text from Jerome's
Commentarioli, and the text implicitly takes the literal sense of the biblical passage to refer to Saul. A number of glosses in Pal. lat. 68 are
introduced as *spiritaliter*.[250] In the heading to Psalm 113, the mystical
heading from the St Columba series is introduced as *spiritaliter*, the
earlier heading (presumably taken as the literal one) being taken as *Vox
Dauid de priscis*.

Instead of *spiritaliter* the gloss often uses the term *allagoricae*, with
no apparent difference in meaning, for example '*cum habitantibus
Cedar*' (Ps. 119.6). *Haec est uox filiorum Sarrae uxoris liberae contra
filios Agar ancellae; allagoricae, id est haec est uox filiorum aeclesiae
contra filios sinagorae.* Or again on Ps. 119.7; '*cum his qui oderunt
pacem*'...*id est cum Saul et socis eius...* (citing the Julian Epitome);
*allagoricae: non sufficit apud aeclesiam habere pacem cum pacem
habentibus, sed cum his qui oderunt pacem desideral ut sit pacifica.*
The margin here has *M*, which stands for *moraliter*, the moral sense
being the equivalent of the spiritual for the compiler. In a gloss on Ps.
131.1 *allagoricae* is contrasted with *iuxta historiam*. '*Memento Domine
Dauid*'...*Quidem hunc salmum, Dauid regi conuenire* secundum histo-

247. McNamara (ed.), *Glossa in Psalmos*, p. 99.

248. *OIT*, lines 312-320, pp. 30-31.

249. See McNamara (ed.), *Glossa in Psalmos*, p. 234. This text of Pal. lat. 68
introduces a passage from Jerome's *Commentarioli in Psalmos*, although the connection of Jerome's text with the allegorical (spiritual) interpretation of the psalm is
hard to see. In any event, Jerome understood the psalm as a direct prophecy of
Christ.

250. E.g. Pss. 44.10, 11, 13; 64.10; 66.7; 67.13, 18, 31; 73.12, 13-17; 75.6; 112.9.

riam *dicunt... Allagoricae autem Christo hic salmus coaptatur.*[251]
The term *moraliter* is used often instead of *spiritaliler* or *allagoricae*.
The interpretation thus described is often contrasted with the historical
understanding, for example, Ps. 86.4 (abbreviated as *Mor*) introducing a
text from Jerome, which follows on an excerpt for the Epitome,
described in the margin as *hist* (that is, *historialiter*). We have a second
occurrence in text alone (abbreviated again as *Mor*) at Ps. 119.1. Occasionally *moraliter* is written in both text and margins,[252] abbreviated as
M.; at other times *M* (once *Mor*, but *-or* later) in margins with another
term such as *aliter* in text.[253] In a few instances we have *M* (*moraliter*)
in the margins without any corresponding term in the text.[254]
    A study of the occurrences of *Moraliter* in Pal. lat. 68 shows that,
apart from the gloss on Ps. 44.2, the compiler uses the term as the equivalent of *spiritaliter* or *allagoricae*. This is the older use of *moraliter*
(or of its equivalent *tropologice*).[255]

12.2. *Emphasis on the Historical Sense*
Throughout the entire gloss the emphasis is laid on the historical or literal sense of the psalms, that is, the interpretation which sees them as
primarily speaking of events of David's day or of later Old Testament
Jewish history. The tradition which the gloss enshrines is aware that
this is the manner of viewing the psalms found in the work we now call
the Julian Epitome, the source it uses principally and to which it occasionally refers as 'the historical commentary', *historialiter.*[256] The gloss

251. McNamara (ed.), *Glossa in Psalmos*, respectively pp. 266 (Ps. 119.6-7), 281
(Ps. 131.1).
    252. As in fol. 3v (p. 106); 10r (at Ps. 67.31, p. 140); fol. 18v (at Ps. 864, p. 183);
fol. 22r (at Ps. 95.7, p. 201); fol. 37v (at Ps. 119.4, p. 265); fol. 38r (at Ps. 121.2,
second exposition, p. 268); fol. 42r (at Ps. 134.7, p. 288).
    253. With *aliter* in text at Ps. 81.7; and especially in the second exposition of Pss.
121 (twice) fol. 38r, 122, 123 (twice), 124, 126, 127, 128, 130, 131, 132, 133, 136;
with *allagoricae* in text at Ps. 119.4, 6; with *spiritaliter* in text at Ps. 67.26.
    254. As at Pss. 67.7, 17, 24, 32; 68.22; Ps. 70 heading; 73.13; 86.4 (twice), 5
(twice); 109.3; 129: heading, 6.
    255. St Jerome, for instance, uses the term *tropologia* in the sense of *allegoria*;
see A. Penna, *Principi a carattere dell'esegesi di s. Gerolamo* (Scripta Pontifici
Instituti Biblica, 102; Rome: Biblical Institute Press, 1950), p. 116; also H. de
Lubac, *Exégèse médiévale: Les quatre sens de l'ecriture*, prem. partie, II (Paris,
1959), pp. 551-55.
    256. In the margins at Pss. 44.13 and 86.4, through the abbreviation *hist*. This

can also interpret the psalms of Christ and of Christian life but is aware that this is the spiritual, allegorical, moral, (tropological) interpretation.[257] This is the Antiochene and Theodorean manner of interpreting the psalms. Yet it would be inexact to say that the interpretation of the gloss is Theodorean, since it lays far more emphasis on interpreting the Psalms of David and his times than Theodore does.

The following is the nature of the historical interpretation of the gloss.

12.2.a. *The Text Interpreted of David and his Contemporaries*. The bulk of the historical interpretations in the gloss concerns David and his contemporaries: *Samuel* (40.12; 109.1 (bis), 3, 4; 118.105, 114); *Saul* (several references);[258] *Saul cum semini suo* (39.15); *Saul et domum (domus) eius* (42.1; 52.6; 58.6); *pro erumnis Saul* (heading of 54, 63, 120, 140); *Saul et Abisolon* (96.10); *Saul cum socis (suis)*[259] (several texts); *montes Giluae* (on death of Saul);[260] *David* (several references);[261] *David cum, socis suis* (several references);[262] *Agag* (109.1

same abbreviation is found in the margins at Ps. 109.15 to indicate a 'historical' interpretation in the commentary. The text of 109.3 introduces the historical interpretation as *iuxta historiam*. The exegesis of Ps. 44 is described thus: '*Haec quae sequntur conueniunt Salomon historialiter, et Christo spiritaliter, et sancto moraliter*' (McNamara, *Glossa in Psalmos*, p. 99). This 'historical' interpretation in the heading of Ps. 44 is described as *inertialis historia* and at the end of Ps. 109 (McNamara, *Glossa in Psalmos*, p. 235) as *historialis inhertia*. Otherwise, the terms designating the literal understanding of the text are not given.

257. Thus at Ps. 109.3 on the words *ante luciferum* (109.3) interpreted first as *ante Saul*: '*Spiritaliter haec Christo conueniunt ut Hirunimus dicit*'. *Spiritaliter* also introduces glosses in Pss. 44.10, 11, 13; 64.10; 66.7; 67.7, 13, 18, 31; 73.12, 13-16; 75.6; 112.9. The terms *moraliter* and *allagoricae* in the text (listed above, n. 253) serve the same purpose. Likewise the term *aliter*, in general.

258. Pss. 40, heading; 41.10; 43.8; 49.3; 51.3, 9 (twice); 52, heading, 1; 54.4, 13, 24; 55; heading, 5, 8; 56.2, 4; 57.11; 58.2; 63.7, 11; 64.5; 65.9; 70.4, 23; 73, heading; 85.2; 92.4; 96.5; 107.7; 109.1 (twice), 3; 114.3, 4; 117.3; 118.23. 46, 51, 69, 86, 98, 110, 121, 150, 161; 119, heading, 2, 3; 138.2; 139.11-12; 146.2.

259. 40.3, 6, 8; 53.5, 7, 9; 55.10; 62.10; 65.3, 12; 123.2; 140.10; 146.6. See also index s.v. 'Saul'.

260. Pss. 39.15; 53.7; 55.8; 62.10; 63.9, 10.

261. 40.2, 14 (twice); 41.7, 8; 42, heading; 44.8; 47.3; 49.3, 7, 23; 54.4, 14; 56.4; 57.11; 58.2, heading, 2; 60.7; 62.12; 63, heading; 64.3; 67.7; 69, heading; 71.2; 73, heading; 101.1; 107.3; 108, heading; 109.1, 2; 118.28, 122; 119.5; 126, heading; 142, heading; 143.3; 146.6. See also index s.v. ' Dauid'.

262. Pss. 52.7; 59.6; 63.11; 67.4; 89, heading (*Oratio Dauid pro socis*); 101.14 (*Dauid Pro se et pro socis dicit*); 107.7; 114.6 (*ego et socii mei*); 118.165 (*mihi et*

written as Achab); *Achitophel* (many references);[263] *Abisolon* (several references);[264] *Doec* (that is, Doeg, 51.8; 52.2); *Iob* (that is, Joab, 59.8; 108.6, 8, 11); *Abimelech* (heading 52); *Nouae* (that is, Nob), *sacerdotes in* (41.11; 52 heading; 52.5); *Golia* (143.16, 171, heading); *Philistini* (53.5); *Sephei* (53.5).

12.2.b. *Text Interpreted of the Assyrian Period.* A second numerous group of references in the gloss is to Hezekiah and his age. They are as follows: *Asse/i/ri* (mentioned relatively often);[265] Rasin (45 heading); Ezechia(s) (many references);[266] Sennacherib (*sencarib*) (45.10; 79.14; 139.2, 12).

12.2.c. *Text Interpreted of Babylonian Period, Exile and Return.* The references are as follows: *Babilonia* (several references);[267] *Caldei* (many references);[268] *Nabocodonosor* (79.14; 118.46); *exilium* (118.54, 86, 107); *captiui* and *captiuitas* (mentioned some 13 times in Ps. 118 and in 132 heading);[269] *Susanna et senes* (118.100); *Daniel* (*et tres*

socis meis); 131, heading. See also index s.v. 'Dauid'; McNamara (ed.), *Glossa in Psalmos*, p. 333.

263. Pss. 40.10; 54.10, 14, 22; 108.8, 31; 118.8, 31, 51, 98. In the glosses of the Montpellier Psalter (Unterkircher [ed.], *Die Glossen*), all these psalms (Ps. 118 excepted) are interpreted of the revolt of Ahitophel, who is generally linked with Absalom. See also McNamara (ed.), *Glossa in Psalmos*, index s.v. 'Achitophel'.

264. Pss. 40.10; 54.22, 24; 69, heading; 92.4; 95, heading; 96.3, 5, 10; 108, heading, 2, 6, 9, 31; 114.4; 118.23, 51, 69, 86, 98, 110, 113, 121, 122, 150, 161; 142: heading. Of these only Pss. 118 and 142 are interpreted of Absalom in the Montpellier Psalter.

265. Pss. 40.3; 45, heading; 47.5; 51.8; 52.1, 6; 70.4; 74.7, 9; 75.4, 6; 82, heading; 85, heading, 9; 86.4; 105.41; 114.4; 139, heading; 141, heading; 143, heading, 15.

266. Pss. 40, heading, 2, 4, 6, 8; 52, heading; 53, heading; 60.7; 64, heading; 75, heading; 76, heading; 85, heading; 90, heading, 16; 116.1; 139, heading; 141, heading; 142, heading; 143, heading.

267. Pss. 42, heading; 59, heading; 65, heading; 66, heading; 70, heading, 9; 72.1; 73, heading; 92.1; 94, heading; 100, heading; 101, heading; 118; 28, 54, 81 (heading to subsection); 123.2; 136, heading, 8; 144: heading, 20; 145.9.

268. Pss. 74.7; 105.41, 47; 106.3; 108.6; 117.22; 118.51, 69, 95, 96, 101, 110, 111, 113, 115, 121, 122, 137 (heading to subsection), 150 (heading to subsection), 155, 161; 123.5; 130.1 (*Caldea*); 135.24; 136.8.

269. Ps. 118.107, 116, 117, 133, 143, 145, heading, 153, heading, 154, 161, heading, 166, 169, heading, 174, 176. *Ex persona captiuorum* occurs about nine times in the same psalm, in headings at vv. 33, 41, 49, 57, 73, 145, 153, 161, 169.

Pueri) (118.23; headings of Pss. 97, 113, 130); *reuersio de Babilonia* (in headings of 17 Pss. and also possibly in those of 102 and 114); *Persi*, (105.47; 106.3; 136.8; 144.10); Cyrus (73.5; 136.8); *Medii* (104.47; 106.3; 142.10); Darius (73.5); Zerubbabel (146.2); *post reuersionem* (133.1).

12.2.d. *Text Interpreted of Maccabaean Period*. The references to the Maccabaean period are as follows: *Machabei* (relatively frequently),[270] *Greci* (73.3, 8, 10, 22; 74.7), Antiochus (107.7; 108, heading, vv. 6, 9, 31), Demetrius (73.3); Honias (54, heading); Simon (54.4, 13, 23, 24). The psalms really interpreted of Maccabean times are only Psalms 43, 54, 73, 108. There are references to Roman times in a few passages: *Romani* (106.3; 108.6, 11) Caesar (48.12) Titus and Vespasianus (79.14).

12.3. *Double Historical Reference*

The analysis carried out in the preceding section shows that the compiler's primary interest, or the primary interest of the tradition he represents, was in interpreting the Psalms of David and his contemporaries. Together with this they were also interpreted of events in Jewish history after David's time.

A feature peculiar to the gloss is a double or alternative reference of the same psalm, seeing it to refer to David and his time and/or to later Jewish history, for example, Hezekiah, Assyrians, Babylon, Maccabees. That his double reference was seriously intended is clear from the fact that it is found both in the headings and in the commentary proper. To illustrate by some examples (Ps. 40): '*Salmus Dauid*'. *Pro erumnis a Saul. Vox Ezechiae…'qui intellegit'* (v. 2). *id est Dauid uel Ezechias… 'inimicorum eius'* (v. 3). *id est Saul et sociorum eius; uel Assiriorum.* (Ps. 47) *Vox Dauid accepto regno. Vox Ezechiae…'Quoniam ecce reges'* (v. 5). *id est Assiriorum satrapae; uel reges terrae Israel aduersus Dauid. 'conuenerunt in unum'. id est aduersus Dauid uel Ezechiam.*

12.4. *Interpretation of the Messianic Psalms in Palatino-Latinus 68*

As is well known, Theodore regarded only four psalms as messianic in the strict sense, that is, as direct prophecies of Christ. These were

---

270. In headings to Pss. 46, 58, 59, 68, 82, 107, 108, and 118.33; also in Pss. 43.10, 12, 18; 78.4; 107.7.

Psalms 2, 8, 44, 109.[271] The other psalms understood of Christ in the New Testament he did not regard as directly messianic. The New Testament use of them would be through accommodation, or use by reason of similarity of circumstances. In view of the stress on the historical exegesis of Pal. lat. 68 we are not unduly surprised to find that it understands this latter group of 'messianic' psalms primarily as historical, referring to David's day or to later Jewish history, and only secondarily and *allagoricae* to Christ. Thus in the interpretation of Psalms 67, 68, 71, 108, 117 and 131.

What is surprising is the gloss's 'historical', non-messianic, interpretation of the two psalms (Pss. 44 and 109) taken by Theodore as messianic. In both cases the compiler appears to be transmitting a non-messianic interpretation which he has inherited, but with which he is personally unhappy.

Psalm 44 is interpreted in heading and glosses of David and Solomon. In so understanding the psalm the authority of Jerome, in his interpretation of Ecclesiastes, could be invoked.[272] No such authority could be invoked with regard to Psalm 109, the New Testament messianic psalm *par excellence*. In the gloss this psalm is interpreted of Saul and Samuel. The 'Lord' addressed in v. 1 is Samuel; *'ante luciferum'* is interpreted as *ante Saul*. Only in a spiritual sense (*spiritaliter*) is this particular text understood of Christ: *Spiritaliter haec Christo conuentiunt ut Hirunimus ait...*[273] This non-messianic interpretation is twice in the commentary and twice in the margins designated as 'historical', *hist.* (*historialiter*).[274]

---

271. Although not mentioned as a distinct group by Theodore, this interpretation is found for the individual psalms in his commentary and in the other Antiochene commentary attributed by some scholars to Diodorus of Tarsus, Theodore's teacher. The four are explicitly noted by Cosmas Indicopleustes in his *Cosmographia Christiana*, V, 123-134, published 551 CE; in Wanda Wolska-Conus (ed.), II, *Sources Chrétiennes*, 159, pp. 182-95 (Greek text with French trans.); ET in J.W. McCrindle, *The Christian Topography of Cosmas, an Egyptian Monk* (The Milkuyt Society, 98; London, 1897), pp. 187-94. For the situation in the commentary attributed to Diodorus see J.-M. Olivier (ed.), *Diodori Tarsensis Commentarii in Psalmos*. I. *Commentarii in Psalmos I–L* (CCSG, 6; Turnhout: Brepols: University Press, 1980), pp. lxxxiv-lxxxv.

272. *Commentarius in Ecclesiasten* (M. Adriaen [ed.]; CCSL, 72; Turnhout: Brepols, 1959), p. 250.

273. See McNamara (ed.), *Glossa in Psalmos*, p. 234.

274. McNamara (ed.), *Glossa in Psalmos*, pp. 234-35.

In what appears to be a personal comment, however, in both psalms the compiler rejects the 'historical' interpretation in favour of the messianic one. Thus in Psalm 44: *Totus hic salmus refertur ad Christum...licet ad Salomonem inertialis historia refertur*;[275] or as phrased at the end of the comment on Psalm 109: *Totus his salmus de Christo canitur, licet alii historialem inhertiam* (MS. *in hertiam) in eo contexunt, ut ostendimus.*[276]

Due to the acephalous nature of the manuscript which begins only with Psalm 39, we cannot be entirely certain how the gloss interpreted Psalms 2 and 8. However, in view of the close relationship of Pal. lat. 68 with the Psalter of Charlemagne, we can be reasonably sure that the exegesis was non-messianic as is the case in the Psalter of Charlemagne, and likewise in the *Tituli Psalmorum* of Pseudo-Bede and in the Psalter of Rouen, all three of which present the same tradition of exegesis with regard to these psalms. With regard to Psalm 2, the heading in the *Tituli Psalmorum* of Pseudo-Bede reads:

> *Generalem Dauid querimoniam facit ad Deum, quod regno sibi desuper dato, et gentes et populi Israel inviderent, communem ad omium correctionem dirigens* (*PL* 93, 489C).

The heading in the Psalter of Charlemagne reads:

> *Hic psalmus Dauid. Vox sociorum Dauid iurgentium quod gentes et Absalon persecuti sunt David. Vel vox Ezechiae* (MS: *Ecclesiae*) de *Assiris.*

The marginal glosses on this psalm in the *Hebraicum* of the Rouen Psalter[277] are difficult to read. The interlinear ones, however, are in keeping with the headings just given. '*Gentes*' of v. 1 is glossed as *Philistini;* '*tribus*' (v. 1) as *Abisolon cum socis;* '*aduersum Christum eius*' (v. 2) as *omnis rex Christus dicitur;* '*super Sion*' (v. 6) as *Hierusalem quia Abisolon quaerit;* '*ego hodie genui te*' (v. 7) as *in die electionis in regnum.*

Curiously enough, the glosses of the Montpellier Psalter,[278] otherwise given to messianic interpretation, contain a dual interpretation for Psalm 2: either referring it to Christ or to David, the latter apparently being taken as the 'historical' meaning. Thus, on v. 1: '*Psalmus Dauid.*

275. McNamara (ed.), *Glossa in Psalmos*, p. 99.
276. McNamara (ed.), *Glossa in Psalmos*, p. 235.
277. MS Rouen, Bibl. mun. 24 (A. 41), pages 2, 4.
278. Unterkircher (ed.), *Die Glossen*, pp. 75-77.

Quare fremuerunt' In hoc psalmo continetur manifeste de xpo et de dauid secundum hystoriam.[279] On v. 2: *'Adsteterunt reges terrae': Si in persona xpi...si autem in persona dauid, manifestum est, quia multae gentes aduersus dominum et aduersus xpm eius dauid, quia omnis unctus xps appelabatur.*[280] On v. 7: *'ego hodie genui te': Si ex persona dauid, quando dedit ei dominus potestatem super omnes gentes.*[281]

In the heading for Psalm 8 in the Psalter of Charlemagne we read, after a reference to *'Saul in monte Gelboe': In quo admiratur profeta Dei potentiam per quam gubernat cunctam animalem (*lege: *mundi molem) gratiasque agit qui (sic.* MS*) tantas omnis memoriam habere dignatus est.*

This heading seems to be a corruption of the one found in the *Tituli* of Pseudo-Bede (*PL* 93, 526D):

> *Admiratur propheta Dei potentiam, per quam gubernat cunctam mundi molem, gratiasque agit quod tantus creator hominis memoriam sit habere dignatus est.*

The same reading occurs in the Psalter of Rouen and in the glosses on the psalm itself corresponding to this heading. In both, the psalm is interpreted throughout as a hymn of praise on divine providence.[282]

The question which arises from all this evidence is how explain the origin of this historical interpretation, and likewise the non-messianic interpretation of Psalms 2, 8, 44 and 109 in the early Irish Church.

12.5. *The Origin of Early Irish Historical Psalm Exegesis*

Codex Pal. lat. 68, although the earliest, is but one of many Irish compositions stressing the historical interpretation of the Psalms. In fact, this was the predominant tradition of interpretation in the Irish schools from the beginning down to the twelfth century.[283] We find it in two Hiberno-Latin works on the Psalms from the late eighth century: the *Eclogae tractatorum in Psalterium* and in 'Das Bibelwerk', particularly in the former. It is found in the *Old-Irish Treatise on the Psalter*, and (naturally) in the Ambrosian codex (Cod. Amb. C 301 inf.) with the Latin translation of Theodore's commentary and the Epitome of Julian,

279. Unterkircher (ed.), *Die Glossen*, p. 75.
280. Unterkircher (ed.), *Die Glossen*, p. 75.
281. Unterkircher (ed.), *Die Glossen*, p. 76.
282. Published by De Coninck and d'Hont (eds.), *Theodori*, p. xliii n. 245.
283. See M. McNamara, 'Psalter Text', above pp. 12-129, especially pp. 90-93.

together with the Irish glosses on both translation and Epitome. It is found in the glosses in the Psalter of Southampton from the eleventh century and in the glosses of the so-called Psalter of Caimin from about 1100. The emphasis is evidenced by the central place which the Julian Epitome enjoyed in Irish tradition from about 700–1200. And together with the historical commentary which is the Julian Epitome there must also have circulated in the early Irish Church another 'historical' commentary on the Psalms found in the glosses on Pss. 1.1–16.11 in one branch of the transmission of the Julian Epitome. The central role of this historical approach to the Psalms is also manifested by the special 'historical' psalm headings found in the *Tituli Bedae* and in the so-called Psalter of Charlemagne.

This stress on the historical understanding of the Psalms may be in some way associated with the special Irish interest in the Old Testament in the seventh century and later, an interest that has left its imprint in canonical collections, liturgy, and some other ways.[284] It may have been helped by the presence of at least two historical commentaries in the Irish schools, namely, the Epitome of Julian and the commentary known through the glosses on Psalms 1–16 in one branch of the Epitome transmission. And together with these it is possible that the glosses of the Montpellier Psalter were in some way associated with Ireland.

The existence of Antiochene exegesis of the Theodorean kind in Ireland can be explained through the presence there of the Epitome of Julian and at least of part of the Latin translation of Theodore's commentary. This, however, only explains part of the evidence. Theodore, it would appear, interpreted only 19 psalms as referring to David and his times, much less than the Irish tradition does.[285] The origin of the

---

284. On this see R. Kottje, *Studien zum Einfluss des Alten Testamentes auf Recht und Liturgie des frühen Mittelalters (6.-8. Jahrhundert)* (Bonner Historische Forschungen, 23; Bonn: Ludwig Röhrscheid Verlag, 2nd edn, 1970).

285. For Theodore's division of the Psalms see F. Baethgen, 'Siebzehn makkabäische Psalmen nach Theodor von Mopsuestia', *ZAW* 6 (1886), pp. 261-88; 7 (1887), pp. 1-60 (270-71); Ramsay, 'Theodore of Mopsuestia', pp. 421-51 (436-37); R. Devreesse, *Essai sur Théodore de Mopsueste* (Studi e Testi, 141; Vatican City: Biblioteca Apostolica Vaticana, 1948), p. 70. For the distribution in the Antiochene commentary reckoned by some as the work of Diodorus of Tarsus, see Olivier (ed.), *Diodori*, pp. lxxx-lxxxv, pp. lxxxiv-lxxxv for Davidic Psalms: in the headings of the commentary itself 18 psalms are regarded as being composed about David: Pss. 3, 6. 7, 10, 11, 12, 16, 17, 21, 35, 37, 38, 63, 67, 69, 71, 119, 139.

greater interest in the Davidic interpretation in Ireland awaits an explanation. It may be related to the interpretation found in the glosses of the
Montpellier Psalter. It is not at all clear, however, that this work has
Irish connections. Within Irish tradition the Davidic interpretation may
have been promoted by some special group, such as the *Romani* whom
we have seen defending it for Psalms 52 and 54.[286] This particular
emphasis, in fact, may have originated within the Irish schools themselves.

It is also possible that the dual form of 'historical' exegesis—interpreting a psalm both of David's time and later Jewish history—originated in Ireland. We find it in such Irish sources as Pal. lat. 68 and the
so-called Psalter of Charlemagne. It is also occasionally encountered in
the glosses of the Montpellier Psalter—which may be connected with
Irish tradition.

Such exegetical activity, coupled with an interpretative tradition on
the double historical reference for the same psalm in the Irish schools of
the seventh century, might explain the peculiar Irish theory of a fourfold sense of Scripture—with a twofold historical sense. It is the scheme
which we find formulated in the *Old-Irish Treatise on the Psalter* from
the early ninth century, and in the Hiberno-Latin 'Bibelwerk' from the
late eighth.

The fourfold sense is thus explained in the *Old-Irish Treatise on the
Psalter* (lines 312-20):[287]

> There are four things that are necessary in the psalms, to wit, *the first
> story* (*cétna stoir*) and *the second story* (*stoir tánaise*), the *sense* (*síens*,
> i.e. spiritual meaning) and the *morality* (*morolus*). The *first story* refers
> to David and to Solomon, and to the above-mentioned persons, to Saul to
> Absalom (Abisolon) to the persecutors besides. The *second story* to
> Hezekiah, to the people, to the Maccabees. The *sense* (*síens*) (refers) to
> Christ, to the earthly and the heavenly Church. The *morality* (refers) to
> every saint.

A difficulty arises from the application of this schema in the *Old-Irish
Treatise* itself, in the understanding of the first psalm, where both first
and second stories are understood of David's own day.[288]

---

286. See above, 10.7.
287. *OIT*, pp. 30-31.
288. *OIT*, pp. 36-37; also pp. 14, 18 (diplomatic edition and variants).

The primary story of the psalms refers to the time of David, the second
to Chusai Arachites (*iesu irechitis*: v. 1. *hissu ireichidis*). He it was who
did not abandon him in the time of the persecution, though every one
(else) abandoned him.

The somewhat uncertain text of the *Old-Irish Treatise* is clarified by a
Latin passage in the Introduction to the Psalter in 'Das Bibelwerk', a
work known to be extremely closely related to the *Old-Irish Treatise*. In
the Paris manuscript of the work the relevant section reads as follows:[289]

> HILAR. *'Beatus uir qui non abiit'*. Prima historia *ad Dauid pertinet, qui
> non abiii in consilio sociorum, qui uoluerunt occidere Saul in spelunca,
> quando Dauid dixit: 'Non continguat mihi, ut mittam manum in Chris-
> tum Domini'* (cf. 1 Sam. 26.9, 11). *'Beatus', reliqua*. Secunda historia *ad
> Chusai Arachitam pertinet, qui non exiit in consilium Absalon et Achito-
> fel,*[290] *qui uoluerunt exire post Dauid quando fugit and occidere eum,
> quousque Chusai dissipauit consilium eorum* (cf. 2 Sam. 15.22, 37;
> 16.16; 18; 17.3, 5, 6, 7, 8, 14, 15, especially 15.34, 17.14).

Although the text of the *Old-Irish Treatise* is thereby clarified, the
problem remains, if we take it that the second historical meaning of a
psalm should refer it to Jewish history after David and his times.

The explanation of the anomaly may lie in the fact that the fourfold
sense as given in the theoretical section of the *Old-Irish Treatise* was
not worked through with regard to its implications. The basic belief
may have been that a text could have more than one historical meaning.

12.6. *The Origin of the Non-Messianic Interpretation of Psalms 2, 8, 44, 109*

We may now pass from the question of the historical sense of Scripture
in general in Ireland to the non-messianic interpretation of Psalms 2, 8,
44 and 109 and the reason for this. It may be that some old tradition of
interpretation lies behind the non-messianic interpretation of Psalm 8.
We should not forget that the interpretation we find in the glosses of the
Rouen Psalter does represent the basic meaning of the psalm. This

289. MS. Paris, Bibl. Nat. Lat. 11561, fol. 56v. The corresponding text from the
Munich MS., Staatsbibliothek, Clm. 14276, fol. 100r has been edited by P. O'Neill,
'The Old-Irish Treatise on the Psalter and its Hiberno-Latin Background', *Ériu* 30
(1979), pp. 148-64 (161).

290. It is worth noting that in the Rouen Psalter a gloss on *'non sic impii'* of Ps.
1.4 reads: *id est Agitofel et Abisolon et omnes impii* (p. 2 of MS.).

understanding of the psalm may have originated outside of Ireland and have come to the island with the commentary that was adopted to replace the lost section of the Epitome of Julian (Ps. 1.1–16.11a). The same may be true of Psalm 2. I have, however, failed to find any Christian evidence of either interpretation outside of Ireland—except with regard to Psalm 2 if the glosses of the Montpellier Psalter are regarded as non-Irish.[291] With regard to Psalm 44, later tradition would have Jerome's interpretation of Ecclesiastes to go on. There seems to have been no Christian tradition, however, which interpreted Psalm 109 of any other than Christ.

It is quite possible that the non-messianic interpretation of all four psalms originated in the Irish schools. We know of the Irish scholars' strong emphasis on the historical interpretation of the psalms, and how they sought to understand them in their Jewish Old Testament setting. They may well have had no scruple of doing the same for the four psalms which alone the Antiochene tradition regarded as prophecies of Christ. The basis of the actual interpretation which they gave to these psalms may have been found in references in tradition (in the Theodorean tradition for instance) on the manner in which Jewish tradition interpreted them.[292]

In any event, this particular manner of interpreting the Psalms seems to have been well established in Ireland by 700 CE or so. We find it in Pal. lat. 68, the *Tituli Psalmorum* of Pseudo-Bede and in the so-called Psalter of Charlemagne—all independent of one another. By the time the gloss in Pal. lat. 68 was put together it was well established and not

291. See above, 3.12.d. Unterkircher (ed.), (*Die Glossen*, pp. 24-26) thinks that the origins of the work may have been connected with Ireland.

292. Ps. 2 was already interpreted messianically in Judaism, before the Christian era (e.g. the Psalms of Solomon, in Qumran). Theodore, however, reports a Jewish interpretation understanding it to speak of Zerubbabel or David *(Argumentum* to Ps. 2, De Coninck and d'Hont [eds.], *Theodori*, p. 10). Theodore also notes that the Jews interpreted Ps. 44(45) of Salomon and his wife (*Le commentaire de Théodore de Mopsueste sur les Psaumes (I–LXXX)* [ed. R. Devreesse; Studi e Testi, 93; Vatican City: Biblioteca Apostolica Vaticana, 1939], pp. 277-78). While this information is not reproduced in the Epitome of Julian, a similar interpretation was given by Jerome in his commentary on Eccl. 1.1 (M. Adriaen [ed.], *S. Hieronymi Presbyteri Commentarius in Ecclesiastes* [CSEL, 72; Turnhout: Brepols, 1969], p. 250). The Theodorean commentary on Ps. 109 transmitted in the Epitome of Julian (De Coninck and d'Hont [eds.], *Theodori*, pp. 351-52) records the Jewish opinions which understood the psalm of Abraham's servant or of David himself.

to the liking of the compiler himself. Nonetheless, it persisted and is found again in the glosses of the tenth-century Rouen Double Psalter.

12.7. *Psalm 118 in Palatino-Latinus 68*

While it is not clear how Theodore interpreted Psalm 118, he probably understood it to refer to the exiles in Babylon. The Epitome of Julian has a lengthy introduction to the Psalm in which it is clearly taken as speaking of the Babylonian captivity: *Ea quae in Babilone gesta sunt psalmo praesenii argumento sunt...*[293] In 1919 L. Mariès[294] published a Greek preface to this psalm which he believes was the work of Diodorus of Tarsus. The author of this preface interprets the psalm as spoken by the exiles in Babylonia and is in part very similar to the *argumentum* of this psalm in the Epitome.

In comparison with the lengthy preface, the comment on Psalm 118 in the Epitome is extremely brief—just one third longer than the comment on the preceding psalm which has only 29 verses as against the 176 of Psalm 118. Some verses are glossed together in just a few lines (for example, 1-5a, 5b-8a, 33a-39a, 50b-56). Verses 89 to 96 (all the *Lamed* section) get merely eight words and from v. 89 onwards the comment is practically non-existent. The Epitome in its present form gives the impression of not representing the original abbreviation.[295]

In contrast with this the comment on Psalms 118 in Pal. lat. 68 is artistically arranged. Each subsection is prefaced by it own special

293. De Coninck and d'Hont (eds.), *Theodori*, p. 362.

294. L. Mariès, 'Extraits du commmentaire de Diodore de Tarse sur les Psaumes: Préface du commentaire—prologue du Psaume CXVIII', *RSR* 9 (1919), pp. 79-101; preface to Ps. 118 in pp. 98-101. The Diodoran authorship is also defended in the definitive edition of this commentary, Olivier (ed.), *Diodori*, 1980. The *Argumentum* of the Epitome (De Coninck and d'Hont [eds.], *Theodori*, p. 362, 1-11) should be compared with the 'Diodorean' Preface, Mariès, 'Extraits', pp. 98, 21-24; 100, 6-11. On Diodorus and the commentary see also M. McNamara, 'Antiochene Commentary on the Psalms: By Diodore of Tarsus?', *Milltown Studies* 10 (1982), pp. 66-75.

295. The Epitome, however, provides the *argumentum* for Ps. 118 in the Hiberno-Latin *Eclogae tractatorum in Psalterium* (MS., Munich, Staatsbibliothek, Clm 14715, fol. 53v (almost verbatim as in the Epitome of Julian, De Coninck and d'Hont [eds.], *Theodori*, p. 362, ll. 1-11). The Rouen Psalter (pp. 251-71) on the other hand, does not use the Epitome at all for Ps. 118. All the left-hand margin and interlinear glosses are, instead, from Cassiodorus, although glosses from the Epitome are resumed again at Ps. 119.

headings and the comment itself is much more complete than the Epitome. It occasionally has texts from the Epitome, but for the greater part it has a fuller commentary, and one which is in keeping with the heading of the Epitome's understanding the text of the exiles in Babylon. This fuller commentary of Psalm 118 is also found in the left-hand marginal glosses of the so-called Psalter of Caimin,[296] written in Ireland about 1100. The Psalter of Charlemagne has the same layout and the same introductions to the subsections as Pal. lat. 68. It appears, then, that Pal. lat. 68 conserves a tradition of exegesis on Psalm 118 found in few other texts.

12.8. *Treatment of the Gradual Psalms in Palatino-Latinus 68*
In the Hebrew text each of the psalms in Psalms 119–133 has as heading *šir la-ma'alot*, 'a song for the *ma'alot*'. It is now accepted that the *ma'alot* in question were the caravans or the pilgrimages to Jerusalem. Before this explanation came to be accepted four or five theories on the meaning of the Latin heading *Canticum Graduum* (and of its Greek equivalent in the Septuagint) were current. Most of these already existed in Patristic times.[297]

One was that the gradual psalms were 'songs of the stairs' or 'of the steps', intended to be sung by Levites on the 15 steps that led from the court of the Israelites to that of the women. This explanation is found as an alternative one (*aliter*) in the Epitome (Ps. 120); and also in Pal. lat. 68 in the heading to Psalm 119.

Another opinion (and quite compatible with the former) was that the Hebrew word referred to the return of the Jews from Babylon. This was the manner in which these psalms (with the exception of Ps. 119) were understood in the Antiochene school[298] and by the author of the Epitome[299] (except that Pss. 120 and 130 are understood principally of the exile).

296. MS. A I at the Franciscan Library, Dún Mhuire, Killiney, Co. Dublin. See McNamara, 'Psalter Text', pp. 245-49.
297. For a brief history of interpretation see F. Hockey, '*Cantica graduum*: The Gradual Psalms in Patristic Tradition', *Studia Patristica* 10, part I, F.L. Cross (ed.), pp. 355-59. Henri Rondet, 'Saint Augustin et les Psaumes des Montées', *Revue d'Ascétique et de Mystique* 41 (1965), pp. 3-18.
298. See Ramsay, 'Theodore of Mopsuestia', p. 437; the Antiochene Introduction published by Mariès, 'Extraits', p. 85; also Olivier (ed.), *Diodori*, pp. lxxxi-lxxxii, and in the edition of the Greek prologue, p. 5.
299. De Coninck and d'Hont (eds.), *Theodori*, pp. 365-77.

A third opinion, very common among Christian writers, was that these psalms speak of the gradual ascent of the Christian or the soul to God. We find this understanding of the psalms in Pal. lat. 68 in a text borrowed from Jerome in the heading to Psalm 119.[300]

The *Tituli Psalmorum* of Pseudo-Bede (*PL* 83, 1084-1092) are heavily dependent on the Epitome for all the Gradual Psalms, with the exception of Psalm 121. For the greater part they merely reproduce its text. The same is true, but to a lesser extent, of the so-called Psalter of Charlemagne.

Matters are different in this regard in Pal. lat. 68. More than in any other section, the tradition in Pal. lat. 68 is caught between the 'historical' and spiritual interpretations. A peculiar feature of the treatment of these psalms in the gloss is that for the greater part they are given a complete additional spiritual interpretation—one that appears to have been evolved by the compiler in the course of the composition itself. In Psalm 119 the second spiritual interpretation is given within the comment on individual verses: vv. 1, 4 (introduced as *moraliter* in both cases and also with *M* in margin at v. 4), and in vv. 6-7 (introduced in the text in both cases as *allagoricae* with *M* in the margin). Likewise in Psalm 120 (vv. 1, 3, 6) with the rubric *aliter* in text and *M* (*moraliter*) in the margin. In 121 the alternative, spiritual, interpretation is given in two blocks (vv. 2-4 and 5-9, likewise in 131) while in the other psalms it comes entirely at the end of the other exposition. This spiritual exposition, as already noted,[301] is heavily dependent on Augustine's *Enarrationes*, although Augustine's own words are rarely used.

In the historical exposition no particular line seems to be followed. The catena does not dwell much, either in the headings or actual commentary, on the Antiochene exegesis referring these psalms to the Babylonian captivity and the return. In the introduction to the entire group the psalms are said to refer to David's trials from Saul (*Dauid in erumnis Saul*). This phrase recurs in the headings of Psalms 120 and 128 (with *pro erumnis*), but only after the Antiochene headings. In the headings and glosses of seven of the psalms (Pss. 121, 122, 123, 126, 127, 128, 132) reference is made to the captivity and return. There are no historical references in the headings or glosses of Psalms 125, 129, 130 or 133 and dependence on the Epitome is very slim in the gloss's treatment of the gradual psalms. The Epitome becomes a major source

300. See McNamara (ed.), *Glossa in Psalmos*, p. 264.
301. Above, 11.3.e.

again only in Psalm 136. In these psalms, then, both in the reduction of Theodorean material and the inclusion of the spiritual exposition, Pal. lat. 68 is different from the remainder of the commentary. Future research may reveal the reason for the change of the manner of exposition followed by Pal. lat. 68 for these psalms.

13. *Conclusion*

13.1. *The Date of the Manuscript*
After almost a century of interest in Codex Pal. lat. 68, we are still uncertain as to the exact date of its transcription. In the first description of the manuscript in 1886, by H. Stevenson Jr, after consultation with I.B. de Rossi, assigned it to the eighth century. This dating was soon contested by some scholars who preferred a ninth-century date. Later a virtual consensus emerged on an eighth-century origin.

13.2. *Date of Original Composition*
We seem to be on more solid ground with regard to the date of the original composition. Both the vernacular glosses and the forms of the names Edilberict and Berictfrid in the colophon indicate an early eighth-century date.[302] The source analysis itself agrees with this, since the latest work used seems to be Adamnan's *De locis sanctis*,[303] which was most probably composed c. 683–86 CE.

13.3. *Relation of Present Manuscript to Original Composition*
Although the present manuscript appears to be younger than the original composition, it seems to reproduce faithfully both the colophon and the glosses of the original work, or one very close to it. While Edilberict would appear to be a scribe rather than the compiler of the original gloss, the forms of his name and that of his father indicate that he wrote early in the eighth century, and some of the vernacular glosses, on philological grounds, are to be assigned to the same period. It appears that most if not all of the vernacular glosses formed part of the original composition, and are not later insertions into the text from the margins. What we have in Cod. Pal. lat. 68, then, seems to be a work originally compiled c. 700 CE, and transcribed by Edilberict early in the eighth century. This has been recopied at least more than once together

302. See above, pp. 165-70.
303. See above, 11.3.h.

with the colophon and vernacular glosses. What additions were made to the text in the course of its transmission is difficult to say. It may be that part at least of the left-hand marginal source annotation, and possibly the *diple*, are later additions and even from different periods and scholars.

13.5. *Place of Origin of Codex Palatino-Latinus 68*
We are also in a state of uncertainty with regard to the scriptorium in which our present codex was transcribed. While a case could still be made out for a scriptorium in Ireland, a number of scholars believe that it was rather in Northumbria.

13.6. *Place of Composition of Original Text of Palatino-Latinus 68*
The vernacular Irish and Northumbrian glosses, and the name of the Northumbrian scribe Edilberict, seem to indicate that the work originated in an area where there were both Irish and Northumbrian scholars, that is, either in Ireland or Northumbria and most probably in one of the monastic schools of the *parruchia Columbae*. From Bede we know of the Irish (Iona) presence in Northumbria and of the presence of English (Anglian) scholars in the Irish schools down through the seventh century.[304] The analysis of the contents of the work reinforces this conclusion.

13.7. *The Gloss Stands in the Irish Exegetical Tradition*
The sources used, the exegetical emphases and certain 'Irish symptoms' indicate that the gloss on the Psalms in Pal. lat. 68 belongs to the Irish (and Irish-Northumbrian) tradition of exegesis, which in these points is distinct from the European and from the exegesis of the Roman Church in Britain.

About one third of the commentary material is drawn from the Epitome of Julian's translation of Theodore of Mopsuestia. With the exception of one small fragment in MS. Bodley 826 (S.C. 2715), copied in Normandy in the eleventh century, both the full translation of Theodore's commentary and the Epitome have been transmitted solely through Irish sources (Cod. Amb. C 301 inf.; Cod. Taurinensis Univ. F.

---

304. See Bede, *Historia ecclesiastica gentis Anglorum*, III, 3, 5, 27; C. Plummer (ed.), *Venerabilis Baedae opera historica* (2 vols.; Oxford, 1896), I, pp. 131-32, 135-38, 192. See also C. Jones (ed.), *Bedae opera de temporibus* (Cambridge, MA, 1943), p. iii.

iv. i, fasc. 5-6; Pal. lat. 68; *Eclogae tractatorum in Psalterium*; the 'Bibelwerk'; the Double Psalter of Rouen and the corresponding Dublin fragment) and in works that can presumably be connected with North-umbria and Ireland such as the *Tituli Psalmorum* of Pseudo-Bede and the so-called Psalter of Charlemagne.[305] If we had only the evidence of the Latin glosses for the cultural setting of the work, we would think of the early Irish schools. The Irish and Northumbrian glosses confirm the evidence drawn from the use of the Epitome of Julian.

Together with this we have in the gloss some other rare sources used also in other Hiberno-Latin exegetical works, for example, Letter 23 '*Ad Dardanum*' of Pseudo-Jerome.[306] To this we may add the almost certain use of Adamnan's *De locis sanctis.*[307]

To this evidence we may add the presence in the gloss of certain 'Irish symptoms', that is, themes, terms, expressions and so on charac-teristic of Irish works either in themselves or in the frequency of their use.[308] As examples of such 'Irish symptoms' in Pal. lat. 68 we may instance the stylized connection of one psalm (or subsection of Ps. 118) with the preceding one through *haeret*,[309] comparison through *more*,[310] the theme of the triple martyrdom,[311] expressions such as *lex naturae, lex literae.*[312] To these we may add the explicit emphasis on the histori-cal sense of Scripture and the contrast made between it and the spiritual sense.

This evidence is made stronger by the explicit mention of the *Romani*,[313] who were evidently an identifiable group in the tradition to which this commentary is heir. It is natural to see in these the *Romani* of the seventh-century Irish Church.

305. See above, 10.8.
306. See above, 11.3.g.
307. See above, 11.3.h.
308. On such 'Irish symptoms' in Hiberno-Latin exegetical texts see Bischoff, 'Wendepunkte', pp. 202-11.
309. Cf. Bischoff, 'Wendepunkte', p. 206.
310. Cf. Bischoff, 'Wendepunkte', p. 207.
311. In gloss to Ps. 44.9. See note 19 in Apparatus II, McNamara (ed.), *Glossa in Psalmos*, p. 100.
312. In gloss to Ps. 148.6. See note 9 in Apparatus II; McNamara (ed.), *Glossa in Psalmos*, p. 307.
313. See above, 10.7.

13.8. *The Significance of the Gloss in Palatino-Latinus 68*

The gloss in Pal. lat. 68 is a text of a certain significance for a variety of reasons. One reason is that, coming as it most probably does from c. 700 CE, it is a relatively early composition by Irish ecclesiastical standards. While most of its patristic texts are elsewhere known, the evidence it provides still merits consideration—at least for the history of transmission of the texts in question. With regard to the Epitome of Julian, the text of Pal. lat. 68 is probably the oldest we possess and, even though in many instances its readings are inferior, it is of importance as evidence for the state of this text in one line of transmission at about 700 CE. It is also of importance that already by that time the Epitome was regarded as a work of Jerome.

The gloss is evidence for the early existence of Letter 23 'Ad Dardanum' of Pseudo-Jerome, thus indicating a pre-Carolingian date for this work.[314] The text which coincides with the Gospel of Pseudo-Matthew[315] seems to argue for a pre-800 date for this apocryphal work. Of much more importance, however, is the evidence which the gloss provides for the life and scholarship of seventh- and eighth-century schools in Ireland and Northumbria. The existence of both Old Irish and Old English (Northumbrian) glosses would seem to indicate the presence of scholars of both traditions in the same school and the spontaneous use of both languages in the study of the biblical text.

The gloss is of major importance for a knowledge of the manner in which the Psalms were taught and studied in Irish schools about the year 700 CE. What is more significant, however, is that the gloss seems to represent a native exegetical activity that was already mature and even old. It could well represent the exegetical activity of the Irish and Northumbrian schools of the mid-seventh century. Mention of the views of the *Romani* would fit in well with this. An analysis of the exegesis of the work, with its twofold historical reference of the psalms and its special understanding of the messianic psalms, indicates that we are in the presence here of a fairly well thought-out system of exegesis. And since the compiler on two occasions[316] expresses himself ill at ease with the interpretation, he is most probably the transmitter of a tradition which was older than his own day.

It would be informative if we could identify the schools in which this

314. See above, 11.3.g.
315. In gloss to Ps. 148.7, McNamara (ed.), *Glossa in Psalmos*, p. 308.
316. Pss. 44 and 109; see above, 12.4.

creative exegetical activity was carried out. The indications are that they were of the *parruchia* of St Columba in Northumbria and Ireland, and possibly also in Iona.

The psalm interpretation of Pal. lat. 68 is but part of a larger system of interpretation, one found again in other related texts such as the glosses of the Double Psalter of Rouen, the 'Bibelwerk', the *Tituli Psalmorum* of Pseudo-Bede and the glosses of the so-called Psalter of Charlemagne. This all represents a rather self-contained system that could only have been worked out over a period of time. As well as having been transmitted in the schools of Ireland and Northumbria, the system itself may have been thought out there.

13.9. *Later History of Palatino-Latinus 68*
There are many things we would like to know about the gloss now found in the acephalous *manuscriptum unicum* of Pal. lat. 68. Did more than one copy of it once circulate? Was it used in the schools of Northumbria alone? Or of those of Ireland alone? How did it find its way to the Continent? Was it read on the Continent, or copied there? Did it in any way influence other Continental writings?

To most of these questions we have no answers. We can presume that a copy of the work circulated in Ireland. This seems indicated by the evidence of the glosses of the so-called Psalter of Caimin, written in Ireland, and probably at Clonmacnois, about 1100 CE. All that now exists of this Psalter is a portion of the text of Psalm 118 and glosses on it. Most of the glosses in the left-hand margins of the manuscript coincide almost verbatim with the text of Pal. lat. 68, a remarkable coincidence given the very special nature of the glosses of the latter on this particular psalm. It seems clear from this that either a sister copy of Pal. lat. 68, or a text very similar to it, continued to circulate in certain places in Ireland four hundred years after the composition of the original.

What was the history of our present text of Pal. lat. 68 before it was taken to the Continent and after it was taken there is difficult to say. Its exegetical approach would probably not have appealed to the prevailing Continental mentality[317] and may have lain unused in a Palatinate library until taken to Rome in 1623, where it again lay unnoticed for over

317. On Western lack of interest in Antiochene exegesis see B. Smalley, *The Study of the Bible in the Middle Ages* (Oxford: Basil Blackwell, 3rd edn, 1983 [1952]), p. 19.

250 years before being brought to the attention of scholars by H. Stevenson Jr in 1886. It is a work that merits attention today as a witness to hidden trends in the interpretation of the Psalter in the early Middle Ages.

1. *The Christian Use of the Psalms*

The subject matter of this paper is tradition and creativity in early Irish psalm exegesis. The tradition in question will in the first instance be the tradition of the Western Church which the Irish Church can be presumed to have inherited. The Western Church, however, was in good part heir to the Christian tradition of the East, in particular to that of Alexandria, though not exclusively so. I shall begin this essay, then, with a brief survey of the use and study of the Psalms in the Church during the patristic period.[1]

1.1. *The Jewish Heritage and the Early Church*[2]

An inherent problem with the Psalter in the Church at any period is that it is the prayer book of the synagogue that has become the prayer book

---

1. Summaries of this subject in L.G. Walsh, 'The Christian Use of the Psalms according to the Tituli Psalmorum of the Latin Manuscripts' (unpublished thesis, University of St Thomas, Rome, 1963); L.G. Walsh, 'The Christian Prayer of the Psalms According to the Tituli Psalmorum of the Latin Manuscripts', in Placid Murray (ed.), *Studies in Pastoral Liturgy*, III (Maynooth: The Furrow Trust; Dublin: Gill and Son, 1967), pp. 29-73, and separately as a booklet under the same title (Dublin 1967); Pierre Salmon, *Les 'Tituli Psalmorum' des manuscripts latins* (Collectanea Biblica Latina, 12; Rome: Abbaye de Saint-Jérôme; Cittá del Vaticano: Libreria Vaticana, 1959), pp. 9-39; P. Salmon, 'The Interpretation of the Psalms during the Formative Period of the Office', in P. Salmon (ed.), *The Breviary through the Centuries* (Collegeville: The Liturgical Press, 1962), pp. 42-61; various studies on the general theme 'L'Antico Testamento nella Chiesa prenicena', *Augustinianum* 22 (fasc. 1 and 2, 1982); M. Simonetti, 'L'interpretazione patristica del Vecchio Testamento fra II e III secolo', *Augustinianum* 22 (fasc. 1 and 2, 1982), pp. 7-33; K.J. Torjesen, 'Interpretation of the Psalms: Study of the Exegesis of Ps. 37', *Augustinianum* 22 (fasc. 1 and 2, 1982), pp. 349-55.

2. Some examples of the relationship of Christian to Jewish tradition in N.R.M. de Lange, *Origen and the Jews: Studies in Jewish-Christian Relations in Third-Century Palestine* (University of Cambridge Oriental Publication; Cambridge

of the Church. While in some instances the Psalms are timeless prayer, in others they can be used meaningfully as Christian prayer only by reinterpretation in a Christian sense, and this at times cannot easily be done without violence to their original meaning. The most recent attempt in the Church to present the Psalter as a Christian prayer book is the Roman Catholic Breviary (*Liturgia Horarum*, Rome, 1972), a work in which certain psalms or verses of psalms found offensive to pious ears have been omitted and in which each psalm is preceded by a brief heading giving it a Christian reference, superscriptions generally taken from the New Testament.

The Psalms is the Old Testament book most cited in the New Testament.[3] Jesus himself used the Psalms during his own lifetime, some of them in such a manner as if he took them as prophecies of himself (e.g. the use of Ps. 109 in Mt. 22.44; 26.24 and parallels; Ps. 8 in Mt. 21.16). He used Psalm 21 as he hung on the cross (Mt. 27.46; Mk 15.34). St Luke tells us (Lk. 22.44) that after his resurrection he told his disciples that everything written about him in the Law of Moses, the Prophets and the Psalms had to be fulfilled. The Psalms chiefly used of Christ in the New Testament writings are Psalms 109; 8; 21; 2 (Vulgate numbering throughout). In these cases the entire psalms are taken as messianic. Apart from these there are verses of other psalms understood as prophecies of Christ or of his mission.

By the year 200, if not earlier, the Christian Church was using the Psalter as its own prayer and song book.[4] This intensified the desire to see in the Psalms prophecies of Christ. The christological interpretation

1976); *idem*, 'Origen and the Rabbis on the Hebrew Bible', in E.A. Livingstone (ed.), *Papers Presented to the Sixth International Conference on Patristic Studies held in Oxford 1971, part 3, Tertullian, Origenism, Gnostica, Cappadocian Fathers, Augustiana* (Studia Patristica, 17; Berlin: Akademie Verlag, 1976), pp. 117-21. See also A. Marmorstein, 'Judaism and Christianity in the Middle of the Third Century', *Hebrew Union College Annual* 10 (1935), pp. 223-63.

    3.   The New Testament texts in question are noted in *Novum Testamentum Graece et Latine* (E. Nestle [ed.]; Stuttgart: Privilegierte Württembergische Bibelanstalt, 1954), pp. 662-65; *The Greek New Testament* (Ed. K. Aland, *et al.*; 3rd corrected edition; Stuttgart: United Bible Societies, 1966), pp. 897-98, 905-906.

    4.   See Walsh, 'Christian Prayer' (booklet), p. 7 n. 5, with references; Balthasar Fischer, 'Le Christ dans les psaumes', *Maison-Dieu* 27 (1951), pp. 86-113, revised form of 'Die Psalmenfrömmigkeit der Märtyrerkirche', in A. Heinz (ed.), *Die Psalmen als Stimme der Kirche: Gesammelte Studien zur christlichen Frömmigkeit* (collected essays of Balthasar Fischer; Trier: Paulinus Verlag, 1982), pp. 15-35.

of the Psalms, however, had already become commonplace in the Church before then.

By New Testament times a corpus of tradition about the Psalms, their origin, their transmission history and their interpretation can be presumed to have existed among the Jews. This continued to be developed during the early Christian centuries and influenced such Christian scholars as Origen and Jerome. The third and fourth centuries, in fact, were a period in which Jewish exegetical activity flourished, some of it now directed against the Christian interpretation of the Scriptures. Since there was direct contact between Jewish and Christian scholars in Palestine and Antioch, it is not surprising that Jewish interpretations should be mentioned, and at times adopted, by some Christian scholars. In fact, some of the material concerning the Psalms found in Origen and in the Psalm Preface is basically Jewish tradition.[5]

1.2. *Christological Interpretation: The School of Alexandria*

Origen (died 253), the first great Christian scholar, was also the first to give a continuous interpretation of the Psalms. His approach to the Psalms was in keeping with his ideas on the sense of the Scriptures in general, and of the Old Testament in particular, that is, the Spirit of God dictated the text of the Scriptures.[6] However, for Origen, what is written, the *littera*, is the sign of certain mysteries, the image of divine realities. Thus, the New Testament mystery is hidden, prefigured, in the Old Testament. To remain in the letter is to end in, or fall into heresy. 'Anyone wishing to understand the Scripture according to the letter would be better to class himself among the Jews than among Christians. Whoever wishes to be a Christian and a disciple of Paul must listen to Paul who says that the Law is spiritual' (Origen, *Hom. in Gen.* 6.1; *PG* 12, 195 AB). For Origen, and the Alexandrian school, all Scripture did have a literal sense. The important matter for the followers of this school, however, was to penetrate beneath the letter to the spirit, to the spiritual sense.

It is necessary to make special mention of Origen because of the deep influence exercised by his writings on later Psalm exegesis, both in the

5. See, for instance, de Lange , 'Origen and the Rabbis', pp. 119-20.

6. On Origen's exegesis see M. F. Wiles, 'Origen as Biblical Scholar', in P.R. Ackroyd and C.F. Evans (eds.), *The Cambridge History of the Bible*. I. *From the Beginnings to Jerome* (3 vols.; Cambridge: Cambridge University Press, 1970), pp. 454-89; see also Simonetti, 'L'interpretazione patristica', pp. 25-31.

East and West. Another writer worthy of mention is Eusebius of Caesarea (c. 263–340), the church historian who wrote an extensive commentary on the Psalms which was translated into Latin by Eusebius of
Vercelli (died c. 371). Although dependent on Origen, Eusebius is interested in the larger questions of content, literary genre, original historical
setting and literal meaning of the Psalms.[7]

1.3. *The School of Antioch: Diodorus, Theodore, Chrysostom, Theodoretus*

The real founder of the exegetical school of Antioch seems to have
been Diodorus,[8] later to become Bishop of Tarsus in 378 (died 393).
Two of his most famous students (about 370–75) were John Chrysostom
and Theodore of Mopsuestia. His school is called by the church historian Sozomen an asketerion, probably a monastery in which young
people were given an intellectual and moral training before they moved
elsewhere, whether to adopt a more severe monastic or ascetical life or
become priests for the pastoral ministry.[9]

The church historians Socrates and Sozomen note that the avoidance
of allegory and the literal explanation of the Scriptures were features of
Diodorus's exegesis.[10] We have no clear evidence from history that
Diodorus wrote a commentary on the Psalms. However, in a series of
studies from 1914 onwards[11] L. Mariès and others have claimed to have

---

7. Cf. Salmon, *Les 'Tituli'*, p. 17.

8. We know absolutely nothing of the nature of the exegesis of Lucian, for
long believed to have been the founder of the School of Antioch; see M. Simonetti,
La crisi ariana nel IV secolo (Studia Ephemeridis Augustinianum, 11; Rome: Institutum Patristicum Augustinianum, 1975), pp. 19-20; M. Simonetti, 'Le origini dell'
Arianismo', *Rivista di storia e letteratura religiosa* 7 (1971), pp. 317-30.

9. Cf. R. Leconte, 'L'Asceterium de Diodore', in *Mélanges Bibliques rédigées
en l'honneur de André Robert* (Paris: Bloud & Gay, 1957), pp. 531-36.

10. Socrates, *Historia Ecclesiastica* 6.3, *PG* 67, 668; Sozomen, *Historia Ecclesiastica* 8.2, *PG* 67, 1516A.

11. L. Mariès, 'Aurions-nous le commentaire sur les psaumes de Diodore de
Tarse?', *Revue de philologie, de littérature et d'histoire anciennes* 35 (1911),
pp. 56-70; *idem*, 'Le commentaires de Diodore de Tarse et de Théodore de Mopsueste sur les psaumes', *RSR* 5 (1914), pp. 246-51; *idem*, 'Extraits du commentaire
de Diodore de Tarse sur les psaumes: Préface du commentaire—Prologue de
psaume CXVIII', *RSR* 9 (1919), pp. 79-101; *idem*, *Etudes préliminaires à l'édition
de Diodore de Tarse sur les psaumes* (Paris: Société d'Edition 'Les Belles Lettres',
1933). English translation of both preface and prologue by E. FitzGerald, 'Antiochene Commentary on the Psalms: By Diodorus of Tarsus? Preface to the Com-

identified a commentary on the Psalms by Diodorus in a number of Greek manuscripts. The first section (Pss. 1–50) of this commentary, together with the introduction, has been published,[12] and has a text that is remarkably like that of Theodore in all essentials. The Preface to the entire work, and the special preface to Psalm 118, give a clear statement of the principles governing Antiochene exegesis, and the persons and events to which the major groups of psalms are to be referred.

Theodore's commentary is known partly through the original Greek text and partly through the Latin and Syriac translations and adaptations. Both Theodore and the commentary recently presented as that of Diodorus maintained all the psalms were composed by David and that only four of them (Pss. 2, 8, 44, 109, LXX and Vulgate numbering) are direct prophecies of Christ. The others are to be understood as moral, didactic psalms or as referring to some event of Jewish history, such as David's time, the Assyrian (Hezekiah), Babylonian (exilic) or Maccabaean periods.[13]

Both John Chrysostom and Theodoretus of Cyr are representatives of the Antiochene School but declined to go along with what they must have considered the excesses of Theodore (and Diodorus) regarding the messianic psalms. In the introduction to his commentary (*PG* 80, 859CD) Theodoretus tells us that his aim is to avoid the excesses of both allegorism and literalism. Among the Christian communities, he tells us, he found some who indulged inordinately in allegory while others so adapted prophecy to historical exposition that their interpretation agreed more with the Jews than with children of the faith—a fairly

mentary and Prologue to Psalm 118', *Milltown Studies* 10 (1982), pp. 76-86. On Diodorus and the commentary see also M. McNamara, 'Antiochene Commentary on the Psalms: By Diodore of Tarsus?', *Milltown Studies* 10 (1982), pp. 66-75.

12. J.-M. Olivier (ed.), *Diodori Tarsensis Commentarii in Psalmos*. I. *Commentarii in Psalmos I–L* (CCSG, 6; Turnhout: Brepols, 1980), with full bibliography on earlier research.

13. For the distribution of the psalms in Theodore's commentary see F. Baethgen, 'Siebzehn makkabäische Psalmen nach Theodor von Mopsuestia', *ZAW* 6 (1886), pp. 261-88; 7 (1887), pp. 1-60 (at 270-71); R.L. Ramsay, 'Theodore of Mopsuestia and St Columban on the Psalms'; 'Theodore of Mopsuestia in England and Ireland', *ZCP* 8 (1912), pp. 421-51; pp. 452-96 (at 436-37); R. Devreesse, *Essai sur Théodore de Mopsueste* (Studi e Testi, 141; Vatican City: Biblioteca Apostolica Vaticana, 1948), p. 70. For the practically identical distribution in the Antiochene commentary attributed to Diodorus see Olivier (ed.), *Diodori*, pp. xxx-xxxv.

obvious reference to Theodore's exegesis. These see prophecy in more psalms than in the four accepted as messianic by Theodore. Yet neither Chrysostom nor Theodoretus has any difficulty in seeing Psalm 8 as containing both teaching on the salvation of the world and on the providence of God as well as a prophecy on the Incarnation.[14]

1.4. *The Latin Fathers*

The majority of the Latin Fathers were influenced directly by the Greek and Eastern tradition. Hilary (died c. 367), a contemporary of the great Athanasius, lived for a time in the East. His exegesis is in the tradition of Origen, Eusebius and Athanasius.[15] Eusebius of Vercelli (died c. 371), already mentioned, was exiled for a while to Palestine. He visited Antioch and Asia Minor before returning to rule his diocese. Ambrose (c. 339–97), made Bishop of Milan in 374, came from a noble Roman family and received a good education in rhetoric and law. On becoming bishop, he devoted himself to theological studies, especially to reading the Greek Fathers.[16] Jerome belongs to many traditions and to both East and West. He got his secular education in Rome, and first set out for the East and reached Antioch in 373, and was back there again for a protracted stay in 382 when he probably attended the exegetical lectures of Apollinaris of Laodicea. He came under the influence of Jewish masters, of Origen, and was in communication with the Cappadocian Fathers— Basil and the two Gregories.[17] Augustine of Hippo (354–430) follows a

14. Comment on Psalm 8, *PG* 55. Thus also Theodoretus, *In Psalmum VIII*, 1, *PG* 80, 913C.

15. On Hilary's Psalm exegesis cf. C. Kannengieser, 'L'éxègese d'Hilaire', in *Hilaire et son temps* (Actes du Colloque de Poitiers, 29 septembre–3 octobre 1968; Paris 1969), pp. 127-42 (133-34); on Hilary's influence on Western exegesis: *idem*, 'L'héritage d'Hilaire de Poitiers. I. Dans l'ancienne Eglise d'Occident et dans les bibliothèques médiévales', *RSR* 56 (1968), pp. 435-50; for influence of Origen see E. Goffinet, *L'utilisation d'Origène dans le commentaire des psaumes de saint Hilaire de Poitiers* (Studia Hellenistica, 14; Leuven: Publications Universitaires, 1965).

16. See Salmon, *Les 'Tituli'*, pp. 22-23; Salmon, 'The Interpretation', pp. 45-46.

17. For Jerome's career and work see J.N.D. Kelly, *Jerome: His Life, Writings, Controversies* (London: Gerald Duckworth, 1975); F. Cavallera, *Saint Jérôme: Sa vie et son oeuvre* (Spicilegium Sacrum Lovaniense, Etudes et Documents, Fasc 1-2; Leuven; Paris: H. Champion, 1922); A. Penna, *Principi e carattere dell'esegesi di S. Gerolamo* (Scripta Pontificii Instituti Biblici, 102; Rome: Biblical Institute Press, 1950); H.F.D. Sparks, 'Jerome as a Biblical Scholar', in Ackroyd and Evans (eds.), *Cambridge History of the Bible*, I, pp. 510-41 (bibliog. pp. 596-97).

spiritual interpretation almost exclusively in his voluminous *Enarra-tiones in Psalmos*. For Augustine the Psalms are spoken by Christ (*in persona Christi*) or speak of Christ, the whole Christ, head and members.[18] Cassiodorus (c. 490–583) is one of the most recent of the major Western writers on the Psalms. Although he presents his work *Expositio Psalmorum* (completed about 548) as an abbreviation of Augustine's *Enarrationes*, he has used other writers besides.

1.5. *Antiochene Influence in the West*[19]

Antiochene influence made itself felt in Western Europe in different ways, chiefly however through the Latin translation of Theodore's commentary on the Psalms, through an Epitome of this work, and through an introduction to the Scriptures by Junilius Africanus. There were, probably, also other ways in which the influence of Antioch made its presence felt in Western exegesis.

1.5.a. *Latin Translation of Theodore's Psalm Commentary*. All that is preserved of this Latin translation of Theodore is to be found in two manuscripts of Irish provenance: Codex Amb. C 301 inf. of the Ambrosian Library, Milan, and MS F.IV.1, fasc. 5-6 of the Turin University Library[20] and in a fragment inserted into the Oxford MS, Bodl. 826 (S.C. 2715).[21] The two Italian manuscripts are of the ninth century and came from the Library of Bobbio. In these we have the full translation of the commentary on Pss. 1.1–16.11 (Cod. Amb. C 301 inf., fol. 14a–39d; Turin, F.IV, 1) and portion of the commentary on Pss. 17–40.13a.

18. On this point see Walsh, 'Christian Prayer', pp. 33-45; Salmon, *Les 'Tituli'*, pp. 24-25; Salmon, 'The Interpretation', pp. 46-47. See also G. Bonner, 'Augustine as Biblical Scholar', in Ackroyd and Evans (eds.), *Cambridge History of the Bible*, I, pp. 541-63, 597.

19. M.L.W. Laistner, 'Antiochene Exegesis in Western Europe', *HTR* 40 (1947), pp. 19-32; *idem*, *Thought and Letters in Western Europe A.D. 500–900* (London: Methuen, 2nd edn, 1957), index s.v. Antiochene; B. Smalley, *The Study of the Bible in the Middle Ages* (Oxford: Basil Blackwell, 3rd edn, 1983 [1952]), pp. 14-20.

20. Critically edited by R. Devreesse in *Le commentaire de Théodore de Mop-sueste sur les psaumes (I–LXXX)* (Studi e Testi, 93; Vatican City: Biblioteca Apostolica Vaticana, 1939); also in L. De Coninck with M. d'Hont (eds.), *Theodori Mopsuesteni Expositionis in Psalmos Iuliano Aeclanensi interprete in latinum versae quae supersunt* (CCSL, 88A; Turnhout: Brepols, 1977).

21. Cf. M. Gibson, 'Theodore of Mopsuestia: A Fragment in the Bodleian Library', *JTS* 21 (1970), pp. 104-105.

The Oxford fragment, with part of the commentary on Ps. 13.6-7, was copied in Normandy in the eleventh century. The Latin translation is believed to have been made by the Pelagian Bishop, Julian of Eclanum (died c. 460). Although only the translation for the commentary on Psalms 1–40 is now known to exist, a translation of the entire commentary can be presumed to have once circulated. Even though what we now have has been preserved almost exclusively in Irish circles, the Commentary probably once had a broader circulation. The Oxford fragment would seem to indicate this.

1.5.b. *The Epitome of Julian's Translation of Theodore's Commentary.*[22] This is an abbreviation and in part adaptation of the Latin translation of Theodore's commentary. It is extant only for Ps. 16.11b onwards. The opening section of the Epitome apparently got lost and was supplied in one branch of the translation (that represented in Cod. Amb. C 301 inf.) by the full Latin translation of Theodore and in another (that represented in the glosses in the Double Psalter of Rouen) by a completely different commentary with a literal or historical exposition.[23] Apart from two exceptions (glosses in the Montpellier and Vercelli Psalters, and section in the manuscript of a commentary on Psalms 78 and 82 by Remigius of Auxerre), the Epitome has been transmitted directly and indirectly (through excerpts, and such like) in sources of Irish provenance. These sources, in probable order of composition, are as follows: the catena in Vatican MS Pal. lat. 68 from about 700 CE (excerpts);[24] the historical sections of the *argumenta* in *De titulis Psalmorum* falsely attributed to Bede (eighth century)[25] and in the related headings in the so-called Psalter of Charlemagne (Paris BN MS lat.

22. Critical edition by De Coninck and d'Hont (eds.), *Theodori Mopsuesteni Expositionis in Psalmos Iuliano Aeclanensi interprete in Latinum versae quae supersunt* (CCSL, 88A; Turnhout: Brepols, 1977).

23. The different sources for the glosses of Pss. 1.1-16, 11a in the Double Psalter of Rouen noted by the present writer in and clearly demonstrated by De Coninck and d'Hont (eds.), *Theodori*, pp. xliii-xliv.

24. M. McNamara (ed.), *Glossa in Psalmos: The Hiberno-Latin Gloss on the Psalms of Codex Palatinus Latinus 68 (Psalms 39:11–151:7)* (Studi e Testi; Vatican City; Biblioteca Apostolica Vaticana, 1986).

25. These headings reprinted in *PL* 93, cols. 477-1098, from Heerwagen's 1563 Basel edition of Bede; study by B. Fischer, 'Bedae de titulis psalmorum liber', in J. Autenrieth and F. Brünholzt (eds.), *Festschrift Bernhard Bischoff zu seinem 65 Geburtstag* (Stuttgart: Hiersemann, 1971), pp. 90-110.

13159) of the late eighth century; the *Eclogae tractatorum in Psalter-ium*;[26] and in the introduction to the Psalter in the one-volume commentary (from Genesis to the Apocalypse) designated 'Das Bibelwerk' by Dr Bernhard Bischoff[27] (both late eighth century); Cod. Amb. C 301 inf. (c. 800–850); in the glosses in the *Hebraicum* section of the Double Psalter of Rouen (Rouen, Bibl. Mun. MS 24 [A.41]) from Ps. 16.11b onwards and in Dublin fragments of its sister codex (Dublin, Trinity College, MS H 3 18)[28] of the tenth century, and in some glosses in the so-called Psalter of Caimín (Franciscan Fathers Library, Killiney, Co. Dublin, MS A 1), from c. 1100 CE.[29]

1.5.c. *The* Instituta regularia divinae legis *of Junilius Africanus.*[30] Junilius, a native of Africa, held the office of Quaestor of the Sacred Palace in Constantinople. About 551, at the request of Primasius, Bishop of Hadrumetum, he compiled his work, *Instituta regularia divinae legis* which was a Latin version of a short introduction to the Bible, composed by Paul the Persian (that is, Syrian), whose acquaintance Junilius had made at Constantinople. The little work represents the basically Antiochene scriptural views of the Syriac school of Nisibis and Theodore's exegesis of the messianic psalms. The work must have been reasonably widely read in the Middle Ages. In 1880 Heinrich Kihn edited the Latin text from 13 manuscripts, one of which (St Gall 908) he dated to the eighth century. In 1947 M.L.W. Laistner[31] listed 23 manuscripts of the work, ranging from the early eighth (BL Cotton Tib. A. XV, fol.

---

26. On this see M. McNamara, 'Psalter Text and Psalter Study in the Early Irish Church (A.D. 600–1200)', pp. 19-142 of the present volume.

27. See B. Bischoff, 'Wendepunkte in der Geschichte der lateinischen Exegese irn Frühmittelalter', *SE* 6 (1954), pp. 169-281 (211, 223-30); trans. by C. O'Grady, 'Turning Points in the History of Latin Exegesis in the Early Middle Ages', in M. McNamara (ed.), *Biblical Studies: The Medieval Irish Contribution* (Proceedings of the Irish Biblical Association, 1; Dublin: Dominican Publications, 1976), pp. 88, 97-102.

28. Published by L. Bieler and G. MacNiocaill, 'Fragment of an Irish Double Psalter with Glosses in the Library of Trinity College Dublin', *Celtica* 5 (1960), pp. 28-39.

29. See McNamara, 'Psalter Text', pp. 50-51 of the present volume.

30. In *PL* 68, cols. 15–42; critical edition from 13 MSS by H. Kihn, *Theodor von Mopsuestia und Junilius Africanus als Exegeten* (Freiburg: Herder, 1880), pp. 465-528.

31. Laistner, 'Antiochene Exegesis', pp. 24-26.

175-180, South England) to the fifteenth century, the majority, however, from the eighth–tenth centuries. (Kihn's eighth-century date for Sangallensis 908 he regards as far too early.) Aldhelm used a copy of the work. It appears that copies of it were also available in Irish libraries: there are citations from it in eighth- and ninth-century Irish texts.[32]

1.5.d. *Glosses in the Montpellier and Vercelli Psalters*. Glosses in the Psalter of Montpellier (Montpellier, Faculté de Médecine MS 409; written at Mondsee before 788) and of Vercelli (Codex LXII of Chapter Library, mid-ninth century) have been edited by Franz Unterkircher.[33] Both sets of glosses are basically the same. The commentary they represent has Antiochene connections, although its exegesis in general is strongly christological. A few of the glosses have been identified as depending on the Epitome of Julian.[34] Occasionally, although there is no verbal connection with the Epitome, the historical reference is Antiochene and of the type found in Theodore, for example, to Hezekiah (Ps. 19), Babylonian captivity (Pss. 41, 72, 83, 136), the return from captivity (Pss. 101, 125, 146), Maccabean times (Pss. 43, 73, 78). (The Diodoran commentary, we may note, understands most of these psalms in like manner.) Together with this, there are instances in the glosses of the Montpellier and Vercelli Psalters where the Psalms are interpreted of later Jewish history but in a manner different from that of Theodore (or, we may now add, Diodorus) for example, Psalms 36 (of Babylon), 40, 41, 42, 65, 72 (of Maccabaean times; in Theodore and Diodorus Ps. 40 of Assyria; the others of Babylon). Occasionally the glosses give more than one historical reference, for example, to Babylon and Maccabaean times (Ps. 41, in glosses only, not in heading), to Saul and Maccabees (Ps. 42; Babylonian in Theodore and Diodorus).

There appears to be a direct reference to the Antiochenes (called *Syri*) and their exegesis in the heading to Psalm 50, the *Miserere*. Despite the biblical heading, which takes this psalm as Davidic and concerning

32. In the *Eclogae tractatorum in Psalterium*, in 'Das Bibelwerk' and in the *Old-Irish Treatise on the Psalter*; cf. McNamara (ed.), *Biblical Studies*, pp. 226, 229 n. 42, p. 255.

33. F. Unterkircher (ed.), *Die Glossen des Psalters von Mondsee (vor 788) (Montpellier, Faculté de Médecine MS 409)* (Spicilegium Friburgense, 20; Freiburg: Universitätsverlag, 1974).

34. Cf. De Coninck and d'Hont (eds.), *Theodori*, pp. xliv-xlv.

David's sin with Bathsheba, Antiochene tradition regarded it as a prayer of the captive people in Babylon (thus Theodore and Diodorus). The heading in the commentary of the Psalters of Montpellier and Vercelli disagrees with this: *Manifeste de Dauid dicitur, sicut titulus eius docet. Syri autem hunc psalmum ex persona eorum qui erant in Babylonia dicunt, quia tulerunt titulos de psalmis.*[35] The heading of this psalm and the accompanying commentary have been transmitted independently in Codex Monte Cassino 57, and were published in 1897 by G. Morin.[36] The authorship of this comment on Psalm 50 has been, and still is, a matter of dispute. Some (for example, A. Vaccari) have ascribed it to Jerome and taken it as evidence of his acquaintance with Antiochene exegesis.[37] Its original setting seems to have been where it stands in the larger commentary we are considering, and provides further evidence that this was composed in circles in the Latin Church consciously conversant with Antiochene exegesis. What these circles were has yet to be identified. For reasons other than its Antiochene connections, Franz Unterkircher believed it was composed in Ireland.[38] Certain characteristics of the exegesis found in these glosses are also found in Irish sources. Thus, for instance, the emphasis on interpreting the psalms of David: his persecution by Saul—(Pss. 62, 85, 140, etc.); his flight from Saul, his return to reign after Saul's persecution and Absalom's revolt (Pss. 80, 114). This, however, scarcely amounts to proof of Irish origin: Irish tradition may have been influenced by the tradition enshrined in this commentary even if the work itself originated outside Ireland.

1.5.e. *Unidentified Antiochene-type Commentary on Psalms 1–16*. It has been noted earlier in this study that although the glosses on the *Hebraicum* of the Double Rouen Psalter from Ps. 16.11b onwards are drawn from the Epitome of Julian as found in the Milan Codex Amb. C 301 inf., those on the opening section (Pss. 1.1–16.11a) are not from the

35. De Coninck and d'Hont (eds.), *Theodori*, p. 216.

36. G. Morin, 'Appendix', *Sancti Hieronymi Presbyteri Tractatus Sive Homeliae Anecdota Maredsolana* 3 (1897), pp. 421-23; reproduced in *PL Supplementum* 2, II, pp. 324-26.

37. Cf. A. Vaccari, 'Titoli dei salmi nella scuola antiochena', *Biblica* 9 (1928), pp. 78-88 (83-85). See also McNamara, in a review of F. Stegmüller and N. Reinhardt (eds.), *Repestorihem Biblicam Medii Aevi* (Madrid: Consejo Superior de Investigaciones Científicas, 1979) in *Irish Theological Quarterly* 48 (1981), pp. 278-79.

38. Unterkircher (ed.), *Die Glossen*, pp. 23-26.

corresponding section of the Milan Theodorean commentary. These glosses, it would appear, represent portions of a hitherto unidentified commentary in the literal tradition of Antioch, although not that of Theodore or Diodorus. For these same psalms, and it would appear corresponding in content to these glosses, we have a series of historical psalm headings. This series for Psalms 1–16 has been transmitted to us in the Psalter of Rouen itself, in the work entitled *De titulis Psalmorum* erroneously attributed to Bede, and in the headings of the so-called Psalter of Charlemagne. Many of these headings also refer the psalms to later Jewish history, but not in the same manner as in the commentary of Theodore. The glosses of some of the psalms, in so far as they are decipherable, correspond to the headings. Some of the expository excerpts on Psalms 1–16 in 'Das Bibelwerk', given under the rubric *Iosepus*, are identical with the glosses on the Rouen Psalter.[39] Since excerpts from the Epitome of Julian for Ps. 16.12 onwards in 'Das Bibelwerk' are also under this same rubric *Iosepus*, it is clear that the Epitome text it drew on was completed for Pss. 1.1–16.11a in the same manner as that used for the Rouen Psalter. Only after much more work has been done on these Rouen glosses will we be able to determine its place in the history of Antiochene exegesis in the West.

Antiochene exegesis did not suit the temper of medieval Europe, and for this reason was neglected. As Beryl Smalley notes,[40] enough material existed in the early Middle Ages to enable a Latin reader to learn at least the principles of Antiochene exegesis and to experiment with them for himself, if he wished. Some of the early Irish scholars availed themselves of this opportunity. But they were alone in doing so. The Antiochenes in fact were generally neglected. The fate of the text of the Julian Epitome that got included in the exposition of Psalm 82 in Remigius's commentary, as well as another non-verbal quotation from the same commentary, is symptomatic of this neglect: neither passage was taken up in the *Glossa Ordinaria* although his commentary was extremely popular and used by the compilers of the *Glossa*.

---

39. All the texts of 'Das Bibelwerk' under the heading *Iosepus* are noted, and those on texts of Psalms 1–16 edited, in McNamara (ed.), *Glossa in Psalmos* (Introduction n. 231).

40. Smalley, *Study*, pp. 19, 17.

1.6. *Psalm Prefaces: East and West*

The great commentators of both East and West prefaced introductions to their commentaries on the Psalms, treating of the principles governing their exegesis among other things. Together with this, we have some early 'introductions' to the Psalter which were never intended as prefaces to commentaries. Some of the great writers such as Jerome also wrote letters on individual points of psalm interpretation. The commentary ascribed to Diodorus has a general introduction with detailed information on the Antiochene principles of psalm exegesis.[41] Much of this is repeated in the introduction to Psalm 118 in the same commentary.[42] No Greek text of a preface to Theodore's commentary is known. In the Latin translation of the comment on Ps. 15.4 Theodore speaks of collections of peculiarities of Hebrew speech which he had made in the preface: *quod quidem inter proprietatum collectiones in praefatione signauimus.*[43] An Old Irish gloss (M1. 37a15) on *praefatione* says: 'that has not come down to us, for this is an epitome'.[44]

During the Middle Ages older Psalm prefaces were being copied and new ones composed. Dom D. de Bruyne has published 84 such psalm prefaces from mediaeval Latin manuscripts,[45] a few of which are, however, really psalm headings. An analysis of these works shows the older influences that were still operative. These prefaces may also give an idea of certain, less usual, methods of exegesis, for example, that which asks whether *omnes psalmi proprie ad David pertinent aut omnes ad Christum, an sunt aliqui, qui ad utrumque pertinent* ?[46] ('[Whether] all the Psalms refer in the time sense to David or whether they all [refer] to Christ, or whether there are some that refer to both').

---

41. Olivier (ed.), *Diodori*, pp. 3-8. The preface was already published, with French translation, by Mariès, 'Extraits', pp. 82-89.

42. The introduction to Psalm 118, with French translation, also published by Mariès, 'Extraits', pp. 90-101.

43. Devreesse, *Le commentaire*, pp. 94, lines 1-4; De Coninck and d'Hont (eds.), *Theodori*, p. 77, lines 90-94.

44. *Thes. Pal.*, I, p. 95.

45. D. de Bruyne, *Préface de la Bible latine* (Namur: A. Godenne, 1920), part VIII, pp. 42-117.

46. de Bruyne, *Préface*, no. 28, p. 81, lines 12-17; S. Berger, *Les préfaces jointes aux livres de la Bible dans les manuscrits de la Vulgate* (Paris, 1902), no. 115.

1.7. *Psalm Headings*

Already in the Hebrew Bible headings were inserted before the Psalms, in part containing directions for the choir but also attempting to identify the historical situation that first occasioned the particular psalm's composition. In the Greek Septuagint translation and in the Latin ones these biblical headings tended to be multiplied.

In an effort to aid the use of the Psalter as Christian prayer new headings were composed for each psalm. These headings are especially frequent in Latin Psalter manuscripts, from which Dom Pierre Salmon has published six full series of then.[47]

The tradition of interpretation behind these headings is sometimes very old. Some of them take their inspiration from one individual commentator (Origen, Eusebius of Caesarea, Jerome, Cassiodorus). Others have names of noted churchmen attached (for example, Augustine of Canterbury), or go back to various isolated traditions.

The Syriac Church rejected the biblical psalm headings altogether and inserted in their stead headings dependent on the Syriac translation of Theodore's commentary.[48] There is also a series of Latin Theodorean headings, transmitted in Irish sources, which depends on the Epitome of Julian. Together with this, as noted already, we have for Psalms 1–16 psalm headings of an historical nature, of the Antiochene kind but not in the Theodorean tradition of exegesis. We shall consider these in greater detail later.[49]

1.8. *Latin Psalm Translations*

Basic to all study of the Psalter is the text, in the original or in translation. By the second century at least there was a Latin translation of the Psalter. These old Latin versions are collectively known as the Vetus Latina. One of these was the *Psalterium Romanum*, once widely used in England and traditionally used in St Peter's Basilica, Rome, whence the name.[50]

Jerome himself tells us that while in Rome (c. 384) he corrected an

47. Salmon, *Les 'Tituli'*.

48. W. Bloemendaal (ed.), *The Headings of the Psalms in the East Syrian Church* (Leiden: E.J. Brill, 1960).

49. See below 2.3.b.

50. Edited by R. Weber, *Le Psautier Romain et les autres anciens psautiers latins* (Edition critique; Collectanea Biblica Latina, 10; Rome: Abbaye de Saint-Jérôme; Vatican City: Libreria Vaticana, 1953).

Old Latin text of the Psalter. What became of this amended text, we cannot say. Later, having settled at Bethlehem (c. 386–89), Jerome made another emendation of the Psalter, using for the purpose the critical work done by Origen on the Greek translation, and like Origen using the critical signs of asterisk and obelus. This emendation was destined to become the official text of the medieval Church. Because of its early acceptance as such in Gaul it came to be called the *Gallicanum*.[51]

Between 389 and 392 Jerome translated the Psalms directly from the Hebrew (for him the *Hebraica Veritas*) into Latin. This version is known as *Psalterium iuxta Hebraeos*, or the *Hebraicum*.[52]

2. *Tradition and Creativity in Early Irish Psalm Exegesis*

2.1. *Irish Psalter Texts*[53]

2.1.a. *The Old Latin Texts in Ireland.* Dr Ludwig Bieler has shown that the Psalter text used by St Patrick was the Old Latin, of the type used in Gaul.[54] There is no trace in his writings of Hieronymian Psalter readings. We cannot say which Psalter text was used by St Columba of Iona (died 597). Adomnán says that the saint died while copying the following words of Ps. 33.11: *inquirentes autem Dominum non deficient omni bono.*[55] This is the Old Latin text; the *Gallicanum* has *minuentur* for *non deficient*. One would scarcely be permitted, however, to draw any conclusion as to Columba's Psalter from this evidence, which may say more about some later Psalter than about Columba's. Apart from an occasional reading in the catena on the Psalms in Codex Vaticanus Pal. lat. 68, Old Latin Psalter texts and readings in Ireland are noticeable by their absence. All the evidence indicates that the new rendering now known as the *Gallicanum* had replaced the Old Latin by 600 or so.

51. Critical edition, *Liber Psalmorum ex recensione Sancti Hieronymi cum praefationibus et epistula ad Sunniam et Fretelam* (Biblia Sacra iuxta Latinam Vulgatam Versionern ad Codicum Fidem, 10; Roma: Vatican Polyglot Press, 1953).

52. Edited by H. de Sainte-Marie, *Sancti Hieronymi Psalterium iuxta Hebraeos* (Collectanea Biblica Latina, 11; Rome: Abbaye de Saint-Jérôme; Vatican City: Libreria Vaticana, 1954).

53. For this section see McNamara, 'Psalter Text', pp. 19-142 of this volume.

54. L. Bieler, 'Der Bibeltext des heiligen Patrick', *Biblica* 28 (1947), pp. 31-58; 236-63, at 244-45, 257 for Psalter text.

55. A.O. Anderson and M.O. Anderson (eds.), *Adomnan's Life of Columba* (London: Nelson, 1961), 3.23, p. 524.

2.1.b. *The Gallican Psalter Text in Early Ireland.* The Gallican Psalter text must have been brought to Ireland during the sixth century at the latest. There is a tradition (first recorded it would seem in Manus O'Donnell's *Life of Columcille*) that the text now known as the Cathach was copied by Colum Cille and that the copying of it was the cause of the battle of Cúil Dremne[56] in 561. The story is an unlikely one. Earlier forms of this story say that the book in question was a Gospel Book, not a Psalter. Besides this, there is evidence that the Cathach was written in the seventh, rather than in the sixth century.[57] The critical signs of the asterisk and obelus as used in the Cathach indicate that it has been edited against the specifically Irish family of *Hebraicum* texts.[58] Its text, then, represents textual criticism carried out in Irish schools, and not a direct copy of a continental model, as the tradition by Manus O'Donnell would have it.

We can presume, however, that the Gallican text was taken to Ireland during the life of Columba (521–97), if not earlier. The earliest evidence of its presence in Ireland is probably in the Springmount Bog wax tablets, which may be dated at about 600 CE.[59] The tablets contain the Gallican text of Psalms 30, 31 and part of 32, and were probably used to introduce students to the arts of reading and writing. The next oldest Gallican text we possess is the Cathach, coming probably from c. 630–50.

---

56. Cf. A. O'Kelleher and G. Schoepperle (eds.), *Betha Colaim Chille: Life of Columcille compiled by Maghnas Ó Domhnaill in 1532* (Urbana: University of Illinois, 1918; repr. Dublin Institute for Advanced Studies, 1994). The tradition of the copying of a book borrowed from Finnén of Druim Finn is given in §168; the identification of the book as the Cathach in §178. For a fuller discussion of 'St Finnian's Book' see H.J. Lawlor, 'The Cathach of St Columba', *PRIA* 33 C (1916), pp. 413-36 (307, 329). W.M. Lindsay, 'Palaeographical Notes' (*PRIA* 33 C [1916], pp. 397-403) and Lowe, *CLA* II, no. 226, find a sixth-century date palaeographically acceptable; so also, more recently, B. Schauman, 'Early Irish Manuscripts: The Art of the Scribes', *Expedition* 21 (1979), pp. 31-47, at 37-38 for the date of Cathach.

57. D.H. Wright assigns a date of c. 630, cf. 'The Tablets from Springmount Bog, a Key to Early Irish Palaeography', *American Journal of Archaeology* 67 (1963), p. 219.

58. See below 4.2.a.ii.

59. See Wright, 'The Tablets', and McNamara, 'Psalter Text', pp. 19-142 in this volume. Schaumann, 'Early Irish Manuscripts', p. 37, however, says that the archaic script used in the tablets argues against a date as late as the seventh century. A sixth-century date would not be unreasonable.

Once introduced, the Gallican text soon displaced the Old Latin completely. In the *Old-Irish Treatise* on the Psalter (c. 800), it is spoken of as if it were the accepted translation[60]. In the Old Irish glosses in the Milan Commentary (Cod. Amb. C 301 inf.), from about 800 CE, the Gallican text is taken as the criterion for determining deviant Psalter readings.[61] We have the Gallican text in the following Irish Psalters (apart from the Cathach, already mentioned):[62] BL MS Vitellius F XI (c. 920); the Gallican section of the Double Psalter of Rouen (Rouen, Bibl. Publique, MS 24, A. 41), from the tenth century, and in the fragments of the sister codex of this in Dublin, Trinity College, MS H 3 18, fols. 2*-3*; in MS Vat. Lat. 12910 of the eleventh century; in the Southampton Psalter (St John's College, Cambridge, MS C. 9), of the early eleventh century, in the abbreviated psalter of the Irish *Liber Hymnorum* of the late eleventh century; in the so-called Psalter of Caimín from c. 1100; also probably in the BL MS Cotton Galba A.V of the twelfth century. To these we may add two later and Cistercian manuscripts: the Coupar Angus Psalter, Vatican MS Pal. lat. 65 (c. 1170) and the Psalter of Cormac, BL MS Add. 36929 (c. 1150–1200).

In reconstructing the original text of the *Gallicanum* the Benedictine editors place the Cathach (with the siglum C) and the text of the Rouen Psalter (with the siglum I) as the third and fourth respectively of their five basic manuscripts. These two texts which are very closely related constitute a family apart among Gallican texts. Apart from these peculiarities, this family contains a text very near to Jerome's original emendation.[63]

A feature of the Cathach is that it contains the critical signs of asterisk and obelus which Jerome used in his original correction of the Latin in accord with the Hebrew—following the lead given by Origen. In the introduction to this rendering (*Psalterium Romae dudum positus emen-*

---

60. See, e.g., lines 329-342: 'What is the translation that is on the psalms?... The translation of the Septuagint (= *Gallicanum*), truly, that is the one which is on the psalms... Jerome corrected it under dagger and asterisk', *OIT*, pp. 32-33.

61. See some of the evidence in McNamara, 'Psalter Text', pp. 102-103 of this volume. Occasionally in these glosses the *Gallicanum* is called 'the Septuagint'.

62. On these texts see McNamara, 'Psalter Text', with summary, pp. 102-103 of this volume.

63. See the Benedictine critical edition of the *Gallicanum*; *Liber Psalmorum* (Rome: Vatican Polyglot Press, 1953), pp. xii—xiv, and D. de Bruyne, 'La réconstruction du psautier hexaplaire latin', *RBén* 41 (1929), pp. 297-324.

daram) Jerome appealed to scribes not to copy his corrected Psalter text without these critical signs. Despite this, the signs were very often omitted: only one of the five basic manuscripts used by the Benedictine editors of the *Gallicanum* (that is, Codex Reginensis Latinus 11) uses most of them. Medieval Gallican manuscripts, notably those of the Alcuin recension, do have obeli and asterisks. In many instances, however, these do not represent Jerome's original, but rather a later collation of the *Gallicanum* against Jerome's rendering from the Hebrew—the *Hebraicum*.[64]

In the Cathach there are about 19 occurrences of the obelus and 21 of the asterisk—the former we may recall indicating passages in the Septuagint (and Jerome's Latin corrected text) but not in the Hebrew, the asterisk indicating a word or words not in the Septuagint but added from the Hebrew. Only in two instances (Pss. 33.10; 84.11) does the obelus in the Cathach correspond to an obelus in Jerome's original. As Dom Henri de Sainte-Marie has noted in his excellent critical edition of Jerome's rendering from the Hebrew, 10 of these critical signs in the *Cathach* reveal their true origin, which is a revision of the *Gallicanum* against the Latin text of the *Hebraicum*. More precisely still, this revision is against the specifically Irish family of *Hebraicum* texts—of which I shall speak presently. The Irish family is characterized by certain omissions—sometimes omission of a single word, other times of an entire phrase. For instance in the Cathach the entire phrase *et opera manuum tuarum dirige super nos* of Ps. 89.17 is *sub obelo*, indicating that it is regarded as having been absent from the Hebrew text. In fact, it is in the original Hebrew text and in the original *Hebraicum*, Jerome's Latin rendering of this. The phrase, however, is absent from the Irish family of *Hebraicum* texts, represented by the three basic manuscripts AKI, to which we can also add the (Irish) Edinburgh Psalter, Edinburgh, University Library MS 56. The presence of the obelus in the Cathach at Ps. 97.5 and 91.11, 95.9 is to be explained in the same manner.

The purpose of the 21 asterisks in the Cathach is less easy to explain. Nine of them correspond to asterisks in Jerome's original, as reconstructed by the Benedictine editors. Five of the other instances would qualify for an asterisk, being on material which is in the Hebrew but not in the Septuagint. In these instances, however, no asterisk is given in

64. See further de Sainte-Marie, *Sancti Hieronymi*, pp. xxiii-xxiv; McNamara, 'Psalter Text', pp. 107-10 of this volume.

the Benedictine edition of the *Gallicanum*. Comparison with the *Hebraicum* may have guided the person who inserted the asterisks in these cases. The remaining seven texts in the Cathach set off by an asterisk present a greater problem, in that the asterisk comes before words that are in the Septuagint. In five of these, in fact, the words under asterisk are found in all texts: the original Hebrew, the Septuagint, the Old Latin and *Gallicanum* (thus at Pss. 34.15; 58.6; 65.7; 85.4; 103.7). In one of these (Ps. 65.7) the words in question (*in aeternum*) is also *sub asterisco* in Codex Reginensis (R), the chief manuscript of the *Gallicanum*, although erroneously, it would appear, in the opinion of the Benedictine editors. It may have been in the exemplar of the Cathach, or the Cathach may have inserted it from comparison with a manuscript of the R type. In another instance of the seven (Ps. 49.7) the word in question (*et*) is absent from an Old Latin and one *Gallicanum* text and is *sub asterisco* also in Codex Abbatiae Sangallensis 20, of the *Gallicanum*. Unless the insertion of the asterisks in this latter group of texts was capricious, their presence in the Cathach may be explained through 'correction' of the underlying Gallican text against some faulty Gallican or Old Latin manuscripts.

The evidence provided by this use of the obelus and asterisk, particularly the former, in the Cathach indicates the existence of a critical textual approach to the Psalter text in Irish schools, and this already in the sixth century or the early seventh at the latest. From the Old Irish glosses in the Milan Commentary we know that a critical interest in textual matters was also evident in the late eighth or early ninth centuries.[65] From these glosses we see that the Irish glossator was interested in the quality of the Latin text of the commentary, in the nature of the biblical text it employed and the instances in which it deviated from the text which for him was authoritative, that is, the *Gallicanum* which he occasionally calls the Septuagint.

2.1.c. *Jerome's rendering from the Hebrew (the* Hebraicum*) in Early Ireland.* We have copies, or fragments, of the *Hebraicum* rendering as used in Ireland in the following texts:[66] the Codex Amiatinus (with siglum A), from about 700 (but before 716); Karlsruhe, Cod. Augiensis XXXVIII (with siglum K), from the ninth century; Paris BN MS Fr.

---

65. McNamara, 'Psalter Text', pp. 106-107 above.
66. On these MSS see McNamara, 'Psalter Text', with summary in pp. 104-105 above.

2452, from the late ninth century; the Double Psalter of Rouen (Rouen, Bibl. Municipale MS 14 [A. 4]), of the tenth century (given the siglum I and already mentioned in relation to the Gallican texts) and its Dublin sister codex in Trinity College MS H 3 18, fol. 2*-3*; the Edinburgh Psalter (about 1025 CE) and the Psalter of Ricemarch, Dublin, Trinity College MS 50 (A. 4 20) (soon after 1055).

In the history of the transmission of the *Hebraicum* we have an Irish family of texts, represented by the manuscripts AKI, in the order of antiquity of the manuscripts.[67] In the order of the purity of the texts as representatives of the Irish *Hebraicum* tradition this order should be reversed, the Rouen Psalter being the most faithful representative of the original Irish *Hebraicum* text.

As already noted, this Irish family is characterized by certain omissions, sometimes of single words, other times of entire phrases. The fact that the insertion of the obeli and asterisks into the Cathach is in dependence on this Irish family indicates that the *Hebraicum* itself must have come to Ireland during the sixth century at the latest. It still remains to be determined whether it was taken to Ireland in what is now its peculiar Irish form or whether this developed in Ireland itself. The use of an Irish text in the Codex Amiatinus indicates that it was being used in Northumbria in the early eighth century. The same family had a wider influence in Europe later through the form of text found in K.[68]

2.2. *Psalm Prefaces and Prologues used in Ireland*
2.2.a. *Jerome's* Scio quosdam, Psalterium Romae dudum positus *and Pseudo-Bede's* Dauid filius Jesse. We know that the early Irish schools used at least these three psalm prefaces. All three are found as prefaces to the Milan Commentary, Cod. Amb. C 301 inf., and are heavily glossed in Old Irish.[69] This latter fact indicates that they were used in the Irish schools.

Jerome's preface *Scio quosdam* (Cod. Amb. C 301 inf., fol. 2c-3a) is introduced as the work of Jerome: *Incipit prologus Hirunimi ad Suffronium…* The same work introduces his second preface (cols. 2a-b) as: *Incipit praefatio psalmorum in Christo Iesu Domini nostro*, with *Hieronimi* interlineated in another hand after *praefatio*. The preface *Scio quosdam* is also cited at length in the Prologue to the Psalter in the

---

67. de Sainte-Marie, *Sancti Hieronymi*, pp. xxii-xxvi.
68. de Sainte-Marie, *Sancti Hieronymi*, pp. xli-xliv.
69. Text in *Thes. Pal.*, I, pp. 7-10.

Hiberno-Latin *Eclogae tractatorum in Psalterium.*[70]

The Pseudo-Bede Preface has as title, *incipit* and *explicit*: (fol. 2b-c): *incipit prologus psalmorum. David filius Iessae...deabsalma lxxu, alleluia xxi. canticum graduum xii.* D. de Bruyne[71] has published two variant recensions of this preface from the MSS, both with a longer ending. These three prefaces were widely used in the Western Church.

2.2.b. *St Basil's Psalm Preface in Rufinus's Latin Translation.* In the Milan text (Cod. Amb. C 301 inf., fol. 3a-4a) we have the Psalm Preface of St Basil in Rufinus's Latin translation, but here attributed to Jerome: *Incipit praefatio psalmorum uel laus psalterii. Hirunimus dicit: Omnis scriptura diuinitus inspirata...* It ends: *...uideamus tandem quid etiam ipsa psalmi indicentur initia.* This Preface of Basil (*PG* 29, 210; 31, 1723-26) was commonly attributed to St Augustine (*PL* 36, cols. 63-66). Although there appears to be an echo of it in the Introduction to the Psalter in the Hiberno-Latin Commentary on the entire Bible from the late eighth century, called by Dr Bernhard Bischoff 'Das Bibelwerk',[72] the fact that the Milan text has no Irish glosses seems to indicate that this particular preface was not much used in the Irish schools.

2.2.c. *Psalm Introduction in Irish Commentaries.* Together with these psalm prefaces received from the outside, we also have some introductions to the Psalter composed in the Irish schools themselves. The Preface to the *Eclogae tractatorum in Psalterium,*[73] as the very title of

---

70. M. Sheehy (ed.), Appendix III reprinted above pp. 124-31. It is without ascription in the Munich MS of the *Eclogae*, but attributed to Hiero(nimus) in the St Gall MS.

71. The longer recensions published by de Bruyne end: *...cantica graduum numero XV. Psalmus primus nulli adsignatus est, quoniam omnium est; deinde quis alius intellegitur in primo nisi primogenitus ut merito inscriptio non fuerit necessaria; deinde quia ipse psalmus christi mentionem facit et aduersus christum eius exponendo personam, inscribendi causum omnino non habet. Ordines historiae inmutatos legimus et in titulis psalmorum; sed psalmi non secundum historiam, sed secundum prophetias leguntur. Ita ordinem psalmorum turbare non potest ordo titulorum. Psalmi omnes qui inscribuntur ipsi dauid, ad christi pertinent sacramentum, quia dauid dictus est christus.*

72. Cf. Sheehy in n. 284 to the edition of the Introduction to the Psalter in 'Das Bibelwerk', in Appendix IV to McNamara, 'Psalter Text', pp. 134-35 in this volume. The preface has been edited from two manuscripts (BL Vep. A 1 and Angers 14) by de Bruyne, 'Préface', pp. 72-73; Berger, *Les préfaces*, no. 91.

73. Partial edition from imperfect Munich MS by Sheehy (ed.), as Appendix III

the work suggests, is in the nature of a series of excerpts from other authors, mainly Cassiodorus but also Hilary, Isidore and Junilius as well as some pseudonymous writings and occasional items, it would appear, from Irish ecclesiastical tradition. The Introduction to the Psalter in 'Das Bibelwerk'[74] also cites from some accepted patristic sources on the Psalms but is much more under the influence of what may be called the Irish approach to the Psalms and is very closely related to the Introduction to the Psalms in the *Old-Irish Treatise* on the Psalter which was composed a little later (c. 800).

2.2.d. *An Antiochene Introduction to the Psalter.* The chief source for Irish commentary material was the full Latin translation of the Commentary of Theodore of Mopsuestia and the Latin Epitome of this. It is possible, as we have seen,[75] that Theodore's commentary was accompanied by a preface or introduction, as the Greek commentary attributed to Diodorus was. However, no Latin translation of any such work is known. One can only speculate whether any Latin psalm preface along the principles of Antiochene exegesis was used in the West or in Irish schools. Future research may throw light on the subject. The fact, however, that in Cod. Amb. C 301 inf. the Antiochene Commentary material is preceded by prefaces of another nature would seem to indicate that no appropriate Antiochene one was known to exist. The denial of any knowledge of such a preface in the Milan glosses (Ml. 37a15) serves to reinforce this.

2.3. *Psalm Headings in the Early Irish Church*
2.3.a. *The Mystical Series of St Columba.* The series of mystical psalm headings most widely used in Medieval Latin Psalter texts is Series I of Dom Pierre Salmon's edition. He calls it 'Série de Saint Columba', because the oldest text in which it is found is the Cathach of St Columba.[76] In Dom Salmon's opinion all of the numerous witnesses to this series derive, through England, from a text being used in Ireland in the sixth century. What the history of this series before this time was is another matter. The four chief texts used by Dom Salmon for his edi-

to McNamara, 'Psalter Text', pp. 124-31 of this volume.
    74. Edited by Sheehy, Appendix IV to McNamara, 'Psalter Text', pp. 132-42 of this volume, from Munich MS.
    75. See above, 1.6.
    76. Salmon, *Les 'Tituli'*, pp. 45-74.

tion are the Cathach (C), the Codex Arniatinus (A), which for the Psalter has the 'Irish' text of the *Hebraicum*, the 'mystical' section of the Argumenta of the work *De titulis Psalmorum* wrongly ascribed to Bede, and Codex Augiensis CVII (tenth century) from Karlsruhe (with siglum R). Like Codex Amiatinus, R also has the 'Irish' *Hebraicum* text and is very closely related to A. Despite the fact that its Psalter text is the *Hebraicum*, it has the Gallican biblical psalm headings of the Irish Cathach Gallican family, and both A and R have Series I of the mystical headings which are generally associated with Gallican Psalters. Another manuscript which we may associate with the above is the so-called Psalter of Charlemagne (Paris, BN MS lat. 13159) of the late eighth century in which all the introductory material, including the mystical psalm headings, is in the central Irish tradition.[77] The earliest witness to this tradition as found in the Psalter of Charlemagne is the introductory material in the incomplete catena on the Psalms (beginning imperfectly with Ps. 39.11b) from about 700 CE found in the Vatican MS Pal. lat. 68.[78]

The Columba series of psalm headings is noted for its christological orientation.[79] The greater portion of the psalms are taken as spoken by Christ, the Church or the Apostles: *Vox Christi, Vox Ecclesiae, Vox apostolorum*. Only 24 are placed on the lips of the psalmist prophet himself, and then generally as direct prophecies of Christ.

It has been noted that this series has roots in very early Christian tradition. On a number of instances Tertullian's treatment of individual psalms is related to this series. Comparisons have also been made between this series and the exegesis of Origen (e.g. in Pss. 7, 8), Justin (Ps. 13), the baptismal liturgy (Ps. 22), the *Enarrationes* of St Augustine (Pss. 48, 50, 56, 60, 86, 90, 115).

While some of the sources for this series can be traced back to the third century, there is no evidence of the existence of the series as such earlier than the Cathach. It is clear that the series was being used in Ireland in the sixth century. Whether it was actually composed in Ire-

---

77. For this MS see Lowe, *CLA*, V, no. 652; K. Gamber, *Codices liturgici latini antiquiores* (Spicilegii Friburgensis Subsidia, 1.II; Freiburg: Universitätsverlag, 1968), no. 1619, pp. 584-85; F. Masai, 'Observations sur le Psautier dit de Charlemagne (Paris lat. 13159)', *Scriptorium* 6 (1952), pp. 299-303; Fischer, 'Bedae de', pp. 96-97.

78. McNamara (ed.), *Glossa in Psalmos*.

79. See Salmon, *Les 'Tituli'*, pp. 51-52.

land in the sixth century or earlier, or was introduced already made from outside, remains uncertain. The possibility of its being compiled in some Irish monastery or school cannot be ruled out. If it was composed there, the richness of Irish tradition and the degree of creativity in the Irish schools during these early centuries of Christianity in the island were far greater than we have been accustomed to accept.

2.3.b. *Theodorean, Antiochene and Historical Psalm Headings.* We are on surer ground with regard to the creativity of the early Irish schools in the matter of the historical psalm headings we find in such works as the catena on the Psalms of Codex Pal. lat. 68, the *De titulis Psalmorum* of Pseudo-Bede, in the so-called Psalter of Charlemagne and in the Double Psalter of Rouen.

In the question of these historical headings we must distinguish between Theodorean headings (depending on the Epitome of Julian) and other historical headings not depending on the Commentary of Theodore or the Julian Epitome. There is a series of headings on Psalms 17–150 which depends on the Epitome of Julian. Together with this, for Psalms 1–16 there exists a historical series of psalm headings which is not drawn from, nor dependent on, the Theodorean commentary. Then again, and together with these two series, we have, especially in the catena of Pal. lat. 68 and in the so-called Psalter of Charlemagne, a series of historical headings, but not Theodorean. These headings for the greater part understand the psalms of David and his times. These different series of historical psalm headings are intimately connected with the actual exegesis of the psalms which we find in the expository glosses of the Vatican catena and the Double Psalter of Rouen.

The Theodorean and historical psalm headings in the pseudo-Bedan *De titulis psalmorum*[80] were first printed in Heerwagen's *editio princeps* of Bede's works (1563), as part of the composition *In Psalmorum librum exegesis.*[81] In this work the exposition of each psalm is divided into three sections: (a) a brief *argumentum*, (b) an *explanatio* dealing with the psalm in general, followed by (c) the *Commentarius* proper. The *Commentarius* goes only as far as Psalm 121, while the *argumenta* and *explanationes* cover the entire Psalter.

It has been shown that this composition in three sections is entirely

80. For a study of these see Fischer, 'Bedae de Titulis psalmorum liber', pp. 90-110; also Ramsay, 'Theodore of Mopsuestia', pp. 453-56.

81. Reproduced in *PL* 93, cols. 477-1098.

arbitrary and in part due to the editor of the *editio princeps*. The *Commentarius* has nothing to do with Bede. It has been shown to be the work of the twelfth-century writer Manegold von Lautenbach.[82] The *argumenta* and *explanationes* once circulated independently of the *Commentarius* and are found in the two manuscripts, Munich Clm 14387 (ninth century) and Paris, BN MS lat. 12273 (tenth century). In both these texts the *argumenta* for all the Psalms come first, after this comes further material on the Psalms (explanation of *sela, interpretatio psalterii artis*, that is, explanation of difficult words in the Psalter, and *Interpretatio nominum Hebraeorum*). After this come the *Explanationes*.

The *Explanationes* are really a summary of the introductions which Cassiodorus prefixed to his commentary on the Psalms. This summary was apparently made by Bede.

The *Argumenta* are composite, comprising two, and sometimes three parts. Section (a), a historical heading, is present for every psalm except Psalm 87, and almost invariably stands first. It is the section that interests us here, and I shall return to it presently. Section (b) gives the mystical explanation, and is none other than the Irish St Columba Series which I have just considered. Section (c) when present, gives a brief moral application drawn from the works of Arnobius or Jerome.

Section (a), the historical heading, interprets the given psalm of some event in Old Testament history: of David's time, of Hezekiah or the Maccabees. From Psalm 17 onwards, with few exceptions, all these historical headings of Pseudo-Bede are dependent on the Epitome of Julian, at times reproducing even its wording. The headings for Psalms 1–16, although giving the literal, non-messianic, non-christological meaning of the text, are not Theodorean. These historical headings in *De titulis psalmorum* are all connected with a particular form of exposition of the Psalms, the historical approach which I shall consider in greater detail later.

The catena on the Psalms of Cod. Pal. lat. 68[83] contains introductory material of a historical nature regarding the understanding of the Psalms. The chief source of inspiration for the historical headings in the catena is the Epitome of Julian or more precisely the *argumenta* prefixed to the

82. Cf. H. Weisweiler, 'Die handschriftlichen Vorlagen zum Erstdruck von Ps. Beda, *In Psalmorum librum exegesis*', *Biblica* 18 (1937), pp. 197-204.

83. This question is considered in greater detail in the introduction to McNamara (ed.), *Glossa in Psalmos*.

exposition proper in the Epitome. The Epitome has influenced the headings of the catena in two ways. In many cases the headings of the catena
reproduce verbatim the text of the Epitome, while in others the substance of the heading in Pal. lat. 68 is that of the *argumentum* of the
Epitome, although the wording is different. In some instances the heading of the catena contains only a mere reflection of the Epitome.

Together with the heading reproducing or reflecting the text of the
Epitome and Theodorean exegesis there is in the catena of Pal. lat. 68
another series of headings interpreting the Psalms as speaking of David
and his times. Sometimes both kinds of headings are found for the same
psalm. On some occasions the Davidic interpretation of the psalm has
influenced the very biblical psalm heading, for example, Psalm 46: *Vox
Dauid accepto regno* (= Davidic reference). *Vox plebis post reuersionem; siue (in tempore) Machabeorum carmen istud tamquam tri-
umphale praecinnitur diui(i)ctis quippe gentibus uel Iudeis praeuarica-
toribus* (= Julian Epitome). Or again Psalm 47: *Vox Dauid accepto
regno pro gratiarum actione* (= Davidic reference). *Vox Ezechiae. Esti-
mationem hominum ignorantium Deum arguit* (Julian Epitome).

These examples, taken somewhat at random, could be multiplied. As
headings they reflect a particular kind of exegesis interpreting the
psalms both of David and later Jewish history, exegesis found in the
expository glosses of the catena. The headings themselves are as creative as the particular form of interpretation itself, which I shall consider later.

I have already spoken of the so-called Psalter of Charlemagne (Paris,
BN MS lat. 13159) in relation to Series I (the St Columba Series) of
mystical psalm headings. All the introductory material to the Psalms in
this Psalter, written hastily and with many errors of transcription c.
795–800, is very closely related to that found in the corresponding
introductory material in the Vatican catena just now considered. This
holds true in a particular manner for the historical headings, both Theodorean and non-Theodorean. The heading of Psalm 42 which I give
here is typical of this relationship.

Psalter of Charlemagne	Catena in Cod. Pal. lat. 68
In finem psalmus Dauid. Gratulatio reuertentis in regnum; uel queralla Dauid pro Saul. Vox plebis in Babilonia. Vox Christi ad passionem et Ecclesiae ad Christum.	*In finem salmus Dauid. De gratulatione reuersonis in regnum; uel querela Dauid pro Saul. Vox plebis in Babilonia. Vox Christi ad Patrem. Vox aeclesiae.*

With regard to this historical material there are differences as well as resemblances of which to take note. Both texts have peculiar biblical headings with reference to David proper to themselves. With regard to the Theodorean material, both draw what they have of it from the Julian Epitome. In a number of instances the material from the Epitome in both the catena and the Psalter is identical, both in the wording and in the amount borrowed. In other cases, however, the text of the Psalter of Charlemagne draws more extensively on the Epitome than does the catena. With regard to the other historical headings not drawn from the Epitome found in the catena, some but not all of these are found in the Psalter of Charlemagne.

It is evident that the tradition preserved in the introductory material of the so-called Psalter of Charlemagne is intimately related to that found in the catena of Pal. lat. 68. Both represent the same tradition which appears to be unique in the Western Church and to be that of the schools of Ireland and of the Celtic Church in Northumbria.

There are historical psalm headings on Psalms 1–16 in the Psalters of Rouen, Charlemagne and in Pseudo-Bede's *De titulis Psalmorum*. In the Double Psalter of Rouen, written in Ireland in the tenth century, the texts of both the *Gallicanum* and the *Hebraicum* are glossed, this latter much more so than the *Gallicanum*. It has been recognized for some time that the marginal gloss on the *Hebraicum* derives from the Theodorean commentary of the kind found in Cod. Amb. C 301 inf. We now know that this Milan Commentary of Cod. Amb. C 301 inf. fol. 14a-146, is actually composite, the first part (on Pss. 1.1–16.11a) being a full Latin translation of the commentary of Theodore of Mopsuestia whereas the remainder (on Pss. 16.11b to the end) is but an Epitome of the Latin translation, a translation now generally believed to have been made by Julian of Eclanum.[84] This Epitome, it would appear, once existed for the entire Psalter, but became imperfect through the loss of the entire opening section. In the tradition represented by the Milan Codex, this loss was made good by inserting in its stead the text of the full translation of Theodore's work.

A check of the Rouen glosses on Psalms 1–16 has shown that the

84. On this point see Devreesse, *Le commentaire*, p. xxvi; A. Vaccari, 'Nuova opera di Giuliano eclanese: Commento ai Salmi', *La civiltà cattolica* 67 (1916), pp. 578-93; A. Vaccari, 'Il salterio ascoliano e Giulano eclanese', *Biblica* 4 (1923), pp. 337-55; and more recently De Coninck and d'Hont (eds.), *Theodori*, pp. xv-xxxvii.

glosses on the portion before Ps. 16.11b are not from the Theodorean commentary, whereas those on verses from 16.12 onwards are drawn from the Julian Epitome. These glosses on Pss. 1.1–16.11 reveal portions of an otherwise unknown commentary, giving a sober, literal interpretation of the biblical text. Unfortunately, only parts of the glosses in question can be read with any degree of certainty, due to the fact that the handwriting is extremely small and that the close binding has made part of the glosses on the left-hand margins illegible. These difficulties are somewhat compensated for by the occurrence of the text of a few of these glosses in the section on the Psalter in the late eighth-century work known as 'Das Bibelwerk'.

I have studied the historical headings in the Rouen Psalter and find that for the greater part they agree almost verbatim with those in the pseudo-Bedan *De titulis psalmorum*. The identity is all the clearer in the rare heading on Psalm 13, although it should also be noted that in one instance (Ps. 12), the heading in the Rouen Psalter agrees with that of the Psalter of Charlemagne, rather than with Pseudo-Bede. Most of the historical headings for Psalms 1–16 in the Rouen Psalter are in the pages with the *Hebraicum*, although one or other is in the facing page with the *Gallicanum* text.[85]

In so far as can be ascertained, these historical psalm headings of Pseudo-Bede and the Rouen Psalter are designed to go with the kind of commentary revealed by the glosses on these same psalms found in the *Hebraicum* of the Rouen Psalter. Basically the same tradition of psalm headings is found in the so-called Psalter of Charlemagne for Psalms 1–16. Because of the importance of this series I publish here (as an Appendix) all three series of historical psalm headings. With the exception of those from the Psalter of Charlemagne for Psalms 2,[86] 3[87] and 4[88] and Psalm 8[89] of the Rouen Psalter, only those from Pseudo-Bede's *De titulis psalmorum* have been published before.

---

85. It has yet to be determined whether some of these argumenta were added later, from MSS such as Clm 14387 or Paris, BN MS lat. 12273; cf. De Coninck and d'Hont (eds.), *Theodori*, p. xliv n. 248.

86. Published already by Salmon, *Les 'Tituli'*, p. 32.

87. Published already by Salmon, *Les 'Tituli'*.

88. Published already by Salmon, *Les 'Tituli'*.

89. Published, together with accompanying commentary, by De Coninck and d'Hont (eds.), *Theodori*, p. xliii n. 245.

2.4. *Psalm Commentaries of the Early Irish Church*

2.4.a. *Non-Antiochene Commentaries in Ireland.*[90] While the material at our disposal has not as yet been sufficiently analysed to permit us draw a complete picture of the commentary material available to early Irish scholars, we have good reason to believe that for the interpretation of the Psalms they had copies of the following works: the *Commentarioli*, and probably also the *Tractatus sive Homeliae in Psalmos*, of Jerome; the *Enarrationes in Psalmos* of Augustine, or an abbreviation of them; the *Formulae spiritalis intellegentiae* and *Instructionum libri duo* of Eucherius of Lyons; Paterius's collection of expositions from the works of Gregory the Great known as *Liber testimoniorum Veteris Testamenti*;[91] the introductions to the psalm commentaries of Hilary and Cassiodorus[92] and very probably their commentaries as well; works of Isidore relating to the various subjects encountered in the Psalter.

For our purpose here this general list, based on the evidence of extant Irish commentaries, will suffice. A more detailed study of the subject would need to specify how widespread the use of any particular commentary was, when its use was first attested, and if possible in what part of Ireland. In general we can say that by the year 800 the works noted above were available in Irish monastic libraries.

2.4.b. *Theodore and Junilius.* We may justly presume that at one time the Latin translation of the complete commentary on the Psalms by Theodore of Mopsuestia was available in the Western Church, at least in certain centres of learning. All that is now extant of this full trans-

---

90. On this subject see McNamara, 'Psalter Text', above pp. 90-93. See also C. Stancliffe, 'Early "Irish" Biblical Exegesis', in E. Livingstone (ed.), *Papers Presented to the Sixth International Confederation on Patristic Studies held in Oxford 1971, part 1: Inaugural Lecture, Editiones, Critica, Philologica, Biblica, Historica* (Studia Patristica, 12; Berlin: Akademie Verlag, 1975), pp. 361-70.

91. Paterius's work is cited extensively under the rubric Gregor(ius) in the section on the Psalter in 'Das Bibelwerk'.

92. The earliest series of excerpts from Cassiodorus's *Expositio Psalmorum* seems to be that in the Hiberno-Latin *Eclogae* (cf. McNamara, 'Psalter Text', above p. 58). The ninth-century Cassiodorus MS Laon, Bibliothèque de la Ville 26 (with Irish glosses) appears to contain only prefatory material from Cassiodorus, not the complete commentary or even part of it; see J.W. Halpern, 'The Manuscript of Cassiodorus' Expositio Psalmorum', *Traditio* 37 (1981), pp. 388-96 (390-91).

lation are sections of the commentary on Psalms 1–40. As already noted[93] almost all of this is written in Irish hands and comes from Irish monasteries. In Turin, Bibl. Univ. MS F. IV,1, fasc. 5-6 of the eighth to ninth century we have the continuous exegesis of Pss. 13.7–16.15 (fasc. 6, fol. 1-6a), the *Argumentum* for Psalm 37 (fol. 6c-d), a series of interpretations of different verses of Pss. 17.1-4, 13a (fasc. 5, fol. 7-14a). In the Milan Cod. Amb. C 301 inf. (c. 800) we also have sections of the full translation of Theodore's commentary in fols. 4a22-13d20 (fragments of the commentary on Pss. 17.17–40.13a).

In the same codex, in fol. 14a-39d we have the full translation of Theodore's commentary on Pss. 1.1–16.11, preserved for us in its entirety because it was used to make good the lost portion of the Epitome of Julian's translation of Theodore's commentary.

In the present state of research we cannot see how widely the full text of Theodore's commentary was known in the Irish schools—apart from the section on Pss. 1.1–16.11 of the Milan Commentary that is. Neither the Turin nor the other Milan fragments with the full translation are glossed in Old Irish, a fact that would tend to indicate that they were not used in the Irish schools.

The full commentary on the Psalms (Cod. Amb. C 301 inf. fol. 14a-146) including the Epitome from Ps. 16.11b onwards is, on the contrary, heavily glossed. It has been shown[94] that for the commentary on the Psalter from Ps. 16.11b onwards, Theodore was known not through the full translation but through the Epitome. All Antiochene (Theodorean) comments on these Psalms found in the catena of Codex Pal. lat. 68, in the *Eclogae tractatorum in Psalterium*, in 'Das Bibelwerk', in the glosses in the Montpellier and Vercelli Psalters and in the Rouen Psalter, and in the historical psalm headings already studied, are from the Epitome, not from the full translation, even in sections where this is still extant. The fact that so many Hiberno-Latin texts from the early eighth century (Pal. lat. 68) to about 1100 (the so-called Psalter of Caimín) excerpt from the Epitome or are dependent on it, proves beyond reasonable doubt that this Theodorean commentary must have been the basis

93. Above, 1.5.a. See in Devreesse, *Le commentaire* and De Coninck and d'Hont (eds.), *Theodori*.
94. Cf. De Coninck and d'Hont (eds.), *Theodori*, pp. xxix-xlv.

for psalm instruction in practically every monastery in Ireland and in Celtic Northumbria.

Although none of the extant manuscripts of Junilius comes from Ireland, the citations from his work, under his name in the *Eclogae*,[95] in 'Das Bibelwerk'[96] and anonymously in the *Old-Irish Treatise*,[97] would seem to indicate that at least some Irish libraries had copies of his work.

2.4.c. *The Historical Psalm Commentary on Psalms 1.1–16.11 in the Rouen Psalter.* A judgment on the real nature of the commentary contained in the glosses on Pss. 1.1–16.11a in the *Hebraicum* of the Double Psalter of Rouen will be possible only after these have been published in full. The historical headings from this commentary (published below as an Appendix) are almost always practically identical with those of the pseudo-Bedan *De titulis psalmorum*. The glosses on Psalm 8 published by Lucas De Coninck and Maria Josepha d'Hont[98] agree with the non-messianic heading to this psalm. The glosses of the other psalms in this section are probably in keeping with the historical headings as given in the Rouen Psalter.

This is the case in Psalm 9. This according to the historical heading can be interpreted as David's prayer giving thanks that his son's evil designs were not put into effect, but it might also be taken as Hezekiah's words on the destruction of the Assyrian army. The glosses follow this dual reference, for example, on the opening word '*Confitebor*': *Praesentibus beneficis praeterita tua munera mihi recordor, hoc est confesio Dauid pro gratiarum actione dum non perpetrauit Abisolon quae cogitauit contra Dauid.* A feature of this exegesis is the close manner in which it follows the biblical psalm heading: '*In finem pro occultis filii psalmus Dauid*'. Likewise on '*in aequitate*' of v. 9: *id est in morte inimicorum, id est Abisolon cum sociis et in uiuificatione amicorum Dauid et sociorum.* The other reference of the title is also present

---

95. See above 1.5.b and Sheehy (ed.) in Appendix III to McNamara, 'Psalter Text', pp. 126-27 in this volume. In the St Gall MS of the *Eclogae* (Stiftsbibliothek MS 261), 154 *Iunili(us)* is mentioned by name.

96. Above 1.5.b and Sheehy (ed.) in Appendix IV to McNamara, 'Psalter Text', p. 135.

97. Above 1.5.b and McNamara, 'Psalter Text', in this volume, p. 53 n. 63.

98. De Coninck and d'Hont (eds.), *Theodori*, p. xliii n. 245.

in the glosses, for example, on '*increpasti gentes*' of v. 6: (*Per angelum Domini?) qui uno impetu clxxxu milia occidit et regem superbum per suos filios occidit* (cf. 2 Kgs 19.35-37 = Isa. 37.36-38) *uel ad Abisolon cum hoste suo conuenit.* There is a similar reference to Senacherib in the gloss on '*iudicabit*' of v. 9. Likewise with regard to Psalm 3. Whereas the biblical psalm heading is here quite precise (*Psalmus David cum fugeret a facie Abessalon filii sui*), a heading followed by Theodore in his exposition, both the heading and glosses of the Rouen Psalter interpret the psalm as appropriate to Hezekiah when surrounded by the Assyrian army. An interlinear gloss on '*multo dicunt animae meae*' of v. 2 refers us to the context of 4 Kings 18 and Isaiah 37, with the account of precisely this matter.

Only when a sufficient amount of the glosses on this section of the Psalter of Rouen have been published will we be able to set about situating the commentary revealed in the context of early Irish and non-Irish exposition of the Psalter.

2.4.d. *Irish Commentary Material on the Psalter.* The early Irish Church inherited both the general Alexandrian and Western tradition as well as the Antiochene. At an early date Irish scholars were compiling commentary and expository material of their own on the Psalms, material that reflects the exegetical approach of their schools.

The earliest of these commentaries is the catena on the Psalms in Codex Vaticanus Palatino-Latinus 68, composed about 700 CE but in part reflecting the earlier exegesis of Irish schools. About a third of its glosses are derived from the Julian Epitome. It stresses the historical approach and combines references to David's times with those to later Jewish history. From the later eighth century we have the *Eclogae tractatorum in Psalterium* which in its expository section draws mainly from the Epitome of Julian as supplemented for Pss. 1.1–16.11 in the Milan Commentary. From about the same period we have the section on the Psalter in 'Das Bibelwerk'. This section draws on the Epitome, supplemented for Pss. 1.1–16.11 as in the Rouen Psalter glosses, but also depends very much on Cassiodorus. It is a very good witness to the rather specific Irish approach to the Psalms which I shall consider in the next section. In this it is closely related to the *Old-Irish Treatise* on the Psalter from about 800–50. From roughly the same period come the numerous Old Irish glosses on the Latin text of the Milan Commentary (Cod. Amb. C 301 inf.) and on the psalm prefaces of Jerome and

Pseudo-Bede. The Old Irish glosses on the Theodorean commentary adhere closely to what the Latin text itself has to say—an indication of how seriously these Irish scholars set about understanding it. From later periods we have the glosses on the Rouen Psalter and the so-called Psalter of Caimín.

Commentaries are only as creative as the exegesis they carry. By reason of the underlying expository approach, we can say that the earlier Irish commentaries are creative, while those of later times (the glosses in the Psalters of Rouen and Caimín) are carriers of this exegesis.

2.5. *Early Irish Exegesis: Tradition and Creativity*

2.5.a. *The General Christian Christological Interpretation in Ireland.* The early Irish Church inherited the general Christian Christological interpretation of the Psalms. That this tradition was cherished in Ireland is evident from the psalm headings of the Cathach which are christological in orientation. We find this same series in other psalters and commentaries used in Ireland or connected with Irish tradition, for example, the catena of Codex Pal. lat. 68, the Codex Amiatinus, the Double Psalter of Rouen. In the *Old-Irish Treatise* on the Psalter (lines 320–28) 12 items prophesied in the Psalms are listed:

> Of what did the prophecy of the Psalms foretell? Not difficult. Of the birth of Christ and of his baptism, and of his passion, and of his resurrection, and of his ascension, and of his sitting at the right hand of God the Father in heaven, of the invitation of the heathen to the faith, of the thrusting of Judah into unbelief, of the increase of every virtue, of the spurning of every injustice, of the malediction of sinners, of the coming of Christ to judge the quick and the dead.[99]

---

99. *OIT*, pp. 30-33. Twelve mysteries are itemized in this list. An Old Irish gloss on *ut impleam uerbum Dei* of Col I, 1: 25 (Wb. 26d9; *Thes. Pal.*, I, p. 670) speaks of the seven things that have been prophesied of Christ. These are itemized as follows in the *Scúab Chrábuid* in *Otia Merseiana* 2 (ed. K. Meyer; 1900–1901), p. 97; C. Plummer (ed.), *Irish Litanies* (London: Henry Bradshaw Society, 1925), pp. 42-43: 'his birth, baptism, crucifixion, burial, resurrection, ascension, coming of the last judgment'. Plummer's edition lists eight mysteries, the first being probably a later addition. Thus also the introduction to the Psalter in 'Das Bibelwerk' (BN lat. 11561, fol. 56ra-b): *Modo, vii. quae leguntur de Christo, id est: natiuitas, baptismum, passio, sepulchrum, resurrectio, ascensio, aduentus ad iudicium et reliqua*, a passage all the more noteworthy in that the surrounding texts, but not this, depend on Cassiodorus, *In Psalterium Praefatio* 1 in M. Adriaen (ed.), *Cassiodorus, Expositio Psalmorum* (CCSL, 97; Turnhout: Brepols, 1958), pp. 3-5; *PL*, 70, cols. 9-10.

The commentaries of Augustine, Hilary, Cassiodorus, and Jerome would have kept the early Irish schools conversant with this general Christian exegesis.

2.5.b. *The Fourfold Sense of Scripture.* About the year 800 the *Old-Irish Treatise* on the Psalter thus expressed a theory about the senses of Scripture:

> There are four things that are necessary in the Psalms, to wit, the first story (*cétna stoir*), and the second story (*stoir tánaise*), the sense (*síens*) and the morality (*moralus*). The first story refers to David and to Solomon and the above mentioned persons, to Saul, to Absalom, to the persecutors besides. The second story to Hezekiah, to the people, to the Maccabees. The sense (refers) to Christ, to the earthly and heavenly Church. The morality (refers) to every saint.[100]

The three Irish terms *stoir* (*historia*, literal or historical meaning), *síans, síens* or *séns* (*sensus*, mystical meaning) and *moralus* (*morale*, moral interpretation) must have established themselves by 800 CE as they are also found in the Old Irish glosses on the Milan Commentary. Two points should be noted about these terms and this fourfold scheme. First: the Latin term *sensus* (from which the Irish *síans, siens*, and *séns* are derived) with the meaning: 'the mystical sense of Scripture', seems to be restricted to Hiberno-Latin texts—at least as a general usage. Outside of such texts I have found it only twice (in Jerome).[101] It is found regularly with this meaning in Hiberno-Latin texts.[102]

Hilary, in *Instructio Psalmorum* no. 6 (CSEL, 27: 1893), p. 7 also lists seven things prophesied in the Psalms: *haec septem quaedam signacula, quae de corporalitate eius, et passione et morte et resurrectione et gloria et regno et iudicio Dauid de eo in psalmis prophetat.*

100. Cf. *OIT*, pp. 30-31, lines 312-19.

101. In G. Morin (ed.), *Commentarioli in Psalmos* 47.14 (CCSL, 72; Turnhout: Brepols, 1969), p. 124; cf. also on the same text M. Adriaen (ed.), *S. Hieronymi presbyteri Commentarius in Ecclesiasten* 11.8 (CCSL, 72; Turnhout: Brepols, 1969), p. 266. All references are to the CCSL edition unless otherwise stated.

102. Hiberno-Latin texts seem at times to have replaced such terms as *prophetia, allegoria, anagogia* of their sources with *sensus*, e.g., the text of the *Eclogae* and 'Das Bibelwerk' to be cited later; *Utrum secundum historiam an secundum sensum legendi sunt psalmi*, which would appear to depend on a text such as that cited in n. 71 above: *psalmi non secundum historiam sed secundum prophetias leguntur.*

The second matter meriting attention is the assertion that the Psalms have a twofold historical sense. This is something I have not found outside of Irish texts. Yet it seems to have been strongly embedded in the Irish tradition by the year 800. We find it asserted again in the same *Old-Irish Treatise* in its incomplete exposition of Psalm 1: 'The first story (*cétna stoir*) of the Psalms (evidently this particular psalm is intended) refers to the time of David; the second (*in tánaise*) to Chusai Arachitis (*iesu irechitis*; *varia lectio: hissu ireichidis*). He it was that did not abandon him at the time of persecution, though everyone else abandoned him.' The same twofold historical sense for this psalm is found in the section on the Psalter in 'Das Bibelwerk', a work, as already noted, very closely related to the *Old-Irish Treatise.*[103]

> Hilar. *'Beatus uir qui non abiit'. Prima historia ad Dauid pertinet, qui non abiit in consilio sociorum, qui uoluerant occidere Saul in spelunca, quando Dauid dixit: 'Non contingat mihi ut mittam manum meam in Christum Domini'* (cf. 1 Sam. 26.11, 23). *'Beatus' reliqua. Secunda historia ad Chusai Arachitam pertinet, qui non exiit in consilium Abisolon et Achitophel, qui uoluerunt exire post Dauid quando fugit et occidere eum, usque Chusai dissipauit consilium eorum* (cf. 2 Sam. 15.34; 17.14).

We seem to have a further reference to a twofold historical sense in psalm interpretation in unidentified sayings attributed to Ambrose, Jerome and Hilary preserved in the two later eighth-century Hiberno-Latin texts—the *Eclogae tractatorum in Psalterium* and in the section on the Psalms in 'Das Bibelwerk'. In the latter text we read as follows.[104]

> AMB(ROSIUS). *Utrum secundum historiam an secundum sensum legendi sunt psalmi? Secundum sensum legendi sunt psalmi ut Ambrosius dicit: 'Si toto affectu inuestigaueris psalmos multum laborem arripies. Nam etiam intellectu historico duplici sensu latent (Eclogae: duplices sensus latent uel habent)'. Hieronimus: 'Historico intellectu inuestigaui psalmos et certas personas in his consideraui'. Item dicit: 'Me ideo diuino labori reddidi et inserui psalmo(s) historico ordine'. Hilar(ius). 'Psalmos lege historico intellectu ubi diuersos modos inuenies'.*

---

103. Cited from BN MS lat. 11561, fol. 56va; same text cited from the other MS of this work, Munich, Staatsbibliothek Clm 14276, fol. 100r, by P. Ó Néill, 'The Old-Irish Treatise on the Psalter and its Hiberno-Latin Background', *Ériu* 30 (1979), pp. 148-64 (161).

104. M. Sheehy (ed.), in McNamara, 'Psalter Text', Appendix IV, above p. 133.

The point made in the observation attributed to Ambrose seems to be that from the point of view of the historical interpretation (*historico intellectu*), the Psalms have a twofold sense—presumably the *prima historia* (*cétna stoir*) and the *secunda historia* (*stoir tánaiste*) of the other texts. The entire passage, with its erroneous ascriptions, is very probably a composition of the Irish schools.[105]

This view on the twofold historical sense of the Psalms, a twofold historical reference, appears to have developed in Ireland itself, as I hope to show later. The theory which we find formulated in the later eighth century probably arose out of a practice of so regarding the Psalms which was a feature of Irish exegesis from at least 700.

2.5.c. *Emphasis on the Historical Sense of the Psalms.* All Christian tradition would assert that the Psalms, as the entire Old Testament and indeed the entire Bible, had a historical sense, a literal meaning—the *littera* as it was called. Where differences would arise was on the emphasis to be placed on this as against the 'inner' or spiritual meaning. One patristic and classical attitude came to be expressed in the comment on Ps. 67.14: *Pinnae columbae deargentatae et posteriora dorsi eius in pallore auri.* The *argentum* was *littera*, the historical sense; the *aurum* the inner meaning, the *sensus*, mystical or spiritual sense. Thus Jerome:

> *Et licet sit pulchritudo etiam iuxta litteram scire quae legas, tamen uis decoris omnis in sensu est. Exterior itaque uerborum ornatus in argenti nomine demonstratur: occultiora uero mysteria in reconditis auri muneribus continentur.*[106]

In this presentation, both the *littera* and *sensus* or *occultiora mysteria* (mystical sense) were both to be respected. The latter, however, was the gold.

---

105. Compare the opening words, however, with the text of the full psalm preface *Dauid filius Iesse* given above in n. 71; see also n. 102.

106. In the Hiberno-Latin commentary on Luke (2.24) of MS Vindobon. lat. 997 we have a similar text: *Plerumque columba diuinarum scripturarum figuram tenet, quando dicitur: 'pennae columbae deargentatae usque auri'. Quid argenti color nisi eloquentiam diuinae historiae significat. Per auri autem formam sensum triplicem spiritalem indicat, id est, tropologiam, anagogen, allegoriam* (J.F. Kelly [ed.], *Scriptores Hiberniae Minores*. II. *Commentarius in Lucam. Commentarius in Iohannem* [CCSL, 108C; Turnhout: Brepols, 1974], p. 18, lines 219-23).

This view is also found in a Hiberno-Latin commentary on Lk. 2.24. Quite the opposite approach was taken in the exposition on the Psalms. This, in part at least, was due to the influence of Theodore's commentary. In an Old Irish gloss in the Milan commentary (Ml. 14c17)[107] we read: 'It is the history (*instoir*, i.e., the literal or historical sense) that is most desirable for us to understand'. The glossator says that he and those of like mind were prepared to leave to others 'the exposition of the sense and the morality (*séns ⁊ moralus*), if it not be at variance with the history that we relate' (Ml. 14d10).[108]

This is but a theoretical assertion of an approach found already in our earliest psalm commentary from the Irish Church, that is, the catena in Codex Pal. lat. 68. In this the exposition is predominantly historical. Deviations from this, especially in the form of christological exegesis, are often explicitly introduced with the rubric: *Spiritaliter*, that is, a mystical interpretation, not the literal meaning intended by the author. The predominance of material of a historical nature in our extant Irish commentaries on the Psalms is evidence of the same interest in the literal exposition rather than the mystical, allegorical or spiritual one.

2.5.d. *Interest in Jewish Traditions on Exegesis of Messianic Psalms.*

The Jewish interpretation, or even varying Jewish interpretations, of the Psalms accepted by Christians as messianic are occasionally mentioned by the Church Fathers. In this way, and possibly also in other ways, Jewish exegesis could have become known to mediaeval scholars. It appears that certain sections of the early Irish Church were sufficiently interested in these traditions to include them in their own writings. Thus in the psalm headings of Pseudo-Bede for Psalm 21 we find inserted, after that of Theodore, the following text from Jerome's *Commentarioli*:[109]

> *Aliter: Iudaei de Esther hunc psalmum putant esse cantatum, quod videlicet ipsius periculo et intercessione apud regem sit populus Israel a morte laxatus.*

From the Commentary of Theodore and the Julian Epitome it could be learned that the Jews interpreted Psalm 2 of Zerubbabel or of

---

107. *Thes. Pal.*, I, p. 13.
108. *Thes. Pal.*, I, p. 13.
109. In *PL* 93, cols. 589D; Jerome, *Commentarioli in Psalmos XXI*, p. 198.

David;[110] that they apparently understood Psalm 44 of Solomon's wife[111] and believed that the speaker in Ps. 109.1 is either Abraham's servant or David himself.[112] The Irish glossator in the Milan Commentary faithfully represents the meaning of the Latin text, yet notes the reference of Psalm 2 to Zerubbabel or David (Ml. 16a17, 18, 16b5) and the mention of Abraham's servant in the commentary on Psalm 109 and the manner in which the biblical text should be understood if the Jewish position were adopted (Ml. 127d3, 4, 5, 6).[113]

From Jerome's commentary on Eccl. 1.1 Western scholars could learn that Jerome himself once believed that both Psalms 44 and 71 *secundum historiam* were written concerning Solomon (thus accepting the Jewish understanding of them), even though they belonged to prophecy about Christ and the Church (*ad prophetiam Christi et Ecclesiae pertinentes*).[114] We shall see that this tradition, too, was known to early Irish scholars. How much more of Jewish interpretation was known in the West, or at least in certain streams of Western tradition, it is difficult to say. In view of the animated debates between Christians and Jews, particularly during the fourth and fifth centuries,[115] it would not be

110. Cf. Devreesse, *Le commentaire*, pp. 7-8 and in index s.v. *Iudaei*; De Coninck and d'Hont (eds.), *Theodori*, pp. 10, lines 19-34.

111. Devreesse, *Le commentaire*, pp. 277-78 and in index s.v. *Iudaei*; De Coninck and d'Hont (eds.), *Theodori*, p. 201, lines 119-24; p. 203, lines 179-80.

112. De Coninck and d'Hont (eds.), *Theodori*, pp. 351-52.

113. *Thes. Pal.* I, pp. 16-17 for Ps. 2; pp. 434-35 for Ps. 109.

114. Jerome, *Commentarius in Eccelesiasten* 1.1, p. 250. This work composed about 389 CE comes from a period when Jerome was under the influence of Jewish rabbinic exegesis; see Kelly, *Jerome*, pp. 150-51.

115. Jewish traditions in the works of the Fathers have been the subject of many studies. Thus, for Jerome, M. Rahmer, *Die hebräischen Traditionen in den Werken des Hieronymus: Quaestiones in Genesim* (Breslau, 1871); *idem, Die hebräischen Traditionen in den Werken des Hieronymus: Die Commentarii zu den 12 kleinen Propheten*, 1-11 (Berlin, 1902); L. Ginzberg, 'Die Haggada bei den Kirchenväter. VI. Der Kommentar des Hieronymus zu Jesaja', in *Jewish Studies in Memory of G.A. Kohut* (New York, 1935), pp. 279-314; S. Krauss, 'The Jews in the Works of the Church Fathers. VI. Jerome', *Jewish Quarterly Review* 6 (1894), pp. 225-61; C. Siegfried, 'Midraschisches in Hieronymus und Ps. Hieronymus', *Jahrbücher für protestantische Theologie* 9 (1883), pp. 346-52; F. Stummer, 'Beiträge zu dem Problem: Hieronymus und die Targumim', *Biblica* 18 (1937), pp. 174-81; J.M. Lagrange, 'S. Jérôme et la tradition juive dans la Genèse', *RB* 7 (1898), pp. 563-66 (on Genesis); A. Vaccari, 'I fattori dell'esegesi Geronimiana', *Biblica* 1

surprising if more of Jewish tradition than is commonly believed was known in the mediaeval West.

2.5.e. *The Messianic Psalms 15 and 21 in Irish Tradition.* According to Theodore Psalm 15 was composed by David in thanksgiving after he had defeated the surrounding nations. The whole psalm, he says, is sung in the person of the people, for whose benefit the power of the enemy was broken.[116] At the end of his exposition Theodore confronts the problem of the Apostle Peter's use of v. 10 as a direct prophecy of Christ in Acts 2.25-31 (to which one might add Paul's use in Acts 13.35-37). Although his language is somewhat obscure, Theodore's position seems to be that in this passage the blessed Apostle shows that the text of the psalm in question was fulfilled in the person of Christ—how exactly he does not say, but apparently typically:

> *Non ergo ab apostolo testimonium hoc usurpatum est, sed causae suae redditum: nam fuerat uidelicet a propheta praedictum, et ideo conuentienter est personae Domini uindicatum; nam prius in similitudine dictum fuerat et figura. Proprie ergo et secundum uerum intellectum, qui*

(1920), pp. 458-80; pp. 470-77 for 'la tradizione ebraica' (*Scritti di erudizione e di filologia*, II [Rome, 1958], pp. 147-70, 159-66). For a detailed examination of Jerome's use of Jewish traditions in *Hebraicae quaestiones in Genesim*, see C.T.R. Hayward, *Saint Jerome's Hebrew Questions on Genesis: Translated with Introduction and Commentary* (Oxford: Clarendon Press, 1995). See also V. Aptowitzer, 'Rabbinische Parallelen und Aufschlüsse zur Septuaginta und Vulgata', *ZAW* 29 (1900), pp. 241-52. Jews were numerous in Antioch in Diodorus's and Chrysostom's time and actively proselytized. It is to be presumed that the messianic prophecies would have formed part of the Jewish-Christian debate. For the background to John Chrysostom's anti-Jewish sermons see P.W. Haskins, in the introduction to St John Chrysostom, *Discourses against Judaizing Christians* (Fathers of the Church, 68; Washington, 1979), pp. xxi-lxxii. For the Jews at Antioch cf. C.H. Kraeling, 'The Jewish Community at Antioch', *Journal of Biblical Literature* 51 (1932), pp. 130-60 (154-60 for Christian period); also M. Simon, 'La polémique antijuive de saint Jean Chrysostome et le mouvement judaïsant d'Antioche', *Annuaire de l'Institut de Philologie et d'Histoire orientales et slaves* 4 (1930), pp. 140-53; S. Krauss, 'Antioche', *Revue des études juives* 45 (1902), pp. 27-49.

116. Devreesse, *Le commentaire*, pp. 90-100; De Coninck and d'Hont (eds.), *Theodori*, pp. 75-81. On Theodore's exegesis of Ps. 15, see L. Pirot, *L'oeuvre exégetique de Théodore de Mopsueste 350–428 après J. C.* (Scripta Pontificii Instituti Biblici; Rome: Biblical Institute Press, 1913), pp. 247-49; Devreesse, *Essai*, p. 72.

ipsis rebus impletus est, Domino conuenit, ad quem eum pertinere imple-
tae sine dubio res loquuntur.[117]

Theodore's non-messianic interpretation of this psalm was censured in the second Council of Constantinople (553) and by the *Constitutum* of Pope Vigilius. The passage picked out for special condemnation was the ending of his exposition in which he treats of Peter's use of v. 10.[118]

The Old Irish glosses on the Milan commentary repeat Theodore's exposition, as this was understood by the glossator at any rate, for example, Ml. 38a3 (on *ab apostolo*): '*Aliter* the apostle did not apply it (i.e. the biblical text) according to the sense in which the prophet uttered it'.[119] Likewise, Ml. 38b4 (on *redditum*): 'i.e. he applies it to support the saying that was uttered through congruence to the cause on which he was engaged'.[120] Or Ml. 38c5 (on a *profeta praedictum*): 'i.e. that of which he (= the prophet Psalmist) applied it is different to that of which Peter uttered it'.[121]

The tradition represented in the psalm headings of Pseudo-Bede,[122] and in the Psalters of Charlemagne and of Rouen differs from that of Theodore in understanding the psalm as a prayer of Hezekiah in relation to his illness. To this the Psalter of Charlemagne adds a further historical heading, taking the psalm as sung by David on the restoration of his inheritance. Here, then, we have two further distinct historical and non-messianic interpretations of Psalm 15.

The glosses of the Rouen Psalter also have a non-messianic interpretation, understanding the psalm to speak of Hezekiah or of both Hezekiah and David or Saul. Thus, the interlinear gloss to '*tu es qui restitues hereditatem meam*' (v. 5): *uel restitues post mortem Saul uel Ezechiae post infirmitatem suam.* To '*laetatum est cor meum...*' (v. 9): *quod corde conceptum est foris in labia eructat.* On '*in inferno*' (v. 10): *in*

117. Devreesse, *Le commentaire*, p. 100; De Coninck and d'Hont (eds.), *Theodori*, p. 81.

118. See Pirot, *L'oeuvre*, pp. 248-49; Devreesse, *Essai*, p. 248. Devreesse notes that the Council's citation of Theodore's comment on Ps. 15.10 is unfaithful and tendentious. Council and *Constitutum* texts in Devreesse, *Le commentaire*, pp. 99-100.

119. *Thes. Pal.*, I, p. 99.

120. *Thes. Pal.*, I, p. 100.

121. *Thes. Pal.*

122. See texts below.

humiliatione uel in sepulchro. The important verse 10 is glossed as follows: '*non dabis...*': *...tuis muneribus et re (...) unctione ornasti... (res)tituti(one) uitae reparabis.* '*Sanctum tuum*' is glossed interlineary as *Dauid uel Ezechias.* The gloss for '*notas milti fecisti uias uitae*' is: *manifestabis quomodo (?) disperala uita per tuam potentiam restituitur uel reuelasti mihi quod Saul non occidisset me.* The gloss for '*cum uultu tuo*' is: *...conspectum tuum in templo laetitia plenus ero semper quae et animo cogitatione et corporis habitu ostenditur uel auerso uultu tuo inimicis hoc est Sauli et amicis* (corr. from *inm—*) *eius.* The origins of this sustained non-messianic interpretation of Psalm 15, which is quite distinct from that of Theodore, remain to be determined. In the dual reference to David and later Jewish history (in this case Hezekiah) it is reminiscent of the kind of exegesis we find in the catena of MS Pal. lat. 68, which unfortunately begins only at Psalm 39.

Theodore understood Psalm 21 to speak of David persecuted by his son Absalom.[123] It was not composed of Christ, nor in the literal sense is it a prophecy of Christ or his passion. How could the sinless Christ say: 'Far from my salvation are the words of my sins' (v. 2)? If different verses of the psalm are applied to Christ by the Evangelists, says Theodore, this is by accommodation, because of the similarity of circumstances. *Quod enim psalmus nullatenus conuenit Domino certum est. Neque enim erat Domini Christi, qui peccatum iron fecit...dicere: 'Longe a salute mea uerba delictorum meorum'.*[124]

Comparing the account of Christ's Passion with this psalm led St Augustine to say: *Passio Christi tam evidenter quasi euangelium recitatur.*[125] The psalm was universally accepted as a prophecy of Christ's passion in Christian tradition, apart from Theodore and the author of the commentary recently published under the name of Diodorus.[126]

---

123. Devreesse, *Le commentaire*, pp. 120-22; De Coninck and d'Hont (eds.), *Theodori*, pp. 107-12. On Theodore's exegesis of Psalm 21 see also Pirot, *L'oeuvre*, pp. 251-54; Devreesse, *Essai*, pp. 72-73.

124. Theodore's position as expressed by the *Constitutum* of Vigilius and Council II of Constantinople; text in Devreesse, *Le commentaire*, pp. 120-21 footnote. Theodore's own text has: *Qui uolunt hunc psalmum in Domini persona, ex hoc loco praecipue conuincuntur non paruum temeritatis incurrere. Quomodo enim potest accipi quia hoc de se Dominus dixerit: longe a salute mea et reliqua* (De Coninck and d'Hont (eds.), *Theodori*, p. 108; Devreesse, *Le commentaire*, p. 120.

125. *Enarratio II in Psalmum XXI*, no. 2, in E. Dekkers and J. Fraipont (eds.), *Enarrationes in Psalmos I–L* (Turnhout: Brepols, 1956), p. 123.

126. Olivier (ed.), *Diodori*, pp. 126-37.

Theodoret of Cyr and John Chrysostom, of the Antiochene school, reverted to the traditional interpretation. Even Junilius lists the division of the clothes (Ps. 21.19) among the 26 Old Testament prophecies concerning Christ.[127] Theodore's non-messianic interpretation of psalms was condemned in the Second Council of Constantinople and in the *Constitutum* of Vigilius.

The interpretation of Theodore is mollified somewhat in the Epitome of Julian by the introduction of the biblical heading, followed by a statement that Jesus's words on the cross tell us to whom this psalm should be referred.[128] This, however, is immediately and somewhat awkwardly connected with Theodore's position on the literal meaning of the psalm:

> *Domini ultima in cruce oratio docuit ad quem debeat hic psalmus referri, qui tamen suis temporibus habuit figuram illius historiae quae narrat Dauid coniuratione Abessalon in aerumnas coactum, in quibus positus hoc carmen uice orationis cecinit.*

As is his wont, the Old Irish glossator tries to bring out the meaning of the Latin text.[129] A gloss on the biblical text says that David sang this psalm concerning events that occurred the morning before Christ's passion and of his passion after that (Ml. 44bl). The same idea is repeated in a gloss on *docuit* of the new heading. A gloss on *suis temporibus*, however, says: 'i.e. when this psalm was first sung it is appropriate to David when he complained with regard to Absalom, according to the literal sense (Ml. 44b4).[130] It refers to Christ according to the mystic sense (*madurúin*)' (44b6).[131]

Both Pseudo-Bede (*PL* 93, col. 589D) and the Psalter of Charlemagne have the Theodorean interpretation, understanding it of Absalom's revolt. However, as already noted,[132] the pseudo-Bedan *De titulis Psalmorum* adds as an alternative the Jewish interpretation, understanding the psalm of Esther.

---

127. In *Instituta regularia divinae legis* 1.22, *PL* 68, col. 3SA; Kihn, *Theodor*, p. 518.
128. De Coninck and d'Hont (eds.), *Theodori*, p. 108.
129. Cf. McNamara, 'Psalter Text', pp. 106-107 above.
130. *Thes. Pal.*, I, p. 125.
131. *Thes. Pal.*, I, p. 125.
132. Cf. above p. 275-76.

2.5.f. *The Messianic Psalms 2, 8, 44 and 109 in Irish Tradition.* These are the only four psalms taken by Theodore of Mopsuestia as direct prophecies of Christ.[133] Theodore's interpretation is reproduced faithfully in the full Latin translation and in the Epitome of Julian and in texts dependent on these, for example the *Eclogae tractatorum in Psalterium.*[134] There is, however, another Irish tradition in which none of these psalms is interpreted as a direct prophecy of Christ. This tradition is found especially in the so-called Psalter of Charlemagne for all four psalms; in the catena of Codex Pal. lat. 68 for Psalms 44 and 109 (the only two in the extant section of the catena); the pseudo-Bedan *In titulis Psalmorum* and in the Psalter of Rouen for Psalms 2 and 8. The evidence is as follows.

Psalm 2. Theodore, citing the words of Peter (Acts 4.24-25) and Paul (in Hebrews, 1.3, taken as Paul's), takes this psalm as a direct prophecy of Christ. Going on the same words of Peter, Jerome reckons any interpretation other than the christological temerarious.[135]

Theodore notes current Jewish interpretations, which understood the psalm either of Zerubbabel or of David.

Curiously enough, the glosses of the Psalters of Montpellier and Vercelli, generally given to christological interpretation, both in the heading and the glosses interpret the psalms both of Christ and of David.[136] *In hoc psalmo continetur manifeste de xpo et de dauid secunduni hystoriam* (on v. 1). In the pseudo-Bedan *In titulis Psalmorum*, in the headings of the Psalter of Rouen and the Psalter of Charlemagne the psalm is understood of David—in the first two as a plaint of David that the Gentiles and foreign nations have invaded Israel, in the last as the voice of David's comrades to the effect that the nations and Absalom have persecuted David.[137]

The left-hand marginal glosses in the Rouen Psalter are difficult to read. However, a number of the interlinear ones are in keeping with the Davidic interpretation, especially as given in the heading of the Psalter of Charlemagne. Thus (p. 2) on *'gentes'* (v. 1): *Philistini; 'tribus'*

---

133. On this point see Kihn (2.5.d), pp. 143, 454-64; Pirot, *L'oeuvre*, pp. 238-47; Devreesse, *Essai*, pp. 76-78.

134. See the opening words on Ps. 2 edited by Sheehy; above pp. 128-29.

135. Jerome, *Commentarioli in Psalmum* 2.1, p. 181.

136. Unterkircher (ed.), *Die Glossen*, pp. 75-77.

137. See appendix to this article.

(*Gallicanum*: *populi*): *Abisolon cum socis; 'aduersum Christum eius':
omnis rex christus Domini uocatur,* (p. 4). *'Sion montem'* (v. 6):
Hierusalem quia Abisolon quaerit; 'Dominus dixit ad me' (v. 7): *reg-
nare faciam in omnes qui te resistere uolunt; 'ego hodie genui te': in
die electionis in regnum; 'beati omnes'* (v. 13): *Dauid cum sociis.*

Psalm 8.[138] The Old Irish glosses in the Milan Commentary reflect
the Theodorean christological interpretation on this psalm faithfully. I
reproduce below the heading to this psalm as found in Pseudo-Bede, the
Psalter of Rouen and the Psalter of Charlemagne.[139] In all three it is
regarded as non-messianic, and as a prophetic admiration of the divine
power, and providence and a thanksgiving for God's concern for
people. We are fortunate in that the glosses on this particular psalm in
the Rouen Psalter are very clear and legible. They agree fully with the
heading and are in no way messianic or christological.

Psalm 44.[140] From Psalm 17 onwards almost all the historical headings of the *argumenta* of Pseudo-Bede are drawn from the Epitome of
Julian. They are of little help, then, for ascertaining the non-Theodorean
interpretation of Psalms 44 and 109. The loss is here made good, however, by the presence of both headings and expository glosses of the
catena of MS Pal. lat. 68, with which exegetical approach the headings
of the Psalter of Charlemagne agree.

The heading of the Psalter of Charlemagne reads:

> *'In finem psalmus Dauid' de se ipse et Salomon. Et 'de his qui commula-
> bunt' de exilio in requiem. 'Ad intellectum filiis Chore'. Ex Patris per-
> sona profeta de Christo hunc psalmum (pre -?; text faded) dicit. Qui
> uerbum suum ante secula de utero profunde diuinitatis in sui manifesta-
> tionem scientiam paternam omnibus monstrans eructauit.*

In this heading we have combined a historical interpretation understanding the psalm of David and Solomon and another form of exegesis
seeing in it a prophecy of Christ. The first part of the text just quoted
coincides practically verbatim with the heading in Pal. lat. 68, while the
second part is similar in tone. MS Pal. lat. 68 reads:

---

138. For Theodore's interpretation see Pirot, *L'oeuvre*, pp. 242-47.
    139. Below. The heading and glosses of the Psalter of Rouen on this psalm have
been published by De Coninck and d'Hont (eds.), *Theodori*, p. xliii n. 245.
    140. For Theodore's interpretation see Pirot, *L'oeuvre*, pp. 244-45.

'*In finem salmus Dauid'. id est de ipso et Salomone. 'Pro his qui commotabuntur'. id est de exilio in requiem. 'Ad intellectum filis Chore canticum pro dilecto'. id est de regno iusti. De Christo et aeclesia... Totus
hic salmus refertur ad Christum de quo Pater in euangelio loquitur: 'Hic
est Filius meus dilectus', licet ad Salomonem inertialis historia refertur.
Vox Dauid de Salomone. Vox Patris de Filio qui est Verbum.*

In these headings we find juxtaposed two contrasting interpretations
of the psalm: one taking it as spoken by David of himself and Solomon,
or of Solomon alone; the other, citing Jerome's *Commentarioli*[141] on
this psalm, saying it refers to Christ alone and describing the 'historical'
reference (*historia*) to Solomon as *inertialis*, 'inept'. This judgment on
the historical interpretation is evidently from the pen of the compiler.

The expository glosses contain the 'historical' interpretation depre-
cated in the introduction. In these the psalm is referred in the literal,
historical sense to Solomon and only *spiritaliter* to Christ, as explicitly
stated in v. 3: *Haec quae sequntur conueniunt Salomon historialiter et
Christo spiritaliter.* Again on v. 8: '*prae consortibus suis*'. *id est Salomon secus filios Dauid; spiritaliter: Christus secus apostolos.* Likewise
on v. 10: '*Adstetit regina*'. *id est filia Faraonis* (cf. 1 Kgs 3.1), *siue
regina austri quae uenit...audire sapientiam Salomonis...; spiritaliter:
'Adstetit regina'. id est Christo aeclesia gentium.*

The compiler had access to the Epitome of Julian from which he
drew a number of his glosses on this psalm. Likewise, the introduction
to the psalm shows the compiler personally agreed with the messianic
interpretation, found in Theodore. It seems fairly obvious that in the
body of the exposition he is transmitting a form of non-messianic exegesis with which he personally disagrees. This non-messianic interpretation may have originated in the same understanding of the psalm
which we find in Jerome's commentary on Ecclesiastes (Eccl. 1.1).[142]
Much more likely, however, it is but part of a larger pattern of approach
to the understanding of the messianic psalms, specifically those considered as prophecies of Christ by the tradition inherited ultimately from
Antioch and Theodore.

Psalm 109.[143] In view of the New Testament evidence, it is difficult

---

141. Cf. Jerome, *Commentarioli in Psalmum* 46.1, p. 209.

142. Jerome, *In Eccles.* 1.1, p. 250.

143. See D.M. May, *Glory at the Right Hand: Psalm CX in Early Christianity*
(SBLMS; Cambridge: Cambridge University Press, 1973). For Psalm 109 (110) in
Judaism see P. Billerbeck, 'Exkursus 18: Der 110. Psalm in der Altrabbinischen

to see how this psalm could in Christian tradition have received anything but a messianic interpretation. It is, however, given a non-messianic interpretation in the heading of the Psalter of Charlemagne and in
the catena of Pal. lat. 68. The heading in the Psalter of Charlemagne
reads:

> *In finem psalmus ad Dominum. Hic psalmus de Dauid loquitur. De ini-*
> *micis suis canitur. Vel Dauid loquens ad Samuel. Vel uox Damasci Elea-*
> *zari serui Abraham. Spiritaliter: Caro Christi de persona Christi. Hic*
> *psalmus pharisei profetatum. Vox Ecclesiae de Patre et Filio.*

Sections of this heading seem to depend on the Epitome of Julian, for
example, the reference to Abraham's servant, to the Pharisees, *Caro*
Christi de persona Christi.[144] The designation of the messianic interpretation as spiritaliter, however, indicates that the exposition represented by this heading must have interpreted the psalms 'historically':
of David, Samuel or Abraham's servant.

The catena of Pal. lat. 68 has no heading for this psalm. Right
throughout the expository glosses, however, the psalm is interpreted
'historically': of David, Saul and Samuel. An appropriate heading
would be *Dauid loquens ad Samuel*—found in the Psalter of Charlemagne. The person who speaks in v. 1 is Saul; the Lord addressed
(*domino meo*) is Samuel. '*Ante luciferum*' is interpreted as *ante Saul.*
The text then goes on to say that in the spiritual sense the psalm refers
to Christ: *Spiritaliter haec Christo conueniunt ut Hirunimus ait*, after
which a series of christological interpretations are given. And as if to
emphasize the fact that this understanding of the text is allegorical, in
the margin it is marked by *M*, that is, *Moraliter*, which for the greater
part in the catena means *allegorice*. Immediately after these allegorical
interpretations, the text is again interpreted of Samuel and of the land of
Canaan. This exegesis is introduced in the text as *secundum historiam*
and in the margin as *hist. Tu es sacerdos in aeternum* is interpreted
aliter as referring to Christ, after which (at v. 5) the glosses revert to the
non-messianic interpretation, designated in the margin as *hist.* And
then, at the very end of the exposition, comes a statement similar to that
found in the heading of Psalm 44: *Totus hic salmus de Christo canitur,*

Literatur', in H. Strack and P. Billerbeck (eds.), *Kommentar zum Neuen Testament*
aus Talmud und Midrasch, IV, 1 (Munich: Beck, 1928; repr. 1961), pp. 452-65.
  144. De Coninck and d'Hont (eds.), *Theodori*, pp. 351-52.

licet alii historialem inhertiam (MS: *in hertiam*) *in eo contexunt, ut ostendimus*—which I render: 'although some, as we have shown, give it an inept historical interpretation'.

Evidently here once more we are in the presence of a form of exegesis which the compiler (or possibly a later scribe) considered it his duty to transmit but with which he personally disagreed. The origin of this non-messianic interpretation remains to be determined. It may have arisen from a reflection on the remark found in the Epitome of Julian that the person of David is intended in v. 1. It could possibly have also arisen from a tradition influenced by a Jewish interpretation which understood the psalm as God's words to David that he would reign after Saul.[145] But even if these influences were present it seems likely that this non-messianic exegesis of Psalm 109 is but part of an overall pattern of interpretation of the traditional messianic psalms, an approach which may well have been the work of the Irish schools themselves.

2.5.g. *Davidic Interpretations and Double Historical Reference in Irish Exegesis.* In the Theodorean interpretation which the Irish schools inherited through the Epitome of Julian only 19 psalms were interpreted as referring to David and his times.[146] In contrast to this, a marked feature of the early Irish tradition is the frequency of the Davidic references, especially in the tradition represented in the so-called Psalter of Charlemagne and the catena of Codex Pal. lat. 68. There is also strong emphasis in the Davidic interpretation on the Psalms in the commentary represented by the glosses of the Montpellier and Vercelli Psalters, edited by Franz Unterkircher.[147] A further feature of both the catena and the headings of the Psalter of Charlemagne is the combination of a reference to both David's times and to later Jewish

---

145. This interpretation is also found in Jewish sources, e.g., the Targum (Aramaic translation) of the psalm, which reads: 'The Lord promised (lit., said) in his Word to set me as Lord over all Israel but said to me: "Turn and wait for Saul...until he dies...after this I will set your enemies as your footstool".' In the *Midr. Ps.* this interpretation is ascribed to Rabbi Jehuda ben Shallum the Levite (c. 370 CE).

146. Thus, e.g., Pirot, *L'oeuvre*, p. 279; Devreesse, *Essai*, p. 70 who lists 16 referring to the life of David (not reckoning Ps. 71 as Pirot does), to which he adds 8 of a moral and religious nature.

147. Unterkircher (ed.), *Die Glossen.*

history.[148] We find this both in the headings and glosses of the catena of Codex Pal. lat. 68. It is also present in the interlinear glosses of some of the psalms in the first section (Pss. 1–16) of the Psalter of Rouen. This Davidic interpretation is so strong in the Psalter of Charlemagne and the catena of Pal. lat. 68 that it has occasioned the introduction of special headings referring to David, or of special references to David into the biblical psalm headings themselves.

As examples of readaptation of biblical psalm headings in favour of a Davidic reference we may instance a few of many: Psalm 43—biblical heading: *In finem filiis Core ad intellectum*; Pal. lat. 68 and Psalter of Charlemagne: *In finem salmus Dauid*. Psalm 75—Biblical heading: *In finem in laudibus psalmus Asaph canticum ad Assyrios*; Pal. lat. 68 and Psalter of Charlemagne: *In finem de laudibus salmus Asaph pro uictoria Dauid et pro uictoria Ezechiae*; Psalm 120—Biblical heading: *Canticum graduum*; Pal. lat. 68 and Psalter of Charlemagne: *Canticum gradum. Vox Dauid pro erumnis Saul*.

In keeping with this interest in David, very frequently in the headings of the psalms in both works we meet such words and phrases as *Vox Dauid, Vox (Oratio) Dauid pro (de) socis (suis), Vox Dauid in exilio, pro erumnis (a) Saul, de Saul, Querela Dauid pro Saul*, and so on. In line with this, the bulk of the historical interpretations in the expository glosses of the catena are of David and his contemporaries: Samuel (Pss. 40.17; 109.1, 3, 4; 118.105, 114), Saul (several references), *Saul cum semini suo* (39.15), *Saul et domus (domum) eius* (42.1, 2; 52.6; 58.6), *Saul et Abisolon* (96.10), *Saul cum socis (suis)* (several texts; also in glosses of Psalter of Rouen, Pss. 1–16), *montes Giluae* (on death of Saul), 39.15; 53.7; 55.8; 62.10; 63.9, 10), *Dauid cum sociis suis* (several references), Agag (109.1, Achitophel and Abisolon (many references for each), Ioab (59.8, 108.6, 8, 11), *sacerdotes in Nob* (41.11, 52.5), *Golia* (143.16), *Philistini* (53.5), *Sephei* (53.5).

The conclusion to be drawn from this evidence is that there must have been at least one stream of tradition in the early Irish schools in which strong emphasis was placed on interpreting the psalms of David and his times. Such an interpretative tradition would have taken the biblical psalm headings very seriously as guides towards the meaning intended by the sacred writer.

---

148. This point is considered in greater detail in the introduction to the critical edition of MS Pal. lat. 68 in McNamara (ed.), *Glossa in Psalmos*.

A matter worthy of study in this regard is the possible relation between this Davidic interpretation and interest shown in the biblical psalm titles in the *Old-Irish Treatise* on the Psalter, and in the closely related introduction to the Psalter in 'Das Bibelwerk'. Equally worthy of study is the interest shown in the number of psalms composed by David or connected with David, Solomon and their contemporaries according to the biblical Psalm titles. The evidence of the Psalm Preface *Dauid filius Jesse* and the Old Irish glosses on it is also relevant here. All this probably reflects exegetical activity of the early Irish schools. The composition of the biblical psalm headings tended to be attributed to Ezra after the return from Babylon, rather than to David or his contemporaries.[149] The number of Davidic psalms (*psalmi David*) given in the sources varies: 74 according to 'Das Bibelwerk',[150] 113 according to the *Old-Irish Treatise*.[151] According to the preface *David filius Jesse, VIIII fecit ipse Dauid, XXXII non sunt suprascripta, LXII in Dauid.*[152] An Old Irish gloss on this last number LXXII says: 'i.e. which suit and are ascribed to the person of David.[153]

With regard to the importance ascribed to the biblical headings, 'Das Bibelwerk', deriving the word *titulus* from a Greek word supposed to mean *incendium* (the *Old-Irish Treatise* has *titio*, 'a firebrand', and *titan*, 'sun'), says it lights up the meaning (of) the psalm that follows on it (*quia incendit intellectum psalmum sequentem*).[154]

A further point to be noted with regard to the number of Davidic psalms is the principle that the psalms without superscription in the Psalter (given as 14 in number in 'Das Bibelwerk', 32 in the Preface *David filius Iesse*) are regarded as being governed by the heading of the preceding psalm. Psalms recognized as having Davidic headings, or anonymous psalms preceded by Davidic psalms, may have been a factor in the early Irish interpretation of psalms as referring to David.

149. See *OIT*, lines 207-217; Ezra gathered the Psalms in one book and 'wrote and arranged its title before every psalm' (*OIT*, pp. 28-29); cf. 'Das Bibelwerk', Sheehy (ed.), above p. 125. The tradition concerning the role of Ezra in establishing the order of the Psalms is found in Origen and in Jewish sources; see de Lange, *Origen*, p. 119.

150. M. Sheehy (ed.), above p. 125.

151. *OIT*, pp. 24-25.

152. *Thes. Pal.*, I, p. 8.

153. *Thes. Pal.*, I, p. 8.

154. Text of 'Das Bibelwerk' in Sheehy (ed.), above, p. 132; *The Old-Irish Treatise*, lines 269-71, in *OIT*, pp. 30-31.

A second feature of early Irish psalm exegesis is the double historical reference given to a number of psalms. We find this in the psalm headings of the Psalter of Charlemagne and of the catena on the Psalms in Codex Pal. lat. 68, and also occasionally in the glosses in the Psalter of Rouen for Psalms 1–16. That the double historical reference was taken seriously in the interpretation is clear from the fact that it is found both in the headings and expository glosses of the catena just mentioned. To illustrate by just two of the many examples:

Psalm 40—heading: '*Salmus Dauid*'. *Pro erumnis a Saul. Vox Ezechiae*... Expository gloss—'*qui intellegit*'. (v. 1). *id est Dauid uel Ezechiae...'inimicorum eius*' (v. 3). *id est Saul uel sociorum eius; uel Assiriorum.*

Psalm 47—heading: *Vox Dauid accepto regno. Vox Ezechiae*... Expository gloss: '*quoniam ecce reges (congregati sunt)*' (v. 5) *id est Assiriorum satrapae; uel reges terrae Israel aduersus Dauid:* '*conuenerunt in unum*' (v. 5) *id est aduersus Dauid uel Ezechiam.*

The explanation of this phenomenon seems to lie in the desire to bring together two distinct modes of historical exegesis, the one understanding the Psalms as speaking of David and his times, the other looking on them as referring to events of later Jewish history. The latter form of exegesis would be basically that of Theodore.

It was possibly from the convergence of these two traditions that the theoretical presentation of the twofold historical sense of the Psalms (the first story and the second story), which we find in 'Das Bibelwerk' and the *Old-Irish Treatise* on the Psalter, emerged.[155] This may have been formed during the course of the eighth century, since the basis for it was already present in the tradition found in the Vatican catena on the Psalms, a work compiled about 700. The theory of the twofold historical sense as put forward in the introduction of the *Old-Irish Treatise* proper seems to envisage the subject matter of the second 'history' as being later Jewish history (Hezekiah, the people, the Maccabees). Yet the example of the 'second story' given both in the *Old-Irish Treatise* and in 'Das Bibelwerk'[156] is taken from the time of David (*Chusai Archites*). This may mean no more than that the theory was badly applied with regard to Psalm 1.

155. On this see above, 2.5.b.
156. Text given above, 2.5.b.

2.5.h. *The* Romani *and Early Irish Psalm Interpretation.* The *Romani* were a well-defined group in seventh-century Ireland especially as proponents of the Roman celebration of Easter during the Paschal controversy from about 630 onwards.[157] They appear to have been a scholarly group, at least in part. A scholar of the *Romani* is mentioned in connection with computation tables.[158] *Romani* are also mentioned in the *Collectio Canonum Hibernensis*[159] (made at the beginning of the eighth century) and in the Canons of Adomnán.[160]

It is interesting to find *Romani* mentioned with regard to biblical exegesis. Our chief source of evidence for this is the catena of Pal. lat. 68. The same texts are found in the introductory material in the so-called Psalter of Charlemagne, where, however, it is obvious that the Continental scribe was occasionally at a loss to understand the Irish original on which he appears to have depended. The occurrences are as follows:

> (Psalm 49). *'Deus deorum Dominus... In finem salinus Dauid.'* De mirabilibus mundi hic salmus ad Iudeos conponitur qui uirtutem neglegentes solas curarent hostias ligalium iusionum; in priore salmo sermonem ad omnes direxit, in praesenti ad Iudeos tantum. Vox spiritus de aduentu Christi. Hic salmus secundum Romanos de iudicio futuro canitur.

The first part of this heading *De mirabilibus...ad Iudeos tantum* is drawn for the greater part from the Julian Epitome. The mystical heading seems to understand the psalm of the first coming of Christ. The understanding of the *Romani* disagrees with this. Actually, the understanding of the *Romani* has nothing exceptional about it. It is that found in Series I *De aduentu Christi propheta dicit et de iudicio futuro* and is similar to the heading of Series III: *Vox apostolica de secundo Christi*

---

157. On the *Romani* of the Paschal controversy see L. Gougaud, *Christianity in Celtic Lands* (London: Sheed & Ward, 1932; repr., Dublin: Four Courts Press, 1993), pp. 185-201; J. Kenney, *The Sources for Early History of Ireland: Ecclesiastical* (Columbia University Press, 1929; later reprints; Dublin: Four Courts Press, 1997), p. 216; K. Hughes, *The Church in Early Irish Society* (London: Methuen, 1966), pp. 103-10; K. Hughes, *Early Christian Ireland: Introduction to the Sources* (London, 1972), pp. 75-80. See also Ó Néill, 'Old-Irish Treatise'.

158. Thus, for instance, in MS Würzburg M.p.th. f. 61, in an additional folio (fol. 29) added to a Hiberno-Latin biblical commentary; text in *Thes. Pal.*, II, p. 285.

159. H. Wasserschleben (ed.), *Die irische Kanonensammlung* (Leipzig: Verlag von Bernhard Tauchnitz, 2nd edn, 1885), pp. 62, 159, 163, 183, 211.

160. Cf. L. Bieler (ed.), *The Irish Penitentials* (SLH, 5; Dublin Institute for Advanced Studies, 1963), p. 254.

aduentu. It is simply impossible, with the little information at our disposal, to determine why the *Romani* understood the psalm in this way. It may have something to do with a theory of interpretation and may be connected with the biblical psalm heading, which for this psalm in the genuine Gallican and *Romanum* tradition is *Psalmus Asaph*, although Pal. lat. 68, with other Gallican and *Romanum* texts take it as a Psalm of David—*in finem salmus David.*[161]

> (Psalm 52). *'Dixit insipiens... In finem.' Salmus David de Saul. Intellegentia Dauid pro Abimelech. id est pro choro. Vox Ezechiae de Rabsace, et de his temporibus quae in illis gesta sunt.* Secundum Romanos *pro insidis Saul et occissione sacerdotum in Nouae (cant)atur. Vox Christi de Iuda traditore.*

(The Psalter of Charlemagne has: ...*occisione sacerdotum in nouo cantico*—an obvious failure of a Continental scribe to make sense out of the Hiberno-Latin spelling *in nouae = in Nobae = in Nobe,* of his original.)

The genuine biblical heading for this psalm in the Gallican and *Romanum* tradition is *In finem pro Melech intellegentiae Dauid.* The tradition represented by Pal. lat. 68 (and the so-called Psalter of Charlemagne) has read *Salmus Dauid de Saul* into the biblical heading. For *Melech* Pal. lat. 68 has *Abimelech,* as have many other MSS. We simply cannot say what reading the Psalter of the *Romani* had. Their interpretation, however, does not follow the Theodorean one or the Epitome of Julian which understands the psalm of Hezekiah and the Assyrian general (cf. 2 Kgs 18.17, etc.). They interpret it rather of the slaughter of the priests of Nob (*Nouae*) mentioned in 1 Samuel 21–22. David's visit there and to the priest Achimelech (called Abimelech in Pal. lat. 68 and other corrupt texts) is the subject of the biblical heading for the preceding psalm (Ps. 51). It may well be these two psalm headings which had the *Romani* opt for the reference to David and his times rather than to later Jewish history. Their interpretation had been read into the very biblical psalm heading of Psalm 52 (*Salmus Dauid de Saul Intelle-*

---

161. See, e.g., the words of Eucherius, *Instructio in Salonium,* in C. Wotke (ed.), *S. Eucherii Lugdunensis opera omnia, pars 1* (CSEL, 31; Vienna, 1894), p. 89, cited in the introduction to the Hiberno-Latin work, *Eclogae tractatorum in Psalterium* (M. Sheehy [ed.], in McNamara, 'Psalter Text', Appendix III, above p. 124. *Quid sibi uult illud quod frequenter in psalmorum titulis inscribitur: 'In finem psalmus Dauid'? Responsio: quod psalmi in finem mundi bonorum repromissionem respiciunt...*

gentia...pro Abimelech) and is also found in the explanatory glosses,
e.g. vv. 1, 3, 5, 6, 7).

> (Psalm 54). *'Exaudi Deus orationem... In finem in carminibus intellectus Dauid.' Vox Honiae sacerdotis expulsi de sacerdotio a regibus Grecorum quod emit Simon quidam propincius Honiae; inde Honias fugit in Aegiptum et Deum ibi coluit iuxta mores Hierusolimorum. Hic salmus* secundum Romanos *pro erumnis Saul cantatur. Vox aeclesiae de Christo.*

In interpreting the psalm as speaking of the persecution of David by
Saul, rather than of Onias and Maccabaean times as the Theodorean
tradition and the Epitome do, the *Romani* may once again have been
guided by the biblical heading of the preceding psalm which connects
Psalm 53 with the report of the Ziphites to Saul that David was hiding
among them. They may even have been influenced by the mention of
David in the heading of the present psalm. The glosses, we may note,
seek to combine this *Romani* interpretation with the Theodorean one at
least as far as v. 9. From v. 10 onwards a third form of interpretation
enters, understanding the psalm of Ahitophel's counsel and Absalom's
revolt—the manner in which the psalm is understood in the glosses of
the Montpellier Psalter.[162]

It is obvious that the *Romani* referred to in these texts were a clearly
identifiable group in the communities in which the catena of Pal. lat. 68
was compiled, or at least in which the tradition it enshrines was formed,
which in the view proposed in the present writer's opinion was in
Columban monasteries of either Ireland or Northumbria.

The period of the activity of the *Romani* would be 630 to 670 or so.
This would suit admirably other items of evidence concerning the age
of the tradition behind the catena in Pal. lat. 68. This, on the evidence of
the Old English glosses it contains and of its use of Adomnán's *De
locis sanctis*, appears to have been compiled about 700. But even then
the non-messianic interpretation of Psalms 44 and 109 seems too much
for the compiler—an indication that this form of exegesis had come
into existence some time previously.

2.6. *Summary and Conclusions: Psalter Text and Study in Ireland 500–800 CE*

In conclusion we may bring together considerations arising from the
study of the various topics in the course of this chapter and examine

---

162. Unterkircher (ed.), *Die Glossen*, pp. 226-30.

what light these can shed on the attention paid to the text and interpretation of the Psalter during the early centuries of the Church in Ireland.

2.6.a. *Psalter Text: Tradition and Creativity 500–600 CE.* It appears that during the sixth century the *Gallicanum* text of the Psalter was the subject of critical attention in Irish schools. The evidence for this derives from the text of the Cathach which was most probably written about 630–50 CE. Dom Henri de Sainte-Henri has shown that the critical signs of obelus and asterisk in this Psalter are evidence of a critical collation of the *Gallicanum* text against Jerome's rendering from the Hebrew, and furthermore against the specifically Irish text of the *Hebraicum*. It is hardly presuming too much to maintain that the critical work in question was being carried out during the sixth century. The evidence scarcely permits us to determine how widespread such critical interest in the Psalter text was in Irish schools during the period.

A sixth-century, or early seventh-century revision of the *Gallicanum* text against the Irish family of the *Hebraicum* implies that this latter text must have been brought to Ireland during the sixth century at the latest. We cannot say whether the specifically Irish family of *Hebraicum* texts reached Ireland in the form later transmitted by Irish sources or whether these peculiarites arose in Ireland itself.

2.6.b. *Irish,* Cathach, *Series of Mystical Psalm Headings: Sixth Century.* This series, as we have seen, has roots as far back as the third century. We have no earlier evidence of its existence as a series, however, before its use in the Cathach of St Columba. While we can conclude that it was being used in Ireland in the sixth century at the latest, we cannot as yet say whether it was put together in Ireland or came ready made from outside. Composition in Ireland would imply a rich tradition of christological psalm interpretation in the island during the sixth century or earlier.

2.6.c. *Emphasis on Davidic Interpretation of Psalms: Before 700 CE.* The early Irish schools inherited the christological interpretation of the Psalms from the generally accepted Christian tradition, and from such commentaries as those of Jerome, Augustine, Hilary and Cassiodorus. This Christian and christological interpretation has strongly influenced the Columba Series of Psalm headings.

Through the Latin translation of Theodore of Mopsuestia's commentary and the Epitome of this they inherited the historical interpretation of Antioch, in which many of the psalms were interpreted of Jewish history after David's time, especially of the times of Hezekiah, the Babylonian Exile, the restoration and of Maccabean times. However, together with this, and independent of the influence of Theodore or the Epitome, there must have flourished in Ireland a tradition interpreting the Psalms of David and his times. Furthermore, this tradition must have existed well before 700 CE since it is attested to both in the catena on the Psalms of Codex Pal. lat. 68 and in the headings of the Psalms in the so-called Psalter of Charlemagne, which was written on the Continent about 795–800, but is heavily dependent on tradition that had come from Ireland.

2.6.d. *Dual Historical Interpretation of the Psalms: before 700 CE.* Another point that emerges from analysis of the catena on the Psalms in Pal. lat. 68 and the headings of the Psalter of Charlemagne is that there existed in Irish schools well before 700 a tendency to combine two distinct historical interpretations, and refer them individually either to David's time or to later historical events. It is a dual form of reference as typical of these Irish sources as it appears to have been unknown outside of them.

2.6.e. *Exegetical Activity of the* Romani*: c. 630–700 CE.* The material at our disposal gives little or no information as to places or persons involved in Irish exegetical activity during these early centuries. It is a rare stroke of fortune that we have come across the mention of the exegetical activity of *Romani* and this with regard to the Psalms.

These *Romani* must have been an easily identifiable group in their day, and one may justifiably identify them with the *Romani* of the Paschal controversy, and thus consider the period of their activity as c. 630–700 CE. From the limited evidence provided, their chief interest seems to have been in understanding the Psalms of David and his time. They may have been rather typical of a number of groups in Irish schools at this period. One very interesting aspect of this limited evidence is that it reveals for us a questioning exegetical activity in Irish schools, a preparedness to disagree with accepted positions on the understanding of the Psalms.

2.6.f. *Literal, 'Historical' Interpretation of Messianic Psalms before 700 CE.* From tradition the early Irish Church would have inherited the christological interpretation of the entire Psalter. From the Commentary

of Theodore and the Epitome of this it would have known of the tradition reducing the number of directly messianic psalms to four. And yet,
despite all this we find attested before 700 CE a tradition which interpreted the entire Psalter as non-messianic in the literal, 'historical'
sense, that is which refused to admit that any of the psalms was originally intended as a prophecy of the Messiah in the literal sense. This is
an approach to the Psalter of which I know no evidence in Christian
tradition outside of Irish sources. The tradition must have been current
in the Irish schools in question before 700 CE since in the catena of
Codex Pal. lat. 68 composed about that date, we find the compiler
objecting to it. He records this interpretation with regard to Psalms 44
and 109 but personally dissociates himself from it and professes his
preference for the direct messianic interpretation of these psalms.

2.6.g. *Origin of Historical Interpretation of Psalms Found in Irish
Sources.* All this brings us to the final question: How much of this
interpretation of the Psalms not attested in non-Irish sources originated
in the Irish schools themselves? In other words: How creative was early
Irish Psalm exegesis?

It is, of course, technically possible that the early Irish schools inherited the non-messianic interpretation of the psalms in question and that
they also inherited a tradition interpreting the Psalms of David and his
times—even the tradition giving a dual historical reference. It seems
much more likely, however, that most, if not all, of this exegetical
activity originated within the Irish schools themselves during the seventh century, if not earlier. We have seen the positions being adopted
by the *Romani* in relation to the meaning of the Psalms. It is legitimate
to presume that there was much more of such exegetical activity. Once
in possession of two historical interpretative traditions—the Davidic
and the Theodorean—it would have been natural to combine them. The
interest in interpreting the Psalms of David and his time, which was so
obviously a feature of early Irish consideration of the Psalms, could
naturally lead to interpretation of even the so-called messianic psalms
of David and his time.

This is to suppose that within the early Irish schools there was a self-
articulating tradition of Psalm interpretation. The dual historical interpretation, which was a practice during the seventh century, would lead
during the eighth to the theoretical presentation of the twofold historical
sense of the Psalms—first story (*cétna stoir*) and second story (*stoir*

tánaise), *prima historia, secunda historia*—which we find in the *Old-Irish Treatise* and the related 'Das Bibelwerk'. The theory has not been properly worked through, since its application to Psalm 1 is not quite in keeping with the theoretical presentation of it in the introduction.

2.6.h. *Possible Outside Influences on Early Irish Psalm Exegesis.* Early Irish Psalm exegesis, as other forms of ecclesiastical learning, presumably took place in the monastic schools. In fact, more than any other biblical book the Psalms, by reason of their use in the divine office, were central to the monastic system. It is surprising, then, to see such stress placed on the historical interpretation, attempting to understand the Psalms in a setting of Old Testament history. It was an approach scarcely calculated to aid the use of the Psalms as Christian prayer. One would expect that the early Irish monastic Church inherited rather than created such a system of interpretation. It is one that seems alien to Western monasticism.

We do know a form of monasticism, however, in which precisely this form of approach was at home. It was that lived by Diodorus, Theodore's teacher, in his school at Tarsus—the monastic school or *asketerion*.[163] What little we know of this comes from the church historians Socrates and Sozomen in the account of the education received by John Chrysostom. Both John and Theodore (to become Bishop of Mopsuestia later), ardent aspirants after perfection, entered the *asketerion* under the guidance of Diodorus and Carterius.[164] The former, Socrates continues, wrote many treatises in which he limited his attention to the literal sense of Scripture, avoiding all that was mystical.[165] Thus also Sozomen.[166] From the Church historian and theologian Theodoret[167] we learn of Diodorus's special interest in psalmody. He tells us that Diodorus and his companion Flavianus, while not yet priests at Antioch, were the first to divide the choir into two parts and to teach the people to sing the Psalms of David antiphonally; with lovers of the divine word

---

163. See above, 1.3.

164. Socrates, *Hist. Eccl.* 6. 3 (*PG* 67, 665B); Sozomen, *Hist. Eccl.* 8. 2 (*PG* 67, 1516A). For John Chrysostom's education in the school of Diodorus see C. Baur, *John Chrysostom and his Time*. I. *Antioch* (trans. Sr M. Conzaga; London: Sands, 1959), pp. 89-103.

165. Socrates, *Hist. Eccl.* 6. 3 (*PG* 67, 665B).

166. Sozomen, *Hist. Eccl.* 8. 2 (*PG* 67, 1516A).

167. *Hist. Eccl.* 2. 19 (*PG* 82, 1060C).

they would spend the night in singing psalms to God.

We can presume that Diodorus would have taken the same love and the same devotional practice with him to the school or *asketerion*. This *asketerion*, as noted earlier,[168] was apparently a religious community directed by Diodorus before he became a bishop in 378. It was probably a monastery in which children and young people were given an intellectual and moral formation before they moved elsewhere, either to enter monasteries of strict observance or become priests devoted to the pastoral ministry.

This information may possibly be supplemented by a passage from the Preface to the Antiochene commentary on the Psalms which its editors believe is from the pen of Diodorus himself. But even if Diodorus is not the author, the text is none the less important as evidence for the use of a commentary like that of Theodore's as an aid to prayer. In the Preface to this Antiochene commentary we read:

> Of this scripture so necessary, I mean the Psalms, I have reckoned it fitting to make a succinct exposition, as I myself have received: of the arguments proper to each psalm and to give an interpretation that is literal. In this manner, the brothers when they chant the Psalms will not be dragged away by the words, nor because they do not understand them will they occupy their minds with other things. On the contrary, because they understand the sequence of what is said they will chant with understanding (cf. Ps. 46.8, LXX), as it is written, that is, from the depths of their intelligence and not merely externally—with their lips.[169]

These words, introducing a commentary parallel to that of Theodore, tell us that the historical interpretation being presented was intended as an aid to prayer and apparently for monks in choir. This may have been the tradition of the *asketerion* of Diodorus.

The *asketerion* of Diodorus and Antioch in its turn was probably only a reproduction of an institution already in existence in the Syrian Church, notably in that of Edessa, where there existed the strict ascetical life of the anchorites and the freer form of life in the Christian schools of the same kind as in the *asketerion* of Antioch. It may well be that some form of this monasticism also existed in the West and that Irish monastic practice and education was influenced by it.

---

168. Above, 1.3.
169. Olivier (ed.), *Diodori*, pp. 4, 33-42; Mariès, 'Extraits', pp. 82-85.

APPENDIX

Historical Headings of Psalms 1–16 in the Psalter of Rouen,
Pseudo-Bede and the Psalter of Charlemagne

PSALMUS 1

ROUEN PSALTER, Psalm 1 (p. 2, top margin, legible only in part)
In ... docet quae merces bona opera et quae...et de Ioseph posse intelligi qui cor-
pus Domini sepelibit et de his qui ad spectacula...
PSEUDO-BEDE (*PL* 93, 483BC)
Omnes generaliter ad studia virtutum incitat, simul adjungens quae merces bona,
quae mala gesta sequatur. Tertullianus in libro de Spectaculis asserit hunc
psalmum et de Joseph posse intelligi, qui corpus Domini sepelivit, et de his qui ad
spectacula gentium non conveniunt.
PSALTER OF CHARLEMAGNE
Illegible for this psalm.

PSALMUS II

ROUEN PSALTER (p. 1; as heading to the *Gallicanum* text)
Generalem Dauid querimoniam facit in Deum, quod regno suo sibi dato, desuper et
gentes et populi Israel inuiderent, commonem ad omnes dirigens coreptionem.
PSEUDO-BEDE (*PL* 93, 489C)
Generalem David querimoniam facit ad Deum, quod regno sibi desuper dato, et
gentes et populi Israel inviderint, communem ad omnium correctionent dirigens.
PSALTER OF CHARLEMAGNE
Hic psalmus Dauid. Vox sociorum Dauid iurgentium quod gentes et Absalon perse-
cuti sunt Dauid. Vel uox Ecclesiae (lege: *Ezechiae*) *de Assiris.*

PSALMUS III

ROUEN PSALTER (p. 3; on right-hand margin of page with *Gallicanum*)
(Pote)st Ezechiae conuenire qui circumdatus Assir(io) exercitu Dominum inuo-
cau(erit).
PSEUDO-BEDE (*PL* 93,494C)
Potest Ezechiae conuenire qui circumdatus Assyrio exercitu Dominum invocaverit.
PSALTER OF CHARLEMAGNE
In titulo psalmi istius docetur quae causa Dauid compulserit ita orare quod
praedierit Absalon filii sui... Nec minus temporibus Ezechiae regis conuenit qui
circumdatur Aziriorum exercitu Domini.

PSALMUS IV

PSALTER OF ROUEN (p. 5; right-hand margin of page with *Gallicanum*)
Ezechiae de auxil(io) corrip(iens) (menda)cio confi(dent) (only left-hand portion of
gloss visible; remainder illegible due to close binding).
PSEUDO-BEDE (*PL* 93, 501A)
*Ezechias contra aemulos suos de auxilio Domini gloriatur, corripiens eosdem, ne in
mendacio confidant, sed desinentes a malis cogitationibus, semper Deo serviant.*
PSALTER OF CHARLEMAGNE
*Psalmus Dauid ex persona Ezechiae contra emulos suos de auxilio Domi gloriantes
hoc carmen componitur. Ac deinde hos dicit corripere uidetur ne in mendatio confidunt* (2 manu:—*ant*)*, sed disinant malis cogitationibus et Domino semper uiuant.
Utilariter* (interl., 2 manu: Ut Hilarius) *dicit: Hic psalmus cantauit Dauid de Abisolon et Acitofel.*

PSALMUS V

PSALTER OF ROUEN (p. 5; right-hand margin of page with *Gallicanum*)
Ezechias post (...) talent gratias a(git...) et adorat in (templo)
PSEUDO-BEDE (*PL* 93, 506B)
Ezechias post infirmitatem gratias agit Domino et adorat in templo.
PSALTER OF CHARLEMAGNE
In hoc psalmo ostenditur persona Ezechiae.

PSALMUS VI

PSALTER OF ROUEN (p. 8; left-hand margin)
Ezechias infirmatus inuocat Dominum (...)is fragillitatem naturae humanae.
PSEUDO-BEDE (*PL* 93, 511B)
Ezechias infirmatus invocat Dominum, causans fragilitatem humanae naturae.
PSALTER OF CHARLEMAGNE
*In hoc psalmo formatur oratio Ezechiae in sua infirmitate uocantis Dominum (?)
clamantisque infirmitas naturae humanae.*

PSALMUS VII

PSALTER OF ROUEN (p. 9; right-hand margin of page with *Gallicanum*)
*Ezechi(as) ab hos(tibus) calumniatus (et a suis) proditus Domino su(p)licat inprae-
cat(us) iudicium eius in eos (qui mendaciter innocen(tiam) accusabant. Vox Dauid
uel Christi ...*
PSEUDO-BEDE (*PL* 93, 515B)
*Ezechias ab hostibus calumniatus, et a suis proditus, Domini supplicat, imprecatus
eius judicium in eos qui mendaciter innocentiam accusabant.*
PSALTER OF CHARLEMAGNE
Psalmus istius sensus et titulo praenotatur. Que querellam istam Domino cantauit

pro uerbis Chusi filii Iemini quem Ebrei Saulem esse aestimant. Vel in hoc psalmo praedicitur quod Ezechiae hostibus clamantibus et a suis proditus et a nobis rebus defamatus depraecatur Deum loquutus sit de iuditium eos qui mendaciter innocentem accusant.

PSALMUS VIII

PSALTER OF ROUEN (p. 12; left-hand margin, continued interlineary)
Admiratur propheta potentiam Dei per quam gubernat cunctam mundi molem gratiasque agit quod tantus creator hominis memoriam habere dignatus est.
PSEUDO-BEDE (*PL*, 93, 52413)
Admiratur propheta Dei potentiam, per quam gubernat cunctam mundi molem, gratiasque agit quod tantus creator hominis memoriam sit habere dignatus.
PSALTER OF CHARLEMAGNE
Leticia cum inimici conculcamur. Aut Saul in monte Gelboe. In quo admiratus (lege: *-atur*) *profeta Dei potentiam per quant gubernat cunctam mundi molem gratiasque agit qui lantam* (corr. in MS from *-as*) *omnis* (lege: *hominis*) *memoriam habere* (*h* interl.) *dignatus sit.*

PSALMUS IX

PSALTER OF ROUEN (p. 15; left-hand margin)
Orat Dauid Dominum pro dolosis cogitationibus filii sui gratias agens quod eas non sequeretur effectus. Vel Ezechias de interritu Assirii exercitus.
PSEUDO-BEDE (*PL* 93, 529A)
Orat Dominum David pro dolosis cogitationibus filii sui, gratias agens quod eas non sequeretur effectus. Potest et Ezechiae congruere gratias agenti post Assyrii exercitus interitum.
PSALTER OF CHARLEMAGNE
Psalmus istius tituli ita inscribitur: Pro ocultis Abselon. Depraecatus est Deum gratiasque Deo reddidit qui eos affectus potentie Deo proibente non secutus sit. Siue persona Ezechiae ostenditur gratias agentis Deo post excidium Assirii exercitus qui tanta in populum Dei molestus est. Vox Ezechiae dicentis laudes de Christo.

PSALMUS X

PSALTER OF ROUEN (p. 21; left-hand margin)
Conuenit Dauid fugienti Saulem et habitanti in deserto Iudae uel Ezechiae.
PSEUDO-BEDE (*PL* 93, 544A)
Verba David quando Saulem fugiens in desertis est habitare compulsus.
PSALTER OF CHARLEMAGNE
Hic psalmus sub persona Dauid intellegitur quando fugerit a facie Saulis et in desertis ludae habitare conpulsus est. Siue et umbra quaedam in tempore Ezechiae deprehenditur quando insistententes (!) *Assiriis rogabatur ab amicis suis ut fuga(ret* added interl.*) se ipsi liberaretur et populum urbem demitteret. Sic de Ezechia* (corr. from *-e*) *narrat: Quare inquis me conpellitis ad fugam cum ab eo*

locum ubi Dominus rogantibus se auxilium adferre solet. Si uero de Dauid intelle-
gatur ipse dicet: Inter me Saul et omnis exercitus eius habitare in patria non sinat.
Et (?) errabundus et uagus more auium et bestiarum huc illucque discurrem tunc ab
eo praesolem Dominum in quo confidens insidias eorum non timebo.

PSALMUS XI

PSALTER OF ROUEN (p. 23; left-hand margin above *Salua*)
*Ex persona Dauid canitur (*interl.*) quod in tempore eius omnis defecerit sanctus,*
uel querela Ezech(iae) quem quidem principes sui (continued interl.) *Assiris pro-*
diderunt et consilium cum hostibus habentes (?) sibi dolore loquibantur.
PSEUDO-BEDE (*PL*, 93, 547A)
Ex persona David canitur quod in tempore eius omnis defecerit sanctus, et diminu-
tae sint veritates a filiis hominum.
PSALTER OF CHARLEMAGNE
In progeniae Dauid. Vel die iudicii. Psalmus Dauid. Iste psalmus ex persona Dauid
*cantatur qui in templo (*lege: *quod in tempore) eius omnis defecerit sanctus et*
deminute ueritatis a filiis hominum. Vel querella Ezechiae quem quidam principes
Assirii suo prodiderunt et con(si)lium (??*) cum hostibus abentes sibi dolore (*lege:
dolose) loquebantur.

PSALMUS XII

PSALTER OF ROUEN (p. 23 *Hebraicum*; left-hand margin above *Usquequo*)
Ezechias depraecatur Dominum ne obliuiscatur illum Dominus.
PSEUDO-BEDE (*PL* 93, 550C)
Ezechiae preces ab Assyriis obsessi.
PSALTER OF CHARLEMAGNE
Hic psalmus depraecatio Dauid pro erumnis Saul. Inde ait ad Dominum: Usquequo
in f(inem). Psalmus Dauid. Ex persona Ezechiae psalmus iste formatur. Quidam
depraecatus sit ne diutius obliuiscatur illum Dominus nec permittat manibus inimi-
corum suorum concludi ne maiorent insultando (—tioni interl. above*—ando)*
*superbis si me agintur (*lege: *agitur).*

PSALMUS XIII

PSALTER OF ROUEN (p. 24; right-hand margin of *Gallicanum* page)
Pro eo quod est insipiens in Ebreo nabal posit(um) est (unde) et Abigal de uiro suo
Nabal dixit: Vere secundum nomen suum insipiens est, reliqua.
PSEUDO-BEDE (*PL* 93, 552BC)
Pro eo quod est insipiens, in Hebraeo Nabal positum est, unde et Abigail de viro
suit Nabal dixit: Vere secundum nomen suum insipiens est. Haec Ezechias contra
Rapascen loquitur.
PSALTER OF CHARLEMAGNE
Hic psalmus pro erumnis Saul cantauit Dauid. In finem psalmus Dauid. Psalmus
iste hoc idem resonat que ueniens Asirius per legatos ad Ezechiam (corr. from—

*em) loquutus sit ut non speraret in Dauid (dd; lege: Deo) suo uel deos qui dicertar-
ent gentium in nihilum radactos esse commemorat. De Iudeorum et gentium populo
quo dicunt de Saluatori nostro non est Deus.*

PSALMUS XIV

PSALTER OF ROUEN (p. 25; right-hand margin of *Hebraicum*; apparently in different hand)
*Verba sunt populi in captiuitate Babiloni(ae) optantis reditum ad patriam enumer-
antisque quibus meritis ad hanc peruenire*
PSEUDO-BEDE (*PL* 93, 556B)
*Verba populi in captivitate Babyloniae optantis reditum ad patriam, enumeran-
tisque quibus meritis ad hanc pervenire queat.*
PSALTER OF CHARLEMAGNE
*Hic psalmus de portatione arche Domini de Cariatharim et de consumatione taber-
naculi Moysi et Aron Dauid cantauit. Vel populi manentes in captiuitate Babilonia
oblantisque habitationem reuerti enumeratque quantis bonis quisque merebitur ad
ista bona perueniri.*

PSALMUS XV

PSALTER OF ROUEN (p. 27; left-hand margin and interlinearly)
*Ezechias in egritudine (Domin)um depraecatur et de reparatione uitae gratulatur et
quod humanarum rerum non sit egenus exponitur.*
PSEUDO-BEDE (*PL* 93, 55713)
*Ezechias in aegritudine Dominum deprecatur, et in vitae suae reparatione gratu-
latur, et quod humanarum rerum non sit egens, exponitur.*
PSALTER OF CHARLEMAGNE
Tituli inscriptio ipsi Dauid. Hoc psalmo de restauratione hereditatis cantauit Dauid.
Siue psalmus iste ex persona (*-a* corr. from *-e*) *Ezechie in egritudine Deum depre-
cantis canitur.*

PSALMUS XVI

PSALTER OF ROUEN (p. 25; left-hand margin)
...deuotum cor hab(entem) (apparently in different hand).
*...psalmo Dauid Dominum (de)praecatur et auditu dig(num) faciat quem ini(mici)
gratis persecuti sunt.*
PSEUDO-BEDE (*PL* 93, 56113)
*Deprecatur Dominum David, ut se devotum cor habentem, auditu dignum faciat,
quem inimici gratis impugnabant.*
PSALTER OF CHARLEMAGNE
*Psalmus Dauid pro erumnis Saul. In hoc psalmo Deum deprecatur ut audire digne-
tur se faciat quem inimici gratis, non odio, persequentis. Hoc ergo petit ut deuotum
cor habentem Dominus adiuuetur.*

Some Affiliations of the St Columba Series
of Psalm Headings: A Preliminary Study

1. *Introduction: Earlier Research*

The Cathach of St Columba contains the Gallican (Vulgate) Latin Psalter. The manuscript as we now have it has only 58 of the original 110 (or so) folios, with the text of Pss. 30.10–105.13 (in the Vulgate numbering). Each psalm is preceded by a rubric, added by the scribe who wrote the Psalter text, and in spaces left blank to receive them. These rubrics contain (a) the Vulgate biblical psalm headings, (b) followed occasionally by an indication on when the particular psalm is to be read (*legendus ad*), and (c) what appears to be a liturgical note regarding the use of the psalm (the order of [b] and [c] can be reversed), and (d) a heading giving for the greater part the spiritual or mystical meaning of the psalm. Only some of the psalms (18) have *legendus ad*; fewer still what for the moment may be called 'a liturgical note'. We may note that the date of the Cathach manuscript is not quite certain. While some would assign a sixth-century date,[1] from Columba's own day, others prefer a seventh-century dating, from 630–50 or so. In any event, the manuscript is our earliest document on the psalms from the Irish Church.

2. *Early Irish Psalm Study 560–750 CE*

2.1. *Commentary by Columbanus on the Psalms (c. 560–90 CE)*
Columbanus was born in Leinster, probably in 543. His biographer Jonas tells us that at an early age Columbanus went to study under Sinilis (probably St Senell of Cleenish, Lough Erne in County Fermanagh),

---

1.   Thus, for instance, most recently, M. Werner, 'Three Works on the Book of Kells', *Peritia* 11 (1997), pp. 250-326 (252): 'the Cathach of Columba (Dublin, RIA, MS s.n.), a manuscript written perhaps during the second half of the sixth century'.

a man renowned among his contemporaries for his piety and his knowledge of the sacred scriptures. From Sinilis Columbanus went to the monastery of Bangor on the shores of Belfast Lough. He left Ireland for the Continent probably in 590. Jonas also tells us that at a youthful age Columbanus expounded the book of Psalms in elegant language (*elimato sermone*). This may have been while he was still with Sinilis, but in any event before he left Ireland. This commentary seems to have been taken by Columbanus to the Continent and is probably the work referred to in the ninth-century St Gall catalogue as *Expositio sancti Columbani super omnes psalmos uolumen I*, and in the tenth-century Bobbio catalogue as *Expositio sancti Columbani in psalmos II*. It has apparently been since lost. Since Columbanus's Psalter text is mainly Vulgate (Gallican),[2] the biblical text commented on in this commentary was also presumably the Gallican. While we can surmise but little about the sources used, and say nothing about the exegetical approach of Columbanus in this commentary, it is likely that he would have known some of Jerome's commentaries on the psalms, and also the works of Augustine. The simple fact that a commentary on the psalms was composed in Ireland in the mid-sixth century indicates the existence of an early solid study of the Psalter in Irish schools.

2.2. *Commentary on the Psalms in Vatican Codex Palatinus Latinus 68 (c. 700)*[3]

This commentary (*glossa*) on the psalms (imperfect by reason of the loss of the text on Pss. 1.1–39.11), with glosses in Old Irish and Old English (Northumbrian dialect) was probably compiled about 700. It represents a well-formed exegetical tradition (in fact at least two such traditions) which began at least half a century earlier. As sources it uses the Epitome of Julian's translation of the commentary of Theodore of Mopsuestia, Jerome's *Commentarioli in psalmos*, apparently also his *Tractatus siue homiliae in psalmos,* his *Liber interpretationis hebraicorum nominum,* and his letters nos. 30 and 73; Augustine's *Enarrationes*

---

2.   See G.S.M. Walker (ed.), *Sancti Columbani Opera* (Dublin: Dublin Institute for Advanced Studies, 1957), pp. lxix, 216; M. McNamara, 'Psalter Text and Psalter Study in the Early Irish Church (A.D. 600–1200)', above p. 19-142 (86-89).

3.   M. McNamara (ed.), *Glossa in Psalmos: The Hiberno-Latin Gloss on the Psalms of Codex Palatinus-Latinus 68 (Psalms 39:11–151:7)* (Studi e Testi; Vatican City: Biblioteca Apostolica Vaticana, 1986). Introduction to the edition reprinted above pp. 165-238.

in Psalmos, or more probably an abbreviation or epitome of them; Eucherius's *Formula spiritalis intellegentiae* and *Instructionum libri II*; Letter 23 'Ad Dardanum' of pseudo-Jerome and Adomnan's *De locis sanctis*.

2.3. *'Davidic' Commentary on the Psalms (630–50 CE?)*[4]

In Pal. lat. 68 the bulk of the historical interpretations concerns David and his contemporaries.[5] This was probably drawn from a full Hiberno-Latin commentary understanding the psalms to speak principally of David and his times. This I here refer to as the 'Davidic Commentary'. The Epitome of Julian's translation most probably originally covered the entire work. We now have it only from Ps. 16.11 onwards; the opening section has been lost and all our extant copies derive from an imperfect original. The missing section was made good in two different ways: (1) in the Milan Commentary in Codex Amb. C 301 inf. by the full translation of Julian (and so also in the Hiberno-Latin *Eclogae tractatorum in psalterium*); (2) by another historical, but Davidic, commentary. This is found principally in the Double Psalter of St Ouen (Rouen Bibl. mun. 24 [A.41]; s. x), but also in the Hiberno-Latin Reference Bible. We can presume that this was known as an independent work to the compiler of the commentary in Pal. lat. 68, and was thus in circulation thus by 700 and earlier.

2.4. *The* 'Tituli Psalmorum' *of Pseudo-Bede (c. 700 CE)*

These headings, printed with a commentary in no way connected with them, in *PL* 93, 477-1098, are found in MSS Munich Clm 14387 (s. ix), Paris BNF lat. 12273 (s. x); also in Paris BNF lat. 2384 (s. ix) and Rheims 118 (s. ix). This series of *Tituli Psalmorum* is composite, with first a historical heading often drawn from the Epitome of Julian, but other times (especially for Pss. 1–16) fitted to suit the commentary of the 'Davidic Psalter'. There follows a heading with the spiritual sense, in the tradition of the Columba series. On occasion there is a heading with the moral application.

---

4.   L. De Coninck (ed.), *Incerti Auctoris Expositio Psalmorum I:1–XVI:11a iuxta litteram* (Kortrijk: Katholieke Universiteit Leuven, 1989) (part 1, introduction; part 2, the text).

5.   See McNamara (ed.), *Glossa in Psalmos*, pp. 59-60.

2.5. *Abbreviation of Augustine's* Enarrationes in Psalmos *(c. 650 CE?)*
Source analysis reveals that the commentary of Pal. lat. 68 draws among other works on the *Enarrationes* of Augustine, or on an abbreviation of these. This is particularly clear for an alternative exposition on the gradual psalms. None of these texts is ascribed to Augustine. On one occasion in the commentary a text dependent on Augustine is ascribed to a certain *Hilarius*, and on two occasions similar texts are accompanied in the margins by the letter *h*, by which *Hilarius* is probably intended.[6] The evidence seems to indicate that a work by Augustine, or an abbreviation of Augustine, circulated in early Ireland under the name of Hilarius. This Hilarius might well be an Irish scholar who had made an abbreviation (or epitome) of Augustine's *Enarrationes,* or had compiled an exegetical work heavily dependent on the *Enarrationes.*[7]

2.6. *Julian's Translation of Theodore of Mopsuestia's Commentary on the Psalms, and the Epitome thereof (500–650 CE?)*[8]
It is not clear whether Julian made his translation of Theodore's commentary before or after he had to resign his episcopal see in 418. When,

6. See McNamara (ed.), *Glossa in Psalmos*, pp. 53-54.

7. One of the sources used by the author of the *Félire Oengusso* (Epilogue 137-140) was 'the *Sensus* of pious Hilary' (*séis Elair*), mentioned together with the tome of Ambrose, the *Antigraph* of Jerome, the *Martyrology* of Eusebius; W. Stokes (ed.), *The Martyrology of Oengus the Culdee* (London: Henry Bradshaw Society, 1905), p. 270. The *Sensus* (*séis*) is the name of some book by Hilary, presumably believed by the compiler of the *Félire* to be one of the great Fathers of the Church. He probably identified him with Hilary of Poitiers, known as the author of the *Tractatus in Psalmos.* However, it is possible that the book in question was by an Irish author, and that the *Sensus* in the title reflected the belief that it concentrated on the spiritual sense (in Hiberno-Latin *sensus*; in Irish *síans*, *séns*, *séis*). In the introduction to the Psalter in the Reference Bible and in the *Eclogae tractatorum in psalterium* there are citations from a certain Hilarius on the spiritual and historical interpretation of the psalms, which cannot be traced to Hilary of Poitiers. The Hilary in question may have been an Irish writer on psalm interpretation.

8. L. De Coninck and M.J. d'Hont (eds.), *Theodori Mopsuesteni Expositionis in Psalmos Iuliano Aeclanensi interprete in latinum uersae quae supersunt* (CCSL, 88A; Turnhout: Brepols, 1977). For Julian's work see among others M.-J. Rondeau, *Les commentaires patristiques du psautier (IIIe–Ve siècles).* I. *Les travaux des Pères grecs et latins sur le psautier: Recherches et bilan* (Orientalia Christiana Analecta, 219; Rome: Pontifical Institutum Studiorum Orientalium, 1982), pp. 175-88. P. Ó Néill believes that the anonymous epitomiser of Julian's translation

or by whom, the epitome of this was made we cannot say. It may have been during Julian's own lifetime. While we can presume that there once was an epitome of the entire commentary, all we have at the moment is that for Ps. 16.11 onwards. The opening section must have got lost, and in the manuscript transmission is replaced by the full translation of Theodore in one branch (Codex Amb. C 301 inf.; the *Eclogae tractatorum in psalterium)*; in another (Double Psalter of St Ouen, MS Rouen, Bibl. mun. 24 [A. 41]; the Reference Bible) by a quite different historical commentary interpreting the psalms principally of David and his contemporaries (the 'Davidic Psalter'). The epitome in both traditions must have come to Ireland at an early date. It is used in the commentary of Pal. lat. 68 (650–700?), in the *Tituli psalmorum* of pseudo-Bede (c. 700), in the *Eclogae tractatorum in psalterium* and in the Reference Bible (750–800).

2.7. *The* Glosa Psalmorum ex Traditione Seniorum *(c. 600 CE)*[9]

This commentary on the psalms is dated to c. 600 or the early seventh century: it cites Gregory the Great (died 604) and a text from it, used in the *Breviarium in Psalmos*, is found in a Luxeuil manuscript (now in Hannover, Kestner Museum, Cul I 48) from the beginning of the eighth century. The commentary originated in France, probably southern France and in Provence. The author cites by name Augustinus, Hieronymus, Eusebius, Eucherius, Benedictus and Gregorius. The only one of these authors to be used extensively is Augustine (the *Enarrationes*). All we find from the others in general are single phrases or sentences to a given word. Boese says there is no trace of an influence from Irish or Insular exegesis in the *Glosa*, nor from Cassiodorus. He believes the work originated in monastic circles, and represents early monastic currents of the Rhone area (such as Provence sea coast: Lerins, linked with

worked in a Latin-speaking area (perhaps Southern Gaul or Spain), possibly in the sixth century and that both the full translation by Julian and the epitome of this reached Ireland perhaps by the second half of the seventh century; see P. Ó Néill, 'Irish Transmission of Late Antiquity Learning: The Case of Theodore of Mopsuestia's Commentary on the Psalms', in *Ireland and Europe: Texts and Transmission* (Dublin: Four Courts Press, forthcoming).

9.   H. Boese (ed.), *Anonymi Glosa Psalmorum ex traditione seniorum. I. Praefatio un Psalmen 1–100* (2 vols.; Aus der Geschichte der lateinische Bibel, 22; Freiburg: Herder, 1992); H. Boese (ed.), *Anonymi Glosa Palmorum ex traditione seniorum. II. Psalmen 101–150* (2 vols.; Aus der Geschichte der lateinische Bibel, 25; Freiburg: Herder, 1994).

monastic centres at Marseille, Lyon, the Jura area around the Lake of Geneva, even as far as Agaunum-Saint Maurice in Valais).

There is a variety of approaches with regard to the understanding of the psalms in the *Glosa*: the psalms are understood as speaking of David himself against his enemies, of Christ against the Jews, the Church against the heretics, every Christian in temptation and trial. The exegesis is predominantly christological and ecclesiological. We are frequently given the persons regarded as speaker in a given psalm, or a given psalm verse, and often introduced with the term *Uox*, 'the voice of'. Often a psalm is understood as having a number of speakers, as seems indicated by the context.

Soon after the original composition, and in the second half of the seventh century (650–700), the *Glosa psalmorum* was heavily drawn on and combined with texts from Jerome's *Commentarioli* and *Tractatus*, and some other as yet unidentified sources, to form the *Breviarium in Psalmos*.[10] The *Glosa psalmorum* is also used for the marginal glosses on Pss. 1.1–16.10 in the Stuttgart Psalter (Stuttgart, Würtemberg. Landesbibl., Cod. Bibl. 2° 73; mid ninth century), and in other Psalters besides.[11]

Evidence is now emerging that the *Glosa psalmorum ex traditione seniorum* was apparently known and used in Ireland in the later seventh and in the eighth centuries. L. De Coninck has indicated a possible influence of it on the comment on Ps. 2.1 in the 'Davidic Psalter' (c. 630–50?) as preserved in the Rouen manuscript.[12] The commentary in Pal. lat. 68 also seems dependent on the *Glosa psalmorum* in Ps. 52.2.[13] There is clear dependence on the *Glosa psalmorum* evident in introductory material to the psalms in the Psalter of Charlemagne (792–800), a manuscript in which much of the introductory material represents a

10. See Boese, *Die alte 'Glosa Psalmorum'*, pp. 76-82. The view that the dependence is the other way around, with the *Glosa Psalmorum* dependent on the *Breviarium*, is most unlikely.

11. See Boese, *Die alte 'Glosa Psalmorum'*, pp. 87-92.

12. Psalter of St Ouen, De Coninck (ed.), *Incerti*, part I, pp. x-xi and part II, 6, 41: *QUARE TURBABUNTUR GENTES. Quid, inquit, similitudine canis in me latratis?;* Boese (ed.), *Anonymi*, p. 11: <ET POPULI MEDITATI SUNT INANIA>. *Inter fremere et meditari differentia est, quia fremere canum est, meditari populis.*

13. Pal. lat. 68, Ps. 52.2, McNamara (ed.), *Glossa in Psalmos*, p. 114: *CORRUPTI SUNT. id est a lege et bono naturae* (same gloss on *declinauerunt* of verse 4); McNamara (ed.), *Glossa in Psalmos* (Ps. 52.2); Boese (ed.), *Anonymi*, I, p. 221: *CORRUPTI SUNT de lege bonae naturae.*

tradition very closely related to that preserved in the commentary of
Pal. lat. 68. There is verbal agreement in many instances.[14] The Psalter
of Charlemagne was written on the Continent, in a centre with Irish
connections. It is not clear whether the influence of the *Glosa psalmorum* is to be explained through Continental or Irish connections, since
the introductory material dependent on the *Glosa psalmorum* is not in
the Pal. lat. 68 commentary.

3. *Partial Analysis of Columba Series of Tituli Psalmorum*

3.1. *Indication of Speakers: Uox...*

In the St Columba series (series I) most of the titles consist of a
speaker, addressing some other person regarding some particular matter. A characteristic of series I is that, when not indicated as the prophet
(that is the psalmist), the speaker is introduced as 'The voice of...',
Uox, for example, *Uox Christi, Uox ecclesiae, Uox apostolorum.* Salmon[15] has noted that in many instances Tertullian is related to this
series I. Among other things Tertullian asserts on a number of occasions that Christ has spoken through the mouth of the prophets (among
whom he includes the psalmists), for example, *Accipe nunc et Filii
uoces de Patre... Item ad Patrem in psalmo 71... Sed et omnes paene
psalmi Christi personam sustinent.*

This use of *uox* in psalm titles is probably old. It is also found frequently in series II, known as 'the series of Saint Augustine of Canterbury', found in the MS BL Cotton Vespasianus A.I ('The Psalter of St
Augustine of Canterbury'), copied in England in the eighth century, and
in other manuscripts; in St Gallen codex 110, written at Verona

---

14. See the critical edition of the introductory material for Pss. 40–151 by
K. Ceulemans, 'Scotti (?) anonymi Tituli psalmorum in psalterio Caroli Magni traditi (= cod. paris. BN lat. 13159). Argumenta, opschriften en woordverklaringen bij
psalmen 40–151. I. Inleiding, kritische tekstuitgave en vertaling'. II. Tekstkritische
aantekeningen en inhoudelijke commentaar' (Dissertation for Licentiate in Greek
and Latin classics, Katholieke Universeit Leuven, 1997). For a non-exhaustive list
of the (verbal) agreements with the *Glosa Psalmorum ex traditione seniorum* see
Ceulemans, 'Scotti anonymi', I, p. xxx, instancing Pss. 62.5; 79.15-17, 20; 91.12;
97.6-10; 99.5-7; 100.21-26; 103.8-9; 104.24; 106.6-8; 109.6-10; 110.4-5; 111.8-9;
112.5-6; 117.6-9.

15. P. Salmon, *Les 'Tituli Psalmorum' des manuscrits latins* (Collectanea Biblica Latina, 12; Rome: Abbaye de Saint-Jérôme; Vatican City: Libreria Vaticana,
1959), p. 53.

(apparently 796–99), and in other manuscripts. This series II probably originated in Italy. The use of *uox* is also found in series III, a series inspired by St Jerome (especially by the *Commentarioli in Psalmos* for the gradual psalms). The earliest witness to this series is a ninth-century text. A number of the psalm titles are also thus introduced in series VII, a series with the text of Cassiodorus as abbreviated by Bede, edited by Salmon from three manuscripts, the earliest of which is the ninth century.

What, if any, precedent the Columba series had in this use of *Uox* in the title remains to be determined. It is worth noting, however, that use of the term *uox* in the sense found in the Cathach headings is frequent in the *Glosa psalmorum ex traditione seniorum*, but in the body of the commentary and for individual verses rather than as headings, which are not found in this commentary. Thus for instance for Psalm 2.

> verse 2: *QUARE FREMUERUNT GENTES. Hic uox prophetae dicit 'quare', ac si dicat: sine causa...* verse 3: *DISRUMPAMUS UINCULA EORUM. Hic tres uoces sunt: apostolorum, angelorum et Iudaeorum.* Verse 8: *POSTULA A ME: uox patris ad filium.*

Similarly on Psalm 4.2.

> *CUM INUOCAREM TE: hic uox Christi et uox ecclesiae;* verse 3: *FILII HOMINUM USQUEQUO GRAUI CORDE? Uox ecclesiae ad Iudaeos increpando loquitur.*

The Speakers

Uses	References
Uox Christi (45 occurrences):	3; 6; 10; 12; 14; 15; 23; 30; 34; 40; 41; 50; 51; 53; 54; 55; 58; 68; 70; 72; 73; 74; 76; 77; 83; 85; 87; 88; 100; 101; 104; 106; 108; 114; 117; 118; 119; 122; 126, 137, 139, 145, 147, 149, 150.
Uox Christi de Judeis:	58; 77; 106; 108.
Uox Christi separated from *de Judeis* by intervening words (*ad patrem, ad apostolos, in passione*):	3; 30; 34; 72; 88; 104; 118.
Uox Christi ad Patrem (17 occurrences):	3; 6; 12; 15; 53; 55; 70; 72; 73; 83; 85; 88; 100; 118; 122; 137.
Christus, without *uox* or with words intervening between *Christi* and *ad Patrem*	16; 58; 87.

Uses	References
Christus ad Patrem.	5.
Uox Ecclesiae (39 occurrences):	8; 22; 48; 61; 62; 64; 69; 71; 75; 81; 82; 90; 91; 93; 95; 96; 97; 102; 103; 105; 107; 109; 110; 111; 112; 120; 121; 124; 128; 130; 132, 134; 136; 138; 140; 143; 144; 146.
Uox ecclesiae in futuro,	133.
Propheta	4; 7; 19; 25 (*p. de se*); 32; 35; 38; 43; 49; 57; 66; 67; 127.
Propheta ad patrem	20; 29; 131.
Uox Apostolorum (13 occasions):	45; 46; 59; 65; 78; 79; 98; 99; 116; 123; 125; 135; 148.
Uox apostolorum ad populum:	65; 99; 148.
Uox Pauli (5 occurrences):	50; 56; 60; 63; 115.
Uox apostolica (5 occurrences):	66; 84; 86; 89; 113.
(Uox apostolica) ad nouellum populum	84.
(Vox apostolica) ad Dominum	89.
(Vox apostolica) de ecclesia	86.

3.2. *Examination of Some Specific Headings*

3.2.a. *Psalm 1*: De Joseph dicit, qui corpus Christi sepeliuit. This heading ultimately depends on a text of Jerome, actually cited in the *Tituli Psalmorum* of Pseudo-Bede in the heading to this psalm: *Tertullianus in libro De Spectaculis adserit hunc psalmum de Joseph posse intellegi qui corpus Domini sepeliuit, et de his qui ad spectacula gentium non conueniunt.*[16] There is no need to postulate direct dependence of the Columba series on Jerome, however. It could have come to the author of the Columba series *Tituli* from a commentary. The introductory comment on Psalm 1 in the *Glosa psalmorum ex traditione seniorum* has:

> *Interrogandum est, iste psalmus in cuius persona cantatur aut quis est 'beatus uir'. Alii uolunt dicere quod in persona Ioseph fuisset cantatus qui corpus Christi sepeliuit; alii in persona sancti Petri aut in persona uniuscuiusque sancti.*

3.2.b. *Psalm 2*: Legendus ad euangelium Lucae. Uox Patris et apostolorum et Christi. *Ad caput scribendum.*

See below at 3.1.

16. G. Morin (ed.), Jerome, *Commentarioli in Psalmos* (CCSL, 72; Turnhout: Brepols, 1959), p. 179.

3.2.c. *Psalm 3*: Uox Christi ad Patrem de Judeis dicit. The Columba heading can be explained by the content of the psalm, in a Christian or christological interpretation or application. The psalm begins: *Domine, quid multiplicati sunt qui tribulant me.* The heading takes the speaker as Christ, addressing the Father (*'Domine'*). The *Judei* would be the *omnes aduersantes mihi* of v. 8.

Practically all the elements of this Columba series heading are found in the *Glosa psalmorum,* which, however, caters for a variety of interpretations. It takes the speaker in v. 1 as *Uox Dauid et uox Christi et uox ecclesiae et uniuscuiusque sancti... Contra Dauid filius suus... contra Christum Iudas uel Iudaei...[C]ontra Christum...multiplicati sunt, quia toti Iudaei et...Iudas cum turba Iudaeorum contra ipsum uenit.*[17] Likewise on *Dentes peccatorum conteruisti* of v. 8: *principes Iudaeorum uel 'dentes' doctores hereticorum et uerba ipsorum.*[18]

This is a different christological interpretation to that given in the *Old-Irish Treatise* on the Psalter, where Psalm 3 is understood as speaking of the resurrection of Christ after three days.[19] This interpretation is based, undoubtedly, on v. 6 of the psalm: *Ego dormiui, soporatus sum, exsurrexi.*

3.2.d. *Psalm 15*: Uox Christi ad Patrem. Thus also the *Glosa psalmorum* on the opening words (v. 1): *CONSERUA ME DOMINE, QUONIAM IN TE SPERAUI. Uox Christi ad patrem in passione in persona hominis adsumpti.*

3.2.e. *Psalm 16*: Christus de Judeis dicit ad Patrem. *Glosa psalmorum* on Psalm 16 has: *Iste psalmus cantatur ex persona Christi contra Iudaeos...* And on v. 3: *PROBASTI COR MEUM DEUS. Uox Christi ad Patrem.*

3.2.f. *Psalm 26*: Ad eos qui primum ingrediuntur, in dominicum. Legendus ad lectionem Esaiae prophetae *(65,13; Vet. lat.):* ecce qui seruiunt tibi bona manducabunt.

See below, 3.3.b.

17. Boese (ed.), *Anonymi,* I, pp. 14-15.
18. Boese (ed.), *Anonymi,* I, p. 16.
19. *OIT,* pp. 26-27: '*Domine quid* [Ps. 3]. It is fit that the psalm which tells of the resurrection after three days should be in the third place.'

3.2.g. *Psalm 32*: Psalmus Dauid. Propheta cum laude Dei populum hortatur. *Psalmus Dauid* is the biblical title. The speaker here, as on 16 occasions, is the (psalmist) prophet. With the Cathach heading proper we may compare the *Glosa psalmorum ex traditione seniorum: EXULTATE IUSTI IN DOMINO. Propheta hortatur sanctos, ut laudent dominum: exultate iusti.*

3.2.h. *Psalm 34*: Uox Christi in passione de Judeis dicit. With this we may compare *Glosa psalmorum* on v. 1: *IUDICA DOMINE NOCENTES ME. Uox Christi in passione et uox ecclesiae in tribulatione...iudica: iudicium discretionis rogat, uel 'iudica' id est discerne inter me et Iudaeos et inter ecclesiam et persecutores.*

See also 5.3.d.ix below.

3.2.i *Psalm 35*: Propheta cum laude opera ipsius Judae dicit. The Cathach manuscript is defective here. This heading, and the surrounding text, is missing. The heading, however, is well attested in the manuscript tradition.

The speaker is the prophet. So also in series II, III and VI. The element *cum laude* may refer to the praises of God in 35.6-10.

The *Glosa psalmorum* in its comments makes reference to *populus Iudaicus*. On what text of the psalm the reference to Judas is based is not clear. Some of the others of the psalm series, however, have a reference both to Judas and *populus Iudaicus*, so that here the Columba series probably represents an established reference of the psalm. Thus in series II: *Accusatio prophetae de populo iudaico*; series III: *Propheta in spiritu de Juda et de populo Judaeorum.*

3.2.j. *Psalm 39*: In finem psalmus Dauid. Patientia populi. We can take *patientia* here to mean 'expectation', or 'patient awaiting', of salvation. The idea seems to be that the psalm, or a text of the psalm, speaks of the patient expectation of the (Jewish) people of the salvation to come. The title is based on the opening words *Expectans expectaui* (in the Vetus Latina *sustinens sustinui*). We may compare the text of the *Glosa psalmorum* on v. 1: *EXPECTANS EXPECTAUI DOMINUM: Uox prophetae in persona ecclesiae loquitur. Quia praeuidebat propheta Christum per spiritum sanctum uenturum esse in carne, propterea dixit 'expectans expectaui dominum' ac si dicat: sustinens sustinui.*

3.2.k. *Psalm 44*: Legendus ad euangelium Matthei, de regina Austri. Propheta pro Patre de Christo et Ecclesia dicit. The first section, with *legendus*, will be treated of later (5.3.c.vi below).

With regard to the heading proper, the speaker is taken to be the (psalmist) prophet. This was one of the psalms generally taken, even in the Antiochene tradition, as a prophecy of Christ. In the words of Jerome, as cited in the commentary of Pal. lat. 68: *Totus hic salmus refertur ad Christum de quo pater in euangelio loquitur: 'Hic est filius meus dilectus'.*

The Cathach (C) actually reads *ad Patre*. It is better retain the critically established reading *pro Patre* than emend C to *ad Patrem*. The word *pro* is probably to be understood as 'in the place of', *in persona*.

3.2.l. *Psalm 52*: Legendus ad euangelium Matthei. Increpat Judaeos incredulos operibus negantes Deum. Both the sections apparently are intended to go together, and will be treated of below in 3.3.l.

3.2.m. *Psalm 54*: In finem intellectus in carminibus Dauid. Uox Christi aduersus magnatos Judeorum et de Juda traditore. The first section is the biblical heading.

Christ is presented as the speaker, whether of the entire psalm or only sections of it is not clear. In the Christian interpretation, Christ is clearly the speaker of vv. 13-15, which would naturally be interpreted of Judas's betrayal of Christ. The *Glosa psalmorum* (as Augustine) has different speakers for different sections. In the opening section we have *uox ecclesiae*. It says that v. 13 refers to Christ, and says that v. 14 is *uox Christi: TU UERO HOMO UNIANIMIS DUX MEUS ET NOTUS MEUS: uox Christi de Iuda*. It also interprets v. 15 of Judas: *Qui simul mecum dulces capiebas cibos*, and at v. 16 says that as far as this we had the Lord's voice (*Usque hic uox dominica; postea propheta adnuntiat de peccatoribus*). At v. 16 (with reference to a plurality, *super illos*) the speaker, the *uox*, is understood to change to become that of the prophet, speaking of the earth swallowing up Core and Abiron. Who the 'mighty ones of the Jews', *magnatos Judeorum*, in the mind of the author of the *tituli* of Columba were, is not easy to determine, as his specific tradition is lost to us.

3.2.n. *Psalm 56*: In finem psalmus Dauid cum fugisset a facie Saulis in spelunca. Uox Pauli post resurrectionem. The connection of this psalm with the resurrection may be through the biblical title, the fuller form of which (also found in Pal. lat. 68) reads: *In finem ne disperdas Dauid in tituli inscriptione cum fugeret (C: fugisset) a facie Saul in spelonca.* The *Glosa psalmorum* (dependent on Augustine) connects the *tituli inscriptio* with the title on the cross. David in the cave, that is in the lower part of the earth, prefigured the human body, where majesty was hidden in Christ's body, with a citation from Paul (1 Cor. 2.8): 'Had they known, they would never have crucified the Lord of glory'. Verse 10 is understood as words of Christ, referring to his resurrection: *CONFITEBOR TIBI IN POPULIS, DOMINE, hoc est postquam resurrexero.*[20]

3.2.o. *Psalm 57*: In finem ne disperdas Dauid in tituli inscriptione. Propheta de senioribus Judeorum dicit. The first section gives the biblical heading. However, it may be intended to go along with the *titulus* proper, and in fact the *titulus* may have been formed from it.

The prophet (psalmist) is given as the speaker, and the biblical title is taken as part of his prophecy. He speaks concerning the elders of the Jews—presumably in their relation with Christ.

In the Christian interpretation both *in finem* and *Dauid* of the biblical psalm headings are understood of Christ. The words 'Do not destroy for David an inscription of a title' are connected with the request of the Jewish high priests (*pontifices*) to change the title (*titulus*) of the cross, to which Pilate replied: 'What I have written, I have written' (Jn 19.19-22). This is the interpretation of the biblical title in the *Glosa psalmorum*.[21] The same *Glosa* interprets 57.2 *iusta iudicate filii hominum* by reference to the Pharisees and the question on paying tax to Caesar in Mt. 22.16. Verse 7 (*Deus conteret dentes eorum in ore ipsorum*) is interpreted in relation to the same episode on the tax. *Dentes* is then further interpreted of the elders of the Jews: *(MOLAS LEONUM): dentes incidunt et molares molunt. Dentes plebs Iudeorum subiecta, molares seniores id est principes eorum, CONFRINGET DOMINUS ambos.*

3.2.p. *Psalm 58*: In finem ne disperdas Dauid in tituli inscriptione quando missit Saul et custodiuit domum eius ut interficeret eum. Uox Christi de Judeis ad Patrem. The first section is the biblical title. That the speaker is Christ is understandable, given the title. Inclusion of *de Iudeis* in the title may derive from an interpretation of Saul such as that

20. Boese (ed.), *Anonymi*, I, p. 238.
21. Boese (ed.), *Anonymi*, I, p. 235 (for Ps. 56).

found in the *Glosa psalmorum: Per Saul regnum Iudaeorum intellegitur. Misit Saul custodire domum Dauid, miserunt Iudaei ut custodirent sepulchrum dominicum.*[22] The presence of direct address 'O Lord' (*Domine*) makes the address to the Father obvious. In the *Glosa psalmorum* there is a variety of speakers, one of them *Christus ad Patrem.* Thus v. 2; *ERIPE ME...uox Christi ad patrem et uox ecclesiae ad Christum.*

3.2.q. *Psalm 101*: Uox Christi et Ecclesiae cum ascendisset ad Patrem. Here this psalm is interpreted of the ascension of Christ. In the Irish Reference Bible it is interpreted of Christ's resurrection:

Quintum sigillum de resurrectione, ut: *Tu exsurgens Domine misereberis Sion* (Ps. 101.14), Christus soluit, ut angelus dicit: *Non est hic, surrexit enim* (Mt. 28.6) et reliqua.

3.3. *Examination of Texts with 'Legendus Ad'*
Eighteen psalms have *Legendus (ad)*: 2; 26 (OT); 27 (OT); 40 (OT); 43; 44; 45; 46; 47; 49; 50 (OT and NT); 52; 68 (OT and NT); 83; 90; 105 (OT); 106 (OT); 129 (OT)

In the Columba series of psalm headings there are 18 occurrences of the phrase *legendus ad*, followed by an indication of some biblical book, or a section or verse of a biblical book, generally from the New Testament (12 of the 18; Old Testament 8, two with both Old and New Testament—Pss. 50; 68). For Psalm 26 I have cited a specific text in the book of Isaiah, and for 44 and 90 specific sections of Matthew and Mark, and in Psalm 50 some specific text of the Acts of the Apostles. A question arising is whether *legendus ad* indicates liturgical usage, or has some other explanation.

It does not appear that *legendus ad* in the Cathach (at least in a number of instances) points to the use of the other book in question in a liturgical service. I here examine each of the occurrences.

3.3.a. *Psalm 2*: Legendus ad euangelium Lucae. Uox Patris et apostolorum et Christi. Ad caput scribendum. Why this psalm is indicated to be read in association with St Luke's Gospel is not clear. It may that the text of Ps. 2.7 *Dominus dixit ad me: Filius meus es tu* is cited twice in Luke (3.22; 9.35) as words of the Father at Christ's baptism and at the

---

22. Boese (ed.), *Anonymi*, I, p. 244.

transfiguration. With regard to the other elements (*uox apostolorum et Christi*), they are parallelled in the *Glosa psalmorum ex traditione seniorum* as we shall see.

In the *Glosa psalmorum* there is a variety of speakers identified within this psalm. For v. 1 (*Quare fremuerunt*) we have the prophet: *Hic uox prophetae dicit 'quare', ac si diceret: sine causa.* There are three speakers for v. 3: the apostles, angels, Jews: *DISRUMPAMUS UIN-CULA EORUM. Hic tres uoces sonant: apostolorum, angelorum et Iudae-orum. Apostoli disruperunt uincula hoc est legalia legis.* In vv. 6 and 7 Christ is the speaker: *EGO AUTEM* (v. 6)*: uox Christi...DOMINUS DIXIT AD ME: FILIUS MEUS ES TU. Uox Christi ad patrem.* The Father is speaker in vv. 7b and 8: *EGO HODIE GENUI TE: uox paterna ad filium...POSTULA A ME: uox Patris ad filium.*

An explanation of the ending *Ad caput scribendum* has led to a variety of opinion, whether possibly a mere scribal direction or an indication that Psalms 1 and 2 are to be taken as a single psalm. The *Glosa psalmorum* probably explains its presence, and in the latter direction. The Preface to the *Glosa psalmorum* ends with the remark that among the Hebrews psalms without title are taken as a single psalm, and then considers Psalms 1 and 2 in this regard: the Hebrews wanted these two psalms taken as one, since they have no title and one (Ps. 1) begins and the other (Ps. 2) ends with a blessing. Christ has consequently willed that this book begin not regarding a fight, repentance or persecution, but regarding himself, because it has been said: 'In the head of the book it has been written of me'. *'In capite libri dictum est de me', quia ipse est caput omnium patriarcharum et omnium prophetarum et omnium scripturarum, et sic erat dignum, ut iste liber hoc est psalterium de capite inciperetur.*[23] At the end of the comment on Psalm 2 the *Glosa psalmorum* reminds us of what has been said in the preface that for the Hebrews Psalms 1 and 2 are taken as a single psalm.

3.3.b. *Psalm 26*: Ad eos qui primum ingrediuntur, in dominicum. *Leg-endus ad lectionem Esaiae prophetae (65.13; Vetus Latina): ecce qui seruiunt tibi bona manducabunt.* Both sections of this heading are, apparently, to be taken together. Salmon (whose reading is given above) punctuates with a pause (a comma) between *ingrediuntur* and *in domi-nicum.* This is probably a wrong understanding. We should, rather,

---

23. Boese (ed.), *Anonymi*, I, p. 8

understand *dominicum* in one of its genuine senses as: 'the church (*kyriakon*); the place where the faithful assemble, gather together',[24] and render: 'To those who enter the community of believers for the first time'. This psalm, headed *Dauid priusquam liniretur* (variant: *ungueretur*), and beginning: *Dominus illuminatio mea et salus mea quem timebo?* is about enlightenment by God and of confidence in God, expressing belief on seeing the good gifts of the Lord in the land of the living (v. 13).

Thus understood, the link with Isa. 65.13 is natural enough. The dominant theme of this psalm and the context of Isa. 65.13 are similar. There appears to be a question here of a devotional connection between the two passages. As P. Salmon, the editor of the Columba series had already pointed out,[25] for the citation of Isa. 65.13 the text used is the Old Latin translation.

The link between the psalm with entry into the Christian community, the anointing at baptism and the enlightenment of faith, is easily made. For Augustine (*Enarratio* 1 in Ps. 26) the speaker is the neophyte coming to faith: *Tiro Christi loquitur, cum accedit ad fidem.*

3.3.c. *Psalm 27:* Legendus ad lectionem Danihelis prophetae. De Judeis Christo dicit. We are not told whether the reference is to the entire book of Daniel or only to a specific text, one that would come to the mind of the reader of Psalm 27 (or to the mind of one listening to it read). The series may have a specific text of the psalm in mind, for instance Ps. 27.1...*et adsimilabor descendentibus in lacum.* This would bring to

24. For this meaning see A. Blaise, *Dictionnaire Latin-Français des auteurs chrétiens* (Turnhout: Brepols, 1954), p. 292.
25. Salmon (*Les 'Tituli'*, p. 58) notes that the text of Isaiah cited is the Old Latin (Vulgate: *ecce serui mei comedent*), and rightly so. However, it agrees fully with no known VL text whether of direct transmission or ecclesiastical citation. As God is the speaker all texts (as Vulgate) have *mihi*, not *tibi*. The nearest is the OL of the European (E) type: *qui seruiunt mihi manducabunt* (with a variant: (*qui) esurient (!) tibi bona epulabuntur*). The addition of *bona* is found only in a variant in the Victorius Marianus's 1566 edition of Jerome's commentary on Eccl. 10.16 ('e codicibus Florentinis et Brixianis'); see the critical edition in M. Adriaen (ed.), *S. Hieronymi presbyteri Commentarius in Ecclesiasten* (CCSL, 72; Turnhout: Brepols, 1969), p. 341. The addition of *bona* may be through an influence of Isa. 1.19. The variant *tibi* for *mihi*, as stated, is found only in the Tituli Psalmorum series I. For the evidence see R. Gryson (ed.), *Vetus Latina: Die Reste der altlateinischen Bibel* 12. II. *Esaias. Ed. Fasc. 10 (Is 61,10–65,23)* (Freiburg: Herder, 1997), p. 1584.

mind the narrative of Daniel in the lions' den of Dan. 6.7, 15-23 (or Dan. 14.30-37). We would again have probably a devotional linking.

3.3.d. *Psalm 40*: *Legendus ad lectionem Esaiae prophetae.* Uox Christi de passione sua et de Juda traditore. Why the link of this psalm with the reading of the book of Isaiah? Is is intended that the psalm accompany a liturgical reading of the entire book of Isaiah? This is unlikely. The link may well be to Hezekiah's illness and the Canticle of Hezekiah in Isaiah 38. This psalm is so interpreted in the Antiochene tradition (Milan Commentary and the Hiberno-Latin commentary [c. 700] in Pal. lat. 68).[26]

3.3.e. *Psalm 43*: Hic exomologesim. *Legendus ad epistulam Pauli ad Romanos.* Propheta ad Dominum de operibus eius paenitentiam gerens pro populo judaico. Psalm 43 is read in relation to the letter to the Romans apparently because Ps. 43.22 is cited in Rom. 8.36 ('For your sake we are being killed all the day long; we are regarded as sheep to be slaughtered').

The (psalmist) prophet is given as the speaker. He addresses the deity as Lord rather than as God, even though this psalm is addressed to God (God rather than Yahweh, the Lord, as this is in the so-called Elohistic collection of psalms, where the divine name Yahweh/Lord is not used). The *Glosa psalmorum* stays closer to the biblical text, for example, v. 3. *MANUS TUAS GENTES DISPERDIDISTI...propheta loquitur ad deum.*[27] Inclusion of *de operibus eius* comes from the opening verse: *Deus auribus nostris audiuimus et patres nostri adnuntiauerunt nobis* opus quod operatus es *in diebus eorum.* The great deed is what God has done for his people from the Exodus and the settlement in Canaan onwards, narrated in the first part of the psalm (vv. 2-9). This could be described as a confession of thanks and praise. In fact the commentary in Pal. lat. 68 sees fit to link the opening words of this psalm with v. 4 (42.4) of the preceding one: *Confitebor tibi in cithara.*[28] One may ask whether the opening word of the St Columba title *Hic exomologesim* simply expresses the same thing: *Hic confessio.*

What is intended by the closing phrase *paenitentiam gerens pro populo judaico* is not clear. It may refer to the end of the psalm (vv. 10-25)

26. See McNamara (ed.), *Glossa in Psalmos*, pp. 92-93.
27. Boese (ed.), *Anonymi*, I, p. 182.
28. See McNamara (ed.), *Glossa in Psalmos*, p. 96.

which speaks of the changed fortunes of the Jewish people, even though they have not forsaken the Lord. If so the Latin may possibly be rendered: 'expressing regret for the Jewish people'.

3.3.f. *Psalm 44*: *Legendus ad euangelium Matthei, de regina Austri. Propheta pro Patre de Christo et Ecclesia dicit.* Psalm 44 is said *legendus* ('to be read') at the place of the Gospel of Matthew speaking of the Queen of the South, that is, Mt. 12.42; this apparently through the link *Adsetit regina a dextris tuis* of Ps. 44.10. See also 3.2.k above.

3.3.g. *Psalm 45*: *Legendus ad lectionem Actus apostolorum.* Uox apostolorum. Psalm 45 is *legendus* at a reading in the Acts of the Apostles. What text of Acts goes with this psalm, or with some specific verse of this psalm, we are not told. The psalm is about the great things God does, how he gladdens the holy city (of Jerusalem). The living tradition that gave birth to this heading would have the specific texts in mind. It probably refers to the joy of the early church as described in Acts, or the great deeds of God, manifested in the coming of the Holy Spirit in power (Acts 2; 10.44).

3.3.h. *Psalm 46*: *Legendus ad lectionem Actus apostolorum. Uox apostolorum postquam ascendit Christus ad Patrem.* Like Psalm 45, Psalm 46 is also *legendus ad lectionem Actus Apostolorum*, but after Christ's ascension. The connection here is clear. Ps. 46.6 says *Ascendit Deus in iubilo*. The connection is with the ascension of Christ as described in Acts 1, an association explicitly made in the *Glosa psalmorum*.[29]

3.3.i. *Psalm 47*: *Legendus ad Apocalipsin Johannis. Figura Ecclesiae Hierusalem futurae.* Psalm 47 is one of the Songs of Zion, about the city of God. It can be linked with a number of texts on the heavenly Jerusalem in the Apocalypse of John, even though no such association is made either in the *Glosa psalmorum*, or in Pal. lat. 68.

3.3.j. *Psalm 49*: *Legendus ad euangelium Matthaei. De aduentu Christi propheta dicit et judicio futuro, increpatio Judeorum.* (We may compare the reference to the judgment with the last item in the list of the *Old-Irish Treatise* on the Psalter; see below 4.5).

29. Boese (ed.), *Anonymi*, I, pp. 198-99.

The title regards the psalm as a prophecy on the coming of Christ and on the judgment to come. Both sections of the title may in fact be intended to go together: the coming of Christ to judge. This title would depend on vv. 3-5: *Deus manifeste ueniet...aduocabit caelum desursum et terram discernere populum suum...Congregate illi sanctos meos.* This could easily be connected with the judgment scene in Matthew's Gospel. The association, in fact, is made in the *Glosa psalmorum ex traditione seniorum:*

> DISCERNERE POPULUM SUUM *id est in futuro iudicio, quando dicturus erit: Ite maledicti in ignem aeternum, et ad sanctos: Uenite benedicti in uitam aeternam (Matt 25:41, 34).* CONGREGATE ILLI SANCTIS EIUS: *propheta hortatur sanctos angelos, unde in euangelio dicit: Mittet filius hominis angelos suos et congregabit electos suos a quattuor partibus mundi et rlq.*[30]

3.3.k. *Psalm 50 (Tibi soli peccaui). Legendus ad lectionem Esaiae prophetae et lectionem Actus apostolorum ubi Paulus eligitur.* Uox Christi pro populo paenitente et uox Pauli ad paenitentiam. There is a possible link of Ps. 50.6 (*Tibi soli peccaui*) with Isa. 53.9 (*Qui peccatum non fecit*) and Ps. 50.9 (*super niuem dealbabor*) with Isa. 1.18 (*Si fuerint peccata uestra sicut fenicium, uelut nix dealbabuntur*) as in *Glosa psalmorum* in both cases.[31]

The connection with Actus Apostolorum presents a problem. If by the 'election' of Paul, his conversion is intended, one of the three conversion narratives of the Acts of the Apostles is the text in question (Acts 9.1-19; 22.4-16; 26.9-18; Paul a *uas electionis,* 9.15). The reference, however, may possibly be to God's call to set Paul aside for the Gentile mission (Acts 13.1-3), an action accompanied by prayer and fasting.

3.3.l. *Psalm 52: Legendus ad euangelium Matthei.* Increpat Judaeos incredulos operibus negantes Deum. In *Anonymi Glosa psalmorum ex traditione seniorum* this psalm is understood of the Jews, with special reference to the parable of the talents in Mt. 25.25-30. Thus, v. 2: DIXIT INSPIENS IN CORDE SUO: NON EST DEUS. 'Dixit inspiens' *populus Iudaicus siue diabolus: non est deus, ac si dicat; non est Christus filius dei.* Mt. 25.28.30 is cited on Ps. 52.4 and Mt. 25.25 on v. 6. Thus:

---

30. Boese (ed.), *Anonymi,* I, pp. 208-209.
31. Boese (ed.), *Anonymi,* I, pp. 214, 216.

INUTILES FACTI SUNT. Inutilis dicitur qui non operatur aliquid boni, unde dicit in euangelio: Tollite itaque talentum ab eo... (Mt. 25.28, 30).[32] Likewise on v. 6: *ILLIC TREPIDAUERUNT TIMORE UBI NON ERAT TIMOR. Tres sensus hic habet, de illa pecunia commendata, unde dicit: et timens abiit et abscondit pecuniam domini sui* (Mt. 25.25); *sic de Iudaeis sicut dixerunt: Uenient Romani et tollent nostrum locum et regnum* (Jn 11.48).[33] With regard to the *Glosa psalmorum ex traditione seniorum* we may also note its comments on v. 2: *CORRUPTI SUNT de lege bonae naturae*. This same verse (and also *omnes declinauerunt simul* of v. 6) is glossed in practically identical fashion in the Hiberno-Latin *Glossa in Psalmos* of Pal. lat. 68 (*a lege et bono naturae*), and it is very probable that in this the Glossa of Pal. lat. 68 is dependent on the tradition found in the *Glosa psalmorum ex traditione seniorum*.

3.3.m. *Psalm 68: Legendus ad lectionem Jonae prophetae et ad euangelium Johannis*. Uox Christi cum pateretur. The mystical heading *Uox Christi cum pateretur* is very apt. Psalm 68 (69) is a christological psalm par excellence, in fact the psalm most cited and referred to in the New Testament, in particular with reference to the passion of Christ. Citations from the psalm are most frequent in John's Gospel. These New Testament citations may be noted here. The texts are as follows: v. 4 in Jn 15.25; v. 9 in Jn 2.17; v. 10 in Jn 2.17; v. 21—see Mt. 27.34; vv. 22-24 in Rom. 11.9-10; v. 24 in Rev. 16.1; v. 25 in Acts 1.20. For Jn 19.28-29 see v. 22. The reading of the psalm in conjunction with John's Gospel (or specified texts from it) is then very understandable.

The psalmist begins by saying that he is in deep waters; the waters have come up to his throat ('soul' in the Vulgate); he is stuck in the mud, the deep; he has come into the depth of the sea. By reason of these opening verses, use of the psalm in conjunction with the book of Jonah—particularly Jonah's prayer from the belly of the whale—from the depths of the sea is quite understandable.

In the *Glosa psalmorum* commentary there is a reference to interpretation through the history of Jonah, through Christ's passion, and there are frequent quotations from and references to the Gospel of John. Thus on v. 2.[34]

32. Boese (ed.), *Anonymi*, I, p. 222.
33. Boese (ed.), *Anonymi*, I, p. 223.
34. Boese (ed.), *Anonymi*, I, p. 291.

SALUUM ME FAC, QUONIAM INTRAUERUNT AQUAE USQUE AD ANIMAM MEAM. *Multi dicunt istam historiam in persona Ionae; tamen potest. Ionas figurat Christum, mare populum Iudaicum, uenter caeti sepulchrum, tres dies et noctes passionem Christi, unde dixit: Potestatem habeo ponendi animam meam, et potestatem habeo iterum resumendi eam in resurrectione tertia die. 'Saluum me fac deus': uox Christi ad patrem in passione.*

3.3.n. *Psalm 83: Legendus ad euangelium Matthei.* Ad eos qui fidem sunt consecuti ; uox Christi ad Patrem de Ecclesia. Christ is taken to be the speaker in this psalm. He addresses his Father concerning the Church. That, in the spiritual sense at least, the psalm concerns the Church was probably a widespread belief. It fits in well with central references in the psalm to the Lord's *(tua) tabernacula, atria, domus.* The psalm would be very suitable for those who had recently been received into the Church—as expressed in the words of the title: *Ad eos qui fidem sunt consecuti.*

The precise reason why this psalm should be suggested as a reading for Matthew's Gospel, or for select verses of it, is not clear. Possibly it was because Matthew was the 'ecclesiastical Gospel', speaking explicitly of the Church (*ecclesia*). Certain verses of the psalm could also be connected with specific sections of Matthew, as they are in the *Glosa psalmorum ex traditione seniorum*, for example, 83.11: 'I have chosen to be abject in the house of my God, rather than to dwell in the tabernacles of sinners', associated in the *Glosa* with Mt. 16.27: 'What does it profit a man if he gains the whole world and suffer the loss of his soul'; or again, v. 12: 'God loves justice and truth': ...'truth because *he renders to everyone according to his work'* (Mt. 16.27).[35]

3.3.o. *Psalm 90*: Uox Ecclesiae ad Christum. *Legendus ad Euangelium Marci ubi temptatur Christus.* Psalm 90.11-12 contains the well-known words used by Satan when tempting Christ: 'He has given his angels charge over you, to keep you in all your ways. In their hands they shall bear you up, lest you dash your foot against a stone'. The text is cited in the temptation narratives of Matthew (4.6) and Luke (4.10-11). Mark has no temptation narrative, but says (Mk 1.12-13) that after his baptism Jesus was driven into the desert by the Spirit, where he was 40 days and 40 nights and was tempted by Satan. Psalm 90 is an apt text to be read in conjunction with this passage of Mark.

35. Boese (ed.), *Anonymi*, I, pp. 380-81.

3.3.p. *Psalm 105*: Uox Ecclesiae ad apostolos. *Legendus ad Exodum.* Psalm 105 is one of the 'historical psalms'. It tells of Israel's unfaithfulness to the Lord in Egypt, at the Exodus, at the Red Sea, in the desert wanderings, before entry into Canaan, and in Canaan. The background to most of the contents is the biblical book of Exodus, which is thus an obvious biblical text for reading with this psalm.

3.3.q. *Psalm 106*: Uox Christi de Judeis. *Legendus ad Judicum et Numeri libros.* Psalm 106 (107) is a thanksgiving hymn, with an invitation to different groups of redeemed to thank God for salvation. One group made their way out of the desert; another group are prisoners. It could be construed by some as in the same spirit as the preceding Psalm 105, and thus a historical psalm, with the books of Judges and Numbers as background. In fact in the *Glossa in Psalmos* of Pal. lat. 68 some of the verses are so interpreted (although the central line of interpretation followed is that of the Julian Epitome of Theodore of Mopsuestia referring the psalm to the people's return from Babylon). Thus, 'in a place without water' of v. 4 is understood as the desert; 'led into the right way' of v. 7 is glossed: 'into the land of promise, in which Israel is'; 'because they had exasperated the words of the Lord' is glossed: 'they were against the words of God, in the spies at Anathema (= Horma), with the exception of Joshua and Caleb' (see Num. 14.45; 21.3). The words 'they were afflicted' of v. 39 is first understood of the (Babylonian) captivity (with Julian-Theodore apparently), and then, in what appears to be an independent tradition, of the time of the Judges: *In tempore Iudicum haec mala facta sunt.*[36] Likewise, 'contempt was poured upon them' of the following verse is first understood of the fact that they had to serve others, and then because they were ruled by a woman, such as Deborah (*uel mulier dominari ut Debora*),[37] again in the period of the Judges (see Judges 4–5).

3.3.r. *Psalm 129*: *Legendus ad lectionem Jonae prophetae.* Psalm 129 is the *De profundis,* 'Out of the depths have I cried to you, O Lord'. Its use in conjunction with the reading of Jonah, particularly Jonah's prayer from the belly of the whale (Jonah 2), in the depths of the sea, would have been indicated.

36. See McNamara (ed.), *Glossa in Psalmos*, p. 228.
37. McNamara (ed.), *Glossa in Psalmos*, p. 228.

I have examined the texts containing the phrase *Legendus ad* in greater or less detail. The evidence seems to indicate that there is no need to postulate here any fixed liturgical setting for these psalms, with the other biblical books of which they speak intended as set readings. If anything I think we should see here a devotional linking of psalm texts to the other books or texts, somewhat analogous to the well-known linking in Irish tradition through such words or phrases as '*haeret*' (Pal. lat. 68, etc.) and '*coniungitur ad*'.

The headings with *legendus ad* presume the reading of a number of books of the Old and New Testaments; from the Old Testament: Exodus (Ps. 105), Judges and Numbers (106), Isaiah (in general? 40), Isaiah 65.13 (26), Daniel (27), Jonah (68, 129); from the New Testament: Matthew (Pss. 49; 52; 83; de regina Austri, Mt. 12.42; Ps. 44); Mark (Mk 1.12-13; Ps. 90); Luke (Ps. 2); John (with Jonah, Ps. 68); Acts of the Apostles (Pss. 45; 46; Actus Apostolorum ubi Paulus eligitur, Ps. 50); Epistle of Paul to the Romans (Ps. 43); Apocalypse of John (Ps. 47).

3.4. *Examination of Texts with Mention of 'Judei'*

In the following tituli mention is made of *Judei* in a variety of ways (*de Iudeis, de populo judaico, increpat Judeos*): titles for: Psalms 3, 4, 7, 9, 11 (13), 16, 27, 30, 34, 38, (43), 49, 52, 54, 57, 58, 77, 81, 82, 88, 93, 104, 106, 108 (113), 118, 125.

On Judas: 35, 40, 51

3.4.a. *Psalm 3*: Uox Christi ad Patrem *de Judeis* dicit. On this heading see above, 3.2.c.

3.4.b. *Psalm 4*: Propheta *increpat Judeos*. With this heading we may compare text of the *Glosa psalmorum*, where, however, the speaker is the Church, *ecclesia*, not the prophet. Thus in v. 3: *FILII HOMINUM USQUEQUO GRAUI CORDE? Uox ecclesiae ad Iudaeos increpando loquitur... QUAERITIS MENDACIUM... Aliter: 'utquid diligitis uanitatem?' Iudaeos increpat qui dicebant: Patrem habemus Abraham...* Likewise on *scitote* of v. 4 and *irascimini* of v. 5: *Uox ecclesiae ad Iudaeos: hoc scitote uos Iudaei.*[38]

---

38. For both references see Boese (ed.), *Anonymi*, I, p. 18.

3.4.c. *Psalm 7*: Propheta dicit ad Christum *de inimicis Judeis* et de diabolo. The speaker is given as the (psalmist) prophet. The *Glosa psalmorum ex traditione seniorum* also notes the prophet as speaker, for example, at v. 2: *DOMINUS DEUS MEUS, IN TE SPERAUI. Uox prophetae.* The inclusion of *de inimicis* is probably due to v. 6: *Persequatur inimicus animam meam.* The enemy can be variously identified. In the *Glosa psalmorum ex traditione seniorum* we have (according to Augustine), for David Saul, for Christ the Jews or Judas. In the same gloss *lacum aperuit* of v. 16 is interpreted as Achitophel against David, Judas or the Jews (*Iudei*) against Christ.

3.4.d. *Psalm 9*: Ecclesia laudem dicit Christo, *de Judeis* et de principe demoniorum. In the *Glosa psalmorum ex traditione seniorum* the speaker of the psalm in general is the Church, although there is an occasional reference to the prophet as speaker. That the chief content of the psalm is praise is already clear from the opening words: *Confitebor tibi Domine,* glossed as follows in the *Glosa psalmorum ex traditione seniorum*.[39] *Uox ecclesiae. Trina confessio hic sonat id est peccatorum, martyrum et gratiarum actio siue laus, ut in euangelio ait: Confitebor tibi pater...*

Verse 4 speaks of *inimicus*, which gives us, apparently, *de Judeis et de principe demoniorum* of the Columba series title. The *Glosa psalmorum ex traditione seniorum* understands as *diabolus* and speaks later in the comment on the psalm of *Antichristus*. The comment on v. 5, however, mentions the Jews: *QUONIAM FECISTI IUDICIUM MEUM. Uox ecclesiae, ac si dicat: aperte gentes elegisti et reprobasti Iudaeos.*

3.4.e. *Psalm 11*: Christus pro passione sanctorum suorum dicit et *de Judeis*. There is mention of the Jews also in the heading to this psalm in Series II (*De morte et resurrectione Christi et de fallacia Judeorum*). The opening reference to the suffering of Christ's holy ones probably depends on v. 6: *Propter miserias inopum et gemitus pauperum nunc exurgam, dicit Dominus,* which the *Glosa psalmorum,* following on Augustine (*Enarratio* in Ps. 11.6), interprets through the gospel accounts of Christ's compassion on the multitudes. For both, however, the speaker in v. 6 is the Father: *Uox patris est.*

---

39. Boese (ed.), *Anonymi*, I, p. 40.

3.4.f. *Psalm 13*: (*Dixit insipiens*) Uerba Christi ad diuitem interrogantem se. *De populo judaico*. We may compare the *Glosa psalmorum ex traditione seniorum*. *DIXIT INSIPIENS IN CORDE SUO*. *Tria genera hic intellegimus: Iudaeorum, hereticorum, philosophorum, qui dixerunt in corde suo: NON EST DEUS*. Or again on. v. 6: *QUONIAM DOMINUS IN GENERATIONE IUSTA EST*, in populo Christiano et Iudaeorum fuit, quia ex ipsis carnem assumpsit.

3.4.g. *Psalm 16*: Christus *de Judeis* dicit ad Patrem. We may compare the text of the *Glosa psalmorum ex traditione seniorum* on the biblical heading: *ORATIO IPSI DAUID... Iste psalmus cantatur ex persona Christi contra Iudaeos et ex persona ecclesiae contra hereticos*.[40] The fact that the psalmist addresses the Lord ('*Domine*') explains the reference to the Father, and the *Glosa psalmorum* on the psalm more than once makes mention of *Uox Christi ad Patrem*.

3.4.h. *Psalm 27*: (*Ad te Domine clamabo, Deus meus*) *De Judeis* Christo dicit. Presumably the speaker intended is the prophet, speaking to Christ. We may compare *Glosa psalmorum ex traditione seniorum* on v. 2: *EXAUDI DEUS DEPRECATIONEM MEAM, DUM ORO AD TE*. *Orauit Christus in cruce pro toto mundo, pro Iudaeis et pro apostolis*.

3.4.i. *Psalm 30*: (*In te Domine speraui*) Hic fidei confessio credentium Deum; uox Christi in passione *de Judeis* dicit. The first part *Hic fidei confessio credentium Deum* is in substance (but not in expression) the same as in the *Glosa psalmorum*: *Uox ecclesiae*.

The next section of the heading (*Uox Christi...*) derives from v. 6, glossed as follows in *Glosa psalmorum ex traditione seniorum*: *IN MANUS TUAS COMMENDO SPIRITUM MEUM: uox Christi ad patrem in passione quando commendauit animam suam et dixit: Pater, in manus tuas commendo spiritum meum*.

The nature of the psalm gives ample opportunity of referring to the Jews, who are often named in the *Glosa psalmorum ex traditione seniorum*, for example, v. 12: *FACTUS SUM OBPROBRIUM UICINIS MEIS: uox Christi et uox ecclesiae. Domino Iudaei multa obprobria dixerunt, et heretici et persecutores dicunt ecclesiae*; on v. 13: *SICUT UAS PERDITUM: sic habuerunt Iudaei Christum*.

40. Boese (ed.), *Anonymi*, I, p. 66.

3.4.j. *Psalm 34*: (*Iudica Domine nocentes me*) Uox Christi in passione *de Judeis* dicit. See also above 3.2.h.

We may compare the heading and glosses of the *Glosa psalmorum ex traditione seniorum*: I*UDICA DOMINE NOCENTES ME. Uox Christi in passione et uox ecclesiae in tribulatione.*

As with Psalm 30 there is ample opportunity in the psalm for reference to Christ's persecutors and enemies, and reference to the Jews. This we find in the same *Glosa psalmorum*, for instance on v. 1: I*UDICA DOMINE NOCENTES ME. Uox Christi in passione et uox ecclesiae in tribulatione…iudica: iudicium discretionis rogat, uel 'iudica' id est discerne inter me et Iudaeos et inter ecclesiam et persecutores;* likewise on v. 4*: QUI COGITANT MIHI id est daemones, Iudaei uel persecutores;* v. 15. *ADUERSUS ME LAETATI SUNT. Laetati sunt Iudaei quando Christum adprehenderunt.*

3.4.k. *Psalm 38*: Propheta *increpat Judeos* qui diuitias habent et nesciunt cui dimittunt. This heading seems to presuppose a detailed moral understanding of the psalm. While the *populus Iudaicus* is mentioned at least twice in the *Glosa psalmorum* on this psalm (vv. 2 and 9) it is as enemies of Christ, not in the sense intended in the Columba series gloss.

3.4.l. *Psalm 43*: (*Deus auribus nostris audiuimus et patres nostri adnuntiauerunt nobis opus quod operatus es in diebus eorum et in diebus antiquis*). Hic exomologesim. Legendus ad epistulam Pauli ad Romanos. Propheta ad Dominum de operibus eius paenitentiam gerens *pro populo judaico.* As already noted, Psalm 43 is read in relation to *Epistula ad Romanos* apparently because Ps. 43.22 is cited in Rom. 8.36. The speaker is the (psalmist) prophet. The prophet as speaker is also highlighted in the *Glosa psalmorum ex traditione seniorum*, for example, v. 3: *MANUS TUA GENTES DISPERDIDIT…propheta loquitur…* (v. 4) *NON ENIM IN GLADIO SUO: propheta dicit.* The prophet is speaking *de operibus*, that is the *opus quod operatus es* (O God) of v. 1. The *Glosa psalmorum* stresses this word, and cites the prophet Habakkuk (1.5): *ego opus operor in diebus uestris*, which is immediately identified as the *opus* prophesied by Isa. 7.14: *Ecce uirgo concipiet*. The prophets have heard from the patriarchs of the great works God has performed for his people, named in the *Glosa* as *populus Iudaicus.*

The words *penitentiam gerens* of the title cause some difficulty, since in the psalm the Jewish people are presented as the innocent ones, punished without cause, a view to which the *Glosa* remains faithful. As already noted (5.3.c.v above), the Latin *paenitentiam gerens pro populo Judaico* may possibly be rendered: 'expressing regret for the Jewish people'.

The words *hic exomologesim* of the title also present some difficulty. As noted above (5.3.c.v), in this context *exomologesim* may simply mean *confessio*, confession of God's glory. It may, however, be a liturgical rubric covering some penitential rite, to which also the *paenitentiam agens* occurring later in the title may refer.

3.4.m. *Psalm 49*: Legendus ad euangelium Matthaei. De aduentu Christi propheta dicit et judicio futuro, *increpatio Judeorum* (See also the *Old-Irish Treatise* on the Psalter; no. 12 and last of list; below 4.5).

As already noted, the reason for the reference to Matthew's Gospel may be by reason of the final judgment scene in Matthew 25. The speaker here is the (psalmist) prophet. The *Glosa psalmorum ex traditione seniorum* also notes the same, for example, v. 5: *CONGREGATE ILLI SANCTOS EIUS: propheta hortatur sanctos angelos...*; v. 14: *IMMOLA DEI SACRIFICIUM LAUDIS... Uox prophetae admonet sanctos...* The interpretation of the psalm as speaking of the judgment to come is a natural one, founded on the text. Thus also in the *Glosa psalmorum*, for example, v. 3: *DEUS MANIFESTE UENIET hoc est ad diem iudicii*. Likewise, the gloss on v. 4: *CAELUM fecit hoc est sanctos* DISCERNERE POPULUM SUUM *id est in futuro iudicio*. The *increpatio Judeorum*, 'rebuking of the Jews', is contained in the psalm itself, if by 'Jews' God's people is understood. Thus in v. 7, with the comment of the *Glosa psalmorum*: *AUDI POPULUS MEUS ET LOQUAR TIBI ISRAHEL: uox dei patris ad populum Iudaicum loquitur.*

3.4.n. *Psalm 52*: (*Dixit insipiens*). Legendus ad euangelium Matthei. *Increpat Judaeos* incredulos operibus negantes Deum. As already noted, the reference is probably to Mt. 25.25-30. The heading can be compared with the comment of the *Glosa psalmorum* on v. 1: '*Dixit insipiens*' populus Iudaicus uel diabolus: non est deus, ac si dicat: non est Christus filius dei'. Likewise on v. 4: *INUTILES FACTI SUNT. Inutilis dicitur qui non operatur aliquid boni.*

3.4.o. *Psalm 54*: Uox Christi *aduersus magnatos Judeorum* et de Juda traditore. See above, 3.2.m.

3.4.p. *Psalm 72*: Uox Christi ad Patrem *de Judeis*. All the elements of this heading could find a basis in the psalm and we can presume that in point of fact it does depend on a full commentary on this psalm known to the compiler of the Columba Series, who was probably Irish. The ending *de Judeis* is well attested in the manuscript tradition. It is omitted only in the related texts, the *Glossa in Psalmos* of Pal. lat. 68 and the Psalter of Charlemagne (BN lat. 13159).

I have failed to find a commentary of the kind presupposed by this Columba heading, with Christ as speaker (to the Father) and central reference to the Jews. It was clearly not that of Augustine who understood *Asaph* of the biblical heading as *synagoga*. For him the speaker, the *uox*, in this psalm is the synagogue. Thus in his *Enarratio* on Psalm 72, no. 4: *Cuius est psalmus? Asaph. Quid est Asaph?... Asaph Synagoga interpretatur. Uox est ergo Synagogae*. Not just the synagogue responsible for Christ's death, Augustine continues, but also the synagogue in the broader sense, the synagogue which offered gifts to God. The *Glosa Psalmorum ex traditione seniorum* follows Augustine's understanding of Asaph. The chief speaker is the synagogue, *Uox synagogae*, again in Augustine's broader sense. There are a few passing references to *Iudaei*, in the sense of God's people, the *synagoga*. Thus, on v. 8: *INIQUITATEM IN EXCELSO LOCUTI SUNT...id est heretici, Iudaei et falsi fratres* Or again on v. 14: *FUI FLAGELLATUS TOTA DIE...Iudaei non intellexerunt, quod deus illis bona faciebat, propterea flagellati erant.*

3.4.q. *Psalm 113*: Uox apostolica *cum Judeis* increpat idola. The heading corresponds to the central theme of the psalm. The sense seems to be that the Jews, as well as the message of the apostles, condemn idol worship. The heading is similar to that of Series III: *Uox apostolorum miracula apud Judeos facta retexens, idola damnat.*

3.4.r. *Psalm 118*: Uox Christi ad Patrem et apostolorum de aduersario et *de Judeis*, et de passione sua et de aduentu suo et iudicio eius et regno. See below, 4.6.

3.5. *Examination of Tituli to the Gradual Psalms in Series I*
In a study of the psalm headings it is important to pay attention to the one designated as speaker (*Uox*), the person or persons addressed, the reason why one and other is used, and the tradition on which the choice depends.

An examination of the *Tituli* in the gradual psalms or Psalms of Ascents (Pss. 119–133, each headed in the Latin tradition as *Canticum Graduum*) from these points of view is indicated. Various views as to the principles governing the understanding of this collection were current. One (the Antiochene tradition) was that these in the main referred to the Babylonian exile. Another was that these 15 psalms were so called because they were sung by the Levites on steps in the ascent to the Temple. A third view was that the ascent referred to was the believers' ascent to God.[41] This interpretation is found in the *Commentarioli* of Jerome.[42] Augustine also has a developed spiritual interpretation of these psalms.[43] In the words of Jerome, cited in the introduction to the collection in the Hiberno-Latin commentary Codex Palatinus Latinus 68: *XV graduum salmi per quosdam profectus nos ad summa perducunt, ut in Dei atris possumus dicere: 'Ecce nunc benedicite Dominum omnes serui Domini'* (Ps. 133.1; last psalm of collection). Eucherius is in the same tradition (dependent on Jerome apparently). These 15 psalms, he tells us, are called Psalms of Ascents in that *nos per quosdam profectus ad sublimia spiritalium rerum prouectione perducant.*[44]

The treatment of these psalms in the *Glosa psalmorum ex traditione seniorum* is heavily dependent on Augustine. There is an introduction to the group at the introduction to Psalm 119.[45] As prefigurations the compiler notes the 15 steps to the temple and the ladder of Jacob. He glosses *Canticum graduum* at Psalm 119 as *id est canticum ascensionis.* As one alternative theory of interpretation he gives:

> *Aliter: 'canticum graduum' hoc est ascensionis de morte ad uitam, de tenebris ad lucem, de ignorantia ad scientiam, de uitiis ad uirtutes et reliqua. Unde in alio psalmo dicit: Ascensiones in corde suo disposuit in conualle lacrimarum... Uallis humilitatem significat, mons uero celsitudinem. Est ergo mons quo ascendere debemus hoc est Christus de conualle plorationis hoc est de uita praesenti ubi per exemplum illius tribulationes sustinemus*[46]

---

41. See McNamara (ed.), *Glossa in Psalmos*, pp. 70-74.

42. Jerome, *Commentarioli in Psalmos*, in Ps. 119, pp. 235-36.

43. See H. Rondet, 'Saint Augustin et les Psaumes des Montées', *Revue d'Ascétique et de Mystique* 41 (1965), pp. 3-18.

44. C. Wotke (ed.), Eudorius, *Instructionum lifer* I (CSEL, 31; Vienna, 1893), p. 100, lines 14-16.

45. Boese (ed.), *Anonymi*, II, pp. 136-37.

46. Boese (ed.), *Anonymi*, II, p. 136.

One branch of Irish tradition followed the Antiochene interpretation as found in Julian's Epitome of Theodore. Another branch of Irish tradition, as found in the commentary in Pal. lat. 68 and in the Reference Bible, stressed the spiritual understanding.[47] An abbreviation of Augustine's *Enarrationes* on these psalms is found as a spiritual interpretation in Pal. lat. 68. The abbreviation apparently circulated as the work of a certain Hilarius, quite possibly an early (seventh-century?) Irish scholar.[48]

The St Columba series of headings to the gradual psalms merits consideration within this Latin tradition.

3.5.a. *Psalm 119*: Uox Christi Ecclesiae. The opening Psalm 119 has as title in the chief manuscripts (AR): *Uox Christi Ecclesiae*. While there are a number of variants, most contain the element *Uox Christi*. The choice of speaker seems ill chosen. Pal. lat. 68 also has as title *Uox Christi* but in the comment of v. 1 has a different speaker: *aeclesia ex tribulatione clammore cordis ad Christum clammat*. Augustine's interpretation is also found in the *Glosa psalmorum*. Thus on the opening verse: *Uox ecclesiae est, quae clamat de angustia praesentis uitae.*[49] On *Quid detur tibi* of v. 3: *Uox dei est ad ecclesiam*;[50] on *cum his qui oderunt pacem* of v. 7: *ecclesia dicit.*[51]

The Church features prominently in the Columba headings to these psalms (it is mentioned in 10 of the 15: 119; 120; 121; 124; 126; 127; 128; 130; 132; 133).

3.5.b. *Psalm 120*: Uox Ecclesiae ad apostolos. The title of Psalm 120 'I have lifted my eyes to the mountains' is *Uox Ecclesiae ad apostolos*, the Church speaks to the apostles. The speaker is the Church, which has lifted up her eyes to the mountains, understood as the apostles, as in Pal. lat. 68, citing Eucherius: *ad montes, id est ad prophetas et ad apos-*

---

47. See McNamara (ed.), *Glossa in Psalmos*, pp. 70-72; M. Mac Conmara (M. McNamara) (in Irish), 'Sailm na nGrád (Sailm 119-133/120-134) i Stair Iosrael agus i Stair na hEixigéise', in M. Mac Conmara and É. Ní Thiarnaigh (eds.), *Cothú an Dúchais: Aistí in Omós don Athair Diarmuid Ó Laoghaire S.J.* (Dublin: An Clochomhar, 1997), pp. 81-93 (89-92 for Irish tradition).

48. See above, 2.5.

49. Boese (ed.), *Anonymi*, II, p. 137.

50. Boese (ed.), *Anonymi*, II, p. 138.

51. Boese (ed.), *Anonymi*, II, p. 139.

tolos et reliquos sanctos. Likewise Augustine on *montes* of Ps. 124.2, cited in Pal. lat. 68: '*montes*'. *id est profetae et apostoli et doctores.*[52] The same interpretation, under the influence of Augustine, is also in the *Glosa psalmorum*, but not as clearly or as succinctly as in Eucherius and the *Glossa* as found in Pal. lat. 68.[53]

3.5.c. *Psalm 121: Uox Ecclesiae ad apostolos.* That the Church is speaker here is easily understood, and is explicitly stated by Augustine (*Enarrationes*), in a text given in abbreviated form in the Hiberno-Latin Vatican *Glossa in Psalmos*, with the marginal reference 'M' (Mora-liter), but most probably from an abbreviation of Augustine (possibly by an Irish scholar Hilarius): *Laetata est aeclesia quae dicta sunt ei a patriarchis et prophetis et ceteris doctoribus per ueterem canonem et nouum, quia omnes hoc dixerunt: IN DOMUM DOMINI IBIMUS; non in templum sed in aeclesiam.*[54] The apostles could be seen included among the *ceteri doctores* of the New (Testament) canon.

In the *Glosa psalmorum ex traditione seniorum* (dependent on Augustine) the speaker is rather the prophet (the psalmist), but concern-ing the apostles, preachers and teachers and the Church. Thus on v. 3: *STANTES ERANT...Praeuidebat propheta per spiritum sanctum succes-sores hoc est sanctos apostolos uel qui praedestinati erunt et futuri in sancta ecclesia.*[55]

3.5.d. *Psalm 122:* Uox Christi ad Patrem. This is the reading of Sal-mon's critical edition, and may well be the original one. The Cathach text is missing. Manuscript K has *Uox Apostolorum.* The Psalter of Charlemagne has *Uox Ecclesiae ad Christum,* a combination found in no other series. The alternative gloss of the Irish *Glossa in Psalmos* (introduced as Mor = *Moraliter,* and probably from Hilarius) assumes that God the Father is the person addressed in the biblical text: the speaker's eyes are lifted AD TE (to God), rather than to the mountains (= the apostles). While the Irish *Glossa in Psalmos* gives no spiritual heading for this psalm, the alternative gloss on v. 1 appears to under-stand the speaker as the Church rather than Christ, and in this it agrees with the first part of the heading of the Psalter of Charlemagne: *AD TE*

---

52. McNamara (ed.), *Glossa in Psalmos*, p. 273.
53. See Boese (ed.), *Anonymi*, II, p. 140.
54. McNamara (ed.), *Glossa in Psalmos*, p. 267.
55. Boese (ed.), *Anonymi*, II, p. 141.

LEUAUI OCULOS. id est non ad montes sed ad semetipsum Dominum, quia perfectior est aeclesia quando hoc dicit quam quando leuat oculos ad montes.[56] The *Glosa psalmoprum ex traditione seniorum* as usual depends on Augustine. It regards the opening words *Ad te leuaui* as *uox ecclesiae,*[57] and makes no mention of *uox Christi* and has no reference to the Father (*pater*).

3.5.e. *Psalm 123*: Uox apostolorum. This seems the best attested and the original reading. MSS K and *i* (*i* = Psalter of Charlemagne) have *Uox Ecclesiae*, to which MS *i* adds: *ad Christum.* The Vatican *Glossa in Psalmos* has the same reading as *i* and the glosses with the spiritual sense (dependent on Hilary's abbreviation of Augustine) follow this understanding: *NISI QUIA DOMINUS. id est manifeste confitetur aeclesia...* The *Glosa psalmorum*, dependent on Augustine, takes the speaker as the Church (*uox ecclesiae*),[58] has no instance of *uox apostolorum*, and in fact makes no mention of the apostles. The tradition of the Columba series (*Uox apostolorum*) is close to that found in the series II of psalm headings (representing an Italo-Insular [English?] tradition), in which the gradual psalms are interpreted as 15 steps in the ascent to God: '(Ps) 123. *QUINTO GRADU apostolorum et martyrum uoces pronuntiat.*'

3.5.f. *Psalm 124*: Uox Ecclesiae. A spiritual interpretation similar to that of this heading is found in Pal. lat. 68, dependent on an abbreviation of Augustine's *Enarrationes: QUI CONFIDUNT IN DOMINO SICUT MONS SION...SION. id est aeclesia inmobilis in fide.* The *Glosa psalmorum ex traditione seniorum*[59] also depends on Augustine, but does not speak of the Church at all. It dwells rathers on Jerusalem as *uisio pacis.*

3.5.g. *Psalm 125*: (*In conuertendo Dominus*). Uox apostolorum de impiis Judeis. So also in the headings of Pal. lat. 68 and the Psalter of Charlemagne, both of which add: *et infidelibus conuertentibus.* I cannot say which text of the psalm led to the identification of the speaker as the apostles (also found in Series III), nor why the psalm is said to be about the unfaithful Jews. This interpretation is not found in Pal. lat. 68.

56. McNamara (ed.), *Glossa in Psalmos*, p. 270.
57. Boese (ed.), *Anonymi*, II, p.142.
58. Boese (ed.), *Anonymi*, II, p. 142.
59. See Boese (ed.), *Anonymi*, II, pp. 145-45.

Inclusion of the Jews is in keeping with the heading for Psalm 118 (see 4.6 below). The *Glosa psalmorum*, as usual, depends on Augustine. The speaker is given as the prophet (psalmist). Thus on the opening words: *In conuertendo Domino captiuitatem Sion*, we are told that Zion is Jerusalem, the eternal Zion. *Quomodo aeterna Sion? Quomodo captiua Sion? In angelis aeterna, in hominibus captiua. Captiuitas Iudeorum in figura fuit in Babylonia, et post LXX annos figura reuersus est ille populus ad ciuitatem suam.* It is doubtful, however, that a text such as this explains the Columba Series heading.

3.5.h. *Psalm 126*: (*Nisi Dominus aedificauerit domum*). Uox Christi ad futuram Ecclesiam. The title takes the psalm to be spoken by Christ to the future Church (in heaven). While Augustine does not make Christ the speaker, he interprets of the Church on earth and of the heavenly Church (a teaching also found in Pal. lat. 68). In vv. 3-4 (*merces fructus uentris...*) Eucherius sees a reference to the future resurrection: *postquam dederit dilectis suis somnum, ostendit quae futura sit resurrectio illa sanctorum.*[60] The *Glosa psalmorum*[61] has little to offer by way of background to this Columba Series heading.

3.5.i. *Psalm 127*: (*Beati omnes qui timent Dominum*). Propheta de Christo et de Ecclesia dicit. For Augustine this psalm is about the Church, but also about Christ. The prophet speaks of many (*beati omnes*) who are one (*beatus es*) in Christ. *Uxor tua sicut uitis* (v. 3) is addressed to Christ; his *uxor,* Christ's spouse, is the Church. In his *Enarratio* on this psalm Augustine recalls and develops his understanding of *filii excussorum* of the preceding one (Ps. 126.4) as sons of the prophets. In this psalm the prophet is again speaking. Augustine's text may have occasioned inclusion of the reference to the prophet in the heading. The substance of Augustine's interpretation (without reference here to the *filii excussorum*) is given in Pal. lat. 68.[62] In the *Glosa psalmorum*[63] the speaker in the opening words is the Church: *BEATI OMNES QUI TIMENT DOMINUM. Uox ecclesiae.* With reference to Augustine by name *uxor* of v. 3 is understood of the Church: *UXOR TUA...Uxor Christi sua ecclesia intellegitis.*

---

60. *Instructionum liber* I, p. 101, ll. 23-25.
61. In Boese (ed.), *Anonymi*, II, pp. 149-51.
62. McNamara (ed.), *Glossa in Psalmos*, pp. 277-78.
63. Boese (ed.), *Anonymi*, II, pp. 151-53.

3.5.j. *Psalm 128*: Uox Ecclesiae. This understanding of the psalm is that found in Augustine.

> *Many a time have they fought against me from my youth up.* The Church speaks of those whom she endures, and as if it were asked, 'Is it only now?' The Church is of ancient birth: Since the time saints were first called the Church has been on earth. At one time the Church existed in Abel only, and he was assailed by his evil and incorrigible brother Cain'.

The *Glosa psalmorum* is equally dependent on Augustine. Citing Augustine by name it glosses the opening words as follows: SAEPE EXPUGNAUERUNT ME A IUUENTUTE MEA. *Ecclesia loquitur de illis quos sustinet. Numquid modo? Olim est ecclesia a iuuentute, hoc est ab* Abel.

3.5.k. *Psalm 129: De profundis clamaui ad te Domine. Legendus ad lectionem Ionae prophetae* (No mystical heading). For consideration of the reading in conjunction with Jonah see above 3.3.r. According to the comment in *Glosa psalmorum* this psalm *secundum historiam de Iona potest intellegi.*[64]

3.5.l. *Psalm 130*: Uox Ecclesiae rogantis. As Augustine explains at length, and as summarized in Pal. lat. 68,[65] the speaker here is one person, Christ and the Church: *totum Corpus Christi hoc dicit.* The Church also features in the *Glosa psalmorum*, dependent as usual on Augustine. The speaker in the opening verse is the prophet (psalmist), but regarding the Church: DOMINE NON EST EXALTATUM. *Uox prophetae in persona ecclesiae.*[66] Verse 2 make a comparison of a weaned child towards its mother. For the *Glosa* (with reference to Augustine) the mother is the Church: *mater ecclesia est.*[67]

3.5.m. *Psalm 131*: Propheta ad Patrem de Christo dicit. This psalm on David and his work for the Lord is taken as spoken by the prophet (inspired by the Holy Spirit being understood) to the Father concerning Christ. Thus in general in the 'spiritual' interpretation, as in Pal. lat. 68: *Allagoricae...Christo hic salmus coaptatur. 'MEMENTO'. id est Deo Patri dicit Spiritus.* In the *Glosa psalmorum* the speaker is the prophet

---

64. Boese (ed.), *Anonymi*, II, pp. 155-56.
65. McNamara (ed.), *Glossa in Psalmos*, p. 281.
66. Boese (ed.), *Anonymi*, II, p. 159.
67. Boese (ed.), *Anonymi*, II, p. 159.

(psalmist). Thus in the comment on the opening words (*MEMENTO DOMINE DAUID...uox prophetae*)[68] and a number of times on other *lemmata*. Once (citing Augustine) it speaks of the words being addressed to the Father (v. 10: *PROPTER DAUID. Hoc Deo Patri dictum est*),[69] and concerning Christ (v. 16: *SACERDOTES TUI INDUANT SALUTARI, hoc est Christum*).

3.5.n. *Psalm 132*: *(Ecce quam bonum)* Uox Ecclesiae orantis. Augustine understands this psalm to speak of the entire Church, as well as of monks. In the main dependent on Augustine, in the spiritual interpretation of the psalm the *Glossa in Psalmos* of Pal. lat. 68 understands it of the unity of the Church, through the gift of the Holy Spirit. Specific to the Columba series title is that the speaker of the psalms is given as the Church. The *Anonymi Glosa Psalmorum* depends heavily on Augustine. The speaker, however, is not the Church but the prophet (psalmist): *ECCE QUAM BONUM. Uox prophetae.*[70]

3.5.o. *Psalm 133*: Uox Ecclesiae in futuro. Finally, we have Psalm 133 (*Ecce nunc benedicite Dominum*), the last of the Psalms of Ascent, with as title 'the voice or chant of the Church in the future eternal bliss'. This, in Jerome's understanding of the Psalms of Ascents, is the culmination of the journey: the Fifteen Degrees have led us on the summit 'so that we may be able to say in the courts of the Lord: "Behold, now, bless the Lord, all servants of the Lord",' cited, as I have already said, in Pal. lat. 68 at the beginning of this collection of the gradual psalms.[71]

3.5.p. *Conclusion.* If any conclusion is to be drawn from the above analysis it would seem to be that for the gradual psalms the Columba Series of psalm headings does not appear to follow any single known psalm commentary or exegetical tradition. While there are points of contact with the exegetical tradition found in the *Glossa in Psalmos* of Codex Pal. lat. 68, this is not sustained throughout. For the headings for these gradual psalms the Columba Series seems to be less close to the *Glosa psalmorum* than it does in other sections.

68. Boese (ed.), *Anonymi*, II, p. 160.
69. Boese (ed.), *Anonymi*, II, p. 163.
70. Boese (ed.), *Anonymi*, II, p. 164.
71. In Boese (ed.), *Anonymi*, II (p. 167) for Ps. 133 the speaker is the prophet (psalmist): *Ecce nunc...propheta hortatur*).

4. Examination of the Psalter Prophecies of Christ
in the Columba Series

4.1. *General Old Testament Prophecies of Christ*

At an early period in the Church a doctrine developed regarding seven things believed to have been prophesied of Christ in the Scriptures. It seems likely that this belief grew from reflection on the seven seals mentioned in the Revelation of John 5.1-3. In most instances they are not explicitly connected with the psalms alone, although in some texts they are. I here give some of these texts from the early Church, from a Latin tradition that appears to be Irish or related to Irish tradition (*Das Bibelwerk*, *Catechesis Celtica*), from Irish tradition as found in the *Scúap Chrábaid* and the *Old-Irish Treatise* on the Psalter. I then pass on to consider what information we can glean on the subject from the St Columba Series of psalm headings itself.

4.1.a. *St Irenaeus (c. 130–c. 200 CE)* Irenaeus:

> We believe in the Holy Spirit who through the prophets foretold God's plan: the coming of our beloved Lord Jesus Christ, his birth from the Virgin, his passion, his resurrection from the dead, his ascension into heaven, and his final coming from heaven in the glory of his Father, to recapitulate all things, and to raise all people from the dead, so that by the decree of his invisible Father, he may make a just judgment in all things.[72]

This gives us six items of prophecy which became commonly accepted in Christian tradition:

1. the coming of our beloved Lord Jesus Christ
2. his birth from the Virgin
3. his passion
4. his resurrection from the dead
5. his ascension into heaven
6. and his final coming from heaven in the glory of his Father, to recapitulate all things, and to raise all people from the dead, so that by the decree of his invisible Father, he may make a just judgment in all things'.

---

72. *Aduersus haereses* 1.10.1; *PG* 7, 549-550A.

4.1.b. *Hilary (c. 315–367 CE).* In the prologue to his *Tractatus super Psalmos* (no. 6) Hilary speaks of the faith of Christ as key of the psalms. He cites Apoc 3.7 which speaks of Christ, the holy and true, who holds the key of David. Hilary then goes on to list the seven seals (*signacula*) through which Christ is prophesied in the psalms.

> *Clauem igitur Dauid habet, quia per haec septem quaedam signacula, quae de corporalitate eius, et passione et morte et resurrectione et gloria et regno et iudicio Dauid de eo in psalmis prophetat.*

This gives us the following list:

1. de corporalitate eius
2. et passione
3. et morte
4. et resurrectione
5. et gloria
6. et regno
7. et iudicio.

This list is similar to that given by Irenaeus, but in Hilary the prophecies (seals) are taken to be contained in the Psalter.[73]

4.2. *The Seven Prophecies of Christ in* Das Bibelwerk *and* Catechesis Celtica
We may now pass from the earlier Christian to Hiberno-Latin tradition, where we find the seven things prophesied of Christ are itemized, the Old Testament text for one each cited, together with the fulfilment text in the New Testament. The first of these texts is in the Reference Bible (c. 800), in the course of a comment on the seven seals of Apoc. 5.1-3. The second text occurs in the *Catechesis Celtica* (the title given to a

---

73. We may also note the list of seven prophecies on Christ (without reference to the Apocalypse) which Ambrose says are contained in the Psalter: 'What others announced in enigmas seems to have been promised quite openly to this prophet alone (i.e. David), namely that the Lord Jesus would be born of his seed, as the Lord told him: "One of the sons of your body I will set on your throne" (Ps. 131[132].11). Thus, in the book of psalms not only is Jesus born for us: he accepts too his saving bodily passion, he dies, he rises from the dead and ascends into heaven and sits at the Father's right hand.' (M. Petschenig [ed.], Ambrose, *Explanatione super psalmos*, XII [CSEL, 64; Vienna, 1919], p. 7; in the praises of the Psalter, as part of the comment on Ps. 1).

collection of mainly homiletic items in the Vatican Codex Reginensis 49; late tenth century), in an item wholly devoted to the seven seals in Apoc 5.1-3.

4.2.a. *Text of the Reference Bible.*[74] *Et uidi in dextera sedentis super thronum librum intus et foris signatum VII sigillis et nemo potuit aperire librum neque in caelo neque in terra neque subtus terram* (Apoc. 5.1-3). *Vidi in dextera,* id est Christi dextera est qua mundum fecit et redemit. *Librum intus et foris signatum. Librum* Uetus Testamentum significat. *Intus et foris.* id est, in historia et sensu. Item de humanitate et diuinitate Christi. *Sigillis VII.* id est, vii quae de Christo principaliter leguntur, id est natiuitas et reliqua. Ideo sigillati in Ueteri quia nemo potuit scire *Ecce uirgo concipiet* (Isa. 7.14; Vulg.) et reliqua usque Christus natus fuit de uirgine. Haec sunt VII sigilla in Ueteri Testamento.

De natiuitate Christi, ut est: *Ecce uirgo in utero* (Isa. 7.14; VL), et reliqua Christus soluit quando natus est, ut dicitur: *Natus est nobis hodie conseruator salutis nostrae* (Luc. 2.11; VL), et reliqua.

Secundum sigillum de baptismo, ut est: *Transiuimus per ignem et aquam* (Ps. 65.12), et reliqua, Christus soluit, ut Iohannes dicit: *Ecce ego debeo baptizari a te* (cf. Mt. 3.14), et reliqua.

Tertium sigillum de passione eius, ut: *Sicut ouis ad occissionem ductus* (cf. Isa. 53.7), et reliqua, Christus soluit, ut: *Inclinato capite tradidit spiritum* (Jn 19.30).

Quarto sigillo de sepulchro eius, ut: *Sepulchrum eius erit honorabile* (Isa. 11.10); item: *Inter mortuos liber* (Ps. 86.6) soluit Christus ut: *Cum Ioseph accepisset corpus Iesu inuoluit illud in sindone mundo* (cf. Mt. 27.6).

---

74. MS Paris BN lat. 11561, fol. 207r; Munich, Clm 14277, 322r. The texts of the Reference Bible (MS Paris, Bibl. Nat. lat. 11561, fol. 207r; Munich, Clm 14277, fol. 3222) and of the *Catechesis Celtica* (Ms Vatican Library, Reg. Lat. 49, fol. 40vab) has been edited by M. McNamara, 'The Affiliations and Origins of the Catechesis Celtica: An Ongoing Quest', in T. O'Loughlin (ed.), *The Scriptures in Early Medieval Ireland: Proceedings of the 1993 Conference of the Society for Hiberno-Latin Studies on Early Irish Exegesis and Homiletics* (Instrumenta Patristica, 31; Steenbrugge: Abbatia S. Petri; Turnhout: Brepols, 1999), pp. 179-203 ('Appendix: Texts on the VII Sigilla', pp. 199-203).

Quintum sigillum de resurrectione, ut: *Tu exsurgens Domine misere-*
beris Sion (Ps. 101.14), Christus soluit, ut angelus dicit: *Non est hic,*
surrexit enim (Mt. 28.6) et reliqua.

Sexto sigillo de ascensione, ut: *Sede a dextris meis* (Ps. 109.1), et
reliqua, Christus soluit, ut: angelus dixit: *Quemadmodum uidistis eum*
euntem in caelum (Acts 1.11) et reliqua.

Septimum sigillum de aduentu eius, ut dicit: *Deus noster manifeste*
ueniet (Ps. 49.3) soluit <Christus> ut Petrus dicit: *Elementa igne ardes-*
cent in aduentu Domini (2 Pet. 3.12).

In this passage we have the list:

1.   de natiuitate Christi
2.   de baptismo
3.   de passione eius
4.   de sepulchro eius
5.   de resurrectione
6.   de ascensione
7.   de aduentu eius.

We find an identical list in the introduction to the comments on the
psalms in the same Reference Bible, in its praises of the Psalter. There
we are told that among other things the Psalter contains the seven things
prophesied of Christ: *Modo .vii. quae leguntur de Christo, id est: nati-*
uitas, baptismum, passio, sepulchrum, resurrectio, ascensio, aduentus
ad iudicium et reliqua.[75] This is practically the same list as in the longer
text of the same work on the seven seals of Apoc. 5.1-3.

This text is interesting in that, unlike the surrounding passages, it
does not depend on Cassiodore, and also because there is a rather close
relationship between the section on the psalms in the Reference Bible
and the *Old-Irish Treatise* on the Psalter.

4.3. *The Seven Seals and the Prophecies of Christ in the* Catechesis
Celtica[76]

Uidi in dextera sedentis super thronum librum scriptum intus et foris,
signatum sigillis VII. Uidi in dextera, hoc est in Christo quia ipse est
dextera Dei per quam cuncta constituit et totum genus humanum
redemit, uel in potentia Dei Patris, uel in sapientia Christi. *Librum.*
Utrumque testamentum propterea unus liber est, quia nec nouum sine

---

75. MS Paris BNF lat. 11561, fol. 56ra-b.
76. Cod. Reg. lat. 49, fol. 40vab.

ueteri nec uetus sine nouo esse potest. Nam uetus nuntius est et uelamen noui et nouum adimpletio est et interpretatio ueteris. *Scriptum intus et foris.* Per scriptionem intimam diuinitatem intelligimus, ut est illud: *In principio erat Uerbum* (Jn 1.1); et per scriptionem foris ostendimus incarnationem Christi, ut est illud: *Christi autem generatio* (Mt. 1.18); siue dicitur: *liber iste scriptus intus et foris. foris* per historiam, *intus* autem per sensum spiritualem, uel *foris* <per sensum> litterae simplicem adhuc infirmantibus congruentem, *intus* quia uisibilia promittit; uel *foris* quia mores aeclesiae in terra propter rectitudinem preceptorum suorum disponit, *intus* quia caelestia pollicetur.

Signatum, id est conclusum sigillis VII. Hoc est, conceptione Christi et natiuitate et passione et sepultura et resurrectione et ascensione et de aduentu eius. Sigilla in profetis pronuntiata sunt. Claues uero in nouo quibus aperiuntur sigilla.

De conceptionis sigillo Esaias dicit: *Ecce uirgo in utero concipiet et pariet filium, et uocabitur nomen eius Emanuel* (Isa. 7.14). Clauis est, cum dicitur: *Aue Maria gratia plena* (Lk. 1.28) et reliqua usque *tui* (cf. Lk. 1.42).

Sigillum de natiuitate ut: *Nascetur homo de semine Iuda et dominabitur omnibus gentibus* (cf. Gen. 49.10; Num. 24.19). Clauis est: *Natus est uobis hodie conseruator salutis, qui est christus* (Lk. 2.11; VL).

Sigillum de passione: *Sicut ouis ad occisionem ductus est* (cf. Isa. 53.7). Clauis est: *Crucifigentes eum, diuiserunt sibi uestimenta eius* (cf. Mt. 27.35).

Sigillum de sepultura: *Erit sepulcrum eius honorabile* (Isa. 11.10). Clauis est: *Ioseph ab Arimathia accepit corpus Iesu* (cf. Mt. 27.57, et par.).

Sigillum de resurrectione: *Non dabis sanctum tuum uidere corruptionem* (Ps. 15.10). Clauis est: *Surrexit Christus sicut dixit uobis* (Mt. 28.6).

Sigillum de ascensione: *Quis est iste rex gloriae? Dominus uirtutum ipse est rex gloriae* (Ps. 23.10). Clauis est: *Uiri Galilei, Quid hic statis aspicientes in celum? Quemadmodum uidistis eum euntem in celum, sic ueniet* (Acts 1.11).

Sigillum de aduentu eius: *Deus manifeste ueniet, Deus noster, et non silebit. Ignis in conspectu eius ardebit, et in circuitu eius tempestas ualida* (Ps. 49.3). Nondum apertum est. Non enim clauis (fol. 40vb) eius adhuc reperitur.

This gives the following list:

342   *The Psalms in the Early Irish Church*

Signatum, id est conclusum sigillis VII. Hoc est,
1. conceptione Christi
2. et natiuitate
3. et passione
4. et sepultura
5. et resurrectione
6. et ascensione
7. et de aduentu eius.

Another text of the same *Catechesis Celtica* (fol. 32r) gives a different list when narrating the stages by which the wall of separation between God and humanity was broken down. The final stage was the eleventh: '*XI, in Christo, per VII, quae profetata sunt de illo, id est natiuitas, babtismum, crux, sepultura, resurrectio, <ascensio et iudicium>*.' There was evidently a great variety in the listing of the seven 'seals' in question.[77]

4.4. *The Prophecies of Christ in the Irish Writing* Scúap Chrábaid
The *Scúap Chrábaid*, the 'Broom of Devotion', is one of the most famous old Irish prayers. It was probably composed in the late eighth century.[78] It has the following list of the things prophesied of Christ:

77. Other examples can be given from the Irish *Liber de numeris*, under the number VII.21: *Natiuitas Christi...eiusdem Christi babtismum...passio et crux Christi...Iesu Christi sepultura...Christi resurrectio...Christi in caelis ascensio... Christi aduentus in iudicium*; cited by R. McNally, 'Der irische Liber de Numeris: Eine Quellenanalyse des pseudo-isidorischen Liber de numeris' (Inaugural-Dissertation zur Erlangung des Doktorgrades der Philosophischen Fakultät der Ludwig-Maximilians-Universität zu München; Munich, 1957). Likewise in the Hiberno-Latin text *Ex dictis sancti Hieronimi*, no. 10 (ed. R. McNally; CCSL, 108B; Turnhout: Brepols, 1973), p. 226: *...septem...quae Christo conueniunt... Aduentum eius, baptismum, passionem, sepulturam, resurrectionem, ascensionem et aduentum posteriorem eius ad iudicium*.
78. See J. Kenney, *The Sources for Early History of Ireland: Ecclesiastical* (New York: Columbia University Press, 1929), pp. 725-26. K. Meyer (ed.), in 'Stories and Songs from Irish MSS. VI. Colcu ua Duinechda's Scúap Chrábaid, or Besom of Devotion', *Otia Merseiana* 2 (1900–1901), pp. 92-105 (97), and in C. Plummer (ed.), *Irish Litanies* (London: Henry Bradshaw Society, 1925), pp. 42-43. Plummer's edition (in the text entitled 'Litany of Jesus, II'), while invoking Jesus' mercy 'for the sake of the seven things that were prophesied for Thee on earth,' actually lists eight, the first ('Thy Conception') being probably a later addition.

1. his birth
2. baptism
3. crucifixion
4. burial
5. resurrection
6. ascension
7. coming of the last judgment.

4.5. *Psalms Prophesy of Christ in the Introduction to the* Old-Irish Treatise *on the Psalter*

Treating of the psalms as prophecy, the *Old Irish Treatise* on the Psalter[79] (lines 320-28) has the following:

> Question. Of what did the prophecy of the psalms foretell? Not difficult. Of the birth of Christ and of his baptism, and of his passion, and of his resurrection, and of his ascension, and of his sitting at the right hand of God the Father in heaven, of the invitation of the heathen to faith, of the thrusting of Judah (*de indarbiu Iuda*) into unbelief, of the increase of every justice, of the spurning of every injustice, of the malediction of sinners, of the coming of Christ to judge the quick and the dead.

This gives us a list of 12 prophecies, six of the traditional seven, with an additional six inserted between the traditional sixth and the seventh.[80]

1. Of the birth of Christ
2. and of his baptism
3. and of his passion
4. and of his resurrection
5. and of his ascension
    a. and of his sitting at the right hand of God the Father in heaven
    b. of the invitation of the heathen to faith
    c. of the thrusting of Judah (*de indarbiu Iuda*) into unbelief;
    d. of the increase of every justice
    e. of the spurning of every injustice
    f. of the malediction of sinners
    g. of the coming of Christ to judge the quick and the dead.

---

79. *OIT.*
80. We may recall the list in the introduction to the psalms in the Reference Bible: *de natiuitate Christi*; *de baptismo*; *de passione eius*; *de sepulchro eius*; *de resurrectione*; *de ascensione*; *de aduentu eius*, etc.

Some of those extra headings of the *Old-Irish Treatise* can be compared with Columba series headings. Thus, for instance:

> *Old-Irish Treatise* no. 7: *of the invitation of the heathen to faith*. Compare the Columba series: 8, *de fide omnium credentium;* 14, *Uox Christi quam dicit fidelibus;* 42, 83, *Ad eos qui fidem sunt consecuti;*

> *Old-Irish Treatise* no. 8, *of the thrusting of Judah (de indarbiu Iuda) into unbelief.* Compare with Columba series: 54, *Uox Christi aduersus magnatos Judeorum et de Juda traditore;* 51, *Uox Christi ad Judam traditorem;* 40, *Legendus ad lectionem Esaiae prophetae. Uox Christi de passione sua et de Juda;* 35, *Propheta cum laude opera ipsius Judae dicit* (= The prophet speaks of Judas and also praises God; = describes content or application of psalm).

> *Old-Irish Treatise* no. 9, *of the increase of every justice.* Compare with Columba 19. *Propheta operantem hortatur;* 23, *Confirmatio populi credentis...uox Christi diligentibus se.;* 32, *Propheta cum laude Dei populum hortatur* [See *Glosa psalmorum*, Ps. 32: *propheta hortatur sanctos, ut laudent dominum*]. We may also note the headings speaking to 'the people' (= the new people of God?): *ad nouellum populum:* 84, 145; *ad populum:* (32), 65, 98, 99, 102 (*ad populum suum*), 138, 145, 148.

4.6. *The Psalms as Prophecies of Christ in the Columba Series*

We cannot say whether the tradition within which the Columba series arose knew of the seven matters prophesied of Christ in the Old Testament, if not in the psalms, or whether this tradition had some other theory on the Christian interpretation of the psalms, and of the link established by the psalms between the Old and the New Testament. Two texts lead one to believe that the tradition knew of some theory. There is evidence of this in two texts, in the titles to Psalm 18 and Psalm 118, the first furthermore referring to the latter.

Heading Psalm 18. *De aduentu Christi per quem reseratur psalmus CXVIII, ibi coniungitur nouum et uetus testamentum.* ('Concerning the coming of Christ, by which Psalm 118 is unlocked; there the New and the Old Testament are joined together').

Here Psalm 18 is understood as referring to the coming of Christ. This seems to be an unusual interpretation for this psalm, but may be connected with an understanding of v. 6 ('he, as a bridegroom coming out of his bride-chamber') as referring to Christ's birth from Mary's womb. Thus Augustine, *Enarratio* on Ps. 18.6 (*'tanquam sponsus procedens de thalamo suo': et ipse procedens de utero uirginali...exultauit sicut fortissimus*) and Series V of the *Tituli Psalmorum*, said to be inspired by Origen, but here close to Augustine: *quod ipse uirginalem thalamum ingressus processerit occulta hominum deleturus*. We may also note the *Anonymi Glosa Psalmorum ex traditione seniorum* on Ps. 18.3 (*Dies diei...nox nocti): Secundum sensum dies Christus, et aliter dies apostoli...Aliter: 'nox' profunditas scripturarum in prophetis nuntiare* (variant reading in MSS VL: *pronuntiant) profundidatem Ueteris Testamenti*.

The second part of the Columba title seems to say that Psalm 118 is unlocked by being understood of the coming of Christ, and further that in Psalm 118 the Old and the New Testaments are joined together. I have failed to find any such understanding of Psalm 118 (the long alphabetic psalm of 176 verses, 8x22, on the Law). The tradition behind the Columba series may have known a sustained christological under-standing of each of this psalm's 22 sections.

The Columba series heading to Psalm 118 seems to contain part of a tradition with principle or theory of psalm interpretation. This heading reads: Psalm 118. *Uox Christi ad Patrem et apostolorum de aduersario et de Judeis, et de passione sua et de aduentu suo et iudicio eius et regno.*

This gives us the following:

1. de aduersario
2. et de Judeis,
3. et de passione sua
4. et de aduentu suo
5. et iudicio eius
6. et regno.

These six headings contain some of the emphases we find in the Columba series, three of which are found together in the heading to Psalm 49: '*Legendus ad euangelium Matthaei. De aduentu Christi pro-pheta dicit et de judicio futuro, increpatio Iudeorum.*'

Thus we have:

1. *de aduersario* (Ps. 118); *aduersus diabulum* (Ps. 143); *Propheta dicit ad Christum de inimicis Judeis et de diabolo* (Ps. 7); *de Judeis et de principe demoniorum* (Ps. 9); *de diab-ulo* (Ps. 12); *aduersus diabulum cum satellitibus eius* (Ps. 143).

2. *et de Judeis*, titles for: Psalms 4; 7; 9; 11 (13); 16; 27; 30; 34; 38; (43); 49; 52; 54; 57; 58; 77; 81; 82; 88; 93; 104; 106; 108;

113; 118; 125; (135). See in detail section 5.3.d above. *Propheta dicit ad Christum de inimicis Judeis et de diabolo* (Ps. 7); *de Judeis* (Pss. 9; 54); *Christus pro passione sanctorum suorum dicit et de Judeis* (Ps. 11); *Christus de Judeis* (Ps. 16); *De Judeis Christus dicit* (Ps. 27); *uox Christi in passione de Judeis dicit* (Pss. 30; 34); *increpat Judeos* (Pss. 4; 38; 52); *Increpatio Judeorum* (Ps. 49); *De (pro) populo judaico* (Pss. 13; 43). (Note also use of verb *increpat* with regard to other persons and things: *diuites increpat* (Ps. 48); *cum Judeis increpat idola* (Ps. 113); *increpat idola gentium* (Ps. 134). On Judas: Psalms 35; 40; 51

3. *et de passione sua* (Pss. 21; 30; 34; 59; 63; 68; 87; 118); *uox Christi in passione de Judeis dicit* (Pss. 30; 34)
4. *et de aduentu suo* (Pss. 18; 49; 67; 76; 118)
5. *et iudicio eius* (Pss. 49; 74; 118)
6. *et regno* (Pss. 118; 150); see also 29; 56; 100; 126; 133; 149; 150: *Uox Christi post saeculum deuictum in regno suo laetantis.*

5. *Some Reflections and Conclusions*

This examination of series I, the St Columba series, of psalm headings has been provisional. Only about one third of the whole (53 out of 146; Pss. 24; 92; 141; 142 are without a heading) has been examined. This is a first attempt to analyse the evidence in an effort to determine the tradition or traditions in which the series stands. Some conclusions seem to emerge.

1. The notes regarding the reading of the particular psalms (*Legendus ad*) seem to be designed to connect the psalm in question, or a verse from it, with some other biblical text, book or books. These notes probably do not reflect a liturgical setting, nor give evidence that the particular book or books were read in the liturgical assembly.

2. The Columba series of psalm headings appears to presuppose the full exposition of a particular psalm, and at times make sense only when seen within this fuller tradition.

3. As far as can be ascertained from the examination made above, this tradition is that of the Latin Church.

4. In many instances, there is a particularly close relationship with the exegetical tradition as found in the Latin *Glosa psalmorum ex traditione seniorum* composed about 600, and later widely used in Europe.

5. With regard to the bearing of the analysis on the date to be assigned to the Columba series of psalm headings, a date of c. 620–50 would suit if we presume that the headings depend on the *Glosa psalmorum*. The date would also fit in with other data from the Cathach, such as the use of the critical signs of asterisk and obelus.[81]

6. However, such a conclusion is not at all required by the evidence. For one thing the *Glosa psalmorum* cannot be presumed to be an original production without a prehistory. While there is a relationship between the Columba series and the *Glosa psalmorum* tradition in a number of psalms, this is not the case for all the headings. There are a number (probably many) of cases where the Columba series is not in the tradition of the *Glosa psalmorum*. Before any definite conclusion could be drawn, the differences as well as the similarities between the two traditions should be examined. Furthermore, even in cases of similarities, direct influence of the *Glosa psalmorum* on the Columba series need not necessarily be presumed. The exegetical tradition, or exegetical traditions, now enshrined in the *Glosa psalmorum* could have been known in Ireland and the Continent before the *Glosa* was composed about the year 600.

7. The evidence for a relationship between the Columba headings and the *Glosa psalmorum ex traditione seniorum* is such that I believe it should be taken into account together with the palaeographical, artistic and other evidence for a sixth-century dating. What now seems indicated is an examination of all 146 headings of the Columba series in an effort to situate them in the exegetical tradition of the Western, and if needs be the Eastern, Christian tradition.

6. *Series I*

Ed. P. Salmon; *Les 'Tituli Psalmorum' des manuscrits latins* (Collectanea Biblical Latina, 12; Rome: Abbaye Saint-Jérome; Vatican City: Vatican Library, 1959).

Asterisks (*) mark headings examined in more or less detail in this essay (the number of asterisks indicating examination under more than one heading),

---

81. See McNamara, 'Psalter Text', above p. 30.

1*   *De Joseph dicit, qui corpus Christi sepelivit.*

2**   *Legendus ad evangelium Lucae. Uox Patris et apostolorum et Christi. Ad caput scribendum.*

3*   *Uox Christi ad Patrem de Judeis dicit.*

4**   *Propheta increpat Judeos.*

5   *Christus ad Patrem.*

6   *Uox Christi ad Patrem.*

7*   *Propheta dicit ad Christum de inimicis Judeis et de diabolo.*

8   *Uox Ecclesiae laudem dicit Christo de fide omnium creden-tium.*

9*   *Ecclesia laudem dicit Christo, de Judeis et de principe demoniorum.*

10   *Uox Christi.*

11*   *Christus pro passione sanctorum suorum dicit de Judeis.*

12   *Uox Christi ad Patrem de diabolo dicit.*

13*   *Verba Christi ad divitem interrogantem se. De populo judaico.*

14   *Uox Christi quam dicit fidelibus. Interpellat Patrem.*

15*   *Uox Christi ad Patrem.*

16*   *Christus de Judeis dicit ad Patrem.*

17   *David in similitudinem Christi dicit.*

18*   *De adventu Christi per quem reseratur psalmus CXVIII, ibi coniungitur novum et vetus testamentum.*

19   *Propheta operantem hortatur.*

20   *Propheta de Christo rege dicit ad Patrem.*

21   *Verba Christi cum pateretur.*

22   *Uox Ecclesiae post baptismum.*

23   *Confirmatio populi credentis; portae quas dicit peccata vel inferni; uox Christi diligentibus se.*

24   Nothing. No heading.

25   *Propheta de se testatur.*

26**   *Ad eos qui primum ingrediuntur, in dominicum. Legendus ad lectionem Esaiae prophetae (65,13; Vet. lat.): ecce qui servi-unt tibi bona manducabunt.*

27**   *Legendus ad lectionem Danihelis prophetae. De Judeis Christo dicit.*

28   *Ad superpositionem diei sabbati Paschae, postquam consum-mata est Ecclesia Christi.*

29   *Propheta ad Patrem et ad Filium dicit de Pascha Christi futura; Ecclesia orat cum laude.*

30*   *Hic fidei confessio credentium Deum; uox Christi in passione de Judeis dicit.*

31   *Post baptismum uox paenitentium.*

32*   *Propheta cum laude Dei populum hortatur.*

33   *Uox fidei per jejunium.*

34**   *Uox Christi in passione de Judeis dicit.*

35*   *Propheta cum laude opera ipsius Judae dicit.*

36   *Huic hortatur Moysem ad fidem demonstrans salutem Ecclesiae, credentem monet ad fidei firmamentum.*

37   *Hic confessio insapientiae, virtus ad salutem.*

38*   *Propheta increpat Judeos qui divitias habent et nesciunt cui dimittunt.*

39*   *Patientia populi.*

40*   *Legendus ad lectionem Esaiae prophetae. Uox Christi de passione sua et de Juda traditore.*

41   *Ante baptismum uox Christi est.*

42   *Ad eos qui fidem sunt consecuti.*

43**   *Hic exomologesim. Legendus ad epistulam Pauli ad Romanos. Propheta ad Dominum de operibus eius paenitentiam gerens pro populo judaico.*

44**   *Legendus ad evangelium Matthei, de regina Austri. Propheta pro Patre de Christo et Ecclesia dicit.*

45*   *Legendus ad lectionem Actus apostolorum. Uox apostolorum.*

46*   *Legendus ad lectionem Actus apostolorum. Uox apostolorum postquam ascendit Christus ad Patrem.*

47*   *Legendus ad Apocalipsin Johannis. Figura Ecclesiae Hierusalem futurae*

48   *Hic divites increpat qui ad inferna descendunt cum mortui fuerint ; uox Ecclesiae super Lazaro et divite purpurato.*

49**   *Legendus ad evangelium Matthaei. De adventu Christi propheta dicit et judicio futuro, increpatio Judeorum.*

50*   *Legendus ad lectionem Esaiae prophetae et lectionem Actus apostolorum ub Paulus eligitur. Uox Christi pro populo paenitente et uox Pauli ad paenitentiam.*

51   *Uox Christi ad Judam traditorem.*

52*** *Legendus ad evangelium Matthei. Increpat Judaeos incredulos operibus negantes Deum.*

53   *Uox Christi ad Patrem.*
54*   *Uox Christi adversus magnatos Judeorum et de Juda tradi-*
       tore.
55   *Uox Christi ad Patrem.*
56*   *Uox Pauli post resurrectionem.*
57*   *Propheta de senioribus Judeorum dicit.*
58*   *Uox Christi de Judeis ad Patrem.*
59   *Uox apostolorum quando Christus passus est.*
60   *Uox Pauli apostoli de Christo dicit.*
61   *Uox Ecclesiae.*
62   *Uox Ecclesiae de Christo.*
63   *Uox Pauli de passione Christi.*
64   *Uox Ecclesiae ante baptismum paschalismatum.*
65   *Uox apostolorum ad populum.*
66   *Propheta monet credentes. Uox apostolica.*
67   *Propheta adventum Christi adnuntiat.*
68*   *Legendus ad lectionem Jonae prophetae et ad evangelium*
       Johannis. Uox Christi cum pateretur.
69   *Uox Ecclesiae ad Dominum.*
70   *Uox Christi ad Patrem.*
71   *Uox Ecclesiae de Christo ad Dominum.*
72   *Uox Christi ad Patrem de Judeis.*
73   *Uox Christi ad Patrem.*
74   *Uox Christi de judicio futuro.*
75   *Uox Ecclesiae ad Christum.*
76   *Uox Christi ad Patrem.*
77   *Uox Christi de Judeis.*
78   *Uox apostolorum post passionem Christi.*
79   *Uox apostolorum de Ecclesia ad Dominum.*
80   *Ad Pentecosten. Uox apostolorum.*
81   *Uox Ecclesiae de Judeis.*
82   *Uox Ecclesiae ad Dominum de Judeis et de vitiis hominum.*
83*   *Legendus ad evangelium Matthei. Ad eos qul fidem sunt con-*
       secuti; uox Christi ad Patrem de Ecclesia.
84   *Uox apostolica ad novellum populum.*
85   *Per jejunium. Uox Christi ad Patrem.*
86   *Uox apostolica de Ecclesia.*
87   *Uox Christi de Passione sua dicit ad Patrem.*
88   *Uox Christi ad Patrem de Judeis.*

89   *Uox apostolica ad Dominum.*
90*   *Uox Ecclesiae ad Christum. Legendus ad Evangelium Marci ubi temptatur Christus.*
91   *Uox Ecclesiae.*
92   Nothing. No heading.
93   *Uox Ecclesiae ad Dominum de Judeis.*
94   *Uox Chrisi ad apostolos.*
95   *Uox Ecclesiae vocantis.*
96   *Ad confessionem prophetia; uox Ecclesiae ad adventum Christi.*
97   *Uox ecclesiae ad Dominum et ad apostolos.*
98   *Uox apostolorum ad populum.*
99   *Uox apostolorum ad populum.*
100   *Uox Christi ad Patrem de requie sanctorum.*
101   *Uox Christi et Ecclesiae cum ascendisset ad Patrem.*
102   *Uox Ecclesiae ad populum suum.*
103   *Uox Ecclesiae laudat Dominum, opera eius narrans fideli populo suo.*
104   *Uox Christi ad apostolos de Judeis.*
105*   *Uox Ecclesiae ad apostolos. Legendus ad Exodum.*
106*   *Uox Christi de Judeis. Legendus ad Judicum et Numeri libros.*
107   *Uox Ecclesiae, ad superpositionem.*
108   *Uox Christi de Judeis.*
109   *Uox Ecclesiae de Patre et Filio.*
110   *Uox Ecclesiae de Christo cum laude.*
111   *Uox Ecclesiae de Christo.*
112   *Uox Ecclesiae quam dicit de fidelibus suis.*
113   *Uox apostolica cum Judeis increpat idola.*
114   *Uox Christi est.*
115   *Uox Pauli apostoli.*
116   *Uox apostolorum.*
117   *Uox Christi de se dicentis.*
118*   *Uox Christi ad Patrem et apostolorum de adversario et de Judeis, et de passione sua et de adventu suo et iudicio eius et regno.*
119*   *Uox Christi Ecclesiae.*
120*   *Uox Ecclesiae ad apostolos.*
121*   *Uox Ecclesiae ad apostolos.*
122*   *Uox Christi ad Patrem.*

123* *Uox apostolorum.*
124* *Uox Ecclesiae.*
125* *Uox apostolorum de impiis Judeis.*
126* *Uox Christi ad futuram Ecclesiam.*
127* *Propheta de Christo et de Ecclesia dicit.*
128* *Uox Ecclesiae.*
129* *Legendus ad lectionem Jonae prophetae.*
130* *Uox Ecclesiae rogantis.*
131* *Propheta ad Patrem de Christo dicit.*
132* *Uox Ecclesiae orantis.*
133* *Uox Ecclesiae in futuro.*
134 *Uox Ecclesiae operantibus quae increpat idola gentium quod nulla sunt.*
135 *Uox apostolorum ad synagogam.*
136 *Uox Ecclesiae.*
137 *Uox Christi ad Patrem.*
138 *Uox Ecclesiae ad populum conlaudans Deum.*
139 *Uox Christi est.*
140 *Uox Ecclesiae.*
141 Nothing. No heading.
142 Nothing. No heading.
143 *Uox Ecclesiae adversus diabolum cum satellitibus suis.*
144 *Uox Ecclesiae ad Christum.*
145 *Uox Christi ad populum.*
146 *Uox Ecclesiae et apostolorum ad novellum populum.*
147 *Uox Christi ad Ecclesiam.*
148 *Uox apostolorum ad populum.*
149 *Uox Christi ad fideles de futuro et de resurrectione.*
150 *Uox Christi post saeculum devictum in regno suo laetantis.*

THE PSALTER IN EARLY IRISH MONASTIC SPIRITUALITY

1. *Scope of this Essay*[1]

In this essay I intend to examine the role of the Psalter in early Irish monastic spirituality, that is during the pre-Norman period 432 to 1200 CE or so. A new era in the Irish Church began in the twelfth century with the advent of religious orders from the Continent. I concentrate on monastic spirituality. Though the sources at my disposal for this study cannot beyond doubt be described as monastic, the presumption is that in the main at least they originated in monasteries. And even though one or other text may describe a non-monastic devotional practice, what is said regarding the Psalter or divine office holds also for the monastic system.

The place of the divine office in the Irish monastic system can be approached from a variety of angles: for example, the number of hours, the psalms used at individual hours (the *cursus psalmorum*), the prayers and canticles.[2] In this essay, however, I confine my attention to just one aspect of the subject, namely the use of the psalms and the manner in which these were interpreted and studied.

---

1.   Some of the positions regarding the Psalter in the early Irish Church given in this paper are worked out in greater detail in some of my other studies as follows: 'Psalter Text and Psalter Study in the Early Irish Church (A.D. 600–1200)', pp. 19-142 in this volume); *Glossa in Psalmos: The Hiberno-Latin Gloss on the Psalms of Codex Palatinus Latinus 68 (Psalms 39:11–151:7)*. Critical Edition of the Text together with Introduction and Source Analysis (Studi e Testi, 310; Vatican City: Biblioteca Apostolica Vaticana, 1986) (Introduction, pp. 165-238 in this volume); 'Tradition and Creativity in Early Irish Psalm Exegesis', in P. Ní Chatháin and M. Richter (eds.), *Ireland and Europe: The Early Church* (Stuttgart: Klett-Cotta, 1983), pp. 338-89, pp. 239-301.

2.   On this see M. Curran, *The Antiphonary of Bangor* (Dublin: Irish Academic Press, 1983).

2. *Sources for the Study*[3]

In this study I shall use information drawn from a variety of sources. We are fortunate, indeed, in that we are exceptionally well informed on the Psalter and its place in the early Irish Church; more so, in fact, than for any other book of the Bible, including the Gospels.

To begin with we have Psalter texts. What is probably the oldest specimen of writing from Ireland (outside texts in Ogham) is found in some wax tablets with portions of the texts of Psalms 30–32. These tablets, now in the National Museum of Ireland, Dublin, were found in Springmount Bog, County Antrim, and were probably originally used as school exercises to initiate students through the psalms, as was customary, into the arts or writing and reading. They date from about 600 CE. Somewhat later than this (from about 630 CE) is the Gallican Psalter, together with psalm headings, in the manuscript known as the Cathach of St Columba, now in the library of the Royal Irish Academy, Dublin. We have further Psalters, or portions of Psalters, with the Gallican text of Irish origin dating from the ninth, tenth, eleventh and twelfth centuries—about seven in all. Some of these have the biblical text only; others are glossed in Latin to a lesser or greater degree. Notable in this regard is the Double Psalter now in Rouen (MS. Rouen, Bibl. Bibl. Publ. 24 [A.41], with the texts of the *Gallicanum* and the *Hebraicum* on facing pages, both with glosses. It was written in Ireland in the tenth century. There are fragments of a contemporary sister-codex of this in Dublin.

We also have texts of Irish origin with Jerome's Latin translation from the Hebrew—known as the *Hebraicum* or *Psalterium iuxta Hebraeos*. We have three full copies of this, with fragments of a fourth. They date from the eleventh and twelfth centuries. In the ninth century on the Continent Irish scholars interested themselves in the Greek text of the Psalter. We have, in fact, a letter by an Irishman working in the Milan area on the translation of the Psalter from Greek into Latin. It was intended to accompany an emendation of the Latin Psalter in accordance with the Greek, which unfortunately has been lost. We also have a text of a Greco-Latin Psalter by an Irishman, and a complete Greek Psalter, with a colophon in Greek saying it was copied by Sedulius Scottus ...*sêdylios skottos egô egrapsa.*

---

3.   See especially McNamara, 'Psalter Text', above in this volume, pp. 19-142.

We have a number of works from early Ireland concerning the interpretation of the Psalms. These early Irish scholars used the translation made by Julian of Eclanum (died after 454 CE) of the commentary of Theodore of Mopsuestia (died 428 CE), at least for Psalms 1–40, and also an Epitome of this Julian translation but not from Julian himself. The first section of this Epitome (for Pss. 1.11–16.11) seems to have been lost and it was replaced by a text with similar historical exegesis. In the Milan Codex Amb. C 301 inf. we have the Epitome, together with the full translation of Theodore's commentary on Pss. 1.1–16.11, and also sections of the commentary on Pss. 1–40. In the Turin MSS, Univ. Library F.IV, I, fasc. 5-6 we have further sections of the same translation. The Milan manuscript was written about 800–50 CE. Together with the Latin text it contains a rich body of glosses in Old Irish on the Latin texts. In the Vatican Codex Pal. lat. 68 we have a catena on the Psalms composed in Ireland or Northumbria (in a monastery of the St Columba union) about 700 CE, with excerpts from the Epitome of Julian, but also from works of Jerome, Eucherius, Augustine (under the name of Hilary) and some others. This work is incomplete, beginning with Ps. 39.11d.

From the late eighth century we have two catena-like compositions with commentaries on the Psalter accompanied by introductions. These are the *Eclogae tractatorum in Psalterium* and the section on the Psalter in the one-volume commentary on the Bible named *Das Bibelwerk* by Dr Bernhard Bischoff.[4] The *Eclogae* in the introduction excerpts from Hilary, Isidore, Augustine, Josephus, Junilius, Eucherius, Cassiodorus, Jerome and Ambrose, and in the commentary proper principally from the Epitome of Julian for Ps. 16.12 to the end, and from the full Latin translation of Theodore's commentary for the opening section. It also cites from Jerome's commentaries (*Commentarioli* and *Tractatus*) and from his translation from the Hebrew (the *Hebraicum*). In the introduction to the Psalter in *Das Bibelwerk* we have texts from Hilary, Isidore, Jerome, Cassiodorus and some other unidentified sources. In the commentary we have texts from Eucherius, Cassiodorus, Gregory (i.e.

---

4.   Bernhard Bischoff, 'Wendepunkte in der Geschichte der lateinischen Exegese im Frühmittelalter', *SE* 6 (1954), pp. 169-281; trans. C. O'Grady, 'Turning-Points in the History of Latin Exegesis in the Early Middle Ages', English translation in M. McNamara (ed.), *Biblical Studies: The Medieval Irish Contribution* (Proceedings of the Irish Biblical Association, 1; Dublin: Dominican Publications, 1976), pp. 74-160 (97-102).

Paterius's arrangement of Gregory's comments on the Psalms), the Julian Epitome (cited as a work of *Iosepus*) for Pss. 16.12 onwards and supplemented by a historical commentary, quite different from Theodore's, for the opening section (again presented as *Iosepus*). It also cites from some unidentified, but apparently Hiberno-Latin, commentary attributed to Hilarius. From about 800–50 CE we have the extensive Old Irish glosses on the Latin texts in Codex Amb. C 301 inf., already mentioned. From about the same period we have a portion of a *Treatise on the Psalter in Old Irish*, consisting of an introduction and part of the commentary on Psalm 1. Both sections are closely related to the Latin text of *Das Bibelwerk*. From the tenth century we have the extensive glosses in the Double Psalter of Rouen, of which mention has already been made, and the corresponding Dublin fragments. The glosses on the *Hebraicum* text are from the Epitome of Julian, supplemented for Pss. 1.1–16.12 by glosses from the same historical commentary used for this purpose in *Das Bibelwerk*. Other glosses on the *Hebraicum* are drawn from Cassiodorus. Augustine's works seem to have provided glosses for the *Gallicanum* text. In the so-called Psalter of Caimin, from about 1100 CE, we have portion of the biblical text of Psalm 118 (the *Beati*) in the *Gallicanum* rendering, with the corresponding text of the *Hebraicum* at the top, and right-hand marginal glosses drawn from Cassiodorus. The numerous glosses on the left-hand margins are almost verbatim identical with the text of Pal. lat. 68, although there are occasional glosses from the Epitome of Julian.

The early Irish Church also used certain psalm prefaces. Three of these are heavily glossed in Old Irish in the Codex Amb. C 301 inf., evidence of their study in the Irish schools. These are the two prefaces of Jerome—*Scio quosdam* (to the *Hebraicum*) and *Psalterium Romae dudum positus* (to the *Gallicanum*) and that falsely attributed to Bede, *David filius Iesse*. The same Milan codex also has St Basil's psalm preface in Rufinus's translation: *(Hieronimus dicit): Omnis scriptura divinitus inspirata*. The fact that it has no Irish glosses seems to indicate that it was not used in the Irish schools.

Psalm headings, *tituli psalmorum*, were very much a feature of medieval psalm study and devotion. Dom Pierre Salmon has edited six series of these from medieval Latin manuscripts.[5] The first, and most

---

5. P. Salmon (ed.), *Les 'Tituli Psalmorum' des manuscrits latins* (Collectanea Biblica Latina, 12; Rome: Abbaye Saint-Jérome; Vatican City: Vatican Library, 1959).

widely used, of the six is the series of mystical psalm headings from the Cathach, and consequently entitled 'the Series of St Columba'. It was early used in Ireland, if it did not originate there. Another series of psalm headings that was early used in Ireland, and most probably originated either in Ireland or the Celtic Church in Northumbria, was that entitled *De titulis Psalmorum* falsely ascribed to Bede (in Migne, *PL* 93, 483-1098). This work combines historical headings, mainly dependent on the Epitome of Julian, with the St Columba series, to which a moral application is occasionally added. The same combination of historical and mystical headings is found in the introductory material prefixed to each psalm in the so-called *Psalter of Charlemagne* (Ms. Paris, Bibl. Nat. lat. 13159), composed on the Continent between 795 and 800 CE, and in this material dependent on Irish tradition.

Early Irish Devotion to the Psalter

Apart from the manuscripts bearing texts of the Psalters or commentaries on it, we have abundant evidence for the central role of the Psalter in Irish monastic life and Irish devotion from other Latin and vernacular Irish sources.

Monastic rules pay attention to it from various points of view, especially from that of the recitation of the divine office. Columbanus (died 615 CE) treats of this in the seventh chapter of his 'Monks' Rule' (*Regula Monachorum*)[6]. The 'Rule of Ailbe'[7] from the Old Irish period 600–900 CE, gives personal devotion to the divine office, with special attention to the *Beati* (Ps. 118), as part of the life of the monk: 'Lection and celebration (of the divine office) with invocation of the Son of God... The diligent fulfilment of the canonical hours' swarms of rules are enumerated' (vv. 20, 22). 'Let him be constant at prayer; his canonical hours let him not forget them... A hundred genuflections for him at the "Beati" at the beginning of the day before his questions, thrice fifty (psalms) dearer than (other) works, with a hundred genuflections every hour of vespers' (vv. 16-17).

The text known as 'The Monastery of Tallaght'[8] has much to say on

---

6. In G.S.M. Walker (ed.), *Sancti Columbani Opera* (SLH, 2; Dublin Institute for Advanced Studies, 1970), pp. 122-43.

7. J. O'Neill (ed.), 'The Rule of Ailbe of Emly', *Ériu* 3 (1907), pp. 92-115.

8. E.J. Gwynn and W.J. Purton (eds.), 'The Monastery of Tallaght', *PRIA* 29C (1911), pp. 115-79.

the practices of the *Céli Dé*, of their use of the psalms and in particular of the *Beati*. The *Beati* was used in a variety of devotional practices, especially in conjunction with the *Magnificat* and the Hymn to St Michael. 'The Monastery of Tallaght' text dates from about 840 CE. From the roughly contemporary 'Teaching of Mael Ruain'[9] we learn of the practice of Muirchertach mac Olcobhiar, erenagh of Clonfert, of saying the *Beati* 12 times in place of the 150 psalms, because he knew that there were more of the monks or penitents who knew the *Beati* by heart than knew the Psalms.

The same Psalm 118, *Beati immaculati in via*, 'Blessed are the undefiled in the way' was also used as protection on a journey (by reason of the inclusion of the term in its opening words) and was also believed to have special efficacy for freeing souls from torment.[10] In some manuscripts of the Psalter each of the 22 subsections is set off and has a special decorated initial letter as if it were a separate psalm. In the Psalter of Charlemagne each subsection of it has special introductory material, as is also the case in the early catena of Codex Pal. lat. 68. The so-called Psalter of Caimin may never have contained more than this sole psalm with its glosses.

From the documents connected with the *Céli Dé* movement of the early ninth century we can glean a little further information on the place of the psalms in Irish devotion and study. It appears that occasionally instruction accompanied the recitation of the psalms. One *Céli Dé* leader is represented as asking another, Mael Ruain of Tallaght, whether it would be enough to recite 50 psalms (that is, daily, not the entire Psalter) if there chanced to be instruction along with them. Mael Ruain replied that he considered the whole contents of the Psalter as not too much of a task.[11] Each brother had different tasks to perform in a monastic community, but the additional labour of each on top of this was the 'Three Fifties' (an Irish title for the entire Psalter). The 'Rule of the *Céli Dé*',[12] is interested in the rights (as well as the obligations) of a cleric in smaller churches and parishes. He had the right to sustenance. As obligations he had to administer the rites of baptism and communion

---

9. E. Gwynn (ed.), in *The Rule of Tallaght, Hermathena* 44 (second supplemental volume) (1927), pp. 2-63; no. 37, 22f.

10. See C. Plummer (ed.), *Vitae Sanctorum Hiberniae* (2 vols.; Oxford: Clarendon Press, 1968 [1910]), I, p. clxxix, and n. 2.

11. Gwynn and Purton (eds.), 'The Monastery of Tallaght', p. 133.

12. Gwynn (ed.), *The Rule of Tallaght*, no. 58, pp. 80-81.

and intercessory prayer for the living and the dead, and Mass every Sunday and every chief solemnity (*primshollamhan*) and every chief feast: 'celebration of all the canonical hours, and chanting of the hundred and fifty psalms daily', unless hindered by teaching or hearing confessions.[13] Teaching and study is again stressed a little later in the same Rule of the *Céli Dé*. There should be a bishop in every chief state in Erin for various offices, including the setting of boys and girls to study and piety: 'for if boys do not study at all seasons the whole church will die, and there will be no belief but black paganism in the land of Erin'. Offering one's children to God to study is regarded as offering tithes. Study began with the Psalter, and the teacher was entitled to the rewards of his labours. In the words of the same rule:

> Any one moreover with whom the boys study who are thus offered to God and to Patrick has a claim to reward and fee at the proper seasons, namely, a milch-cow as remuneration for (teaching) the Psalms with their hymns and canticles and lections, and the rites of baptism and communion and intercession, together with the knowledge of the ritual generally, till the student be capable of receiving Orders... The milch-cow is made over immediately after the student has publicly proved his knowledge of the Psalms and hymns, and after the public proof of his knowledge of the ritual the fee and habit are due. Moreover the doctor or bishop before whom proof in the Psalms has been made is entitled to a collation of beer and food for five persons the same night.[14]

The psalms, we can see, were a matter for the classroom as well as for the choir. But the one does not appear to have taken from devotion to the other. Mystical reasons were advanced why each of the canonical hours was celebrated. Thus, for instance, in an Irish text now in Trinity College, Dublin (MS 1336 or H.3.17):[15] 'Sext, for then Adam sinned and then Christ was placed upon the Cross...' Similar or identical ideas are put at much greater length, and in prose and verse, in a tractate on the Canonical Hours in the *Leabhar Breac*.[16] This text, in Gaelic, seems to have been composed in the eleventh or twelfth century. The ideas

---

13. Gwynn (ed.), *The Rule of Tallaght*, no. 58, pp. 80-81.

14. Gwynn (ed.), *The Rule of Tallaght*, no. 62, pp. 82-83.

15. R.I. Best (ed.), 'The Canonical Hours. H. 3. 17. Cid ara ndéntar ceilebrad isna tráthaib-sea...', *Ériu* 3 (1907), p. 166.

16. R.I. Best (ed.), 'The Lebar Brecc Tractate on the Canonical Hours', in O. Bergin and C. Marstrander (eds.), *Miscellany presented to Kuno Meyer* (Halle a.S.: Max Niemeyer, 1912), pp. 142-66.

behind these texts are already present in the Antiphonary of Bangor (late seventh century).

Neither the obligation of recitation nor the association of the Psalms with the classroom seems to have diminished genuine love for the Psalter. On the contrary, this love probably increased the desire to learn more about the meaning of the Psalms. The monks could scarcely conceive of a Christian, much less a monastic, life without the canonical praises of the Creator. This shows through in such a composition as the *Navigatio Brendani*.[17] In this work, with its account of the chanting of the divine office, the prolonged fasts and such like, the institutions and practices of monastic life in an Irish environment are faithfully reproduced. The author is painting a picture of an ideal monastic life. His purpose was not solely, nor even primarily, to describe the wonders of the ocean.[18]

We find the same love of the Psalter in a poem by the scholar monk Máel Ísu Ua Brollcháin (died 1086), who got his monastic training in Armagh in the north of Ireland but later journeyed south to the monastic school of Lismore where he chanced on the old and tattered copy of the Psalter through which at the age of seven he had been initiated into reading and writing and the secret mysteries of the work. He addresses the tattered manuscript as Crinóc—'Dear little, old thing' in a poem, part of which reads:

> Crinóc, lady of measured melody,
> > not young, but with modest maiden mind,
> together once in Niall's northern land
> > we slept, we two, as man and womankind.

> You came and slept with me for that first time,
> > skilled wise amazon annihilating fears
> and I a fresh-faced boy, not bent as now,
> > a gentle lad of seven melodious years...

> Your counsel is ever there to hand,
> > we choose it, following you in everything:

17. C. Selmer (ed.), *Navigatio Sancti Brendani Abbatis from Early Latin Manuscripts (with Introduction and Notes)* (Publications in Mediaeval Studies; Notre Dame: University of Notre Dame Press, 1959; reprint Dublin: Four Courts Press, 1989).

18. For this judgment see J. Kenney, *The Sources for the Early History of Ireland. I. Ecclesiastical* (Columbia University Press, 1929; repr. Dublin: Four Courts Press, 1997), p. 415.

> love of your word is the best of loves,
>   our gentle conversation with the King...

> Seeking the presence of elusive God
>   wandering we stray, but the way is found,
> following the mighty melodies that with you
>   throughout the pathways of the world resound.

> Not ever silent, you bring the word of God
>   to all who in the present world abide,
> and then through you, through finest mesh,
>   man's earnest prayer to God is purified.[19]

The substance of the sentiments found in this vernacular Gaelic poem (so beautifully rendered by Professor James Carney) reflects the praises of the Psalter as expressed in the earlier Christian psalm prefaces, both of East and West. Máel Ísu may well have been dependent on one of them, for instance on Cassiodorus's words as abbreviated in the Preface to the Psalter in *Das Bibelwerk*: 'O truly glittering book, radiant speech, remedy of the wounded heart, honeycomb of the interior man, the image of things spiritual, language of virtue; it bows down the proud and raises up the lowly'.[20] Máel Ísu, in any event, had pondered deeply on the place of the Psalter in monastic and Christian life.

We find similar evidence for the place of the Psalter in monastic and clerical life in the Lives of the Irish Saints,[21] the testimony here being all the more eloquent in that it is incidental. These again note that seven was the usual age to begin learning and reading. They speak of the daily round of devotion comprised in the celebration of the canonical hours, and make mention of individual hours. We read of the Psalter being sung antiphonally on a journey, for example, in the *Vita sancti Carthagi*, par. 9.[22] The chant was so sweet that St Mochuta was spellbound by it. Never had he heard such sweet singing as he had from those holy clerics.

Irish vernacular secular literature also makes mention of the central role of the Psalter to monastic life. The twelfth-century composition known as *Agallamh na Seanorach*, 'The Colloquy of the Elders', tells

---

19. J. Carney (ed. and trans.), *Medieval Irish Lyrics Selected and Translated* (Dublin: The Dolmen Press, 1967), pp. 74-79, and pp. xxvii-xxviii.

20. Latin text edited by M. Sheehy in McNamara, 'Psalter Text', Appendix IV above p. 129.

21. See references in Plummer (ed.), *Vitae Sanct. Hib.*, I, pp. cxiv-cxvi.

22. Plummer (ed.), *Vitae Sanct. Hib.*, I, pp. 172-73.

how Caoilte and Oisin, the remnants of the ancient Irish Fenian warriors wore permitted to live on to experience the advent of Patrick and Christianity to Ireland. In one of the episodes Caoilte encounters two Christian priests, two eminent presbyters of St Patrick's *familia*. In true clerical fashion they were 'performing all the order of the serene dominical canon (that is, reciting or chanting the divine office), with mutual praising of the Creator'. In the same text we read of three young clerics who came out fishing, saying their prescribed hours as they fished, their 'euphonic readings' as Caoilte describes them. Caoilte inquires as to the reason why the eight canonical hours are recited daily and is told by the priest Colman that it is for the cleansing for the eight faults that cleave to body and soul in every man. The text goes on to spell this out. 'Prime against immoderate gluttony; Tierce against anger born of many causes...pleasant and profitable Vespers we oppose to sore despair... Matins of God's atoning Son, against enslaving sullen pride. Mayest thou, O judicial King, O Jesus, save me for the sake of the eight!'[23]

The use of the Psalter does not appear to have been confined to pious clerics. It features also in the *Aislinge Meic Conglinne* ('The Vision of Mac Conglinne'),[24] a satire of Irish society, both clerical and lay, composed about 1100 CE. It tells of the journey of the goliardic cleric Ainér MacConglinne from the north of Ireland to the monastery of Cork in the south. In the guest house of Cork, Ainér is said to have taken down his book satchel, brought out his Psalter, and to have begun saying his psalms. And, so the story continues, it is recorded that the scholar's voice was heard a thousand paces beyond the city, as he sang his psalms through spiritual mysteries, in laud and stories and various kinds, in diapsalms and synpsalms, and sets of ten, with poems and canticles at the end of each fifty. Later, we read, Ainér preached to his hosts, presumably on the Psalter: 'he washed his hands, took his book satchel, brought out his Psalter and began preaching to his hosts'. Texts such as this can be very indicative on the role of the Psalter in the medieval community, and possibly in the parish community as well as in the monastic.

The degree to which the Psalter had passed beyond the monastery

23. English translation by Standish O'Grady in *Silva Gadelica*, II (2 vols.; London: Williams & Norgate, 1892), pp. 176-78.

24. K. Meyer (ed.), *Aislinge Meic Conglinne: The Vision of Mac Conglinne* (London, 1892), pp. 12-13, 58-59, translation reprinted in T.P. Cross and C.H. Slover (eds.), *Ancient Irish Tales* (London, 1936), pp. 554-55, 570.

and ecclesiastical settings in mediaeval Ireland is further evidenced by the fact that the term itself (*saltair* in Irish) has come to designate even secular compositions, for example, the Psalter of Cashel which is a legal tract. The ancient Irish warrior Fionn Mac Cumhaill was believed to have been a prophet. It is, presumably, because of this that he is made to refer to himself as 'the first psalmist of the Gael'.[25] That psalmody was identified in the popular mind with Christian praise of God is neatly expressed by the words addressed in the sixteenth-century poem of the Fenian hero Oisin to awake from sleep to the new Christian age: 'Oisin, long has been your sleep; rise up, and listen to the Psalms.'[26]

After these preliminaries on the subject we can now proceed to examine the evidence on the place of the Psalter within the early Irish monastic system.

4. *The Spiritual Interpretation of the Psalms*

a. *The Psalter in the Divine Office*

One of the principle uses of the Psalter in Irish monastic tradition, as indeed in all monastic tradition, was of course as the core of the divine office. In a monograph soon to be published, Michael Curran, M.S.C. makes a study of the divine office in early Ireland, drawing especially on the evidence of the *Antiphonary of Bangor*.[27] What is said in this section draws almost exclusively on this study.

As far as can be ascertained, the divine office in Ireland was structured as: psalmody, prayer, reading. With regard to the five day hours (that is, *secunda, tertia, sexta, nona, vespertina*), and combining the date from the *Rule* of Columbanus and the Antiphonary, we can say that the structure of each of them was as follows: (1) three psalms; (2) *Gloria in excelsis* at Vespers; (3) Collect; (4) *Oratio communis*. In the *Navigatio Brendani* set psalms are twice given as follows for the three psalms of the day hours: Sext, Psalms 66; 69; 115; None, Psalms 129; 132; 147; Vespers, Psalms 64; 103; 112; *Vigilia matutina* (= *secunda*, Prime), Psalms 50; 62; 89; Terce, Psalms 46; 53; 114.

---

25. E. MacNeill (ed.), *Duanaire Finn*, no. 34, in *Duanaire Finn: The Book of the Lays of Finn*, part 1 (Irish Texts Society, 7; London: Irish Texts Society, 1908), pp. 85, 199.

26. G. Murphy (ed.), *Duanaire Finn*, no. 57, in *Duanaire Finn: The Book of the Lays of Fionn*, part 2 (Irish Texts Society, 38; London: Irish Texts Society, 1933), pp. 204-205.

27. See Curran, *Antiphonary*.

Michael Curran notes that the psalms used for Terce, Sext and None in this system are well chosen to express the traditional understanding of these hours of prayer as commemorations of the passion, death, descent, and final triumph of Christ. In the psalms for Terce (Pss. 45, 53, 114) the central theme is the glorification of Christ, following his total trust in God throughout his passion and death.

Fr Curran goes on to note that there is agreement between the office we find in the *Navigatio* and that of Columbanus and the Antiphonary of Bangor in so far as their description of the psalmody of the day hours goes. This permits us to surmise that the office of the *Navigatio* was not confined to just one monastery and that even in the seventh century the day hours at Bangor were celebrated as described in the *Navigatio Brendani*. He also remarks that this singular office originated in an insular development of a tradition which goes back ultimately to the writings of Cassian and possibly to the monasticism of southern Gaul. The psalms chosen for morning prayer and Prime (or *secunda*) were those already assigned to the conclusion of the morning prayer vigil and to the *novella solemnitas* in the East at the end of the fourth century as this is described by Cassian. Furthermore, the choice of psalms for the hours of Terce, Sext and None was determined by the Christian interpretation of these hours, as found in Cassian and other early authors.

In this case, we may note, a certain Christian interpretation of these psalms would be ascertained by their set place in the divine office and by the tradition within which this was formed and maintained. The particular understanding of the psalms in question would, presumably, be brought to mind as they were read within the tradition which believed a particular canonical hour was celebrated at that particular hour rather than at another one—to use the words of the *Leabhar Breac* treatise on the canonical hours.

That such a tradition of interpretation existed in Ireland may well be so. As far as I can ascertain, however, we do not have actual documentary evidence of this interpretation of the psalms in question in the material that has come down to us. But this is not a definitive argument that the particular line of interpretation did not exist. The Irish tradition of christological interpretation we are now to consider was formed before the divine office as found in the *Navigatio Brendani* was compiled.

b. *Irish Christological Psalm Interpretation*
We have two major texts on the presence of the spiritual and christological interpretation of the Psalms in early Ireland. The first is found in the introduction to the *Treatise on the Psalter in Old Irish*,[28] the other in the St Columba series of psalm headings. The former text comes immediately after the treatment of the different meanings to be found in the psalms. It is stated that there are two historical senses or meanings in the psalms, a spiritual meaning and a moral one. The spiritual meaning refers to Christ, to the earthly and the heavenly Church, while the moral meanings refers to every saint. The text continues:

> Of what did the prophecy of the psalms foretell? Not difficult. Of the birth of Christ and of his baptism, and of his passion, and of his resurrection, and of his ascension, and of his sitting on the right hand of God the Father in heaven, of the invitation of the heathen to faith, of the thrusting of Judah into unbelief, of the increase of every justice, of the spurning of every injustice, of the malediction of sinners, of the coming of Christ to judge the quick and the dead.[29]

Here we are presented with a list of 12 items prophesied in the Psalms, five more given by St Hilary in his introduction to the Psalter (*Instructio Psalmorum* no. 6),[30] namely: Christ's humanity (*corporalitas*), passion, death, resurrection, glory, kingdom and judgment. Irish tradition also lists seven things prophesied of Christ: his birth, baptism, crucifixion, burial, resurrection, ascension and his coming to the final judgment. This list is found in the early Irish text, the *Scúap Chrábaid* ('Broom of Devotion'), possibly from about 650 CE,[31] and Irish litanies.[32] The longer list in the *Old-Irish Treatise* tends to spell out what it had just before given as the spiritual and moral meanings of the Scripture.

---

28. *OIT*.

29. *OIT*, pp. 30-33.

30. A. Zingerle (ed.), Hilary, *Tractatus super Psalmos* (CSEL, 22; Vienna, 1891), p. x.

31. K. Meyer (ed.), 'Stories and Songs from Irish MSS. VI. Colchu na Duindechda's Scúap Chrábaid or Besom of Devotion', *Otia Merseiana* 2 (Liverpool, 1900–1901), pp. 92-105 (97). In an Old Irish gloss on *ut impleam verbum Dei* ('that I might fulfil the word of God') of Col. 1.25 in a Würzburg manuscript (*Thes. Pal.*, I, p. 67), we are told that this means 'the seven things that have been prophesied of Christ'. What these are is evidently presumed known. The gloss is from about 750 CE. See also Meyer, *Aislinge* in *OIT*.

32. C. Plummer (ed.), *Irish Litanies* (London: Henry Bradshaw Society, 1925).

We have already spoken of the St Columba series of psalm headings, found as headings to the psalms in the Cathach of St Columba. It must have been used in Ireland during the sixth century at the latest. Its history cannot be traced back beyond the earliest text in which it occurs, that is, the Cathach. We do not know whether it was composed in Ireland or elsewhere. In any event it has its roots in very early Christian tradition. It has some of the interpretations of the psalms found in Tertullian's writings and also has connections with the writings or interpretations of Justin, Origen, the early baptismal liturgies, and the *Enarrationes* of Augustine. It has some references which appear to be to liturgical observances. We are still unable to situate it exactly in any particular liturgy. It may have been originally composed to go with a Psalter text used in the divine office or in other liturgical observances.

This Columba series is noted for its christological orientation. The greater part of the psalms are taken as having been spoken by Christ, the Church or the apostles, and if some are placed on the lips of the psalmist-prophet (as 24 are) it is generally for the purpose of prophesying of Christ. Thus: 'The voice of Christ to the Father' (Pss. 3, 12 etc.), 'The voice of Christ to the Church' (115), 'The voice of the Apostles when Christ suffered' (59), 'The voice of the Apostles after Christ ascended to the Father' (46), 'The voice of the Church to the Lord' (69), 'The voice of the Church after baptism' (22), 'The Church gives praise to Christ' (9), 'The prophet warns believers' (66), 'The apostolic voice' (66).

Headings such as these would have facilitated the use of the psalms as Christian prayer. And together with this widely used series of St Columba, Irish Psalters also have some introductory material from such writings as the commentary of Cassiodore which would serve the same purpose.

The commentary material being used in Ireland, and which I have already listed, would also be of help as in it there are some references on the testimony the psalms bore to Christ and to Christian life. However, it would be quite misleading to regard the Irish commentary material as christologically oriented. In fact, the exegetical writings being used in Ireland and even those composed there differ markedly from other medieval commentaries on the psalms such as those of Alcuin, Florus Diaconus, Paschasius Radbertus, Prudentius of Troyes, Remigius of Auxerre and Walafrid Strabo. These commentaries were avowedly allegorical. They were of the sort that would serve as aids to the liturgical use of the psalms. Irish commentaries, on the contrary, were of a different sort. Their authors shied away from this kind of exegesis and when they used it they most often brought it explicitly under the control of the literal sense, which they regarded as primary.

5. *The Primacy of the Literal Sense*

It may be that allegorical exegesis was practised to a greater extent in Ireland than is evident from our extant commentary material. In the introduction to the Psalter in *Das Bibelwerk*, composed about 800 CE, the question is asked: 'Should the Psalms be read according to the historical (i.e. literal) or mystical sense?'[33] The answer given is that they should be read according to the mystical sense, as Ambrose says: 'If you seriously study the Psalms you will take on a hard task, since approached from the historical point of view they have a twofold meaning'. This is followed by citations attributed to Jerome, and Hilary on the historical approach to the psalms. Even here, then, despite the text attributed to Ambrose, the stress is on the historical approach, with mention of a twofold historical sense. In fact, *Das Bibelwerk* itself in its treatment of the first psalm gives a first historical meaning and a second historical meaning (both on David's day) to this psalm, followed by a spiritual, mystical, meaning (on Christ) and finally a moral meaning. The introduction to the *Eclogae tractatorum in Psalterium* is roughly contemporary with the *Bibelwerk*, and there the same texts on how the psalms are to be read are found again.[34] The stress in the *Eclogae* is clearly on the historical approach. The primacy on the historical sense is put more forcefully in the Old Irish glosses on Julian's Latin translation of Psalm 1 of Theodore's commentary. Irish tradition referred to this translation and the Epitome as the 'historical' commentary. One Old Irish gloss on Psalm 1 says that it is the historical sense (in Irish *stoir*)[35] which is the most desirable to understand. Other glosses immediately following remark that other interpreters of the Psalms may draw out other senses from them, that is, the spiritual (mystical, christological) and the moral, provided these are not at variance with the basic,

33. Sheehy (ed.), Appendix IV in McNamara, 'Psalter Text', p. 132 in this volume.

34. Sheehy (ed.), Appendix III in McNamara, 'Psalter Text', pp. 126-27 in this volume.

35. *Thes. Pal.*, I, p. 13.

historical understanding. This approach, then, clearly subordinates all senses to the primary, historical, one. This same point is made again in glosses on Psalm 21 in the same Milan Text.[36] Here the Epitome of Julian had modified somewhat in its heading the non-messianic interpretation of Theodore, an interpretation found in the body of the comment of Psalm 21 as distinct from the introductory material. An Irish gloss on the text says that according to the historical sense (*stoir*) the psalm refers to David when he complained with regard to Absalom; it refers to Christ, however, according to the mystic sense. So much for the situation about 800 CE. From the catena in Codex Pal. lat. 68, composed about 700 CE, we gather that the subordination was by then old. In the body of this work's comment on Psalm 44, the psalm is understood not of Christ but of Solomon. A comment on Ps. 44.1 consequently runs: 'What follows refers to Solomon historically, to Christ spiritually, and morally to the saint'. The non-messianic exposition of Psalm 109 in the same catena is no different. Thus, on Ps. 109.3 *'Before the dawn'*, that is ('historically speaking', understood) before Saul; in the spiritual sense these words refer to Christ, as Jerome says. A text of Jerome is then cited, but one which this doctor would have taken as the literal, not the spiritual, meaning of the verse.

Many more texts could be added to strengthen what has here been said as to the theoretical subordination of the spiritual to the historical (literal) meaning. The point will, however, become clearer still from a consideration of the actual exegetical material and the exegesis of the messianic psalms within this.

6. *Historical Commentary Material in Ireland*

The bulk of the Irish commentary material on the Psalms, listed in the second section above, is mainly concerned with the historical interpretation. This is especially the case with the Theodorean material in the Milan and Turin texts. This also holds true for the catena-like commentary in Codex Pal. lat. 68 from 700 CE, and likewise the commentary section of the *Eclogae tractatorum in Psalterium*, which culls mainly from the commentary of Theodore and the Epitome of Julian. This historical commentary is also excerpted from in the commentary section of *Das Bibelwerk*, and even in sections where *Das Bibelwerk* is not giving

---

36. *Thes. Pal.* I, p. 125.

historical exegesis it is not necessarily allegorical; it is also interested in obscurities in the biblical text which show through in the Latin translation. The Irish glosses on the Milan commentary in Cod. Amb. C 301 inf. is as historically oriented as the Latin text upon which it comments. The glosses on the Double Psalter of Rouen are in good part from the historical Julian Epitome and the equally historical commentary that supplements this for Psalms 1–16. The glosses in the so-called Psalter of Caimin are for the greater part almost identical with texts from Pal. lat. 68. The introductory material in the so-called Psalter of Charlemagne and the historical section of the *Tituli Psalmorum* of Pseudo-Bede tell the same story. The only apparent reason for this preponderance of historical commentary material seems to be an Irish predilection for this type of exposition. It was not that no other sort was known to them. They did have access to the commentaries of Jerome and Cassiodorus, and to others (such as Augustine's) it would also appear. But when they use these it is as subsidiary sources to the works of historical interpretation, whether these were from Antioch or elsewhere. The Irish Psalm commentary catenae are selective in keeping with the interests of the early Irish schools.

7. Irish Exegesis of the Messianic Psalms

The primacy accorded to the historical meaning can be seen especially in the manner in which the traditionally accepted messianic psalms were interpreted in Irish tradition. The tendency in the Church, both East and West, from early times has been to multiply the number of messianic psalms or to regard all the psalms as prophecies of Christ, or at least as speaking of him. This went beyond the New Testament evidence which uses only a certain number of psalms, or of psalm verses, as speaking of Christ.

We know that the Antiochene Theodore of Mopsuestia did not regard this New Testament evidence as in all cases requiring Christians to believe that the psalms or verses in question were composed as direct prophecies of Christ. Theodore actually regarded only four psalms as directly messianic, in the sense that they were intended in their original composition as direct prophecies of Christ. These 4 were (in the Septuagint and Vulgate numbering) Psalms 2, 8, 44 and 109. Such psalms as Psalms 15 and 21 were explicitly excluded from his list.

The Epitome of Julian follows Theodore's interpretation except that it tries to mollify his understanding of Psalm 21 by introducing the Latin biblical psalm heading and by referring the reader to Christ's words on the cross for the original intention of the psalm.

Throughout, the Old Irish Milan glosses on Theodore's commentary and the Epitome of Julian reproduce the meaning of the originals, even with regard to the ending of Theodore's exposition of Psalm 15, which is not altogether clear. One Old Irish gloss says: 'The apostle (i.e. Peter) did apply the Psalm according to the sense in which the prophet (i.e. the original psalmist) uttered it'.[37] We have already considered the Old-Irish gloss on Psalm 21 of the Epitome (6.5 above).

It is curious that this Antiochene position should be accepted so wholeheartedly in the early Irish Church. What is much less easy to understand, however, is that there was also another tradition of exegesis in the same Church that went far beyond the position of Theodore, and in practice denied the existence of any messianic psalm at all! This tradition of exegesis is actually very well represented in our sources. It is found is glosses on the Rouen Psalter, in the introductory material of the so-called Psalter of Charlemagne, in the Pseudo-Bedan *Tituli Psalmorum* and in the commentary found in Codex Pal. lat. 68. For instance, Psalm 15, not accepted as messianic by Theodore, is accepted as non-messianic also in the glosses of the Rouen Psalter—glosses that are quite independent of either Theodore or Julian. These glosses understand the psalm as referring either to David or to Hezekiah after his illness. This, too, holds true for the key verse, v. 10: 'You shall not permit your holy one see corruption'. The Pseudo-Bedan *Tituli* understand the Psalm of Hezekiah: 'A Prayer of Hezekiah in relation to his illness'. The Psalter of Charlemagne combines both: 'Hezekiah or David on the restoration of his inheritance'.

In the glosses of the Rouen Psalter Psalm 2 is interpreted of David. This is also the case in the headings of the Pseudo-Bedan *Tituli* and of the so-called Psalter of Charlemagne.

The catena of Codex Pal. lat. 68 begins only with Psalm 39. We need have no doubt, however, but that the lost section was along the tradition found in the glosses of the Rouen Psalter and in the headings of Pseudo-Bede and the Psalter of Charlemagne. In Psalms 44 and 109 the catena in Pal. lat. 68 has a detailed and sustained non-messianic interpretation. Psalm 44 is understood in the historical sense as referring to Solomon;

---

37. *Thes. Pal.*, I, p. 99.

only in the spiritual sense would it refer to Christ. Psalm 109 is understood of David and his contemporaries (Saul and Samuel) in the historical sense; of Christ only in spiritual sense. A very interesting feature
of the exposition put before us in the catena is that by the time the work
was compiled the non-messianic interpretation must have been well
established. Although the non-messianic interpretation is recorded in
detail, twice we are told in the text, either by the compiler or a copyist,
that it is a wrong interpretation and that the true one is the christological. The dissenting hand writes: 'This entire Psalm refers to Christ,
although some interpret it ineptly in a historical manner' (to which is
added for Ps. 44 'as referring to Solomon'). This takes us into a new
dimension in early Irish Psalm exegesis.

8. *Creative Seventh-Century Irish Psalm Exegesis*

There are indications in our sources that the seventh century was a
creative one for Irish psalm exegesis and that in the course of that century special positions were worked out specifically with regard to the
historical exegesis of the Psalms. The Davidic and Antiochene primary
reference of the Psalms, the messianic interpretation took positions
which would lead in time to the formulation of the fourfold sense of
Scripture we find in texts from about the year 800 CE.

The exposition of the Psalms we find in Codex Pal. lat. 68 provides
us with a more or less fixed point from which to start. This work was
compiled about 700 CE. We arrive at this date on the one hand by its
almost certain use of Adamnan's *De locis sanctis*, composed about
683–86 CE, and on the other by the presence of Northumbrian glosses
which are regarded as being no later than the early eighth century. We
have seen that the compiler of the work was reproducing, recording, not
creating. He disagreed with some of what he recorded—supposing that
the observation in the exposition of Psalms 44 and 109 is the compiler's. We can legitimately presume that the material in the catena is a
half-century or so older than 700 CE. This would take us to 650 CE or
so, a date that records well with the mention of *Romani* in the text. The
Romani of the Paschal controversy were active about this date.

One noteworthy feature of the exposition of the catena is the combination of a twofold historical reference for individual psalms. A number
of them are seen to refer either to David and his time or to later Jewish
history—this second reference often being that of the Antiochene

school. The first, Davidic, reference seems to represent some other school of interpretation, one which tended to understand the psalms as referring in the first instance to David and his period, particularly to his trials from Saul and Absalom. We cannot say whether this form of exegesis came to Ireland from outside (as the Antiochene interpretation did), or whether it was developed in Ireland. Whether one or the other, it appears that a group called the *Romani* favoured it. The exegetical opinions of this group are mentioned three times in the catena (in the introductory material for Pss. 49, 52 and 54) and twice their interpretation took the particular psalm to speak of David and his trials from Saul.

The radical and non-messianic interpretation of Psalms 2, 8, 44 and 109 seems to have been unknown in Christian circles outside of Ireland. There is a good probability that with regard to Psalms 2, 44 and 109 at least the non-messianic understanding was arrived at in Ireland itself by scholars working on Jewish traditions transmitted to them in the commentaries of Theodore and Jerome and in the Epitome of Julian. Jerome in one of his works interpreted Psalm 44, in accord with Jewish tradition, as referring to Solomon. Theodore records Jewish interpretations of Psalms 2 and 109. Irish writers, with their love for nature poetry, could easily see Psalm 8 for what it really is: a species of nature poem, in praise of divine providence and human dignity.[38]

Finally with regard to the senses of Scripture: the dual historical reference—to David's day and later Jewish history—is recorded in the exposition of Pal. lat. 68 but not worked into a theory. The acceptance of this dual reference could easily lead to the peculiar formulation of the fourfold sense of scripture we find in the *Old-Irish Treatise* on the Psalter, composed in the early eighth century. The formulation is as follows:

> There are four things that are necessary in the Psalms, to wit, the first story (*stoir* = historical meaning), the second story, the sense (*síens* = spiritual or mystical sense) and the morality (= moral sense). The first story refers to David and to Solomon and to above-mentioned persons, to Saul, to Absalom, to the persecutors besides. The second story to Hezekiah, to the people, to the Maccabees. The sense (= spiritual sense) (refers) to Christ, to the earthly and heavenly church. The morality (refers) to every saint.[39]

38. In *PL* 93, col. 489C.
39. *OIT*, pp. 30-31.

What is peculiar to this is not that it has a fourfold sense of Scripture. Such a schema was common and became accepted later in the well-known quatrain on *littera, allegoria, morale, anagogia.* What is unique here is the twofold historical sense, the first referring to David and his time, the other to later Jewish history. This seems Irish. And it is not something just said here in passing. We find reference to a multiple (or twofold) historical sense in the introductions of both the *Eclogae* and the Psalter section of *Das Bibelwerk*—both Hiberno-Latin works roughly contemporary with the *Old-Irish Treatise.* Furthermore, the twofold historical sense is worked out in great detail in the exposition of Psalm 1, both in the *Old-Irish Treatise* and in *Das Bibelwerk.*

I believe the explanation lies in an inner development within Irish exegetical learning, arising from the confluence of two independent historical traditions of interpretation.

9. The Biblical Psalter Texts in Ireland

What has just been said on Irish exegetical activity should not be divorced from the evidence available to us on the fortunes of the biblical Psalter text in Ireland.

St Patrick's Psalter text was Old Latin, of the type being used in Gaul. We can presume that the Old Latin was also the first Psalter text to be used in Ireland. This, however, must have soon been superseded by Jerome's revision known as the *Gallicanum* (also referred to as the Vulgate text), of which we have a number of Irish manuscripts (see 5.2 above). Two Irish manuscripts, in fact, are among the five basic ones used by the Benedictine editors for the critical edition of the *Gallicanum.* One of these two, the Cathach, is provided by the critical signs of obelus and asterisk used by St Jerome in his original revision to indicate the relationship this bore to the original Hebrew. As noted already, we also have Irish manuscripts of Jerome's Latin rendering from the Hebrew—the *Hebraicum* as it is called. There are, in fact, Irish families both of the *Gallicanum* and *Hebraicum*, the latter characterized principally by certain omissions. These are mostly brief, even of single words. Sometimes, however, an entire phrase is omitted, as in Ps. 89.17. Dom Henri de Sainte-Marie has shown that the use of the obelus in the Cathach does not always represent Jerome's original revision—where it indicated matter in his rendering (and in the Septuagint) absent from the original Hebrew. Sometimes these Cathach obeli represent a revision not against the Hebrew original but rather a revision of the *Gallicanum* text against Jerome's Latin translation of the Hebrew (the *Hebraicum*) and specifically a revision against the Irish family of the *Hebraicum* in places where this differs from Jerome's original rendering. A clear example of this is the obelus in the Cathach at Ps. 89.17. It marks a section absent, not from the Hebrew nor Jerome's rendering of this, but rather from the Irish *Hebraicum* family.

Since the Cathach appears to have been written about 630 CE, the evidence indicates that the *Hebraicum* in its Irish text from must have existed in Ireland by 600 CE at the latest and also that a revision of the *Gallicanum* text against it must have been carried out by that time. This seems to argue towards the exercise of textual criticism in Ireland during the sixth century. How extensive or widespread this was we cannot say. Future research may throw more light on the matter.

We may also note that this interest in the asterisks and the obeli continued to exercise the attention and the curiosity of Irish scholars and copyists. They are treated of in the introductions of the Psalter used in the Irish schools and are reproduced in some of the later Irish texts.

10. *Origins of a Tradition*

From what has been said it is clear that the early Irish monastic approach to the Psalter differed in certain significant ways from that of Europe. We naturally ask how this approach to the Psalter made its way to Ireland, and if it did not come from abroad what factors led to its emergence in Ireland. The natural solution would be to postulate influence from abroad. In this case we have to seek a form of monasticism in which there was similar emphasis on the historical approach to the Psalms. This, I believe, we find in Antioch in the days of Diodorus (fourth century).[40] We know from the theologian and Church historian Theodoretus of Cyr (*Hist. Eccl.* 2.19) that even before his ordination as a priest, or before he had founded his school, Diodorus had a special interest in the choral recitation of the psalms. We can presume that this same interest continued even after he had founded his monastic community (asketerion). We also know of Diodorus's position on the interpretation of the Scriptures and of his rejection of allegory. A commentary of his on the Psalms would be along non-allegorical principles.

40. See M. McNamara, 'Antiochene Commentary on the Psalms By Diodore of Tarsus? Introduction', *Milltown Studies* 10 (1982), pp. 66-75.

Presumably his explanation of the Psalms to members of his monastic community would have been the same. As long ago as 1905 a Greek commentary was discovered which presents Antiochene exegesis and sets forth the principles of this in a general introduction to the Psalter and in a special prologue to Psalm 118. A number of serious scholars (but not all) believe this commentary is the work of Diodorus. Whatever of this point, the introduction tells us that the commentary, written in strict adherence to Antiochene principles, was intended for members of the monastic community as an aid to the proper recitation of the divine office, to help them sing the psalms with understanding (Ps. 46.8). I cite a portion of the preface here:

> I have thought fit to give a brief exposition of this most necessary work of Scripture, the Psalms, as I myself have received it, an exposition of the subject-matter of each psalm and their literal interpretation. In this way the brethren, when they are singing the psalms will not be merely carried along by the stream of words nor, from lack of understanding, find their minds occupied with other thoughts; rather by grasping the sequence of thought in the words they will sing 'with understanding' as it is written (Ps. 46.8, Septuagint), that is from the depths of their minds and not with lip-service and superficial sentiments.[41]

We do not known how long Diodorus's approach to the Psalms continued to exist in Antioch or the Greek world. It seems to have been radically diluted by the end of Theodoretus's life. The Syriac Church, however, took Theodoretus's psalm interpretation as their own. He became their master, *the* Interpreter. His commentary was translated into Syriac to be transmitted into our own day. The close affiliations between the monastic school system of Diodorus and Syria (Edessa) may have helped here. We do not know if the Latin West knew any form of monasticism akin to that of Diodorus. But this commentary came West, to be transmitted in Ireland in the far West as it was in Syriac on the eastern borders of Christianity. It may be that some form of monasticism similar to the Syriac helped transmit the peculiar approach to the Psalter from the East, whether it be Edessa or Antioch, to Ireland. Future research may tell.

---

41. Translation of general preface and prologue to Ps. 118 by E. FitzGerald, 'Antiochene Commentary on the Psalms: By Diodore of Tarsus? Preface to the Commentary and Prologue to Psalm 118', *Milltown Studies* 10 (1982), pp. 76-86 (77).

11. *Conclusions*

In conclusion we may return to the title of this essay and ask again what was the place of the Psalter in early Irish monastic spirituality. We can say that its role was central, if complex. With the rest of Christendom, the Psalter was regarded as God's word, the book in which he conversed with men and women, the songs in which God first praised himself, the mirror of the soul, the soul's guide to God. Few early Irish monks would not agree with the words of Máel Ísa Ua Brollcháin:

> Your counsel is ever there to hand,
> > we choose it, following you in everything,
> love of your words is the best of loves,
> > our gentle conversation with the King.

They knew that through the Psalter 'the mighty melodies of God's praise throughout the pathways of the world resound'. They could regard the Psalter as the voice of Christ addressing his Church, or the voice of the Church addressing Christ. They could give rein to the affections of their heart. However, they also honoured a tradition that bade them pay respect to the head and the principles of historical exegesis, to respect and reverence both the biblical text and its interpretation. They seemed to have sought to bring together in theory and to actively apply in practice the rational and the affective approach to the Psalter. To this end they invented the series of multiple psalm headings such as we find in the *Tituli Psalmorum* ascribed to Bede. These first gave the historical meaning or reference. On this there followed the mystical or spiritual meaning, generally with reference to Christ. After this there sometimes followed a moral reference. This approach to the Psalms must have been used to a greater extent than the extant sources would lead us to believe, since we find it applied to preaching and found in the very structure of eleventh-century Irish homilies.

This ancient approach to the Psalms is not without relevance to their use in our own day. The revised Breviary, too, seeks to combine respect both for the original meaning and reference of the psalms with their use as Christian prayer. This it does in the general introduction and in the special headings to the psalms and canticles. The new series of psalm headings, mainly from the New Testament, seeks to facilitate the use of the psalm or canticle as Christian prayer; another heading gives the genre of the composition.

Old psalm prefaces delighted in saying that all human life was in the Psalter, life in all its complexity. This, too, is what we find in the Irish approach to this most beloved of books: it sought to combine the various elements that come together in it, past and present, head and heart.

CHRISTOLOGY AND THE INTERPRETATION OF THE PSALMS
IN THE EARLY IRISH CHURCH

1. *Introduction*

The theme of this present symposium is Christology. If there is one subject which immediately brings us to the question of biblical hermeneutics, particularly with regard to the understanding of the Old Testament, it is Christology.

The origin, the person and the mission of Christ have been understood against the background of the Scriptures. Christ fulfilled what was written of him in the Law, the Prophets and the other writings. The New Testament theologians draw liberally on the Hebrew Scriptures in their presentation of who Jesus Christ was. Later New Testament writings develop the content of earlier New Testament texts for the same ends. The development of Christology during the early Christian centuries used the Scripture in a variety of ways. It was the matrix from which a newer presentation of Christ's work grew. It served as a background against which Christian theologians could bounce their ideas, and draw terminology, in their reflections on the mystery of Christ. They easily saw their newer formulations as the inevitable outcome of what the Scriptures say, and almost inevitably came to see their newly formulated doctrine as the message intended by Scripture. Development in Christolology meant often going beyond old formulations which had been found inadequate.

The history of Christology tells us of the differences between the attitudes of the school and church of Antioch and those of Alexandria, the former showing a reluctance to adopt new doctrines.

Any theory on the development of Christian doctrine must of necessity come to terms with the relation of later developments to Scripture, and must perforce take up a position on the literal meaning of the Bible, on whether there are other senses of Scripture beyond the literal, and if so how do these relate to the literal sense.

J.H. Newman did this in 1845, in his *Essay on the Development of*

Christian Doctrine, in his treatment of the Syrian school of theology, of Antioch, Diodorus and Theodore of Mopsuestia in particular. This essay he reproduces in his later work *The Arians of the Fourth Century*.[1] Writing of the origins of Arianism he has this to say:

> [T]he immediate source of that fertility in heresy, which is the unhappy distinction of the Syrian Church, was its celebrated Exegetical School. The history of that school is summed up in the broad characteristic fact, on the one hand that it devoted itself to the literal and critical interpretation of Scripture, and on the other that it gave rise first to the Arian and then to the Nestorian heresy. *In all ages of the Church, her teachers have shown a disinclination to confine themselves to the mere literal interpretation of Scripture. Her most subtle and powerful method of proof, whether in ancient or modern times, is the mystical sense, which is so frequently used in doctrinal controversy as on many occasions to supersede any other.* In the early centuries we find this method of interpretation to be the very ground for receiving as revealed the doctrine of the Holy Trinity. Whether we betake ourselves to the Ante-Nicene writers or the Nicene, certain texts will meet us, which do not obviously refer to that doctrine yet are put forward as palmary proofs of it.[2]

What is meant by the 'mystical' (or 'spiritual') sense of Scripture is no clearer today than it was in John Henry Newman's time. It is a question that is constantly recurring, and is still a matter of debate. The biblical evidence itself indicates that we exercise caution in this matter. That biblical texts had an original, literal, sense is clear. But with the passage of time, and well within the biblical period itself, what precise meaning a text conveyed, or was intended to convey, to the original recipients would in a number of cases have been lost, and the original setting forgotten. This seems to have been the case in particular with regard to the Psalms. The texts were transmitted within a community of faith, faith in a God living and active. They were reused as inspirational, thus in a sense reinterpreted, within such a faith community. The original meaning of texts may have been lost, but the God who once inspired them was still leading his believing community forward. Earlier texts and unwritten traditions could have been understood in the light of a later deeper revelation, and for this reason rephrased. While the later

1. J.H. Newman, *An Essay on the Development of Christian Doctrine* (London, 1845; reproduced in later editions, 1878, 1890), pp. 284-96; *The Arians of the Fourth Century* (London, 3rd edn 1871 [1853]), pp. 403-15.

2. J.H. Newman, *The Arians of the Fourth Century* (London, 6th edn 1890), p. 404 (italics added).

rephrasing could be true doctrine, it is debatable whether such expressions of doctrine can aptly be called the sense, 'mystic', 'spiritual' or otherwise, of the earlier expression in text or in oral tradition. To illustrate by some examples: In reply to a query by Jesus concerning his identity, Peter replied according to Mark (8.29) and Luke (9.2): 'You are the Christ (Messiah)' (in Luke: 'the Christ of God'). This would appear to have been the earlier formulation. According to Mt. 19.16 Peter's reply is: 'You are the Christ (the Messiah), the Son of the living God'. This later formulation in Matthew can hardly be taken as being the 'mystic' sense of the earlier expression as found in the other two Gospels. The later understanding can hardly be accepted as being derivable from the earlier by some set of hermeneutical rules. It came, in Christ's words (Mt. 19.17) not 'by flesh and blood', by any human deduction, but by revelation from God. The same can be said of John's christological presentation. This also, I believe, holds true with regard to the trinitarian and christological developments of succeeding centuries. It seems best to respect an original meaning, a literal meaning, for the biblical texts in question and regard later developments for what they are: development of doctrine legitimate when conforming to the Spirit's guidance of the Church rather than as 'mystic' or 'spiritual' senses of Scripture.

Something similar may be said with regard to the fulfilment of the Old Testament in the New, or the christological meaning of the Old Testament. It is clear that the New Testament presents the mystery of Christ as being foretold in the Old. Yet we must take such statements in the light of the central doctrine that Christ is the mystery hidden from preceding generations, and revealed only to the Church by the Spirit. Undue stress on christological interpretation of the Old Testament might rob the mystery of its content.

What has just been said is related to a matter which has been receiving attention for some time past, namely 'the Bible in Academe; the Bible in Ecclesia'. It is not my purpose here to enter in any detail into this question, which is very much a topic of discussion among Catholic and other scholars. What may be of help is to see whether the particular problem is one that has arisen for the first time in the recent past, mainly due to new literary approaches, new archaeological finds, coupled with a general belief and desire that church authority and the concept of revelation be excluded from scientific inquiry. I believe that the problem is an ancient one, arising from the nature of the Bible as

literature and the Church as a believing community reflecting and articulating the central truths of faith. I illustrate this in particular by the
approach to the Psalms in the Antiochene and early Irish tradition.

2. *Interpretation of the Psalms in Antiochene Tradition*

2.1. *The School of Antioch*

The Antiochene exegetical school, originating with Diodorus of Tarsus,
is characterized by its rejection of the Alexandrian allegorical approach
and its insistence on the interpretation of the Bible as literature, and in
accord with the norms of literary interpretation. The aim of such exegesis was what was referred to as 'history', the literal sense of Scripture,
the meaning supposed to have been intended by the original author.
This at times (but very rarely) may have been direct prophecies of
Christ. The later use of biblical texts as referring to Christ or other
Christian truths (for instance future resurrection) would be regarded as
rereading, accommodation or the bringing out of a truth inherent in the
literal sense (which use the Antiochenes referred to as 'theoria', 'the
more lofty theoria'), which sense or senses cannot be alien to the literal
sense (or 'the history'). However, what exactly they meant by 'theoria'
is less easily defined.

The Antiochene position in this matter principally concerns Old Testament texts in their relation to the New Testament and Christian theology. The Antiochene principles of psalm exegesis are formulated in the
commentary on the Psalms by Theodore of Mopsuestia, for long known
to scholars. They are also found in the more recently published general
preface to the psalm commentary and the prologue to Psalm 118, now
more generally believed to be the work of Diodorus of Tarsus, but
which may very well be a later adaptation of the commentary by
Theodore of Mopsuestia.[3] In the East, Antiochene exegesis, and the
commentary of Theodore, was adopted by the Syrian Church, so much
so that one can refer to it as that of the Syrian Church (Syria, including
Antioch).

---

3.   On this commentary see M. McNamara, 'Antiochene Commentary on the
Psalms by Diodore of Tarsus Introduction?', *Milltown Studies* 10 (1982), pp. 66-75;
preface to the Psalm commentary and prologue to Ps. 118 translated by E. Fitz-
Gerald, 'Antiochene Commentary on the Psalms: By Diodore of Tarsus? Preface to
the Commentary and Prologue to Psalm 118', *Milltown Studies* 10 (1982), pp. 76-
86.

2.2. *The Psalms in Antiochene Exegesis*

The real founder of the exegetical school of Antioch seems to have been Diodorus, who became Bishop of Tarsus in 378 (he died 393). The Church historians Socrates and Sozomen note that the literal interpretation of the Scriptures and the avoidance of allegory were features of Diodorus's exegesis. We have no clear historical evidence that he wrote a commentary on the Psalms. However, from 1914 onwards L. Mariès and others have claimed to have identified a commentary on the Psalms by Diodorus in a number of Greek manuscripts.[4] The first section of this commentary (on Pss. 1–50), together with the introduction, was published in 1980.[5] The introduction, together with a special prologue to Psalm 118 had already been published in 1919.[6]

The 'Diodoran' introduction speaks warmly of the Psalms in words reminiscent of Athanasius:

> 'All Scripture is inspired by God...and profitable for teaching...that the man of God may be complete, equipped for every good work' (2 Tim 3.16, 17). And one would not be wrong in maintaining that this eulogy of the Sacred Scripture applies in its entirety to the book of the divine Psalms. For this book does, in fact, teach righteousness gently and mildly to those who are prepared to learn, it reproves the self-willed with solicitude and without harshness, and it corrects all the defects we unhappily fall into inadvertently or deliberately.
>
> But it is not just when we are singing the psalms that we become aware of all this, but rather when we find ourselves in those very situations that make us conscious of our need of the psalms. Blessed indeed are those who need only the psalms of thanksgiving, because their lives are full of happiness. But since, being men, it is impossible for us to escape harsh trials and spiritual crises brought on by factors within or

---

4.   L. Mariès's earlier studies led to his work, *Etudes préliminaires à l'édition de Diodore de Tarse sur les Psaumes: La tradition manuscrite, deux manuscrits nouveaux. Le caractère diodorien du commentaire* (Paris: Les Belles Lettres, 1933).

5.   J.-M. Olivier (ed.), *Diodori Tarsensis Commentarii in psalmos*. I. *Commentarii in Psalmos I-L* (CCSG, 6; Turnhout: Brepols, 1980).

6.   L. Mariès, 'Extraits du commentaire de Diodore de Tarse sur les Psaumes: Préface du commentaire—Prologue du Psaume CXVIII', *Recherches de Science Religieuse* 9 (1919), pp. 79-101. Both the preface and prologue have been translated into English; see FitzGerald, 'Antiochene Commentary', pp. 76-86. Tranlation also in K. Froehlich, *Biblical Interpretation in the Early Church* (Philadelphia: Fortress Press, 1984), pp. 20-21. Whether the work is by Diodorus or not, it is a good introduction to Antiochene psalm exegesis.

external to ourselves, it is a most useful remedy that the soul comes to know when it discovers, already anticipated in the psalms, the subject matter of its converse with God. For the Holy Spirit has communicated in advance every kind of human experience and, with the most blessed David as his intermediary, he has provided us with words appropriate to our experiences and capable of remedying the evils we encounter. Thus the words that we passed over hastily and with superficial attention as we sang the psalms, are then understood and arrest our attention when we find ourselves a prey to anguish and sufferings: the very wound we bear in ourselves calling forth, as it were by nature, its appropriate remedy, and the remedy itself in turn being adapted to our need and affording the antidote to the sufferings we endure.[7]

The author, however, does not feel that the Alexandrian allegorizing is required for this end. On the contrary. He believes that the intelligent liturgical use of the psalms comes from the literal interpretation. The text continues:

> I have thought fit to give a brief exposition of this most necessary work of Sacred Scripture, the Psalms, as I myself have received it, an exposition of the subject-matter of each psalm and their literal interpretation. In this way the brethren, when they are singing the psalms, will not be merely carried along by the stream of words nor, from lack of understanding, find their minds occupied with other thoughts; rather by grasping the sequence of thought in the words, they will sing 'with understanding', as it is written (Ps 46:8; lxx text), that is from the depth of their minds and not with mere lip service and superficial sentiments.[8]

The best representative of Antiochene exegesis is Theodore, later Bishop of Mopsuestia (died 428). Among other works he composed a commentary on the minor prophets and on the Psalms. This latter was a work of his youth, strictly in accord with the principles of his school. He takes David to be the author of all the psalms. Each psalm, he notes, refers to some definite historic situation which is to be determined from a consideration of the psalm as a whole. This situation could be from the life of David himself or from some age subsequent to him. In this latter case David would have seen the future in prophetic vision. Some of the psalms, according to Theodore, refer to events in David's life. In the extant commentary some 80 psalms are referred to the history of Israel from Solomon to the Maccabees (referring to Hezekiah, the

---

7. Translation FitzGerald, 'Antiochene Commentary', pp. 76-77.
8. Translation FitzGerald, 'Antiochene Commentary', p. 77.

Babylonian captivity, the return from Exile, the Maccabees). Despite his views that David saw the future in prophetic vision, Theodore maintained that only four psalms (Pss. 2, 8 44[45], 109[110]) are prophecies of Christ.

Theodore was well aware of the use of Old Testament texts in the New, but refused to take this as an argument that these were all originally intended as prophecies. There is a difference from one text to another, he notes. Referring to adversaries who refuse to make such distinction he writes in his work *Adversus allegoricos* (preserved only in Syriac):

> These insane people have not perceived that the apostles in quoting the sayings of the Old Testament do not quote them in only one way; sometimes they quote them to show their fulfillment, at other times as an example of the exhortation and correction of their readers, or else to confirm the doctrine of the faith, although these sayings were uttered for other purposes according to the historical circumstances.
>
> Now when our Lord applies Psalms 8 and 110 to himself, and when Peter in Acts and Paul in his Epistles apply to our Lord the same Psalms as well as Psalms 2 and 45, they take them in their true sense.
>
> But when our Lord says on the cross: 'My God, my God, why hast thou forsaken me?' and again: 'Into thy hands I commend my spirit,' which saying is found in Psalm 31:6, these words are said by a comparison according to the resemblance of the events, although in their original place their application is different. Now the difference which exists between these things is evidenced with clarity from the context to those who want to know the truth.[9]

It so happened that just as Antioch was loath to depart from the letter of the Bible, so also it did not cherish new formulations in trinitarian or christological doctrines, and was regarded as heretical or favouring heresy. Its exegetical approach was also regarded in the same light, and soon after its flowering under Diodorus (367–71) and his student Theodore it became suspect. It was still so regarded by John Henry Newman, as can be seen from the text cited above at the outset of this article.[10]

---

9.   Cited in D.Z. Zaharopoulos, *Theodore of Mopsuestia on the Bible: A Study of his Old Testament Exegesis* (New York: Paulist Press, 1989), p. 115.

10.   Newman, *An Essay*, pp. 284-96; Newman, *The Arians*, pp. 403-15, at 404.

3. *Theodorean and Antiochene-type Exegesis in Ireland*

3.1. *Theodorean Psalm Interpretation in Ireland*

Theodore composed his five-book commentary on the book of Psalms in Greek for Cedron his brother. When, due to pressure from Augustine of Hippo, Julian, Bishop of Eclanum in southern Italy, was expelled from his diocese in 418 he went East and resided for a while with Theodore's brother. Julian translated Theodore's commentary into Latin, possibly even before 418. This full translation has in part been preserved, mainly through the interest of Irish schools and scribes, in manuscripts from the Columbanus library of Bobbio. The greater part of the Latin tradition of the work, however, is known through an abbreviation (Epitome) where Theodorean and other types of commentary are mingled. This, too, has been preserved mainly through the interest of the early Irish schools.

Codex Amb. C 301 inf. of the Ambrosian Library, Milan contains a complete commentary on the Psalter (referred to occasionally below as the Milan Commentary). In it, for Pss. 1.1–16.11 we have Julian's full translation of Theodore's work, and the Epitome for the remainder. We have excerpts from the full commentary and the Epitome in the Hiberno-Latin *Eclogae tractatorum in Psalterium* ('Excerpts from Commentators on the Psalter') and from the Epitome in the Hiberno-Latin one-volume commentary on the Bible known as the 'Reference Bible' (*Das Bibelwerk*)—both of the mid or late eighth century. We also have many excerpts from the Epitome in the tenth-century *Double Psalter of St Ouen* (now in Rouen). In these Irish works we find the Antiochene and Theodorean approach to the psalms. For a detailed analysis of the relevant texts, see Appendices I and II below.

3.2. *Davidic Psalm Interpretation in Ireland*

Analysis of the psalm commentaries in Irish manuscripts, however, indicates that the Irish tradition has gone beyond this Antiochene and Theodorean exegetical approach towards another which tends to interpret almost all the psalms as referring to David and the events of his life. In this form of commentary, which I shall call 'Davidic', none of the psalms, not even any of Theodore's four, is interpreted as prophecies of Christ, but all of them tend to be understood as having been composed concerning David and his times.

Our evidence concerning its existence is as follows. It is found in the

Hiberno-Latin commentary on the Psalms, extant imperfectly (only for Ps. 39.11 to the apocryphal Ps. 151) in Codex Vatican Pal. lat. 68, a commentary composed apparently in Ireland or Northumbria about 700. The exegesis itself must have existed in Irish circles somewhat earlier, from c. 650 or so. In this commentary there are references to the exegetical activity of a group called 'Romans' (*Romani*), and the examples given of this activity concern a Davidic interpretation of the Psalms, even though not that found in the commentary itself. These *Romani* may have been the same as the Irish group active in the debate about Easter about 630 or so. The 'Davidic' interpretation is also presupposed in the so-called psalm headings of Pseudo-Bede (*Bedae Tituli Psalmorum*) which seem to have been composed in Ireland or Northumbria about 700. An almost identical series of psalm headings is found in the so-called Psalter of Charlemagne (found in the manuscript Paris, Bibliothèque Nationale lat. 13159), written in France between 792 and 800, having behind it the Northumbrian-Irish tradition.

For Psalms 1–16 both the headings and the 'Davidic' commentary presupposed by these headings are found in the Double Psalter of Saint Ouen (or the Double Psalter of Rouen), written in Ireland in the tenth century and now in Rouen, Bibliothèque municipale MS 24 (A.41).[11] This double Psalter has on the right-hand side the Latin Vulgate Psalter text known as the *Gallicanum*, accompanied by glosses, generally of a spiritual nature, interpreting the psalm as speaking of Christ, the Church, and Christian life. On the left-hand side, opposite this, we have Jerome's Latin translation from the Hebrew, known as the *Hebraicum* or *Iuxta Hebraeos*. This is accompanied by glosses giving the 'historical' interpretation of the psalm. These are drawn mainly from the Epitome of Julian's Latin translation of Theodore, but for Pss. 1.1– 16.11a (and occasionally elsewhere) from the 'Davidic' commentary.

We cannot say if this novel 'Davidic' form of psalm exegesis originated in Ireland-Iona-Northumbria or came to Ireland from the outside. From our present point of view its ultimate origins are of less significance. What matters is that it was at home in Ireland, at least in certain circles, and continued at least in part right down to at least the tenth century (See Appendices).

---

11. This section of the Rouen glosses has been edited in a provisional form by L. De Coninck, *Incerti auctoris expositio Psalmorum I:1–XVI, 11a iuxta litteram* (2 vols.; Kortrijk: Katholieke Universiteit, Leuven Campus Kortrijk, 1989). Pars prior: Praefatio editoris; Pars altera: Textus.

3.3. *Theodore's Commentary on Psalms 2 and 8 in Ireland*

3.3.a. *Psalm 2: Theodorean Interpretation.* The full text of Julian's Latin translation of Theodore's commentary on Psalm 2 has been preserved in the Milan Codex Ambrosianus C 301 inf. (from the Bobbio Library). There are also extensive excerpts from the full translation in the Hiberno-Latin *Eclogae tractatorum in Psalterium*, composed about 750–75.

This is one of the psalms which Theodore interpreted as directly messianic. He avails of the exposition to express his views on the humanity of Christ (*homo susceptus/assumptus, persona suscepti hominis*). Study of the nature and orthodoxy or otherwise of Theodore's christology received a certain new impetus with R. Devreesse's publication of his psalm commentary in 1939.[12] Opinion was divided as to the orthodoxy of the christological views in this commentary. In his analysis of this commentary E. Amann showed the same sympathy for Theodore's basic orthodoxy as he had already shown in relation to Theodore's homilies. In his view, the reason why people condemned Theodore for Nestorianism is that they made a kind of bogeyman of the expression *homo assumptus*.[13] With regard to Theodore's exegesis of Psalm 2 Amann remarks: 'Provided that one excludes all prejudice, and defines clearly what is meant by *homo assumptus*, all these explanations of Theodore can be taken in good part'.[14] Amann concedes that Theodore occasionally did not watch carefully enough over his vocabulary; on another occasion he used a rather poor figure to express the mystery of the ineffable union. But Amann is clearly convinced that his basic thought is sound.[15] The opinion of other reviewers of the commentary were less benign. J.M. Vosté finds it impossible not to see expressed in Theodore's psalm exegesis the doctrine of union by mere inhabitation, from which results the divinity of the Man Christ by mere exterior, honorific designation. As Vosté sees it, for Theodore the mystery of the Incarnation supposes no more than a moral union of grace and honour

---

12. R. Devreesse, *Le commentaire de Théodore de Mopsueste sur les psaumes (I–LXXX)* (Studi e Testi, 93: Vatican City: Biblioteca Apostolica Vaticana, 1939).

13. E. Amann, 'Un nouvel ouvrage de Théodore de Mopsueste', *Revue des Sciences Religieuses* 20 (1940), pp. 491-526 (520).

14. Amann, 'Un nouvel ouvrage', p. 516.

15. On this point, and for a review of reaction to Devreesse's edition of the commentary, see F.A. Sullivan, *The Christology of Theodore of Mopsuestia* (Rome: Gregorian University Press, 1956), pp. 20-22 (21).

between the 'man assumed' and the Word. Thus the Christ is born and dies as mere man; in reality he is no more God than are the faithful, who are temples of the Holy Spirit and adoptive sons of God, having become by grace *divinae consortes naturae.*[16]

Already in the *argumentum* to this psalm, Theodore notes that as well as being a prophecy of Christ's passion, the psalm has a second main theme: *Indicat etiam ius imperii et potentiam dominationis insinuat, quam super omnia, post resurrectionem,* homo *a Deo* susceptus *accepit.*[17]

The theme is repeated in the exposition of v. 6a (*Ego constitutus sum rex ab eo*): Susceptus *itaque* homo *ius super omnia dominationis accipit ab inhabitatore suo, Verbo suo.*[18] Likewise, on the same verse: *De hoc ergo et in praesenti propheta Dauid loquitur, id est* suscepto homine *a Deo Verbo...*[19] Again on the same verse: *alia constant Deo, alia* suscepto homini *conuenire.*[20] *Comprobatur...quod dictum est Ego autem constitutus sum rex ab eo, ad* assumptum hominem *pertinere...Si quis uero dicat a Patre collatum esse homini, non a Verbo, non est ulla diuersitas utrum a Deo an a Patre* homo assumptus *sit tanto honore donatus.*[21]

16. J.M. Vosté, 'Théodore de Mopsueste sur les Psaumes', *Angelicum* 19 (1942), pp. 179-98 (191). There was a similar reaction by F. Diekemp in his review of Devreesse's edition in *Theologische Revue* 40 (1941), pp. 156-59. Diekamp's criticism was replied to by A. Vaccari in the essay 'In margine al commento di Teodoro Mopsuesteno ai Salmi', *Miscellanea Giovanni Mercati*, I (Studi e Testi, 121; Vatican City, 1946), pp. 175-98. A. Grillmeier, *Christ in Christian Tradition: From the Apostolic Age to Chalcedon (451)* (London: Mowbray, 1965), has serious doubts about the orthodoxy of Theodore's Christology. He writes: '[t]he *Homo assumptus* formula seems inevitably to put Theodore's christology on the accidental level. It was precisely because of it that he had to swallow the greatest insults, so that he was regarded as a *Paulus (Samosatenus) redivivus*, as a proponent of an anagogic christology, teaching two persons and two sons, in short of the adoptionist christology which was seen to be embodied in Paul of Samosata. Theodore's language, in fact, all too often gives the impression that the union in Christ was achieved by the assumption of an already self-sufficient man' (pp. 347-48).

17. In L. De Coninck with M.J. d'Hont (eds.), *Theodori Mopsuesteni Expositionis in Psalmos Iuliano Aeclenensi interprete in latinum versae quae supersunt* (CCSL, 88A; Turnhout: Brepols, 1977), pp. 10, 7-8.

18. De Coninck and d'Hont (eds.), *Theodori*, pp. 13, 142-43.

19. De Coninck and d'Hont (eds.), *Theodori*, pp. 13, 147-48.

20. De Coninck and d'Hont (eds.), *Theodori*, pp. 13, 164-65.

21. De Coninck and d'Hont (eds.), *Theodori*, pp. 13, 172-76.

3.3.b. *Old Irish Glosses on Theodore's Commentary on Psalm 2*. The Latin Codex Ambrosianus is heavily glossed in Old Irish (from about the year 800). The glosses often refer to 'the Manhood of Christ', 'the Godhead of the Son': 'the Manhood of Christ' Ml 16a3 (on *dominationis* of the *argumentum*); 'when the Godhead assumed Manhood' (*anarróet deacht doinact* [MS: *donacht*], Ml 16a4 (on *Homo [a Deo susceptus]* of the *argumentum*); 'through the death of the Manhood of Christ' (*tri bas doinachtae crist*, 16d2; nothing corresponding in Latin); 'of the Manhood of Christ that the Godhead assumed' (*doinachtae crist araroét indeacht*), Ml 17a8, on text: *ex persona suscepti hominis* on v. 16a); 'of the·Manhood of Christ' (17a11, on *[de]. suscepto [homine]* of text); 'from the Godhead of the Son' (on *[suscepto homine a] Deo [Verbo]* of text). On the text *alia constant Deo, alia suscepto homini conuenire*, it glosses *Deo* as 'i.e. to the Godhead of the Son' (17b21), and *suscepto* as 'i.e. to the Manhood of the Son' (17b22). There is a lengthy Irish gloss on the word *Deo* of the text *non est ulla diuersitas utrum a Deo...Homo adsumptus*: 'though it be from the Godhead of the Son or from the Godhead of the Father that the Manhood of the Son assume that which He hath assumed, it matters not' (?; Irish text: *ní hisuidiu*; something seems lacking in text) (Ml 17c3). At the end of his commentary on v. 6a Theodore notes his concern to exclude the opinion of those who assert *per hoc minorem unigenitum Filium a parte deitatis accipere*. The Irish gloss on *(per) hoc* runs: 'this is what the heretics say, that the Godhead of the Son is less than the Godhead of the Father, for it is from the Father that the Son has received power: he then who receives is less than he from whom it is received, and he who is endowed than he who bestows it' (17c7).

With regard to the Latin text of Theodore's commentary a question naturally arising is whether in the West the commentary was transmitted merely as a literary document without any attention being paid to its particular presentation of Christology. This is a distinct possibility, as we do not know what, if any, influence Theodore's presentation of Christology had in the West. A further question is the weight to be attributed to the content of the Irish glosses, whether, that is, they are to be regarded merely as attempts to convey the sense of the Latin text, or whether they are evidence for a late eighth-century Irish interest in Theodorean Christology.

3.3.c. *Psalm 8: Theodorean Interpretation*. As already noted, this present psalm, Psalm 8, is one of the four taken by Theodore as a direct prophecy of Christ. We have his full commentary on this psalm in Latin translation in the manuscript, Milan, Ambrosian Library (Amb.) 301 inf. We also have small sections of the Greek original. Theodore introduces his commentary on the psalm as follows:

> In this psalm the blessed David, filled with the spirit of prophecy, speaks in advance of the incarnation of the Lord and says of him those things which were later fulfilled in deed. Thus indeed is the boldness of Jewish contradiction checked. For it is clear that these words *Out of the mouths of infants and sucklings you have perfected praise* (Greek rendering, 8:2) have in very deed been fulfilled in the Lord when events bore testimony to the prophecy and to what was prophesied (Mt. 21.16; see also 1 Cor. 15.25-28; Heb. 2.6-8).[22]

Theodore interpreted the psalm as speaking in prophecy of the divinity and humanity of Christ.[23] We shall now consider the Latin translation of his commentary on vv. 5-8, together with the Irish glosses on it, in three distinct sections.

3.3.c.i. *Theodorean Commentary on Psalm 8.5-8 in Milan Codex Amb. C 301 inf. Section 1*

> (Ps 8:5a–8a), *Quid est homo quod memor es eius usque sub pedibus eius.* Vnus atque idem et Deus Verbum, cui principia psalmi constant, et homo his, quae inseruimus, dictis esse signatur, cuius memor est et quem *uisitat* et quem *minuit paulo minus ab angelis, quem honore coronat et gloria* et quem *constituit super opera manuum suarum.* In quo quanta sit naturarum diuersitas hinc ostenditur, quod eius, cuius Deus meminisse dignatus est, ita humilis est condicio atque mediocris, ut collata haec in illam, quae diximus, beatus Dauid stupeat ac et miretur. Nam cum dicit *Quid est homo quod memor es* et reliqua, naturae nostrae aperte indicat uilitatem et quae non sit tanti meriti, cuius debeat Deus ita meminisse, ut unitam sibi etiam titulo honoris exaequet: ob hoc enim propheta Dei bonitatem cum stupore miratur, quoniam ita humilem uilemque naturam in consortium suae dignitatis asciuerit. Deum ergo esse Verbum qui *memor fuerit*, qui *uisitauerit*, qui imminuerit hominem paulo minus ab angelis, qui gloria et *honore coronauerit*, ostensum est sufficienter. Qui

---

22. Latin text, and sections of Greek original, in Devreesse (ed.), *Le commentaire*, p. 42; Latin text in De Coninck and d'Hont (eds.), *Theodori*, pp. 37-38.

23. On this see R.A. Norris, *Manhood and Christ: A Study in the Christology of Theodore of Mopsuestia* (Oxford, 1963); Sullivan, *Christology*.

uero sit iste homo, in quem tanta beneficia collata sunt, ab apostolo
Paulo discamus dicente: *Testatus est autem quodam loco qui, dicens,
Quid est homo quod memor es eius usque sub pedibus eius*, et adiungens
dicit: *Eum, qui paulo minus ab angelis minoratus est, uidimus Jesum
propter passionem mortis gloria et honore coronatum.*[24]

3.3.c.ii. *Irish Glosses on Theodorean Commentary (Section 1) in Milan
Codex.* The Milan Latin text of the commentary on Psalm 8 is very
heavily glossed in Old Irish (from c. 800 CE) and the purpose of these
glosses seems to be to give the sense of Theodore's text. They consequently speak repeatedly of 'the Godhead and the Manhood of the
Son'.[25] Here are some examples: 25c2 (on *Deus*): 'the Godhead'; 25c3
(on *Verbum*): 'the Manhood'; 25c5 (on *humilis est*): 'it is shown that
the manhood is lowly according to nature because it is the Godhead that
remembers it and helps it'; 25c8 (on *quae non sit tanti meriti*): 'i.e. the
substance (*afolud*) of the Manhood'.

3.3.c.iii. *Text of Theodorean Commentary (Psalm 8.5-8, Section 2) Censured in* Constitutum *of Pope Vigilius).* Part of Theodore's commentary
on Ps. 8.5-8 was cited in Latin translation for censure in the *Constitutum* of Pope Vigilius (553 CE). It is substantially the same as that
which is still extant in the full translation of Julian of Eclanum. The following is the text of Julian's translation, as found in the Milan Commentary:

> Grandis itaque differentia inter Deum Verbum et susceptum hominem
> lectione psalmi praesentis ostenditur; quae etiam nouo quoque Testa-
> mento similiter indicatur: nam Dominus in Euangelio quae inter prin-
> cipia psalmi dicta sunt praesentis sibi competere demonstrat, in quibus
> plane totius creaturae factor ostenditur, cuius magnificentia, impleta
> omni terra, transcendisse caeli spatia perhibetur; Apostolus uero sequen-
> tia de homine Iesu, qui tantis beneficiis ostensus sit, dicta esse confirmat.
> Manifestum ergo est quod aliam diuinae Scripturae nos doceant Dei
> Verbi esse substantiam et aliam *hominis suscepti* naturam, multamque
> inter utrasque esse distinctionem; nam alia *memor* est, alia memoria
> digna censetur et alia quidem *uisitat*, alia beata dignatione uisitationis
> efficitur; alia etiam in hoc benefica est si *ab angelis paulo faciat min-
> orem*, alia uero etiam beneficium accipit si angelorum fastigio non
> aequetur; et haec quidem *coronat gloria* uel *honore*, haec autem insigni

---

24. Devreesse (ed.), *Le commentaire*, p. 45.
25. See glosses on this psalm in *Thes. Pal.*, I, pp. 44-51.

capitis decoratur; *haec constituit super omnia opera manuum suarum, pedibus* assumptae *cuncta subiciens*, ista uero assumitur, ut dominetur his quae prius subiecta non habuit.[26]

3.3.c.iv. *Irish Glosses on the Censured Text:* Ml 25d1 (on *multamque inter utrasque*): 'i.e. both the Godhead and the Manhood of the Son'; 25d2 (on *memor*): 'i.e. the Godhead'; 25d3 (on *memoria*): 'i.e. Manhood'; 25d6 (on *et [haec quidem]*): 'i.e. the substance (*folud*) of the Godhead'; 25d7 (on *haec [autem insigni]*): 'i.e. substance (*folud*) of Manhood'; 25d9 (on *ista [uero adsumitur]*): 'i.e. the Manhood'.

3.3.c.v. *Theodorean Commentary on Psalm 8.5-8 in Milan Codex Amb. C 301 inf. Section 3*

Cum ergo audimus Scripturam dicentem aut honoratum esse Iesum, aut clarificatum, aut collatum illi esse aliquid, aut accepisse super omnia dominationem, non Deum Verbum intellegamus, sed *hominem susceptum*, et, siue a Patre haec in eum collata siue a Deo Verbo dixerimus, non errabimus, quia id dicere Scripturae diuinae sumus magisteriis eruditi.[27]

3.3.c.vi. *Irish Glosses on Theodorean Commentary (Section 3) in Milan Codex:* 25d10 (on *[in eum] collata*): 'i.e. the Man that assumed (*arároét*) Godhead'; 25d11 (on *non errabimus*): 'i.e. whichever we say from which the Manhood has received all that it has received, i.e. whether from the Godhead of the Father or from the Godhead of the Son'; 25d12 (on *id dicere*): 'i.e. that it, to wit, the Divine Scripture says it, namely, this, that we are not wrong whichever we say'.

3.4. *Concluding Remarks on Theodorean Christology in Irish Circles*
A number of questions need to be confronted with regard both to these Latin texts and the Irish glosses on them.

The theology of the texts represents the thinking of the Antiochene Theodore. We do no know how much, if at all, his translator Julian shared Theodore's christological concerns or viewpoints.

We know that in the early seventh century Northern Italy was divided with regard to Theodore, to the Three Chapters and to the stance taken by Pope Vigilius. It would be interesting to know whether Theodore's

26. Text reproduced as in De Coninck and d'Hont (eds.), *Theodori*, pp. 40-41, 99-141. Latin text of Vigilius's *Constitutum*, of Amb. C.301 inf and Greek text in Devreesse, *Le commentaire*, pp. 46-47.
27. De Coninck and d'Hont (eds.), *Theodori*, pp. 41, 142-48.

commentary in Latin translation was part of this debate, whether Theodore's christological views, as distinct from his right to his good name, were held in Northern Italy. One would like to know whether Columbanus was aware of the nature of the christological issues involved, even though he criticized Vigilius for not being sufficiently vigilant with regard to the Three Chapters.

It is not clear to what extent the Irish glossator was aware of the christological issues involved in the Latin text being commented on— for instance on the acceptability or otherwise of such terms as *homo susceptus* or *homo assumptus*. The fact that he tends to speak simply of the 'Godhead of the Father', 'the Godhead of the Son', and of 'the humanity of the Son' would seem to indicate that the glossator was not interested in the theological questions as such. If he were he would probably have given a more nuanced presentation with more attention to the implications of the terms.

While a command of the christological issues involved on the part of the Irish glossator is not to be presumed, the glosses, I believe, merit deeper consideration in order to see whether they contain evidence of Christological reflection in the early Irish schools that produced them.

4. *The Christological Interpretation of the Psalms in the Early Irish Church*

In a general manner in what has preceded, and more specifically in the Appendices, I lay stress on the evidence for the historical, non-christological, interpretation of the psalms in the early Irish Church. My reason for so doing was that I believe this aspect of the question is not widely known.

This approach to the psalms would have been very much a matter for the classroom. The emphasis on the historical approach in no way indicates an absence of a devotional one and of a christological interpretation. Both were very much facets of the early Irish Church.[28] The central position of the Psalter in the divine office and in private devotions is sufficient proof of this approach. Down through the centuries the praises of the Psalter were proclaimed by the great patristic writers and their teaching made available in special psalm prefaces. Most

---

28. For this devotional approach and christological interpretation see M. McNamara, 'The Psalter in Early Irish Monastic Spirituality', above, pp. 353-77 of this volume.

notable among these is the Introduction to the Psalms by St Athanasius and the praises of the psalms by St Ambrose and St Hilary of Poitiers. All human life was seen as reflected by the Psalter; it was a mirror of the soul. It was a guide for every soul seeking God. Cassiodorus wrote along these lines in the introduction prefaced to his commentary on the Psalter, and sections of this introduction are excerpted into the introduction to the comments on the psalms in the Hiberno-Latin one-volume commentary commonly known as the 'Reference Bible'. The work was compiled some time before the year 800 and probably on the Continent, if not by an Irishman at least under strong Irish influence and especially in the section on the Psalms. In this introduction the Psalter is addressed as follows: 'O truly glittering book, radiant speech, remedy of the wounded heart, honeycomb of the interior man, the mounted picture of things spiritual, language of virtue. It bows down the proud and raises up the lowly.' Such a vision of the Psalter must have been deeply reflected on by the Irish scholar monk Máel Ísu Ua Brollcháin (who died 1086) in a poem of his only recently discovered and identified for what it is. Máel Ísu had got his monastic training in Armagh (in the north of Ireland; 'in Niall's northern land'), where at the age of seven he began to learn the rudiments of reading and writing from a Psalter. He later journeyed south to the monastic school of Lismore, where he came across the now tattered old Psalter with which he began his career. In his poem, full of tender love for the book, he addresses this old Psalter as 'Crínóc', 'Dear little, old thing'. It is clear that for him God was present in the Psalter, giving through it spiritual advice and manifesting his divine will. The relevant sections of the poem run:[29]

> Crínóc, lady of measured melody.
>   not young, but with modest maiden mind,
> together once in Niall's northern land
>   we slept, we two, as man and womankind.
>
> You came and slept with me for that first time,
>   skilled wise amazon annihilating fears
> and I a fresh-faced boy, not bent as now,
>   a gentle lad of seven melodious years...

29. In the translation of J. Carney, *Medieval Irish Lyrics Selected and Translated* (Dublin: The Dolmen Press, 1967), pp. 74-79 (74-77); introduction pp. xxvii–xxviii.

Your counsel is ever there to hand,
  we choose it, following you in everything:
love of your word is the best of loves,
  our gentle conversation with the King...

Seeking the presence of elusive God
  wandering we stray, but the way is found,
following the mighty melodies that with you
  throughout the pathways of the world resound.

Nor yet silent, you bring the word of God
  to all who in the present world abide,
and then through you, through finest mesh,
  man's earnest prayer to God is purified.

The oldest Irish approach to the psalms was most probably a christo-logical one. It is that found in what is known as the St Columba Series of Psalm Headings, preserved in the Psalter known as the Cathach of St Columba (Columcille), a manuscript now in the Royal Irish Academy, Dublin. While a tradition attributes this to Columcille of Iona (died 597), a date apparently palaeographically possible, it is more likely that the text was written about 630–50 or so. In this Psalter each psalm is preceded in red by a heading intended as an aid to the Christian prayer of the psalms. Of the six known series of psalm headings this is the oldest and the most widely attested. The oldest of the manuscripts carrying it is the Cathach itself. The series can be presumed to have been compiled well before the date of the Cathach, and must have been used in Iona and Ireland in the time of Columcille himself. It is uncertain whether the series originated in Ireland and was compiled elsewhere. This Columba series is noted for its christological orientation. The greater portion of the psalms are taken as spoken by Christ, the Church or the apostles, or are placed on the lips of the prophet-psalmist (as 24 psalms are) concerning the person or work of Christ. Thus, for instance: 'the voice of Christ to the Father' (Pss. 3; 12; etc.), 'the voice of Christ to the Church' (Ps. 115), 'the voice of the apostles when Christ was suffering' (Ps. 59), 'the voice of the apostles when Christ ascended to the Father' (Ps. 46), 'the voice of the Church to the Lord' (Ps. 69), 'the Church gives praise to Christ' (Ps. 9), 'the prophet announces the coming of Christ' (Ps. 67), 'the prophet cautions believers' (Ps. 66).

It is very likely that this christological interpretation of the psalms represents the approach of Columcille of Iona. It seems that he had a particular interest in the Scriptures, and especially in the Psalms and the wisdom books, and in their interpretation according to the approach of Cassian. The evidence for this comes from works written apparently very soon after his death and by persons who knew the saint. One is the *Amra Choluimb Chille*, 'The Elegy of Colum Cille', attributed to Dallán Forgaill. The poem is a very early one, probably written about the year 600, three years after Columcille's death.[30] In its praises of the saint the *Amra* says in stanza 5:

> He ran the course which runs past hatred to right action.
> The teacher wove the word.
> By his wisdom he made glosses clear.
> He fixed the Psalms,
> he made known the books of the Law,
> those books Cassian loved. He won battles over gluttony.
> The books of Solomon, he followed them.
> Seasons and calculations he set in motion.
> He separated the elements according to figures among the books of the Law.
> He read mysteries and distributed the Scriptures among the schools...

Without going into detail, here we have an indication of the influence of Cassian, and of Columcille's activity with regard to the Psalms, the wisdom books (Proverbs, Ecclesiasticus, Wisdom). We have similar evidence of the influence of Cassian and of the wisdom books in the near-contemporary Irish work from Iona, the *Aibgitir Chrábaid*, the Alphabet of Piety.[31] While John Cassian (c. 360–435) cannot be classed as a biblical commentator, a particular approach to biblical interpretation, one of a spiritual, allegoristic kind, characterizes his writings. He has also given us an expression of the fourfold sense of Scripture which became classical in the West: first the *historica interpretatio* and the *intellegentia spiritalis*, the latter being subdivided into *tropologia, allegoria* and *anagoge* (*Collationes* 14.8).[32]

---

30. On this see T. Owen Clancy and G. Markus, *Iona: The Earliest Poetry of a Celtic Monastery* (Edinburgh: Edinburgh University Press, 1995), pp. 97-128 with notes 239-48. See also P. Ó Néill, 'The Date and Authorship of *Aibgitir Chrábaid*: Some Internal Evidence', in P. Ní Chatháin and M. Richter (eds.), *Ireland and Christendom: The Bible and the Missions* (Stuttgart: Klett-Cotta, 1987), pp. 203-15, at 207-208.

31. See Ó Néill, 'The Date', esp. pp. 208-10.

32. See V. Codina, *El aspecto cristologico en la espiritualidad de Juan Casiano* (Rome: Pont. Institutum Orientalium Studiorum, 1966), esp. chapter 3, 'La theoria', pp. 74-104, and 'Los cuatro sentidos de la Escritura', pp. 105-15.

Irish tradition knew that the Psalms belonged to the third section of the Hebrew canon, the *Hagiographa* or Sacred Writings, not to the Prophets. From another point of view, however, the Psalms were classed as prophecy since they prophesied about Christ and of the New Testament. Thus in the *Old-Irish Treatise* on the Psalter from about 800 CE.[33] The same text goes on to ask:

> Of what did the prophecy of the psalms foretell? Not difficult. Of the birth of Christ and of his baptism, and of his passion, and of his resurrection, and of his ascension, and of his sitting at the right hand of God the Father in heaven, of the invitation of the heathen to faith, of the thrusting of Juda into unbelief, of the increase of every justice, of the spurning of every injustice, of the malediction of sinners, of the coming of Christ to judge the living and the dead.[34]

5. *Origin and Development of Irish Christological Psalm Exegesis*

The earliest approach to the Psalms in Ireland was probably the allegorical one. It would have been that of St Columba of Iona (d. 597), and that represented by the Columba Series of Psalm Headings. Not long afterwards, and in the course of the seventh century, if not already present in Columba's time, two quite distinct forms of historical exegesis are known to have been practised in Ireland and in the area of Irish influence in Northumbria. One is Antiochene exegesis in the tradition of Theodore of Mopsuestia. This approach was already well established by 700. How the translation of Theodore's psalm commentary, and of the Epitome based on it, reached Ireland is hard to say. It seems likely that it was through Northern Italy. It is likely that it was here that this Latin translation and adaptation of Theodore's commentary was preserved. The Irish may have come into contact with it through the monastery of Columbanus at Bobbio (Columba the Younger, d. 615). Possibly it was known to Columbanus himself, although there is no evidence of this from his writings. From Bobbio it may have made its way to Ireland, and from Ireland, as a heavily glossed school text, back again to Bobbio, in what is now the Codex Ambrosianus C 301 inf. This, however, is far from certain. In the Hiberno-Latin Psalm commentary preserved in Vatican manuscript Palatinus Latinus 68, compiled in Ireland or Northumbria about 700, mention is made of persons

33. *OIT*, pp. 22-23.
34. *OIT*, pp. 30-33.

called *Romani* interpreting stated psalms in a historical sense as referring to David and his times. If the *Romani* in question are those of the
Paschal controversy this would indicate the existence of a historical
Davidic form of psalm exegesis in Ireland about the year 632. This
would fit the evidence well, since the same commentary in MS Pal. lat.
68 from about 700 contains a combination of Davidic and Theodorean
historical psalm interpretation.

In the course of the seventh century two major approaches to the
Psalms were brought into contact, the allegorical and the dual historical
mode of interpretation. We also have evidence that in the course of the
seventh century in Ireland and Northumbria attempts were made to
respect both approaches and even to give a theoretical formulation to
both. This issued in the series of composite psalm headings known as
the *Tituli Psalmorum Bedae*, probably put together about 700. For each
psalm the *Tituli* has both an *Argumentum* and an *Explanatio*. The *explanationes* depend almost exclusively on the introductions with which
Cassiodorus prefaced each psalm in his large commentary. The *argumenta*, though brief, can be divided into three sections: (a) an historical
explanation, in which the psalm in question (unless of a general nature,
as is Psalm 8) is understood as referring to the trials of David, to Hezekiah or the Maccabees; (b) a section, introduced by *aliter*, giving the
mystical meaning; (c), when present, gives the moral application. Section (a) depends for the greater part on the Epitome of the Theodorean
commentary or on the Davidic commentary; section (b) simply reproduces the Columba Series of Psalm Headings; section (c) draws on
Jerome or Arnobius. The later Irish tradition of psalm exegesis will be
heavily dependent on the synthesis arrived at by the end of the seventh
century.

In the commentary in Pal. lat. 68, from about 700, a historical
approach in many of the psalms interprets the particular psalm of David
and his times, and also of later Jewish history, for instance Hezekiah or
the Maccabees. This is united with a mystical interpretation or application in the tradition of the Columba Series of Psalm Headings. In good
part dependent on this earlier practice, in the course of the eighth century, it would appear, a specifically Irish fourfold sense of Scripture
was put together with a twofold historical sense, a mystical sense (in
Irish *sens/sians* or *rún*; in Hiberno-Latin *sensus*), and a moral sense. We
find this in the introduction to two Hiberno-Latin compositions on the
Psalms, the *Eclogae tractatorum in psalterium* (from about 730–50)

and the 'Reference Bible' (about 750–90). It is also in the introduction to the Psalms in the *Old-Irish Treatise* on the Psalter, from which I cite:

> There are four things that are necessary in the Psalms, to wit, the first story [in Irish *stoir* = historical meaning], the second story, the sense [*síens* = mystical meaning]and the morality. The first story refers to David and to Solomon and to the above-mentioned persons, to Saul, to Absalom, to the persecutors besides. The second story to Hezekiah, to the people, to the Maccabees. The mystical sense (*síens*) [refers] to Christ, to the earthly and heavenly Church. The morality to every saint.[35]

In the Irish exegetical literature the importance of both the literal and the spiritual senses was kept in mind, and sometimes one could be put forward as more important than the other. This at times depended on the immediate source being used. A favourite text in regard to the importance of the spiritual sense was Ps. 67.14 ('If you sleep among the midst of [inheritance drawn by] lots, you shall be as the wings of a dove covered with silver, and the hinder parts of her back with the paleness of gold,' Douay Version). A Hiberno-Latin commentary on Lk. 2.24 (from about 780) reads:

> For the greater part, the dove carries a figure of the divine Scriptures, when it is said: 'The feathers of the dove are of silver' as far as 'of gold' (Ps 67:14). What does the color of silver signify but the eloquence of the divine historical meaning? By the form of gold, however, it indicates the threefold spiritual sense, that is tropology, anagogy, allegory.[36]

We find a similar tradition in the Hiberno-Latin commentary on the Psalms in Codex Pal. lat. 68 of the Vatican Library. There this same Ps. 67.14 is first considered historically, then allegorically:

> 'The feathers of the dove.' That is, you are as elegant, O tribe of Juda, as the feathers of the dove. 'Dove.' that is the ark... Spiritually: 'If you sleep in the midst of inheritances (drawn by lot).' That is, believing in two Testaments, in either Testament you will find the Holy Spirit; *and*

---

35. See *OIT*, pp. 30-31.

36. *Plerumque columba diuinarum scripturarum figuram tenet, quando dicitur: 'Pennae columbae deargentatae' usque 'auri' (Ps. 67.14). Quid argenti color nisi eloquentiam diuinae historiae significat? Per auri autem formam sensum triplicem spiritalem indicat, id est, tropologiam, anagogen, allegoriam.* Latin text in J.F. Kelly (ed.), *Commentarius in Lucam e codice Vindobonense latino 997* (= *Scriptores Hiberniae Minores* [CCSL, 108C; Turnhout: Brepols, 1974], p. 18 [with reference to Gregorius Magnus, *Mor. in Iob* 18, *PL* 76, cols. 50A, and to Cassianus, *Conlatio* 8.3 (CSEL 13), pp. 218-20]).

> *although there is beauty according to the letter* (= literal interpretation),
> *nevertheless the spiritual meaning is more elegant.* Consequently, the
> external ornamentation of the words is shown by the name of silver; the
> mysteries of hidden things, however, are contained in the concealed gifts
> of gold.[37]

In another context, the literal sense is clearly seen as the more important, in fact as indispensable. Thus in an Old Irish gloss on Julian's
translation of Theodore's comment on Psalm 1, in the Milan Commentary: 'it is the history [i.e. historical sense] that is most desirable for us
to understand' (Ml 14d7).[38] In another text the glossator says that his
own task, the task of one interested in the primary meaning of the text,
is the literal sense; examination of the other senses is for others, but
these must not go against the literal sense: 'it is thus that we leave to
them the exposition of the sense and the morality, if it be not at variance with the history that we relate' (Ml 14d10).[39]

The stress on the literal or spiritual and christological senses varied
through the centuries in Irish commentaries on the Psalms. The earliest,
Pal. lat. 68, is strongly historical with, however, inclusion of the spiritual and christological dimension. The Milan commentary, being a
Latin translation and part adaptation of Theodore's commentary, is
avowedly historical. The Irish glosses on this seem principally interested in bringing out the sense of the Latin text and do not attempt to
impose another interpretation on it. Greater attention to the spiritual and
christological interpretation in the *Eclogae tractatorum in psalterium*

---

37. *'Si dormiatis...' id est propter dominationem omnium tribuum. 'Pennae
columbae'. id est decorassa (= decorosa) es, o tribus Iuda, ut pennae columbae...'columba'. id est arca... Spiritaliter. 'Si dormiatis inter medios cleros'. id est
duobus credens testamentis inuenies in utroque testamento Spiritum Sanctum; et
licet sit pulchritudo iuxta litteram, tamen decorosius est sensus; exterior itaque
uerborum ornatus in argenti nomine demonstratur; ocultorum uero misteria in
reconditis auri muneribus continentur.* Latin text in McNamara (ed.), *Glossa in
Psalmos*, p. 138. The Latin text cites Jerome, *Commentarioli in Psalmos on Ps. 67*
(ed. G. Morin in CCSL, 72; Turnhout: Brepols, 1959), pp. 214, ll. 8-15.

38. In *Thes. Pal.*, I, p. 13.

39. In *Thes Pal.*, I, p. 13. On the senses of Scripture in Irish texts, see further M.
McNamara, 'The Irish Tradition of Biblical Exegesis, AD 550–800', in S. van Riel,
C. Steel and J. McEvoy (eds.), *Iohannes Scottus Eriugena: The Bible and Herme-
neutics* (Proceedings of the Ninth International Colloquium of the Society for the
Promotion of Eriugenian Studies held at Leuven and Louvain-la-Neuve June 7–10,
1995) (Leuven: University Press, 1996), pp. 25-49 (43-45).

and more so (with greater use of Cassiodorus) in the Psalms section in the 'Reference Bible' (both mid or late eighth century). The tenth-century Double Psalter of St Ouen gives the spiritual interpretation on the Vulgate Psalter (the *Gallicanum*) on the right-hand sides and the historical interpretation on Jerome's translation from the Hebrew (the *Hebraicum*) on the left-hand pages facing this. The glosses on the later Southampton Psalter (beginning of eleventh century), although as yet not fully examined, seem to give much more place to the spiritual interpretation of the psalms.

6. *Irish Psalm Interpretation and Some Modern Hermeneutical Concerns*

This consideration of the interpretation of the messianic psalms, or of the christological application of the psalms, in Irish tradition reveals that some of the concerns of exegesis over the past 200 years were already there in part in the early Church and in medieval Ireland. I shall briefly consider a few of them here.

6.1. *Primacy of the Literal Sense*

All Christian tradition admitted, at least in theory, that Scripture had a literal, as distinct from spiritual sense, and that this literal sense was fundamental. In practice, however, exposition according to the literal sense was not much practised. The Christian meaning of the Old Testament, or the implications of the text of both Testaments for Christian living were of greater interest.

The Irish tradition stressed the literal meaning. A further feature of one branch of the tradition is the consideration of the text of the Psalms without any reference to the New Testament or Christian living. This is noticeable in particular with regard to Psalms 2, 15 and 21.

6.2. *A More than Literal Sense of Scripture?*

Consideration of many psalm texts, as Old Testament texts in general, without finding in them any intrinsic reference to a future redeemer or to Christ, raises the question whether we should speak of a more than literal sense of Scripture (whatever this might mean). If Psalm 44(45) is a marriage song, without any forward glance, can we say that an apparently stray remark such as 'Your throne, O God, endures forever' (v. 6) had a depth of meaning beyond that which the poet psalmist would have conceived of, with reference even to Christ's divinity (see Heb.

1.8)? Similar questions can be raised with regard to Psalm 21 (in the Davidic interpretation), to Psalm 109 (110) and others. And if we refuse to admit that it had such a dimension, how can the Old Testament text be linked with the mystery of Christ? I merely raise the question. And to raise it, and appreciate it, gives us an understanding of the positions of Origen, Alexandria and Antioch. Can we truly say that (to use Newman's term) Scripture has a 'mystical' sense? Or should we opt for some other term in our attempt to understand the place of Scripture, the Book of the Covenant, in the working out of God's plan? Perhaps we should look on the Bible, the Old Testament in particular, as enjoying a life of its own, even though inspired by God, as a text to be first understood in its own time, and on more than one instance foreign to our way of thinking. The God of whom Scripture speaks continued to reveal himself, and later tradition often used old categories and old terms to describe the new revelation of the divine, sometimes without inner continuity between the old text and new revelation. The problem was sensed by the Antiochenes. Perhaps their *theoria* explanation has still something, possibly even a good deal, to offer.

6.3. *Bible in Academe, Bible in Ecclesia*
Study of the Bible as a historical and literary text and use of the Bible as a sacred book at the centre of the believing communities, the Bible in Academe and the Bible in Ecclesia, are features of our own day. They present problems on how to formulate a theory in which both are seen as complementary rather than as opposed. The facts and the problem are not new. They were perceived in the school of Antioch. In this sense the academic approach was regarded as a requirement for a proper liturgical use of the psalms of David. The command 'Sing praises with understanding,' *psallite sapienter* (Ps. 46.8), was regarded as possible only when combined with literal and historical interpretation. The same could be said to have held true in the Irish tradition. The members of the religious community using the Double Psalter of St Ouen would find the historical exposition in Jerome's translation from the Hebrew on the left-hand pages, and facing this the spiritual interpretation on the Vulgate *Gallicanum* text.

While knowledge of this tradition will scarcely solve our present-day problems, awareness of tradition might contribute a sense of perspective.

APPENDIX I

*Irish Historical Non-Messianic Davidic Interpretation
of Psalms 2 and 8*

1. *Psalm 2 in the Double Psalter of St Ouen (Rouen Psalter)*
I have already spoken above (in 7.3.b) of this 'Davidic' commentary on the Psalms,
found for Pss. 1.1–16.11 on the left-hand side on the Double Psalter of St Ouen
(Rouen Bibl. mun. MS 24 [A.41]), in glosses on the *Hebraicum*. It has a special
heading (found also in the *Tituli* of Bede and in the introductory material to Psalm 2
in the so-called Psalter of Charlemagne). Both in the heading and in the expository
glosses, the psalm is interpreted entirely in a non-christological manner.

Heading
David makes complaint of a general nature to the Lord that the pagan nations and
the peoples of Israel are envious of his kingdom given to him from above, [thus]
addressing a common admonition to all.
    The voice of David's companions accusing Absalom and the voice of the Jewish
people concerning the Assyrians, and the voice of Hezekiah.

Interpretative Glosses (biblical text indicated by italics)
(v. 1). *Why shall the [pagan] nations be agitated?* Why, he says, like a dog, do they
bark at me?
And the tribes meditate empty things? Why do you think up an empty plot, [since]
you cannot expel him whom God helps?
the tribes. Absalom and his companions. *vain things.* David's flight.

(v. 2) *The kings of the earth rise up.* Those are said 'to stand' who rise up for war.
and the leaders will act together. They act of set purpose that they may expel me.
together. of a single purpose.
against the Lord and against his Christ. [text in part illegible]…and they desire to
destroy the law.
his Christ. Every king is called a 'Christ of the Lord', for no one accepts… [text in
part illegible] unless God [or: the Lord] permits.

(v. 3) *let us break asunder their chains.* [text uncertain…] they say: The chains of
the kings of the peoples of Israel who reduce us to slavery.
their chains. the voice of David and of his companions.
let us cast their snares from us. After the manner of untamed calves.

(v. 5) *in his anger.* In a lighter punishment.
and in his rage he will throw them into disorder. May he so throw them into disorder that they do not know what to do or what to speak; that is in a more severe
punishment.

(v. 6) *For I have installed [orditus sum] my king…* [text illegible]
Sion. Jerusalem, which Absalom wants to have.

(v. 7) *The Lord said to me: You are my son.* [text in part illegible]…the king's [son?]…the Lord has decreed,…not only, but he has wished that he […], where he says; 'He will call on me, "You are my father" as far as "I will set him" ' [Ps. 88.27-29].
today I have begotten you. [At the t]ime in which I shall make you rule over all who want to oppose you.
today. In the day of your election to the kingdom.

(v. 8). *Ask of me and I will give you [the pagan] nations as your inheritance.* [Although] a father may have many [sons], nevertheless to one alone is it [gran]ted that anything he may ask is never denied.
and the ends of the earth [as] your possession. The [seven] nations of Canaan and among [text illegible]…and the men of Syria as far as the Euphrates.
and [as your] possession. It is useless for them to expel me when God gave me as inheritance the land of promise.

(v. 9). *You shall rule them with a rod of iron.* So that you subdue all by rigour.

(v. 10). *Now, therefore, have understanding, O kings.* Acquire understanding so that you may do what is most certainly in your inter[est] [*text slightly uncertain*].
Now, therefore. The voice of David or of the Holy Spirit.
understand. your lord.
be instructed you judges of the earth…

(v. 11). *And exult in trembling…*
[serve the Lord] in trembling. Because ambivalent service proceeds either from hatred of the master or from servile wickedness.

(v. 12) *Adore.* Correct your way of acting towards David, rendering the right of kingship to him.
[lest] he be angry. By reason of the persecution of me.
lest you perish from the way. It is a debt owed to nature that those who serve under discipline minister.
from the way. From the place of battle in battles against David.

(v. 13) *when after a while his fury blazes up.* [When] indignation erupts, blessed are those who hope in him…
Blessed are those who hope in him. David with his companions.
Blessed. David's conquering men.
in him. Not in his own strength.

2. *Psalm 8 in the Double Psalter of St Ouen (Rouen Psalter)*

In his work *Theodore of Mopsuestia on the Bible*[40] D.Z. Zaharopoulos notes that Theodore's interpretation of Psalm 8, as applied in his commentary 'is strange to the original meaning of this Hebrew hymn because the most distinctive elements in it are the majesty and glory of God as revealed in the calm of an oriental night, and the place of man in the scheme of creation'. However, given the New Testament use it is not surprising that the christological interpretation was nigh well universal in the Christian Church. This is what we have in all the psalm headings series.

Together with this, however, there was another historical and non-christological interpretation, even though not widely attested. We find it in the psalm headings of Pseudo-Bede (used, and probably compiled in Northumbria, eighth century or earlier).[41] Thus, the heading to this present Psalm (Ps. 8): 'The prophet admires God's might, by which he governs the whole mass of the world and gives thanks that such a great Creator has deigned to be mindful of man'. An entire commentary to this heading has been preserved in the glosses of the Double Psalter (*Gallicanum* and *Hebraicum*) now in Rouen (France) but written in Ireland in the tenth century.[42] The gloss on Psalm 8 is as follows:

(v. 1). *O Lord...* The gods of the heathen are in their own lands, but the name of our God is made known throughout the whole universe.

(v. 2). *from the mouths of babes...* No age, no human life ceases from praising you. All creation should praise the Creator.

babes and sucklings. that is, those who cannot speak, who are tender and are being breast fed. This came about at the Red Sea when everyone sang 'Let us sing to the Lord' (Exod. 15.1) ...

What is man? When the Creator is so great and created things so many, why should man deserve to be helped?

Man. or David.

You remember. You give him a kingdom.

Or the son of man... Human nature is weak, but through your mercy you visit it.

You make him a little less than God. You have placed him in the third grade below yourself. First the angels, then humans are set in glory...

You give him power over the works of your hands. The whole world with its equipment has been handed over to mankind.

---

40. Zaharopoulos, *Theodore*, p. 48.

41. On the pseudo-Bedan psalm headings see M. McNamara, 'Tradition and Creativity in Early Irish Psalter Study', in pp. 239-301, at 261-64; see also p. 298 (in this volume).

42. On this commentary see McNamara, 'Tradition and Creativity', pp. 268-70. The 'historical' commentary for these psalms has been provisionally edited by De Coninck, *Incerti*; Ps. 6, pars altera, pp. 20-21.

(v. 6). *You have placed all things under his feet...sheep and cattle...* Not only things of the land but also things of the sky and of the sea have been given for his use.
Beasts of the field. Goats and pigs and such like, or the wild beasts which feed through the fields.
In all the earth. Just as the discourse began by the admiration of your might, thus at the end it has magnificently praised that same might.

The significance of this ending is that the author notes the *inclusio* technique of the psalms, a technique also common in Irish poetry, where it is known as *dúnadh* 'a closing', 'shutting', 'in prosody a technical term for closing or ending a poem with the word with which it begins' (see *Contributions to a Dictionary of the Irish Language*, D, col. 450). The same point is made in the Old Irish Milan gloss on the verse (Ml 26b10): 'As this psalm begins with praise and admiration of the Lord, it is thus moreover that it is concluded, even as the poets do with us.'[43]

With the gloss on v. 6 ('goats and pigs and such like'), compare the ancient Irish hermits' delight in such animals, for example, Marbhán to Guaire: 'I have a hut in the wood (v. 8)... Around it tame swine, goats, young pigs, wild swine, tall deer, does...' (v. 16).[44]

APPENDIX II

Messianic Psalms, other than Psalms 2 and 8, in the Irish Tradition

1. *Psalm 44 (45)*
a. *Psalm 44 (45) Theodorean interpretation*
Theodore's exposition of Psalm 44 (45) has been preserved in Greek.[45] We do not have a full Latin translation; only the Epitome. The psalm is taken throughout as a prophecy of Christ and his Church: the *regina* of v. 7a is *ecclesia*. The Irish glosses on the Milan codex tend to follow the Latin, but make the references to the Church more explicit (with seven references, mostly from v. 10 onwards). To give one example, on *ibi* of v. 13b: *Filiae Tiri in muneribus. Multo honore apud potentes quosque et ibi* (sic MS; *lege tibi*) *ipsa uicinitate compertos habebitur*, the Milan gloss first corrects and then comments: 'or *tibi*, i.e. O primitive Church of the apostles' (*a eclais cétnaide inna napstal*) (Ml 65d14). The expression *primitiua ecclesia* is found in Hiberno-Latin texts. The present example helps us identify *ecclesia primitiua* in question as that of the New Testament period.

43. *Thes. Pal.*, I, p. 51.
44. See G. Murphy, *Early Irish Lyrics Eighth to Twelfth Century* (Oxford: Clarendon Press, 1956; repr. Dublin, 1998), p. 13.
45. Devreesse, *Le commentaire*, pp. 277-306.

b. *Psalm 44 (45): Davidic interpretation*

The composite biblical heading for Psalm 44 (45) ends: *canticum pro dilecto*, in Hebrew *sîr yedîdôt* (*yedîdôt* apparently being a feminine plural of *yedîd*, 'beloved'). Jerome understood the related Hebrew word *yedîdî* ('my beloved') as a name for Solomon, and in his commentary on Ecclesiastes[46] interpreted the entire psalm of Solomon. This is also how the Irish Davidic interpretation found in Pal. lat. 68 understands it. Thus in the heading (as in that of the so-called Psalter of Charlemagne): Salmus Dauid. *id est de se ipso et de Salomone*. And again: prae consortibus tuis (v. 8). *id est Salomon secus filios Dauid*. Adstetit regina (v. 10). *id est filia Faraonis, siue regina Austri quae uenit a 54v v finibus terrae audire sapientiam Salomonis*. Adducentur regi (v. 15). *id est Salomoni uirgines de Aegiptis*. Post eam. *id est filiam Faraonis*. The text is also interpreted of Christ and the Church, but this exposition is generally introduced as *spiritaliter*. The compiler himself is evidently quite unhappy with the form of interpretation he is about to consign to writing, since on v. 2, *eructuauit*, he says: Totus hic salmus refertur ad Christum de quo Pater in euangelio loquitur: *Hic est filius meus dilectus*, licet ad Salomonem inertialis historia refertur.

Yet despite this, a few lines further on we read: *Haec quae sequntur conueniunt Salomoni historialiter, et Christo spiritaliter, et sancto moraliter*.

2. *Psalm 109 (110)*

a. *Psalm 109 (110) Theodorean interpretation*

No copy of the Greek text of Theodore's commentary on Psalm 109 (110) has come down to us, nor has any part of the full Latin translation. All we have is the Epitome of the Latin translation. The introductory words inform us that the Lord himself in the Gospel interpreted this psalm of himself to the Pharisees. The exposition,[47] which is not extensive, interprets the entire psalm of Christ, and introduces a theological element on the relationship of the Son, or of *Verbum*, to the Father. In the comment on the opening words *Dixit Dominus Domino* usque *meis* in the Epitome two interpretations of the Jews are rejected: one taking the speaker as Abraham's servant, the other as David, describing what God had said to Abraham at the time he was prepared for war.[48]

The Irish glosses, as is usual, concentrate on bringing out the meaning of the Latin text. One (Ml 127d3) identifies Abraham's servant as 'a servant who went from Abraham to woo Rebecca for Isaac.' The next gloss (Ml 127d4) interprets v. 1, with Abraham as the intended speaker: *Dixit .i. seruus* (the speaker is Abraham's servant); *dominus .i. deus pater* (i.e. Abraham's servant said that God the

46. M. Adriaen (ed.), *S. Hieronymi presbyteri Commentarius in Ecclesiasten* (CCSL, 72; Turnhout: Brepols, 1959), p. 250.

47. De Coninck and d'Hont (eds.), *Theodori*, pp. 351-53.

48. *Cessant ergo falsae opiniones Iudaeorum, qui aut Abrahae serui personam de domino suo loquentem introduci putant, aut ipsum Dauid, quid Deus Abrahae in procinctu belli dixerit, describentem intelligi uolunt* (De Coninck and d'Hont [eds.], *Theodori*, pp. 351-52).

Father said); *domino .i. abrachae* (i.e. the lord who is addressed is Abraham). The gloss goes on to note (as the Latin Epitome being glossed does) that such an inter-pretation is false. The next gloss (Ml 127d5) tells what the understanding would be if David were speaker, in the second Jewish interpretation: the subject of *dixit* is David; *Dominus* is *Deus Pater; domino* is Abraham, i.e. David said (in this psalm): God the Father said to Abraham, David's master. With the Latin Epitome, the gloss adds: 'such an understanding, indeed, is error'.

There are also Irish glosses on the christological exposition of the Latin text, with reference to the Manhood and the Godhead of the Son, as in the glosses on Psalms 2 and 8. The Latin commentary, with christological interpretation, says: 'The prophet calls Christ Lord according to divinity' (*secundum divinitatem*). An Irish gloss on *secundum (diuinitatem)* has: 'That is the true sense' (Ml 127d7). Another text of the commentary says: 'The Lord (*Dominus*) is said to sit so that his kingdom and domination be indicated by those words, according to the text (Ps. 9.5b): 'You are seated (*sedes super thronum qui iudicas iustitiam*) on the throne, you who judge justly'. A composite Latin and Irish gloss on *Dominus* runs: 'that is, *Christus secundum carnem*, i.e. for it is not necessary to say it to his Godhead for he is of equal authority with God the Father already' (Ml 127d8). The next gloss, on *super* reads: 'i.e. it is said to him with respect to his Manhood' (Ml 127d9).

Immediately after the citation of Ps. 109.5b, the Epitome text, with Theodorean theology, continues:

> Filio ergo Pater aequalitatem honoris communicat, iudicandi quoque tradit et communicat potestatem. Honoris communio Homini per Verbum collata *cons-essionis* nomine *a dextris*, praestantioribus in nobis partibus, indicatur; qui locus utramque naturam in Christo contestatur; non enim donatur nisi homini potestatis aequatio, et e regione non asciscceretur in societatem tantae dignitatis si solus homo esset.[49]

There are a number of Irish glosses on this text, all apparently intended to explain the sense of the Latin. Two to be combined into one, on the text from *(ergo) Pater* to *iudicandi* read: 'i.e. He gives equal honour with Himself and with the Godhead of the Son to the Manhood of the Son' (Ml 127d10–11). An extensive gloss on *(partibus), indicatur* reads: 'i.e. the Godhead and the Manhood of Christ are indicated through the passage of the narration that he speaks of here, to wit, *sede a dextris*, for he says that to the Manhood, and that that would not have been said to it, were it not that the Godhead dwelt in it' (*manipad deacht duatrub indi*) (Ml 127d14). On *[nisi] homini* we have the gloss: 'i.e. to the Manhood of Christ' (Ml 127d16).

b. *Psalm 109 (110) Davidic interpretation*
The commentary in Pal. lat. 68, in the literal exposition, is a full non-christological exposition, interpreting the psalm as spoken by David of Saul and of himself. Thus:

---

49.   De Coninck and d'Hont (eds.), *Theodori*, pp. 352, 19-25. Text and Irish glosses in *Thes. Pal.*, I, pp. 434-37.

Dixit dominus. Vox Dauid; id est Saul (the voice is that of David; the 'lord' he refers to is his lord Saul, who is the speaker in what immediately follows).

> *Domino meo.* id est Samueli. *Sede a dextris meis.* id est Saul Samueli dixit postquam interficit Achab pinguissimum Amalech [Achab = Agag; see 1 Sam. 15.32-33]. *inimicos tuos.* id est gentes circumstantes. *Uirgam uirtutis tuae.* Vox Spiritus Sancti; id est Dauid. *ante luciferum.* id est ante Saul…secundum historiam *dominare in medio.* id est inter genera Cannan. *tecum principium.* id est uictoria in die belli…*in splendoribus sanctorum.* id est in Samuele qui lux huius mundi fuit. *ante luciferum genui te.* id est Samuel; …iurauit *Dominus.* id est in uisionibus Samuelis promisit uictoriam de hostibus. *Dominus a dextris tuis.* id est adiuuabit te in praelio. *reges.* id est reges gentium. *de torrente in uia bibit.* id est in exilio bibebat aquas (the reference apparently is to David's flight before Absalom).

As was the case at the beginning of the exposition of Psalm 44 (45), so at the end of the exposition of Psalm 109 (110), the compiler says: *Totus hic salmus de Christo canitur, licet alii historialem inhertiam in eo contexunt, ut ostendimus.*

3. *Psalm 15 (16) in Irish Exegesis*
a. *Psalm 15 (16) in Antiochene Exegesis (Diodorus and Theodore)*
We have an Antiochene commentary on the Psalter, which may be the work of Diodorus of Tarsus, teacher of Theodore of Mopsuestia.[50] The exposition of Psalm 15 (16) in this work is basically the same as that found in Theodore's commentary. Theodore's own commentary has been preserved partly in the original Greek; mainly, however, in the full translation of Julian of Eclanum in Codex Amb. C 301 inf.[51] In his brief introduction he says that Psalm 15 (16) is for the same occasion as the preceding one, namely that it gives thanks for the destruction of the surrounding nations, which David himself defeated with divine aid. The psalm, then, was sung (composed) in the person of the whole people (of Israel). Theodore seems to interpret vv. 9–10 of Israel. 'My flesh' (lxx) of v. 10 is for the entire person; 'rests in safety', that is, Israel in safety in her own soil. The 'holy one' of v. 10 who shall not see corruption is Israel, 'holy' in comparison with the Gentiles and shall not be corrupted by the iniquity of her adversaries. Theodore notes Peter's use of this in Acts 2.31, and his understanding it of the resurrection of Christ. Theodore sees this use by Peter in keeping with the original meaning of the text (although Theodore's words seem far from clear):

> We must note here that the blessed apostle Peter is reported in the book of Acts to have used the sayings of this psalm as if they had been spoken about Christ. However, it must be made known that even in Acts this psalmic utterance is understood by Peter as it was understood by the psalmist. In Acts, of course,

---

50. See Olivier (ed.), *Diodori*, pp. 66-75; 76-86.

51. Latin text preserved in Milan, Codex Amb. C 301 inf., and also in Turin, University Library F.IV,1, fasc. (in part damaged by fire in 1904; MS from Bobbio). De Coninck and d'Hont (eds.), *Theodori*, pp. 75-81; Devreesse, *Le commentaire*, pp. 90-100.

the psalmic text is quoted with a more stimulating force and in accordance with its true signification. What I mean is that this psalmic utterance as far as its verbal literalism is concerned has received its issuance in the Lord Christ. The apostle applied this biblical testimony to the Lord Christ because the issuance of the new circumstances had pronounced it more fittingly suited to him.[52]

Theodore's (non-messianic) interpretation of this psalm was condemned by the *Constitutum* of Pope Vigilius and the Fifth Council of Constantinople 553 CE.[53]

(i) *Early Irish Interpretation of Psalm 15 (16): The Milan Commentary and Old Irish Glosses (c. 800 CE).* In the Irish manuscript Amb. C 301 inf., written by the Irish scribe who signed himself 'Diarmuid' we have the full Latin text of Julian's translation. The Old Irish glosses (from c. 800 CE) in general try to bring out the sense of the Latin text, for example, on Peter's use of it (in Theodore's text cited above): 'it was not the apostle who first uttered this text. Another possible meaning: the apostle did not apply it according to the sense in which the prophet uttered it' (Ml 38v3).[54] Or again on the Latin *causae suae redditum* (rendered above as 'fittingly suited to him'): 'i.e. he (the apostle Peter) applies it to support the saying that was uttered through congruence to the cause on which he was engaged' (Ml 38c4); or a little later, 'that of which he applied it is different to that of which Peter uttered it' (Ml 38c5). Obviously there was difference of opinion among the eighth-century scholars as to whether Peter used the text in its original sense, in the sense intended by the original author of the psalm.

(ii) *Early Irish Interpretation of Psalm 15 (16): In the Glosses in the Double Psalter of Rouen (Ireland tenth century).* In the Latin glosses on this psalm in the Double Psalter (*Gallicanum* and *Hebraicum*) of Rouen we have a further non-messianic interpretation of this psalm, quite different from that of Theodore of Mopsuestia. This Psalter text and glosses were written in Ireland in the tenth century and later taken to France. In this interpretation the entire psalm is understood principally as referring to the sickness of King Hezekiah (Isa. 38; 2 Kgs 20). It is given in the special heading as being the prayer of Hezekiah in his illness, and is interpreted in the brief comments as such.

(Heading) In his illness Hezekiah beseeches the Lord and gives thanks for having been restored to health, and expounds that he has not been deprived of earthly goods.

(v. 9a) *Wherefore is my heart glad.* When I see that you give your gifts lavishly, my heart rejoices in you.

---

52. Translation in Zaharopoulos, *Theodore*, p. 148.
53. Relevant text of *Constitutum* in Devreesse, *Le commentaire*, pp. 99-100.
54. *Thes. Pal.*, I, p. 99.

And my flesh has dwelt confidently. I have so much confidence in you that I believe that I shall be restored to strength in this cure. Or (another possible sense of the text is): (I rejoice) in the hope of receiving the kingdom of David.

(v. 10a) *You shall not leave my soul in hell.* You will not allow me, to whom you have decided to give so many happy things, to go to death.
In hell. i.e. in lowliness (humiliation) or in the grave.
(v. 10b) *Nor allow your holy one to see corruption.* You have adorned (me) with gifts and with the royal anointing; (you will grant me) restored health.
(Your) holy one. that is, David or Hezekiah.
(v. 10c) *You shall show me the path of life.* You shall show how a life already despaired of can by your power be reintegrated; or (another possible meaning): you revealed to me that Saul would not kill me.
The fullness of joys before your face... I will be full of joy in your presence in the temple at all times, which is manifest in the thought of the heart and the clothes of the body; or: you will turn away your face from (my) enemies, that is Saul and his friends.

4. *Psalm 21 (22) in Irish Exegesis*

An examination of the treatment of Psalm 21 in the various forms of the Theodorean and Irish historical exegesis is interesting and informative from the point of view of the present study.

This psalm, *Deus Deus meus*, recited by Christ on the cross, is headed in the Vulgate *In finem pro adsumptione* [MS I of the Irish Vulgate, has *pro susceptione]* *matutina psalmus Dauid.*

In the genuine Theodorean commentary (as preserved in Latin translation in fragments in Milan and Turin, deriving from Bobbio), David is said to have sung (= composed) this psalm 'as he found himself in the trials that had been brought on him by Absalom' (*in tribulationibus quae illi ab Abessalon illatae fuerant constitutus.*[55] In the Epitome an attempt is made to combine this historical understanding with a christological reference: Christ's final prayer on the cross has taught us to whom we should refer this psalm, *qui tamen suis temporibus habuit figuram illius historiae quae narrat Dauid coniuratione Abessalon in aerumnas coactus, in quibus positus hoc carmen uice orationis cecinit.*[56]

The Irish glossator in the Milan commentary is faithful to this christological interpretation of the Latin Epitome. Thus, a gloss on the title *pro susceptione* reads: 'i.e. of the wending that Christ went to the house of the priests, to wit, to the house of Annas and Caiaphas, and of his coming to Pontius Pilate, afterwards in the morning before the Passion, it is of that that David sang this psalm, and of his passion that Christ suffered after that *ut dicitur in tractatu libri Marci secundum Hieronymum*' (Ml 44b1).[57] The end reference is to the Commentary on Mark, which this

---

55. De Coninck and d'Hont (eds.), *Theodori*, pp. 107, 1-2.
56. De Coninck and d'Hont (eds.), *Theodori*, pp. 108, 2-5.
57. *Thes. Pal.*, I, p. 125.

same scribe Diarmuid also glossed; see the Latin text in *PL* 30, 639C. A gloss on *docuit* ('taught') of the Epitome says: 'i.e. it is of the passion of Christ that David sang this' (Ml 44b2). The Theodorean interpretation, however, is not forgotten. On *Diviserunt sibi vestimenta mea* usque *meam* the Epitome has a historical and 'mystical' interpretation: *haec omnia captis Hirusolimis a coniuratione Abisolon circa Dauid constat impleta. Euangelista autem in Deo pro rerum similitudine hoc testimonio usus est, sicut et in aliis ostendimus.*[58] The Irish glossator is alert to the dual reference. In a gloss on *haec omnia* he says: 'i.e. by Absalom to take the kingship in his father's stead' (Ml 44d29). He has the following gloss to *rerum similitudine*: 'i.e. the figure of the mystic sense *(fris inrúin)*' (Ml 45a2), the sense intended being, it would appear, that what happened to David was a figure of Christ in his passion. The Irish gloss (on *ostendimus*) is fuller. It runs: 'i.e. that the figure in accordance with which the prophet uttered it, and the mystic sense *(indrún)* with which the evangelists apply it, are different'.

The *Tituli* of Bede *(PL* 93, 589) have a dual historical reference—first to David, in Absalom's conspiracy and then to Esther, going on a Jewish interpretation recorded by Jerome, *Commentarioli in Ps XXI,*[59] without any spiritual heading. The heading in the Psalter of Charlemagne makes more explicit the reference in the Theodorean heading, referring it to Absalom's taking over David's harem *(concubinas)*: *Hic psalmus: Dauid cantauit cum suscepisset Absalon concubinas sibi in coniugium* (cf. 2 Sam. 16.21-22).

The gloss on Ps. 21.19 *(diviserunt sibi uestimenta mea)* in the *Hebraicum* of the Double Psalter of Rouen is in keeping with this explicit heading: David's *vestimenta* are his harem—*Dauid: decem concubinas eius rapuerunt*.

The identification of the clothes as women *(concubinae)* may have an exegetical history behind it which has not yet been fully studied. We find something similar in the Jewish interpretation of Zech. 3.3, in which the visionary says he saw Joshua the high priest 'clothed with filthy garments.' Why Joshua was so clothed required an explanation. The Babylonian Talmud, *Sanhedrin* 93a, explains it through the illicit marriage of his sons: 'His (that is Joshua's) sons married wives unfit for the priesthood and he did not protest' (the reference being to Ezra 10.18 which says that four sons [= descendants] of Joshua the son of Jozadak and his brothers married foreign wives). A tradition such as this probably lies behind the Aramaic (Targum) translation of Zech. 3.3, where 'garments' are identified as 'wives unsuitable for priesthood' (= priests), rendering: 'And Joshua *had sons who were unsuitable for priests*' (literally: 'for the priesthood'). The same principle of translation is followed through in Zech. 3.4-5 where the Hebrew text: 'Remove the filthy garment from him', is rendered as : 'Speak to him and let him drive out from his house the wives who are unsuitable for priests' (literally 'for the priesthood'), and 'They clothed him with garments' of the Hebrew text as: 'they made him marry a wife who was suitable for a priest' (literally: 'fit for the priesthood'). This understanding of Zech. 3.3 is found substantially in Justin's *Dialogue with Trypho* 116.3 (c. 155–

---

58. De Coninck and d'Hont (eds.), *Theodori*, p. 131.
59. *Commentarioli in Psalmos*, in Ps. 21, p. 198.

60 CE), with the difference that Jesus (= Joshua) is said to have married a harlot. It is also found in Jerome's commentary on Zechariah, where Joshua (with others) is mentioned as having taken a foreign wife.[60] It may be that the equation of clothes with spouses has drawn inspiration from the custom of claiming a wife by casting one's garments over her (Deut. 27.20; Ruth 3.9; Ezek. 16.8). It might also be (as in Justin) that the equation is not restricted to wives, and that it may have had more widespread application than for the sole text of Zech. 3.3-5. The equation clothes/women found in the Hiberno-Latin commentary of the Double Psalter of St Ouen may, then, be a remnant of a more widespread ancient exegetical tradition.

5. *Psalm 30 (31), verse 6a in Irish Exegesis*
Verse 6 of this psalm ('Into your hands, O Lord, I commit my spirit') was recited by Jesus on the cross (Lk. 23.46) and by Stephen at his martyrdom (Acts 7.59). In contrast to Psalms 2, 8, 45, and 110, Theodore does not find in this New Testament citation an argument that the text was originally intended as a messianic prophecy. A disciple of his could write:[61]

> But when our Lord says on the cross: 'My God, my God, why hast thou forsaken me?' and again: 'Into thy hands I commend my spirit' which saying is found in Psalm 31.6, these words are said by a comparison according to the resemblance of the events, although in their original place their application is different. Now the difference which exists between these things is evidenced with clarity from the context to those who want to know the truth.

The exposition in the Epitome of Julian's translation is almost identical:

> *In manus tuas, Domine,* usque *meum*. Utitur hac uoce Dominus in patibulo tamquam apta, non tamquam propria: quia concinebat <ad> causam, non quia praedixerat passionem.[62]

The Irish gloss on the text (on *tamquam propria*) renders faithfully the sense of the Latin of the Epitome, but seems to leave responsibility for the view with the 'historical commentator', whose viewpoint the glossator himself may not have shared. It reads: 'i.e. for it was not for that that the prophet uttered it according to the literal truth, says the (historical) commentator' (Ml 50a8). The word rendered as

---

60.   For examination of the Talmud and Targums texts see L. Smolar and M. Aberbach, *Studies in Targum Jonathan to the Prophets* (The Library of Biblical Studies; New York: Ktav; Baltimore: The Baltimore Hebrew College, 1983), p. 25; R.P. Gordon, *Studies in the Targum to the Twelve Prophets* (VTSup, 51; Leiden: E.J. Brill, 1994), pp. 108-11; K.J. Cathcart and R.P. Gordon, *The Targum of the Minor Prophets* (translated, with a Critical Introduction, Apparatus, and Notes; The Aramaic Bible, 14; Wilmington, DE: Michael Glazier; Edinburgh: T. & T. Clark, 1989), pp. 191-92. For the texts of Justin and Jerome, see Gordon, *Studies*, pp. 109-10; Cathcart and Gordon, *The Targum*, pp. 191-92.

61.   Isho'dad of Merv, *Introduction to the Psalms*; cited in Zaharopoulos, *Theodore*, p. 115, as part of a long citation from J.M. Vosté, 'L'œuvre exégétique de Théodore de Mopsueste', *Revue Biblique* 29 (1929), pp. 544-46.

62.   In De Coninck and d'Hont (eds.), *Theodori*, p. 136.

'historical commentator' is *stoirier*, from *stoir*, 'history', or 'historical sense of Scripture.' It is found only in the Milan glosses, and may here have the slightly pejorative sense of 'historical commentator' (who does not pay attention to the christological reference of the text).

6. *Psalm 31 (32).1b–2 in Irish Exegesis*

Psalm 31 (32).1b–2 *Beati quorum remissae sunt iniquitates et quorum tecta sunt peccata. Beatus vir cui non inputabit Dominus peccatum* are cited by Paul in Rom. 4.6-8, to add weight to his point that human works by themselves are useless for obtaining pardon from God. The Latin translation of Theodore's commentary is extant partly in the full rendering, as well as in the Epitome.[63] The psalm is taken as a poem on the cure of Hezekiah from his illness. The Epitome comments on vv. 1b-2 as follows: 'Et quorum *usque* peccatum. *Usurpat Apostolus hos uersus aptos magis actioni suae quam prophetice in illam causam directos*'. The Old Irish Milan glosses on the text make the same point. Thus, on *apostolus*: Ml 50d16: 'i.e. it is in the book of the apostle'; on *actioni suae*, l50d17: 'i.e. on account of their aptness to the doctrine that he preached'; on *prophetice*, Ml 50d18: 'i.e. for the prophet did not utter it with respect to that to which the apostle applies it, says the commentator (*stoirier*)'—again using the rare term *stoirier*, 'historical commentator,' possibly to distance himself from his position.

7. *Psalm 68 (69) in Irish Exegesis*

Psalm 68 (69) is one of the psalms most frequently quoted in the New Testament. The citations range over the entire psalm, with a concentration on the psalmist's prayer for revenge against his enemy in vv. 22-28. The texts are as follows:

v. 4	Jn 15.25
v. 9	Jn 2.17
v. 10	Jn 2.17
v. 21	See Mt. 27.34
vv. 22-24	Rom. 11.9-10
v. 24	Rev. 16.1
v. 25	Acts 1.20

According to Theodore, in the Greek text and the Epitome of Julian's translation,[64] the poem is written in a spirit of prophecy on the time of the Maccabees and its discourse is quite appropriate for the persons and events of that age. Commenting on v. 22 (*Et dederunt in escam meam fel, et in siti mea potauerunt me aceto*) the Epitome has:[65]

---

63. Devreesse (ed.), *Le commentaire*, p. 142; De Coninck and d'Hont (eds.), *Theodori*, pp. 139-42.

64. Greek text, Devreesse (ed.), *Le commentaire*, pp. 447-59; Epitome, De Coninck and d'Hont (eds.), *Theodori*, pp. 251-55.

65. De Coninck and d'Hont (eds.), *Theodori*, p. 253.

> *Usus est hoc euangelista testimonio cum de Domini passione loqueretur; quod*
> *quidem ad iudaicae profertur impietatis indicium: non in tempore Passionis*
> *prodita, sed longe a diuina Scriptura ac multo ante predicta; probatur ergo*
> *magis similibus aptata esse negotiis quam propria singulorum.*

The Irish glosses to the Milan Codex on this psalm are not expansive. Two, however, note Theodore's position.[66] A gloss on *similibus* (Ml 86d16) has: 'i.e. in
respect to appropriateness he applies it to the Passion, namely, *dederunt rl.*' A gloss
on the concluding word, *singulorum*, reads: 'i.e. for it was not first sung to them'
(Ml 86d19a), i.e. 'to those who were crucifying Christ' (Ml 86d19).

Irish tradition as represented in the commentary of Pal. lat. 68 (from c. 700)
attempts a multiple exegesis. The comment is prefaced by corresponding titles: *Pro*
erumnis Saul. Vox Ionae de sua persona. Vox plebis in captiuitate. Sed Dauid de
tempore Machabeorum profetali spiritu hoc carmen scripsit. Vox Christi in pas-
sione. Its comment on v. 22 is brief, first giving a Davidic interpretation, and then
noting Jerome's position:

> *Et dederunt in escam meam fel.* Id est si ad Dauid: omne quod manducabam in
> exilio pro felle reputabam; Hirunimus: Ex hoc testimonio intellegitur quod ad
> Christum salmus iste refferi debeat.[67]

8. *Psalm 71 (72) in Irish Exegesis*

The biblical title of this psalm refers it to Solomon ('For Solomon'; *In Salomonem*).
We possess the Greek text of Theodore's commentary[68] and the Epitome of Julian's
translation.[69] Theodore notes that some would refer part of the psalm to Solomon
and part to Christ. For Theodore the psalm is not simply about Solomon; it includes
his reign and also predicts future events. The Irish glosses on the Milan codex do
not go beyond the content of the Latin text. In the Pal. lat. 68 commentary, the first
heading is that David predicts that Solomon is to reign. The mystical heading gives
it as the voice of the Church to the Father. Next we are told that Jerome says that
the psalm in its proper sense refers to Christ, a point made again in the commentary
of v. 5 (*et permanebit cum sole*), with a citation from Jerome's *Commentarioli* on
the passage.

9. *Psalm 108 (109) in Irish Exegesis*

Psalm 108 (109).8 (*Et episcopatum eius accipiat alter*) is used by Peter of Judas's
betrayal (Acts). In the Epitome of Julian's translation it is taken throughout as .
referring to the Maccabees, without even a mention of the use of v. 8 in the New

---

66. In *Thes. Pal.*, I, p. 290.

67. McNamara (ed.), *Glossa in Psalmos*, p. 142. The reference is to Jerome, *Commen-*
tarioli, on this verse (pp. 216, lines 13-15). Theodore's position on v. 22 is also given in the
Constitutum (ch. xxv) of Vigilius (reproduced in Devreesse [ed.], *Le commentaire*, pp. 454-
55).

68. Devreesse (ed.), *Le commentaire*, pp. 469-77.

69. De Coninck and d'Hont (eds.), *Theodori*, pp. 260-62.

Testament. The same is true of the Irish Milan glosses on the text. In the introductory material to the commentary in Pal. lat. 68 it is first understood as the voice of David concerning his son Absalom, and then of the Maccabees. Next we are told that the psalm contains 30 curses, which are fitting for Judas the betrayer on account of the 30 pieces of silver. The comment on v. 8 takes *episcopatus* to mean *principatus*, and *accipiet* (sic MS) *alter* as *id est Ioab pro Achitophel, uel Salamon pro Abisolon*. No mention is made of the New Testament use of the verse.

10. *Psalm 131 (132) in Irish Exegesis*

The biblical heading of this psalm simply has *sîr ha-ma'alot, Canticum Graduum*. It asks God to remember David and all his concerns for the ark and the tabernacle. In the Antiochene tradition it (with the other gradual psalms) was interpreted of the Babylonian exile, this particular one being taken as a ground for future hope for the exiles. The Milan Commentary (the Epitome of Julian's translation of Theodore) follows the Antiochene approach.

The Hiberno-Latin *Eclogae tractatorum in Psalterium* for the glosses on this psalm draws almost exclusively on the Epitome of Julian. The 'Reference Bible' psalm section has nothing on Psalm 131 (132).

In the early Irish commentary found in Pal. lat. 68 the central exegesis followed is Davidic: the psalm is taken as speaking of David and his time: the psalm was sung by David, as if in the person of his comrades requesting that the ark be taken from Kiriat-Jearim to Holy Zion, and also concerning the prophetic promises made to Samuel concerning David. Thus the 'historical' heading. Next comes another application: 'The prophet (David) says (this) to the Father concerning Christ.' The glosses remind us again that 'historically' (*secundum historiam*) the psalm speaks of what was to happen to David and (citing Jerome, in his *Tractatus* on this psalm that 'it can be applied allegorically to Christ' [*Allagoricae Christo hic salmus coaptatur*]. The exposition ends with a full spiritual interpretation (dependent on Augustine), understanding the psalm of Christ and of the Church.

The Irish glosses on the Milan text tend to follow and explain the sense of the Epitome of Julian, thus being in the Antiochene tradition. At one point, however, the glossator seems to forget his usual habit of giving terse comments on the Latin text. On the *lemma* to be commented on in v. 14: *Haec requies mea in saeculum saeculi (hic habitabo quoniam elegi eam)* the glossator remarks: 'This is the verse that Jerome sang as he went into Bethlehem, namely *haec requies, etc.*' The scribe (possibly Diarmuid, and even the Diarmuid known as *scriba et anachoreta* of Castledermot) may have himself been a hermit, anxious to have completed his tour of duty transcribing these glosses, and only too anxious to return to the peace of his hermitage—like Jerome of old in Bethlehem.

THE IRISH AFFILIATIONS OF THE *CATECHESIS CELTICA**

1. *Designation*

The *Catechesis Celtica* is the name given to the contents of Codex Reginensis Latinus 49 of the Vatican Library, and is but the Latinization of the French title 'Catéchèses celtiques' given to the varied contents of the manuscript by Dom André Wilmart, when he published about one third of the work in 1933.[1]

Wilmart considered this title the most appropriate one for the contents of the collection. The genre of the collection, he notes, is hybrid and difficult to define. In it, one is in an intermediate and almost indistinct zone, half-way between direct preaching and didactic commentary. None the less, on rereading in succession the pieces chosen for inclusion by the compiler, one cannot fail to get the impression that his precise aim was to furnish priests involved in the ministry with varied expositions which would permit them to preach on the Gospel reading of the day. Thus, through these catecheses we are introduced to the ill-digested learning of a versatile exegete and also to the popular faith of a Christian community in the process of formation.[2] In the catalogue of the Vatican Reginensis collection of manuscripts, published in 1937, Wilmart avoids use of his earlier designation and describes the contents of Codex Reginensis 49 as: 'Commentaries and Homilies, principally of parts of the Gospels, and some excerpts'.[3] The title, however, remained

---

* This essay was originally published in a volume of the periodical *Celtica*, dedicated to Professor Brian Ó Cuív; now dedicated to the memory of Professor Ó Cuív, who died 14 November 1999. This paper is the text of the Statutory Public Lecture delivered in Trinity College, Dublin, 8 September 1989.

1. A. Wilmart, OSB, *Analecta Reginensia: Extraits des manuscrits latins de la Reine Christine conservés au Vatican* (Studi e Testi, 50; Vatican City: Biblioteca Apostolica Vaticana, 1933).

2. Wilmart, *Analecta Reginensia*, p. 33.

3. Andreas Wilmart (ed.), *Codices Reginenses latini*. I. *Codices 1-250 recensuit et digessit* (Vatican City: Biblioteca Apostolica Vaticana, 1937), pp. 112-17 for

and has been extended by Fr Robert McNally and later writers to such other presumed Hiberno-Latin collections of homilies as those of Cracow and Verona.

2. *Contents of Vatican Codex Reginensis Latinus 49*

A colophon gives the scribe's name as *Guilhelm: Finit. Amen. Guilhelm scripsit hunc librum. Deo gratias* (f. 53). The Codex is numbered as (folios) 1-54, but there is no f. 5. The order of the folios in the present manuscript is disturbed and the text must be read in the sequence: ff. 1-2, 4, 3, 7, 6, 8-23, 32-47, 24-31, 48-54. There have also been some mistakes in transcription along the history of transmission, with portions of some texts copied erroneously as parts of other ones.

In the manuscript itself there is no clear division between the individual pieces. For this reason the division is left to the editors, who can differ on their separation of the material into individual items. Thus, whereas Wilmart divides the contents into 46 items, McNally in his unpublished edition of the text finds 57. The editor is helped on occasion in his efforts by the presence of headings to some items, for example, *Incipit umelia de oratione dominica* (f. 9 v); *Omelia in Dominica Palmarum* (13 r); *Omelia in Cena Domini* (16 v); *De Cena Domini id est de capitulo VI* (17 r); *Hoc ad solemnitatem Paschae conuenit* (18 v); *In nomine Dei Summi* (20 v, 30 r), and the final item headed *De die domi(ni)co* (f. 53). Together with these headings there is occasionally other introductory material which seems to indicate the beginning of a new item, such as the place in the Eusebian Canons of the Scripture pericope to be commented on. This information is occasionally accompanied by the number of the chapter in question, thus: 14 r (Palm Sunday); 24 r (Lk. 11.27-8); 25 v (Mt. 13.45-6); 27 v (Mt. 21.10-11); 29 r (Mt. 12.42); 30 r (Mt. 21.1-11); 30 v (Lk. 2.1-20; Christmas Day); 37 r (Mt. 10.16); 39 r (Mt. 6.33); 40 v (Lk. 13.6-9); 42 v (Mt. 9.10-13); 43 v (Jn 14.1-2); 47 r (Lk. 2.21).

Sometimes we have, without indication of Canon or chapter, a Scripture passage to be commented on, apparently indicating the beginning of a new item, thus: 35 v (Mt. 16.34), 40 v (Lk. 13.6-9). Together with these headings and openings, we are aided in our separation of the pieces by certain formal and formulaic endings, for example, *Finit*

Cod. Reg. 49: 'Commentarii et homiliae, maxime de partibus Evangeliorum, excerptaque nonnulla' (p. 112).

(10 v, first exposition of the *Pater noster*); *Finit. Amen* (11 v, second exposition of the *Pater noster*); ...*per infinita secula seculorum. Amen* (16 r); *ipsi gloria et imperium in secula seculorum. Amen* (16 v); ...*qui cum Patre et Spiritu sancto uiuit et regnat in secula seculoram. Amen* (17 r); a similar prayer for eternal union with God *in secula seculorum. Amen* (47 r, two distinct items; 47 v; 51 r).

The argument for distinct items is strengthened when a given piece has both a heading, introduction and an ending. However, even with these aids we are at times left in doubt with regard to the exact division or the original intention of the compiler in this matter. Thus in 16 r we have one exposition of the narrative of Jesus' entry into Jerusalem rounded off with the ending: *Semperque laetamur et conregnemus cum illo in perpetua uita per infinita secula seculorum. Amen,* which is followed immediately (without heading) by another exposition of the same text: *Moraliter. 'Duo discipuli', id est doctores cum fide et opere.* This moral exposition is, in the tradition to which I believe the *Catechesis Celtica* belongs, but the normal continuation of treatment of the text in accord with the different senses of Scripture.[4] This, in turn, is followed by an ending: *ipsi gloria et imperium in secula seculorum. Amen,* after which comes (16 v) a homily headed *Omelia in cena Domini.* Sometimes when an item is not marked off by either heading or ending it can be identified as a unit by means of the subject matter, as in the case of 9 r (comment on Ps. 1); 11 v (order of reading of the canonical Scriptures in St Peter's Church, Rome); 18 v, section of a penitential; to which we may add two collections on various subjects (both preceded by sections with formulaic ending), that is, 20 r and 49 v.

3. *History of Research*

According to slips preserved in the Vatican Library, Codex Reginensis Latinus 49 has been consulted between 1913 and 1973 by 28 different scholars, including: W.M. Lindsay (10 April 1915), K.W. Hughes (5 April 1951), B. Bischoff (17 April 1958; 3 March 1962), R.E. McNally (16 September 1960; 17, 21 October 1968). It was consulted too late by W.M. Lindsay for inclusion in his major works *Early Irish Minuscule Script* (Oxford 1910), *Notae Latinae* (Cambridge 1915).[5] There is a

---

4. See further below, 6.1.
5. Nor is it mentioned in his other study: W.M. Lindsay, 'Breton scriptoria:

marginal gloss *guor/cher* (written in two parts, one above the other) in f. 21 r to the word *summitas (fracta est summitas inferni cum resurgerent mortui)*. Attention had been drawn to this gloss by H.M. Bannister, in the work *Paleografia musicale Vaticana*, who read it as *quor cher* and regarded it as Irish. Lindsay communicated his new reading (*guor cher*) of the gloss to J. Loth, who published a study of, it, together with a facsimile of the page carrying it. He regarded the gloss as Cornish rather than Breton.[6]

In May 1932, in preparation for his work on the cataloguing of the Reginensis Collection, Wilmart wrote to Loth, informing him of the existence of two further glosses in the manuscript, that is, *trapen* over the Latin word *capite* in f. 32 v and another of uncertain reading in f. 50, that is, *he be* (with a stroke over the final *e*) above the Latin word *elimosina*, which Wilmart expanded as *he ben* (less likely *he ber*). In the same letter he remarked that the Celtic origin of the collection is evident, and that the copyist of the present text (writing in the tenth century, or at earliest towards the end of the ninth) reproduced unaltered an earlier collection, one probably put together in the eighth. With regard to the provenance of MS 49 Wilmart remained uncertain. In his own view there were three possible points of origin from the palaeographical point of view: Cornwall or Wales; Brittany (*Bretagne Armoricaine*, his preference); or Fleury-sur-Loire. In the same letter Wilmart also remarked that the text of Luke 21–20 in the manuscript was entirely in the Celtic tradition as known to us through the manuscripts DELO (read: Q)R, except for 2.11, where for (*quia natus est uobis hodie) saluator (qui est Christus Dominus*) Reginensis 49 has: (…) *conseruator* (…) and adds *saluasti*. Wilmart asks whether *saluasti* here might not be another gloss. Loth published this correspondence in 1933.[7]

The codex next attracted attention in 1933 when Wilmart published about one-third of it (in XIV 'Catéchèses') together with an introduction of five pages.[8] He took our present copy to be from the tenth century, most likely from the first half. However, behind this tenth-century

Their Latin abbreviation-symbols', *Zentralblatt für Bibliothekswesen* 29 (1912), pp. 264-72.

    6.   J. Loth, 'Une glose britonnique du Xe siècle', *RC* 36 (1915–16), pp. 411-12.

    7.   J. Loth, 'Une glose brittone inédite du IX–Xe siècle: une autre origine douteuse', *RC* 50 (1933), pp. 357-62.

    8.   Wilmart (ed.), *Analecta Reginensia*, pp. 29-34.

collection he saw an original which he believed was very similar—apart from the vernacular glosses and errors of transcription—to an original to be situated approximately towards the end of the eighth century and located in the British Isles, either in Cornwall or Wales. In his introduction Wilmart does not seriously consider the possibility, much less the likelihood, of Irish origin. He sees a clear 'Celtic' link in the biblical text of the Gospels used in the 'Catéchèses'. It is that of the 'Celtic' family, represented by the manuscripts DELQR, L being the Lichfield Gospels, probably written in a Welsh centre. He notes that the Gospel text used in the 'Catéchèses' is not particularly close to L, which he takes as a possible indication of Cornish rather than Welsh origin. He makes no mention of the fact that D (the Book of Armagh) and R (the Rushworth or Mac Regol Gospels) and presumably Q (the Book of Kells) are Irish. Another link 'with the Celtic race and Insular bias'[9] he sees in the indiscriminate use of the Apocrypha. He instances the Gospel according to the Hebrews, certain *profetica verba*, the signs before Doomsday, the colourful description of the three Magi, the wonders worked on Sunday.

The first of the 'Catéchèses' published by Wilmart was one headed '*De cena Domini*'. Dom J. Huyben soon pointed out to Wilmart that the sources of this were to be found in the writings of Paschasius Radbertus. That same year Wilmart published an essay on the matter. This catechesis is but a résumé of Paschasius's large commentary on Matthew's Gospel and of his treatise *De corpore et sanguine*.[10] It would indicate a date in the later ninth century for this particular text of the catechesis, and for the entire corpus if all the material is of the same date.

In 1936 the Bollandist Paul Grosjean made a very thorough study of the section of the 'Catéchèses celtiques' published by Wilmart and advanced very strong reasons for concluding that they are not without Irish connections.[11] In this remarkable study Grosjean modestly tells us that he wishes to draw attention to certain details in the catecheses which appeared to him, in their cumulative force, to indicate at least

---

9. 'la race celtique et les partis pris insulaire', Wilmart (ed.), *Analecta Reginensia*, p. 32.

10. A. Wilmart, 'Une source carolingienne des catéchèses celtiques', *RBén* 45 (1933), pp. 350-51.

11. P. Grosjean, 'A propos du manuscrit 49 de la Reine Christine', *Analecta Bollandiana* 54 (1936), pp. 113-36.

certain relationships with Ireland.[12] What he presents us with, in fact, is a thorough examination of the portion of the *Catechesis* published by Wilmart, indicating the relationship with the Irish language, and with Irish tradition, both vernacular and Latin. In his introductory section he notes the three glosses discussed by Joseph Loth: *guorcher, tra pen, he ben*, the first of these indicating Cornwall rather than Wales or Armorica. He disagrees with Loth's understanding of the second gloss, which makes little sense in the context, and prefers another with the meaning 'in favour of'. The third expression *he ben* (after which he puts a question mark), he notes, could be Breton or Cornish; the matter is not as yet clear. Grosjean compares peculiarities of the catecheses' Latinity with Irish tradition: *pascha modicum, haeres Christi, aliena non immolanda sunt Deo, filius vitae, veteris legis, creator omnium elementorum, familia caeli et terrae, gradus angelorum, initium* (in an absolute sense of 'beginning of Lent'); the use in verbs with infinitive in *-are* of the subjunctive in *-a-* instead of in *-e-* (e.g. *negamus* for *negemus*).

He goes on to note the resemblance in ideas and literary expression between the catecheses and Irish literature of the Middle Ages. In this section he stresses in particular the close relationship between the catecheses and the homilies in the *Leabhar Breac* and the material in the glosses of the Gospels of Máel Brigte. He mentions especially the use of the stereotyped *peroratio*, rigorously adhered to in Irish homilies. He instances a very close connection between one text of the *Catechesis Celtica* (ed. Wilmart, p. 111 lines 55-61), and the *Leabhar Breac*. The *Catechesis* text reads: (*Beati qui habitant cum Abel et Enoc et Noe) cum Abraham et Isac et Iacob, cum Moise et Aaron et Iesu filio Nun, cum XII profae(tis) cum XII apostolis, cum omnibus sanctis ab initio mundi usque ad finem, cum IX ordinibus angeloram, cum patre et filio et spiritu sancto, in pace et laetitia, in puritate et in iuuentute, sine fame et nuditate, cum abun(dantia) omnis boni sine ullo malo, circa regem iuuenem, largum, pulchrum, aeternum. Rogamus deum omnipotentem ut mereamur possidere illam beatitudinem in saecula saeculorum. Amen.* Grosjean notes that the beginning of this passage is cited in almost the exact same way by the glossator of the Gospels of Máel Brigte. This glossator, be he Máel Brigte or someone else, appears to have had before him different collections of homilies. According to Grosjean, the citation he has from the *Catechesis Celtica* leads one to

---

12. Grosjean, 'A propos', p. 118.

believe that Reginensis 49 itself, or a similar collection, was in the library of the glossator of the Máel Brigte Gospels (in Armagh itself if Máel Brigte was the glossator).

Grosjean also notes the relationship of the Apocryphal elements of the sections published by Wilmart and Irish tradition (i.e. the Magi, miracles at Christ's birth, Longinus, the *octo pondera de quibus factus est Adam,* the *IIII familiae quae ascribentur in iudicio,* the signs before Doomsday, the text *De die dominico*).

Grosjean concludes his essay by noting that the 'Catéchèses celtiques' are not without relationship with Ireland, but prudently remarks that we know only one third of the work and that the sections remaining unpublished might well destroy hastily construed hypotheses. He follows this remark by recalling the role played by the *Céli Dé* reform (eighth and ninth centuries) in the Irish Church. One can suppose, he notes, that this, like all reforms, would have been accompanied by a renewal in preaching. The date of the *Céli Dé* also fits in well with the aim assigned by Wilmart to the compilation of the *Catechesis Celtica,* a collection designed to aid preachers in their task.

I hope to show later that the unpublished sections admirably bear out Grosjean's surmises regarding the catecheses' relationship to Irish tradition, and in particular to the *Leabhar Breac* and the glosses of the Gospels of Máel Brigte.

Grosjean's study appeared too late to have influenced Wilmart in his treatment of Codex Reginensis 49 in his catalogue of the Reginensis Collection published in 1937.[13] This does not go considerably beyond his earlier 1933 work in *Analecta Reginensia* apart from noting that the homily *De cena Domini* (ff. 17-18 v) depends on Paschasius Radbertus. He notes that in Mt. 6.33 (ff. 39-40 v) the Codex has the Book of Armagh reading *prestabuntur,*[14] and that there is an infinite number of abbreviations according to the custom of the Irish.[15] The glosses show, however, that the book belonged to the British (Breton), not the Irish (Scottic).[16]

---

13. Wilmart, *Codices Reginenses.*

14. Wilmart, *Codices Reginenses,* p. 115.

15. Wilmart, *Codices Reginenses,* p. 117: 'Compendiorum infinitus est numerus, ex hibernorum consuetitudine adhibitorum et quae nunc lectorem multum docent'.

16. Wilmart, *Codices Reginenses*: 'Quapropter Brittonum liber erat, non Scottorum'.

McNally worked on the manuscript in the Vatican Library in the early and late 1960s and was preparing an edition of it for publication. He edited one text from it, *De die dominico*, in 1973.[17] In the preface he speaks of Vat. Reg. 49 and its contents:[18]

> The Vatican Codex, Reg. lat. 49...can be dated to the late ninth or early tenth century and is...Breton, perhaps Welsh. The script, a remarkable combination of Carolingian minuscule and insular abbreviations, seems to confirm the probability of Breton origin. The manuscript contains the only extant copy of the *Catechesis Celtica*, a collection of homilies, intended for liturgical use in a Celtic setting. Since its contents are composite in nature, it is impossible to date the work as a whole, though beyond doubt some of the component pieces of this collection are authentic specimens of early Celtic piety and representative of its oldest and purest traditions.

In a note to this he adds:

> With respect to Wilmart's scholarship, his edition of the *Catechesis Celtica* should be reworked with proper care for the source-analysis and the reproduction of the complete text. A careful study of the whole work will yield remarkable conclusions on the spirituality of the Old Celts (Irish?). My edition of this work is nearing completion.

McNally died in 1978, but before his death he had completed the transcription of the entire manuscript and provided it with a source-analysis.

McNally's rather thorough source-analysis has relatively few Hiberno-Latin or Irish references: Pseudo-Isidore, *Liber de numeris*; Pseudo-Bede, *Collectanea*; Pseudo-Jerome, *Expositio IV evangeliorum, In Matthaeum, In Lucam, In Ioannem;* Scotus Anonymus, *In Lucam* (the Vienna Commentary on Luke); Scotus Anonymus, *In epistolas Catholicas*; for specific texts the *Collectio canonum Hibernensis* (on the *Pater noster*); the *Leabhar Breac* and the Cracow Homily Collection (being prepared for publication by himself).

Frederic Mac Donncha has made an intensive study of a set of Middle Irish homilies, found in the *Leabhar Breac* and elsewhere. In 1972 he successfully completed a PhD dissertation (National University of Ireland) on the subject.[19] In a study of these homilies, published in

17. R.E. McNally, *Scriptores Hiberniae Minores*, I (2 vols.; CCSL, 108B; Turnhout: Brepols, 1973).
18. McNally, *Scriptores*, I, pp. 178-79.
19. F. Mac Donnchadha, 'Na hoimilí sa Leabhar Breac (LB), Lebor na hUidre

1976, he noted the relationship between the *exordia* and the *perorationes* in them and elements in the *Catechesis Celtica* (which he believed to be most likely of Irish origin).[20] He also noted that many questions about these homilies must remain unanswered until the various Hiberno-Latin scriptural commentaries are all published (to which he could have added the Hiberno-Latin homiletic material).[21]

In the early 1980s Giovanni Maria Vian published an interesting and informative survey of the contents of Codex Reginensis Latinus 49, accompanied by a history of research on the *Catechesis Celtica*.[22] A concluding English summary to the essay in Italian seems to favour Irish, rather than Cornish, origin.

A decisive turn in the direction of research in this general area came about a little later through the studies of Jean Rittmueller, both in her doctoral dissertation on the *Leabhar Breac* homily *In cena Domini* and on the sources of the corresponding glosses in the Gospels of Máel Brigte.[23] Her doctoral dissertation concentrated on the study of the homily *In cena Domini* in the *Leabhar Breac*. This is in the form of a commentary on Mt. 26.17-30. She studies the commentaries on this passage in Irish tradition in writings from the seventh century down to the twelfth—from the Manchanus Gospel glosses of the mid-seventh century to the glosses of the Gospels of Máel Brigte (1138 CE; MS British Library Harley 1802). In all there are seven distinct Irish texts. Behind the central Irish tradition she finds Jerome's commentary on Matthew and the Manchanus glosses, jointly giving rise to the basic outline of exegesis for Mt. 26.17-30. Within this tradition she situates

(LU), Leabhar Mhic Carthaigh Riabhaigh (LMC) agus i Vita Tripartita Sancti Patricii (VTP) (nó Bethu Phátraic): a mbunús, a n-údar agus a ndáta' (PhD dissertation, National University of Ireland, 1972).

20. F. Mac Donncha, 'Medieval Irish Homilies', in M. McNamara (ed.), *Biblical Studies: The Medieval Irish Contribution* (Proceedings of the Irish Biblical Association, 1; Dublin: Dominican Publications, 1976), pp. 59-71, esp. 64-65.

21. Mac Donncha, 'Medieval Irish Homilies', p. 71.

22. G.M. Vian, 'Le catechesi celtiche pubblicate da André Wilmart', *Romanobarbarica* 6 (1980–81), pp. 145-59.

23. J. Rittmueller, 'The *Leabhar Breac* Latin and Middle-Irish Homily *"In Cena Domini"*: An edition and source analysis' (PhD dissertation, Harvard University 1984; Ann Arbor: University Microfilms International); J. Rittmueller, 'The Gospel Commentary of Máel Brigte Ua Máeluanaig and its Hiberno-Latin Background', *Peritia* 2 (1983), pp. 185-214; J. Rittmueller, 'Postscript to the Gospels of Máel Brigte', *Peritia* 3 (1984), pp. 215-18.

the *Catechesis Celtica* homily *De cena Domini*, which she tentatively assigns to the eighth–ninth century. She shows that the assumed dependence of the *Catechesis Celtica* homily and the Máel Brigte Gospel glosses on Paschasius Radbertus is not the explanation of their similarity. Among the Máel Brigte Gospel glosses there are a number marked as '*Man*', obviously considered as deriving from a writer thus abbreviated. The natural expansion of the abbreviation in an Irish context would be 'Manchianus' or 'Manchanus', and there was a noted Irish exegete of this name in the mid-sixth century. Bischoff could not accept the identification because of the presumed dependence of the *Man* glosses on the Eucharist on Paschasius Radbertus.[24] Rittmueller has now shown that the Irish tradition in question is quite independent of Paschasius. They both depend on common sources (Jerome's commentary on Matthew and the *Verba seniorum* on a eucharistic miracle). On occasion also Paschasius has been proved to depend on Irish sources and, in fact, on one of the sources carrying the Irish exegetical synthesis on Mt. 26.17-30.

I have dwelt on Rittmueller's contribution at some length as I believe what she has established with regard to the homily *De cena Domini* and its exegesis of Mt. 26.17-30 may well hold good for the use of Matthew's Gospel in other homilies of the *Catechesis Celtica* and other Irish sources, for example, the *Leabhar Breac*. Matthew's Gospel, in fact, was the chief text used in Irish homilies and we are fortunate in having various Hiberno-Latin commentaries on it from the seventh to the twelfth centuries. This exegetical tradition may help us in locating the exposition of the *Catechesis Celtica* collection in place and time.

A major contribution to the study of the *Catechesis Celtica* to be noted here is that of An tAthair Diarmuid Ó Laoghaire, in a conference given in 1984 and published in 1987.[25] He notes further points of con-

24. B. Bischoff, 'The "Man" glosses (Manchianus?) of the Gospel Book of London B.M. Harley 1802', appendix to his essay 'Wendepunkte in der Geschichte der lateinischen Exegese im Frühmittelalter', *SE* 6 (1954), pp. 274-79; English translation by Colm O'Grady, 'Turning-Points in the History of Latin Exegesis in the Early Middle Ages: A.D. 650–800', in McNamara (ed.), *Biblical Studies*, pp. 145-49. On this question see Rittmueller, 'The Gospel Commentary', pp. 200-14; Rittmueller, 'The *Leabhar Breac*', pp. 277-94, with notes.

25. D. Ó Laoghaire, 'Irish Elements in the Catechesis Celtica', in P. Ní Chatháin and M. Richter (eds.), *Ireland and Christendom: The Bible and the Missions* (Stuttgart: Klett Cotta, 1987), pp. 146-64.

tact between the contents of the collection and a variety of Irish texts: the Irish *Liber de numeris*, the Cracow Conferences, the Lambeth Commentary, the *Old Irish Treatise* on the Psalter, the *Collectio canonum Hibernensis* and others besides. One notable contribution is Ó Laoghaire's treatment of one of the presumed Breton or Welsh glosses, namely the gloss on *Elimosina*. The text (f. 50 r a 21) in the manuscript reads: *elimosina dei mei opus la* (with stroke over *a*) and *.i. he be* interlineated above *elimosina*. As transcribed by Wilmart, this reads:[26] *Elimosina dei mei opus la(udat)*, with gloss on *elimosina* given (as the reading appeared to him) as: *I(dest) he be(n)*. He also admits that the expansion of *la* to *laudat* is but a conjecture. Ó Laoghaire has brought to our attention what appears to be the real reading for this passage, that is, that found in the *Collectio canonum Hibernensis* XIII.2: *Elimosina hebraice, Dei mei opus latine intellegitur*. The separation of *b* from *e* in the *Catechesis* text seems due to the need to avoid the upper extension of the letter *s* of *elimosina*. The extra (final) *e* (clear in the manuscript) may be due to a copyist's error or misunderstanding of the original. That the text of Codex Reginensis Latinus 49 should be read in accord with the *Hibernensis* text is rendered all the more probable in that we have here an 'etymology' in the Hiberno-Latin tradition. That the basically Greek word *elimosina* should be taken as Hebrew is not surprising. *Eli* in Hebrew means 'My God' (cf. Mt. 27.46); *mosina* could easily be connected with the Hebrew *ma'aseh* 'work'. The Bretonic glosses are thus reduced to a maximum of two. Some years later Jean Rittmueller published a new description of the work (Vat. Reg. lat. 49) and gave a table of its textual parallels with the *Liber questionum in evangeliis*.[27] In 1994 the present writer made a detailed study of the sources and affiliations of the work.[28]

In what follows I shall examine the Irish affiliations of the *Catechesis* from different points of view: biblical text used, exegetical tradition involved, homiletic material, apocryphal material.

26. Wilmart (ed.), *Analecta Reginensia*, p. 108, line 32.

27. J. Rittmueller, 'MS Vat. Reg. Lat. 49 Reviewed: A New Description and a Table of Textual Parallels with the Liber questionum in evangeliis', *Sacris Erudiri* 33 (1992–93), pp. 259-305.

28. M. McNamara, 'Sources and Affiliations of the Catechesis Celtica (MS Vat. Reg. Lat. 49)', *Sacris Erudiri* 34 (1994), pp. 185-237.

4. Catechesis Celtica *and Irish Biblical Text*

My examination of this topic is necessarily limited by the Irish (Latin) biblical text known to us in the present state of investigations.[29] For the Old Testament we have only the Psalter. With regard to the New Testament we have ample evidence for the Four Gospels, while for the remainder we are confined for the greater part to the text of the Book of Armagh, with an additional text from the Pauline Epistles and some evidence from the commentaries for the Catholic Epistles.

4.1. *The Psalter Text*[30]

From the time of Jerome onwards the Western Latin Church used three texts of the Psalter: the Old Latin (Vetus Latina; sometimes referred to simply as the *Romanum* [abbrev. Ro]), the Latin text revised by Jerome against the Greek and Hebrew, known as the *Gallicanum* [abbrev. Ga], and Jerome's translation direct from the Hebrew, known as the *Hebraicum* or *Iuxta Hebraeos*. Both the *Gallicanum* and the *Hebraicum* were known and used in Ireland and, as the Benedictine editors of the critical editions of both have shown, Ireland had a distinct family both of *Gallicanum* and *Iuxta Hebraeos* texts. The specifically Irish family of the *Gallicanum* is found in the manuscripts given the sigla C and I, that is, the Cathach of St Columba (MS in the Royal Irish Academy) and the Double Psalter of Rouen (MS, Rouen Bibliotèque publique 24 [A 41]).

I have counted some 99 Psalter texts in the *Catechesis Celtica*. In 54 of these the text employed is identical with both that of the Old Latin (*Romanum*) and the critical edition of the *Gallicanum*, and they are consequently without significance for our purpose. Likewise with 31 others in which the text used is identical with the critical edition of the *Gallicanum*, even though this does not coincide with the Old Latin. It seems obvious that the compilers' Psalter text was the *Gallicanum*, not the Old Latin.

29. On this see M. McNamara, 'The Text of the Latin Bible in the Early Irish Church: Some Data and Desiderata', in P. Ní Chatháin and M. Richter (eds.), *Ireland and Christendom: The Bible and the Missions* (Stuttgart: Klett Cotta, 1987), pp. 7-55.

30. On this see M. McNamara, 'Psalter Text and Psalter Study in the Early Irish Church (A.D. 600–1200)', pp. 19-142 in this volume.

What is significant are the texts which agree with none of these. In the *Catechesis Celtica* we have 13 such texts, disagreeing with the critical edition of the *Gallicanum* but agreeing with the readings of the specific Irish family of the *Gallicanum*. It is of little significance that the specific CI reading may also be an Old Latin text. This is evidence of contamination of the *Gallicanum*, not direct use of the Old Latin (or *Romanum*). The texts are as follows:

18.5	(*exiit* [two occurrences], for *exiuit*);
26.4	(*petiui*, for *petii*);
26.4	(*omnibus diebus*, for *omnes dies* of *Gallicanum*);
27.5	(*distrue [illos et non edificabis eos]* for *destrues i. et non aed. eos* of Ga; Ro has: *destrue il. nec aed. eos*);
32.2-4	(*conlaudatio; psallite ei*);
32.7	(*in utrem*);
43.23	(*obdormis*);
43.26	(*adiuua nos Domine*; two occurrences);
49.3	(*ardebit*; CI only with Ro);
83.11b	(*quam habitarem*, CI only);
91.14	(*[in atriis] domus [Dei]*; I with Ro);
145.7	(*soluet*);
146.6	(*humiliat*, only I, with Ro).

4.2. *The Gospel Text*

We know of some 30 Irish Gospel manuscripts, and some other texts not written in Ireland related to these. One of these texts, *Usserianus priimus* (with symbol r[1]) has the Old Latin Gospel text. Another, the Book of Durrow, has the Vulgate text. A number of the manuscripts have not as yet been fully examined from the point of view of textual character. The majority of those which have, however, present a mixed text of both Vulgate and Old Latin readings. During the latter part of the last century and the opening years of this one, scholars have identified a group of manuscripts which carry such a mixed text, manuscripts known by their symbols as DELQR, that is, the Book of Armagh (Codex Dublinensis), British Library Egerton 609 (probably written in Brittany), the Lichfield Gospels (probably written in a centre at the Welsh border), the Book of Kells (Codex Cennanensis), and the Rushworth or Mac Regol Gospels (most probably written at Birr). These texts do not constitute a family, as they do not descend from a common original. Since the group cannot be assigned to any particular country, but have representatives from Ireland, Wales and Brittany, they are often (if not generally) referred to as 'the Celtic Gospels'. It should be noted that a number of other Irish works have the same characteristic readings as this group but have not as yet been adequately examined.

The *Catechesis Celtica* has an abundance of Gospel texts, especially from Matthew, the Gospel most frequently commented on in the homilies. For the most part, these are longer passages, first cited in full and then commented on with repetition of the key texts. Together with this there are many brief Gospel texts cited throughout the homilies and the other different items.

For the purpose of my study here I can take the established Vulgate text as my point of reference. What must interest us is the total number of deviations in reading from the Vulgate text and their textual affiliations in so far as this is ascertainable.[31] I have counted 333 such deviations: 173 for Matthew, 6 for Mark, 79 for Luke and 75 for John. I have failed to trace the origin of quite a number of these readings. They do not feature in the extensive apparatus of Wordsworth and White's critical edition of the Vulgate. Some of them could be Old Latin readings, others simply adaptations made by the homilist. (This latter possibility, however, is something not lightly to be presumed.) My chief interest here is the relation of the texts to Irish tradition, principally to that of the mixed Irish or Celtic group DELQR, and related texts.

In this we must distinguish between the different Gospels. One notable feature of the citations from Matthew's Gospel in the *Catechesis Celtica* is the high proportion of the deviations from the Vulgate which coincide with the DELQR group. In fact, of the 173 deviant readings in question, 85 (almost half of them) are from this DELQR group. None of the deviations in the texts from Mark's Gospel seems to belong to the DELQR group, while a few (but not too many) of those from the Gospels of Luke and John do.

It is clear that the form of Gospel text for Matthew, in particular, used principally by the compiler or compilers of the collection, was of the DELQR type. The longer passages could be pages from one of these manuscripts, or of another similar to them. Wilmart rightly took this

---

31. M. McNamara, *Studies on Texts of Early Irish Latin Gospels (A.D. 600–1200)* (Instrumenta Patristica, 20; Steenbrugge: Abbatia S. Petri & Dordrecht: Kluwer Academic Publishers, 1990), pp. 215-43. I edit the entire body of *Catechesis Celtica* Gospel texts which show disagreement with the Vulgate, and where possible I note their affiliations.

text as one of the clearest guides for identifying the contents of Vat. Reg. 49 as 'Celtic'. He noted that the biblical text used was not particularly close to L (presumably representing the Welsh text), and took this as a further reason for favouring Cornwall (rather than Wales) as place of origin.

At the present stage of research it is very difficult to speak of a Welsh or a Breton form of Gospel text. To do so it is not sufficient to list the Gospel manuscripts written in these regions. We must also try to trace the use of a given text in the region's literature.[32] Egerton 609 (E) seems to have been written in Brittany, but we do not have evidence that it was a text form actually used there. In fact, we know relatively little, as yet, of the Gospel text of Brittany.

An examination of the *Catechesis Celtica* Gospel texts reveals a preponderant correspondence with the readings of the Irish texts DRQ. Much more analysis, however, is required before we can say whether the Gospel text at the disposal of the writer or writers was nearer to any one particular known Gospel manuscript.

All the texts of the *Catechesis Celtica* which differ from the standard Vulgate or Old Latin versions are not of the DELQR type. The compiler(s) had certainly a very special text for Lk. 2.11 which occurs a number of times in the homily on the Gospel for Christmas Day and also outside of it. The text of Lk. 2.11 reads: *quia natus est uobis hodie conseruator salutis qui est Christus Dominus in ciuitate Dauid* quae dicitur Bethlehem. The Vulgate and general Old Latin text has: *quia natus est uobis hodie Saluator qui est Christus Dominus in ciuitate Dauid.* This text (*conseruator salutis*) is found again in the (presumed Hiberno-Latin) Vienna Commentary on Luke (in MS Vind. lat. 997).[33] This is the reading of the Old Latin (Irish) text *Usserianus primus*, found also in Sankt Paul, Carinthia,[34] fragment (MS 23.3.19 with siglum), the final words *quae dicitur Bethlem* being found only in the latter.

I have given here the evidence for Irish affiliations in the Gospel text of the *Catechesis Celtica*. This does not prove categorically that these

32. We have one such study: L.H. Gray, 'Biblical Citations in Latin Lives of Welsh and Breton Saints differing from the Vulgate', *Traditio* 8 (1952), pp. 389-97.

33. J. Kelly (ed.), *Scriptores Hiberniae Minores* (CCSL, 108C; Turnhout: Brepols, 1974), p. 15, line 84.

34. D. de Bruyne (ed.), 'Deux feuillets d'un texte préhieronymien des Evangiles', *RBén* 35 (1923), pp. 62-80.

homilies are of Irish origin. Before a final conclusion is reached other aspects of these biblical citations will need to be examined. One is the use of a liturgical *incipit* in pericope as if it were part of the biblical text, treating it as a *lemma* for comment. Thus for Jn 2.1 we have: *In illis diebus die tertio*,[35] with later comment on the opening words added only for liturgical purposes. Fr B. Fischer informs me that division of Gospel texts with words such as these inserted in the text itself is a feature of Gospel manuscripts written in Brittany.

A further point worthy of note regarding the Gospel text of the *Catechesis Celtica* is a presumed knowledge of the Greek text and the citation of part of Mt. 28.1 in Greek in the homily on the resurrection headed *In nomine Dei summi. Amen*. The Greek is actually cited in the course of a grammatical discussion on the gender of (the Latin) *uesper, uespere, uesperum, uespera*, the corresponding Greek word (to these Latin neutrals) being introduced as feminine.

> '*Vespere sabbati*'. *Id est, graeca nomina sunt uesper et uespere et uespera, et interpretantur finis uel defectio. Et femini (ini) generis est in greca uespere, nam sic est in euangelio greco:* ΟΨΕ [above this: *id est uespere*] ΤΗ [above this: *id est, hac*] CABBATOY [above this: *id est, sabati*] ΤΗ [above this: *id est, qua*] ΕΠΙΦΟC [above this: *id est, lucescit*] ΕΙC [above this: *id est, in*] MOYAN [above this: *primum*] CABBATON [above this: *id est, sabatorum*]. *In quo apparet quod* opse *femininum nomen est,* te *uero femininum pronomen est. Quidem autem uolunt uespera, non uespere, hie dici debere. Quidem dicunt quod uespere commune est uel masculinum et femininum* (f. 20 v).

The significance of the evidence on a knowledge and use of the Greek text has yet to be evaluated. Its use in the *Catechesis Celtica* must be examined in conjunction with the presence of essentially the same Latin text, and two of the words of the Greek text, in the eighth-century Hiberno-Latin commentary on Matthew entitled *Liber questionum in euangeliis*. I shall return to this point below.[36]

---

35. Wilmart (ed.), *Analecta Reginensia*, p. 72.

36. See below, 8.6.d, p. 438. The text of the *Catechesis Celtica* just cited, with more of the Greek text than in the *Liber questionum in evangeliis*, is identical with a text from the commentary attributed to Frigulus, printed in *PL* 102, col. 1120. J. Rittmueller believes that the *Liber questionum in evangeliis* draws heavily from Frigulus's commentary on Matthew. See Rittmueller's introduction to her critical edition of *Liber questionum in evangeliis* (CCSG; Turnhout: Brepols, forthcoming). A critical edition of Frigulus's commentary from a single manuscript is in preparation. This manuscript, however, lacks the ending and the comment on Mt. 28.1. For

4.3. *The Text of the Pauline Epistles*

For an evaluation of the affiliations of the text of the Pauline Epistles we have only the text of the Book of Armagh (with siglum D in Vulgate manuscripts; no. 61 for Beuron Old Latin) and of the Würzburg manuscript Universitätsbibliothek M. p. th., f. 12 (with siglum W).[37]

There are numerous citations from Paul in the *Catechesis Celtica*. Their textual affiliations, however, have not been studied in any depth. A number of the citations from Romans agree with the Book of Armagh readings against the Vulgate. Thus:

> 2.4 (*ignoras, bonitas*); 2.5 (+ *tu autem*; *cor impenitens*, for *im. cor*); 9.26 (*uocabitur*; Vg: dictum est); 9.25 (*dilectam dilectam*; Vg: *misericordiam consecutam*, twice); 11.20 (*sta*); 11.33 (*inscriptalia*, D: *inscrutabilia*; Vg: *incomprehensibilia*); 13.2 (*appropinquauit*; Vg: *adpropiauit*).

There is an extensive citation from Romans in a comment on Mt. 7.12 ('The Golden Rule') which agrees verbatim with D as distinct from the Vulgate and other texts. In the course of the comment Rom. 12.9-10 is cited as follows: *Exsecrantes malum adherentes bono caritatem fraternitatis inuicem benigni honore motuo praevenientes.*[38] The Vulgate has: *odientes malum adhaerentes bono caritatem fraternitatis inuicem diligentes honore inuicem praeuenientes.*

Only D has the variant *exsecrantes*, with no Old Latin support. It too, alone in Vulgate texts, has the variant *benigni* for *diligentes* (although some Old Latin texts do have it) and *mutuo* (*motuo*) for *inuicem* (with the Ambrosiaster, Augustine and Sedulius Scottus).

Beyond these texts from Romans there does not appear to be any close connection between the many *Catechesis* Pauline citations and the Book of Armagh. More detailed study is required to ascertain the exact textual affiliations of the Pauline text used by the compiler.

---

a description of the Frigulus commentary and of the use of Frigulus in the *Liber questionum in evangeliis*, see J. Kelly 'Frigulus: An Hiberno-Latin Commentary on Matthew', *RBén* 91 (1981), pp. 363-73. See also J. Rittmueller, 'Sources of the *Liber questionum in evangeliis*: The Redactors Adaptation of Jerome's Commentarius in Matthaeum and Augustine's De Sermone in Monte', in T.O. Loughlin (ed.), *The Scriptures and Early Medieval Ireland: Proceedings of the 1993 Conference of the Society for Hiberno-Latin Studies on Early Irish Exegesis and Homiletics* (Instrumenta Patristica, 31; Steenbrugge: Abbatia S. Petri; Turnhout: Brepols, 1999), pp. 241-73.

37. See McNamara, 'The Text', pp. 49-51.

38. Wilmart (ed.), *Analecta Reginensia*, p. 83.

4.4. The Text of the Catholic Epistles and Apocalypse

For the Irish textual tradition for the Catholic Epistles we have again the Book of Armagh, and a small fragment of text for 2 Peter from Bobbio, now in Turin. The indirect transmission is found in the two early Hiberno-Latin commentaries on these Epistles.[39]

Walter Thiele[40] has examined the Irish tradition and notes that the biblical text of the section of the *Catechesis* published by Wilmart, together with that of the Hiberno-Latin commentaries, tends to agree with the text of D. There are relatively few citations from these seven Epistles in the entire compilation. I have counted eight from James; thirteen from 1 Peter, two from 2 Peter, six from 1 John, and find it hard to situate them within the Latin Bible.

There are about 32 citations from the Apocalypse in the *Catechesis*. These, once again, I have been unable to situate within the Latin tradition. They do not appear to agree either with the Vulgate text or that of the Book of Armagh.

4.5. Conclusion on Biblical text of the Catechesis Celtica

In the matter of citations from the Psalms and the Gospels the *Catechesis Celtica* has evident affiliations with Irish tradition. The same is true with regard to some citations from Romans. Any view on the origins of the compilation must take this evidence into account.

On the other hand, no solution regarding origins will convince until it explains all the phenomena of the work's biblical text, the deviations from Irish traditions and its affiliations with other recognizable ones (if such is the case), as well as the Irish connections.

An indication of the importance of the biblical citations in the matter of determining origins can be seen in one of the texts from the *Catechesis* published by Wilmart.[41] This is text IX, a commentary on Mt. 7.11. It opens with a reference to an earlier writing of the author (*sicut prius scripsi*), which leads Wilmart to suspect the entire piece is from some (unidentified) source.[42] He tentatively mentions Gildas the Wise and *De excidio et conquestu Britanniae*. No definite sources have thus far been identified. Any theory of origins, however, will have to reckon with

39. See McNamara, 'The Text', pp. 51-52.
40. W. Thiele, *Epistolae Catholicae Vetus Latina: die Reste der altlateinischen Bibel* 26 (Freiburg, 1956–69), p. 22.
41. Wilmart, *Analecta Reginensia*, pp. 83-85.
42. Wilmart, *Analecta Reginensia*, p. 83 nn. 2, 7.

Irish-type elements in the biblical text, for example, the addition of *bona* in Mt. 7.12, Ps. 32.7 (*utrem*), and the extensive Book of Armagh-type text of Rom. 12.9.

5. Catechesis Celtica *and Irish Exegetical Tradition*

5.1. *Comment on Psalm 1*[43]

One of the unexpected items in the *Catechesis Celtica* is its expostion of Psalm 1 in its entirety (f. 9 r-v). This is quite out of keeping with the other items in the collection. The greater part of the commentary on Psalm 1 is paralleled in other Irish sources. This is all the more significant in that early Irish psalm exegesis had clearly defined characteristics of its own, which sets it off from the general psalm exegesis of the Western Church, indeed from psalm exegesis as generally known to us. This Irish exegesis of Psalm 1 is found in a number of sources: The *Old-Irish Treatise* on the Psalter[44] (from c. 800 CE), the Irish 'Reference Bible' (in Hiberno-Latin; from c. 750–800), the *Eclogae tractatorum in Psalteriun*, in Hiberno-Latin (from c. 750 CE), in the Double Psalter of Rouen (Psalter of St Ouen or St Evreult), written in Ireland in the tenth century, with expositions on both the text of the *Gallicanum* and of the *Hebraicum*, the former being 'historical', literal, as distinct from the spiritual, found in glosses on the *Hebraicum*.[45] A peculiarity of this Irish exegesis was the finding of a twofold historical (literal) reference for the Psalms, the first referring it to David and his times, the second (at least in theory) to later Jewish history (Hezekiah, Assyrian, Babylonian or Maccabean times). It matters little that items of this Irish exegesis can be traced to earlier sources. If found in combination with other Irish elements, the supposition is that the entire body of exposition is Irish.

---

43. On the Psalms in Irish tradition, see McNamara, 'Psalter Text', also M. McNamara, 'Tradition and Creativity in Early Irish Psalter Study', pp. 239-301 in this volume; pp. xxx-xx for the twofold historical sense and Ps. 1.

44. *OIT*, pp. 32-37.

45. Preliminary publication of the glosses on the *Hebraicum* by L. De Coninck, *Incerti auctoris expositio Psalmorum I:1–XVI:11A iuxta litteram* (Kortrijk: Katholieje Universiteit Leuven Campus Kortrijk, 1989), Ps. 1 in pars II, pp. 4-5.

5.1.a. *The Psalm's Title. Catechesis Celtica*

Beatus uir. *Ubi est titulus? Non habet titulus quia ipse est titulus omnium psalmorum. Aliter: Ideo non habet titulum quia de Christo narrat.*

Old-Irish Treatise[46]

Question. Why has this psalm no title? Not difficult. *Ideo primus psalmus non habet titulum, quia titulus omnium psalmorum est. Primus psalmus*, says Bede, *titulum non habet quia capiti nostro Domino Salvatori de quo absolute loquitur non debuit proponi.*

5.1.b. *Division of the Psalm*
Catechesis Celtica

Tria in hoc psalmo continentur: diffinitio, increpatio, laudatio. Primo currit diffinitio hominis iusti a loco ubi dicit: Beatus uir *per II uersus usque Dauid dicit:* Erit tamquam lignum (i.e. vv. 1-2 incl.). *Currit enim laudatio hominis iusti per V uersus usque Dauid dicit:* Non sic impii (i.e. v. 3). *Postquam sequitur item uersus II de hac laudatione, ubi dicit: non sic usque dum dicit* peribit (vv. 4-6).

Old-Irish Treatise[47]

Some of the numbers of the commentators say that the three things which are found in the psalms are found in this psalm alone, to wit, *vox definitionis*, 'the speech of definition', *vox consolationis*, 'the speech of consolation', *vox increpationis*, 'the speech of rebuke'. *Primus psalmus titulus est omnium psalmorum, quod in eo continentur tres voces omnium psalmorum, i.e. vox definitionis, vox consolationis, vox increpationis.* This is *vox definitionis* in it, from Beatus uir *usque* die ac nocte. This is *vox consolationis* in it, from die ac nocte *usque* prosperabuntur. This is *vox increpationis* in it, from prosperabuntur *usque in finem.* Twelve verses in it.

The verses in question are to be understood in the older sense, not in the sixteenth-century and current meaning, in which the psalm has six verses.

The same tradition of the division of this psalm is found in the right-hand margins of the *Gallicanum* of the Double Psalter of Rouen. There in the right-hand margin to *Beatus uir* we have *diffi(initio)*; opposite *die*

46. *OIT*, pp. 32-33.
47. *OIT*, pp. 32-35.

ac nocte we have *consul(atio)*; opposite *prosperabuntur* we have *increp (atio)*.

5.1.c. *First and Second Literal Exegesis*. The text of the *Catechesis Celtica* proceeds to give what, in effect, is the first literal interpretation of v. 1, according to the Irish fourfold sense pattern. The text runs:

> Beatus uir. *id est Usai, filius Arachi*. Impiorum. *id est Achitophel et familia Abisolon. Impius, qui nihil pie agit... Aliter*. Beatus uir. *id est Dauid*. Impiorum. *id est filiorum Zarabiae, qui uoluerunt occidere Saulem, id est Ioab et Usai et Assael, qui impii dicuntur, quia contradicebant semper consilio eius...* Diei. *id est quando Saul fuit in spelonca*. Nocte. *quando salutauit Dauid Saul post motatam lanceam, dormitante Saul.*
> Item. Beatus uir. *De Ionatha dici potest. Secunda intentio semper historialiter de Iosa dicitur, id est quod pedinet ad Dauid. Quod autem pertinet persecutoribus Dauid, Assiriis et Babilonis, maxime ad Nabacodonosor, intentione secundae historiae et ad Sincharib deductum inuenies.*

The entire passage is anything but clear with regard to its exact meaning. It speaks of a *secunda intentio*, of an *intentione secundae historiae* without any prior reference to a *prima intentio*. The lack of clarity may be due to later use of an exegetical tradition, only imperfectly understood. The text and historical references become clearer when situated within the early Irish framework of interpretation and of this Psalm 1 in particular.

We have, first, the theory of the fourfold sense of the Psalms (in particular Ps. 1) as given in the *Old-Irish Treatise* on the Psalter:[48]

> There are four things that are necessary in the psalms, to wit, the first story, and the second story, the sense and the morality. The first story refers to David and to Solomon and to the above-mentioned persons, to Saul, to Absalom, to the persecutors besides. The second story to Hezekiah, to the people, to the Maccabees. The meaning (*síens* = spiritual or mystical sense) (refers) to Christ, to the earthly and heavenly church. The morality (*morolus*) (refers) to every saint.

A little further on, this theory is applied to the interpretation of the Psalms, in particular Psalm 1, as follows:[49]

48. *OIT*, pp. 30-31.
49. *OIT*, pp. 36-37.

The first story (*cétna stoir*) of the Psalms refers to the time of David; the second (*in tánaise*) to Chusai Arachitis (*iesu irechitis*; variant reading: *hissu ireichidis*). It was he who did not abandon him at the time of persecution, though every one (else) abandoned him.

The same exposition is found in the section on the Psalter in the 'Reference Bible', a work closely related to the *Old-Irish Treatise*. In words attributed to a certain Hilar(ius), most probably an early Irish expositor on the Psalms, the twofold historical sense is thus applied to Ps. 1.1:[50]

> *Hilar.* Beatus uir qui non abiit. *Prima historia ad Dauid pertinet, qui non abiit in consilio sociorum, qui uoluerunt occidere Saul in spelunca, quando Dauid dixit:* Non contingat mihi ut mittam manum meam in Christum Domini (cf. 1 Sam. 26.11, 23). Beatus reliqua. *Secunda historia ad Chusai Arachitam pertinet, qui non exiit in consilium Abisolon et Achitophel, qui uoluerunt exire post Dauid quando fugit et occidere eum, usque Chusai dissipauit consilium eoram* (cf. 2 Sam. 15.34; 17.14).

The text of the *Catechesis Celtica* obviously belongs to this Irish tradition of exegesis. For some reason as yet unknown, however, it uses the term *intentio* (in the meaning of 'sense') instead of 'story' (*stoir*) and *historia* (i.e. 'historical meaning') of the *Old-Irish Treatise* and the 'Reference Bible'.

5.1.d. *Psalm 1 Interpreted of Joseph (of Arimathea).* The *Catechesis* text goes on to interpret Psalm 1 (in the historical sense presumably) of Joseph of Arimathea who buried the body of Jesus. This interpretation, too, is found in almost all Irish texts.[51]

5.1.e. *Psalm 1 Interpreted Spiritually of Christ.* The *Catechesis* text continues: *Aliter. De Christo semet ipso psalmus iste cantatus est secundum ueritatem.* By *ueritas* in this text 'the mystical sense' or 'spiritually' is most probably to be understood. It corresponds to the *síens* of the *Old-Irish Treatise*, and *sensus* of Hiberno-Latin texts.[52]

5.1.f. *Psalm 1 Interpreted Morally of Every Saint.* The *Old-Irish Treatise* in its fourfold sense says that the morality (*morolus*) of the psalms

---

50. See text in McNamara, 'Tradition and Creativity', pp. 272-73 above.

51. E.g. the Columba Series of Psalm Headings; the *Tituli Psalmorum* of Pseudo-Bede (*PL* 93, col. 483B), the Irish Reference Bible.

52. On this see McNamara, 'Tradition and Creativity', pp. 271-72 above.

(Ps. 1 is principally if not solely intended) refers to every saint. The *Catechesis* text goes on without special introduction to say: Beatus uir. *id est unusquisque sanctus.*

As part of this moral exposition it comments on v. 3 as follows:[53]

> Et erit tamquam lignum *quod est in paradiso Adae. Quomodo est istud lignum non Hieronimus dicit. Lignum, quod inter aquas bene crescit, (est) in quo IIII flunt: formositas, fructuositas, uiriditas et semper frondosum. Item de ligno Hieronimus dicit. Lingua ebreica lignum illud mochal [sic] dicitur. Nihil ueterescit in eo, sed cotidie innouatur fructus eius; siue non defluit folium ab eo et non defecit fructus eius.*

A text corresponding to the greater part of the above is found in a gloss to this verse in the *Hebraicum* section of the Rouen Psalter (written in Ireland in the tenth century). Theodore of Mopsuestia and Jerome interpreted this entire psalm as containing moral teaching rather than history or prophecy, and the glosses in the Rouen Psalter are in this same line of exegesis. The gloss on v. 3 reads:

> Et erit tanquam lignum transplatatum. *Hoc lignum nochul [sic] uocatur quod inter aquas bene crescit; huic ligno III sunt: uiriditas fructuositas et semper frondosum est; sic huic uiro conuenit uiriditas uirtutum, fructuositas in filiis, et senium in hereditate florida.*

There are a few other brief interpretations of the psalms in the *Catechesis* corresponding with Irish psalm interpretation, but none in so sustained a fashion as we find for Psalm 1.

5.2. *Interpretation of Genesis 1*[54]

In Codex Reginensis 49, ff. 18 v - 20 r we have an item headed 'Hoc ad solemnitatem paschae conuenit'.[55] It comes after a homily and an exposition on the narrative on the institution of the Eucharist (Mt. 26.20-30). The item is actually a homiletic exposition on the creation narrative of Gen. 1.1-26 read at the Easter Vigil. It is thus introduced in the *Catechesis*:

> *Haec autem lectio quam sancta eclesia ad sanctificationem huius noctis constituit, conuenientiam in se et magnum profectum continet nobis.*

---

53. In De Coninck, *Incerti*, pars altera, p. 4, lines 30-34.

54. For Genesis 1 in Irish tradition see M. McNamara, 'Celtic Christianity, Creation and Apocalypse, Christ and Antichrist', *Milltown Studies* 23 (1989), pp. 5-39, esp. 5-16.

55. Wilmart, *Analecta Reginensia*, pp. 39-44.

> *Conueniens autem erat ut principium in principio, et natiuitas in natiui-*
> *tate ac babtismum in babtismo legeretur. Sicut namque in hac lectione*
> *principium mundi monstratur, ita in hac sollemnitate resurrectionis*
> *Christi initium noui testamenti aeclesia ostendit.*

The text is actually an exposition of this creation narrative according
to a threefold sense, historical, spiritual and moral, although it is not
formally laid out as such. It has an ending of the kind frequently found
in Irish homiletic and semi-homiletic compositions:

> *Et postea in montem sublimem regni caelestis subleuabuntur, ubi erit*
> *uita sine fine, letitia sine tristitia, iuuentus sine senectute, sanitas sine*
> *dolore, lux sine tenebris; ubi non uidebitur inimicus et non audietur nisi*
> *spirituale carmen laudis Domini nostri Iesu Christi; ubi non odorabitur*
> *nisi suauissimus (odor); ubi non gustabitur nisi dulcedo; ubi dabuntur*
> *praemia sempiterna sanctis eternis cum eterno Deo in secula seculorum.*
> *Amen.*

The exposition itself seems very closely related to the exegesis of this
section which we find in such works as the 'Reference Bible', the *Commemoratio Geneseos*, the commentary on Genesis 1–3 in MS Sankt
Gallen, Stiftsbibliothek 908,[56] and in some other sources besides. The
homiletic exposition of the *Catechesis* seems to follow the commentary
material very closely indeed: the *lux* of Gen. 1.2 is *lux pallida* or the
angels; the firmament of Gen. 1.3 is *caelum aereum uel glaciale et
iacinthimum uel celum igneum*. In both, the exposition is according to
the threefold sense. The moral interpretation of *duo luminaria* in both is
fides et opus. These are but a few, almost random, examples of sustained correspondence between the catechetical homily and the commentary material.

Only detailed analysis will reveal how close the connection really is
and whether other influences are present in the *Catechesis* beyond that
of the commentaries on the Hexameron. That this exegetical synthesis
on the six days of creation was very much at home in early and later
medieval Ireland is proved by a comparison of the strictly exegetical
Latin material with works in Irish, and with Latin works of demonstra-
bly Irish origin.

---

56. On this text, see now C. Wright, 'Apocryphal Lore and Insular Tradition in
St. Gall, Stiftsbibliothek MS 908', in P. Ní Chatháin and M. Richter (eds.), *Ireland
and Christendom: The Bible and the Missions* (Stuttgart: Klett Cotta, 1987),
pp. 124-45.

5.3. *Exegetical Glosses on the Canticle of Solomon*[57]

In the *Catechesis Celtica* there is neither exegetical or homiletic commentary on the Canticle of Canticles. There are, however, in the collection, a number of citations from this book, principally in a homiletic treatment of Lk. 11.27-28 ('Blessed is the womb that bore you'). 1 have counted 30 texts of Canticles in the various homilies and half of these (15) carry exegetical material from the commentary of Apponius on this work, more precisely from the abbreviation of Apponius's commentary on Canticles. This abbreviated commentary on Canticles was used in Ireland; in fact it was the only commentary on Apponius known to have been used there. It is the sole source for the commentary on this biblical work in the 'Reference Bible' and in the Hiberno-Latin Marburg (Marburg, Staatsarchiv Hr. 2, 11) fragmentary commentary on Canticles as well. We know from their Rule that this book of the Canon was held in high regard by the *Céli Dé*.

In this instance, as elsewhere, the *Catechesis Celtica* is using exegetical material current in the early Irish Church.

6. Catechesis Celtica *and Irish Homiletic Tradition*

In this section I shall consider homiletic material in the *Catechesis Celtica* which I consider related to corresponding vernacular Irish and Latin material in the *Leabhar Breac*. Where possible this material will also be compared with Hiberno-Latin exegetical material. In this section I concentrate on material having to do with the liturgical celebrations of Holy Week and Easter.

In the Codex Reginensis 49 this is found together in ff. 13 r b - 23 v b, 32 r (ff. 24-31 are displaced in the binding). The collection opens with a text entitled *Omelia in dominica die palmarum* (f. 13 r), in which priests are presented as being directed to preach Christ's great deeds

---

57. Apponius's commentary, and the later abbreviation of this, have been critically edited by B. de Vregille and L. Neyrand, *Apponii in Canticum Canticorum expositio* (CCSL, 19; Turnhout: Brepols, 1986). For Apponius's commentary in Irish tradition see M. McNamara, 'Early Irish Exegesis: Some Facts and Tendencies', *Proceedings of the Irish Biblical Association* 8 (1984), pp. 71-73; and *idem*, 'New Critical Edition of Apponius and Hiberno-Latin Studies', *Proceedings of the Irish Biblical Association* 11 (1987), pp. 93-96; also de Vregille and Neyrand, *Apponii in Canticum*, pp. xxxviii-xliii (pp. xxxix-xl for the *Catechesis Celtica*).

and miracles to some undefined audience which is exhorted to listen and put the message into practice:

> *Et idcirco, fratres karissimi, sicut necesse est sacerdotibus uirtutes et mirabilia quae fecit Iesus narrare uobis, ita et uos debitis humiliter audire et in corde firmiter tenere, in actus et in opere uoluntarie perficere.*

This text is on the curing of the blind men at Jericho (Mt. 20.29-34). It has what appears to be a formulaic ending (...*caelestia dona quae semper manent in caelo*, f. 14 r). This is followed by the continuation of the biblical passage (Mt. 21.1-17), its place in the Eusebian Canons being indicated in the left margin. This text begins with a small capital. The biblical text is rich in DELQR readings. The comment begins in Irish fashion through *heret*. (Cum appropinquassent *heret* egredientibus illis ab Iericho.) This text gives what appears to be the 'historical' interpretation of the pericope, even though no explicit mention is made of this. Another exposition of the same pericope follows immediately on this (15 r) and without heading. This section ends with a *peroratio* (*Illud autem scire et intellegere debetis, fratres carissimi*), ending in formulaic fashion: *Semperque laetemur et coregnemus cum illo in perpetua uita per infinita secula seculorum. Amen* (f. 16 r). Immediately, in the same line, as heading, there follows: *mora(liter)*, formally introducing the next section, beginning a new line and with small capital, as the moral exposition of the same pericope. This, too, has a formulaic ending (16 v ...*ipsi gloria et imperium in secula seculorum. Amen*).

Immediately on this there follows (16 v) another piece entitled *Omelia in cena Domini* (addressed to *fratres karissimi*). This is on the Gospel for the washing of the feet (Jn 13.1-14), in which only the *lemmata* commented on are cited. It has a formulaic ending (...*qui cum Patre et Spiritu sancto uiuit et regnat in secula seculorum. Amen*). There follows another section (f. 17 r), headed in the right-hand margin as *De cena Domini, id est de capitulo VIo* (written *de capitulo / uio*). It contains the pericope Mt. 26.20-30, on the institution of the Eucharist. This has a formulaic ending (f. 18 v).

This is followed immediately by a brief section from a penitential. Then comes another section headed *Hoc ad solemnitatem paschae conuenit* (18 v), which opens by noting that Holy Church has arranged this reading for the sanctification of this holy night. The reading is Genesis 1, here provided with a commentary, of which I have already treated. It has a formulaic ending (20 r: *cum eterno Deo in secula seculorum.*

Amen). A rather brief section, with some unrelated items follows. Then come a number of sections on the Gospel resurrection narratives. The first (20 v) is headed: *In nomine Dei summi*, opening: Vespere autem sabbati *usque* in hodiernum diem, that is, the resurrection narrative of Mt. 28.1-15. It is a long section without any apparent structure, one which I shall consider in greater detail below (8.b.c). Following on it (22 v, last line) we have a new piece beginning with a small capital: *Vespere sabbati*. Although not formally introduced as such, the nature of this new exposition indicates that it is the spiritual interpretation of the same pericope. The next small capital, and apparently the next division, is in f. 23 v: *Duo sepelierunt Christum, id est Ioseph et Neco-dimus...* The true beginning of this section, however, is to be found a few lines earlier: *Moraliter: sepulchrum Domini sanctam aeclesiam significat*. We thus have a threefold exposition of the resurrection narrative of Matthew, in accord with the historical, spiritual and moral senses of Scripture. In 23 v another section follows (23 v, 32 r), on the praises of Easter Sunday, ending: *Ipse est dies specialiter in quo erit pasca magnum in fine mundi, quando Dominus sedebit in sede maiestatis sue, iudicaturus humanum genus reddens unicuique iuxta opera sua.*

In the *Leabhar Breac* the Passion and Resurrection material is all together, but separated from the homilies on Palm Sunday (*Domnach na hImrime*, p. 40.a 26), Spy Wednesday (Judas's betrayal, p. 44 a), the homily *In cena Domini* (p. 48 b 18). The section on the Passion of the Lord is in pp. 160-72. The treatment is principally on the Passion (Good Friday), to which is subjoined, with separate heading, a homily on the resurrection of Christ (Easter Sunday) and another untitled homily on the incredulity of Thomas (Low Sunday). The entire body is preceded (pp. 157 b 31–159 b 51) by a piece on the corresponding holy places in Jerusalem, from Bede's summary of Adomnan's *De locis sanctis* (taken down from the description of Arculf). It is headed: 'Here commences an account of the holy places which are in the Eastern world around Jerusalem, and around the holy places also, as related by Bede, the illustrious chief historian'. Next comes a section entitled *Pasio Domini nostri Iesu Christi incipit* (pp. 160 a–163 b). This is an Irish version of the Gospel of Nicodemus. Next (pp. 163 b 21–169 b 42) comes another item headed: 'The second version of the passion of the Lord here according to Matthew'. This is a paraphrase of Mt. 26.36–27.10, with some apocryphal and foreign elements, from Gethsemane to the death

of Judas, called 'the incidents of the even and the morning of the next
day' (Good Friday). At p. 166 a 4 there is a break and a new part begins
with the heading: 'The third account here' (*In tres gné inso*). This is
really a continuation of the preceding paraphrase of Matthew (with
some apocryphal additions). This continues the narrative of Matthew
until the death of Christ and has a formal ending, with a prayer to God
to protect Matthew (p. 167 a 52).

There immediately follows, with special capital but without heading,
another section in Irish, being an abbreviated paraphrase of the Gospel
narratives (but mainly of Matthew 28) of the resurrection and post-
resurrection appearances of Christ. There then follows a fourfold exposition of this according to the plain (historical), spiritual, moral and
anagogical senses, these presented explicitly as such (*etargna staraide,
etargna fhollus; etargna siansaide, i. runda ⁊ infhoilsigi, mad iar sians;
etargna bésta; iar n-anagóig*).[58]

After the anagogical exposition there follows an exhortation to celebrate the Easter festival, followed by a text on the day of judgment
(p. 169 b 41).

A section of a bilingual homily for Good Friday follows (pp. 169 b
43–170 a 20), left incompleted, two and a quarter inches of blank space
being left for its completion. After this there follows an Irish translation
of the apocryphal *Descensus ad Inferos*, being the second part of the
Gospel of Nicodemus.

Here it is worth noting that exposition according to the multiple sense
of Scripture is a feature in common between the homiletic material in
the *Leabhar Breac* and Codex Reginensis latinus 49. There is this difference, however, that while the *Leabhar Breac* homilies are clearly
structured according to the multiple sense exposition, with an indication
of where one type of interpretation ends and the other begins, only
occasionally is mention made in the *Catechesis Celtica* of a multiple
exposition. This is all the more noteworthy in that the exegetical exposition of the *Liber questionum in euangeliis*, on which the *Catechesis
Celtica* texts very often depend, is predominantly in accord with the
historical, spiritual and moral senses of Scripture.

---

58. R. Atkinson (ed.), *The Passions and the Homilies from the Leabhar Breac*
(Todd Lecture Series, 2; Dublin: Royal Irish Academy, 1887), pp. 137-41.

6.1. *The Homily on the Lord's Supper*

Jean Rittmueller has made a detailed study of the sources of the homily *In cena Domini* of the *Leabhar Breac*[59] and has shown conclusively that it stands in an Irish tradition that can be traced from Manchianus in the seventh century, down through the Hiberno-Latin commentary on Matthew entitled *Liber questionum in euangeliis* of the eighth century to the glosses of the Máel Brigte Gospels of 1138. The *Catechesis Celtica* homily and the commentary of the 'Reference Bible' on the institution narrative of Matthew belong to this same tradition, as do some other texts.

6.2. *Homiletic Material for Palm Sunday*

The *Catechesis Celtica* introductory material on the cure of the blind men of Jericho (Mt. 20.29-34) need not detain us here, since there is no text corresponding to it in the *Leabhar Breac*.[60] It is, however, worth noting that the Gospel reading (Mt. 27.1-17) on which the *Leabhar Breac* homily for 'Riding Sunday' (i.e. Palm Sunday) is based is the continuation of the text on the blind men of Jericho.

The *Catechesis Celtica* homiletic material that follows (on Mt. 21.1-17) is related to Irish tradition and to the bilingual homily of the *Leabhar Breac* in a number of ways. To begin with, together with the indication of the Eusebian Canons it has as heading *In nomine Dei summi*. These dedicatory words, as McNally notes, while not in themselves a conclusive proof of Hiberno-Latin presence, are symptomatic of its influence.[61] Then again, the homily has the DELQR biblical text. Its exposition, too, in accord with a multiple sense of Scripture, is like that of the *Leabhar Breac* homily—in both cases the historical, spiritual, moral senses are treated. The relationship is closer than this, since right through all three sections, but through the first two in particular, there is a correspondence in the actual exposition of the text. Likewise, both have a relationship to other Irish exegetical texts (e.g. the glosses of the Máel Brigte Gospels), even when not related to one another. A detailed study of the kind performed by Rittmueller would be required to do justice to the relationship. Here I can only cite a few examples:

---

59. Rittmueller, 'The *Leabhar Breac*'.
60. See Atkinson, *Passions and Homilies*, pp. 168-71, 419-25.
61. See below, n. 66.

(i) *Statim inuenietis asinam*

CatCelt: *id est prescientia Spiritus sancti quod inuenitur asina, quod II equi, quod alligata esset, quod dimmetetur.*

LB: *Iesus per praescientiam spiritus sancti intellexit quod inu-eniretur asina, et quod alligata esset, et quod duum animalium numerus inueniretur, quodque dimitt[er]entur.*

In the spiritual exposition:

(ii) *Betfage*

CatCelt: *id est domus maxillae interpretatur, quod significat eclesiam in qua ruminant sacerdotes misteria legis...*

LB: *quod interpretatur domus maxillarum, signat ecclesiam in qua ruminantur sacra mysteria scripturarum.*

(iii) *Duo discipuli*

CatCelt: *...siue chorum apostolorum cum duobus legibus;*

LB: *signant duas leges, i.e. Uetus et Nouum (Testamentum).*

In the moral exposition:

(iv) *Intrauit Iesum in templum*

CatCelt: *id est ipsum hominem qui templum Dei est;*

LB: *exprimit homini (!) cum sit templum Dei.*

The relationship between the *Catachesis Celtica* and the *Leabhar Breac* could best be illustrated by printing both in parallel columns. It runs right through, especially in the spiritual exposition.

When we turn from a comparison of the *Catechesis Celtica* with the *Leabhar Breac* text to a comparison with the Hiberno-Latin commentary *Liber questionum in euangeliis* we find a continuous correspondence between the two. So close, in fact, is this in the historical and spiritual exposition that one may legitimately ask if the compiler of the *Catechesis Celtica* had the *Liber questionum in euangeliis* as a direct source. That he had seems clear from the very opening of the exposition, which in both texts is as follows: Cum appropinquassent (Mt. 21.1) *heret* egredientibus illis ab Iericho (Mt. 20.29), that is, the Irish technique of linking contextual texts through the word heret.

The introductory *Catechesis* material on the cure of the blind men at Jericho also follows the *Liber questionum in euangeliis* exegesis. Thus, in this homiletic material on Palm Sunday we have a tradition stretching from the seventh century to the twelfth, from the *Liber questionum in euangeliis* to the Máel Brigte Gospel glosses through the *Catechesis Celtica* and the *Leabhar Breac* homilies.

6.3. Catechesis Celtica *homiletic material on Christ's Resurrection*
The first item in this section is the homiletic treatment of Genesis 1, the reading for the first part of the Easter Vigil. This, as we have seen, is closely related to Irish exegetical tradition. After this comes the homiletic treatment of the Gospel for the Easter Mass, that is, Mt. 28.1-15: '*Vespere autem sabbati' usque 'in hodiernum diem*' as the opening words put it. For grammatical purposes 28.1a is also given in Greek capitals, as follows: ΟΨΕ ΤΗ CΑΒΒΑΤΟΥ [Greek text has: σαββατων] ΤΗ ΕΠΙΦΟC [*sic*! Greek has: ἐπιφωσκουση] ΕΙC ΜΟΥΑΝ [= μίαν] CΑΒΒΑΤΟΝ. Next there is a homily of rather unusual kind, headed *In nomine Dei summi. Amen.* It has no obvious unifying principle of exposition, taking a variety of approaches to the text and apparently introducing items foreign to the central theme. In this it differs from the first exposition of the text in these homilies. It is obviously intended by the compiler as the historical interpretation of the biblical pericope but has little in common with the *Leabhar Breac*'s historical exposition of the same passage. We shall consider this first exposition in greater detail below because of its very special Irish affiliations, albeit from other points of view. Matters are different with regard to the connection between the *Catechesis Celtica* and the *Leabhar Breac* in the spiritual exposition of the Gospel passage. To illustrate by some examples:

CatCelt: Vespere sabbati. *id est in fine ueteris testamenti*;
LB: 'The evening of the sabbath' denotes the completion and termination that overtook the Law on the coming of the Gospel.
CatCelt: Duo Mariae. *IIae aeclesie*;
LB: 'The two Marys who were seeking Christ at the grave' denote the two Churches that are seeking the Lord today in the New Testament—the Church of the faithful Jews, and the Church of the chosen Gentiles.
CatCelt: Angelus. *id est Christus, Dei Filius et hominis, ueniens in carnem, consulans sanctas animas cum lenitate dicens:* Venite ad me omnes:
LB: 'For an angel came from heaven': this denotes the Saviour Jesus, whose name in the Scripture is 'the Angel of great counsel', coming from heaven to earth at the pleasure of the heavenly Father, to help and deliver men...

CatCelt: Accedens reuoluit. *id est in carnem ueniens litterae duritiam ammouit*;

LB: '...he pushed the stone from the grave', means, mystically, when Christ came into the body, He put away the hardness and severity of the teaching of the Law, through the clemency and gentleness of the teaching of the Gospel.

CatCelt: Videte locum. *id est, credite humanitatem sed incircumscriptam assumite diuinitatem*;

LB: 'Come and see the place', i.e. the humanity, as being the place and dwelling of the Son in his divinity.

In the *Leabhar Breac* text the moral exposition is followed by a passage on the praises of Easter Day, with an exhortation to honour it.

> 'Beloved brethren,' says the sage, 'let us today celebrate the festivity of the Easter; this festival fully deserves its honour and celebration at the hands of all the faithful.' This feast is directed to be honoured in three ways... And though all feasts fully deserve their celebration and honour in these three ways, still more does this festival; for in it is the assembling together of the folk of heaven and earth; it is the festival alike of the Old and New Testament; it is the peculiar feast of the heavenly Father; the feast of the Lord's resurrection; the feast which surpasses all others; the honoured and venerable festival of the people of heaven and earth, is this festival of Easter. For many are its wonders and marvels: in it the angel passed over the houses of the children of Israel; ...in it Christ arose from the dead, after binding the devil in hell; in it the souls of the righteous of the five ages of the world came out of hell into paradise; in it will be the famous day, the Day of Judgement.
>
> (The text goes on to describe this great Day of Judgment at some length.)[62]

In the *Catechesis Celtica* the moral exposition is also followed by one, or perhaps two, pieces with an exhortation to celebrate Easter, singing its praises, and dwelling on the marvels done and yet to be done on that day.

> *Facta sunt in hac die multa beneficia, quia in hac die resurrexit Christus, Filius Dei uiui post uastationem inferni, et solutionem humani generis de ore diaboliet de peccato Adae. Et in hac die debemus laetari, quia dies mirabilis est, dies uenerabilis, dies solemnis, dies lucis et iustitiae, dies principalis, dies salutis humani generis, dies laudabilis, dies magnae gloriae, dies resurrectionis Domini nostri Iesu Christi. Resur-*

62. *Leabhar Breac*, p. 169 a; Atkinson, *Passions and Homilies*, p. 390 (Irish text, pp. 141-42).

rectio Christi in caelo et in terra ueneranda est, quia per illam nostra resurrectio facta est (f. 32 r).

This is immediately followed by a further *praeconium paschale*:

> *Solemnitas ista uenerabilis est per totas aeclesias mundi, id est solemnitas resurrectionis Christi Filii Dei uiui altissimi a mortuis, quia omnes sollemnitates, quae sunt in anno, annumerantur Christo, sunt quasi fructus mirandi et pulchri inter flores... Ista tamen solemnitas paschae prae omnibus specialiter pertinet Christo, nam etsi ueneranda fuerit dies uaticinationis Christi quam profetae uaticinauerunt...uenerabilior et altior est haec solemnitas resurrectionis Christi quae ueneratur in caelo et in terra... Hic est dies in quo est maxima laetitia et exultatio familiae caeli. Hic est dies in quo fecit Deus Pater caritatem et pacem inter homines terrae et familiam caeli. Ipse est dies specialiter in quo erit pasca magnum in fine mundi, quando Dominus sedebit in sede maiestatis sue, iudicaturus hamanum genus reddens unicuique iuxta opera sua.*

There are no glosses on this section of the Gospel of Máel Brigte. When we turn to the *Liber questionum in euangeliis*, once again we find the same tradition as in the *Catechesis Celtica*. This is continuous in the spiritual exposition, but is also present in the literal interpretation, as we shall see in the next section. It is a fair assumption that here again the compiler of the *Catechesis* was using the LQE or a commentary almost identical with it.

6.4. *The Easter Homily* 'In nomine Dei Summi. Amen' *and its Manchianus Glosses*

I now return to the Easter homily, or homilies, in ff. 20 v–23 v. I have earlier (8.6 above, introduction) described the *Catechesis Celtica* sections on the resurrection narratives as lacking any apparent structure. It seems clear, however, that the first section in the folios indicated above contains a triple exposition (historical, ff. 20 v–22 v; spiritual, 22 v infra–23 v; and moral, 23 v) on the resurrection narrative of Mt. 20.1-15, although this original plan has not been respected in the present layout of the manuscript.

The first of these homilies, which must have been intended as the historical exposition, is headed '*In nomine Dei summi. Amen*' (ff. 20 v–22 v) and is of special interest to us for a variety of reasons. For one thing, we find in it the only sure Breton or Cornish gloss *guor cher* (f. 21 r). On the other hand it contains very strong indications of Irish affiliations, even of Irish origin, not least being the source indication *Man.* and the heading.

In this homily, by way of exception almost as far as Codex Reginensis 49 is concerned, we have the presumed sources indicated in the margins, and occasionally in the text. The marginal notations are (in order of occurrence): *hir*(unimus), *Ag*(ustinus), *Man*(chianus?), *Sedo*(lius; *Carmen paschale*), *Amb*(rosius) (twice), *hir*(unimus) (twice), *Man*, *Ag* (twice), *hir* (twice). In the text itself *Arcul.* (= Arculfus) is indicated as a source: '*De forma tegovii et aeclesiae rotondae Arcul. refert*' (= Adomnan, *De locis sanctis* I.2, 1-14). In this part there is also clear dependence on the *Liber questionum in euangeliis*, a dependence that is more pronounced in the spiritual and moral expositions that follow on it.

The historical exposition begins by a treatment of the opening word *uespere* (Mt. 28.1), which presents an obvious problem if taken to mean 'evening', since Christ's resurrection was in the early morning. The exposition opens with a long text on this and related forms, taken from the grammarian Virgilius Maro, a text already cited by the seventh-century anonymous Irish writer from the circles of Cummian, in his work *Pauca de ratione conputandi secundum solem et lunam.*[63] It reads:

> *Est etiam uesper, uespere, uesperum, uespera. Hic casus nominatiuus quadruplex est cuius differentia hoc erit, quod uesper quidem dicitur quoties sol nubibus aut luna ferruginibus quacumque diei uel noctis hora contegitur. Et hoc meritum est ut* (sic!; Virgilius Maro: hoc neutrum ut) *uesper, -is, -ri, -em, -er, -re declinetur. Nominatiuo uespere uocatur ab hora nona, sole discessum inchoante. Sed hoc nomen non declinatur: Vesperum cum, sole occidente, dies deficit, et sic declinatur: uesperum, -i, -o, -um, -um, -o. Vespera est cum lucis oriente aurora nox finitur, et sic declinatur: uespera, -ae, -ae, -am, reliqua. Cauendum est ne aut uesper aut uesperum aut uespera pluralem numerum habeant* (Virgilius Maro: habere putentur).

63. Text of Virgilius Maro in *Virgilio Marone Grammatico, epitomi ed epistole* (critical edn ed. G. Polara; trans. L. Caruso and G. Polara; Nuovo Medievo, 9; Naples: Lignori, 1979), pp. 186, 188. Text of *De ratione conputandi* ed. D. Ó Cróinín in *Cummian's Letter De controversia paschali* (ed. by M. Walsh and D. Ó Cróinín; together with a related Irish computistical *Tract De ratione conputandi* ed. D. Ó Cróinín; Studies and Texts, 86; Toronto: Pontifical Institute of Mediaeval Studies, 1988), p. 133. I am grateful to Professor Louis Holtz for having pointed out the source of this quotation to me in 1990. I note that he had done so to D. Ó Cróinín in 1983.

This text is immediately followed by another in which the Greek text of Mt. 28.1a is cited for the purpose of showing that *opse*, the presumed Greek for *uespere*, is feminine.

In this first and historical exposition the homilist is concerned with the harmonization (*concordantiae*) of the resurrection narratives of the Gospels. The *Man.* texts tend to occur in contexts of Gospel harmony (*concordantiae*).

The first of the *Man.* references comes soon after the initial grammatical considerations, and considers the different Marys mentioned in Matthew 28 (f. 20 v b 21-2). The text has the marginal references *Ag* and *Man* immediately under one another (line-ending noted by /):

> *'Venit Ma/ria Magdalena'. id est de Magdalo in Galilea de qua,/ ut Marcus dicit, iecit Dominus VII demonia. 'Et altera/ Maria'. id est uirgo mater Domini. Cessantibus enim car/nis operibus in Domino, mater non dicitur haec.*

The next occurrence (f. 21 r b 6-14) has an explicit reference to harmonization and is on the interval between the arrival of the different women at the tomb:

> *Aliqua distantia de aduentu istarum mulierum uidetur inter euangelistas. Mattheus dicit: uespere; Marcus, uero, Ortu sole. Lucas, ualde deluculo. Iohannes, cum adhuc tenebrae essent. Man*(chianus?) *de hac concordatione dicit sapi*(ens)*: Consummatio noctis uespera est, sicut consummatio diei uespera est. Quando nox consummatur, diluculum est et adhuc tenebre et prima lucescit et statim oritur sol, ut IIII euangelistae in una narratione congruant.* (The manuscript has, without marginal reference: … Man. De hac: concordatione dicit sapi., consummatio…)

The text here ascribed to Man(chianus) sapi(ens), *Consummatio noctis uespera est, sicut consummatio diei uespera est*, would appear to depend on Virgilius Maro's understanding of *uespera* cited above: *Vespera est cum lucis oriente nox finitur.*

A little further on (f. 21 v a) we have a further text, ascribed in the margin to *Man.*, towards the end of which there is a further passage ascribed in the text itself to the same source:

> *Sciendum ob quam causam pauciores angeli in morte Christi quam in natiuitate uidentur. Nascente enim illo legitur: 'Et ecce exercitus caelestis', reliqua. In morte autem III tantum angelis amministrare intelliguntur, quia caelestis rex in terrestria rura ueniens debuerat cum exercitu caelesti uenire ad repugnandas aereas uirtutes. Ascendens autem in caelos iterum cum exercitu uadit sicut legitur: 'Attolite portas principes*

uestras', reliqua. Man. Spelunca sepulchri corporis Christi IIIbus custo-
ditur ad spem resurrectionis confirmandam. id est angelis, IIIbus mulier-
ibus, et apostolis.

Given the evidence of Irish affiliations, it is natural to expand the abbreviation *Man.* as *Manchianus* and to identify the scholar in question with the seventh-century Irish scholar known now from a variety of sources. He is mentioned in the prologue of the Irish pseudo-Augustine's *De mirabilibus sacrae scripturae* (composed 655; *PL* 35, 2175-6): *post patrem Manchianum*, as teacher of pseudo-Augustine. He is presumably the same person as the *Manichaeus* of the printed editions of *De mirabilibus* II, 4, who is mentioned as among the *Hibernien-sium...ceteros sapientes* who are said to have died on a year identifiable as 652. Manchianus is cited in the Hiberno-Latin commentary on the Catholic Epistles (seventh century) as *Manchianus doctor noster* by reason of a comment of his on use of a text of Genesis 15 (*credidit Abraham Deo*) by both the Apostles Paul and James (Jas 2.23).[64] Manch(i)anus's commentary on the narrative of the institution of the Eucharist of Matthew has been excerpted from in the glosses of the Máel Brigte Gospels as *Man., Manchanus.*[65] P. Grosjean and others believe that he is very probably to be identified with Manchán of Liath Mancháin (Lemanaghan) (died 655), while J. F. Kenney and others identify him with Manchianus of Men Droichit (died 652).[66]

Apart from the name of *Man.* (Manchianus), there are arguments for Irish connections, even origin, for this particular homily. To begin with,

64. McNally, *Scriptores*, p. 15: '*Manchianus, doctor noster, hanc rem duorum apostolorum uno exemplo utentium (tractauit), et ad utrasque causas de clasibus uoluit similitudinem ponere que uno eodemque uento mouentur, sed non uno itinere currunt.*'

65. See Rittmueller, 'Gospel Commentary', pp. 200-14.

66. See P. Grosjean, 'Sur quelques exégètes irlandais du VIIe siècle', *Sacris Erudiri* 7 (1955), pp. 67-98 (89); McNally, *Scriptores*, p. ix. D. Ó Laoghaire ('Irish Elements', p. 158) prefers to be more general, stating that the Manchianus in question 'was perhaps one of the two of that name, the first of Men Droichit (652), the other of Liath Manchán (655)'. The arguments in favour of identification with Manchianus of Men Droichit is the identification of the *pater* of the prologue with *Manichaeus* of 11. 4, said to have died in 652, the annalistic obit of Manchianus of Men Droichit: thus J.F. Kenney, *The Sources for the Early History of Ireland*. I. *Ecclesiastical* (New York, 1929; repr. Shannon, Ireland: Irish University Press, 1968; Dublin: Four Courts Press, 1997), pp. 276-77; Walsh and Ó Cróinín (eds.), *Cummian's Letter*, p. 88 n. 225.

the very title '*In nomine Dei summi*' is symptomatic of Irish origins.[67] The interest in grammatical questions in evidence at the beginning of the homily is in keeping with what we know of early Irish commentaries. Some of the sources used in the text have Irish origins or associations. The most noteworthy is the long excerpt from Virgilius Maro Grammaticus, a text also used by Manchianus's Irish contemporary, the anonymous author of *De ratione conputandi*, from the circles of Cummian. Then there is the mention of Arcul(f)'s description of the holy places, that is Adomnan's *De locis sanctis*.[68] It is also to be noted that pseudo-Jerome's commentary on Mark (probably of Irish origin, and possibly from the pen of a certain Cummeanus) is cited at least twice under the name of Jerome. The clear use of the Hiberno-Latin work *Liber questionum in euangeliis* is a further argument for strong Irish connections, if not for Irish origin. The *Man.* glosses and influence of this same commentary on Matthew are also present in the section on the Eucharist in the Máel Brigte Gospels glosses.

There remains the difficulty of the use of the Greek text of Mt. 28.1a. However, the Greek Psalter text of Ps. 39.3 is used in the Hiberno-Latin (and probably sixth-century) pseudo-Hilary commentary on the Catholic Epistles (1 Pet. 1.1).[69] With regard to the Greek text of Mt. 28.1a cited in the *Catechesis Celtica*, it must be noted that the text in question is found in substance, though not verbatim, already in the seventh-century Hiberno-Latin *Liber questionum in euangeliis* (MS Orléans: Bibl. Mun. 65 [2], p. 266). This reads:

> *De nomine uero quod et uespere multi opinantur diuersa. In euangelio*
> *uero greco ita habetur*: ОΨН САВВА, *id est uespere sabbati quae in*

---

67. On this title, see R. McNally, ' "In nomine Dei summi": Seven Hiberno-Latin sermons', *Traditio* 35 (1979) 121-43, pp. 123-24 for the formula: 'The appearance of the dedicatory words, "*In nomine Dei summi*" in early medieval manuscripts, while not in itself a conclusive proof of the Hiberno-Latin element, is symptomatic of its influence'. F.E. Warren had earlier commented on the significance of this formula: 'This short and pious motto which is written on the upper margin of the opening pages of the Bangor Antiphonary seems to have been especially, if not exclusively, used by Irish scribes' (*The Antiphonary of Bangor* [2 vols.; London: Henry Bradshaw Society, 1895], II, p. 35).

68. For the text referred to in the homily, see D. Meehan (ed.), *Adamnan's De locis sanctis* (SLH, 3; Dublin Institute for Advanced Studies,1958), part 1, pp. 42-47.

69. McNally, *Scriptores*, p. 77.

primam sabbatorum. In quo apparet quod ΟΨΗ *femininum nomen est.*
ΤΗ *enim femininum pronomen. Unde quidam uolunt quod uesper com-*
munis generis, id est feminini et masculi…

In this particular homily, we may note, the *Catechesis Celtica* agrees
with the LQE in a number of points with regard to questions concerning
the death and resurrection of Christ (e.g. the length of time Christ was
in the tomb, both citing Augustine as an authority). It is obvious that
both belong to the same tradition, even though here the *Catechesis* is
not dependent solely on the LQE, for one thing, because it cites more of
the Greek text.[70]

That early Irish scholars were interested in the harmonization of the
Gospel passion and resurrection accounts is clear from the 'Reference
Bible', where the greater part of the entry on Mark (12 columns out of
16 in the Paris MS, BN lat. 11561 ff. 156 r–159 v) is devoted to questions on the passion and the resurrection of Christ and the general resurrection. Some of the same sources are used as in the *Catechesis Celtica*
homily, and the contents of one section on the prophecies of the resurrection and the number of hours Christ was in the tomb (drawing on
Augustine for this) are the same in both.

6.5. *Homily for Octave of Easter*
In ff. 32 v–35 v we have a long homily for the Octave of Easter, on the
text of Jn 20.26-31.[71] The *Leabhar Breac* also has a homily, in Irish and
Latin, on this same passage.[72] There are certain similarities between the
two (such as the number of the post-resurrection appearances, the one
to Thomas being the sixth). There are also Irish 'symptoms' in the Latin
of the *Catechesis Celtica*, for example, Low Sunday called *pascha
modicum* (Irish *Mion-Cháisc*). There is no clear relationship, however,
between the *Leabhar Breac* text and the *Catechesis*, possibly because
of the lack of a common exegetical source, as was the case in the homilies on pericopes from Matthew's Gospel.

6.6. *Homily on Christ's Fast and Temptation in the Desert*
The very first item in the *Catechesis Celtica* (ff. 1–3 r) is a commentary
on Mt. 4.1-11, that is, Christ's fast in the desert and his temptation. This

70. See n. 34 above.
71. Wilmart, *Analecta Reginensia*, pp. 47-58.
72. Atkinson, *Passions and Homilies*, pp. 227-34 (Irish text), 465-70 (Latin text,
with English translation of small portion of Irish not represented in the Latin).

is separated by a short piece (f. 3 r-v) from the comment on Mt. 19.16-30 on the call of the rich young man. In the *Leabhar Breac*, after treatment of Palm Sunday (p. 40 a 26) and Judas's betrayal (Spy Wednesday *Cédain in braith*, p. 44 a 1), and immediately before the section *In cena Domini* (p. 48 b 18) comes a section entitled *De ieiunio Domini in deserto* (p. 45 a 7). This is a bilingual homily which originally belonged to the eleventh-century homiliarium.[73] One feature of this *Leabhar Breac* homily is the close manner in which part of it is related to the Latin tradition found in the *Catechesis Celtica*. This is evident in particular in the Latin text, in the *Leabhar Breac* first (i.e. the historical) interpretation of the pericope and also in the final section on the supremacy of almsgiving over mere fasting, and in the remark that the time devoted to fasting is a tithing, a tenth of the 365-day year. Since the Latin texts coincide verbatim and in sequence as comments on the *lemmata* there can be no question of mere accident. The final text found in both works, and in the *Collectio canonum Hibernensis*, strengthens the argument for direct links through some particular homiletic tradition. As examples we have:

> Ductus est, *non inuitus aut captiuus, sed ex uoluntate pugnandi...*Postea esuriit: ...*ne a temptando pauens hostis aufugeret...*in sanctam ciuitatem: *ista assumptio non imbecillitate Dei...sed de inimici superbia, qui uoluntatem Saluatoris necessitatem putat...*si cadens adoraueris me: *arrogans et superbus etiam hoc de iactantia loquitur...*

This particular exegetical text occurs almost verbatim in the Hiberno-Latin *Liber questionum in euangeliis*. Going on the evidence of other texts, the presumption is that the *Catechesis* depends (directly most probably) on the Hiberno-Latin commentary. The same is probably true with regard to the *Leabhar Breac* homily.

In both the *Catechesis Celtica* and the *Leabhar Breac* (in the Irish and Latin texts) we have an item on the seven-week fast, minus the six Sundays in which there is no fast, being one tenth of the year, the Lenten fast being consequently a tithing. In this section the *Catechesis Celtica* text is almost verbatim as that of the *Liber questionum in euangeliis*.

Next after this in the *Catechesis* comes a text to the effect that Christ fasted immediately after his baptism which occurred at the Epiphany

---

73. Atkinson, *Passions and Homilies*, pp. 172-81 (Irish text), 425-30 (Latin text, with translation of small section of Irish not directly from Latin).

(January 6). The present position of the Lenten season in the calendar is
due to the Fathers. There is a similar text in the *Leabhar Breac*, although
not immediately after the treatment of Lent as a tithing. As in other
texts, here too, the *Catechesis Celtica* is almost verbatim like that found
in the *Liber questionum in euangeliis*.

The text on the supremacy of almsgiving over mere fasting comes
almost immediately after that on tithing in the *Leabhar Breac*, whereas
in the *Catechesis* it is separated by a number of texts not drawn from
the *Liber questionum*. The text reads as follows in the *Catechesis*:

> *Debet quoque unusquisque nostrum ieiuinare in istis diebus; etsi non
> ualuerit, manducet cum gemitu et suspirio et dolore animi. Pro eo quod,
> aliis abstinentibus, ille abstinere non potest, et conieuiunare non potest,
> amplius (debet) erogare pauperibus, ut peccata, quae non potest ieiu-
> nando curare, possit elimosinas dando redimere. Bonum est ieiunare,
> fratres; sed melius est elimosinam dare. Si aliquis utrumque potest, duo
> sunt bona. Si uero non potest, melius est elimosinam dare. Si possibilitas
> ieiunandi non fuerit, elimosa sufficit sine ieiunio. Ieiunium uero sine
> elimosa omnino non sufficit. Elimosina sine ieiunio bonum est. Ieiu-
> nium uero sine elimosina nullum bonum est nisi forte ita sit aliquis pau-
> per, ut non habeat omnino quod tribuat. Illi, qui non habuerit, sufficit
> uoluntas bona. Tale ergo ieiunium sine elimosina sicut lucerna, quae
> sine oleo accenditur, fum(ig)are potest, lumen habere non potest. Ita
> ieiunium sine elimosina carnem quidem cruciat, sed caritatis lumine
> minimum illustret.*

In the margin of Codex Reginensis 49 this text is ascribed to *Ag*, that is,
Agustinus. It is, in fact, from Sermon 199 (nos. 2-3 and 6) of St Caesarius of Arles,[74] which with many other sermons of this saint became
falsely attributed to Augustine (as Sermon 142, 3, 1-2; in *PL* 39, cols.
2022-23) in the course of transmission. The *Catechesis* text is composed from two distinct sections (2-3 and 6) of Caesarius's homily. The
central section of it (*Bonum est ieiunium...sufficit uoluntas bona*) is also
in the *Leabhar Breac* text,[75] which, however, we should recall, has more
from Caesarius's homily than that found in the *Catechesis*. The *Collectio canonum Hibernensis* (XIII, 8),[76] in the section on fasting, has an

74. G. Morin (ed.), *Sanctus Caesarius Arelatensis: sermones*, II (CCSL, 104,
Turnhout: Brepols, 1953), pp. 803-807.

75. Atkinson, *Passions and Homilies*, p. 429.

76. H. Wasserschleben (ed.), *Die irische Kanonensammlung* (Leipzig: Verlag
von Bernhard Tauchnitz, 2nd edn, 1885), p. 40.

almost identical text, with, however, some differences. In one branch of the *Hibernensis* tradition the excerpt is attributed to Jerome, in another, to Augustine.

The similarities and differences between these Irish texts may be due to dependence of all on some common homiletic tradition or patristic *florilegium*.

6.7. *Homilies on the Lord's Prayer*

We have seen that the *Catechesis Celtica* has more than one item on the Lord's Prayer, or more exactly a collection of material headed by the title *Incipit umelia de oratione dominica*. It does not appear that the compiler has imposed any great order on this material. Matters are somewhat different with the material on the *Pater noster* in the *Leabhar Breac* (pp. 248 a 45–250 b). This is a bilingual text, the sentences or phrases occurring alternately in Latin and Irish.[77] The text opens with an introduction, followed by a single exposition of the petitions of the *Pater*, after which come comments of various kinds.

Opinion is divided with regard to the date to be assigned to the *Leabhar Breac* text. Frederic Mac Donncha regarded it as part of a homiliarium of the eleventh century. Brian Ó Cuív would date it, from its language, to the end of the Middle Irish period, probably the twelfth century.[78] The piece has been transcribed in later Irish in MS BL Egerton 91 (f. 20; of the fifteenth century). Robin Flower noted that some points in the commentary in the Egerton manuscript are also to be found in the comment on the *Pater* in Mt. 6.5-13 in Harley 1802 (i.e. the Gospels of Máel Brigte). Thus far, scholars have failed to identify the sources of the *Leabhar Breac* text on the *Pater noster*.

It appears that the solution to the quest will come through the newly identified Hiberno-Latin exegetical and homiletical texts. Already, before the material brought to the attention of students by Bischoff, the Latin text of *Leabhar Breac* invited comparison with the commentary

---

77. Atkinson, *Passions and Homilies*, pp. 259-66 (Irish text), 495-503 (English translation of Irish), 503-506 (Latin text).

78. See Mac Donncha, 'Medieval Irish Homilies', p. 61; F. Mac Donncha, 'Seanmóireacht in Éirinn ó 1000 go 1200', in M. Mac Conmara (ed.), *An léann eaglasta in Éirinn 1000–1200* (Baile Átha Cliath [Dublin]: An Clochomhar, 1982), pp. 77-95, p. 79; B. Ó Cuív, 'Some Versions of the Sixth Petition in the Pater Noster', *Studia Celtica* 14-15 (1979–80), pp. 212-22 (212).

on the Pater in Pseudo-Jerome, *Expositio IV evangeliorum*, available in *PL*, 30. Keeping with the aim of this paper, I here begin by comparing the Latin text of the *Leabhar Breac* with that of the *Catechesis Celtica* and then with other related texts.

The relationship of the Latin text with the *Catechesis* is verbatim and manifold, not merely in the exposition of the petitions. In the comment on the opening words we read in both: *Quid lautem filiis carius esse debet quam pater? Quid enim petentibus filiis non dabit pater...ut filii essent, et dicant: 'Pater noster...'* The *Leabhar Breac* text (Latin and Irish) gives six reasons why this Prayer is said (sung) silently. *Sex autem causis haec oratio silenter canitur.* The *Catechesis Celtica* is interested in the point, but gives no list: *Interrogatur hic. Cur silenter hii uersiculi canuntur? (Hoc) multis causis ostenditur.* Obviously, the *Catechesis* compiler has cut short his source. The *Leabhar Breac* text speaks of the Old Testament prefigurations of the *Pater: Haec autem oratio figurata est in scala uisa ab Iacop, in Bethel, cum septem gradibus attingente a caelo usque ad terram... Prophetata est per Isaiam prophetam, dicentem, 'faciet Dominus uerbum breuissimum super terram...'*, to which the *Leabhar Breac* Latin text (and corresponding Irish translation) adds: *uerbum consummans et breuians iniquitates hominum.* The same text is found verbatim in the *Catechesis Celtica*. The passage of Isaiah intended is not quite clear (possibly Isa. 38.7), and the Irish translation interprets somewhat.[79]

This text of the *Leabhar Breac* is followed by a very interesting one: *Hic est malleus ferreus, quo contritus est diabolus, sicut dicitur, 'malleo ferreo conteram soliditatem tuam'.* The Irish text, and apparently translation, of this passage presumes to identify the source of the citation: 'This is the iron hammer by which the power of the devil is broken, as saith Job in the person of the Lord: "I will break your power, O devil, saith the Lord, with an iron hammer"'. The text is also in the

---

79. The text is not Vulgate of Isa. 38.7, which has: *...quia faciet Dominus uerbum hoc quod locutus est*, i.e. making the shadow on Ahaz's sundial turn backwards. The Septuagint translation does not differ significantly. The Irish *Leabhar Breac* translation renders *uerbum* of the Latin as 'prayer': 'The Lord will make a short prayer, by which all their sins and vices shall be forgiven to men' (Atkinson, *Passions and Homilies*, p. 501). The other text which follows, attributed to Job in the Irish translation, cannot be traced. Both 'quotations' may be from a non-biblical source.

Catechesis Celtica as the immediate continuation of that just quoted: *Hic est malleus de quo contritus est diabulus, sicut est malleo ferreo ut concutiam soliditatem tuam.*

The *Leabhar Breac* text connects the seven petitions of the *Pater* with the seven gifts of the Holy Spirit, and with the seven deadly sins. This is also true of the *Catechesis Celtica*. Comparison of the *Catechesis Celtica*, with the *Liber questionum in euangeliis* shows that here again the former is indebted to the latter, in some sections more heavily than in others. The exposition of the Lord's Prayer (Mt. 6.9-13) in the *Liber questionum in euangeliis* is extremely rich (covering pp. 88 to 94 of the Orléans manuscript). There are no less than four different explanations of the passage and various other points of Christian teaching are connected with its seven petitions: the teaching on the paradise of Adam, Adam's person, the seven principal vices, the manner in which the Lord himself fulfilled the seven petitions, the seven days of creation, the six ages of the world (*Sex aetates*), and the seventh age after the judgment. A number of the headings, and the substance of the teaching on them, have passed over into the *Catechesis*. What must also be noted is that the *Leabhar Breac* text has material from the *Liber questionum in euangeliis* not in the *Catechesis Celtica*, such as a number of interpretations of the text of Matthew, which at times agree verbatim with the Latin *Leabhar Breac* text, for example, the interpretation of *regnum* (of *Adueniat regnum tuum*) as *iudicium*, likewise the following: *Cum ergo dicimus in oratione Domenica, get ne nos inducas in temptationum', nonne hic petimus, non temptari sed ut non feramur in temptationes quas sustinere non ualemus* (LB 249 b 32-4).[80] The text of LQE (MS Orléans, p. 90, 3-2 from end) has: *Non hic petimus ut non temptemur sed ut non feramur in temptationes quas sustinere non ualeamus.*

---

80. Atkinson, *Passions and Homilies*, p. 504; in the manuscript the Latin is followed immediately by Irish text: *In tan din atberum is-in ernaigthi choimdetta Et ne .n.ī.d.ī.t. 'a Dé nachar-léic i n-amus', ni hed chuinchemit andsin, na ro-tartaither aimse foraind, acht is ed, na tartaither oir-n aimse dofhulachta no-n-scarut fri forpthecht 7 fri fírinde* (Atkinson, *Passions and Homilies*, p. 263; English translation p. 499: 'When we say in the Lord's prayer:—"O God, leave us not in temptation," we do not thereby ask that no temptations should be put on us, but what we ask is, that there should not be given us temptations beyond our power, which may sever us from spirituality and truth').

The explanation of these phenomena seems to be that both the *Catechesis Celtica* and the *Leabhar Breac* texts depend on the *Liber questionum in euangeliis*, or a text almost identical with it. Direct dependence of the *Leabhar Breac* on the *Catechesis* does not appear indicated by the evidence. The commentary of the kind found in the *Liber questionum in euangeliis* must have been known in Ireland, and have continued to be used there, since it seems to have been employed as a source for the glosses of the Gospels of Máel Brigte, roughly contemporary with the *Leabhar Breac* homily or catechetical text on the Lord's Prayer.

Many more questions remain to be answered with regard to the *Leabhar Breac* text on the Lord's Prayer, for instance, the exact relationship of the Irish version to the Latin. The new Hiberno-Latin material will scarcely bring an answer to all of these, as for instance, the background to the Irish form of the sixth petition: *ní r-lecea sind i n-amus ndofulachtai; ocus nach-ar-léic i n-amus.*[81] However, the newly identified corpus of material of apparently Irish origin or affiliations should help immensely.

7. Catechesis *Homilies on Matthew and the* Liber questionum in euangeliis

In examining the relationship between the *Catechesis Celtica* homiletic tradition and the homiletic tradition of the *Leabhar Breac* I have used the relevant material from the seventh-century Hiberno-Latin commentary on Matthew entitled *Liber questionum in euangeliis*. The use of this commentary established for these sections can be extended to practically all the pericopes from Matthew commented on in the *Catechesis Celtica*, with the exception of the homily on Mt. 20.1-16 (f. 7 v–8 v) which is entirely from Gregory the Great's homily I and II on the Gospels. The historical and spiritual exposition on Mt. 19.16-30 (ff. 3 v and 7 r) draws on it throughout. So also the homily that follows on Mt. 21.33-46. Here, once again, direct use of the *Liber questionum in euangeliis* [LQE] seems indicated by the opening section verbatim identical in both:

> '*Aliam parabolam audite*' (Mt. 21.33) *a loco ubi ait:* '*Accesserunt ad eum principes sacerdotum*' (Mt. 21.23), *reliqua a Matheo sine ulla*

---

81. On these *Leabhar Breac* forms, see Ó Cuív, 'Some Versions', pp. 214, 216.

cuiuisque rei uel personae interpositione sermo contexitur. Potest enim putari (LQE: aestimare) omnia principibus locutum fuisse (LQE: esse) a quibus fuerat de potestate interrogatus, siue hic tacuit breuitatis causa, quod Lucas dixit: 'coepit' inquit, 'dicere ad plebem parabolam', reliqua. 'Homo erat': Dominus noster...

It has been already noted that this same source (LQE) is used for the homily for Palm Sunday (Mt. 21.1-17) and for that on the institution of the Eucharist (Mt. 26.20-30) as well as for the homilies on the resurrection narrative (Mt. 28.1-15). We find the same source used for another homily on Mt. 20.29-34 (ff. 47 v, 24 r).

We may thus say that practically the sole source for the compiler's understanding and exposition of the Gospel of Matthew was the treatment of this Gospel in the *Liber questionum in euangeliis*.

8. *Use in the* Catechesis Celtica *of Apocrypha and Rare Latin Texts*

Wilmart, in his edition of sections of the *Catechesis Celtica*, noted the indiscriminate use made in them of Apocrypha, *prophetica verba*, texts on Doomsday and signs before Doomsday, and suchlike. The use of these he saw as further indication of the Celtic origin of the homilies. We may go further and use this evidence as a strong indication of specifically Irish affiliations.

8.1. *The Magi and the Gospel According to the Hebrews*[82]

In the homily for Low Sunday (f. 35 v), towards the end of the homily, we have a citation from the Gospel of the Hebrews:

> *Item, isti VIII dies paschae in quo resurrexit Christus Filius Dei significant VIII dies post remissionem paschae in quo iudicabitur totum semen Adae, ut nuntiatur in euangelio Ebreorum, et ideo putant sapientes diem iudicii in tempore pascae, eo quod in illo die resurrexit Christus ut in illo iterum resurgant sancti.*

---

82. On this subject see R.E. McNally, 'The Three Holy Kings in Early Irish Latin Writing', in P. Granfield and J.A. Jungmann (eds.), *Kyriakon: Festschrift Johannes Quasten* (2 vols.; Münster: Verlag Aschendorff, 1970), II, pp. 667-90; M. McNamara, *The Apocrypha in the Irish Church* (Dublin Institute for Advanced Studies, 1973; corrected repr. 1984), pp. 54-56, §48. The text is in Wilmart, *Analecta Reginensia*, pp. 73-74.

Different texts from the work entitled 'The Gospel according to the Hebrews' are encountered in Irish sources. One of these is the description of the Magi. A text on these is found, without indication of source, in the *Catechesis Celtica* in a commentary on the Gospel for the miracle of Cana (Epiphany) (Jn 2.1-11):

> *Hodie III magi ab oriente uenientes cum IIIbus muneribus Ihesum Christum dominum nostrum inuenerunt. Haec autem est tractatio nom-(inum) de his tribus magis. Primus eorum senior(um) Melchus nomine, qui erat canus cum barba prolixa et cum coma, tonicam habens iacin-thinam et sagum milleum, et indutus erat calciamentis iachi(n)tino et albo commixtis, opere polimatario uarie compositis. Secundus Caspar nomine, iuuenis imberbis, rubicundus, tonicam millenicam et sagum rub-eum habens, calciamenta iacinthina uestitus, tus secum afferens quasi deo digne deum adhorauit. Tertius Patizara nomine, fuscus, niger, inti-g(er) barbatus, tonicam rubeam et sagum album habens, et calciamentis millenicis indutus, per mirram filium hominis moriturum confessus est. Omnia autem uestimenta eoram sirica erant.*

A slightly different form of this tradition is found in the *Collectanea* of Pseudo-Bede (*PL* 94, 541C-D), probably of Irish origin, and in other Irish sources.

8.2. *The* Liber de gradibus caeli, *Attributed to Gregory the Great*[83]
In the homiletic exposition on Genesis 1 for the Easter Vigil, on Gen. 1.26 the *Catechesis* has:

> *Et nouissime factus est homo ad imaginem et similitudinem Dei. Imago autem in sanctitate et aeternitate anime consistit, ut Gregorius in libro de gradibus caeli dixit; similitudo uero in persecutione et dominatione ostenditur.*

What must be the same work, but attributed to Augustine, is cited in the Hiberno-Latin commentary on Genesis 1–3 preserved in the St Gall manuscript, Stiftsbibliothek MS 609 (*Augustinus in libro de gradibus caeli*).

---

83. See P. Grosjean, 'Le "Liber de gradibus caeli" attribué à S. Grégoire le Grand', *Analecta Bollandiana* 61 (1943), p. 99-103. On the St Gall text 609, see also Wright, 'Apocryphal Lore', pp. 124, 132-33. The text is in Wilmart, *Analecta Reginensia*, p. 41.

8.3. *The Signs of Seven Days before Doomsday*
In f. 52 v of Codex Reginensis 49 there is an item entitled *De diebus VII ante diem iudicii*, with a description of the events to occur on the seven days preceding Doomsday.[84] The greater part of this depends on the apocryphal *Apocalypse of Thomas*. There are citations from this same work in some homilies in a Reichenau manuscript, now at Karlsruhe, homilies which may be of Irish origin. It is clear from the extensive use made of it that the apocryphal work was known to the author of the concluding cantos (153–62) of *Saltair na Rann*. There was an early interest in the signs before Doomsday in Ireland, coupled with a rich development on this particular tradition. While the signs as given in the *Catechesis* are not of the developed kind we find in later texts, the presence of a text dependent on the *Apocalypse of Thomas* can be taken as a further indication of Irish affiliations of the collection of homilies.

8.4. De Die Dominico
The *Catechesis Celtica* text (f. 53 r) entitled *De die dominico* was published by Wilmart.[85] It was republished, together with two other texts, by McNally, one of Breton origin (Orléans 221[193]; Paris BN Lat. 3182), the other (Vatican, Pal. lat. 220) in an Anglo-Saxon hand of the Middle or Upper Rhine. The texts are closely related to the Irish *Epistil Ísu* and the *Cáin Domhnaigh*. If not of Irish origin, the piece entitled *De die dominico* at least has strong Irish affiliations.

8.5. *The Seven Seals: The Seven Things Prophesied of Christ*
In the *Catechesis Celtica* (f. 23 v), in a text in praise of Easter, it is stated that on this day effect is given to the destruction of the seven walls of the sin of Adam and Eve. This destruction had already been going on through history, in Abel, in Enoch and others and finally, as no. 11: *in Christo, per VII quae profetata sunt de illo, id est natiuitas, babtismum, crux, sepultura, resurrectio, (ascensio et iudicium)*.

---

84. On the question in general see McNamara, *Apocrypha*, pp. 128-44 §§104-108; also M. McNamara, 'Airdena Brátha', in *Dictionary of the Middle Ages* (13 vols.; J.R. Strayer [ed. in chief]; New York: Charles Scribner's Sons, 1982), I, pp. 111-12.

85. Wilmart, *Analecta Reginensia*, pp. 111-12; McNally, *Scriptores*, pp. 185-86, with discussion of texts etc., pp. 175-79.

These seven things prophesied of Christ[86] are given in greater detail in a separate item in the *Catechesis* (f. 40 v), this time in a comment on Apoc. 5.1: *Vidi...librum scriptum...signatum sigillis VII.* The comment reads:

> Signatum, *id est conclusum sigillis VII. Hoc est, conceptione Christi et natiuitate et passione et sepultura et resurrectione et ascensione et de aduentu eius. Sigilla in profetis pronuntiata sunt, claues in nouo quibus aperiuntur sigilla. De conceptione sigillo Esaias dicit:* Ecce uirgo in utero concipiet et pariet filium, et uocabitur nomen eius Emmanuel. *Clauis est, cum dicitur: Aue Maria, gratia plena, et reliqua usque tui. Sigillum de natiuitate ut:* Nascetur homo de semine Iuda et dominabitur omnibus gentibus. *Clauis est:* Natus est uobis hodie conseruator salutis, qui est Christus...

The tradition behind them is well attested in Latin literature. It has been traced by E.A. Matter from four manuscripts, with two families: Family A, Karlsruhe Aug CXI, Munich Clm 14423; Family B, Munich Clm. 6407 and Vatican lat. 5096. The piece is connected in these manuscripts with the exegesis of Apocalypse 5.1-5. The tradition may have originated in Visigothic Spain in the sixth or seventh century. The tradition of the seven things prophesied of Christ is found in a number of Irish texts without direct connection with the Apocalypse. They are already listed by Hilary in his *Instructio psalmorum* (the introduction to his

---

86. On the larger question of the origin of the seven seals tradition see E.A. Matter, 'The Pseudo-Alcuinian "De septem sigillis": An Early Latin Apocalypse Exegesis', *Traditio* 36 (1980), pp. 111-37. Some Irish texts listed, McNamara, 'Tradition and Creativity', pp. 363-64 n. 99. With regard to Irish texts we have, apart from the *Catechesis Celtica*, an Old Irish gloss on Col. 1.25 in the Würzburg Codex which speaks of the seven things that were prophesied of Christ (Wb. 26d9); *Thes. Pal.* I, p. 670. These are itemized in the *Scúap Chrábaid* (K. Meyer [ed.], in 'Stories and Songs from Irish MSS. VI. Colcu ua Duinechda's Scúap Chrábaid, or Besom of Devotion', *Otia Merseiana* 2 (1900–1901), pp. 92-105 (97) and by C. Plummer, *Irish Litanies* (London: Henry Bradshaw Society, 1925), pp. 42-43; see also R. McNally (ed.), 'Der irische Liber de numeris: Eine Quellenanalyse des pseudo-isidorischen Liber de numeris' (PhD dissertation, Munich, 1957), p. 117, no. 21; Sermon VII of the series, 'In nomine Dei summi': McNally, ' "In nomine Dei summi" ', p. 143; in the Hiberno-Latin work entitled *Quaestiones uel glosae in euangelio nomine*, items no. 47-48, McNally, *Scriptores*, pp. 143-44; also in the Hiberno-Latin work *Ex dictis S. Hieronimi* nos. 9-10, R. McNally, *Scriptores*, p. 226.

commentary on the Psalms), no. 6, on which much of the Latin and Irish tradition probably depends.[87]

The Latin tradition studied by Matter is really quite different from the developed one we find in the *Catechesis Celtica*. After an introductory paragraph, found in Family A only, citing Apoc. 5.1-5, the seven seals are identified in the traditional manner (*natiuitas, baptismum, crucificatio, sepultura, resurrectio, ascensio, iudicium*). The text then goes on to link the seven gifts of the Holy Spirit with these seven seals, and in the third and final section to link the same seven gifts with the Patriarchs. The *Catechesis Celtica* form of the tradition, which cites both the prophecy and its New Testament fulfilment, is found again in almost identical form in the Hiberno-Latin 'Reference Bible', in the comment on Apoc. 5.1-5. It begins:

> Librum intus et foris signatum. *Librum Uetus Testamentum significat.* Intus et foris. *Id est in historia et sensu...*sigillis VII *qui de Christo principaliter leguntur, id est natiuitas reliqua. Ideo sigillati in ueteri quia nemo potuit scire* Ecce uirgo in utero concipiet *reliqua usque Christus natus fuit de uirgine. Haec sunt VII sigilli in ueteri testamento de natiuitate Christi. Ut est* Ecce uirgo in utero *reliqua, Christus soluit quando natus est, ut dicitur:* Natus est nobis hodie conseruatur salutis nostrae *reliqua. Secundus sigillus de baptismo...* (MS Paris BN 11561, f. 207 r-v)

The form of both is extremely close right through all seven seals. The wording is likewise. With regard to the first, we may note the presence in both texts of the rare and peculiar reading *conseruator* ('Reference Bible', *conseruatur*) *salutis* for Lk. 2.11. The ending of the best-known form of the tradition on the seven seals, with the connection of the seven gifts of the Holy Spirit with the patriarchs is found separately in the *Catechesis Celtica* (f. 3 r-v) and also in the Irish *Liber de numeris* (as VII, 1).

9. *Concepts and Phrases Common to* Catechesis *and Irish Texts*

In this study I have, for the greater part, concentrated on areas which have not been hitherto fully explored. To the evidence for Irish affiliations of the homily collection in Codex Reginensis Latinus 49 which I have given above, we must add that already brought forward by others. This I have given in summary as part of the history of research, namely

---

87. *PL* 9, cols. 236B.

terms and phrases in the Latin text which are unusual in Latin but which correspond to the vocabulary of Irish vernacular texts, especially religious documents. I repeat these here:

> *pascha modicum, haeres Christi, aliena non immolanda sunt Deo, filius vitae, veteris legis, creator omnium elementoram, familia caeli et terrae, gradus angelorum, initium* (in the specialized sense of 'beginning of Lent').

To these others could be added, for example, *sensus* with the meaning of the Irish *sians*, that is, spiritual sense (on Mt. 21.7 and Jn 12.14): *Hic notandum est quod...super utrumque animal sedere non possit... Tamen sensui* (= the spiritual sense) *magis conuenit quod super utrumque animal sedit, quia Dominus II populos supersedit, id est Israelem et gentilem* (f. 14 r); *tres XL*, that is, *tres quadragesimae*, the 'three Lents'.

This list could well be expanded. Such a study, however, is best left to a full examination of the peculiarities of the vocabulary of the *Catechesis Celtica*.

10. *Conclusion*

At the end of this investigation I return to the title of this paper and ask: How Irish is the *Catechesis Celtica*? How Irish are its affiliations?

Let me review the evidence. Although the script is Carolingian and not Irish or Insular, it does have certain Irish or Insular abbreviations, possible pointers to an Insular or Irish original.

In its biblical text there is a fairly strong Irish element in the Psalter text used, and in the Gospel of Matthew, in particular, there is clear evidence of use of the DELQR group of texts, which was at home in Ireland, if not restricted in use to that country. There is also evidence for the use of a text of Romans and of the Catholic Epistles of the kind used in Ireland.

Passing from Bible text to exegesis we find clear evidence of a close relationship between the *Catechesis Celtica* and the Irish tradition of Psalm exegesis, with relation to the understanding of Psalm 1, at any rate. The compiler's understanding of Genesis 1 is also that of the Hiberno-Latin commentaries on the Hexameron, and in so far as one can judge, also that of vernacular Irish literature. What little comment on the Canticle of Canticles the collection has is also that of the commentary of Apponius, a work very much at home in Irish circles.

We have seen that a major source for the compiler, and almost the sole source for the interpretation of Matthew, was the *Liber questionum in euangeliis*. As Bischoff has noted, this was quite an influential work. Much of it has passed over into the Hiberno-Latin one-volume commentary, the 'Reference Bible' (composed towards the end of the eighth century), and into the commentary of Paschasius Radbertus on Matthew. The date of the work's origin is uncertain, but probably the eighth century.

The author whose name was abbreviated by the compiler as *Man.* should, I believe, be taken as the mid-seventh-century Irish scholar Manchianus *sapiens* of Men Droichit, who died in 652, or possibly as Manchán of Liath Mancháin (Lemanaghan), who died in 655. Another author cited by him, namely Pseudo-Jerome on Mark, may also have been Irish. Together with this there are Irish affiliations in other texts he cites by name or uses anonymously: Gregory's *Liber de gradibus caeli*, the Gospel according to the Hebrews, traditions on the Magi, and in points of doctrine in the *Catechesis* known to have been of interest to the early Irish, for example, the seven things prophesied of Christ. Then there is the Latin phraseology, rare, if not unknown, outside of Irish sources but current in Irish texts and at times possibly representing translation from the Irish.

These are all Irish affiliations, to say the least. They may not prove that the *Catechesis Celtica* had an Irish origin, but they must at least be taken very seriously in the consideration of origins. An authoritative, if not final, verdict on provenance can only be given after the arguments in favour and against any particular origin have been duly weighed.

Should one opt for an Irish origin—and in Ireland itself rather than in Irish circles on the Continent—an attempt at a date and place must be made. In the Irish homiletic tradition, the *Catechesis Celtica* would fit well into the development between the compositions of Manchianus of the mid-seventh century and the *Liber questionum in euangeliis* (eighth century), on the one hand, and the glosses on the Gospels of Máel Brigte (1138 CE), on the other. Grosjean mentioned *Céli Dé* circles as a suitable milieu for composition, by reason of this monastic movement's interest in preaching. The use of Apponius's commentary on Canticles by the compiler would further favour this position. We know of the regard in which this book of the canon was held by the Reform monks. *The teaching of Mael Ruain* tells us that 'when a person was at the point of death, or immediately after the soul had left him, the *Canticum*

Salomonis was sung over him. The reason for this practice was that in that canticle is signified 'the union of the Church and every Christian soul' (*ceangal na heaglaise agus gacha hanma Criostuidhe*).[88] I cannot say that the composers of the *Rule of Mael Ruain* got this theory of interpretation from the commentary of Apponius. We may possibly infer as much, though, from a comment on Mt. 21.11: *Hic est Iesus profeta a Nazareth Galilaee* occurring in one of the homilies on Mt. 21.11. Nazareth is first interpreted as *flos munditiae*. The homilist then links it with Cant. 7.12 as follows (f. 28 v):

> *Ciuitas autem in qua Christus nutritur nobiscum cor nostrum est in quo* flores munditiae *bonae cogitationes fiunt quas Deus quaeritur, sicut in Cantico Canticorum dixit:* Videamus, si floruit uinia (Cant. 7.12). *Viniam animam uniuscuiusque dicit in qua flores diuersorum colorum cogitationes diuersarum uirtutum, misericordiae, patientiae, oboedientiae castitatisque et ceterarum uirtutum quas Deus requirit; et sicut coram oculis hominum concupiscibile et pulchrum est in aestatis tempore pomarium cum uariis floribus aut ager cum ditiersis holeribus coloribus conspicere, ita et anima coram Deo cum multarum uirtutum (et) cogitationum (floribus) pulchra est. Igitur in corde nostro per bonas cogitationes (Iesus) nutritur, sicut in Nazareth nutritus est.*

The possibility, or even the likelihood, of a non-Irish origin for the *Catechesis Celtica* also needs to be explored further. The arguments put forward to date have to do with the manuscript Codex Reginensis Latinus 49 rather than with the nature of its contents: the Carolingian script, indicating Continental, not Insular origin, and the three glosses which have been seen to connect it with Cornwall. The value of the first argument still holds good and indicates a Continental origin for the present manuscript. With regard to the three 'Celtic'—presumed Cornish—glosses, one (*he ben*) seems in reality to be no more than a Latin abbreviation (*heb*) for *hebraice*. The most important of the three, that is, *guor cher*, occurs as a marginal gloss in a homily which contains strong indications of Irish origin: the heading *In nomine Dei summi*, citations ascribed to *Man*, who is most probably the seventh-century Irishman Manchianus *sapiens* of Men Droichit or Manchán of Liath Mancháin, clear dependence on the Hiberno-Latin *Liber questionum in euangeliis*, and contact with other Irish sources.

---

88. E. Gwynn (ed.), *The Rule of Tallaght*, *Hermathena* 44 (second supplementary volume) (1927), pp. 18-19, §29.

It may well be that more detailed research will indicate the presence in these catecheses of non-Irish affiliations (in the Bible text, source employment, and other ways), and in so doing give us new insights into the manifold relationships that existed between monks and scholars in Ireland, Britain and on the Continent.[89] Evidence for non-Irish affiliations, however, will need to be concrete, as concrete as that now before us for the Irish affiliations.

89. For more detailed examination of the Irish and non-Irish affiliations of these catecheses, see M. McNamara, 'Sources and Affiliations of the Catechesis Celtica (MS Vat. Reg. Lat. 49)', *Sacris Erudiri* 34 (1994), pp. 185-235; see also *idem*, 'The Affiliations and Origins of the Catechesis Celtica: An Ongoing Quest', in T. O'Loughlin (ed.), *The Scriptures of Early Medieval Ireland (Proceedings of the 1993 Conference of the Society for Hebrew-Latin Studies on Early Irish Exegesis and Homiletics)* (Instrumenta Patristica, 31; Steenbrugge: Abbatia S Peter; Turnhout: Brepols, 1999), pp. 179-203.

INDEXES

INDEX OF REFERENCES

OLD TESTAMENT

Psalms (cont.)

Ref	Pages	Ref	Pages	Ref	Pages
68.5	206	71.5	189, 415	73.20	175
68.9	321, 414	71.6	170	73.22	222
68.10	321, 414	71.8	189	74	175, 204, 309, 346
68.14	212	71.10	174, 179, 181, 182	74.4	176
68.15	212	71.13	170	74.7	221, 222
68.21	321, 414	71.15	192	74.9	170, 176, 189, 213, 221
68.22-28	414	71.17	189	74.54	74
68.22-24	321, 414	72	199, 200, 212, 248, 309, 329	75	197, 221, 286, 310
68.22	97, 208, 212, 219, 321, 414	72.1	200, 221	75.4	221
68.24	212, 321, 414	72.8	329	75.6	206, 218, 220, 221
68.25	321, 414	72.13	189	75.9	189
68.26	212	72.14	329	75.10	189
68.28	130	72.17–73.2	58, 71	75.11	210
68.31	130	72.19	170	76	186, 199, 221, 309, 346
68.34	170	73–76	199	76.8	189
68.35	130	73	198, 200, 204, 205, 208, 213, 220-22, 248, 309	76.9	189
69–70	212			76.11	192, 212
69	199, 204, 220, 221, 226, 310, 363, 366, 395	73.1	189	76.17	175
		73.2	189, 213	76.19	212
		73.3-17	71	77–81	199
69.2	109	73.3	189, 192, 222	77	99, 177, 198, 309, 324, 345
69.4	181	73.5	210, 222		
69.6	78	73.6	74, 182		
69.20	76	73.8	222	77.3	213
70	173, 179, 198, 200, 204, 207, 219, 221, 309	73.9	189	77.6	74
		73.10	189, 222	77.16	100
		73.11	175	77.20	210
70.3	99, 192	73.12	100, 210, 213, 218, 220	77.21	109, 189
70.4	220, 221			77.25	176
70.8	109	73.13-17	218	77.34	213
70.9	192, 221	73.13-16	220	77.35	189
70.20–71.9	71	73.13-14	213	77.37	213
70.20	192	73.13	206, 207, 219	77.38	189
70.23	220	73.14	74, 99, 173, 179, 184, 213	77.43	175
71	196, 223, 226, 276, 285, 310, 415			77.44	179, 191
		73.15	109, 210, 213	77.45	175, 179, 182, 191, 193, 217
71.2	220			77.46	168, 175, 179, 186
71.3	207	73.18	189		

INDEX OF AUTHORS

d'Hont, M.J. 43, 48, 168, 192, 193, 210, 211, 225, 229-31, 246, 248, 249, 251, 265, 266, 268, 269, 276-80, 282, 284, 305, 388, 390, 392, 407-409, 411-14
Diekemp, F. 388
Draak, M. 176
Dümmler, E. 64

Ehrle, F. 83
Ehwald, R. 27
Esposito, M. 28, 59, 62, 64, 78-80

Ferguson, T.S. 159
Finlayson, C.P. 74, 75
Fischer, B. 37, 49, 58, 104, 157, 158, 167, 211, 246, 262, 432
Fischer, B. 240
Fitzgerald, E. 242, 375, 381-83
Flower, R. 55
Fraipont, J. 213, 214, 279
Frede, H.J. 49, 59
Froehlich, K. 382

Gamber, K. 261
Gardthausen, V. 62
Gibson, M. 245
Ginzberg, L. 276
Goffinet, E. 244
Gordon, R.P. 413
Gottlieb, T. 89
Gougaud, L. 21-23, 25, 67, 72, 166, 183, 202, 289
Graham, H. 25
Gray, L.H. 431
Grillmeier, A. 388
Grosjean, P. 421-23, 452, 462
Gryson, R. 317
Güterbock, B. 166, 180-82, 184
Gwynn, E.J. 23, 357-59, 468

Halpern, J.W. 267
Hammerstein, R. 215
Haskins, P.W. 277
Hayes, R. 64, 65
Hayward, C.T.R. 277
Heist, W.W. 21
Hellmann, S. 64, 66

Henry, F. 26-28, 67-69, 72-78, 82-85, 112, 147, 148, 153, 155
Herren, M.W. 59, 61
Hilberg, I. 213
Hillgarth, J.N. 31, 32, 103, 116
Hockey, F. 231
Howlett, D. 61
Hughes, K. 25, 26, 98, 105, 202, 289
Huglo, M. 157

Jones, C. 234
Joyce, P.W. 22, 25
Jubainville, H. d'Arbois de 62

Kannengieser, C. 244
Kelly, J. 433
Kelly, J.F. 399, 431
Kelly, J.N.D. 244, 276
Kenney, J.F. 19, 23, 25, 28, 39, 40, 42, 44, 45, 57, 59, 62, 64, 68, 69, 72, 77, 78, 83, 86, 89, 100, 102, 167, 202, 289, 342, 360, 452
Ker, N.R. 165, 167
Kihn, H. 247, 280, 281
Kottje, R. 226
Kraeling, C.H. 277
Krauss, S. 276, 277
Krusch, B. 45, 46, 86
Kuder, U. 161, 164
Kuypers, A.B. 40

Lagarde, P. de 213, 214
Lagrange, J.M. 276
Laistner, M.L.W. 245, 247
Lambert, B. 215
Lange, N.R.M. de 239, 241, 287
Lawlor, H.J. 28, 29, 34, 76, 107, 109, 158, 254
Leconte, R. 242
Liebart, F. 83
Lindsay, W.M. 28, 29, 39, 59, 166, 178, 254, 419, 420
Loth, J. 420, 422
Lowe, E.A. 26, 28, 39, 42, 45, 47, 156-58, 163, 167, 170, 172, 178, 261
Löwe, H. 25
Lubac, H. de 219

INDEX OF MANUSCRIPTS

Vercelli
Biblioteca Capitolaire LXII: 248-249,
        268, 285

Verona
Cathedral Chapter Library I (I) (Codex
Veronensis; Psalter of Zeno of
Verona): 102

Vienna
Nationalbibliothek MS 1861: 158

Würzburg
Universitätsbibliothek M. p. th. f. 12
(Codex Paulinus): 166, 433

Zurich
Stadtbibliothek Rheinau 34: 158
Stadtbibliothek C.12: 158

JOURNAL FOR THE STUDY OF THE OLD TESTAMENT
SUPPLEMENT SERIES